TOWnsend

A CELEBRATION OF POETS

NORTHEAST 4-6
SPRING 2008

creativeCOMMUNICATION
A CELEBRATION OF TODAY'S WRITERS

A CELEBRATION OF POETS
NORTHEAST 4-6
SPRING 2008

AN ANTHOLOGY COMPILED BY CREATIVE COMMUNICATION, INC.

Published by:

creativeCOMMUNICATION
A CELEBRATION OF TODAY'S WRITERS

1488 NORTH 200 WEST • LOGAN, UTAH 84341
TEL. 435-713-4411 • WWW.POETICPOWER.COM

ISBN: 978-1-60050-177-7

FOREWORD

This edition of our poetry anthology is an important transition for Creative Communication. Since our beginning in 1993, we have called our contest "A Celebration of Young Poets." Having worked with student poets for over 15 years, we realized that the writers who have been accepted to be published are not "young" poets. They are poets. Young or old, they are writers who have proven their worth as poets. These are the poets we celebrate.

We also start this year with a new cover for the anthologies. We are excited about this new look and our new logo of a hand releasing stars. Our logo can represent different things. It could be a teacher or mentor releasing a writer to the world through our publication. It could represent the fact that the stars are limitless and these writers are just starting to shine with their potential. We have become the starting point for thousands of writers and we hope each poet continues to make writing a part of their lives.

What is recorded between these pages is unique. It exists nowhere else in the world and is now recorded forever. Take the time to read what these poets have shared. A part of themselves and their world exists in each poem. Savor it. Enjoy.

Sincerely,
Thomas Kenne Worthen, Ph.D.
Editor
Creative Communication

WRITING CONTESTS!

Enter our next POETRY contest!
Enter our next ESSAY contest!

Why should I enter?
Win prizes and get published! Each year thousands of dollars in prizes are awarded in each region and tens of thousands of dollars in prizes are awarded throughout North America. The top writers in each division receive a monetary award and a free book that includes their published poem or essay. Entries of merit are also selected to be published in our anthology.

Who may enter?
There are four divisions in the poetry and essay contests. The divisions are grades K-3, 4-6, 7-9, and 10-12.

What is needed to enter the contest?
To enter the poetry contest send in one original poem, 21 lines or less. To enter the essay contest send in one original essay, 250 words or less, on any topic. Each entry must include the student's name, grade, address, city, state, and zip code, and the student's school name and school address. Students who include their teacher's name may help the teacher qualify for a free copy of the anthology.

How do I enter?
Enter a poem online at:
www.poeticpower.com

or

Mail your poem to:
 Poetry Contest
 1488 North 200 West
 Logan, UT 84341

Enter an essay online at:
www.studentessaycontest.com

or

Mail your essay to:
 Essay Contest
 1488 North 200 West
 Logan, UT 84341

When is the deadline?
Poetry contest deadlines are December 4th, April 7th, and August 18th. Essay contest deadlines are October 15th, February 17th, and July 15th. You can enter each contest, however, send only one poem or essay for each contest deadline.

Are there benefits for my school?
Yes. We award $15,000 each year in grants to help with Language Arts programs. Schools qualify to apply for a grant by having a large number of entries of which over fifty percent are accepted for publication. This typically tends to be about 15 accepted entries.

Are there benefits for my teacher?
Yes. Teachers with five or more students accepted to be published receive a free anthology that includes their students' writing.

For more information please go to our website at **www.poeticpower.com**, email us at editor@poeticpower.com or call 435-713-4411.

TABLE OF CONTENTS

States included in this edition:

Connecticut
Maryland
Massachusetts
Virginia

Spring 2008 Poetic Achievement Honor Schools

* Teachers who had fifteen or more poets accepted to be published

The following schools are recognized as receiving a "Poetic Achievement Award." This award is given to schools who have a large number of entries of which over fifty percent are accepted for publication. With hundreds of schools entering our contest, only a small percent of these schools are honored with this award. The purpose of this award is to recognize schools with excellent Language Arts programs. This award qualifies these schools to receive a complimentary copy of this anthology. In addition, these schools are eligible to apply for a Creative Communication Language Arts Grant. Grants of two hundred and fifty dollars each are awarded to further develop writing in our schools.

Agape Christian Academy
Alexandria, VA
Linda Cason
Sharon Miser

Albert D Griswold Middle School
Rocky Hill, CT
Barbara Pearce*
Nancy Sullivan*

Ashford School
Ashford, CT
Bernie Schreiber
Mr. Tormey
Charles Wilcox

Battlefield Elementary School
Fredericksburg, VA
Elena Danigelis*

Benjamin Syms Middle School
Hampton, VA
Chautauqua Hopson*

Bensley Elementary School
Richmond, VA
Ms. Casey
Christina Frear
Maria T. MacLaughlin
Karen Struder
Ms. Swann
Mrs. Watson
Ms. Wolfe

Booth Hill School
Trumbull, CT
Mrs. Beers
Mrs. Consolati*
Margret McGovern
Mr. Swetckie

Brookside Elementary School
Dracut, MA
Kathleen Irwin
Mary Ellen McCarthy
Sharon McGrath
Mrs. S. Ninteau

C C Burr Elementary School
Auburndale, MA
    Melyssa Taylor*

C Hunter Ritchie Elementary School
Warrenton, VA
    Susan S. Robertson*

Cape Henry Collegiate School
Virginia Beach, VA
    Tina Howard*

Captain Nathan Hale Middle School
Coventry, CT
    Carla Kennedy
    Adrienne Manzone*
    Laura Myslinski*
    Judy Ripp
    Jeff Spivey*

Chalk Hill School
Monroe, CT
    Ms. Donahue
    Mrs. Fenn
    Mrs. Henn

Charlotte A Dunning Elementary School
Framingham, MA
    Carol Berlin
    Nicholas Botelho*
    Jae Goodwin*
    Cheryl Pennie
    Jane Shapiro
    Donna Treece

Chase Collegiate School
Waterbury, CT
    Thomas Cayer
    Nedra Satin Gusenburg*

Church of the Redeemer Christian School
Gaithersburg, MD
    Toni Morris*

Clark Avenue Middle School
Chelsea, MA
    Mrs. Delaney
    Steve Edelstein
    Mrs. Hijazi*
    Ms. Karll
    Ms. Solano-Franco
    Mrs. Walsh

Clover Street School
Windsor, CT
    Elaine Chartier
    Lisa Thomas*

Coleytown Elementary School
Westport, CT
    Katie Hall
    Rosemary Metke
    Edward Wolf*

Courthouse Road Elementary School
Spotsylvania, VA
    Brenda Nettles
    Michelle Sims

Crestwood Elementary School
Richmond, VA
    Diane Bivins*
    Christine Guerci
    Mali L. Hart

Davenport Ridge School
Stamford, CT
    Mr. Margiotta
    Pam Woodside

E Russell Hicks School
Hagerstown, MD
    Julie Slivka*

E W Thurston Middle School
Westwood, MA
    Joseph Lawlor*
    Mrs. Longoria

Edmond P Talbot Middle School
Fall River, MA
Tracy Duarte*
Mr. Silvia

Forest Avenue Elementary School
Hudson, MA
Mr. Glines
Linda Monstur
Karen Pedevillano
Mrs. Tkachuk

Foxborough Regional Charter School
Foxborough, MA
Amanda Carey
Mr. Pinsoneault
Charlotte Sheer*

Francis Asbury Elementary School
Hampton, VA
Dianne Congrove*

Freetown Elementary School
East Freetown, MA
Mrs. K. Falzone
Ms. Fernald
Mrs. Huling*
Mrs. Michael
Kerrie Sellars

Fuller Middle School
Framingham, MA
Allison Benabdallah*
Kathryn Bucci*
Carol Gay*
Meera Gill

General John Nixon Elementary School
Sudbury, MA
Anderson Manuel*
Mr. Whiting

Gilmore Academy
Brockton, MA
Vilma Andrade
Matthew Kawalec
Jocelyn Young

Grace Episcopal Day School
Kensington, MD
Ann Beirne*
A. Scott

Grace Miller Elementary School
Bealeton, VA
Susan Aylor*
Amy Costanzo
Sherri McMillon

Har-Bur Middle School
Burlington, CT
Nancy Kutz
Martha Lecko*

Hawley Elementary School
Newtown, CT
Stephanie Dunshee*
Melissa Thorpe*

Hebbville Elementary School
Baltimore, MD
Tunia Jackson
Darnell Peaker*

Helen H Hansen Elementary School
Stoughton, MA
Lauren Bechtel
Miss Paulson*
Susan Zbinski

Hindley Elementary School
Darien, CT
Christopher Basta*
Kathy Gale

Homeschool Plus
Norfolk, VA
Carol Martin-Gregory*

Immaculate Heart of Mary School
Towson, MD
Terri Archibald
Kathy Zoppo*

Irving School
Derby, CT
Joseph E. Benedetto*

J F Kennedy Middle School
Natick, MA
Christopher Forest*

Jack Jackter Intermediate School
Colchester, CT
Linda Kurczy
Kathleen Yanez

Jane Ryan School
Trumbull, CT
Marianne Ferrari*

John Ward Elementary School
Newton Centre, MA
Sara McClellan
Naomi E. Singer
Kenneth Waldman*

Leicester Memorial School
Leicester, MA
Evemarie McNeil*

Lincoln Street School
Northborough, MA
Susan Grady
Catherine Simisky

Litchfield Intermediate School
Litchfield, CT
Shelly Hill*
Tara Kraut
Mr. McDevitt*

Long Meadow Elementary School
Middlebury, CT
David Derouin
Dawn G. Dinallo*
Noel Siebern*
Carolyn Smith

Madison Middle School
Trumbull, CT
Allison Roche*

Magnolia Elementary School
Lanham, MD
Mr. R. Allen
Mrs. T. Childress
Camille Dorsey

Mary Walter Elementary School
Bealeton, VA
Patricia Baker*

McCleary Elementary School
New Castle, VA
Karen Jones*

Milton L Fuller Elementary School
Gloucester, MA
Mrs. Carney*

Monelison Middle School
Madison Heights, VA
Ann Harris
Lynette Smith*
Linda Wise*

Mount Hope Christian School
Burlington, MA
Rosemary Schiavi
Mrs. Voss

Munger Hill Elementary School
Westfield, MA
Stephanie Martell
Vicki Stoops

Oakdale Elementary School
Ijamsville, MD
Mona Clawson
Lynne Harris

Our Lady of Mercy School
Madison, CT
Ginna Daniels*

Page Middle School
    Gloucester, VA
        LeeAnn VanVranken*

Plainfield Catholic School
    Moosup, CT
        Julie Fauxbel
        Ms. Fogarty
        Mrs. McIntosh

Quashnet School
    Mashpee, MA
        Mrs. Donovan
        Lucinda McKay

Sacred Heart Elementary School
    Roslindale, MA
        Kathleen Cody*

Sacred Heart School
    North Quincy, MA
        Mrs. Gibbons
        Margaret Hanna*
        Patricia McGowan*
        Mrs. Norris
        Patricia Peck
        Mr. Shea

Salem Church Middle School
    Richmond, VA
        Dorrie Bishop
        Krista Coalson*
        Denise Hattley

School of International Studies at Meadowbrook
    Norfolk, VA
        Andrew Sytsma*

Scotts Ridge Middle School
    Ridgefield, CT
        Linda Haines*

Sinai Academy of the Berkshires
    Pittsfield, MA
        Christine Kleinerman*

Soule Road School
    Wilbraham, MA
        Ellen Schmutte*

Southbrook Academy
    Bridgewater, MA
        Carla Harris
        Deborah Proper

St Christopher's School
    Richmond, VA
        Mrs. Brown
        Ms. DiLucente
        Mr. Echols
        Mrs. Epes
        Ms. Fraine
        Ms. Frischkorn
        Ms. Gehring
        Ms. Grinnan
        Ms. Halladay
        Ms. Hoge
        Paula Jones
        Glorietta Jones
        Cabell Jones
        Ms. Jones
        Ms. Kirk
        Mr. Morgan
        Mrs. Oakley
        Mrs. Prince
        Ms. Sands
        Ms. Vizcaino
        Ann Wilson
        Nancy Young

St Clement Mary Hofbauer School
    Baltimore, MD
        Christine Godlewski
        Linda House
        Janice McIntosh
        Deborah Neidhardt
        Wendy Parker*

St Joseph School
    Webster, MA
        Karen Lefebvre*

St Joseph School-Fullerton
Baltimore, MD
Katherine Diggs*
J. Delores Keefer*
Barbara Owens*
Peggy Radziminski
Helena K. Scher*

St Luke's School
New Canaan, CT
Erin Ablondi
Miss King
Jane N. Olsen
Melissa Zurkowski

St Mary's Primary School
Taunton, MA
Erinn Grasso*
Kristie Pelland*
Linda M. Redmond

St Rose School
Newtown, CT
Bobbie Blizman
Mary Jo Bokuniewicz*
Mrs. Ferri*
Rita Garrett*
Judy Jewell
Tamra Russo
Miss Sideleau
Jeanne Vitetta*

Swampscott Middle School
Swampscott, MA
Mrs. Cardinal*
Irene Dalton

Thoreau Elementary School
Concord, MA
Brad Bennett
Margery Condon
Nancy Dillon
Mary Gallagher
Tom Hourihan
Merrie Najimy

Trinity Christian School
Fairfax, VA
Mrs. Bode
Constance Boltz
Mrs. Butler
Mrs. Datema
Penny Gale
Melissa Knaus*
Miss Locke*
Sindy Quinonez
Kathy Rickwald*
Jennifer Silva

Trinity School
Ellicott City, MD
Linda Meyer
Debby Moulding*

Village School
Marblehead, MA
Stephanie Trainor-Madigan*

Wakefield Forest Elementary School
Fairfax, VA
Karen M. Hickman*

Waller Mill Fine Arts Magnet School
Williamsburg, VA
Sherrie Geyer*

West Frederick Middle School
Frederick, MD
Gillett Palmer
Judith Reilly*

West Woods Upper Elementary School
Farmington, CT
Kerry Jones
Judy Muirhead*
Ms. Wilhelm*

Weston Intermediate School
 Weston, CT
   Linda Allegretti
   Rudd Anderson
   Karen Andrade
   Mrs. Balzi
   Kellie Brown
   Gregory Cannito
   Ms. Casey
   Celeste Coulter
   Kelly Farrell
   Sharon Huynh
   Carolyn Jones
   Mrs. Knudsen
   Geri Leka
   Alison Margo
   Barbara Nardella
   Mrs. Oliver
   Kathy Pando
   Carinne Phoenix
   Renee Tomaselli
   Kendra Verdi

Weston Middle School
 Weston, CT
   Sheila Cooperman*

Whitinsville Christian School
 Whitinsville, MA
   Terry Ebbeling
   Kathleen L. Hudson*

Willis E Thorpe School
 Danvers, MA
   Ms. Burke
   Kristen D'Entremont
   Lorraine M. Errico*
   Lisa Horn
   Miss Lyons
   Kaitlyn MacDonald
   Mrs. Martin

Yeshiva Academy
 Longmeadow, MA
   Lisa Borlen*

Language Arts Grant Recipients 2007-2008

After receiving a "Poetic Achievement Award" schools are encouraged to apply for a Creative Communication Language Arts Grant. The following is a list of schools who received a two hundred and fifty dollar grant for the 2007-2008 school year.

Acadamie DaVinci, Dunedin, FL
Altamont Elementary School, Altamont, KS
Belle Valley South School, Belleville, IL
Bose Elementary School, Kenosha, WI
Brittany Hill Middle School, Blue Springs, MO
Carver Jr High School, Spartanburg, SC
Cave City Elementary School, Cave City, AR
Central Elementary School, Iron Mountain, MI
Challenger K8 School of Science and Mathematics, Spring Hill, FL
Columbus Middle School, Columbus, MT
Cypress Christian School, Houston, TX
Deer River High School, Deer River, MN
Deweyville Middle School, Deweyville, TX
Four Peaks Elementary School, Fountain Hills, AZ
Fox Chase School, Philadelphia, PA
Fox Creek High School, North Augusta, SC
Grandview Alternative School, Grandview, MO
Hillcrest Elementary School, Lawrence, KS
Holbrook School, Holden, ME
Houston Middle School, Germantown, TN
Independence High School, Elko, NV
International College Preparatory Academy, Cincinnati, OH
John Bowne High School, Flushing, NY
Lorain County Joint Vocational School, Oberlin, OH
Merritt Secondary School, Merritt, BC
Midway Covenant Christian School, Powder Springs, GA
Muir Middle School, Milford, MI
Northlake Christian School, Covington, LA
Northwood Elementary School, Hilton, NY
Place Middle School, Denver, CO
Public School 124, South Ozone Park, NY

Language Arts Grant Winners cont.

Public School 219 Kennedy King, Brooklyn, NY
Rolling Hills Elementary School, San Diego, CA
St Anthony's School, Streator, IL
St Joan Of Arc School, Library, PA
St Joseph Catholic School, York, NE
St Joseph School-Fullerton, Baltimore, MD
St Monica Elementary School, Mishawaka, IN
St Peter Celestine Catholic School, Cherry Hill, NJ
Strasburg High School, Strasburg, VA
Stratton Elementary School, Stratton, ME
Tom Thomson Public School, Burlington, ON
Tremont Elementary School, Tremont, IL
Warren Elementary School, Warren, OR
Webster Elementary School, Hazel Park, MI
West Woods Elementary School, Arvada, CO
West Woods Upper Elementary School, Farmington, CT
White Pine Middle School, Richmond, UT
Winona Elementary School, Winona, TX
Wissahickon Charter School, Philadelphia, PA
Wood County Christian School, Williamstown, WV
Wray High School, Wray, CO

Grades 4-5-6

Top Poem Grades 4-5-6

Tears

Tears are symbols,
Petite, little symbols
That crawl on the faces of many.
They show heartaches and heartbreaks,
Melancholy and misery,
Sadness, sadness, and sadness.

Tears are symbols,
Petite, little symbols
That shout about joy and relief.
They leap out of wide eyes
And show cheerfulness and glee,
Happiness, happiness, and happiness.

Tears are symbols,
Petite, little symbols
That break out when pushed too far.
They show impatience and displeasure,
Madness and annoyance,
Anger, anger and anger.

Tears are symbols,
Petite little symbols
That speak in so many languages.

Emily Bamberry, Grade 6
E W Thurston Middle School, MA

Top Poem Grades 4-5-6

The Ocean and Me

The ocean, I feel is like a part of me
For when I dive into this blue blanket
The water swarms about my tiny feet
As it wraps me in a little warm bundle
Holding me tight as if it were my only protection.

For when I hide my face in this deep blue ocean
I only see other life forms
And a whole new world just waiting to be discovered.
The gentle touch of the sand against my soft skin
Is as if it were my pillow
Just waiting for me to lie down my head
And rest there 'til day breaks.

For when I'm with this continuously expanding blue blanket of mine
I feel safe and at home. I feel free.
And when I'm with the ocean in my mind I'm so far apart from the world
That I feel that I'm now free to explore the unexplorable
And change the unchangeable.
I feel that all my problems and burdens float away with the waves
So that I can be in perfect peace and harmony.

The ocean and I become one when we are together
For that is the ocean and me.

Mariana Byrne, Grade 5
Mary Munford Elementary School, VA

Top Poem Grades 4-5-6

Spring Flowers

The smell of cherry roses
fills the weakening air,
I see the timid sun come out
and shine my chestnut hair.

The blue and yellow flowers
awake the sleeping call,
they open up their petals
and hope they will not fall.

The presence of the flowers
makes my heart just soar,
the seeds keep growing and growing
and soon there will be hundreds more.

Lily Harwood, Grade 4
Weston Intermediate School, CT

Top Poem Grades 4-5-6

Come Listen

Come listen
my fingers bouncing
like grasshoppers
over the shiny white keys
pianissimo turns to
FORTISSIMO as fast as a blink
fast, slow, fast, slow
major, minor, major, minor
mindlessly, effortlessly
chords mold into a song
energy filling my fingers
as the air becomes full with
the melody, the harmony
of the song
come listen

Sonia Khurana, Grade 5
John Ward Elementary School, MA

Top Poem Grades 4-5-6

The Silence Tree

There is a tree that is more beautiful than anything there ever was
It has vibrant reds and greens and a silence that is golden
It pulls you in and comforts you and holds others out
This silent sanctuary cannot be disturbed
For its barrier is impenetrable for spirits of hate and fear
Only pure ones of love and hope get to glance its sloping branches
They arch higher than any other and cradle you with care
Enter and come out with the utmost sense of calm
That leads you to a moment of silent peace

Victoria Loughborough, Grade 5
McDonogh School, MD

Top Poem Grades 4-5-6

Dawn Awakening

Dawn.
Opening its
door.
A crack.
to let
light
ooze
in like
Molasses.
It vacuums up
the last specks
Of darkness.
then,
wakes the sun.
To give
light
to the newborn
clouds.
In the fiery
sky

Jack Mendillo, Grade 5
Coleytown Elementary School, CT

Top Poem Grades 4-5-6

Soft Winter

The wind races the leaves
As the deer lift their head
The air is soft
For the bird's journey ahead

The bear creeps back to darkness
As the trees dance to the season's beat
The stream stops its babbling
As the turtle hide their feet

Into the ground mice burrow
A good nest the squirrels seek
As the grass disappears
Only a wolf's eyes will peek

A whole new challenge is coming
What will become of things
We will just have to wait and listen
For a new season's ring

Tommy Nickerson, Grade 6
William J Johnston Middle School, CT

Top Poem Grades 4-5-6

Grandfather

All is quiet.
I squeezed her hand
And wished this plane of hurt would land.

The sky is black
And full with rain.
I hoped the cleansing water would ease my pain.

The flowers in my hand
Dropped soft to the ground.
My sadness was lost,
But it came back around.

I looked at the stone,
When she said not to cry.
I turned away fast
To wipe a tear from my eye.

He would hug me so tight.
I've been here since dawn.
He was here yesterday,
And now he is gone.

Erin Reilly, Grade 6
E W Thurston Middle School, MA

Top Poem Grades 4-5-6

Sun Bridge

Days are pebbles, flung straight into the sea,
Yet each has its pattern, like a red-wooded tree.
Each holds an adventure, be it tepid or tart,
Memories flooding, like a sky-woven dart.

A sun bridge, an arc in the sky,
A piece of ecstasy, to undergo you can fly.
A feeling of bliss, an audacious obsession,
Losing all feeling of dire depression.

Swallow the moon, the honey-gold curls,
The starry night living, the constellations in twirls.
Their ivory afterglow, their radiant scent,
Of small crickets humming, of lives lacking dents.

The treasure of friendship, not enclosed by a box,
It's out there, it's waiting, and you can take it to lock.
This treasure is priceless, not from a vulgar, insipid store,
Friendship is stimulation, it was prepared to adore.

The sun bridge is bawling, but where could it be?
It's not so fortuitous; it's painless to see.
Life is a journey that is flounced from a book,
Just peer around you, take a diminutive look.

Megan Schaller, Grade 4
Jacksonville Elementary School, MD

Top Poem Grades 4-5-6

Little Monks

Stones
Sitting, meditating
On a riverbank
Watching the calm water
Ripple and swirl
As the wind blows
The grass and flowers
Dance and bend
While the stones
Sit and meditate

The sky darkens
Clouds gather
"Plink! Plink!"
Droplets fall from the sky
And land in
The river that
Is alive with ripples
They stain the stones
While they quietly
Sit and meditate
Like little monks

Sea-Jay Van der Ploeg, Grade 5
John Ward Elementary School, MA

Forest Cat

The cat in your house
isn't the same
as the lone forest cat.
He's not your average pussycat,
hunting for himself.
His willowy outline
gliding through the mist.
Fur sleek and soft,
and can be every hue.
But doesn't he know
it is all artificial?

Maggie Voetberg, Grade 4
Cedar Point Elementary School, VA

In the Eyes of Africa

My arenaceous lands
drowned
as a newborn sun's
light projects.
My animal kingdom
bows
in its presence.
My people,
abandoned beds,
ascented into dawns companionship,
now abundant in
chores.
My heart:
free as a wild stallion
roaming my land
my people
my family
my Africa.

Elizabeth Fucigna, Grade 5
Hindley Elementary School, CT

Dance

Dance is my inspiration
It is my sensation
When I jump, I soar in the air
The wind blows through my hair

Clickity, tippity, tappy
The noise makes me so happy
When I have a smile on my face
People know I am in my own place

Turn, swirl, pow
When I turn, I don't know how
How can I stop this dancing?
I just keep on prancing

I just have to swirl and hop
Dance is my thing, I'll never stop.

Grace Terrell, Grade 4
Mapleshade Elementary School, MA

The Swing

Up, Up, and away,
The swing goes
As you touch
Your toes.

The cold breeze
Brushes again and
Again along your
Face.

A feeling of
Happiness is all
Over you, as you
Feel you can
Touch the whole wide world.

You reach your hands out
To touch the trees nearby,
You can't reach…
but you feel happy,
With you, the swing and the birds.

Caroline Lane, Grade 4
King's Highway Elementary School, CT

Bowers School

Bowers School is about being
safe.
Bowers School is about being
responsible.
Bowers School is about being
respectful.
Bowers School is about
learning for the future.
Bowers is about
EVERYTHING.

Taeler Cruz, Grade 4
Bowers School, CT

Nana

Nana
Beautiful, kind
Helpful, creative, generous
She makes everyone happy
Role model

Eileen O'Connor, Grade 5
Sacred Heart School, MA

Monday

M any say it's when the week starts
O ver but others say it's
N ot but to me it's just another
D ay in the wild
A nd adventurous life of
Y oung and old people.

Brooke Young, Grade 6
Monelison Middle School, VA

Easter

Christ did
die, by
and by.
We mourn for Him with Seraphim.
But yet there is hope for his
resurrection
and life.
Through all
crying and
strife.
Jesus did
die, you
need not
cry.
For
souls
are
born
today.

Ben Christenson, Grade 4
Trinity Christian School, VA

Morning Commute

Sun rises
Commuters awake
Trains are screeching
Buses are driving
Commuters buy coffee
They hop on!
And go downtown
Typical morning

William Hart, Grade 5
Sacred Heart Elementary School, MA

Spring Is Here

Spring is here let's celebrate
Spring is here some birthday's are here
spring has sprung because spring is here
let's celebrate!

S prung
P retty
R oses
I mportant
N ice
G reat

I ncredible
S unny

H ot
E xciting
R eal
E xcellent

Makenzie Sevigny, Grade 4
Marsh Grammar School, MA

Hope

Hope is what you feel in your heart
It helps you with a new tomorrow.
Hope gets you through the day and night
Without having a fear or fright.
With hope you can play a game of chance
— WIN or LOSE
It just depends on how much hope you have,
And you are the one to choose!

Emily Caruso, Grade 4
Salem Elementary School, VA

Nature

Nature is like an earth,
where things bloom as a time of birth.

Wind can blow around your face,
And creatures come out from place to place.

There are all kinds of seasons,
With different types of reasons.

This is what nature is all about.

Chase Cauthen, Grade 6
Magnolia Elementary School, MD

Open

It is a warm summer day.
BUT there's nobody outside;
so I went to go explore in the wonderful woods.
It was getting itchy and scratchy and then
I stood there silently.
A bear was crossing my path.

Jacob Swinton, Grade 6
Monelison Middle School, VA

My Dachshund

I love my dog, Jessie, he is the best
I love my dog, Jessie, he can pass any test
That dog loves the water so we call him mud puppy
But we might as well turn him into a guppy!
That dog of mine has won my heart
It will be quite hard to pull us apart.
Even though he has a couple more years
I'm still going to soak in my own tears.
I should forget about those bad thoughts
Instead I'll tell you what I've taught.
I taught him how to howl or sing real good
The way every good dog should
Jessie's fur shimmers in the light
So if you see him, he'll be out of sight!
Did I mention he loves the snow?
If you looked at him, you might already know.
Who's the best dog in the world?
Jessie, of course — haven't you heard?

Alexia Wilson, Grade 5
Clover Street School, CT

Winter

Cold, white snowflakes fall
Peacefully and calmly to the ground
From the cloudy, baby blue sky.
Kids sledding, skiing, and snowboarding too.
Winter is a really exciting time of year,
Christmas is coming soon!

Katie Gramm, Grade 5
St Mary's Primary School, MA

Sunrise

I wake up before the sun peeps over the horizon.
The birds are chirping,
And the bright colors of daybreak
Increase until the whole sky
Looks like a painting by a three year old
Or careless brush strokes.
The warm beams hit my face, refresh me, and tell
Me that a great day is coming.
My dream is interrupted
By the loud earsplitting screech of my alarm,
So I must leave this gorgeous display
And prepare for school.

TJ Gresham, Grade 6
Trinity School, MD

Horses

Run, trot, jump, woo!
Run, run, jump, stop — judge said good!
Saddle off, bridle off, wash down, done!
This is my day with my lovely, horse.

Olivia Pierce, Grade 4
Summit Montessori School, MA

The Old Scarecrow

The empty patch is where I stay,
Without any company, without any play.
Lonely all day, and all night,
I never give the crows a fright.
I'm not scary and I'm not mean,
My creator never finished my seams.
Crispy, crunchy leaves fall,
Like the Statue of Liberty I keep standing tall.
The whispering wind wanders around me
Like a newborn squirrel lost in an enormous oak tree.
No one ever stops by,
Or takes the time to say "hi!".
The faint smell of a perfect pumpkin pie drifts up my nose
As the overgrown grass tickles my toes.
I'm as old as the abandoned barn down the street.
If only I had working feet,
I'd run away from this lifeless place.
Maybe I'll go live in outer space.
But really I'm just an old man made of hay
And this empty patch is where I'll stay.

Stephanie Giblin, Grade 6
Madison Middle School, CT

Ocean

Spraying ocean mist
Strong waves crashing against the shore
A wonderful day
Taylor Brown, Grade 6
Monelison Middle School, VA

The Flute

I hear the wind
like a gentle flute,
the river like a bird soaring
through the air,

In the river, fish
swimming to and fro,
like tiny dancing humans,

A bird near by, telling me,
feel the breeze,
listen to the music
held beneath the river.
Franchesca Pafumi, Grade 6
Memorial School, MA

The Shot!

My heart is beating fast.
I can hear all the people in the bleachers
cheering and shouting.

The whistle blows.
I jump into the air with all my might
and grab the ball.

I start running
as fast as I can.
As I am running,
I wonder, will I get a goal,
or just miss the shot,
and let my team down?

I get to the basket.
I look up.
I take the shot, and
SCORE!!
And that was the winning goal!
Faye Liakopoulos, Grade 6
Swampscott Middle School, MA

Misery

Misery is the color of gray
It sounds like babies moaning
It tastes like food that makes you empty
It smells like dead fish
It looks like rain dropping
It makes you feel like laying on the street
Sneha Jayaraj, Grade 6
Albert D Griswold Middle School, CT

Penguins

Penguins jump, penguins swim, penguins like to do everything.
When penguins swim they get so cool.
When penguins jump they look like a fool.
They float around in the water all day.
Tell me that and I'll just say okay.
While nesting an egg the moms go away.
While the fathers stay at home loafing all about.
Daddy's staying home taking care of me in the freezing winds.
Mother goes out to get food for her little twins.
If the egg is so snuggled close the penguin will feel it start to crack.
The mom is here watching the egg hatch.
She comes up beside daddy to give him a kiss for all of his hard work.
The egg finally opens up to see the world.
What two beautiful penguins they have.
They welcome the baby penguins to their new family
and hug each other so they don't get cold.
They will love each other until they get old.
Kayla Thompson, Grade 6
Irving School, CT

The Battle of the Dragon Cave

In the dark, deep cave,
About 100 feet in,
      The dragon has been sleeping.
Since daybreak he has been snoring gently.
Across the cave lie his chicks.
Through the cave entrance they hear the distant clanking of metal.
By the time the father is up the slayers are in the cave.
Without waiting the slayers rush forward, swords extended.
Except for the commander, who has stayed back.
Between the slits of his helmet he sees his slayers have been killed.
Within the cave the dragon rushes forward, breathing fire.
With fear as his current emotion, the slayer runs from the victorious dragon.
Peter Kobanski, Grade 6
Albert D Griswold Middle School, CT

School

You might think school's a drag. Try and give it a shot.
It doesn't matter if you have A's or D's. Just give it all you've got.

It might seem bad now. But it will pay off in the long run.
Your hand might hurt now. Just wait until you're done.

Don't be a drop out. Go all the way.
It might seem bad now. But you might regret it someday.

You now have success. A perfect dream come true.
You wondered how it happened. It's all because you believed in you.

You can do good or bad. Depending if you believe.
When school's over with, it will be such a relief.

Now you are well educated. You can do what you set your mind to.
It's all because of the one thing you did. You believed in you!
Amanda Varden, Grade 6
Corkran Middle School, MD

The Knight with the Beard

There once was a knight with a beard
He looked kind of strangely weird
He was a big liar
His pants caught on fire
And he was burnt from his feet to his beard.

Grayson Kane, Grade 4
Weston Intermediate School, CT

Mr. Stubbles

I have a kitty named Mr. Stubbles.
He and I love to cuddle.

He likes to lay on my bed.
Sometimes he lays so still I think he's dead.

He makes me so giddy.
I love my kitty!

Caroline Simon, Grade 6
St Joseph School-Fullerton, MD

Snow

I look outside my window,
Seeing white small flakes
Falling from the sky.
What was it I wondered?
Snow it's snow.

I walk outside as the snow whispers to me.
It came down as fast as can be
What a wonderland I thought.
It was softer than sand.
As the snow sprinkled down on me.

Small as pebbles beautiful as the sea.
I thought as it sprinkled down on me.

Bridget Duncan, Grade 5
Soule Road School, MA

Feelings

Feelings
Feelings
Feelings
Colorful feelings
Good sad feelings
Red hot mad feelings
Crying feelings
Angry feelings
Shining sun bright feelings
Happy sad big feelings
Small feelings, too
Hot feelings
Cold feelings
Don't forget excitement feelings
Last of all, best of all, I like happy feelings

Gerdy Burke, Grade 4
C Hunter Ritchie Elementary School, VA

Laila

Laila, when we soar on the swings
your soft, curly, chestnut hair flows in the air
and your chocolate brown eyes twinkle in the sunlight
we both giggle and run to the monkey bars
as we kick wood chips behind us
we hear little birds chirping
Laila, you are smiling whenever we are together
the trolleys screech out, "Laila come play on us,"
you are an angel
sweet, loving, and funny
we always have so much fun together
you are a flower bud
and I am the water trying to help you grow

Val Herman, Grade 5
John Ward Elementary School, MA

The Magic of Words

Words are like the sound of birds you hear in the woods.
Books are like a chest-full of valuable goods.

A book brings you to a magical land,
To beaches of beautiful golden sand.

It takes you to a dragon's lair,
Or to a gladiator pit, fighting a bear.

You become a knight with a shining sword,
Or a slave rebelling against his evil lord.

As you reach the end of the magical land,
You wish for more books to have in your hand.

Timothy Vander Hart, Grade 6
Whitinsville Christian School, MA

Rain Forest Dew

Cheetahs spotted in yellow,
Birds decorated in green,
Lions are roaring loudly,
Bugs are crawling on leaves.

Aryana Miller, Grade 4
C Hunter Ritchie Elementary School, VA

Portal to the Beach

I put you to my ear and heard,
the faint sound of waves,
crashing against rocks.

I closed my eyes and felt the warm sand,
under my feet,
between my toes.

I took in the smell of salt lingering in the air,
and ran for the water,
to find it was not there.

Tasha Kim, Grade 6
Greenwich Country Day School, CT

Ideas

You can imagine anything in a poem.
Here are some ideas;
people,
palm trees,
scientists,
hippos,
rocket ships,
elephants,
kitty cats,
burps,
clouds,
pretzels,
polka dots,
and papers.
Just ideas.

Griffen Massey, Grade 4
Munger Hill Elementary School, MA

The Cat

I eat
I sleep
I sharpen my claws
I chase little mice
My owners applause.
It feels good
to earn my prize,
a bowl of food
at a perfect size.

Lydia Curtiss, Grade 6
Litchfield Intermediate School, CT

Winter in Virginia

Dreary, rainy days
Cold winds blow a symphony
Lonely music plays

Zoe Serratelli, Grade 6
Cape Henry Collegiate School, VA

Money

Money,
Flat, crinkly
Fold, spent, given
Fun to roll in
Smackaronies

Ryan Lino, Grade 4
Freetown Elementary School, MA

Easter at Grandma's!

Arrived at grandma's at 8:00 A.M.
Bought Easter eggs
Counted how many eggs there were
Decided to hide them early
Easter eggs were all hidden by noon
It was fun at grandma's house!

Sanil Patel, Grade 6
Albert D Griswold Middle School, CT

What Is Fawn Hollow?

Fawn Hollow is…
Teachers
Students
Homework
Recess
Fawn Hollow is…
Math
Science
Reading
Poetry
Fawn Hollow is…
Nice teachers
Mean teachers
Strict teachers
Soft teachers
Fawn Hollow is…
The smell of kids after gym
The sound of music in the halls
The sight of art on the walls
The smell of school lunch being made

Kelly O'Meara, Grade 4
Fawn Hollow Elementary School, CT

Would You Rather Be Somewhere…

Would you rather be somewhere…
Where the grass is green
Where the water's clean
Would you rather be somewhere…
Where flowers always grow
Where butterflies flit to and fro
Would you rather be somewhere…
Where no one fights
Where everyone has equal rights
Would you rather be somewhere…
Where everyone has a home
Where no one is alone
Would you rather be somewhere…
Where everyone is filled with joy
Every single girl and boy

Dylan Donahue, Grade 5
Coleytown Elementary School, CT

Mist

The gray blanket sweeps in,
Responding to the whispers of wind.
It settles down, weaving in and out,
In and out,
Until you cannot spy
That rock that was in front of you,
Just seconds ago.
But away it glides,
As swift as it came,
To settle down somewhere else,
That is the way of mist.

Nicolas Moss, Grade 6
Scotts Ridge Middle School, CT

Alone

Being alone
Just by myself
All alone
Nothing to do

When I'm alone
I can't play a game
Unless someone invites me
which doesn't happen very often.

Stuart Lohr, Grade 4
Crestwood Elementary School, VA

Grandma

You are so funny.
Smiles are also beautiful.
Laughs make me cheerful.

Jennifer Martin, Grade 4
Brookside Elementary School, MA

Cats

I like cats and cats like me.
I like cats, can't you see?
They are cute and funny.
They run as fast as a bunny.
They run around the house at night.
And give little critters a scary fright.
I like cats.

Aaron Gray, Grade 4
Grace Miller Elementary School, VA

Kittens

K itties are cute
I da is my kitten
T otally adorable
T hen again playful
E veryone loves them
N obody hates them
S uper duper cuddly

Perry Mullins, Grade 4
Trinity Christian School, VA

The Foul Line

When I step up to the line
I hear a holler and a cry
The line cries out to me
Please don't step on me

When I make the shot
The whole team cheers
For more and more
The last shot of the game
The ball goes in the hoop
And the whole building
Is full of happy and sad.

Tyler Grono, Grade 5
Soule Road School, MA

Peace Rocks

P lan for peace
E nd the war
A bolish the Armies
C are for your enemies
E radicate guns

R emember to respect difference
O pen hearts to new friends
C onsider compromise
K eep cooperating
S ing celebration

Don't fight; have peace.

John Newhall, Grade 5
Marblehead Community Charter Public School, MA

Christian Faith

As a Catholic, there's a way to be
We should live a certain way — each and every day
Honoring God faithfully
Going to church, where I will pray

Forgiveness is a trait I'm thankful for
We should all be clean of soul
Everyone should be that way to the core
If you're not, it will take its toll

Telling the truth is another good thing
In confession the truth we seek
Reading the Bible, His praises we will sing
If we know about God, we will not be meek

We donate money for those in need
In our hymnal we will find a song
For others we will do this very good deed
As Christians we will remain strong

Alex Cvecich, Grade 5
Greenwich Catholic School, CT

It's You I Blame

Mostly you're mean, sometimes you're nice
You should really pay the price
I don't understand why you pick on me
Instead of the others that you see

You're the tornado
And I'm your path
So one, two, three
You do the math

You're such an enigma
It's outrageously insane
So goodbye, farewell
It's you I blame

Caroline Cannon, Grade 6
Weston Middle School, CT

Baseball/Family

Baseball
Determined, athletic
Sprinting, working, playing
Stadium, muscle, gatherings, house
Eating, sitting, relaxing
Nice, peaceful
Family

Brenton Doyle, Grade 4
C Hunter Ritchie Elementary School, VA

Fall Surroundings

Fall is a time when the weather is crisp,
Bold, beautiful, bright colors adorn the trees
Auburn red, goldenrod yellow, amber orange,
And emerald green leaves lying lovely on the ground.
There sits the maple tree leaves like red fire,
Or as yellow as gold.
You could see the bitter nightshade berries as
Yellow as the sun.
In the distance there is an eastern white prickly pine cone.
You could hear two squirrels arguing over acorns.
Then running playfully through the trees
Scampering down gathering brown nuts are two squirrels.
In the crisp night air you can feel the wind
Blowing against your face.
You could smell the aroma of a freshly baked apple pie.
That's fall and all of its beautiful surroundings.

Gabriella Oppedisano, Grade 6
Madison Middle School, CT

Who Am I?

I am a Cameroonian, polite with anyone
I am a waterfall that falls down a hill
I am as strong and confident as a wrestler
I am a soccer ball, round and fast
I am a president that leads my country
I am a moon that goes out at night
I am a computer that calculates everything
I am an ocean that is huge and long
I am as tall as a tree
I am a professional swimmer, rapid as a dolphin
I am a bell that rings at night
I am a bell that gives good news to everyone

Daril Nantchouang, Grade 6
Fuller Middle School, MA

Green

Green is a lazy alligator sleeping
Green is a slow turtle walking
Green is seaweed swaying in the sea
Green is tall grass moving in the wind
Green is a sour Granny Smith apple
Green is a lizard sneaking around
Green is a frog hopping along

Erika Passmore, Grade 4
C Hunter Ritchie Elementary School, VA

Jewels

There are eight jewels,
I know the first,
Topaz is there along with onyx,
Opal comes with diamond
And sapphire with ruby,
Last but not least,
Bright green emerald
With the little jade
Aren't they so cute?

Samantha Bassett, Grade 5
Woodlawn Elementary School, VA

Going to the Ocean

Time to get your flip-flops,
Your sunglasses and your lotion.
Grab your pail and shovel,
We're going to the ocean!
Bring a towel and blanket,
Don't forget your swimsuit,
'Cause we're gonna get real wet!
Let's tan in the sun,
Build a sandcastle,
We're going to have lots of fun!
Let's dance all night,
Have a campfire,
While hanging in the moonlight.
So get your favorite music,
We're gonna have a party!

Elizabeth Mullin, Grade 6
St Joseph School-Fullerton, MD

I Am Me

I am timid,
Meeting new people.
I am gullible,
He tells me to look, nothing is there.
I am proud,
I run the race and win.
I am bold,
I always take a risk.
I am kindhearted,
My family comes first.
I am defiant,
I don't like to listen to my parents.
I am intelligent,
I get A's in math.
I am secure,
I'm with my older brothers.
I am carefree,
It's summer.
I am caring,
I love my friends.

But most of all, I am me.
Anna Munford, Grade 6
Blue Ridge Middle School, VA

Alone

When I am alone
I feel very lonely
Because nobody's there to talk to
So you really can't tell anybody how you feel
So you are just like saying everything over and over in your mind
And you can't do anything with anybody in there.

John David Mora, Grade 4
Crestwood Elementary School, VA

See

The waves race toward me
And finally land gracefully in between my toes
They jump up and down, playing around in the open sea
When they finally reach the shore
They play no more
For the waves die down, you see
The once great wave loses its power and falls onto the sandy ground
The waves go in a cycle
They are born in the sea and come to me
Die but then magically rebirth
One after another
Never ending
And beautifully young and old at the same time
All waves are different and unique in its own way
Just like us people
But not the same
And the waves will never die
Until the very end
But until then
Good-bye waves, good-bye
Don't die waves, don't die

Diamante Bovelli, Grade 6
Bigelow Middle School, MA

The Fallen King

Before the King Oak's countdown hit zero
He had reigned majestically above all his fiefdom.
The King was shelter for all the animals that dwelled below
In hollows and on the ground.

As his guardians grow old new ones develop to the sounds of rhythmic tapping
As the acrobatic acorns jump down the tree for their final act.
They think this is the end but when they crater
Into the ground it is a new beginning.

The wind carries the aroma of autumn
Like a fan blowing the fragrance of fruit.
Levitating leaves sway back and forth in the air
Like an old man sleeping peacefully in a hammock.

When leaf bare, the giant oak strains to hold on,
But with the King's old age the wicked whistling wind took his life away.
There I found him years later, touching his rough bark
Like coarse sandpaper lying on the ground.

Brendan Welch, Grade 6
Madison Middle School, CT

Polluting

The grass is so brown.
It makes me want to frown.
I go around the city.
It is such a pity.

The garbage is piled in a landfill
And creates a big hill.
It has many germs.
It brings many worms.

We use water every day.
And we want it to stay.
We have to stop polluting our air water and soil.
If you don't, we will spoil.

Ryan Covensky, Grade 6
Captain Nathan Hale Middle School, CT

New York City

The bums asking for money
Loud beeping cars
Hot, smoky grilled food
My soothing icy cold drink
The handle as I open the taxi door

Katarina Milic, Grade 4
C Hunter Ritchie Elementary School, VA

About Myself

I am Puerto Rican with curly hair.
I am a person that makes my sister laugh.
I like to play and do splits and do the wheel.
I like to be a teacher when I grow up.
I love the shoes baby pat and echo red.
I like to get cuddly with my Pooh pillow.
I am Puerto Rican with curly hair.

Marielys Berrios, Grade 4
Bowers School, CT

Have You Ever Thought

When you wake up in the morning
And you go to the window
What do you see?
Do you see random objects?
Have you ever thought,
Where all those came from?
Have you ever thought of space?
Where did that come from?
Did you think it just randomly appeared?
Do you think of the trees, the grass, water…
Where did that come from?
Have you ever thought of you?
Where did you come from?
Where did the first people come from?
Did they just appear?
No they came from God.

AJ Paladino, Grade 6
Whitinsville Christian School, MA

Ice Cream

Ice cream has such a nice taste.
I've never seen it go to waste.

It makes things seem so fun,
Unless it melts in the sun.

Ice cream can be soothing after a race.
Because of the coolness on your face.

Ice cream is great, but it can make you hyper.
You might run around like an angry viper.

When you think all is good then comes brain freeze.
And this could make monkeys fall out of trees.

I love how ice cream feels so cold.
Sell it anywhere; I'm sure it'll be sold.

Eddie Bates, Grade 6
Captain Nathan Hale Middle School, CT

The Art Room

You paint in it
You draw in it
You do whatever you want in it.

You think in it,
You work in it
You even build your world in it

You play in it
You build in it
You can even find a friend in it.

And even when you don't have art
You always have it in your heart

Max Messier, Grade 6
Fuller Middle School, MA

Earth

Orbiting
spinning slowly
third planet from the sun
the only known planet with life
alone

Jackie Burke, Grade 5
Marblehead Community Charter Public School, MA

Blue

Blue is a full clear sky
Blue is the little pond full of goldfish
Blue is lake glittering in the sun
Blue is a river with motorboats gliding over its surface
Blue is a bay with salt flying all over its beaches
Blue is an ocean with waves that crash over its shores

Carter Ware, Grade 4
C Hunter Ritchie Elementary School, VA

Bubbles

Bubbles
Fun and clear,
Floating, touching, popping,
A kid's favorite toy,
Sphere.
Séamus Woods, Grade 4
Riderwood Elementary School, MD

Silver Pocket Watch

The moon is silver
Like a giant pocket watch
Soft glimmering light
Giving shreds to everyone
Just at its peak it goes dark
Sally Rose Zuckert, Grade 5
St Luke's School, CT

Gregor

Brave, warrior, funny, protective
Who fears the death of boots
Who needs to protect the Underland
Who gives lots of love
Who believes in abnormally sized bugs
Gregor
Briana Cedergren, Grade 6
Chalk Hill School, CT

My Ocean Trip

The ocean slowly whips past me,
As I float along,
Being perfectly still,
With my head leaned back,
Saltwater surrounding me,
The ocean just to me,
As the waves crash against the shore,
— Reflect —
As the waves crash against the shore,
The ocean just to me,
Saltwater surrounding me,
With my head leaned back,
Being perfectly still,
As I float along,
The ocean slowly whips past me!
Perri Mirabile, Grade 5
Hindley Elementary School, CT

Thoughts

Do not restrict your thoughts,
For when you do,
Your learning ends.
Think openly about others,
When you let your mind free,
Who knows?
Only you…
Jacob Manvell, Grade 4
Salem Elementary School, VA

Spring

Beautiful flowers are growing,
Colorful butterflies are flowing,
Birds make a beautiful sound,
No more snow is found.
Rivers run fast,
The sun comes out at last,
Trees grow tall,
No more leaves fall,
Dandelion fluff blows,
We hold roses up to our nose,
Bushes turn green,
We change thick glass to screen,
    Say hello to Spring!
Katherine Welsch-Lehmann, Grade 4
Weston Intermediate School, CT

How to Sled

Look up the hill,
Watch,
Climb the hill,
Slide down,
Turn,
Tumble,
Twist,
Tackle,
Repeat.
Will Tentindo, Grade 6
Village School, MA

Road Trip

Spring Break has started
It's off to the beach
Down in South Carolina
Good times within reach

Swimming in the pool
Playing football on the beach,
Water gun fights with family
Hear my female cousins screech!

Spring Break has ended,
Say good-bye to the beach,
Back to Virginia
Where teachers will teach.
Rafe Sanders, Grade 5
Mary Walter Elementary School, VA

Butterflies

Butterflies
they flitter, flip, and fly
they tickle your nose
they're like small birds in the sky
when they fly it really shows
the true colors that they hold.
Amanda Balicki, Grade 5
Litwin Elementary School, MA

What Is the Legion?

What is the legion?
defenders of planets,
helpers of helpless,
guardians of worlds,
warriors in battle,
nightmares of evil,
victorious heroes,
a vicious army,
a first class ticket to excitement,
a world of strategy,
powerful heroes,
This is the *Legion of Superheroes!*
Cammy Kimball, Grade 5
Jane Ryan School, CT

Nature Walk

Today I took a nature walk,
The trees were tall and bare.
Without all their exquisite leaves,
The twigs looked like wild hair.

The squirrels were fast and frisky,
They jumped to a great height.
Unfortunately the food they sought,
Was mostly out of sight.

The cardinals wore their coats of red,
They looked just like the British.
The robins came in twos and threes,
And seemed to be so skittish.

The snow plows have been put to rest,
Their winter job is done.
The children now come out to play,
And springtime has begun!
Jeffrey Kurzman, Grade 5
Davenport Ridge School, CT

Words

Majestic creatures on a page,
With voices,
That tell a story
Whispering and screaming,

They give a key for a reader
to unlock,
The Story
Cassie Cohen, Grade 4
King's Highway Elementary School, CT

Winter Snow

Winter snow unique
Blanket of woven crystals
Soft but chilling — brrrr!
Marin Langlieb, Grade 4
Jacksonville Elementary School, MD

There's a Monster Under My Bed!!!

There's something strange beneath my bed,
It wiggles, it jumps, it bobs its head.
It eats my clothes and chews my toys too,
I'd lock your doors before it comes after you!!!
It has a melon-shaped head and drools like crazy…
You could make a fountain out of it if your weren't so lazy!!!
I sneaked and peeked under my bed…
But all I see are its bright yellow eyes
And its melon-shaped head.
I made a plan to get it out…
I tried to catch it but it bit me "ouch!"
I turned on the lights to see what it was,
It was my dog Max and I said, "Oh Max, I love you so much!"

Kendra Lee Graham, Grade 6
Edmond P Talbot Middle School, MA

What Is School?

What is school?
A different place where
learning stares you in the face,
a place of writing
reading and books,
a place of happy
cheerful looks.
A place of friendship
play and fun,
though these feelings
don't apply to everyone,
for some it's a place of boredom and heat,
though for me it is
a wonderful treat.
So what is school?
A different place
where learning stares you in the face.

Anna Nesgos, Grade 5
C C Burr Elementary School, MA

A Day in the Forest

The forest is beautiful, peaceful and clean,
It is the most wonderful sight I have ever seen.
The trees all bend in the wind,
And welcome me as I come in.
The birds sing overhead,
Such a lovely song, it could put me to bed.
The air there is so clean and new,
This is a sight, only taken by a few.
It smells so nice, covered with mist,
It leaves the air clear and crisp.
A stroll through the forest is quite a ball,
It is a nice calm place where you get away from it all.
To be among the animals without a care,
Is quite a time, like going to a fair.
After a day in the forest, where worries lack,
You may never want to go back.

Kate Greenberg, Grade 5
Davenport Ridge School, CT

October

I watch the leaves fall to the ground,
Down, down without a sound.
Brown, orange, yellow, red,
These are the colors that run through my head.
Finally it's Halloween,
One of my friends is dressed as a queen.
Some kids go from door to door,
Dressed as goblins, ghouls and more.
Lollipops, chocolate bars and candy corn,
I hear the wrappers being torn.
The month of October is almost done
By tomorrow November will have begun.

Olivia Holverson, Grade 4
Forest Avenue Elementary School, MA

Thanksgiving

Thanksgiving
I can see people fight over the leg part of the turkey.
I can smell sweet relish ready to be in my mouth.
I can hear spoons picking up delicious foods.
I can taste the smooth gravy lurking around my mouth.
I can touch silverware.
Thanksgiving

Chiaki Santiago, Grade 5
Jane Ryan School, CT

Vending Machine

Shoving in a dollar,
the machine won't accept it.
Finally it takes it.
You type in what you want,
only finding you don't have enough money.
Minutes ticking away,
you decide to ask someone for spare change.
Going from table to table:
"Anything?"
"No!"
"Anything?"
"No!"
Finally a generous person
gives you fifty cents.
You rush over to the Vending Machine,
only to find it's closed!

Matt Benjamin, Grade 6
Fuller Middle School, MA

Snails and Bunny

Snails
Slow, small
Moving, sleeping, sliming
Goo, slime, fur, fuzz
Running, hiding, spying
Fast, quick
Bunny

Jack Larson, Grade 4
C Hunter Ritchie Elementary School, VA

It's Time

It's time somebody told her
she's beautiful
inside and out
she doesn't need that make up
to be very gorgeous
It's time somebody told her
that she's good at everything she does
she shouldn't hide her talents
in that stuffed-up house
It's time somebody told her
she's smart in every subject
she studies
in class
It's time somebody held her
so close
and dear to their heart
It's time somebody loved her
no one ever has
Now, it's time

Mackenzie Satalino, Grade 6
Two Rivers Magnet Middle School, CT

I Tripped Off a Cloud

Slowly rising
Creeping, crawling
Towards the top
Sitting, waiting
In the red roller coaster car
The wheels are
Clicking
Clacking
Moving up
Closer, closer to the
Sky
Near enough to
Touch a cloud
Arms reach
Body plunges

Falling, falling
From the sky
The track is blurred
As we zoom along
Leaving me feeling
Like I just tripped off a cloud

Caroline Waldo, Grade 6
Scotts Ridge Middle School, CT

Tree

Giant
Tall, green
Staring, looking, growing
Strong trunk with branches
Great tree

Sian Lum, Grade 4
Grace Miller Elementary School, VA

Math

Subtraction, addition, multiplication, division.
All these things are very easy; hey, this is easy peasy lemon squeezy.
First there is fractions even pi, mathematic terms like 5+5.
Now anyone can just do math; split in two makes a half.

Simplify, then multiply, and then your answer won't be too high.
Using a formula to get your sum, will save you time over doing 21 times 31.
Dividing isn't so hard; it's just like multiplying backward.
Finally your sum shall come, then you will be number one.

Emily Failla, Grade 6
Scotts Ridge Middle School, CT

Maggie

You are the red in the heart
The light in the night
A tiger caring for her child

You are packed with stories like a book
The scientist who always studies
The A+ on a test

You are the defense for offense, always a team player
The safe hero in every cartoon
A big, strong person; someone I depend on

You are an "on" and "off" storm
You can be either strict or very nice
A dark, scary night or a bright morning

You are a fast Ferrari
Always quick to follow through with things you do
The person who drinks too much soda and gets hyper

You are the magazine that everyone loves
The popular animal at the zoo
The nice, loyal friend that everyone wants

You are the board game on a rainy day
The story that can be read a thousand times and never get boring
The ace on Black Jack

Doug Goldstone, Grade 5
St Luke's School, CT

My Maple Tree

My maple tree stands strong and tall.
Her leaves turn bright orange and reds in the fall.
It's a sight to see as her helicopter seeds fall from the tree.
Her maple syrup sweetens my food.
Her maple candy brightens my mood.
Her branches hold houses where birds build their nests,
And in the spring when the chicks hatch, it's where they can rest.
Her canopy of leaves is an umbrella to all living creatures.
I have come to adore her magnificent features.
She is my Great Maple Tree!

Kristen Delzell, Grade 5
Jack Jackter Intermediate School, CT

Philly

There once was a man named Philly.
Who dreamed he was married to Jilly.
He woke in the night
with a terrible fright
to see he was married to Millie.

Maria Valenzuela, Grade 5
Charlotte A Dunning Elementary School, MA

Dogs

A dog is a heavenly creature,
Kissing and greeting your wonderful teacher.
A dog is a kissing machine,
They can make your face really clean.
A dog is a secret keeper, and won't say a word,
They're so quiet they won't say it to a bird.
A dog is your cutie pie,
Sometimes they can be shy.
A dog is your guard,
They can run around in your yard.
A dog can take hugs,
They are your cuddle bugs.
A dog is your friend,
Your friendship will never end.

Marissa Machado, Grade 4
Freetown Elementary School, MA

Fantastic Fall

Fall is fantastic!
It's the smell of crisp, autumn air.
The maple leaves, crackling, rose red.
The whistling wind is soft to the touch,
while bay brown chipmunks hide in a bunch.
The colorful leaves are blowing all around
like balloons drifting into the sky.
Goldenrod flowers awake from a long night's sleep.
The branches without their leaves are
like cake without icing, totally bare.
The spiky prickers are painful to the touch.
The juicy berries are as red as Santa's rosy cheeks.
The sight of the crumbling rock wall and humongous oak trees
is stupendous with a blanket of frost covering them.
And this is why fall is fantastic!

Linda McAuley, Grade 6
Madison Middle School, CT

Silent Wings

Flying gracefully and soundlessly above the world
The painting of nature seen but not heard
Skimming black marble water with silver tipped wings
So simple but still memories they bring
Silhouetted against pink skies at dawn
All beautiful with grace like a fawn
In the morning they will fly
Canadian geese in the sky

Meghan Dougherty, Grade 5
Booth Hill School, CT

My Sister

My sister is sweet and mean.
My sister is annoying and fun.
My sister is every sister put together
     nice ones, mean ones,
And sometimes in between ones.
My sister is everything I would of wished for
     and everything I wouldn't have wished for.
I love my sister…
SOMETIMES!!!

Sophia Francolini, Grade 5
Forest Avenue Elementary School, MA

Spring's Garden

Rising seas of grass all around
Red-bellied robins cover the ground
Cotton balls hug the silky azure sky
Making way for a rainbow pathway passing by
Sensational scents are sent into my nose
From daffodils, geraniums, and a blushing rose
Clinging to grass are drops of dew
Bees buzz in a garden of hue
Don't you love spring?
I know I do!

Caroline Forster, Grade 5
Booth Hill School, CT

Randy Moss

The wide receiver Randy Moss
Who thinks he is the boss
When he is running he looks like he is in cruise control
And the undefeated season went down the toilet bowl

Dylan Litvinchyk, Grade 6
Captain Nathan Hale Middle School, CT

My Verboten Vacation

During the summer we took a vacation
But, sadly it was not across the nation
To West Virginia was our trip
It was as boring as a paper clip

It was a very long car ride
And I wished so much to go outside
We went to a nasty looking hotel
And I realized there was a horrid smell

Very dirty was the room
I thought it would bring me to my eternal doom
Later on I ate food so cheesy
And it left me feeling queasy

During that night I could not sleep
And this memory I try not to keep
Finally to the beach was a new sensation
Which ended my lousy vacation

Caleb Gross, Grade 6
Immaculate Heart of Mary School, MD

I Know That Spring Is Here

When the flowers bloom,
When the wind is soft,
When gone is the thought of doom,
And the grass isn't rough,
I know that spring is here.

When the air is smooth,
When the sun is out,
When everything is nice and soothed,
And beautiful things begin to sprout,
I know that spring is here.

When I go out to play,
When I am happier than normal,
When I have not a lot to say,
And people aren't all formal,
I know that spring is here.

When you smile at me,
I know that spring is here.

Kimberly Cassidy, Grade 5
Lincoln Street School, MA

Softball

Flying, gliding through
the air swing that
bat then drop it quick!
You better run
Here comes the short-stop
with the ball:
1st base, 2nd, 3rd and
Home Run!

Kelly Majerowicz, Grade 5
St Joseph School-Fullerton, MD

Hamburger

Juicy, flat, fat
Reminds me of pat
Fun on a bun
Yummy yum yum
Tender
Pure as gold
Hits my senses really bold
Always waiting never cold
I hold mine in a choke hold
Better than a banana split
I will never forget it
I'll dig in a bottomless pit
But I'll need a mess kit
And a helmet
But I'll not be separate
Hamburgers are my perfect fit
I ate mine lickety split
What it's gone.

Robbie Clarke, Grade 6
Captain Nathan Hale Middle School, CT

Horses

H uge and happy
O utside jumping fences
R unning wild and free
S trong and speedy
E njoy grazing in the sun
S oft tickly muzzles

Mariah Frost, Grade 4
Leicester Memorial School, MA

Cleats

Chunks of dirt from many fields
Trapped underneath my cleats
All from victorious wins
Never depressing defeats

Dirt isn't all they fill
They're also full of recollections
Like scoring my first goal
Or running in the wrong directions

Since I only use them for two seasons
They get locked up far, far away
Sad, lonely and cold like prisoners
And wait until April before they play

Ani Soultanian, Grade 6
E W Thurston Middle School, MA

Sami

Sami
Kind, caring, sweet, friendly
Who loves her friends
Who fears snakes
Who needs her family
Who gives everything
Who believes good things take time

Sami Sederquest, Grade 6
Chalk Hill School, CT

Inside This

I sway back and forth
Back and forth
I am cold when
all my leaves fall down
The flowers are wilting

The sky is dark
But here comes spring
I am warm
the snow is gone

I am happy again
I have my leaves
All bright and green.
I like being a tree!

Blair Bonifield, Grade 5
Newton-Lee Elementary School, VA

Money

Money —
kids need it,
men crave it,
women want it,
everybody requires it.
It is just a piece of paper.
Every piece of money
has a president's
face on it.
What will they buy with crisp,
cool, papery money.
Money is as flat as a
pancake.
Some people have millions.
You can call them millionaires.
They collect money
to spend,
for its crinkling goodness,
and for its
glory.
Money!

Jimmy Buck, Grade 4
Hawley Elementary School, CT

Lacrosse

As I get out of the car,
I bolt to the field,
So I am not too late.

I hear the crushing of cleats,
And the clashing of sticks.

The college crowd in the stands,
Chant a cheer,
As the ball bolts stick to stick.

Afterwards, the team walks in tandem,
Their dreams have been realized
On this championship field!

Anne Smith, Grade 6
Trinity School, MD

Cats

Cats playing with string
What a tangled mess.

Cats catching mice
To keep them out of my room.

Cats chasing birds
Feathers flying through the air.

Cats love to sleep on the bed
But never in the water.

Catherine Beatty, Grade 4
Freetown Elementary School, MA

The Race Horse

I remember a horse who won races and more,
Never losing or letting down fans galore
Then one day,
He lost.

That horse, he lost, because he fell,
But he got right back up so no one could tell
That his heart hurt.

He loved racing, entering those gates.
So he was sad, but he knew…Retirement waits.

He got sent to a pasture because of his knee
But he loved it, you see.
Because for him, the race was over.
Life would continue amidst the clover.

And he would heal.

Larkin Meehan, Grade 6
West Woods Upper Elementary School, CT

Summer

Summer is as welcome as a flower in a field of weeds,
With children laughing,
Birds singing, and
Hot dogs and hamburgers sizzling
The ice cream tastes sweet
After a run through the summer sun,
Swimming through the salty ocean,
Or just kicking back and relaxing.
The waves are crashing on the beach
While swimmers dash through the waves,
Or just an under the sun's rays.
At the end of the day
All I wish is it could go on forever,
I play for the last couple minutes,
Left in the day.
In the last moments of sunlight,
The sunset comes out to play,
Red, purple, orange, and green,
Complete the day.
The flowers have bloomed
And seven weeks of summer still remain.

Lauren Webb, Grade 6
Trinity School, MD

Grandma's House

Grandma's house is the best place to go
Great Italian food and fried dough
It's the best place to be on a cold winter day
For some soup and a great place to stay
It's a great place to be if you need some love
And you will also get a great big hug
Grandma's house is the best

Olivia Stephenson, Grade 5
St Mary's Primary School, MA

Mystery Man

The mystery man is seen around town,
Without a smile, or even a frown

It seems as though he has nothing at all,
Except some clothes, and maybe a shawl

He walks alone all day and all night,
He shows no emotion, not even in fright

He's the mystery man always in sight,
He's the mystery man, what is his plight?

Brian Yoffe, Grade 4
Memorial-Spaulding Elementary School, MA

Balloons

Balloons are red, balloons are blue
They fly away, and I hope you do,
On a cloud to heave, it's true,
You float away like the ocean,
Smoothly coming to you,
You are floating so sweet in the sky,
When you fly away you become sweet as pie

Starr Woods, Grade 4
Crestwood Elementary School, VA

Strong and Independent

When you get out of a bad relationship
you don't think you can move on,
Then other times you just move too fast
just to lose the pain.
Then it will just happen again,
so things won't be the same.
So don't cry my young child,
he might think you're weak,
But honey you're not!
There will be a much stronger man for you tomorrow,
But be patient don't fall up in sorrow.
We are independent and
we don't need a stuck up-man to care for our every need.

Tamber Pennick, Grade 6
Monelison Middle School, VA

Passion of Love

Black like the wind, white like the snow
all I see is my passion of love,
like a nice summer Sunday day,
all I do is listen and pray for my good, my bad
and don't forget the last one sad,
I also pray for the poor and the rich
but I only wish for one kid,
I would treat him like treasure,
I would treat my wife like diamonds,
all I know is that I'm a new kid at St. Paul
but they still treat me like diamonds and rubies.

Isaiah Shaw, Grade 6
St Paul School, CT

Monkeys

Monkeys have lots of energy they keep
In their little monkey feet
Monkeys jump up and down
They like to play around
Monkeys have a lot of fun
In the very warm, hot sun
Monkeys come out in the day
And try to act in all the plays

Breanna Carpenter, Grade 4
Waller Mill Fine Arts Magnet School, VA

My Big Wish

I wish I were one million eagles
Soaring in the sky
Symbolizing hope and freedom
Conquering all that threaten
Overpowering being endangered
Defeating all that lies ahead
Showing, that all things
Big and small can overcome the
Biggest threat of them all
Extinction

Jenna Patterson, Grade 6
Scotts Ridge Middle School, CT

Two Celestial Bodies

Sun
bright, orange
shining, rising, falling
daytime, sky, nighttime, shadowed
magical, white
Moon

Bethany Marion, Grade 6
Captain Nathan Hale Middle School, CT

Snowplowing

Truck, plow, snow
Plow, snow, sand
Snow, sand, town
Sand, town, DOT
Town, DOT, plow road
DOT, plow road, shovel
Plow road, shovel, tractor
Shovel, tractor, strobe

Joseph Gulia, Grade 6
Chalk Hill School, CT

Winter

W aves of snow
I n fields
N o birds whistle
T eeming with snow
E nter that freezing season
R ight to left people shoveling

Joseph Alindogan, Grade 6
Magnolia Elementary School, MD

Books Are Adventures

Books are adventures that you can be.
Lots of fun.
Good to read,
See new places.
Make new friends.
Sometimes the story never ends…
Once I went into a castle.
Ran from monsters, ghouls, and beasts.
Went to a world of opposites,
Where north was south and west was east.
Traveled through a deep, dark ocean.
Solved a mystery (with help, of course).
Found a magic carpet, then
Rode upon a wild horse.
Saw some cats roam through a forest.
Watched Tom Sawyer paint a fence. Went to Egypt and saw King Tut.
Saw the campers pack their tents…

The ending of a book is the best.
The magic happens there…
So, now let's read another book!
New adventure everywhere!

Noelle Acaso, Grade 5
St Joseph School-Fullerton, MD

Do You Remember

Do you remember, back long time ago
When we stepped through the window, which caused us to grow
Made us who we are, who we are now
It helped us to grow, independent and strong

A window of new beginnings, a doorway to truth
Through all of the hardships, thinking win or lose
Do you remember that journey, that voyage, that quest
That taught us to always do our best

I remember that trip to understanding, I remember it quite well
I also believe, that up to old age, I will remember this journey, I'll remember and tell

Shebati Sengupta, Grade 5
Lincoln Street School, MA

My Cat

My cat's name is Delilah,
She is as cool as can be,
She is so soft
When she rubs against me.
My cat Delilah
She was made for me,
No matter what
She cannot be beat.
My cat Delilah
She is so cool,
I hope in the summer
She does not jump in my pool.

Kathie Williams, Grade 6
Francis Scott Key Elementary/Middle Technology Magnet School, MD

God

God, the Son, died on the cross.
God, the Father, sent his Son to die on the cross.
The Son arose from the dead.
Jesus taught the people about God.
The disciples taught about Jesus, too.
Most of all, Jesus loves us.

Leyla Herrarte, Grade 4
Agape Christian Academy, VA

Night's Transition into Day

The sun rises and warms the earth from the night before
The flowers open and absorb the bright sun
The robins soar
As the sun rises it greets everyone
In the morning everything seems lighter
The day starts anew
The calls of owls in the night seem slighter
The night before the bats flew
When the sun rose valiantly
It scared all the animals of the night away
The transition between them is made subtly
Then the animals of the day came out to play
To see the most beautiful transition on Earth
You must stay up extremely late
It is the most beautiful scene since the day of this planet's birth
This transition is the most exquisite scene to date
When night arrives
The animals of the day scurry away
The blackness thrives
And brings the day to demise

Hunter Warburton, Grade 6
Grace Episcopal Day School, MD

Pickles the Hyper-Active Big Eyed Fish

I saw him swimming
that day with such power and force
that if he didn't turn
he would have smashed into the wall

Every day he would fly under the water
to his underwater palace
where he would swim
around and around again
after getting dizzy from going around
he would dive next to his swan
covered in bright green moss

I could never forget feeding
Those orange flakes of fish food
That he loved,
But those days are over
ever since that hyper-active big eyed fish
died
but, he will always be in my memory

Sean Rogers, Grade 6
Swampscott Middle School, MA

Magma

The precarious magma swirls
cutting through the underbrush
eradicating thousands of years of
nature's hard work
as the magma slowly creeps into the
quiet, unsuspecting village
death alights in peaceful souls
the flowing death liquid
seeps towards its victims
ready to unleash a malicious attack

Jason Ashton, Grade 5
West Woods Upper Elementary School, CT

The Substitute

My Science teacher has the flu
Therefore we have a substitute
An old man who seems to be blind
Or maybe he just doesn't mind
That Julie's passing notes to Toolie
And that Amanda and Miranda are texting
Or that my neighbor Krissy is drawing
Or that Missy is yawning.

I sit there in the middle of it all
Pondering about the mall
I look at the substitute
Who's oblivious to the class
And he closes his eyes and looks like he's snoozing.

R-I-N-G

As people fly out of the room
He snaps awake and says,
"That's all for today."

Jordan Pinsky, Grade 6
Fuller Middle School, MA

The Ocean

The ocean breeze,
Hits me like a soft hand stroking my cheek,
The faint salty smell filling the air around me

I turn toward the sun,
A carpet of light rolls across the ocean,
Hiding the darkness from the world around me

As I turn around,
My footsteps have been claimed by the sea,
Along with the sand castles the other kids had made

As I leave the beach,
I take one last look,
To see the tip of the sun vanish beneath the waves,
Leaving the world in the silent darkness.

Miranda Gish, Grade 6
International School of Boston, MA

School

I think school is important. It is educational. Even though I don't always like it. I think it is important for a good education. One thing I don't like is getting up so early. Other than that I kind of like school. I like how the teachers can be there to help you. School would be a lot different if the teachers could not help you. If teachers couldn't help you school would be terrible. I would try as much as I could to stay home if school was like that. Teachers are like giant talking books. Teachers are also like talking schools but they are helpful talking schools!

Brittnea Sprankle, Grade 6
E Russell Hicks School, MD

The Little Lady in Purple

The little lady in purple lives in my garden. I tend to her every need and in return she stands there and makes my garden lovely. Her purple petals pop out at me, her yellow petals are like confetti and her light green petals are ready to shine. She looks so fair and elegant. The little lady in purple.

Sarah MacKnight, Grade 5
St Mary's Primary School, MA

Afraid of the Cornstalk Watcher

He has hay filled up to his chin, and he doesn't have a name
The black birds caw at him mad as a hatter
He guards the cornstalks all day long, like a security guard watches the doors at the White House
The black fluffy feathered birds fear the cornstalk watcher

The cornstalks sway in the wind, just how an ice skater sways back and forth on the ice
The crisp, crunchy leaves in clusters of three are stuck in between the cornstalks
The maroon leaves are scooped up with a rippled rake so none are left behind

The cutter comes down the hill, so they can pack up the sweet butter corn and send it off to market
First the farmer has to take down the corn stalk watcher
Now the birds sing a sweet song as sweet as candy but…
Now the cutter rumbles down the hill like a stomach when it grows hungry
The bird's sugary sweet song twists into a caw

So, did you guess who I am…?
I'm a scarecrow!

Maggie Donlon, Grade 6
Madison Middle School, CT

Months

The wind will blow the softly fallen flakes of snow,
February 2nd is Groundhog's Day, will it be an early spring or a winter to stay?

The first signs of spring are in the air, the days are warmer and the skies are fair,
Flowers are blooming and the grass is green, what could be lovelier than this scene?

The end of the year is near, many children will not shed a tear,
This is time for children to play because the days and nights of summer are on the way.

The 4th of July is the day to celebrate because the soldiers have great faith,
The summer is quickly coming to the end, I can see the teacher right around the bend.

The new year of school has begun, I can no longer have summer fun,
October 31 is Halloween, many haunted creatures can be seen.

The holidays are here, it is time for fun and cheer,
Christmas is done and now the New Year has begun.

Peter Kvietkauskas, Grade 5
Hebron Elementary School, CT

The 1st Summer Day
Come peace, come happiness,
Bring on the day,
In with the light, and leave with the night,
Summer is here to stay!
Meagan Mitchell and Rachel Lampson, Grade 6
Memorial School, MA

Ten Little Mars Men
Ten little Mars men got a fine;
One went to jail; then there were nine.
Nine little Mars men stayed up late;
One forgot to sleep; then there were eight.
Eight little Mars men went to heaven;
One stayed up there; then there were seven.
Seven little Mars men tried some magic tricks;
One disappeared; then there were six.
Six little Mars men went into a hive;
One got his head stuck; then there were five.
Five little Mars men wanted more;
One got stung; then there were four.
Four little Mars men climbed up a tree;
One fell off; then there were three.
Three little Mars men said the word "moo;"
One could not stop laughing; then there were two.
Two little Mars men went to the sun;
One got fried; then there was one.
One little Mars man went looking for some fun;
He never came back; then there were none.
Gavin Metsack, Grade 5
Ashford School, CT

Saphira
S nake like neck and tail
A sapphire like design to her scales
P owerful, ferocious talons tear and rip
H er huge wings let her glide smoothly
I n times of need she rescues people in danger
R aging fire explodes from her mouth
A fine and heroic young dragon
KayLee Besse, Grade 4
Leicester Memorial School, MA

Twilight
With the stars above my head,
Tell me to rest in bed.

The sun wakes me up every day,
Its smile is so very gay.

And at dusk the moon is bright,
Like a firefly taking flight.

Between night and daylight,
So that is called the very twilight.
Emma Beatty, Grade 5
Foxborough Regional Charter School, MA

Wind
Touching the tree leaves
Twirling and swirling around
Such a gentle wind
Jennilyn Barr, Grade 6
School of International Studies at Meadowbrook, VA

Dots
Down the rain falls
But this isn't rain at all

They were circles oh so round
And the balls bounced on the ground

There were polka dots
Many, I mean lots

Will this madness ever end?
Will it ever descend?

Look animals call
Right where the dots fall

Well that's how animals got their spots
That's how clothes got polka dots!
Vanessa Nguyen, Grade 5
Linscott-Rumford Elementary School, MA

The Beach
New Seabury Beach is my favorite place to be.
I love the way the ocean rolls its shells to me.
Sometimes I hear the sand calling my name.
Then I jump out of bed to take my claim.
The pool waves hello, and sings merrily.
With the sand so hot, and the water so cold,
I always feel like gold.
After the pool it's on to the ocean.
Then to the beach where the water is open.
New Seabury Beach is my favorite place to be.
I love the friendship and adventure with friends and family.
Maddie Ross, Grade 5
Soule Road School, MA

Orange Soda Pop
I woke up one morning,
Went downstairs
Craving a can of orange soda pop.
But I failed to notice my black cat pass by,
And when it rubbed against my leg
I let out a cry.
Down, down,
It went cascading through the air.
I think you know what happened next.
My cat isn't black anymore…
Well, you get the picture.
James Teeling, Grade 5
Occohannock Elementary School, VA

Grr! Grr! Grr!
Growling and growling
Making loud noises
GRR! GRR! GRR!
The panda was as strong as an ox
He was so scary
His teeth were as sharp as a tack
Let's go back! Let's go back!
That panda is as crazy as a lion
Not as playful as a kitten
I'm never coming back again
Samantha Goodwin, Grade 4
Freetown Elementary School, MA

Evil March Winds
Every time I go outside
I really have to hide
Behind a bush or a tree
They're always looking for me.

The evil March winds
They give me evil grins
When they spot me I must hide
Don't go outside!
Lindsay Fucile, Grade 4
Freetown Elementary School, MA

My Black Lab
My Black Lab
She waits in the wind
Waiting to play.
She walks away until
Another day to play.
When she gets to play
She'll love to stay
Alone with you.
Cameron Parmiter, Grade 4
Munger Hill Elementary School, MA

Claireen
There once was a girl named Claireen
she walked around looking mean
she loved to run
and liked to make fun
when she fell and made a big scene.
Kiana Murphy, Grade 6
Monelison Middle School, VA

Running
The breeze against my face
It feels so good
I am like a lion
Chasing its prey
I am the fastest thing around
Until I have to go inside
Robert Lamb, Grade 5
Wakefield Forest Elementary School, VA

Teacher
Teacher
Kind, caring
Helps, listens, friendly
Always cares about us
Mrs. Peck
Kylie Jusseaume, Grade 5
Sacred Heart School, MA

Food Is Fun to Eat
Burgers and fries are fun to eat,
along with pizza, pasta, and chicken feet.
All those foods are fun to eat.
Especially buffalo wings and meat!!!
Kyle Grabowski, Grade 5
Chalk Hill School, CT

Icicles
Icicles melting
Crystals hanging from the eaves
Dripping all day long
Perry Bowers, Grade 6
Our Lady of Mercy School, CT

The Library
The library
Quiet
The library
People reading books
People searching for information

The library
Peaceful
People around to answer your questions
People helping you search for books

The library
Memories
The place that I come to learn
The place that I love
Anna Kennedy, Grade 6
Fuller Middle School, MA

Palmer's Sickness
My brother is sick,
He stays at the hospital,
I feel very sad.

He is infected,
He has Desmoplastic,
It's very scary.

It's like he lives there,
Children's Hospital is good,
He'll get better soon.
Claudelle I. Osias, Grade 5
Sacred Heart School, MA

Ireland
Pretty flowers bloom
Green shamrocks are beautiful
Sparkling nice gold coins
Rodney Dailey, Grade 4
St Gregory Elementary School, MA

Sand
Soft hot beads of sand
Sinking as you walk fast
Sneaking between toes
Gabrielle Kerins, Grade 6
Our Lady of Mercy School, CT

I Don't Want a Bath
I don't want a bath
I haven't done my homework
And we're all out of soap
I can't find my rubber duck
Everyone said the pond water is clean
And when you comb my hair it hurts
You always get the water in my eyes
And there is no bubble bath
I only got dirt on my clothes
There is only food on my hands
All the water is cold
And I took a bath last week
So I'm not taking another
Sean Mula, Grade 6
E W Thurston Middle School, MA

Pumpkin Ted
Once I had a pumpkin named Ted.
He had a vine shaped bed.
I sent him outside
But then he died.
My poor old pumpkin Ted.
Colin Barry, Grade 5
Plainfield Catholic School, CT

Tigers
Tigers
Shocking, perilous
Stalks through jungles
I feel like prey
Alarming
Mitchell Brazier, Grade 4
Trinity Christian School, VA

Reading
I'm stuck in this
sea of words
waiting for the answer to
this unbelievable mystery
except I'm only on chapter 3
Robert Gwinn, Grade 5
Milton L Fuller Elementary School, MA

The British Are Coming

There was a guy named Paul Revere.
He came out one night and said, "the British are here."
When the war began he said, "we must fight."
So he fought all night.
When they were done no one had a tear.
Then they got home and told everyone there is nothing to fear.

Ryan Aylward, Grade 4
Helen H Hansen Elementary School, MA

Summer Begins

Summer is coming quick with a bunch of things to do,
such as, riding a bicycle, hanging out with the family and having
some barbecue.
When school ends, summer begins,
Are you ready to start anew?

Priscilla Lucas, Grade 5
Jacob Hiatt Magnet Elementary School, MA

Advice to a Friend

Dear Friend,
Life is like a hockey game…
Some moments will be hard —
And some will be as easy as passing the puck.
Some moments you will be so close —
Like missing the net by an inch.
But others you'll be off by a mile!
There will be bumps on the ice —
That will make you stumble.
But if that happens…
Come up with a strategy and start again.
Even when moments are tough —
And it seems there is no hope to make a goal
Just get up,
Keep skating,
Be a good sport,
And keep trying your best!
Seek the smooth ice!
Don't ever give up until you win the game!
    Sincerely, Rick Green

Rick Green, Grade 5
Har-Bur Middle School, CT

I Made a Mistake

I went to the pound to get a dog,
I made a mistake…and got a hog.

I went to the mall to get my brother a shirt,
I made a mistake…and got him a skirt.

I went outside to swim in my pool,
I made a mistake…and rode a mule.

I went to my room to call a friend,
I made a mistake…and called The End!!

Jessica DuBois, Grade 4
Freetown Elementary School, MA

A Baseball Game Live

Roar, roar!
Hear the crowd roar!
Here them cheer, cheer for the home team
Hooray, hooray the home team's up to bat!
Awww, awww they cry when their team gets out
Crack, hear the crowd roar, it's another homerun
The home team wins!!
And the crowd goes nuts!!
"It's just another plain loss" grumbles an away fan

Davey Harwood, Grade 6
Summit Montessori School, MA

Spring

When spring comes 'round the corner,
The birds will chirp and sing.
The grass, the sky, the clouds,
The sun will brighten ev'ry thing.
When spring comes 'round the corner,
The butterflies will fly.
When spring comes 'round the corner,
It means that summer is nigh.

Meredith Palmore, Grade 4
C Hunter Ritchie Elementary School, VA

My Dogs

Furry, soft, and oh so cute
Oh my gosh, they're chewing up my boot.

Swoosh, whoosh goes one's tail
Watch out for that pail!

Lick, lick as they lick my face
Come on dogs, let's have a race!

Bark! Bark! goes the dogs
Oh no, don't chase the frogs!

When they go to sleep
I don't hear a peep.

Crash! the dogs wake up
What sleepy pups.

In the cage they go
My dogs with tails that are almost as light as snow.

Abigail Keith, Grade 4
Freetown Elementary School, MA

Birds

Flying, flying in the air
acting like they just don't care,

Listening, listening in the ground
seeing if there's something found.

Chase Del Valle, Grade 5
West Woods Upper Elementary School, CT

Spring Life

S unny
P retty
R oses
I ncredible
N ice
G reat

L ovely
I nnocent nature
F antastic
E xcellent

Angely Gonzalez, Grade 4
Marsh Grammar School, MA

A Twinkle Above Earth

Stars twinkle in the night sky.
They seem to be so high.
A twinkle of light shines very bright.
Put a smile on your face.
Look at the stars pace.
Now you see it.
Now you don't.
If you believe in it, it will show.
If you don't then it won't.

Arjola Tanellari, Grade 6
Irving School, CT

A Friend Is a Sister

My Best Friend,
Has gone away
No longer can I call,
And ask to play.

She lives way down south,
With her mom, dad, and brothers,
But she was always like a sister,
Friends, even our mothers.

We meet in Florida,
A place of the past,
When we go on vacation,
We always have a blast.

I know she'll be back,
But every night,
Even a picture of her,
Gives my heart a delight.

Linnea Thomas, Grade 6
E W Thurston Middle School, MA

The Stars and Moon

Shining oh so bright,
Twinkling in the night,
By sun they are gone.

Shawn Spencer, Grade 4
Riderwood Elementary School, MD

1:00 A.M.

Waking up at 1:00 a.m
There's boom, boom, and flash, flash, there's titter tatter, titter tatter,
boom, boom, flash, flash hiding under your covers,
covering your ears, praying for it to stop,
boom, boom, flash, flash, titter tatter, titter tatter, boom, boom, flash, flash
Then comes a soft boom, and a little flash,
Then I don't hear much, except I hear little birds singing lightly, tweet tweet
There's soft booms now and then, boom…boom…boom…flash…flash
And then I close my eyes and think…think about happy times.
And as soon as I get relaxed, I fall asleep
all is quiet…quiet…quiet
I breathe heavily (huuh)
rain drops falling from the trees, splash, splash, splash
but I don't hear it, because I'm asleep
all is peaceful, little birds tweet tweeting lightly.
Tweet, tweet, splash, splash
All is peaceful, quiet, quiet, quiet
tweet…tweet…tweeeet
the rain is peaceful; all is just so silent
Tweet, tweet, tweet.

Karin Plante, Grade 4
Miscoe Hill Elementary School, MA

The Lake

At the murky lake with black loons and small houses,
The water splashes like it's being slapped by the fin of a whale, with waves
and faint calls by the black and white water birds.
As I dive in the slimy depths,
the taste of bitter, salty water goes in my mouth and nose.
And when I come up there is no wind.
It is as if the air is lifeless.
When I smell the pine trees' scent anywhere,
it reminds me of this special place.

Logan VanDeurse, Grade 5
Foxborough Regional Charter School, MA

A Day in the Life of a Puppy

The salty, crunchy kibble taste, still drifts around in my mouth,
As I look up into the bright blue sky, I see a hamburger shaped cloud,
And I can almost taste the sweet ketchup
A wondrous daydream, suddenly floats into my mind,
Of many, many human foods.
My mind snaps back to the hamburger cloud.
Oh, I long to reach up to get it,
But of course…I can't
I sniff the air, it's fresh and clean.
Almost like my brand new blanket,
Then I spot my master's roses, my master's bright red, roses.
Planted in the soft, chocolate, brown dirt
And a tempting feeling builds up inside me.
A tingling sensation, goes through my small and fragile body,
The time suddenly sped away I don't know how it happened!
But suddenly I see, my masters beloved flowers,
Ripped out of the ground in front of me.

Meghan Shipp, Grade 6
Litchfield Intermediate School, CT

Shy Blossom

Spring is here and it is day,
Why don't you come out and play

Night has fallen and I'm asleep
In my bed across the street

Dawn has come, now wake up
Time to show the world's beauty
Through us

Day is here and I am bored,
Come out and play
Do not snore

But the shy blossom
Was not there
He was in the tummy of
A sly opossum

Shannon Baird, Grade 4
C Hunter Ritchie Elementary School, VA

Dear Cat

Dear Cat
I know when you are happy
Because you purr and shed your fur.
I know when you are sad,
Because you cry every single minute.
I know when you are angry,
When you bite and scratch people.
I know when you are happy again
Because you stop biting and start to purr again.

Brendan Dilbarian, Grade 4
Potter Road Elementary School, MA

Summer

The bees coming out of their hives
The burgers on the grill ready to be eaten
The joyful sounds of kids playing
Corn on the cob my mother makes
I have friends always nearby
I always have friends…
Summer

Jordan Carroccia, Grade 5
Jane Ryan School, CT

Who Am I?

I am a sweet apple that is healthy
I am a white Taj Mahal that shines brightly
I am an answer book that studies for the test
I am like a small tree that grows every day
I am a reminder calendar that remembers birthdays of family
I am like a cute puppy that likes to play
I am like a beach umbrella that loves summer
I am a peaceful ocean that is always silent

Shitalben Patel, Grade 6
Fuller Middle School, MA

Bald Eagle

Soaring white and black
Bird of our independence
Show our liberty

Joshua Varghese, Grade 5
Charlotte A Dunning Elementary School, MA

Views

In the summer
I always swim.
Sometimes I look up
at the swans
soaring right in the wind.
And sometimes
I just look up
and watch the clouds,
oceans of cotton waves.
I see thousands of views.

Daniel Cetlin, Grade 4
South Area Solomon Schechter Day School, MA

Game Winner

The crowd howls happily
as a shooter takes his chances.
Numbers flash furiously as time runs down
while the shooter tries
to concentrate
through thumping bleachers.

His legs wearily wobble,
when he arithmetically aims.

Silence

strikes the crowd
as the ball arches through the air.

Swoop!

and swishes the net
before the silence snaps.
Another win is in the books
for the hero of the day

Matthew Martyn, Grade 6
Trinity School, MD

Who Am I?

I am a counselor helping someone and giving advice
I am like a bright star that shines joyful all the time
I am a mall that shops all the time to the best stores
I am hot as the sun that glows every morning
I am a basketball moving every place and having fun
I am a Boricua that is proud and amused
I am Puerto Rican, happy because
they are people that cook well like I will some day

Arlene Cruz Famania, Grade 6
Fuller Middle School, MA

Dear Spring

Dear Spring,
You are a new
Person in town…

The birds are your toys
Soaring in the sky

When you are angry,
You stomp around
Thunder is heard everywhere
Lightning is your hateful words

But when you smile
The sun shines
It is beautiful out again

Grumpy old Winter
Packs his bags and
You take his place

You are a new person
In town…

Megan Tynan, Grade 6
Chalk Hill School, CT

Ritual Dragon

Smart, fierce
Has fun, plays, runs
Happy, sensitive
Friendly, hyper
Kid

Zach Nadeau, Grade 4
Bowers School, CT

It's Over

I don't hear what I want to hear
I don't see what I want to see
I don't feel what I want to feel
So why am I here.
You said I made you feel special
You said I was the best thing to happen
So why did you leave.
Will I ever see you again
Will you ever come back
NO! It's over.

Sarah May, Grade 6
Monelison Middle School, VA

An Arctic Fox

An Arctic fox as cute as a kitten
Standing still
Facing the dangers of the Arctic
He is as brave as a sabertooth tiger
Seeing the good and bad sights

Bryce Amaral, Grade 4
Freetown Elementary School, MA

Football

In the huddle
calling the play
getting to the line
with five seconds left
calling an audible at the line
"Hike," calls the QB
he drops back
and launches
the ball downfield.
As it soars through the air,
the receivers are running
as fast as they can.
Then the ball descends down
and then you can see
a receiver catches the ball
for a touchdown
and then,
the crowd goes wild!

William Boyd, Grade 5
St Christopher's School, VA

Monkeys/Bananas

Monkeys
weird, smelly
eating, yelling, screaming
brown, nice, patch, stem
falling, rotting, growing,
yellow, delicious
Bananas

Jacob King, Grade 5
McCleary Elementary School, VA

Butterflies

Butterflies soar through the sky,
Everyone is trying to touch the sky.
Let them soar all through the night,
The butterflies say it's all right.
Now's the time to see them fly,
All night all day.
You don't want to go away.
See the butterflies fly so high,
Maybe next time we'll touch the sky.
Butterflies in the sky.
Watch them soar so so high.

Amber Washburn, Grade 5
Rowayton Elementary School, CT

Summer

S wimming in the pool
U nder a shade tree
M ake a brand new game
M ake a new friend
E at lots of fun food
R ide a fast roller coaster

Dudley Dodoo, Grade 6
Magnolia Elementary School, MD

Wolves

Howls pierce the night
The essence of fear trails them
Gray shapes prowl the woods

Nathan Troutman, Grade 4
Trinity Christian School, VA

What Is Poetry?

Poetry is…
What's happening in your time on Earth
Everything around you
Yourself

Poetry is…
Expressing yourself
Feelings
Senses
Not rhyming

Poetry is…
Rhyming
Feeling good about yourself
Telling people who you are
Describing how you live

Poetry is…
How your life is
What's happening in your time on Earth
Everything around you
Yourself

Mikey Nizzardo, Grade 4
Fawn Hollow Elementary School, CT

Candy

What is your favorite candy you may ask?
Well I like
Skipping Skittles
Jumping jelly beans
Beautiful bubble gum
And
Silly Starbursts
But that's just for breakfast
There's also
Elegant eggs
Twirling Tootsie Rolls
Kick Line Kit-Kat
And
Around the room Air-Heads
Those are just for lunch
Happy Hershey's
Marvelous Mento's
Caring chocolates
And
Lovely Lindt
Those are just for dinner

Julia Walsh, Grade 6
E W Thurston Middle School, MA

My House After School
My long homework
My loud brother
My black pencil lead
Fresh air
My hard wood desk

Timmy Colgan, Grade 4
C Hunter Ritchie Elementary School, VA

The Roaring Dragon
The train is a roaring dragon
All who hear him cover their ears
Has one yellow eye that shines in the dark
All stop before him
And let him pass

He screeches so loud
Throughout the land all will hear
He is a metal dragon
That stands so proud
His breath leaves a cloud of smoke behind

His tale is behind him all the time
As a cat is behind a mouse all the time
He will stop at nothing
Until it's his last days

Nazar Kharyna, Grade 6
Swampscott Middle School, MA

Baseball Field
The fast frantically flailing feet of the fans rush
into the stadium.
Something smells scrumptious at the concession stand.
Batters bat beautiful
base hits, and the balls whistle in the air.
Pitchers throw crazy
curve balls that create curiosity among the fans.
Crowds cheer continuously
as the game drags on.
The players play perfectly with the
help of the crowd's enthusiasm.
As the roar of the stadium dies down,
another game falls into the win column at
Oriole Park.

Richard Garry, Grade 6
Trinity School, MD

Skating
S liding across the ice
K eys to jumping, take off, air time, landing
A cold, exciting sport
T umbling down to the ice, ouch!
I ce skating is my favorite sport
N ew levels, new competitions, new Medals
G old medal winner, hooray!

Kayla DiPilato, Grade 5
Leicester Memorial School, MA

Green Beetle
Green beetle sits still
In the oak tree's green leaves
Watching the gold stars

Casey Griffin, Grade 4
C Hunter Ritchie Elementary School, VA

One
A pack of wolves run together across the moonlit plain
Eyes glistening, haunches taut
Fur standing on end.
The leader, Alpha Male
Snarls at the cowering herd —
and barks,
Let us hunt
with the quiet of the night at our feet.

The minor wolf quivering in the frosty night
dare to stray from his leader's might.
Behold — a flick of golden amber eyes —
And Alpha Male is upon him!
Fangs slashing, battle cry in his throat.
It is over in minutes, as the wolf pack recedes
Kicking up a trail of silver dust.
The Leader baying at the moon.
A limp lifeless form lies still in the snow.
A red carnation on its side.

The end of one story
the beginning of another
and wolf pack is content as one.

Madelyne Xiao, Grade 6
West Frederick Middle School, MD

Rain in the Summertime!
Drip,
Drop,
Drip,
Drop,
There goes the rain in the summertime!
What am I supposed to do when it's raining outside?
I'll put my boots on and splash in the puddles.
That's what I'll do all day long.
I wish I could live outside, so when it rains I can play all day!

Emily Stewart, Grade 4
WB Sweeney School, CT

Old History
Here in Williamsburg there is so much history
Some of it is a mystery
It is here where Patrick Henry gave his speech
The Whigs took Virginia beyond the king's reach
So Williamsburg is full of history
come and help unravel the mystery

Brianna Ciuffo, Grade 4
Mary Walter Elementary School, VA

Giant

There once was a girl
Who grew and grew.
She grew so big
She nearly flew.

Emily Gray, Grade 4
Plainfield Catholic School, CT

Shining Stars

Each little star glows
Every night it shines so bright
They twinkle at night

Jacqueline Choi, Grade 5
Sacred Heart School, MA

Summer

Winter's faded, spring is gone,
Birds sing their songs,
And endless nothing falls from the sky,
Raining from the heavens.

The ocean talks to me,
Taking me away to the land of time.
Where my imagination floats,
Making rainbows in the sky.

Paige Belcastro, Grade 5
Soule Road School, MA

Flowers

Fragrant flowers bloom
Where meadows are clear and new
I can smell beauty

Paul Flanigan, Grade 6
Our Lady of Mercy School, CT

The Game

We were finally in the big game
A score that ended with a tie
Would be a crying shame
A quick basket would be the last try

They passed to me, I'd be the one
I would hit a three point from the zone
I blocked the crowd and saw none
It was as if I was in the gym alone

The shot clock was ticking away
I could feel the sweat on my head
How I wished to save the day
"Shoot!" was all I heard the crowd said

Then time to focus and put up the shot
I could only hope and wish
Did it make it or did it not
The only sound was a loud swish!

Kylen Lane, Grade 6
Immaculate Heart of Mary School, MD

How

How do you cry? How do you laugh?
How do you find exactly one half?
How do you receive? How do you send?
How do you live if the world's about to end?
How do you focus? How do you zone out?
How do you find out what someone's all about?

How come we're short? How come we're tall?
How come we all don't go to the mall?
How come we sit? How come we stand?
How come we don't all walk hand in hand?
How come there's a devil? How come there's a God?
How come very few religions don't seem odd?

How many men volunteer? How many women litter?
How many people walk on this earth that always seem so bitter?
How many insects are untrained? How many animals are left to roam?
How many mammals are looking around searching for a home?
How many fish don't lay eggs? How many fish lost them?
How many fish are looking for their babies now, their one and only gem?

These are things that ponder in my mind now
These are things that I must know: how?

Aliyah Hickman, Grade 6
Francis Scott Key Elementary/Middle Technology Magnet School, MD

Quiet

It's easy to catch quiet in the country.
You have to be as quick as a freight train.
It's incredibly easy to find.
You might find it at a seashore after a mighty wave crashes down on the sand.
You might find it in your garden behind a buzzing bumblebee.
You might find it very, very far away beyond the whistle of the wind.
But when you find it put it in a pocket in your heart because it's a piece of the sun.

Meghan Wood, Grade 5
Jack Jackter Intermediate School, CT

Fifty Stars*

In memory of Sgt. Billy Neil

Fifty stars flutter in the icy morning breeze.
Fifty pure white shapes on blue that represent so much.
The mourners listen with heavy coats and heavy hearts.
Everything is still.
Even the birds don't dare to move.
The only voice is the low one that belongs to the minister.
His voice so soft and low and yet it seems to travel so far.
The world itself seems to be listening and hides the sun behind dark gray clouds.
Eyes brimming with tears, they lay dark red and pure white flowers before him.
Then all goes silent.
The silence seems to go on forever both in the ears and in the heart.
Suddenly, loud bangs sound out sending chills down your spine.
Cracking and banging then all at once they are gone.
And it is over.
And it is as though the flag no longer has fifty stars.

Zachary Shapiro, Grade 4
Farmland Elementary School, MD

Sleepover

All of the girls were there.
   Having more fun than ever.
     As the rest of them sleep.
      I stare out the window.
       Looking at the beauty of the forest
        …wondering what would happen.

Cameron Powers, Grade 5
Francis Asbury Elementary School, VA

The Hunting Wolf

I creep across the moor then strike,
   shadow hides me from moonlight.
I am a wolf,
   my jaws snap quickly to kill the squirrel,
I am a wolf.

I leap across the old trunk on the trail of prey,
I snap the neck then dodge
   those deadly hoofs of a frightened deer
     my pack swarming around.

We all eat well but make not a sound
   for we are the hunters of the night.
We are the wolf.

Cameron Bauserman, Grade 4
Evergreen Montessori School, MD

Blue

Blue, it is all over the world
it's on T-shirts, jeans, cars, food, water, books,
pencils, pens, bookbags, and the sky
Blue Blue Blue Blue
Blue!!

Daniel Rivera, Grade 5
Clark Avenue Middle School, MA

If I Were in Charge of the World

If I were in charge of the world
I'd change the word grumpy,
There'd be no old computer games
And NO school.

If I were in charge of the world
There'd be lots of video games,
Deeper pools for diving
And bigger cat chairs for my cat Ming.

If I were in charge of the world
You wouldn't have telemarketing,
You wouldn't have worms,
And you wouldn't have hobos
Or country music.

If I were in charge of the world.

Cali Vaccarello, Grade 5
Charlotte A Dunning Elementary School, MA

Nature, Here and There

From the babbling brook,
That carved the canyon from which I look,
Here comes the mountain breeze,
Which the birds float on with ease,
All the way from the brook to the air,
This is nature, here and there.

Jacob Hale, Grade 5
Winthrop L Chenery Middle School, MA

Nature's Wildlife

Butterflies fluttering far, far away,
Fluttering, fluttering right across the bay!

Birds in the air, flapping their wings,
Flapping their wings above the splashing springs!

In the forest there are many trees,
Swaying their branches in the breeze!

Bumble bees feeding on nectar in flowers,
They keep themselves busy for hours and hours!

Flowers releasing petals in the breeze,
Sometimes they can make me sneeze!

If you glance out the window, everything is in view,
I hope you love nature as much as I do!

Alexa Pomerleau, Grade 6
Tyrrell Middle School, CT

The Yummy, Yummy Ice Cream, Looking Good

Good! Cold, slushy,
melts, soft,
White sprinkles, and yummy, good!

It melts like a milkshake,
Pretty, cone, crunchy
Yummy, yum, good!

It melts in my mouth.
I use my hands, to wipe the ice cream,
I look at the ice cream,
Cause it's yum, yum good, good

I love ice cream!
Yes I do!
Stick it on a plate, or a cone
to eat it after it melts
Your hands get sticky, icky like glue.
Ice cream is so good.
Ice cream is so yummy.
It looks like snow,
if you look at the snow don't think it's ice cream,
Because it's yummy, yummy, good, good.

Lynnette Mojica, Grade 6
City View School, MA

Drugs

I wish I could shut down illegal drugs.
They only turn you into thugs.
Drugs can lead to an addiction.
And that's nonfiction.
This is my mission.
It's a hard position.

Gabriel Alexander, Grade 5
Trinity Christian School, VA

Summer

My favorite season is summer
though it can be a bummer.

All the beautiful roses
In the wind striking poses.

They're all very nice
Like ginger spice.

Natasha Franklin, Grade 6
Monelison Middle School, VA

I Wish I Was the Earth

I wish I was the Earth
And could control all of
The natural disasters.
Saving people from getting hurt
From hurricanes, tornados,
Earthquakes and tsunamis.
Homes that have been destroyed
Land damaged
Families lost
Nowhere to live.

Lydia Strong, Grade 6
Scotts Ridge Middle School, CT

Mountains

Pretty in some ways
Mountains are majestic things
Beauty forever

Ian Currivean, Grade 4
Trinity Christian School, VA

Peace

Peace is like the whiteness of a dove
soaring in the air

Peace looks like rays of the sun
coming down on the earth

It sounds like Martin Luther King
saying his "I have a dream" speech

And it can be noisy but
Peace is always with us.

Shane Harris, Grade 4
St Augustine Cathedral School, CT

Snow Falling

Light as a feather
Graceful as ballerinas
Falling pure and clean

Astin Donovan, Grade 6
Our Lady of Mercy School, CT

Saint Anne

Jochim and I are husband and wife.
I had a baby girl late in my life.
Mary is my daughter's name.
As Queen of Heaven she has great fame.
My grandson's name is Jesus.
He will never leave us.
I love to pray.
July 26th is my feast day.
Have you guessed who I am?
My name is Saint Anne.

Katie Hugo, Grade 4
Angelus Academy, VA

The Bird

He sings like the stars
when suddenly a soft gale
blows by
and gradually gets harder
he tries to protect himself
from the wind
but suddenly
he slips
and yells for help
his claws are cranes
hanging on for dear life
care as ever
not to fall.

Sean Lewis, Grade 5
Chestnut Hill Community School, MA

Monkeys

cute, soft
climbs, walks, plays
They are so cool

Brittanie Fontaine, Grade 4
Brookside Elementary School, MA

Lance Armstrong

Champion
Having cancer
Winning the tour
The best biker ever
Always pushing to be faster
Every day thinking of life
Never gave up
Great inspiration
Champion

Andrew Lydon, Grade 5
J F Kennedy Middle School, MA

Roller Coasters

Roller coasters
Fun, loopy
Fast, down, tunnel
I like the drops
Thrilling

Joshua Baroni, Grade 4
Trinity Christian School, VA

The Poor Hippie

There once was a hippie in red
Who pulled on a long dangling thread.
His pants fell down,
And made him frown
So now he's a hoho instead.

Paul Zukas, Grade 5
Sacred Heart Elementary School, MA

New Years Eve

Yah! New Years Eve!
Bang! Boom! Pop!
Yah! New Years!
Noooooooo
I missed the ball drop!

Julia Barouxis, Grade 4
Munger Hill Elementary School, MA

My Aunt

My great aunt was very ill
She couldn't even remember my name
I was surprised she was with us still
Being without her would not be the same

We visited her many times
But it was time for her to go
That day she died
We walked away so slow

I loved her very much
But she is better off in Heaven
On my heart she had a clutch
It was hard because I was only seven

I wish I could still see her face
But I know she is in a better place

Emily Cowman, Grade 6
Immaculate Heart of Mary School, MD

Moon

The light at night
White
Growing
Shrinking
Shining
Satellite

Alex Sullivan, Grade 6
Quashnet School, MA

The Hour of the Night

The night sky casts a shadow on the street
the wind sweeps the grass
the weeds whisper
All the creatures of the night stir about
fantasies become realities
The trees sigh
their branches scratching
and tapping against your window
The nightmares creep about
dwelling in the shadow
The wind blows moving the trees weeds and grass
they all talk to each other
The ground stirs
and an unearthly light reflects onto us
While around it glows hundreds of tiny little lights
The glowing orb starts to distinguish
and out comes an even greater light
The creatures of the night withdraw from which they came
the nightmares shrivel in the light
Then slowly this orb of fire starts to rise

Ethan Armistead, Grade 6
Cape Henry Collegiate School, VA

The New Day

The sun peeks through the
Misty forbidden blue sky,
Now, the world sees peace.

Amanda Wade, Grade 4
Charlotte A Dunning Elementary School, MA

Sisters

Our faces flush with joy
As we zoom down our orange slide.
We dribble a soccer ball
And laugh when someone gets a goal.
We jump up and down
Anticipating a visit to our far away cousins' house.

At Grandpa's funeral we hug and cry,
And remind each other of good times with him.
When we leave our familiar rooms,
We tell each other it'll be all right.

If the power goes out,
We look up into the sky for sparkling stars,
Until light fills the room again.
We grasp each others hand
On the big roller coaster,
And prepare to scream.

We help each other on
Through hard times and scary times,
And enjoy the good times together.
We are sisters.

Julia Meehan, Grade 4
East Farms School, CT

My Last Good-bye to Grandpa

We were going out in the rain
Shaking rain drops off like wet dogs
We'll be out for a while
You come too
We came to people bunching around an engraved stone
People dressed in black
They all looked like bats
A priest was lecturing; I poked my head up to see
A forest of adult's legs
Many of them crying into puddles of rain
My mom's face looked down at me
The tears in her eyes
Fell like the raindrops in the sky
People's faces cried out to me
WHY? WHY?
Later in the years I realized where I was,
Years ago when I said goodbye at my grandfather's funeral
When I was only four.

Caitlin Farnan, Grade 5
West Woods Upper Elementary School, CT

Santa Is on His Way

Christmas
Presents under the tree
Fresh gingerbread cookies right from the oven
Christmas carols
Minty candy canes
The prickly pines of the Christmas tree
Christmas

Molly Coarse, Grade 5
Jane Ryan School, CT

Stacey

Stacey is my second mother,
my pet yet also my friend.
My goddess with power beyond all.
She walks upon the ground in bleakness of nights
without a fright.
Has been my protector for as long as I can remember,
With strength unmatched.
I will love her for all of my life
and I will keep her in my heart forever.

Salim Jones, Grade 6
Magnolia Elementary School, MD

I Like to Read!

I like reading!
It is fun!
You learn a lot!
Why are you sitting there?
Go grab a book and start reading!
Go find a book that you can read and read it!
You might like it or not,
There are so many books to read!

Tyler Lamotte, Grade 4
WB Sweeney School, CT

Different Books

There are different books —
pleasant books, scary books,
animal books
My teacher bellows
as loud as a stampede
if you don't read.
Books can teach
the unteachable.
You need books.
In your hand,
it's a flat piece of land.
Oh look!
It's mom with my library books!
I can't wait to sink
into a new adventure.
Maxim Donaher, Grade 4
Hawley Elementary School, CT

The Brain

These three little pounds of magic ball
Let me hear my mommy's call
See the dinner table near the wall
Smell the delicious cheese ball
Taste the sausage from the last fall
Touch the tablecloth from the mall
That was a nice dinner after all
Grace Huang, Grade 4
Floris Elementary School, VA

Bravery

Bam! The guns crack
over the salty sea
just like a thunderstorm
about to hit me

As the men rush
to assemble on the deck
the enemy ship approaches
no longer a little speck

My legs turn to jelly
as the battle nears.
Tell my wife I love her.
I'm going to face my fears.

The crossfire commences.
I rush to my post.
I salute to you my friend.
You will see me as a ghost.

The enemy ship taunts us.
I can't believe my eyes.
The gun is pointed at me.
I have met my demise.
Kyle Griffin, Grade 6
Charlton Middle School, MA

Double Dutch

When I hear the ropes go click clack
I think of a train on the tracks

With the fast motion of a motorcycle
It really makes me thing of speed.

Think of how fast I move, like if I were to race a cheetah
Trust me I would be in the lead

My best friend Jada think it's not a sport
compared to her being a cheerleader

I wonder how she would feel if I said that about cheerleading
But I can't because I used to be one

I told her that double Dutch is an extreme sport
So, maybe the next time she'll remember that double Dutch is a true sport!!!!!!
Temitope Akinyemi, Grade 6
Magnolia Elementary School, MD

Happiness

Happiness is a sun up in the sky shining down on you.
Happiness a new flower blooming in the springtime.
Happiness is the late spring turning into summer.
Happiness is a very big smile.
Happiness is a banana along with an apple in a shining red bowl.
Happiness is a glass of lemonade sitting in the refrigerator.
Happiness is kids playing outside having the best time of their lives.
Happiness is a child shouting for joy.
Happiness is a trophy sitting on a stand with confetti falling all around.
Happiness is a yellow highlighter being thrown up in the air.
Happiness is a girl at a birthday party smiling at all her friends.
Jessica Crews, Grade 5
Newton-Lee Elementary School, VA

Brandon

I am a cheetah on the pitchers mound
I am a lion on the playing field
I fit through life like a moth in a room of candles
When I'm on the field I smell the sweaty players
I hit like there is no tomorrow
I hear the balls flying in the air when they come off the bat
When I'm in the field I see the people striking out because of me,
I hear people cheering me on when I bat,
When I pitch I can taste the win over the other team.
I'm terrified when I pitch the ball down the middle,
I fear they are going to hit it over the fence,
My arm is like 5 of the strongest men in the world.
When I'm on defense I play harder than a pro team
When I am pitching I feel the heat when it is the last inning and we are up by one
A man on 1st, 2, 3rd bases loaded, 2 outs.
A home run hitter is up, the pitcher throws it down the middle and BING
The ball flies in to the outfield and center fielder catches the ball.
And the Yankees win the game!
Brandon Figel, Grade 6
E Russell Hicks School, MD

China Mist

Orange and black stripes
Stalking in the mountain mist
Hunting the helpless

Ethan Greenleaf, Grade 5
Foxborough Regional Charter School, MA

The Storm

As I creak my door open,
And walk down the hall,
I hear a tap on the roof,
Of the rain coming down,
It seemed to be singing,
Or telling me something,
I didn't know what,
Then I saw a glimpse of the storm,
The thunder roaring,
The lightning shrieking,
And the water flying about,
The ripples of rain on the window,
Slipping down,
One by one,
As I followed their path down,
I saw puddles all around,
Together looking like a river,
Each droplet splashing,
Every puddle growing,
Water's natural beauty was showing again.

Molly Cohen, Grade 6
West Frederick Middle School, MD

Stars

When I look at the stars
I see pictures
I saw a star
that you can only see
from the other side of the world
I love to look
at stars in the night sky
stars are pretty to me.

Jules Lilienfeld, Grade 4
South Area Solomon Schechter Day School, MA

Mom

Her blond hair
floating in the air
as if shot out of a cannon when she walks us to school
Her brown eyes
look like pools of tea,
the liquid she drinks every morning
to keep awake during the hard days
of cooking and cleaning and taking care of all three of us.
When she sleeps
she looks like a Sleeping Beauty
with a smile on her face.

Robert Shull, Grade 5
John Ward Elementary School, MA

Friends

My friends are the very best.
They are better than the rest.

We all laugh and when we play.
I wish we could be together every day.

They've been my friends since first grade,
Even though other friends we made.

I hope we're friends forever.
And that we will breakup never.

Elizabeth Lelonek, Grade 6
St Joseph School-Fullerton, MD

Ocean City

I've waited so long to go on this trip
And we're almost finally there
I always get hasty to take a dip
And the wind blows through my hair

I love to walk along the beach
And let the current take me in
The sound of the seagulls when they screech
Is funny and makes me grin

It is relaxing to lie under the sun
And sunbathe on my towel
It is so quiet, I feel like the only one
On this beach right now

During the summer I love to be here
Whenever I leave I start to tear

Carlena Zembower, Grade 6
Immaculate Heart of Mary School, MD

Pool Music*

This place
    the always noise being heard
water splashing
    the gates creaking on old hinges
Beach balls bouncing over clear water
            VOCABULARIES
                    of
happy kids
        yippees
            water fights
                    language combinations
as soda cans pop open in people's faces
    an orchestra
        of
Cries from leaving children hitting my ears
        with the always noise of this place
the   POOL!! Is my world.

Katherine Alperin, Grade 5
West Woods Upper Elementary School, CT
*Inspired by Arnold Adoff

Life

Life can be cruel, unhappy, or dull.
Life is good at times
And life is bad at times as well.
Life holds our memories forever.
Life is great for most people
And life is horrible for some people.
Life just goes on and on.
Before you know it,
Your life will be over.
Rima Viradia, Grade 6
Irving School, CT

Basketball Is My Favorite Sport

Basketball is my favorite sport
And I like it when my friends
Help me on the court
I like basketball
Because everyone screams
And everyone knows
We're the number one team!
Rodney Crump Jr., Grade 4
Clover Street School, CT

Tree

Tree oh tree,
always filled with glee.
Throwing your leaves
in autumn like confetti.
Jason White, Grade 5
John F Kennedy School, CT

The Fat Cat

There once was a little old cat
Who dreamed of eating a rat
She made a mistake
And ate a cake
And now she's a little too fat.
Michaelah Nunes, Grade 4
Freetown Elementary School, MA

Big Papi

There is a baseball player Big Papi,
Sometimes he is very sloppy,
He weights about 500 lbs. which is fat,
When he's at the plate holding the bat.
Paul Andreuk, Grade 6
Captain Nathan Hale Middle School, CT

Spring

Spring is cooling
Spring has puddles
Spring has cuddles
Spring has little showers
But lots of pretty flowers
Shenisa Mohammed, Grade 4
Crestwood Elementary School, VA

Try Again Tomorrow

I have a story I need to tell,
About a time, not so well,
When I really have to think in sorrow,
Yes, I'll try again tomorrow.
When nothing could cheer me up,
Not even a cute, little pup,
There's a saying I'll have to borrow,
Yes, I'll try again tomorrow.
My legs are stiff; I think they'll freeze,
My hair is blowing with the breeze,
My arms are still, I could not row,
I'll have to try again tomorrow.
Olivia Heutlinger, Grade 4
Willis E Thorpe School, MA

Troubled

I am troubled
At school
I am loving
To my family

I am bold
When I am pitching
I am reckless
To my brother's room

I am proud
To be an American
I am stubborn
When I do math

I am open minded
To new people
I am carefree
In the summer

I am straight forward
When I think something's wrong
I am troubled
At school!
Caleb Bratcher, Grade 6
Blue Ridge Middle School, VA

Painted Glory

Beautiful buntings
Stationed on the suet feeder
Like a nail in wood.
Gazing in its glory,
A star with elegant eyes.
Resting phenomenally,
Pulling attention
Like a U.F.O in the sky.
So beautiful
He's out of this world.
Shawn Paxton, Grade 5
Chestnut Hill Community School, MA

Joy

Joy is overwhelming and wonderful
Like a fish in a sea of happiness
Joy is soft and calm
Almost as green as grass
Joy is a time for friendship
Like a butterfly floating in the air
Joy has its own life
Like a peaceful birds song
Joy is overwhelming and wonderful
Madalyn Helson, Grade 5
Newton-Lee Elementary School, VA

No One Cares

No one cares!
When I have numerous books,
And it feels like I need a fork lift,
To carry them home,
No one helps me carry them.
No one cares about me,
Or this world,
No one asks me how my day was.
It's a strike to my heart.

This mysterious person,
Carried some books,
I look up at him in the bright sunlight,
We became best friends forever,
I returned the favor,
He couldn't spell,
I helped him study,
We were there for each other,
And we cared for each other,
So there is hope in this world.
Jake Zelinske, Grade 4
Tilghman Elementary School, MD

Flames

The flames do flicker forever on
And ever on they burn.
They consume like something alive;
Beings of fire devouring all in turn.
The matter that they reach
Burns to ash, is suddenly gone
In flames that want more, forevermore,
And flicker ever on.

Heat and kindling and air,
Together when combined,
Produce a creature of rage and flame,
That cares for naught and has no mind.
And when it at last is doused,
With cool water in large supply,
It leaves behind a scar on the Earth
That ne'er in time will die.
Ryan Konopka, Grade 6
Scotts Ridge Middle School, CT

Getting Wooster

Looking at the puppies' faces,
Watching them walk to different places,
I see a puppy walking towards me.
I hope he is part of our family.

He was the calmest of them all.
He came up to me without a call.
I picked him up with such great care.
With my hand I stroked his hair.

He looked at me with soft brown eyes
While whimpering little puppy cries.
I wondered if he was sad.
So I pet him more and he became glad.

I knew for sure he was the one.
His new life with me had just begun.
I knew this puppy needed a name.
I wanted it to be original and not the same.

Sydney Palmer, Grade 6
Immaculate Heart of Mary School, MD

Wrestling

Wrestling is a physical sport.
You may get hurt and go to court.
But don't let that make you stop.
For you will regret it on the spot.

You may become a state champ.
For that go to my dad's camp.
Practice is sometimes boring,
So please don't end up snoring.

My dad will then get mad.
Trust me, that would be bad.
You would then get kicked out.
By my dad with a great shout.

Then you would leave with a frown.
Everyone will think you're a clown.
You shall never become a state champ.
You will leave the camp with a cramp.

You try to come back.
All you get is a quick glance from Jack.
No one else cares to look.
Now you feel like a misunderstood crook.

John Knapp, Grade 6
Captain Nathan Hale Middle School, CT

Snowflakes

Twinkling snowflakes
Descending from the gray sky
Melts into liquid

Jordan Connell, Grade 4
C Hunter Ritchie Elementary School, VA

Harriet Tubman

Harriet Tubman was growing up as a slave,
She worked hard with no money to save.
She was sent to work at Miss Susan's house,
she didn't much like her or her spouse.

She had nowhere to go and no food to be eaten,
So she went back to Miss Susan's where she was beaten.
At six she got separated from Old Rit and Ben,
When she got Bronchitis she was sent home again.

Harriet and other slaves picked a lot of cotton,
They received no pay and their treatment was rotten.
She worked from early in the morning to late at night,
And she would usually work with all of her might.

She tried to help a slave but got hit with a weight,
Her wound was so bad that no one knew her fate.
She recovered in her cabin inside the quarter,
But her wound resulted in a sleeping disorder.

She helped many slaves on their flight to be free,
She died on March 10th at the age of ninety-three.

Matt Carr, Grade 6
Daniel L Joyce Middle School, MA

Christmas

Christmas
See fun and exciting toys
Smell apple pie being baked
hear joyful laughs of kids opening gifts
taste the turkey at the big feast
touch the cold wrapping paper of my gifts,
Christmas.

Samuel Lambert, Grade 5
Jane Ryan School, CT

Little Sister

I was just two years old
When there came a great surprise
I was so excited by what I was told
I could not wait to see it with my own eyes

My mom said, "It is time"
We excitedly rushed to the car
And I found a shiny dime
I was thinking of the special surprise and saw a shooting star

We were all filled with delight
My little sister was born
She was such a beautiful sight
On December 15 morn

She had a pretty face
And she had an amazing name, Grace

Caroline Schertle, Grade 6
Immaculate Heart of Mary School, MD

Stars

I gaze upon
the bright stars
in the sky
I think to myself
that somewhere
somehow

a girl
just like me
is seeing the same bright
ornament in the sky
I wonder

If I'll ever experience
the stars up close
space planets
stars

I look up at the North Star
and see the sky is fading
The biggest most beautiful
star of all is rising
into its rightful place in the sky

Lauren Muller, Grade 6
Swampscott Middle School, MA

My Christmas Surprise

One day it was Christmas morning.
I was very glad.
I just woke up from snoring.
Then I woke up my dad.

Then we all woke up.
And started down the stairs.
Also, I found a cup.
That was filled with lots of hair.

I saw a box that was very big.
Inside the box I heard a sound.
I thought it was a pig.
You're not going to believe what I found.

I looked inside and found 2 cats.
I was very happy it wasn't rats.

Austin Moore, Grade 6
Immaculate Heart of Mary School, MD

Spring

My eyes open as birds chirp
The warmth of the sun in my face
Flowers wake up from a cold winter
Leaves back on the bare trees
Grass as green as emeralds
Shimmers as a new season arrives.

Carrie Mao, Grade 6
Bigelow Middle School, MA

Shakespeare

Shakespeare gold and bold.
Standing out beyond all.
All enemy writers will tremble in his presence.
He's less than a god, but more than a man.
This is my speech and today I make a stand.
The man who wrote "Romeo and Juliet" and "Shakespeare in Love,"
flies to the sky as a beautiful dove.

DeCor Davis, Grade 4
C Hunter Ritchie Elementary School, VA

Let's Take a Walk

Let's take a walk
Down the cold path
Where the colors are as bright as the noon day sun

Walking through the forest is walking through a million sky scrapers.
Feel the raindrops jump a long way down,
The wind blowing them right over our head.

We start running through the sky scrapers,
We trip and fall and land in leaves,
Feel them crushing in our hands
In the leaves we see one little flower;
It smells like a spring day.

I can just taste the pine in the air
The sun comes out and the ground gets warm
Our walk has ended but we will come again.

Caroline Evans, Grade 6
Trinity School, MD

Fish

Under the water surface the fish effortlessly glides,
Briskly moving its fins to a quick precise beat,
Flexibly turns to the side of the bowl
Moving up, down, all around as if it's lost
Blows a tiny delicate bubble,
The fish becomes calm as if it's relaxing after a long boresome day.
Fish.

Sarah Mapelli, Grade 5
West Woods Upper Elementary School, CT

Nine Planets

Mercury, Venus, Earth, Mars, Jupiter, Saturn, Uranus, Neptune, Pluto.
Mercury closest to our sun.
Venus the sweltering planet.
Earth the planet of life.
Mars the red one.
Jupiter the biggest of them all.
Saturn the one with the ring.
Uranus the fifteen moons bright as a star.
Neptune the unlucky one with storms.
Pluto the coldest and smallest.
Put them all together and they make our solar system.

Jeffrey Estrada, Grade 5
Clark Avenue Middle School, MA

Bill Gates

There once was a rich man named Bill Gates.
A lot of people think that he's great.
But usually, all of the honeys,
Like him because of all of his money.

Ryley Blouin, Grade 6
Captain Nathan Hale Middle School, CT

West Virginia State Fair

In stables are animals.
See the food and rides,
They are so tempting, but save money for later.
I can hear the sound of mooing cattle and food frying.
The smell of fresh hot dogs and nachos.
I can almost taste the spicy cheese and fresh chili.
When I got home even though I'm holding a rubber toy
I can still feel the soft fur of cattle.

Ella Switzer, Grade 5
McCleary Elementary School, VA

Summer

You are dying of thirst
Water seems more refreshing than ever
90-105 degree weather with a scorching sun
A tad breeze making you thirstier
You feel like jumping into a swimming pool
Yet there are good parts
No homework or teachers for months
Every last moment of this time free
Endless games of sports
It's the dreaded season of heat but
One of the most lovable times of year
It's summer

Matt Lund, Grade 5
Jack Jackter Intermediate School, CT

Good Advice

Dear friend,
Life is like a flowing river,
With may detours and dams.
The river may be polluted, or at times be abused.
The river will…
Sometimes flood, and sometimes dry out.
There will be hard decisions —
Times when you will be tempted to take the wrong path.
Times when you will have to think outside the box,
And sometimes take the less traveled tributary.
But as long as you believe in yourself,
You will overcome those rapids in your path.
Use your knowledge and anything becomes possible.
Knowledge is the key to success.
Push the limits, and do what has never been done before.
And remember,
Never, ever, give up…
Keep on rowing through the river of life!

Thomas Dudzik, Grade 5
Har-Bur Middle School, CT

My Sister

M y sister who I love dearly
A nnoying, aggravating, but alive and well with a lot to say
D aring, determined to get her way
I ntelligent
S erious
O pen minded, one and only
N ever backs down (Just like her big sister)

Lydia Z. Cuffy, Grade 6
Magnolia Elementary School, MD

Peaceful Land

Mountains very tall,
Tall trees almost touch the sky
Water's peaceful here

Matt Rothermel, Grade 5
Foxborough Regional Charter School, MA

Man O' War*

Pure blinding speed and fiery fire
Lashing out with thunder hooves
Boiling blood runs in his veins, inherited from grand sire
Giant strides swallow the track as he crosses the wire

Red's neck taunt as he is held back
Shaking that noble head in frustration
Resentment towards the freedom he lack
Muscles stretch and pull, as he fights the tack

In the midst of the heat, he is fleet on his feet
Asking for more rein, fighting against the iron bit
Under the tight hold, still no challengers does he meet
Whip resting at his hip, the jockey sits confidently in his seat

Like a hawk soaring through the sky
The wind whistling by, swoosh, swoosh
Almost as if Red knows how to fly
Sir Barton doesn't even come close to tie

Many races has Red run, both short and far
Easily galloping to victory, brightness in his eyes
Conquering the racetrack during the First World War
Because he's Man O' War

Stella Zhu, Grade 5
West Woods Upper Elementary School, CT
*Inspired by Robert Frost

Max

As hours pass it's like you're a year older.
As days roll by, you're getting older by the second.
Months, years go by, it's almost our time to come to an end,
So goodbye my friend, I love I care for you.
The time did come for Max to go.
I was sad that he was gone, but I know we'll meet again.
I love, I care for Max.

Bailey Pereira, Grade 4
Freetown Elementary School, MA

Autumn Days

Leaves of all colors fighting for their lives to hang on to their mother maple tree so they don't crinkle, prune, then die.
The wind shivers along with the trees causing the leaves to fall like raindrops.
I hear the rustling of the trees swaying and the trickling of the small waterfall.
The whooshing crackle of our feet running through leaves blends along with the buzzing of the bees.
The trees fill the woods with the bare branches creating an obstacle course of spikes.
The leaves litter the ground with blotches of color rustled brown, forest green, and burgundy red.
The air crickets talk with a whisper blending with the screaming wind.
The wind withers and carries the leaves on a journey until their landing.
The air smells of burning branches under a bonfire filling the air with a strong but soft scent.
I touched the roughness of the bark on the trees and the softness of the autumn moss.
I see the acorns and pine cones hiding their heads under the leaves like people sheltering their houses.
The birds are humming a tune followed with the beating rhythm of the crickets.
The trees' heads bend by the whooshing of the wind some happy, mad or even sad.
The faint rumble of the tractor in the distance overpowers the whistling of the wind.
Autumn is a peaceful time, it's not too hot or cold but the faint spiraling rush of the wind of my face.

Taylor Puzzio, Grade 6
Madison Middle School, CT

The Ocean and the Rock

The ocean lapped against the land, sending tendrils of foaming water spiraling over the sand.
The jagged rock smirked down at the ocean.
"You are weak," it called.
"Anyone can bend you to their will, whereas I am solid, and powerful."
The ocean looked pitifully at the rock.
"Fool. Don't you know time is on my side?
I am thousands of years old, yet I still shine in the morning light,
I am still beautiful. Where will you be in two hundred years?
Crumbled and horrific. Just wait. You will see."
Many years later, the ocean decided to check up on her old foe.
The rock was a sorry sight.
Whole chunks of stone fell into the sea, other parts were completely eroded.
The once proud boulder was dying.
"Help me," the rock gasped. "I am old and weak. Take pity on a lesser being."
"I cannot do a thing for you," the ocean replied. "If time is against you, you have no chance.
All things solid must crumble, though I will be around forever."
With a final shudder, the rock fell into the sea, sinking to the sandy bottom.
The ocean carried her old foe out into the water, mocking the rock with every wave and splash.

Christine Aucoin, Grade 6
Thomas Blake Middle School, MA

Family

Family is very important in a child's life
Without family you won't have anything
You love your family at home,
but when you take them out in public you just want to pull your hair out
Your family will always be there to protect you from any harm
If you think that your parents are overprotective,
you think that they will always be watching you
They do that for a reason
Sometimes you might get in a fight with your family
and you say you will never talk to them again, you know that will never happen
Your parents yell at you because they love you and want you to learn from your mistakes
If you respect your parents they will respect you back
Your family comes first for everything

Kristina Biblekaj, Grade 6
Irving School, CT

Fish

The fish that swim in a sad little pond,
Are things that I feel bad for.
I can't imagine all they've been through,
I can't imagine what they endure.
Yet I do not think that it is fair,
That one must die each day,
For if people want to cook and eat them,
Do you think they have a say?
They float there week after week after week,
As if very nonchalant.
But I think that they are thinking
That this is not the life they want.

Marina Bates, Grade 6
E W Thurston Middle School, MA

Tears Falling

Tears falling,
Pulled away from family,
From friends,
From hope.
Whips tearing flesh,
Salt poured into cuts,
Tears falling.

Dark feet
Pounding the ground,
They just ran.
Either found or escaped.

This was their lives
On the plantations.
No hope,
No happiness,
Just tears falling.

Erik Galins, Grade 5
Charlotte A Dunning Elementary School, MA

Cousins

My funny cousins always play like lion cubs,
Tussling with one another and
Smiling about the fun they have,
They are gazelles running through the fields.
They dance like leaves twirling to the ground in fall.
Their laughter, cries, and yells delight me.
They are precious gems to me.

Sara Woods, Grade 6
Trinity School, MD

Swim Away

Swim away and you could hear
The ocean waves far from here
The sun is hot, the water is cold
You are playing with summer tools like making sand castles
In the sandy beach.

Nick Chin, Grade 5
Charlotte A Dunning Elementary School, MA

Snow

White pure snowy Alaska
Brown snowy trees
With a cool refreshing smell
And blue birds singing
With every step you take you hear a shuffle
With every handful you feel the soft cold snow

George Saad, Grade 5
St Mary's Primary School, MA

A New School

Before school I filled out a form
And put on my first uniform
I was very anxious and nervous too
But, when I got there I didn't know what to do

That morning I had to wake up a little early
Only to make my hair curly
I didn't ride the bus anymore
So today I entered the car door

I was with my friend who was also new
We helped each other all the way through
My mom picked me up that day
And I couldn't wait to get home and play

When I got home I wasn't mad
Because I realized my day wasn't that bad
I never talked to my old best friend again
But the memories will never end

Brittan Wetzelberger, Grade 6
Immaculate Heart of Mary School, MD

Mountain Ride

Sky Bright Sky Clear
    Wavering shining sun
White capped Peaks Soft Slight Snow
    Click of the bindings
And away we go
    View oh so beautiful
Breathtaking Mountain
    Squint our eyes
And down with speed
    Twisting turning tree confusions
Long and sloping runs
    Exhilarating downward Diamond Rides
Slow down to catch our breath
    Catch the seconds that slip away fast
My heart beating quickly
    Frost tweaked cheeks
We go on down to the very bottom
    Spray the snow into the sky
And watch the fading Twilight
    Disappear over the endless abyss
And finish our day of Skiing

Persis Ticknor-Swanson, Grade 6
Smith College Campus School, MA

Woods

You can camp out there
Animals live in the woods
Is creepy and dark

Deer live in the woods
You can have a nice picnic
People take hikes there

Nicholas Mallozzi, Grade 5
Jane Ryan School, CT

Summer

refreshing pool
summer camp
tanning
umbrellas to keep sun away
vacation time!
summer is surely the best season!

Jessica Markowski, Grade 6
Albert D Griswold Middle School, CT

Monkeys

Swift and steady
All around ready
For what they eat
Bugs and grubs and meat
Some big as a bear
Some small as a hare
Spider thumb monkeys
Both so small
Patas monkey probiscis monkey
Both big and strong

Andrew Curiel, Grade 5
J F Kennedy Middle School, MA

I Am From...

I am from
Nerds
Lenny and Mel
Football
Pizza
Lincoln Park
Winter
Taco sauce
Football cards
P.E.
Virginia

Sam Qualley, Grade 5
Wakefield Forest Elementary School, VA

The Bowling Ball

A bowling ball can hit you hard.
The pain will *never* go away.
Just like when you lose a loved one.
Like a bowling ball hitting you.

Courtney Kiley, Grade 5
St Mary's Primary School, MA

The Teachers Lounge

What do they do in there?
That's what we all wonder
A place of mystery
On which we all try to ponder.

What do they do in there?
Do they think about school?
Do they think of summer days
Like swimming in a pool.

What do they do in there?
Perhaps they go wild
And do things they tell us
That we're not allowed.

What do they do in there?
A question on all of our minds
This may remain a mystery
For the answer we may never find.

Andrea Wong, Grade 6
Fuller Middle School, MA

Bright Glowing Star

You can be what you want to be,
Just go for your dream you will see,
It's your choice you will know,
What you want to be, soon will show,
Think about it, it's not win or lose,
Just be wise in what you choose,
You are special, yes you are,
You will soon be a bright glowing star.

Hayley Bickley, Grade 6
Salem Church Middle School, VA

The Faded Trail to Freedom

There's still time
To disappear
And run away
Or face your fears.

Once you've started,
Don't turn back.
Don't hesitate;
It's time you lack.

They will come after you
As soon as you pause.
They will act very soon.
They will stop your cause.

They know where you are
Or where you will be,
But just keep running;
There's a chance of being free.

Marta Pysak, Grade 6
St Bridget Elementary School, MA

The Elephant

It's a Elephant
Listen Listen
His feet go
Thump Thump
When he steps
The land
Shakes

Cody Wyland, Grade 6
Monelison Middle School, VA

Owl

I am the eyes
and ears of the forest
some say I'm wise
I say they're right
On voles and moles
and mice I feed
In the dead of
night I hoot
The voles and moles run
to their homes but
it's too late I grasp
them with my talons
and fly away
Back to my perch
I wait another day

Spencer Persechino, Grade 6
Litchfield Intermediate School, CT

Spring

Spring's a good time to make a rhyme
To jump, to laugh, to play...
To say hola to warmth, and bye to cold!
It's just fine to play!
Bye to heavy jackets
Hello to shorts and tees!
Ring! Ring!
Bring spring!
Feels so nice and clean everywhere!

Joseph Sheridan, Grade 5
St Joseph School-Fullerton, MD

Awesome Pets

Pets, pets
Pets are cool.
Pets are super kind.
Pets are really behaved.
In the good old summertime.
They like to have fun.
That's just what they will do,
They just want to play
All the time and have fun,
Fun with
You!

Patrick Gagliardi, Grade 5
St Joseph School-Fullerton, MD

Basketball

Basketball is my favorite sport.
Not soccer or baseball, not of that sort.

When I dribbled down the court to score the winning basket,
I went to the bench and the coach said fantastic.

When my mom was driving home I saw writing on the wall.
Then I saw a group of kids playing basketball.

I looked back over at them and said — uh!
Then my mom said go and play, so I walked over and said…
Can I play too?

Gary Miles, Grade 6
Magnolia Elementary School, MD

Dinnertime

Dinnertime is a time to get together
A time to enjoy, not depending on the weather
A time to eat and share your day
No matter how much you have to say
Dinnertime is a time like no other
A time to spend with each other

Sarah Finkel, Grade 4
Weston Intermediate School, CT

Puppies

Puppies
Puppies
Puppies
Cute puppies
Soft, cuddly puppies
Long, fat, noisy puppies
Short puppies
Shy, tiny Newfoundland puppies
Fuzzy, playful poodle puppies
Short, spotted shepherd puppies
Chubby puppies, too
Huge puppies
Wimpish puppies
Don't forget beagle puppies
Last of all, best of all, I like dachshund puppies

Christina Robinson, Grade 4
C Hunter Ritchie Elementary School, VA

My Favorite Books

Books scattered across my bed,
All in different themes,
Every word becomes a thread,
To weave tonight's dreams.

My Blanket that is worn,
Keeps me warm at night,
Hides a book, a little torn,
But it is my comfort and my light.

Ikiah Decas, Grade 5
Foxborough Regional Charter School, MA

Playing Football

Hike!!
I fly across the line.
I dodge, duck, and juke left.

I am open.
The ball comes
Flying towards me.
I jump as high as I can.
Bam!
The ball is in my hands.

I land with great force.
I turn around and run.
My teammate is blocking for me.
I feel a slight pull.
I run even faster and lose whoever was behind me.

I'm 5 seconds away from a touchdown.
All of a sudden d*#! I am tackled
Right on the goal line.
I get up.
I yell as loud as I can, "Wow we won!"

Trevor Kelly, Grade 6
Swampscott Middle School, MA

Ramses the Great

A controlling old king was Ramses the Great.
He built statues and temples at a record-high rate.
But like all pharaohs King Ramses died,
So they built a huge pyramid and put him inside.

Lance Johnson, Grade 6
Captain Nathan Hale Middle School, CT

Honey I Love*

I love a lot of things, a whole lot of things.
Like,
When I bake with my mom,
We make a great cake a lot.
We also eat the cake right up!
But honey, let me tell you, I love that great cake!
I love that great cake!
I love a lot of things, a whole lot of things.
Like,
When I jump into the pool,
I feel so cool when my coach says go as fast as you can.
But honey, let me tell you, I love that cool water on me.
I love that cool water on me.
AND
When I see him rolling over I say,
You look like a bowling ball!
Also, you look like a log.
But honey, let me tell you, I love that rolling dog!
I love that rolling dog!

Devon Tice, Grade 4
Potter Road Elementary School, MA
*Inspired by Eloise Greenfield

Lonely Bird

A lonely bird in upset sorrows
Wishing that some day he too
Could fly through the clouds.

A lonely bird in upset sorrows
Sitting in a nest watching
the sun set.

A lonely bird in upset sorrows
is no longer upset,
he is now soaring through
the clouds.

Melina Gallo, Grade 5
Clark Avenue Middle School, MA

Her Eyes

Kittens
surrounding me
staring
with irresistible
green eyes
too many to choose from
all pleading
for homes
but suddenly
my eyes
meet hers
my mind
is made up

Cara Macdonald, Grade 5
Coleytown Elementary School, CT

Ireland

Green Irish shamrock
Leprechauns singing tonight
Gold shining brightly

Zachary Joseph, Grade 4
St Gregory Elementary School, MA

Girls

Girls, girls everywhere,
Love the fragrance of their hair
Red heads,
Brunettes,
Blondes too,
Also like their designer shoes,
Uggs,
Sneakers,
And high heels that touch the sky,
In stores what they see is what they buy,
Hollister,
Juicy,
Abercrombie,
I wonder if they will ever talk to me?

Daniel Curtin, Grade 6
E W Thurston Middle School, MA

I Am Someone

I'm a person, a human being. I am myself and no other.
I have friends, a family, a life and no one can take them from me.
I won't be treated like a rag doll under the bed.
My personality is a lit candle that never dims.
I am a person, too.

Hanna DeLoe, Grade 5
St Luke's School, CT

Calm and Relaxing

I started
Walking
Down
A stone path
Then
I came
Upon
A foggy
Creek
The wind
Whispered
As I watched
The fish Splash
In the Water
And watched
The butterflies
Flutter
In the breeze

Savannah Smith, Grade 5
Francis Asbury Elementary School, VA

Snorkeling

As I walk down to the beach,
I hear the sand crushing beneath my feet.
As I stand in the sand, I hear waves
crashing against the rocks.
As I bend down to touch a shell,
it feels smooth and slippery.
I stand up to smell the air.
It smells like salt.

The sun shone brightly so I could easily see through the water.
It was like looking through glass.
A rock knocked against my foot.

I looked into the horizon,
I saw kilometers of water.
As my guide walked down, he said that the wind blows really hard.
Soon we were all ready to dive!
I was so excited and scared.
3…2…1… Dive!
I jumped, getting salty water in my mouth.
I saw wonderful fish —
Pear fish, stingray, octopus, squid, and baby eels.
What an amazing experience!

Justin Nathenson, Grade 4
Hawley Elementary School, CT

Stars

Stars are at night,
Only at night,
Because in the day you can't see them,
Because it is cloudy and the sun is very bright.

Mary Gray, Grade 5
Milton L Fuller Elementary School, MA

My Math Teacher Ate My Homework

My math teacher talks about food so much
A tray of brownies she would always clutch

She would talk about pizza
When we do fractions
Munching on protractors
We can't believe her actions

Then one day while collecting homework
She began to devour
Each and every paper
Eating nonstop for an hour

My report card read "F" in math
I felt like a jerk
Telling my dad it's because
My math teacher "ate" my homework

Corey Souza, Grade 6
Edmond P Talbot Middle School, MA

My World

The classroom is silent as we all write.
The whole world is silent
as it spins around at night.

As the flowers bloom
and the bees start buzzing,
it's a wonderful world so come out and play.
We will have fun in every way.

As the teaching time starts,
the comprehension ends.
As the world rests its little head,
I sleep silently in my bed.
As the world spins around again.

Sarah Calamita, Grade 4
Totoket Valley Elementary School, CT

Winter

The snow silently falls from the sky,
Dancing through the air.
The snowflakes grow to thousands,
Covering the flowers with a white blanket,
The plants around now see,
That its time for them to sleep.
Winter is now here.

Molly Isberg, Grade 6
E W Thurston Middle School, MA

Caterpillar Life Cycle

I inch all around,
I have spun a large cocoon,
my new wings stretch wide.

Joshua Fuller, Grade 5
Foxborough Regional Charter School, MA

Baseball

Baseball season is here
It is time to hear some loud cheers!
Baseball is a lot of fun to play.
It makes me want to say "Hooray!"

Watching some teams like the O's and the A's
Makes me want to go
To the park some days.

This home run of a poem was written by Tyrone Murray,
Future Hall-of-Famer!

Tyrone Murray, Grade 5
St Joseph School-Fullerton, MD

What Is the Beach?

The beach is…
Sand in between my toes
Music made out of the beautiful blue waves
Catching crabs
Seagulls up in the air, acting like planes.

The beach is…
Low tide and high tide
Dolphins jumping
Snails moving s…l…o…w
sand bars up to my ankles.

The beach is…
Finding dangerous sand worms
Building sandcastles
Wind blowing in my hair
And the sun setting to rest in the water
for the night.

Carly Klittnick, Grade 4
Fawn Hollow Elementary School, CT

The Lonely Tree

One lonesome tree,
Stands upon a shimmering pool of water,
A bright sunset sits on the horizon,
Turning the water shades of yellow and orange,
The water seems to stretch,
On and on,
Until it meets the pink and red horizon,
All is at peace,

All is silent.

Krista Fernandes, Grade 5
St Mary's Primary School, MA

The Leaf Land

There was once a land
The leaves thought it was grand
They went there to play
They went every day
The leaves had a blast
They went home at last
Back to the trees
With the birds and the bees
They had some fun
But now they are done

Jordan Graham, Grade 5
Mapleshade Elementary School, MA

Happily Never After

When you think of books
Reading is boring
When the teacher starts reading
You start snoring

A cat, a hat
A coat in a boat
It's all so droll
I fell asleep in a root beer float

I know this story, please stop
Harry Potter, I don't care
Cinderella, Goldilocks, Snow White
Rapunzel and her long, long hair

Sleeping Beauty and her prince
Stay asleep if you dare
Mickey, Goofy, Donald, and Pluto
Alice in Wonderland and the hare

Thank God she's almost done
Dalmatians with polka dot fur
Now you're at my favorite part
And they lived Happily Ever After.

Sara Cordeiro, Grade 6
Edmond P Talbot Middle School, MA

War

Vietnam War
Disturbing, unpleasant
Fighting, bombing, dying
Many lives were lost
Civil War

Theresa Liang, Grade 4
Sacred Heart School, MA

Easter

Easter time is here
When Jesus rose from the dead,
Let's all praise the Lord!

Richard Anthony Laue, Grade 4
St Joseph School-Fullerton, MD

Brothers

Little brother
Annoying, crazy
Misbehaving, never loving
Always playing Nintendo
Monkey

Emily Armstrong, Grade 4
Grace Miller Elementary School, VA

Thunderstorms

Treacherously grey!
Hair-raising experience!
Natural disaster!!!!!!

Erin Beckham, Grade 5
Hebron Elementary School, CT

The Cold and Hot Day

Summer
Hot, warm
Running, playing, exhausted
Sky, sun, cold, playing
Snowing, blowing, playing
Cold, white
Winter

Miles Gaither, Grade 4
Ridgeway Elementary School, MD

Liberty

L iving in this world of greed,
I t is something we all need,
B ringing dreams of hope and love,
E xultant countries soar like doves,
R ebelling evil and injustice too,
T his can't be very far from new,
Y ou know there's something we can do.

Conor Freeley, Grade 5
Sacred Heart Elementary School, MA

Soccer

Soccer is the sport I play.
It's my favorite in every way.
I love to score goals.
Sometimes it hits the poles.
I love to win.
So I show a grin.

Katie Dickson, Grade 4
Brookside Elementary School, MA

What Happens in Spring?

Sun so bright and warm
Pretty plants are planted
running streams run across the land
in spring birds sing a very happy song
no snow, no really cold winds to blow
green grass glows in the sun

Sean Powell, Grade 4
Marsh Grammar School, MA

Erupting

Lava
Slides down the side
Of the loud erupting volcano.
Like skiers sliding in snow.

Daniel Speck, Grade 4
Home School, MD

Home Is

Home is a place for family
Jokes being sent back and forth
Everyone laughing
Home is a place for TV
Watching thrilling basketball games
Home is time to play outside
With your friends
Home is a place
For Grandma's fishcakes,
Sister's cupcakes,
Dad's famous oxtail
And Mama's moist pound cake
Home is a place where
You wake up and sleep
Home is
Home is

John Lambert, Grade 5
Clover Street School, CT

Horses of Freedom

Horses can run free
anywhere they want to be
horses are the best

Candace Alexander, Grade 5
Sacred Heart Elementary School, MA

Teachers

Teachers are people
With valuable time.
Who read you books
And poems that rhyme.

They always dress up
Or dress "very formal"
When they see their class talk
They think it's not normal.

They will usually teach math
Or reading the longest.
Just to make sure THEIR class's
Brains are the strongest.

Even though they're in school
For an awfully long while
Every day they manage
To give you a smile.

Kelly Michonski, Grade 4
Munger Hill Elementary School, MA

Poetry

I don't like poetry; I don't like it at all!
Short poems, simple ones or the very tall!
Poetry just isn't my thing
I'd even rather dance and sing!
I don't know when this came about
But as far back as I can remember, I'd shout,
"I don't like poetry; I don't like it at all!"

When I was really little the rhyming made me twitch,
Every time I heard one, I got this terrible itch!
Poetry just isn't my thing
I'd even rather braid string!
Poetry is not for me,
Whenever I write it, people agree!
I don't like poetry; I don't like it at all!

I'm older now and some things haven't changed;
Poetry still gives me a "chill"
But it's really the "Wii" that gives me a thrill!

Nicky Bader, Grade 5
Coleytown Elementary School, CT

Around the World in 5 Seconds

Bet you I can go around the whole world in 5 seconds!
Start timing!
1…
I'm starting from Boston, Massachusetts,
Now I'm going over to Utah.
Hey I'm at Valencia, Spain, can't believe I've gone so far.
2…
I see Greenland from Russia,
I see Europe from Maine,
I see Rhode Island from Egypt,
I see a bunch from this "plane."
3…
So I left you off in Africa,
I'll pick you up in Turkey.
We're traveling over Japan, I feel so lucky!
4…
Hey! I'm back at home. I have to wrap up the poem.
5 seconds, that's it!
That's how long it took me to travel around the world.
Traveling around the world was fun, but now when I am done,
With my journey around the world, I am putting away my globe.

Veronica Podolny, Grade 4
Memorial-Spaulding Elementary School, MA

Spring

Spring is waiting to go out to the world.
Spring is a wonderful time of year.
Spring has flowers of colors and colors you can lay on.
Spring birds chirping like the sound of music!
Spring is fainting as days go by don't be sad be happy
Spring will come next year!

Ashley Holmes, Grade 4
Bowers School, CT

Poetry

Poetry is a passion!
It can be rhyming.
Poetry can depend on your feelings.
It can be sad, happy, mad, silly and serious.
It can be long or;
it can be short.
It can be anything you want it to be.
It makes you calm down.
It can make you feel better when you are sad
Or when you are down.
Poetry is cool.
Some people do not like poetry.
I love poetry.
Poetry is fun!

Taina Quiles, Grade 4
WB Sweeney School, CT

Peaceful Place

Astonishing red and yellow tulips
Reaching out to the spring sun
Water trickling down slowly but smoothly
Flowing and crashing down
Birds sing a little tune

This is my peaceful place

Olivia Nicholson, Grade 5
St Mary's Primary School, MA

Snake

Venom stored in fangs,
Slithering across the ground,
Avoided by all.

Samyukta Mallick, Grade 5
Foxborough Regional Charter School, MA

Lemur

There once was a ring-tailed Lemur,
Who came down with a very bad fever.
When he woke one morning,
And found it very boring,
He took out his shoe,
Which smelled very new
(I don't know if it's true.)

In late afternoon,
When he could see the moon,
He got out some cheddar,
Then felt ten times better.
And then the next day,
(He worked at the circus)
While we were walking he saw us.

We found that his name was Jim
Can you guess how many rings he had with him?

Sean Gilroy, Grade 5
Forest Avenue Elementary School, MA

Spring Our Friend

The worms help the plants
The worm's friends are ants

The black ants are talking
With worms who are walking

"Winter has come to an end
So, springtime will be our friend."
Samuel Woodring, Grade 4
Home School, VA

The Beach

The ocean a beautiful diamond.
The sand smooth on my feet.
The taste of the salty water is a
taste buds worst enemy.
The beach umbrellas
popping out of the ground.
See the seagulls squawking.

This is the place to be.
Claire Di Bella, Grade 5
Oakdale Elementary School, MD

Boring

As boring as reading.
As boring as watching TV.
As boring as sitting.
As boring as looking out a window.
That is how boring studying is.

Reading a dull book.
Watching repeats on TV.
Sitting and doing nothing.
Watching kids play.
That is how boring studying is.
Christian Gonzalez, Grade 5
Clark Avenue Middle School, MA

The Bittersweet Dream

It comes
Dark depths of the night
Deep in sleep it comes
Bittersweet

It's quiet and serene
Your most desirable thoughts
All your memories tingle in your head

They escape as morning approaches
Resting away until night time returns

Bitter and sweet
The bittersweet dream
Gillian Ryder, Grade 6
Weston Middle School, CT

My 11th Birthday

In the middle of June I had a party with a lot of balloons.
It was a luau sleepover when everyone was there we picked clovers.

The morning of the party we ate breakfast oh so fast.
Then we went to White Marsh Mall and shopped all the way down the hall.

Then we went to a store and walked in the door.
I sat in a chair this was it I was there.

Then I got the dot and it marked the spot.
Where I would get my ears pieced when the gun went through I felt queerest.

Every year until now I had a fit this year I did it.
When I went home I had a nice scone.

I'm scared to death of needles but I went through
I thought it would be nice to have a new thing or two.
I'm still happy to this day that I wasn't scared I went all the way!
Kayla Lari, Grade 6
Immaculate Heart of Mary School, MD

Valentine for You

Here is a Valentine for you.
This is my gift to you.

I'll get you candy, you get me flowers. We'll be together forever.
I will never leave you; you will never leave me because we're family.

It's Valentines Day!
Let's say hooray because we're together anyway.
I wish you a Happy Valentines Day!

Sanya Hashmi, Grade 4
Courthouse Road Elementary School, VA

Advice

Dear Brother,
Life is like a bouquet of flowers…
Sometimes you get stuck with the weeds.
But with patience, hard work,
And a helping hand from the sun and rain,
More beautiful blooms will appear!
Other times you get a single rose…
Showering love from that one mysterious crush.
You might get a sunflower…
A sign to bloom and make changes in life.
Or a tulip…
A sign to be cheery and to be with your buds.
Whatever the flower is,
A bouquet will help you win or solve a tricky problem —
You just have to keep picking until you choose the right blossom.
Sometimes you are awarded with a gorgeous bouquet…
Meaning, "Congratulations, you did it!"
Keep on picking those flowers!
    Love, Andie

Andie Stone, Grade 5
Har-Bur Middle School, CT

Victoria

Slowly walking, half staggering,
I go to the window
I watch my cousin gracefully running,
each step as light as a feather.
Off she goes,
skirt swooshing,
hair floating behind her.
She stops at the stream
Carefully takes off her shoes.
Wading in she starts sinking,
the gooey mud creeping through her toes.
Her head tilts back
and gives out a delicate laugh.
Wading further in,
She lies down
her skirt floating up to the surface
the stream willingly supporting her;
slowly her thoughts travel into another world.
I turn and stagger back
my thoughts fuzzy from sleepiness
I return to my comforting bed.

Fiona Ross, Grade 5
John Ward Elementary School, MA

Ed

There once was a boy named Ed
Who loved to eat white bread
He ate and he ate
Put on lots of weight
Before long, he dropped dead.

Johanna Villagrana, Grade 5
Charlotte A Dunning Elementary School, MA

Current America

Wind blows through the willows
And war brews through the land
A new leader is being chosen
And a nation is being unfrozen.
For eight years a Texas leader
Has ruled us full and full
But a portion of the nation
Finds him very, very dull.
Many people would not look or care
If Bush were to simply disappear.
Barrack Obama, John McCain, and Hillary Clinton
Are the Presidential candidates
All of them hope to one day
Drive up to the White House's black gates.
Many mothers shed a tear
As their sons pack to go to the War on Terror in Iraq
For five long years U.S. soldiers have died in Iraq
And sadly only a few have ever come back.
We hope the future of this nation is as great as its past
And that it changes for the better pretty fast!

Andrew Katz, Grade 5
Mapleshade Elementary School, MA

The Time of Fall

Swish, swish scream the oak leaves
As they dance upon the trees
"Help, help!" hollered the oak leaves
"Help us, help us, help us please!"
And then, finally, without a sound
They all silently slopped to the ground
Little children run around
All of them jumping, fun is found
Birch leaves crunch beneath their feet
As cereal does between their teeth
Amber colored foliage is raked into a pile
Crazy kids jump for a while
They smell the pine
It smells so fine
Squirrels scurry taking flight
Just like five o'clock traffic at night
Chipmunks start to go to bed
As fast as a red winter sled
Oak, birch, redwood, stand tall
This is the time, the time of fall

Robert Lancia, Grade 6
Madison Middle School, CT

People

All the people of the world,
Skinny, short, fat and tall,
We're all the same from deep within,
Stout, chubby, lean or thin,
Every race, from every nation,
We're all a part of God's creation.

Erik Kline, Grade 6
Worcester Seventh-Day Adventist School, MA

Bad Traits

The first time I hit my sister
Oh boy it felt so great!

But hitting someone
Isn't such a good trait.

So before I got in trouble
I went to apologize.

But when I went to see her
Tears were pouring from her eyes.

I said I was really sorry
Which made her really glad.

And it was then when I realized
That family is the most important thing in life.

So live your life knowing
That they will always be by your side.

Shyanne Garofalo, Grade 6
Irving School, CT

Spring

Spring is here,
It's time to cheer.

Berry blossoms are near,
Let's get on our gear.

Listen to children playing,
They're looking at clouds passing.
Jessie Gagnon, Grade 5
Brookside Elementary School, MA

The Desert

A dry, barren place.
Sidewinders slither around.
It is very hot.
Alex Reardon, Grade 5
Trinity School, MD

1195

Lockers are great, lockers are good.
They keep everything safe.

But when I'm late,
You never open.

I get mad and start to holler,
and then I kick and try again.

You did not open, I hit you again.
Then…

CRASH! BANG! BOOM!

Everything comes falling out!
No matter what I still love my locker!
Nicole Good, Grade 6
Fuller Middle School, MA

The Mosquitoes

I don't like mosquitoes
Mosquitoes suck your blood
They make you itch
They bug you around
They go pzzzz in your ear
That's why I don't like mosquitoes
Gregory Aasen, Grade 4
Marsh Grammar School, MA

My Pencil

Orange as a basket
Shiny as a Folder
Kind of a fat wood
Sharp as a knife
Kind of thin
Frankie LoBuono, Grade 4
Marsh Grammar School, MA

I Am

I am brave and strong
I wonder if I'm going to die soon
I hear myself crying
I see Jesus
I want my family and me to be safe!
I am brave and strong

I pretend that everything is okay
I feel sad
I touch Jesus
I worry about my family
I cry if one of my family members dies
I am brave and strong

I understand that Jesus loves me!
I say I love my family and myself
I dream that I have a better life
I try to be someone like Jesus
I hope that I see Jesus
I am brave and strong
Amariliz Candelaria, Grade 5
Clover Street School, CT

The Shot

Running down the court
With fans cheering
Pressure holding you down
Opponents closing in
You shoot the ball…
But you miss
Your teammates get the rebound
They pass it back to you
You shoot again…
SCORE
Just before the buzzer.
Shelby Stegmaier, Grade 5
Mary Walter Elementary School, VA

Anything Is Possible

I believe in miracles,
And wishes do come true.
I can wish upon a star,
And I know you can too.

Somewhere over the rainbow,
There is a pot of gold.
I know there is I'm sure there is,
That's what I've been told.

Anything is possible,
If you truly believe.
You must try your hardest,
Always do your best,
And you will achieve.
Daniel Robushi, Grade 5
Davenport Ridge School, CT

Frost Bite

On the mountain
I try to fight
The bitter cold
frost bite
Jillian Scannell, Grade 4
Naquag Elementary School, MA

Dust

I'm in a corner
As you can see
A speck of dust that's sitting with me!
It doesn't talk much to tell you the truth,
It doesn't have a mouth
But it does squeak Dutch.
I use him as an obstacle
Because he doesn't move at all.
But I'm just a bunny,
And he's just dust,
But together we make a dust bunny.
Jacob Kallio, Grade 5
Forest Avenue Elementary School, MA

The Words That Come Out of Me!

There are words like Slavery
That make me want to cry.
I dread to say it
As it soon passes by.

There are words like Faith
That make me feel strong.
If I don't think about it
My understanding will go wrong!
Stephanie Thompson, Grade 4
Long Meadow Elementary School, CT

Alone

When I thought I was lost
And everyone was gone
I looked up
And saw nothing
I put my head back down
I thought of who I left
And who left me
No good thoughts came
But then I thought of
Who I still had
And who stayed
No matter what
I looked up again
And then I saw
Truth
In good or bad
I'm never
Alone
Rachel Spencer, Grade 6
Weston Middle School, CT

Mother's Day

For mothers day I gave you a coupon
For taking care of me on, and on.
You have done so many things,
Including giving me my life
Your love is so powerful,
It cuts like a knife.
What brings joy to my heart is the smell of your cooking,
I even have a taste when you aren't looking.
You read to me King Arthur
Every night beside my bed,
And I think about you
Every night in my head.
Every mother's day
We have a brunch,
We're supposed to just love the mother
But I love the whole bunch.
We do so many things on this day,
At least that's what I say.
But on mothers day, I know what I'll do.
I will give presents, make breakfast,
But most important I will love you.

Daniel Grossman, Grade 6
Charles E Smith Jewish Day School, MD

Summers

Summers seem to blow by,
Like the smell of apple pie.

School is out,
All of the children are running about.

We love to play in the pool,
It's so nice and cool.

I ride my bike,
It's just as good as a hike.

We go to the beach,
Our skin turns to a peach.

Now summer has passed,
It happened way too fast.

Ethan Bossange, Grade 5
Charlotte A Dunning Elementary School, MA

Who Am I?

I am like a soccer ball that plays a lot
I am like the TV that talks too much
I am like a Ferrari car that runs too fast
I am like a whale that can be polite when it needs to be
I am as strong as a lion or the characters of *Dragonball Z*
I am as friendly as a dog
I can be as calm as the beaches of El Salvador
I am as curious as a monkey

Jonathan Alas, Grade 6
Fuller Middle School, MA

Me

I laugh like a hyena
My thoughts soar like a bird
My words run fast like a cheetah
My dreams grow like a puppy to a fully grown dog
New questions leap and jump in and out of my mind
like a kangaroo
My curiosity is like a newborn kitten wanting to explore
My memories are as special to me as a mother's child
New thoughts, ideas, and memories will come
But old thoughts, ideas, and memories will stay,
and some will be lost in my mind
But I will always be me

Molly Helmer, Grade 5
Wakefield Forest Elementary School, VA

Earth

The Earth filled with wild flowers
Breezes as cool as a splash of ocean water
Sand as soft as feathers, sparkle like diamonds
Grass as green as a grasshopper
The sky as blue as the sea
The sun glaring in your eyes
Waves crashing together
Swush, splash, gulp
It is like the Earth is singing
Trying to tell you how beautiful it is
Trying to be a great big ball of happiness
That is the Earth

Alexandra Furtado, Grade 5
Dighton Middle School, MA

Girls

G irlfriends
I nvitations to dinner
R eal kisses
L ong lasting
S chool queens

Ethan Severin, Grade 6
Worcester Seventh-Day Adventist School, MA

Choosing

First I was going to write about a monkey,
Because they are so funky,
And how they swing from tree to tree,
Then I thought how long it would have to be.

Then I would write about a dog,
But my mind was a fog.

Next I would write about a state,
But by the time I finished it would be too late.

So I decided to write about them all,
Now I'm finished I think I'll go to the mall.

Brendan Cabey, Grade 6
E W Thurston Middle School, MA

Raindrops

Pip,
Pip, pip,
Plop
I hear raindrops.
Pitter, patter, pitter, patter,
On the roof the rain spatters.
Sploosh, splash, sploosh, splash,
The giant puddles crash.
Onto the windshield — smash.
Swish, swash, swish, swash,
The windshield wipers wash.
Pip, pip, pip,
Plop.

Hilary Cochran, Grade 6
E W Thurston Middle School, MA

This Little Tree

This little tree
that lives 2 blocks away from me
I go and sit
and talk to it
and people stare at me.
I ask it questions,
things I like to mention,
that I couldn't tell anyone else.
I dance around it
and sing about it
and all my classmates laugh at me.
They say, "Little Marie, Little Marie,
why don't you get some real friends
instead of that boring old tree?"
I shrug it off
because they don't see
that this little tree
comes alive to me.

Valerie Lynn Cedrone, Grade 5
C C Burr Elementary School, MA

There Once Was a Grape

There once was a grape
That dressed like an ape
It swung on drapes
All day 'til it was late
Then it fell down and
Squished itself to bed.

Megan McCrory, Grade 4
Plainfield Catholic School, CT

A Winter Night

Falling snow tonight
Cold breezes freezing the lakes
Snow filling the trees
My hair waving in the cold breeze
How I love winter

Cristina Brouwer, Grade 4
Freetown Elementary School, MA

Sensing Indy

I see Indy shake himself dry when he is done swimming
I see him wag his tail when I get off the school bus
And I see him chew his bone happily

I hear Indy thump his tail on the ground as I walk toward him
I hear my squeaky voice as I make him go crazy
And I hear my love singing out to him as I say goodnight

I feel his soft fur as he snuggles up to me
I feel the sharp pain of his claws cut into me like a sword as he jumps up to greet me
And I feel his love seep into my heart and my love does the same

I smell that swampy smell when he is done swimming
And I smell that musty cave breath as he licks my face

I taste his tongue sneak into my mouth as I kiss his muzzle
That's my Indy!

Madison Lynnworth, Grade 4
Miscoe Hill Elementary School, MA

Spring's Back with a Tune

Birds chirp and sing their sunny tunes
encouraging the flowers to bloom
Pop! Bam! Bing! There's one! And another now two!
Daisies and Roses pop too
clouds depart and the sun shines as if it was a bright shining star.
Now let the Blue Jays sing their sunny tunes
and watch the flowers go…
POP! BAM! BING! The flowers bloom
spring's tune has started AGAIN!!!!!!!

Daniel Satterthwaite, Grade 6
School of International Studies at Meadowbrook, VA

The Telltale Heart

There was an old man with a "vulture" eye.
He hired a manservant to take care of him,
but the old man's evil eye scared him to death.

The manservant was haunted by that colorless eye
everywhere he went.
He loved the old man,
But he loathed his horrifying eye.

The manservant knew he had to do something
To stop that appalling eye from haunting him.
Late at night, he quickly, but quietly, snuck into the old man's room.
The evil eye was wide open.

He put a pillow on the man's face, chopped him up and buried him under the floor
Early in the morning, there was a knock at the door.
It was a policeman. "Neighbors heard screams in the night."
The old man is not in his room.
The manservant heard heartbeats and told the police what he did.
They didn't believe him, so he showed them the old man's still beating heart.

Alex Gardner, Grade 6
St Joseph School, MA

Bananas

Bananas, Bananas,
looking like a sliver of the sun
that had fallen to the ground.
Bananas, Bananas,
a big banana smile.
Bananas, Bananas,
they come in a bunch.
Bananas, Bananas,
what a great thing to munch!

Nathan Jordan Maltz, Grade 4
South Area Solomon Schechter Day School, MA

Colors of the Rainbow

R ed is the color of your heart
O range is the color of leaves falling from a tree
Y ellow is the color of the bright sun

G reen is the color of the sparkling grass

B lue is the color of true spirit
I ndigo is the color of the deep sea
V iolet is the color of a flower blooming

Caroline Kren, Grade 4
Weston Intermediate School, CT

Peace

Peace is like Heaven coming from the sky.
Peace looks like the wind blowing my hair.
It sounds like a baby laughing and it can be wonderful but,
Peace is always next to me

Kaylee Fuentes, Grade 4
St Augustine Cathedral School, CT

One

As my heart beats, as the wind blows,
As I race through fields of lush, green grass,
I feel my heart thumping,
My blood flowing,
My head spinning.
As I lay among the soil and seeds,
Blades of grass whispering in my ear,
I feel the steady beat, of the Earth's lifeline,
Pounding through mine.
As we connect, as my heart beats, and the wind blows,
As I race through fields of lush, green grass,
I feel the land around me,
The hills and the ocean,
I feel the rush of the animals, and the clouds,
The life, flowing through me.
Through my veins,
And through my mind it courses.
Until our hearts share the same beat,
Until our souls blend,
Until, we are One.

Alekhya Chaparala, Grade 6
Oak Hill Middle School, MA

My Dog

If my name was daisy
Just like my dog.
I would be chasing my tail
All day long.

Cody Sullivan, Grade 4
Courthouse Road Elementary School, VA

My Mind

My mind is like a soaring plane with wings that never stop,
It's a cruise ship on the dock that is about to take the sea,
A beautiful bright butterfly with newly colored wings,
A bright white star in the sky,
A bleach white snowflake that has just floated down,
Creativity by my side,
Life is just the start of things my mind can think and do,
My mind is a smart explorer that travels around the world,
The flames of the sun are my ideas afloat,
A boat far out on the sea,
Exploring minds of others,
And that is just the start.

Annie Elwell, Grade 5
Raleigh Court Elementary School, VA

Mona Lisa

Stare into my misty eyes,
That have observed so many lives.

Stare into my mischievous smile,
Over time it has cracked just like an old tile.

You are not the first person to stare,
In awe, in awe at my long brown hair.

People travel from far and near,
Just for a day or two right here.

So many times have I had to move,
Just to end up right here in the Louvre.

I have stood the test of time,
So come, so come and be a guest of mine.

Maddy McKeown, Grade 6
E W Thurston Middle School, MA

Blue

Blue is the summer sky.
Blue is the ocean, but I don't know why.
Blue is a raindrop falling in a puddle.
Blue is some frogs close together in a huddle.
Blue is the color of my brand new sweater.
Blue is the color of my Aunt Janet's letter.
Blue is a teardrop on one's face.
Blue is the sweat after a race.
Blue makes me happy.

Lydia Albrecht, Grade 4
Waller Mill Fine Arts Magnet School, VA

Summer
Summer best of all,
The blooming of the flowers,
Every single hour.
Brea Sasser, Grade 4
Hebbville Elementary School, MD

It's Winter
It's winter and it's really cold
I can feel the wind beating on my face
The snow trembling behind me
Dancing in circles around my head.
Annaleah Ramseyer, Grade 4
Freetown Elementary School, MA

Across the Hudson!
To arms my men
for our country we fight,
giving up is not an option,
upon the middle of the night.

"Across the Hudson!"
Guns and cannons galore,
we fight for our country,
and much, much more.

Hessians are here,
ready and near.

Guns at the ready,
hold straight and steady.

Dawn to dusk,
Hessians ahead,
we fire until,
we know they're dead.
Edward Schildnecht, Grade 5
Hindley Elementary School, CT

Pencils
Are tools of imagination
Allowing you to explore everything
Are keys that are able to unlock doors
Which come upon you in your paths
Are passageways into imagination
Connecting it to the world
Are every color ever invented
And use the colors to make
Powerful imagery
Are secrets that only you
Understand the meaning
Are the beginnings and ends
To the greatest stories ever written
Are utensils for writing
Yet they are so much more
Kellen Dunnavant, Grade 5
Raleigh Court Elementary School, VA

I Made a Mistake
I went to the field to get a ball,
I made a mistake…and went to the mall.

I went to the store to buy a snake,
I made a mistake…and bought a cake.

I went to school to get my friend,
I made mistake…and found the end.
Ethan Moquin, Grade 4
Freetown Elementary School, MA

come with me
come with me
my friend
sing the songs
of the trees with me
then dance
on the mossy ground
then watch
the delicate sun set
then rest on the bed
of flowers I made you
then dream
of you and me
walk on the little dirt path
of mother nature.
Isaac Gotterer, Grade 5
Sinai Academy of the Berkshires, MA

All Alone
Sitting here all alone,
No one calls me on the phone,
Sitting here reading a book,
No one even cares to look,

Walking around the endless bend,
No one to go with not even a friend,
Living like this can be sad,
But sometimes life just turns out bad.
Gabrielle C. Phillipo, Grade 5
Forest Avenue Elementary School, MA

A Recipe for Relaxation
2 cups of gold grains of sand.
Toss in some peaceful music and waves.
A lounge chair.
A yoga mat
Seagulls
Clear blue sky.
Palm trees to shade me.
Shells of pearl.
A girl like me in her gray capris
Relaxing on
This little baked island.
McCala McDonald, Grade 5
C C Burr Elementary School, MA

Fire
Fire
Shines bright
A blazing light
Shimmering in the night
Warms you like
A charm
Fire
Anuj Patel, Grade 5
J F Kennedy Middle School, MA

Hatred
Hatred is black tar on the ground
It sounds like the devil attacking
tastes like month-old pizza
and smells like a swamp
Hatred looks like a snake spitting venom
It makes you feel depressed
John-Paul Colasacco, Grade 6
Albert D Griswold Middle School, CT

Ladybugs
Black spots all over
Antennas on top of head
Wings buzz when flying
Tiny legs to walk on
Black spots all over body
Eyes burning at you
Tiny legs are ticklish
Tiny body buzzes around
Meghan Esposito, Grade 5
Jane Ryan School, CT

School Hallway
When we got out of class
I always dash
So I don't get caught like a bass
By the huge 8th graders

I wish I was outside
So I could scream and hide
And not have died
By the huge 8th graders

If I was here
They would kill me like a deer
With an arrow in my ear
Those huge 8th graders

If they break into
My little den
And steal my pen
I'll be angry at the huge 8th graders

I hate those HUGE 8TH GRADERS!!!
Matthew Nevin, Grade 6
Corkran Middle School, MD

The Calm Sea

I look over the bow and dream that I
am drifting far away from land.
I see the fluffy clouds passing through
the light blue sky.

I feel the cool wind press against my face.
I hear the waves splashing against each other.
I look down and see large and tiny fish
swimming in schools.

I sight a dolphin jumping in the air.
I want to dive in the dark blue ocean
and swim with the beautiful whales.

I take out my seashell and listen to the calm sea.
I smell the fresh air and the seagulls flying past me.
I hear a storm coming, the sky begins to darken.
It begins to rain. Instantly the rain stops.
I see a colorful rainbow.

I hear my friends yelling my name.
I notice I was home the whole time.

John King, Grade 6
Swampscott Middle School, MA

A Weird Walk

This tale may seem odd but is very true
On a walk with my black Cocker Spaniel named Curly
I left with one dog and came back with two!
On a very cold morning I left with my dog
Toward a long walk that was too long to jog
I heard a very loud barking on my way back
I came to a dog that was well out of whack
A little brown beagle that could do no harm
Was chasing a jogger who was in great alarm
I had seen the beagle before and I knew the owners
She asked me to help and what could I do
But let my dog play with the beagle I knew
To my surprise the dog followed me home
When we got nearer I told the dog to come
For I knew it shouldn't roam
It waltzed up my steps and in through the door
This was something I had never seen before
When my mom and I drove the dog to his house in our car
All the owner said was, "Thanks, I guess he went too far."

Michael Rosamilia, Grade 6
Scotts Ridge Middle School, CT

Love

Love is like the wind
You can't see it, but it's there
Like waves in the ocean
You can find it everywhere
Love is like the wind

Luan Cadabia, Grade 5
Charlotte A Dunning Elementary School, MA

Animals

Animals creeping in the dark,
Be very quiet or they'll get scared.
Some are house pets,
While some live in water.
Many are wild in the woods,
Then, there are those who stay out of sight.
Some swing from vines,
As others hang from trees.
Many swim in water,
But most run on the ground.
Some are vicious,
Yet some are delightful,
Some are gigantic,
Others are petite.
Heaven has called some home,
And others continue to surround us with their beauty.

Brooke Towle, Grade 4
Riderwood Elementary School, MD

Miranda

M y game is softball
I love softball. I
R un run run run
A round the bases. I
N ever let a ball go by
D ANG!! She got out.
A nd catch that ball whizzing by your head! I

H it that ball all the way to right field
I mpossible to beat
L ike it?? I
L ove it!!

Miranda Hill, Grade 6
Monelison Middle School, VA

Peace

Peace wonderful peace
A warm summer breeze
The grass swaying back and forth like people
Silence but yet there is sound
A beautiful orchestra playing to the sound of your thoughts
A sight to behold Peace

Ethan Eddy, Grade 5
Marblehead Community Charter Public School, MA

Scared

I walk into school with a smile on my face
I hear the noise inside my head.
The expression on my face turned
Red purple and black
My best friend comforts me till the end
So for now on my life at school has changed
I'm not scared anymore
And my face is the right color

Brianna Tyler, Grade 5
Francis Asbury Elementary School, VA

Summer

S un shining all day
U nder the umbrella on the beach
M e and my friends
M any hot days
E veryone has barbecues
R elax all summer-long!

Anna Pearson, Grade 5
J F Kennedy Middle School, MA

Angel

An angel came down to me
She said that I did not need to cry
If I wanted to see her again
I just had to close my eyes and dream

Kendra Barrera, Grade 5
Clark Avenue Middle School, MA

Silver Swan

A silver swan
Glides
Strides
Over the clear
Translucent
Water
As if ice
Were layered
On top
But as
The
Sun comes up
It all seems to
Stop.

Cameron Hunt, Grade 5
C C Burr Elementary School, MA

Bright and Dark

Day
Bright, sunny
Entertaining, enjoying, learning
Conversation, laughter, stars, moon
Resting, snoring, dreaming
Dark, cool
Night

Nicki Hosey, Grade 6
Captain Nathan Hale Middle School, CT

Revolt

Nat Turner
brave, impatient
killing, revolting, leading
slaves, Virginia, American, rebellion
capturing, convicting, believing
strong, commander
John Brown

Brian Shartzer, Grade 4
Waller Mill Fine Arts Magnet School, VA

Summer's Here

Summer
is here
the best season of all

As I walk down the garden stones and bricks
I can see the rocky dirt path
that leads to the big beautiful bushes of strawberries
I just can't wait
to go pick the berries and eat them in the nice cool summer breeze

Meghan Mulholland, Grade 5
Francis Asbury Elementary School, VA

What Is White?

White is the color of fluffy snowflakes,
And the icing on yummy cupcakes!
White is a cloud in a dream,
And delicious vanilla ice cream.
It is like an endless path.
And bubbles in a bubble bath.
White is the color of a polar bear, paper towels, and a bone.
Also the color of old women's hair, snowy owls, and a sugar cone.
It is the color of marshmallows,
And the beard of old fellows.
The sound of white is the leaves rustling in the breeze.
And white is the tissue you use when you sneeze.
White tastes sweet like sugar so pure.
It is the color that you feel after finding a cure!
White is the color that is truly great…
And a color whose decision you would not debate!

Danielle LaPenta, Grade 5
Har-Bur Middle School, CT

Ode to My Quilt

My mother brought me my quilt
Which was newly sewn from London,
A quilt as soft as a cloud.
I wrapped my body in it as if it were a cloak
Sewn together with stitches of sun and cotton.
A powerful quilt
My body was a butterfly made of cotton,
A monarch
Bright yellow, shot through by one pink thread,
A strong bear, a broad caterpillar,
My body was honored in this way by this powerful quilt.
It was so beautiful.
For the first time my body seemed unacceptable,
Like a freezing beggar,
A beggar unworthy of that woven warmth, of that vibrant quilt.
Nevertheless I resisted the sharp temptation to hide it away as girls hide diaries,
As parents hide presents away for celebration,
My body was a flower bud, becoming more wholesome, by this quilt.
The moral of my ode is this:
Sad becomes happy, and cold becomes warm.
When it is a matter of a quilt stitched with love in the winter.

Crosbie Marine, Grade 5
New Canaan Country School, CT

Cruise Ship

I'm going on a cruise ship,
Have you been on one
Well let me tell you something,
They're lots of fun,
You can go places like Turkey or Maine,
But don't take your kids
That's a real pain.

Matthew Barnett, Grade 4
Memorial-Spaulding Elementary School, MA

Simon Cowell

American Idol judge Simon Cowell
The meanest one, he's just like an owl
Too bad his fashion sense is whacked
He only wears three colored shirts — white, gray, and black.

Sage Dieterle, Grade 6
Captain Nathan Hale Middle School, CT

Wow

Wow that is a big toy
Wow that is a big smile
Why are you smiling
Only because I am near you
Why thank you
Why are you nice to me

Emily Gillin, Grade 4
Courthouse Road Elementary School, VA

Friends

F antastic
R esponsible for fond memories
I ndescribable they're always there
E xcellent
N ever ending fun
D ay by day getting closer
S omething special

Jennifer Billo, Grade 4
Helen H Hansen Elementary School, MA

Stepping Up to Bat

I walk nervously but excitedly to home plate,
My sweaty palms tightly grasp the blue metal bat
And I move my elbows back
I see the pitcher wind up, but can no longer hear the crowd.

The pink gum sticks to the roof of my mouth, not moving —
The balls seems to move in slow motion as it comes to me.
I wait for the bright target to approach the sweet spot,

Then, at the right moment, my whole body tightens
And I lunge into the ball, swinging the bat as fast as I can
The only sound I can hear now is the loud crack of the bat
And my rapid breathing as I spring to get to first base,
The umpire flails his arms quickly calling out "Sa-fe!!"

Angela Baldacci, Grade 6
Swampscott Middle School, MA

Ode to Toaster Waffles

You are so good with buttery syrup
And you are so glad with the circular shape
You are the best breakfast food I like
You smell so good when you come out of our toaster
So I am sorry that I have to eat you

Cameron Eccles, Grade 4
C Hunter Ritchie Elementary School, VA

Laughing

Laughing, laughing all night long,
Laughing 'til the morning's dawn,
Laughing, laughing as you run,
Laughing is so much fun

Laughing, laughing 'round and 'round,
Laughing is such a wonderful sound,
Laughing, laughing because nothing's wrong,
Laughing, laughing on and on

Valerie Morani, Grade 5
Foxborough Regional Charter School, MA

4-Year-Old Princess

"I'm a princess."
Sophie.
4 years old,
But still the greatest little sister
Anyone could ask for.
Her long, gorgeous eyelashes may droop,
Her face may get as red as a tomato when she's livid.
But I don't care.
On December 31, 2002,
She arrived after 9 months.
I could almost hear her saying
"Not now," when she was born.
Her favorite lines are
"One minute!" and "I don't want to."
Or maybe the conversation starter for her,
"Second of all,"
But now, 4.5 years later,
She's talking and walking,
She is so adorable, and she's
More alive than ever.

Stu Krantz, Grade 6
Charles E Smith Jewish Day School, MD

The Sky

The sky has a sun that waves at me
The sky has clouds that look over me
The sky has stars when it is dark outside
The sky makes rain so we go inside
The sky can be cool when it is fall time
The sky can be warm when it is summer time
The sky can make a rainbow that shines before your eyes
The sky, the sky, the sky

Jimmy Kervick, Grade 5
Soule Road School, MA

What I Shall Put in a Box Marked "Friends"

Our swims in the pool its water so blue, the clothes that we shared from Limited Too.
The laughs that we had when we heard something funny, the day we went shopping with tons of money.
The leftovers of tickets of movies we saw, staying up late not sleeping at all.
The cherry shorts I still haven't given back, our matching Hannah Montana sacks.
The happiness we shared having fun, the warm summer days lying in the sun.
The pictures that we giggled at, of you and me in a funny hat, those shoes that I just adored,
the time that we were very bored.
The things I hated that we wanted to sell, you will always be my BFFL!

Emily Roe, Grade 4
Wyngate Elementary School, MD

Autumn Is Everywhere

Autumn is everywhere, all around me.
Leaves are jumping down the tree.
Crimson, nutmeg and emerald are surrounding me.
The foliage flows to the ground like a gymnast tumbling through her routine.
And the prickly pine cones hide under peaceful leaves so crafts people need to dig for them.
Autumn is everywhere.

Autumn is everywhere, the rustling wind picks me up and floats me away like I am in a dream.
The acorns fall from the tree, making a sound like someone cracked her knuckle.
The apple grass brushes over my shoes disguising them, when my shoes shuffle through the grass.
Autumn is everywhere.

Autumn is everywhere I hear the birds chirping with joy.
I smell a fire and roasting marshmallows as I finish my journey through the woods.
I see a rock wall that reminds me of people sitting in the pews during church.
Autumn is everywhere.

Autumn is everywhere, the itchy ivy wears a scarlet disguise, so it is hard to tell what it looks like.
Also, the tough oak trees are so tall no one can touch the top.
I look forward to finishing my woodland walk.
Back home, mom will have apple and pumpkin pie that is moist and steaming with delight.
The pies taste like creamy cups of cinnamon and sugar.
Autumn is everywhere.

Lauren Fitzsimmons, Grade 6
Madison Middle School, CT

Christmas Day

Christmas Day
The tree filled with mysterious presents stacked underneath the evergreen.
The sweet, smelling cinnamon pine cones Mom placed underneath the tree.
My brother unwrapping the presents like a bear digging its claws in the nice, juicy, salmon.
The sweet eggnog on Christmas morning slipping down my mouth as a waterfall down into the river.
My awesome virtual skateboard game slips through my fingers like soft silk and milk.
Christmas Day

Alex Pellerano, Grade 5
Jane Ryan School, CT

Looking Through the Window

Times have changed now looking through the window. From the field of grass to a blanket of gray. A shadowy cover that hides the true earth. Lost in factories and smoke that smother the cities and towns. My window might be fading from the fast coming dark but the atmosphere is tearing ripping wildly apart. Rivers and oceans desolated from destruction. Us people are all but saving the world. If we all could stand back in our shadows looking and seeing what is happening looking through the window.

Julexus Cappell, Grade 5
Keister Elementary School, VA

Sheala

Sheala, Sheala what can I say????
She always makes my day
From the bottom of the toy chest, I never knew
That she could help me overcome the flu,
She's never out of sight
She sleeps with me at night
She has round paws
Not like a real dog's

So Sheala I'll have to say,
you're just ok
oh and she's a stuffed animal —
just by the way!!!

Taahira Boyd, Grade 6
Magnolia Elementary School, MD

The Sun

The sun is as hot as a chile pepper fresh from the garden.
It's as bright as a light bulb, as big as the Earth.
It's as yellow as a dandelion,
It's as round as a brand new baseball,
It warms you like a huge oven in the middle of the desert.

Matthew Medina, Grade 4
Helen H Hansen Elementary School, MA

Dying

Why do people have to die?
Why is it dark
when people die?
All I can see when people die is… crying.
darkness, and rain outside,
All it sounds like is…crying,
one last breath from
the person who is dying.
All I feel is sadness,
one less person to talk to
and I'm a little lonely.
All I see is…shadows,
moonlight during the day,
and darkness.
What do most people die from
Is it cancer?
Is it from smoking?
Is it from sickness?
Is it from age?
Is it from second hand-smoke?
Why do people die?

Hannah Card, Grade 4
Hawley Elementary School, CT

Penguins

Penguins waddle fast
Penguins dive under the deep
In the cold blue sea.

Alex Nguyen, Grade 5
Charlotte A Dunning Elementary School, MA

Summer Fun

S wimming around the pool in the hot sun
U ntil the day ends we never stop to rest
M emories of the good days of summer
M oaning when summer ends
E ntertaining each other for fun
R ings of the ice cream truck make me smile

F un times
U nity, the power of the kids
" **N** ightime" the first day of summer is finished

Jalen Markel Paul, Grade 5
Sacred Heart Elementary School, MA

The Big Colorful Tree

There is a big tree out the window
With three different colors
Green, maroon, and orange
The leaves are swaying in the wind
They are trying to break free
Trying to flutter around in the cool fall wind
Near the church and near the school
And out the window is the big tree with three different colors
Green, maroon, and orange

Tiffany Abbondanza, Grade 5
St Mary's Primary School, MA

Winter

Winter
Fun, cold
Sledding, ice skating, skiing
Ice, fires, friends, scream
Swimming, laughing, water skiing
Warm, thirsty
Summer

Alexis Zuras, Grade 4
C Hunter Ritchie Elementary School, VA

Wild

Magnificent creatures
Throwing all their weight into speed
They are free
They are and always will be
These majestic creatures throw their heads
With the wind
Whinnying to everything behind them
Pounding the sand with what we call hands
Wild, wild west
That is where most of them roam free
Running away from polluted air
Looking at the wind
Feeling the breeze in their mane
One word to describe them
Wild

Eleni Demestihas, Grade 5
Booth Hill School, CT

Spring

Nice weather appears
Flowers pop out everywhere
The sun is shining.
Cari Elizabeth Middlecamp, Grade 4
St Joseph School-Fullerton, MD

People

People.
Man is the most powerful animal.
Too powerful.
They can turn peace to war.
They can turn war to peace.
They can kill millions.
They can save millions.
People are a fearful thing.*

*Line written by Fujita Ryo
Jack Snedaker, Grade 5
Rowayton Elementary School, CT

Gunfire

My friend called me a liar
When there was a loud roar of gunfire.
I could have sworn it hit the door,
But I thought no more.
My world collided when
The secret denied.
It was only
Fire crackers!
Khari Jones, Grade 4
Bensley Elementary School, VA

Water

Water crashing,
Water smashing.
You can see
Fluorescent
Fish and
Amazing whales
That splash
And frolic
All the time.
The coral
Is so beautiful.
The colors
So nice.
The seaweed
Is long
Wavy as always.
Slimy yet
Still beautiful.
So many
Sights to
See in the sea.
Grace Orfanello, Grade 4
St Mary's Primary School, MA

Elvis

A famous singer named Elvis,
when he sang he shook his pelvis,
he rarely had time to spare,
for he always had to do his hair.
Elijah Estes, Grade 6
Captain Nathan Hale Middle School, CT

Money

It is important
Money helps you pay your bills
Kids can use it too
Daniel Powers, Grade 4
Brookside Elementary School, MA

My Locker

Number 1146 is my favorite number.
It is my locker.
Although it's messy, it's still so cool.
It keeps my books and it's always so full.
It goes BANG when I close it,
it goes CREAK when I open it.
With his best buddy the lock,
it keeps all my stuff with luck.
Karla Martinez, Grade 6
Fuller Middle School, MA

Pools

Pools are big
and filled with water.
Fathers go in pools
to play with their daughters.
Lexie LoCoco, Grade 5
Milton L Fuller Elementary School, MA

Boring Forests

The boring forest
With snoring leaves
Among the trees
Mom get me out of here
Oh please oh please
When I sniff the air
It makes me sneeze
And wheeze

Oh Mom just get me out
Of here oh please oh please
It's worse than studying
On a Friday night
And this forest gives me a fright
I get bored and just have
To admit that this family
Trip will have to be fun
Without me
I QUIT!
Rachel Bernui, Grade 5
Newton-Lee Elementary School, VA

Show Horses

Show horses, show horses everywhere,
Beautiful, tight braids in their hair.
Claire Chick, Grade 4
Naquag Elementary School, MA

Bug House

A bug house is a snug house
Maybe under the rug house
No glowing fires or cable wires
Just a comfy cozy bug house
Emmalee Deojay, Grade 5
Plainfield Catholic School, CT

Dreams

Dreams are cool,
Dreams are cruel,
Dreams are different to you.

Dreams are nice
Dreams give advice
Dreams give imagination greatness.

Dreams are smart,
Dreams give you thought,
Dreams always give you a memory.
Dreams
Zach Mastrianni, Grade 5
J F Kennedy Middle School, MA

Yankees

Announcer starts the game
lineup and starting pitcher
A-Rod, Messina, Damon,
Giambi, Matusi, and Jeter.

On the couch I wait anxiously.
The first pitch and play
ready to take on the world
'cause today is opening day.

My remote can take a rest
this channel will not change
until the final out
that decides the winner of the game.

Popcorn, peanuts, and Coke
will get me through each inning
screaming, jumping, and bragging
whenever we are winning.

The Yankees are the best
the Yankees are my team
Word Series victory
is always my season's dream!
Tyler Quinn-Pereira, Grade 6
Edmond P Talbot Middle School, MA

The Life of Harriet Tubman

In the year 1820 a young girl was born,
Her name was Harriet and her parents were torn.
For they had become slaves and they probably knew,
That if things didn't change, she would be a slave too.

Harriet was raised by her folks, Old Rit and Ben,
Who let her be hired out at the young age of ten.
At age twenty-four, Harriet's heart it did grow,
To a man John Tubman and the freedom he did know.

John Tubman was going to betray his fine wife,
And all because Harriet wanted a better life.
Harriet went to the North without John anyway,
And was able to escape the patrollers and keep them at bay.

While she was in the North she met William Still,
And Harriet knew she had found a safe friend in Bill.
She went back to the South for slaves, ten times or more,
And all this she did before the start of the war.

The Civil War began and lasted five long years,
When the North finally won, the slaves began their cheers.
Harriet became a hero to those near and far,
She is remembered this day as one who raised the bar.

Kevin Doherty, Grade 6
Daniel L Joyce Middle School, MA

School

School is for learning,
And sometimes it's fun.
You are always learning,
And you're never done.
School takes up,
Fall, winter, and spring,
But think, of all the money it will bring.
There's a teacher, a principal, and a secretary too,
But the most important person is you!
School starts in the morning at nine,
I know that the day will be fine.

Jane Hickey, Grade 5
Toquam Magnet School, CT

Cat, Rat, Snap

I jump as the cat clashed against my cage
I could feel the hair on my back stand up straight
Falling down into the bedding,
I see my owner come and take me out
I feel comfortable now
that my owner is here to protect me
from that pesky cat
She gives me cheese to comfort me
While I fall into a deep sleep
Feeling my owner's warmth

Abigail Hutton, Grade 6
Litchfield Intermediate School, CT

School Subject

Math is hard, art is boring
When I listen to the teacher
I end up snoring
I can't wait until the bell rings
So I can go do my things

Brandon Jimenez, Grade 5
Foxborough Regional Charter School, MA

Lighting the Menorah

I scratch the match
against the matchbox.
The flame bursts
and I light
the golden menorah.
The eight candles
reflect off the window,
The menorah's bright light makes it hard to see.
The wax from the candles
drips onto the menorah.
Soon the candles
are little stubs
of light
ready to burn
out any second.
Then they flicker…
and go out
but the images
of them melting
on that golden menorah
still is with me!

Anna O'Gorman, Grade 6
Swampscott Middle School, MA

Change

If I could change the world
Everybody would be able to do
What they want

If I were to change the world
Everyone won't have to worry
About war, we would all get along
Everyone would unite under one law
That law is treat everyone fairly

9/11 would be forgotten
We would still have the Twin Towers
Nobody wants to remember those who passed
Nobody will remember the 4 planes

All people would live in a house
Poor or rich
We would all live as one
We all have dreams
To change the world

Sarah Clough-Segall, Grade 6
Glenbrook Middle School, MA

Summer
In the summer air,
Happy birds sing peaceful songs.
In my big window.
Vashaun Burrell, Grade 4
Hebbville Elementary School, MD

Poetry
Poetry is sweet and fine.
It is just a big spotlight.
It makes surrounds beautiful and nice.
I like the fun of it
And thinking of rhymes.
Jenny Hale, Grade 4
Crestwood Elementary School, VA

War
Bombs falling everywhere
Patients, death all over
Volunteers crying
Everyone is running
Explosions all together,
Is fear itself
Loved ones worry, others running
War is scary for all people
It comes to an end
People dead, others alive
Wait to see if he survived.
Corey Leja, Grade 6
Whitinsville Christian School, MA

The World Is White
I wake up one morning,
And gaze out the window,
Attracted by the magnificent sight.

The ground is blanketed with snow,
The branches, slick with ice.

The newly-risen sun is bright,
And reflects off the snow,
Blinding me.

The sky, a deep blue,
Not a cloud in sight,
On this early morning.

All is silent,
Peaceful, relaxing,
It feels like I'm the only one on Earth.

I open the window,
It is brisk, and chilly,
My breaths come in small puffs.
The world is white!
Zach Spitz, Grade 5
Mill Pond School, MA

Baseball…To Me
The smell of hot dogs, in the breeze, as I walk on the field.
Nerves wracked as I step on the mound for the first pitch of the game.
Excitement and relief when we finally get three outs.
Our turn to bat.
Relax, focus, stay back, deep breaths.
Explode to the ball and hear the ping.
Ball floating through the air like a paper airplane in flight.
Run, run, run! SAFE!!!!!!!
Logan Mills, Grade 6
Salem Church Middle School, VA

The Sunset
The sunset is so beautiful tonight
Such pretty colors!
Orange
Purple
Pink
And green
So pretty, so bright, and definitely light!
I'll watch all night until it vanishes into the sky and
I'll wish for another one to come back tomorrow just as bright!
It's so pretty I could sing, it's like a shiny diamond ring!
I'll be singing and dancing or maybe flinging and prancing all night long.
But when it's time to sleep you'll have to say goodnight
To all the light and get cozy under the covers until your all bundled up.
No more singing or dancing, nor flinging or prancing.
It's time to go to sleep.
Goodnight sunset!
Madison Sauter, Grade 4
Miscoe Hill Elementary School, MA

One Great Summer Day
It was dawn one day and the hot sun was
  blazing
    down
      on
       me.
  I was paddling in my canoe in the crystal clear river.
It was so clear I could see my white rope.
  Just as I was paddling a graceful heron swooped down and sat beside me
We paddled all the way back home together.
  I will always remember that sunny day as one great summer day.
Morgen Salyers, Grade 5
Francis Asbury Elementary School, VA

Who Am I?
I am a sun, bright as the light and sugary as the moon
I am a radio that never turns off
I am the sun that goes over my country, the Dominican Republic
I am looking good like my lip gloss
I can be hyper like a dog jumping up and down with a smile on my face
I am a crazy student that always gets in trouble
I am a rat that fits everywhere a person can fit
I can fly like Jordan and I can party like a rock star
Iracely Sanchez, Grade 6
Fuller Middle School, MA

Fall

The wind blowing in my hair
and the leaves crunching under my feet.
The strong sun on my face.
Laughing with my friends under a brown willow tree.
All the colors floating around me
brown, red, orange and yellow too.
I love fall. Don't you?

Margaret A. O'Brien, Grade 5
Lincoln Street School, MA

My Dad

My dad is so sweet,
He buys me tons of treats.

He fills my life with fun,
Always trying to include everyone.

He brings joy and happiness into my life
Every day and every night.

He really cares for me
Including my mommy.

He loves to see me happy
With a big smile on my face.

When I'm depressed and blue
He tries to make me smile so I'll laugh with him too.

When all of his work is done
We'll be having a bunch of fun!

Emily McCarthy, Grade 6
St Joseph School-Fullerton, MD

Cheesy!

Grilled cheese is the sandwich
I like the most
It is grilled in to
Golden buttery toast

You wrap it in foil
350 in the oven
The wonderful taste
You will be lovin'

Oozing from the side
Is melted cheese
Once you finish
You'll ask for "more please"

When you are done
And full with your meal
Clear your spot or
With mother you will deal!

Xavier Benjamin, Grade 5
Church of the Redeemer Christian School, MD

Titanic

Rose sits upon a board floating in the water
Jack is floating with no life preserver
holding on to Rose.
Rose makes a promise never to let go
and to die old and warm in her bed
Jack freezes to death
a boat comes for help
Rose
    lets
        go and swims for her life
Rose is saved
her and 6 others
out of fifteen hundred
and Jack is
        never
            seen
               again.

Maddie Barcomb, Grade 4
Munger Hill Elementary School, MA

A Lady High Up

A lady high up
Not moving or breathing
Almost touching the sky
Standing there so proud and tall
Her green has almost faded
But looks white through the misty air
In the surrounding water boats swish by
On land cars zoom up and down the busy street
Both carry tourists from galore
They have come to see just the lady
Just her
They all look
Then they all think…
What a wonderful lady she is
Yes, she is a wonderful lady

Our Statue of Liberty is a wonderful lady

Marissa Scott, Grade 5
St Mary's Primary School, MA

What Is Autumn?

Dancing flames leaping out of crisp, fallen leaves
The sparkling sun beating on cold air and dewed grass
A spooky walk in the frozen night
A festival of bright Mother Nature
Playful animals lurking in the dim moonlight
A lively graveyard flooded with the dazzling outdoors
The song of children playing happily in the streets
A peaceful stroll in the park
The sound of a rake scraping the grass to grasp fallen leaves
The exploding crowd of a long exciting world series game
That is Autumn

Sam Ditkoff, Grade 4
Weston Intermediate School, CT

School

I go to school
And I act cool
But people think I'm not
They say that I should stop
They say that I'm a fool
Mona Mahmoud, Grade 4
Grace Miller Elementary School, VA

What Is a Horse?

What is a horse?
A horse is…
A loyal companion
A friend to the end
Elegant and graceful
A strong animal, but gentle too

A horse is…
Caring like a mother is to her child
The sun on a sunny day
A good friend
A beautiful animal

A horse is…
Amazing to me
Big and strong
A trusted animal
Wild and free.
Melissa Bokine, Grade 4
Fawn Hollow Elementary School, CT

Hershey Park

Once I entered Hershey Park,
I hear screams and talking.
I'm hit in the face with the smell of
Pizza, hamburgers,
Hot dogs,
And cheeseburgers.

And soon I'm eating
Pizza, hamburgers,
Hot dogs,
And cheeseburgers.

A few minutes later,
I'm holding onto
The safety bar
On the sidewinder.

I go on what feels
Like a hundred rides except
For this one like ferris wheels.
I want to stay
In Hershey Park
The rest of the day.
Nick Rakowski, Grade 5
Oakdale Elementary School, MD

Wind Travels

Wind whistles by me.
It leaves me shaking
like the shivering trees
of Fall.
A striking cold whistle
is a humming song of winter.
A warm breeze pushes
winter to the side.
A blazing sun beam lets
me know it's summer.
Where did the wind go?
Daniela Lopez, Grade 5
Clark Avenue Middle School, MA

Rain

Inky black
Wet like lakes
Makes things grow well
Rain
Alex O'Connell, Grade 5
St Christopher's School, VA

Pencil Poem

A pencil.
A hexagon
Known to man as the
"Use-every-day."
But I think of
a pencil
differently,
like the feel
of silk,
or the smell
of rich chocolate.
The pencil,
Is the shrine,
Of poetry.
Harrison Knapp, Grade 4
King's Highway Elementary School, CT

Peace

Peace is like a big bright flower
in the sky

Peace looks like
a world of happiness

It sounds like a
choir of birds singing and

It can be commotion
sometimes but,

Peace is always in Heaven.
Alloir Gordon, Grade 4
St Augustine Cathedral School, CT

A Day in the Jungle

As I rapidly swing
from tree to tree
I feel the
roughness of them.
I smell the fresh
air as it
bangs against my face.
I see the yummy
bananas and grab
a great big yellow
mushy one from
the tree.
Taylor Rousseau, Grade 6
Litchfield Intermediate School, CT

Birthdays

You eat lots of cake.
You can get lots of presents.
People will be there.
the cake will be delicious.
Your friends will be nice to you.
Samantha Cotto, Grade 4
Battlefield Elementary School, VA

Snow

White and Fluffy
The snow came down
There is white all around
I slip and slide on the ice
A sled would be nice
I sled on a toboggan
The snow comes up and hits my noggin
I love playing with snowballs
It's great when snow falls
As I played in the new fallen snow
My toes and fingers froze
When my day is done
I could not wait until tomorrow
To go and play in the snow
Zachary Kulesza, Grade 6
Whitinsville Christian School, MA

Words Unspoken

I know how I feel about you,
I just don't say.
Is it cause of me?
Or is it just the way,
I think I like you,
I talk to you every day.
Plus a lot of people say,
You feel the same way.
The words for you,
Are just locked up in a cage,
Most likely they are going to break away.
Auseanta Holloway, Grade 6
Benjamin Syms Middle School, VA

Candy Monster

Bubble gum hands that are gooey and sticky.
Rock candy eyes that make your mouth water.
M&M finger and toenails that look extremely delicious.
Rainbow skittles that fall from her hair the size of your head.
A chocolate bunny for a nose.
But even though this monster is delicious,
I'm not so sure it will last!

Wynn Hollis, Grade 5
Hindley Elementary School, CT

Laundry at Sea

Cool, gentle wind blows in my face.
Fresh, linen sheets puff out like sails on a boat.
I twist the crank to tighten the clothesline.
Giant capes ripple in the wind like waves in the sea.
Am I really in my yard?

Ethan Lowman, Grade 5
Wakefield Forest Elementary School, VA

When I Think of My Grandmother

When I think of my grandmother
I see her happiness when she talks to me
I see her sadness when she talks about my cousin
I see her personality when she talks about honesty
I see her delightful smile when she starts laughing at my jokes
When I think of my grandmother
I hear her voice on the phone, sounding like music for my ears
I hear her banging pans when she washes them
I hear her talking about her life when she was little
I hear her singing Christian music
When I think of my grandmother
I smell her hands dirty from the garden
I smell her caramel shampoo
When I think of my grandmother
I taste her "Pamonha," corn and cheese
I taste her "Frango Cairpira," chicken
I taste her desserts like "pudim"
When I think of my grandmother
I feel her hug squeezing me
I feel her amazing hands doing a massage
When I think of my grandmother

Isadora do Carmo, Grade 6
Fuller Middle School, MA

Too Much Homework!

I have too much homework, don't you see —
Reading, math, and social studies
So much science, spelling too —
It is too much homework to do
Book reports, tests, and so much more.
Homework, homework, homework galore!
Homework here, homework there —
Homework is everywhere!

Krista Laforest, Grade 5
Sacred Heart School, MA

Calculator

Life has many options just like a calculator.
You add on things or subtract things from
your life or maybe divide your life into groups.
You may get a remainder that you don't want
so you make it into 1 whole decision. But
soon you may break down like a calculator
or blow up and you can run out of batteries
if you choose the wrong option.

Andy Kossowski, Grade 6
Albert D Griswold Middle School, CT

Spring

In the spring the tender wind laps at my face
All my troubles melt away
In the spring, the summer is holding back its delight
It is a wonderful time as showers give life to all the plants
It's as warm as honey slipping down my throat
Spring is a time of life

Ian Hickey, Grade 5
Booth Hill School, CT

Birds

Birds are so
Intelligent
They have wonderful
Colorful feathers
They look and feel
Sort of soft
I also see them when they flock
When they land they like to eat then take off
So just for a reminder when you see them
Make sure you look and enjoy watching them too

Gabrielle Greenhill, Grade 6
Irving School, CT

TV

I am a TV
I wonder what they are watching
I hear bang, boom, bam inside me
I see them watching me
I want to be a big screen TV
I am happy that they watch my shows
I pretend not to move
I feel warm when I'm turned off
I touch the carpet
I worry they'll replace me for a big screen TV
I cry when I'm turned off
I am young
I understand why they watch me
I say all the words people say on the shows they watch
I dream of being in a better house
I try to be calm
I hope to not be thrown out
I am a TV

Connor Cox, Grade 6
Page Middle School, VA

Emotions

Happy or sad
Glad or mad
Emotions are everywhere
Surprised or bored
Enthusiastic or adored
They are always there
Pain or overjoyed
Excited or annoyed
Emotions are everywhere

Elizabeth Magee, Grade 5
Southbrook Academy, MA

Juggernaut

J ust unstoppable
U nkillable
G reat
G igantic
E nergetic
R eally fast
N othing can destroy it
A bsolutely indestructible
U nlimited
T itanium

David Pease, Grade 5
Ashford School, CT

Life

We are manufactured,
Sent out for a test drive.

We must be oiled,
And gassed.

Eventually, we become old,
And rusty.
Some of our parts stop working.
We have to be fixed.

And after a while,
Our engine stops.

We break down.
Chris Savoca, Grade 6
Scotts Ridge Middle School, CT

Spring

Spring is my favorite time of year,
And now it's finally here!
A week off from school,
Not too hot, but not too cool.
Spring is full of memories,
singing birds, and buzzing bees.
I love Spring!
It's almost like my favorite thing.
Julia McDonald, Grade 4
E Ethel Little Elementary School, MA

Neighbors

Do you know those neighbors?
The ones who play with
Star Wars light sabers
The ones who accidentally lock
their kids out of the house
The ones who go running around the neighborhood screaming about a mouse
The ones who always miss
the bus stop every day
The ones who randomly on their
lawns just sit down and lay
The ones who come to your house
singing Christmas songs
The ones who as a neighborly welcome get you a pair of tongs
The ones who play in your yard
The ones who send you another
person's Christmas card
I know those neighbors all too well
For this poem is about my family and me as well

Natasha Armbrust, Grade 6
Scotts Ridge Middle School, CT

Fire

Its sparks fly like birds, but burning in the air.
Like bees finding pollen from their flowers.
The smell is like ashes burning for heat and brightness.
There are so many shapes in it.
The fire starts glowing… and then I can taste the burning hot heat.
I look at it and can see so many things like bicycle wheels
and triangles in its atmosphere.
I feel warm from its hot, red, fiery color burning in the air.
It fills me with thoughts…what if the burning hot fire could talk?
Michael van der Merwe, Grade 4
King's Highway Elementary School, CT

Feathered Friend

I know he's gone.
My yellow, red, gray, and white feathered friend.
He used to chirp every dawn.
Glide around the house all the time.
My first and last feathered friend.
He chirped when he sat on my hand.
I didn't seem to care when his sharp nail clawed my skin.
I didn't seem to care when he nipped my finger.
I didn't seem to care that I had to take care of him all the time.
I didn't seem to care for those things because he was worth it all.
He really did seem happy.
So very ecstatically and joyful, my feathered friend.
Lost in the abyss of the cold world.
One day he's normal the next day he flees, lost in the wilderness.
I never saw my awesome friend ever again.
He really was a wonderful bird.
So very playful.
All my friends adored him.
Especially me.

Dean Bregman, Grade 6
Charles E Smith Jewish Day School, MD

Soccer Ball

As I pass the ball to my teammate,
they pass back to me.
I am running
as fast as a tiger
making sure that every step counts
as I am tricking people.
It is just me and the goalie.
I shoot the ball
as strong as a kangaroo's legs.
And the ball is as fast as an eagle.
It is spinning really fast and then…

I fell down!

I thought that I missed the goal
but when I looked up at the goalie's face
I knew I made a goal
and my team had won.

WOW!!!!

Raymond Johnson, Grade 5
John Ward Elementary School, MA

Hunting

The woods are calm around me
That plant ahead is sprinkled with doe pee
With a 20-gauge buckshot
Miss I shall not
I am careful with each grunt
For a wrong one could spoil the hunt
I master the sound of the bleat
For if one came out wrong I'd be beat
With a buck-kicker brand choke
My barrel blows smoke
While a buck falls dead
With 8 points atop his head

Carrington Lanier, Grade 5
St Christopher's School, VA

A Carefree Life

A child's life should be grand,
Like playing in the summer sand.
Picking a pumpkin for Halloween Day,
Visiting a farm to ride in the hay.

A child's day should be full of fun,
So go outside and run, run, run.
Get a dog and toss him a stick,
You're guaranteed to have your face licked.

A child's dreams are vivid and wild,
With so much detail they're definitely not mild.
Joy, laughter, giggles, and grins,
Sounds of a child from beginning to end.

Connor Ryan, Grade 5
Homeschool Plus, VA

Shadow

I am your shadow.
I was born in your image
And I live by your side.
My best friend is you of course!
'Cause your life creates mine.
We like to play copycat whenever I'm around.
My worst enemy is your best friend
(he makes you forget I'm always there for you)
I fear the night because
I have to leave you for yet another day
I love you. I love the great blue sky
I get to see when the sun is high.
I'm swinging next to you, laughing, smiling, having a good time.
I'm breathing real air.
But it's just a dream.
(because I'm not really there)

Madeline Bussard, Grade 6
St Stephen Parochial School, MD

The Snowy Day

I am absent today because of the snow
The snow fell at night
It was seven inches deep
On my day off I will have snowball fights
Go sledding and make snowmen
When I come in from the snow I will drink hot chocolate
I look back at my childhood and
Remember the snowflakes looked like stars

Drew Treger, Grade 6
Wakefield Forest Elementary School, VA

Ladybug in Springtime

Ladybug in springtime
crawling rapidly up my trunk
to the leaves that await at my top branches,
rustling when the wind blows.
The squirrels are chattering to each other
trying to find the acorns
they buried under the soil last autumn.
The chatter annoys me
but the ladybug keeps crawling up my brown tattered trunk,
up to the green crispy leaves full of chlorophyll,
covered with aphids from stem to tip
crawling away to not get eaten.
The ladybug comes closer
to the birds roosting happily in my topmost branches.
twittering as they flit from tree to tree
in the bright afternoon sunlight.
The ladybug has reached the leaves
and is munching aphids happily.
As it starts to get dark it gets colder
and the ladybug flies home to her little ladybug children
who have been waiting anxiously throughout the day.

Lydia Elizabeth Field, Grade 4
Hawley Elementary School, CT

An Orange Fish

I swim by the other
colorful fish
and listen to them
wish
that they were
the beautiful
color I am.
Orange.
I ate a snack
and look who
comes back,
A big blue shark
He must have smelt
my tasty food.
I swim and swim
then dive into the
the sand
SWUSH
He can't get
me now

Kristina Fischer, Grade 6
Litchfield Intermediate School, CT

Winter Is Coming

The light glistening white,
Blankets of snow
cover the hills
And valleys all over,
Because winter is coming.

The bears, foxes, bunnies and birds,
Are hibernating
in rest and peace,
Because winter is coming.

We all celebrate and enjoy
Our family and friends.
We have a good time,
Because winter is coming.

"Ha, ha," the children laugh,
Playing in the blanket of snow.
So get our sled, mittens,
Gloves, hat, and coat.
Because winter is here!

Rory Sullivan, Grade 4
Quashnet School, MA

Dogs

Dogs
Soft, active
Drooling, barking, playing
Playful fur ball
Big lap cat

Krista Jenkins, Grade 4
Grace Miller Elementary School, VA

The Beautiful Grand Canyon

The beautiful Grand Canyon
Always shining and glittering
The beautiful orange rocks
Always warm and fantastic
The smell of the great pine trees
Spreads all over the canyon
The orange sand floating like the wind
The Grand Canyon
Great to visit and have fun
The beautiful grand canyon

Edmond Aboukheir, Grade 5
St Mary's Primary School, MA

Tanks

Huge vehicle very powerful
War Zone
Breaks Out
Powerful — Zoom
Army uses them
Green, tan, brown and mean
Metal, Steel and Guns
Fuel and gun powder
Roars like a lion…
A god of War

Christian Wolff, Grade 6
Litchfield Intermediate School, CT

Snowflakes

S mall silly flakes
N autical snowdrifts
O utside for hours
W illy nilly everywhere
F rolicking around
L akes freezing in almost every spot
A mazing bizarre designs
K iller snowballs and forts
E xhilarating snowmen
S now everywhere!

Sarah Moughan, Grade 4
Leicester Memorial School, MA

Cold (A Fictional Poem)

I am here in my temple,
Life, so plain and simple.
I have no one to love,
No one to love me.
I feel cold,
Yet, forgotten,
Telling my own soul,
Never let the dream go!
Although sometimes,
I feel so much like,
I'm nothing,
But invisible.

Mychell Brewington, Grade 5
Perrywood Elementary School, MD

Death

Cold, dark
Fearing, scaring, haunting
It's only a part of life
Afterlife

Walker Field, Grade 5
Soule Road School, MA

Summer

In my backyard
I have a pool,
the water is very clear.
I just watch everything
there is a fence around the pool
and with pink flowers next to it
it is really sunny,
you can hear the pool filter
in the shed
I think to myself
I wonder if I should water those flowers,
the blue sky with the sun in it is perfect

Stephanie Fortune, Grade 4
Southbrook Academy, MA

Water

water
rushing
down the
stream
fast
as a
bull
with
lightning
flashing
in the
sky and
thunder
rumbling
overhead
in the
clouds and
raindrops
dropping
on my
head

Andrew Bombara, Grade 5
C C Burr Elementary School, MA

A Man Named Grime

There once was a man named Grime
He was in jail for committing a crime
He said "What the hay"
And found out a way
To escape from his cell with a lime

Nathan Goldenberg, Grade 4
Weston Intermediate School, CT

The Afternoon Hall

At the end of the day come two twenty-five,
I'm staring at the clock, just barely alive.
The song of freedom finally sounds,
And up out of their seats everyone bounds
But just one thing to stop me: the hall.
The hall is a war, a long battlefield.
Rush hour traffic, where nobody yields.
Slamming lockers, like a shot from a gun.
Crashes, collisions, like from red lights kids run.
Almost to the locker, I round the 1st hall,
Just avoiding being slammed into a wall.
Students everywhere, all around,
Some lying on the floor, some getting a pound.
Dodging and jumping, my life may be at stake,
Another seven yards I think I could make.
Teachers running, yelling, giving a chide
Just a few yards more, I go in for a slide!
Safe at last, I could still make it to band
I turn the dial to find that my locker is jammed.

Mikaela Karlsson, Grade 6
Fuller Middle School, MA

The Moon

A silver dollar in the sky,
Orbiting us and asking why.
Why do you land on me,
Saying we have found destiny?
New rocks, minerals, and more,
Why not leave it for others to explore?
Why leave tracks on my face and stick a flag in its place?
I, the moon, am here in space,
Orbiting the Earth as the Earth orbits the Sun.

Emily Olin, Grade 5
Weston Intermediate School, CT

What Is a Dog?

A dog is…
Someone that will always worship you
The one that jumps in your bed at 5 A.M.
The thing that eats your food when you aren't looking
A friend that is always there.

A dog is…
The thing that jumps in the pool with you
The one that rolls over and makes you rub her tummy
Something that smells as bad as old milk
Someone that's as cute as a baby.

A dog is…
The one that nips at you if they're eating
The thing that gives you kisses as wet as can be
The one that loves you…
The one that you love.

Alyssa Barnett, Grade 4
Fawn Hollow Elementary School, CT

I Like Dogs

Before: I like dogs…but I can't have one, I heard they were
A lot of fun, I would take care of it very well
I will sneak one…
Please don't tell
I will make it follow me
His head sticks out in the breeze
After: I need a piece of tissue because I do
Snoopy did a doo-doo that's not cool
When he does that I get so mad and my mom and dad
Just get so sad
But at least he's cute, that's not bad
When I walk him he runs away
He wants to play I say not today
He's so small with his hotdog shape
And I gotta a cute dog that doesn't look like an ape

Cheyenne Walker, Grade 5
Jacob Hiatt Magnet Elementary School, MA

The Warrior*

A Warrior Heir can beat them all,
Wizards, enchanters, soothseers fall.
He is a kid, Jack's his name,
His destiny to win the game.

Hunted down,
Escaped again,
Poisoned daily by a supposed friend.

Behind a grave,
His sword may lie,
From an ancestor who had the chance to live or die.

A wizard appears, flames aglow,
Can kill the boy who would not go.

Jack's future may be brutally cold,
The face beneath the seeing-glass told,
The story of a young boy's life,
A tale of good, evil, and strife.

Eve Phelps, Grade 5
Hindley Elementary School, CT
Inspired by "The Warrior Heir" by Cinda Williams Chima

Summer Fun

S ummer is the best part of the year
U sing different way to plan the whole day
M y family always goes to New Hampshire
M e, my brother, sister, dad and mom go to Jamaica pond
E ven if it's raining outside, still be happy
R emember it's always fun in summer

F orget about those embarrassing times at school
U nder your house is where you go to cool off
N othing better than a good summer.

Desiree' Marie Smith, Grade 5
Sacred Heart Elementary School, MA

Pollution

Once the last river is polluted
the last tree is cut
and the last fish is caught
we will know that
we can't eat money.
Shakya Adhikari, Grade 4
Summit Montessori School, MA

My Dog

Her little button eyes
Stare me down at night,
When I look at her I see
Something sweet and nice

She's soft and fluffy
And plays ruffy
She never rests and you can
Count on her to make a mess

She has an aggressive bark
And has teeth like a shark

But that's just my dog Elsie,
She's the best.
Imani Powell, Grade 6
Magnolia Elementary School, MD

Fading

Into the fog
Into the steam
Fading faces
Happy, sad, confused, surprised
Everything vanishes into the distance
Into the light
Out of this world
To a place beyond imagination
Explore, take a chance, be free
Love life,
Love friends,
Love love.
Celia Marion, Grade 5
St Luke's School, CT

Summer Fun

S wimming in the pool
U nder the hot sun
M y friends and I
M aking fun out of nothing
E very day's the same
R unning and playing

F astly the days go by
U nstoppable minutes gone
N o more summer fun
Charles Vadala, Grade 5
Sacred Heart Elementary School, MA

Autumn

Wow! Wondrous colors flying through the air like a graffitied plane
So many people laughing everywhere, along every lane

Elections, turkeys, and monsters with candy
All the school free holidays in autumn can sure come in handy

Sunsets of fetching pink, looks as cool as iced apple cider
The most beautiful season, I think as I ride

I smell sassafras leaves, a flavorful lemon scent
I touch tree bark as grooved as an aged park bench

Autumn is a time to smile, not to frown
Fall is a sweet season to crown
Danny Delucia, Grade 6
Madison Middle School, CT

My Months

January is a new year with lots of shouts and happy cheer
February is really sweet you get a Valentine and a treat
March is cold or so I've been told
April has showers which bring May flowers
May honors mothers who think of me and others
In June we get out of school then jump into the swimming pool
On the Fourth of July we see fireworks in the sky
In August we get out of the pool then we get ready for a new year at school
In September my parents celebrate their anniversary a special date
October comes with many treats, lots of costumes and lots of sweets
November it will be my birthday I can't wait for that happy day
December is the very best because of vacation, I get to rest
Tyler Retalic, Grade 5
Charlotte A Dunning Elementary School, MA

I Am a Boy Who Loves to Swim

I am strong and graceful at swimming.
I wonder if I will be a professional swimmer.
I hear the splashes of the aquamarine crystal clear water.
I see the calm porcelain water I am proud of.
I want to be the best swimmer I can be and I will.
I am strong and graceful at swimming.

I pretend I will compete in the Olympics some day.
I feel worthy there is swimming.
I touch the silky arctic water and feel relaxed.
I worry I will injure myself and won't be able to swim ever again.
I cry when I think that too.
I am strong and graceful at swimming.

I understand I probably won't compete in the Olympics when I'm older.
I say, "I'm going to win a gold medal."
I dream I will beat all of the world records of the Olympics.
I try to be better and put more effort into it.
I hope all my friends and family are proud of me.
I am strong and graceful at swimming.
Eddie Kureczka, Grade 5
Hebron Elementary School, CT

The Amazing Color Blue

Blue is the sound of the ocean water!
The sight of a new hot rodder,
And a cloudless sky
In the middle of July!
Blue is the shadow of the snow,
And the feeling you get when you're way down low!
Blue is a jay flying across the sky.
Blue is the color of many an eye!
Blue has the taste of something sweet —
Surely something you would like to eat!
Blue is the color of President Washington's vest,
And the blue ribbon you get when you've done your best!
Blue is a new car racing down the street —
Going so fast it's gone in a heartbeat!

Nick Gauthier, Grade 5
Har-Bur Middle School, CT

Hello Basketball, Goodbye Soccer

Hello quiet foul shots,
Goodbye windy field goals.
Hello 10-foot hoops,
Goodbye wide goals.
Hello orange basketballs,
Goodbye white and black soccer balls.
Hello under-the-legs,
Goodbye doing the rainbow over your head.
Hello shiny basketball shoes,
Goodbye spiky cleats.
Hello soft knee pads,
Goodbye hard shin pads.
Hello squeaky courts,
Goodbye muddy grass.
Hello Basketball, Goodbye Soccer.

Leah Rubinstein, Grade 4
Long Meadow Elementary School, CT

My Sanctuary

My room shows my personality;
it has sports posters, model cars, and trophies
that show my achievements.

My room is my sanctuary,
my place to escape
from teachers, parents, and my sister.

It's where I go to calm down and sometimes to cry.

it's also where I go to laugh
and have fun with my friends;
we play floor hockey with the foam puck
that squeezes into the tiny goal.

My room, my sanctuary, my place to escape
from the world around me.

Max Cohen, Grade 6
Swampscott Middle School, MA

The Leaves

The leaves dance around my head.
They swim through the air like fish in a pond.
They whistle through my mind in an echoing sound.
The leaves brush the top of the sky.
They cough the dust of the seasons past.
They sing in a loud chorus of wind.
The leaves shiver in an instant when wind blows by.
They float in a rhythmic motion when coming from the tree.
They slip by the force of something else.
They rest in the grass on a calm summer day.
They are buried by the bone chilling snow on a winter morn.
The leaves sleep with the clouds as their blanket.

Haley Arnold, Grade 5
Raleigh Court Elementary School, VA

Me and My Brother

Me and my brother went fishing yesterday
We go fishing every day.
Me and my brother had a lot of fun
Even with the shining sun.
Me and my brother went down the hill
To go see the one and only Bill.

Kerry Cline, Grade 6
Home School, VA

The Lonely Dog

Day after day
there sat a lonely dog
Nobody ever looked at it
The kids would come with
their dog but nobody would ever
pay attention to the dog
they would just say "what an ugly dog"

Fru Anyere, Grade 5
Charlotte A Dunning Elementary School, MA

Sailing on the Waves

I sail the seas
on cotton waves.
Cotton waves
make my boat shake.
The cotton waves
take me places
The cotton waves
push me upon the shore.
The cotton waves.

Wes Fixler, Grade 4
South Area Solomon Schechter Day School, MA

Poetry

Paper on your desk
Becomes colorful with words
Meaningful message

Richard Dizon, Grade 6
School of International Studies at Meadowbrook, VA

The Glare

There once was a man with no hair.
His head gave off a very bright glare.
He blinded a man,
Named Superman.
And then he ate a very large pear.

Jacob Mathews, Grade 6
Captain Nathan Hale Middle School, CT

Sandwich

Pink ham, light yellow cheese,
holes in the bread.
Yum! Yum! Yum!
Just looking at the
light chestnut brown crust
makes me want to
Eat it!
It looks
as good as a chocolate sundae!
I reach out to feel it.
Rough, bumpy,
but creamy, and wet
from the mayonnaise.
It smells heavenly and yummy
all mixed together,
Delicious.
When I take a whiff,
it smells like a bakery.
I hear a small voice
Eat me! Eat me! Eat me!
Lunchtime! Yay!

Quinn Karp, Grade 4
Hawley Elementary School, CT

Pollution

I wonder how
I wonder when
Will this world come to an end
They say it's wrong
They say it's not right.
Stop polluting our world
and giving me a fright.
Our world is good
Our world is a delight
Keep it clean so we'll have
A bright sight.

Natalie Saintil, Grade 5
Sacred Heart Elementary School, MA

Autumn

Way up in the trees,
There is lots and lots to see,
Trees that have beautiful leaves,
They fall because of the blissful breeze,
Autumn brings me lots of fun things!

Kayla Cooper, Grade 6
Benjamin Syms Middle School, VA

Daisies

The daisies
Wait
For spring
To come
So they
Can bloom
Into
Beautiful
Flowers
To see
Sunlight again
So people
Can see them
To know
Spring has come
Until winter
Comes again
And they have to say
Goodnight.

Ashley Rose-Marzelli, Grade 4
St Mary's Primary School, MA

I Have a Cat

I have a cat
That people think is fat
But no not me, I don't think so.

I have a cat
That people think is very lazy
But no not me, I don't think so.

I have a cat
That people think is mean
But no not me, I don't think so.

I have a cat
That I will admit is a little fat
But oh how I love him so!

I have a cat
That I will say is a bit lazy
But oh how I love him so!

I have a cat
That I must agree is kind "a" mean
But oh how I love him so!

Hannah DeSousa, Grade 6
Edmond P Talbot Middle School, MA

Beautiful Penguins

Across the polar ice caps
Silently and gracefully
Perfect little penguins
Slide and glide

Samantha Kolbert, Grade 4
Weston Intermediate School, CT

Calls of Spring

Petals falling
Spring is calling
Rain is falling too
I hear the calls of sunshine
But all I see is rain
Sunset's coming
Oh rain just stop falling
Please

Meghan O'Connor, Grade 6
Thomas Blake Middle School, MA

Two Birds

I stare up
At the small,
Chirping bird
In the trees.
The chirping
Is a beautiful
Continuous pattern
That sounds like a song.
The branches sway
With the bird on them.
The wind brisk, as I spot,
Yet another bird
On the ground,
Pecking up
The small bird seed.
Another bird, seems to be calling
Back to the first bird I spotted,
But my eyes,
Cannot see,
The other bird.

Tess Vogel, Grade 4
Hawley Elementary School, CT

Summer

S wimming with friends
U nder a shady tree on a hot day
M ustard and ketchup on hot dogs
M unching on ice cream to stay cool
E verybody playing and relaxing outside
R elax inside if it's too hot outside

Jason Imri, Grade 5
Jane Ryan School, CT

Little Cousins

They might get under your skin
You have to let them win
They talk and talk and talk
You can never make them stop
They copy what you do
They stick to you like glue
But whatever through and through
You know you love them too!

Chelsea Bonanca, Grade 6
Edmond P Talbot Middle School, MA

My Furnace

Clank, clank
Rumble, rumble,
The furnace is
A dinosaur
Its roar is
As loud as
A rocket blasting
Off.
Bang, bang
The warmness inside
Hits the walls fast
Like lightning
Slapping
Small mountains.
Clank, clank
Rumble, rumble

Anna Lafreniere, Grade 4
Braeburn School, CT

Christmas

Share.
Wrap gifts.
Give gifts to the poor.
Sing praises to the Lord.
Celebrate the true meaning of Christmas.
Appreciate the birthday of the Baby Jesus.
Decorate and put a star on the Christmas tree.
Thank the people who give you a lot of gifts on Christmas.
*   *
*   *

Daniel DiCocco, Grade 5
St Clement Mary Hofbauer School, MD

I Am

I am a worried older sister and a "perfect daughter"
I wonder what my siblings think of me
I hear them fighting over me
I see them cherishing me
I want to do well in their lives
I am a worried older sister and a "perfect daughter"

I pretend that I get a reward for being such a good sister
I feel I can be a little bit better
I touch my siblings' hearts
I am a worried older sister and a "perfect daughter"

I understand the way I drive them crazy
I say that they drive me crazy too.
I dream of what all three of us could be someday.
I try to connect with them.
I hope we all turn out all right.
I am a worried older sister and a "perfect daughter"
I am Mary Kate Gibbons

Mary Kate Gibbons, Grade 5
Clover Hill Elementary School, VA

The Average Day in Room 217

I stare at my blank screen,
Bored out of my mind.
My friends also just stare at their screen.
I finally get up to ask a question.
Ms. Makseyn snaps "Sit down!"
And I scurry back to my seat,
To continue writing my report.

But my pencil tip breaks,
And I get up to sharpen it,
"If you value your life, you'd better sit down,"
Comes Ms. Makseyn's voice.
I run for my valued life,
And sit down in my seat.
This is the average day in room 217.

Tristan Smith, Grade 6
Swampscott Middle School, MA

Baseball

When you hit a home run,
You run the bases and have fun.
When you get an out,
Don't you dare pout.
When you hit a double,
You're not in trouble.
When you lose a game,
It is not a shame.
What matters is you had fun,
So, go hit a home run!

Jack Conlin, Grade 4
Helen H Hansen Elementary School, MA

Hero

Everyone has a hero, brave and true.
With a little work you can be one too!
Eat right, be bright, and always get some sleep at night!

"What makes a hero" I hear you ask.
(Don't worry you don't need a mask.)
But first I need you to complete this task.
Stop the robber who stole the peach cobbler!

To the beach you must run! This will be fun.
Look! He's over there, sitting in that foldable chair.
Stop thief! Unhand that tasty treat, and just admit your defeat.

Quick, before he robs the delicatessen
please, oh please teach him a lesson.
Put him in jail!
The judge will set his bail.

You did it! Hooray!
You're a hero now!
Well, at least for today.

Michael Boyle, Grade 4
Helen H Hansen Elementary School, MA

The Washing Machine

My washer is like a summer storm,
Its water can be cold or warm,
It spins and hums and gets you wet,
And sprays your clothes with water jets.
Colin Travis, Grade 6
Benjamin Syms Middle School, VA

Soccer/Skateboarding

Soccer
score, goal
Points, friend, fun
team, winning, 360's, jumping
riding, half pipe, in plant
fun, fast
Skateboarding
Clover Perando, Grade 5
McCleary Elementary School, VA

Winter

The ground is pure white
It is falling out of clouds
It is now winter
Apryl Ogallo, Grade 4
Hebbville Elementary School, MD

Kittens

Kittens
Playful, small
Jumping, clawing, cuddling
A playful creature
Small mammal
Svetlana Gureyeva, Grade 4
Grace Miller Elementary School, VA

Down Down We Go

Jumping off cotton candy clouds
I tumble down,
Down
Down
We wrestle each other
To the ground
A driver peers up at me
Splat
"Oh no"
I'm too late
The wiper swipes me
Off the windshield
Soaring through the air
Like a rocket
Landing in a slush puddle
My face planted in the mush
Vrroom
The sound of engines fill my ears
As night falls, I turn to ice.
Gwyneth McDonald, Grade 4
Braeburn School, CT

My Colors

Dark blue is the color of my soccer jersey
And white is the color of my soccer ball

Orange and black are the official Ridgefield colors
By the way, a few weeks ago I had a pink cast

Look up at the crystal clear, magnificent turquoise sky
But don't look at the blazing eye watering yellow sun

Look down at the smooth, gentle, green grass
Clifford the big, red dog's footprints are there

Gary our hamster has light brown fur
But a juicy, steamy hamburger is dark brown after coming off the grill

Gray makes me feel fuzzy and blurry
But gold make me feel like someone special

Do you have any favorite colors to share?
Daniel Standish, Grade 6
Scotts Ridge Middle School, CT

Snow

The snow is falling on a cold winter day.
You can feel the excitement in the air.
It is like confetti falling when you are at a parade in New York.
They are like small warriors rushing to the battle on the ground.
The snowflakes are as small as ants.
Each one with a unique shape.
One by one the white pieces of snow flutter to the ground
As if they were butterflies.
Thousands of them free fall.
Winter makes a first impression.
Wade Erwin, Grade 5
Wakefield Forest Elementary School, VA

What She Found in Her Lunch!

My friend got lunch from the cafeteria.
It looked like it was covered in bacteria.

It was her sizzling, lumpy, watery, soup.
It looked like a bowl of tan puke.

And the bread was covered in green sticky mold.
And I got a shiver and I turned cold.

The broccoli was covered in cheese.
You could jiggle it and turn it upside down without it fallin' on your knees.

When she drank her milk it was green and sour.
Some kids already had it devoured.

She ended up not eating her lunch.
And the kid next to her had eaten the lunch in one munch!
Heather Strauss, Grade 6
Captain Nathan Hale Middle School, CT

Blue

Blue is a rippling ocean
Blue is the very high sky
Blue is a plump raindrop falling to the ground
Blue is a little blueberry waiting to be eaten
Blue is a baby bluebird waking up
Blue is a blooming violet in June

Juliana Rodgers, Grade 4
C Hunter Ritchie Elementary School, VA

Teacher

My teacher Mrs. Sheer,
is very kind.
She has an opinion
that is different than mine.

If she ever left
it would be bad.
She is my favorite,
I'd be very sad.

Mrs. Sheer helps me out
with anything I need.
I have no doubt
she would never be mean.

Julia Renaghan, Grade 5
Foxborough Regional Charter School, MA

Night Is a Wonderful Time

Night is a wonderful time,
When all of the nocturnal animals come out.
The gleaming moon and stars
Shine brilliantly, on these animals.
The coldness of the night is incredible.
The gleaming stars shine in my room,
Everybody is asleep at night.
Night is a wonderful time.

John Ferguson, Grade 4
Quashnet School, MA

Midnight Message

On the eighteenth of April in seventy-five
Paul Revere took a midnight ride,
He told his friend one by land two by sea,
Up he looked two there be,
Lanterns were hung in the old church tower
As the clock struck the twelfth hour,
The British were on their way
On their ghostly ship across the bay,
When Paul Revere gave a shout
The Minute Men rushed out,
This was the beginning of a terrible war
Which we won so therefore,
We are free to this day
From the British way

Taryn Murphy, Grade 6
Windermere School, CT

Drama

Drama is like a pond of ripples
One big thing starts
Then the ripples get bigger and bigger
Until it gets crazy and it stops
The ripples are my family
And that's how I like it
I am the ripple that starts it and then we boom
Then it's gone and we don't know why we are fighting
I love my family being like that
And especially when it's a big day like a birthday
We can stop right away and celebrate with each other
Anything different would be out of the ordinary

Neil Hailey, Grade 5
Old Bridge Elementary School, VA

Saving Earth

The Earth is a place worth saving.
The world is a planet worth craving.
The ozone keeps the air in.
We need to fight for the earth and win.

The land is not getting smaller.
But our population is getting taller.
The pollution is in the water and air.
I just might never see a bear.

Soon the trees will be cut down.
I think my smile just turned to a frown.
But there is a way to save the earth.
It requires stopping bad habits and giving less birth.

And it may crush people's dreams.
But it may also stop the deadly sun beams.
Also save paper it's right.
Cut fewer trees to save the night.

All I am saying is we need to keep hope.
Just don't mope.
And get off the couch.
And when you do this don't be a grouch.

Chris Reel, Grade 6
Captain Nathan Hale Middle School, CT

Sun

In the morning
The sun enters the sky
On her chariot of light
Shining the blue filled sky
With clouds to comfort her as she approaches
In the afternoon she closes her shutters
As the sky darkens
Stars and the moon enter the sky
And unlock the door of night

Michael Landsburg, Grade 5
C C Burr Elementary School, MA

The Lost Cat

In the field, I can see nothing else but the tall grass swaying in the breeze. I hear my stomach growling and wish I was back at home, with the warmth of the fire engulfing me. The meadow's grass sticks to my fur. The taste of the mouse I had eaten still hangs in my mouth. The smell of the other animals brings fear, or I don't want to come upon a hungry wolf. The sky is turning black, and the cold night starts to close in on the field. The shadowy figure of a mouse takes me over. I pounce and with a squeak the mouse is silent. The fur tickles my whiskers. Surviving can be tough as a lost cat.

Lauren Tourtellotte, Grade 6
Litchfield Intermediate School, CT

Too Hard to Believe

Taking out the old poker table used to be a routine,
Setting it out on their kitchen table,
Watching my Memere and Pepere, they were the best players I've ever seen.
We would laugh and talk all night long and sing a silly song.
As we sat and sang we would look out their glass window and gaze at Arizona's pink sky.
But slowly the cancer started to affect him, which had never happened to him before.
All the laughter felt more like a disaster,
This slowly hit me in such a way.
I went to my room and cried all night long, because it was too painful just to see
And I couldn't even imagine that this was happening. It was too hard to believe.
Now the three longest weeks of my life have gone, and they took the song with them.
Arizona's pink sky started to fade.
The news I have been dreading finally arrived.
His last words in French he was quite the guy.
I felt like I had just lost a tooth I wasn't supposed to,
And there is going to be a gap in my mouth forever.
That gap in my heart will never be replaced. I knew my Pepere wouldn't want me to cry.
But there was no way to stop the tears from rolling down my cheek
I was scared that in each tear a memory would run down my cheek too.
But then I realized that some memories will never die,
Especially the ones you care for and the one that make you cry.

Rachel Citren, Grade 6
Charles E Smith Jewish Day School, MD

Sights of Autumn

When autumn arrives, the crisp air blows in the trees.
Towering tulip trees that touch the sky.
When autumn arrives, multicolored leaves of scarlet, topaz, and pumpkin float in the air.
They twirl to the ground like little dancers.
Aster and goldenrod paint a peaceful autumnal scene everywhere.
Oak trees throw their acorns in all directions.
Tangerine pumpkins and Jack o' Lanterns with glimmering lights make a spooky sight on All Hallows Eve.
Ghosts and ghouls are like a nightmare come true.
Leaves of amber, crimson and golden-yellow settle on the forest floor.
Small crystal clear stones dazzle in the sunlight like mirrors.
When autumn arrives, there are berries on plants galore.
Red berries are like a warning sign to visitors not to eat them.
But there are dangers, look around.
Poison Ivy and Sumac to name a few.
These rash-causing plants are colored scarlet in the fall.
Lightly frosted grasses stand out in the field.
Somewhat spiky pine cones of all sizes love to leap to the ground with a thud.
Oh, the stunning scene autumn creates.
It's all around you.
What more can I say?

Emily Socha, Grade 6
Madison Middle School, CT

Snowmobiling

Skimming over the snow
On a silver and black Polaris
Wind hitting my face
Freezing my cheeks and making my eyes water
Speeding down the trails
Sharing this time with my dad
The noise of the engines roar throughout the woods
I was having so much fun
Until we left

Jon Palczynski, Grade 6
Whitinsville Christian School, MA

OMG

There once was a man named Tim
Who had a friend named Jim
Jumping from a cliff they found
When they hit the ground
It knocked the wind out of them

Will McKeown, Grade 5
Charlotte A Dunning Elementary School, MA

Mother

M akes me feel good about myself.
O ne and only mother that I love.
T he best role model I could ask for.
H elps me when I get stuck on my homework.
E very dream I have she supports me.
R eminds me I can be anything I want to be.

Alison Frye, Grade 5
Wakefield Forest Elementary School, VA

My Mother and Her Knitting Needles

Her knitting needles clinked their way
to the endless route.
They left a path for me to follow.
Mother groans when she messes up,
but fixes it with a big smile that blooms
I watched her every move
on a cozy couch.

Her knitting needles are puppets
that Mother makes them move.
I tried everything to be just like her,
but never as successful as she is.
Her gentle hands seemed to have magic,
like the magic in a fairy tale.

Her knitting needles
twirled, curled, and swirled with the yarn.
I could smell the cinnamon rolls in the oven,
But I still stared at the needles.
I felt a drop of jealousy,
but amazed and proud of my mother.

Akari Miki, Grade 5
John Ward Elementary School, MA

My Guardian Angel

My guardian angel is pure and true.
She goes with me everywhere
And does what I do.
I know she is honest
And a beautiful girl.
Her cheeks are the color of a pink pearl.
With eyes the color of a light blue,
My guardian angel remains pure and true.

Emily Baskin, Grade 5
Soule Road School, MA

Winter into Spring

The fight between winter and spring rages on.
The grass pokes its head above the snow,
The flowers dance in the field,
Trees sway in the refreshing breeze.
The wind whistles a song across the meadow,
Gray storm clouds move out of the blue sky
Plants can finally breathe freely again.
Spring has finally won the battle.

Neil Sun, Grade 5
John Ward Elementary School, MA

The Civility Award

We came out of Room 29,
normally and calm.
I announced to my friend —
"I want to sit with you, you come too."
My teacher went first,
giving the one and only description
of "this winner."
Then she talked
in what felt like slow motion.
S-h-e i-s d-e-f-i-n-i-t-e-l-y a h-a-r-d w-o-r-k-i-n-g s-t-u-d-e-n-t.
Come on…Come on…
"Liz Sherrill"
I sank in my seat.
Me? Me? Is it me?
It was!
My face was tomatoed with red.
All the praises and excitement
were waiting to just burst out of me.
Cheers were overheard from the other end of the hallway.
I had won the award.
I had won the award!

Liz Sherrill, Grade 5
West Woods Upper Elementary School, CT

Happiness

I looked outside
it seemed the trees
were waving at me
made me feel happy
and strange at the same time

Kyle May, Grade 6
Monelison Middle School, VA

Crazy Daisy

There once was a girl named Daisy.
I think she was very crazy.
She would never rest.
She was never the best.
That girl was not at all lazy.

Nick Mariasi, Grade 6
Captain Nathan Hale Middle School, CT

Snow

Down down down it comes
It's cold and white
It's on the ground.

It twirls around me
I dance around
I feel like a heavenly angel.

The snow ball fight
A snow man too
A big fort that is bigger than you.

Emma Walsh, Grade 4
Freetown Elementary School, MA

Spring

Little butterfly,
Flying like the graceful wind
Looking for flowers

Noah Basmaci, Grade 4
St Joseph School-Fullerton, MD

Dream

Dream means a lovely
Thing,

Dream means to be happy and
Sing,

Dream will tell you a lovely
Story,

Dreams will give you all
Your glory,

Dreams make you see
Something,

Dreams make you keep
Bumping,

Dreams know you and what you want
To see,

Just think and think and you'll
Be free.

Carter Violette, Grade 5
Jack Jackter Intermediate School, CT

Cloudy

No!
Cloudy was dead,
Gone forever.
Fallen from the hands of life
To the jaws of death.
I couldn't hold back
My tears of pain.
Cloudy,
My angel fish
Died bravely
Stuck in a shell…
Suffocating.
The bowl
Empty
Except for the shell that killed her.
I was scarred for life that day,
The day,
Cloudy
Swam to the fishbowl in the sky —
Fish heaven.

Olivia Fadus, Grade 4
Hawley Elementary School, CT

Rolf the Golfer

There once was a man named Rolf
Who really liked to golf
Once was hit with a ball
And took a nasty fall
And that's how he lost at a game of golf

Alex Davis, Grade 4
Brookside Elementary School, MA

Intruding

All different colors
running through the forest
Chasing after its prey
It gets into a stalk
It looks like a tiger
just waiting for his fresh kill.
"Why don't you attack it?" I ask.
"I will wait until it is the right moment,"
she answers angrily at me
for intruding
while she is hunting.

Julian Mills, Grade 5
St Christopher's School, VA

My Family

F unny and fantastic
A wesome and angels
M agalhaes and magnificent
I ncredible and inventive
L ovable and laughable
Y es, my family is cool!

Samantha Magalhaes, Grade 4
Freetown Elementary School, MA

Rock Shatter Cliff

Shattering rock,
Falling down to Sheer Stone Valley
Weakening,
Breaking
The hold of the rock
Then grips loosen
Scraping,
Sliding,
Rock splinters
Losing the grasp
Twisting,
Turning.
Then out of nothing
Fireworks explode,
Shards of rock go
Flying, and litter the ground
Of Sheer Stone Valley.

Perry Miller, Grade 5
C C Burr Elementary School, MA

Depressed

I am a weeping willow
I am endangered animals
Screaming to get saved
I am a best friend
Moving far away
I am a compost pile
Rotting in the sunlight
The rain dripping on the sidewalk
The wind
Chopping through the trees
I am depressed

Michaela Gorski, Grade 5
Jack Jackter Intermediate School, CT

Cuddly Mice

Mice
Fluffy, soft
Chew, scurry, sleep
Give themselves warm baths
Cheese lovers

Mikayla Nogueira, Grade 4
Freetown Elementary School, MA

Morning Brings a New Day

Sunup arrives in a glorious fashion,
Erasing the dark with pinks and purples,
Covering the horizon,
But behind it is what people want,
A new day,
Bringing thrills and chills,
Challenges and adventures,
Forget yesterday because,
A new day has arrived!

William Vester, Grade 5
Coleytown Elementary School, CT

Tornadoes

They sky is dark,
The wind is harsh,
And the mud is pale at the marsh.
Thunder crashing,
Lightning flashing
It's all happening so quick.
The clouds are forming a funnel
Like a tunnel,
It's stretching to the ground.
It comes in many shapes,
So shut the drapes and go down in the basement.
It swirls at many miles per hour,
When you spot it you see its great power.
It can be more than a mile wide and long,
It's bigger than doubled King King.
As it roars across the land,
It makes a giant band that's marked into the ground.
When it's over it's safe to come out,
If there's not much damage there's no reason to pout.

Kyra Kabler, Grade 5
Charlotte A Dunning Elementary School, MA

Sailor's Dream

Down by the hill a child awaits,
For his father on the ocean gates.

The thunderous waves show Neptune's rage,
The length of life move page to page.

The crackling thunder, the crackling the sea.
The ship goes under, forever lost to see.

The tear of a child show burning dreams,
The tear of a child yet still gleams.

Mike Ogego, Grade 6
Hoover Middle School, MD

Ode to Family

Oh, family
How thy kindness, compassion and love
Fills my heart with joy
Your forever hugs
That warm my days
Your gentle understanding
With reassuring praise
The core of my life
The absolute bliss
The sunshine on a cloudy day
The gold in the treasure chest
The diamond in the mine
The music in my music box
My inspiration
My one true completion
Oh, family

Sophia Barlotta, Grade 5
West Woods Upper Elementary School, CT

Spinning Eagle

I am spinning out of control
I wonder if I will ever lose focus spinning through the air
I hear people cheering
I see many yards of field
I want to be thrown through the air
I pretend to be a spinning eagle
I feel the wind through my grinds
I touch shoes
I worry about getting crushed
I cry when getting kicked
I am fire through the air
I understand that I will be in pain tomorrow
I say this will be true
I dream of the next game
I try to dream while diving through the air
I hope to be in the next game
I am a football

Yasmene Kimble, Grade 6
Page Middle School, VA

The Pencil Sharpener

"CRACK!" My pencil's tip just broke.
I stuck my hand in my case
and it was just what I feared!
My new pack of number 2's
had sadly disappeared…
and worst of all, during the biggest test of the year!

I tiptoed to the pencil sharpener and shoved it through the hole.
I ground my pencil to a stub and its shavings to the floor.
Nervously, I turned the handle,
getting faster every second.
Finally my pencil was as sharp as it would get!

Sharpening my pencil was something to regret,
because my teacher stood up and said,
"Time to hand in your test!"
I looked on the blank sheet hoping it was a dream,
because I had only gotten up to question number 3!

Amanda Boralessa, Grade 6
Fuller Middle School, MA

Snowman

A jolly black smile in a field of white
Two round charcoal eyes stare with delight
A pair of fragile arms branch out to embrace
A tall top hat with a band of lace
His long nose glows throughout the day
His scarf is wrapped tight to keep the cold away
Buttons run down his long curved figure
Always standing tall despite the weather's vigor
Melting down when spring is near
Until next winter he will disappear

Sarah Baer, Grade 6
Scotts Ridge Middle School, CT

The Baby Blue Bird

The baby blue bird was singing
By my window that day.
The singing was ringing in my ears
And just would not go away.
The bird started to fly,
Waving his arms in the sky.
He started to fly away
And would not come back today.

Alyssa Vito, Grade 5
Soule Road School, MA

Love

Love is a brother and sister
Love is a mom and dad
Love is a teacher a poet a writer
Love is a smile
Love is friends and family
That's what love is.

Julianna Eddy, Grade 4
Weston Intermediate School, CT

Water Fountain

Drip, drip, drop, drop
Falling with a little plop
Tap, tap, tap, tap
Beating like a little rap.

Splish, splish, splash, splash
Coming in fast like a dash
Plink, plink, plink, plink
Flowing down into the sink.

Anni Xie, Grade 6
Fuller Middle School, MA

The Really Old Mouse

Once there was a couple of mice.
Who lived in a white house.
The girl mouse was so old,
she forgot everything that she did
for the past 20 years.
She walked into her living room
and saw the old boy mouse
and said "Who are you?"

Tyler Nadeau, Grade 4
Plainfield Catholic School, CT

William

W ill we overcome our fears?
I s there a way?
L osers is what they call us
L azy is what we are not
I ncredible winners we are
A mazing is what they call us
M y life is now without fear of failure.

William Davis, Grade 6
Magnolia Elementary School, MD

Nature

Nature is beautiful in so many ways,
The wind whistles through the night sky each and every day.

And when the leaves fly, you know fall is here.
When the clouds cry, spring is so near.

When the sun is shining, in the hot summertime day
Bright flashing lights get in your eyes' way.

When you see a thunderstorm you know God is crying and fairly mad.
It makes people fearful and makes people sad.

Nature in all its glory, so magnificent it can be
I love all nature, it's wonderful to me!

Kyle Silverman, Grade 4
Helen H Hansen Elementary School, MA

Earth

Green grasses
crystal blue oceans
Where have they all gone?
Where is our earth that was first created?
Is this it, all the hate and war?
Is this our earth that has turned into pollution and global warming?
Where is the earth that was once a beautiful, peaceful place?

Jesenia Martinez, Grade 5
Milton L. Fuller Elementary School, MA

Black

Black is night,
At a horror movie
Poison berries topped with hatred
A dead rose as black as coal
Evilness trapped in a dark room
No windows
No doors
Light doesn't exist in this world of
Pain
Death
As the crows of the night call the death of sunshine, happiness, my world.

Kristen Betzner, Grade 5
Newton-Lee Elementary School, VA

Devil with an Angel's Voice

My mom left to do some errands and I am alone at home.
I wonder what I will do?
Then I remember the muffins.
Right when I grab one,
an angel on my shoulder says, "Do not take that muffin."
Suddenly, on my other shoulder, a devil appears.
"Eat the muffin!" says the devil.
I rethink it over.
And then I hear the angel say…"OK, eat the muffin."
But little did I know that the devil was imitating the angel's voice.

Nathaniel Golob, Grade 5
Smith College Campus School, MA

My Feelings

Inside of me
I feel like a glimmering piece of gold.
My feelings change
Depending on the experiences I have had.
When I am sad,
My stomach freezes
Like an ice cube.
When I am happy,
My stomach jumps all around.
All the bad stuff
Clears away.
I feel like a
Golden sun.
Sad feels like
Big storm clouds
Lurking inside of me.
Sad floods my body.

Madison Pirone, Grade 4
Hawley Elementary School, CT

Family Commotion

It's quite a commotion around the house,
My sister is crying while in her blouse,
My mom's in the shower washing with soap,
I'm upstairs being a dope,
My dad is cooking while holding putty,
My dog's outside getting all muddy,
And that's what's happening in my house,
Be careful — watch out for my old, lost, pet mouse.

R.J. Clasby, Grade 5
Hindley Elementary School, CT

A Midsummer Beach Day

Little kids all over shivering,
The beaches waves are wavering,
Crying because wanting to go down,
Little crabs are crawling along the ground,
Ants are looking for a small hint of ice cream,
Dolphins are practicing their high scream,
The tiny fish are complaining that they are cold,
People who have chairs, are being fold,
The water has a touch of fog,
In the swamp there are some logs,
The water has a little steam,
The trees have a little lean,
The waves are swaying,
While the children are playing,
Some people are playing with sand boxes,
In the woods there are some foxes,
They are lurking,
The waves are also jerking,
The water has a certain pose,
I hope you now have a lot of "knows."

Kayla Martinez, Grade 5
Holland Elementary School, MA

Playing Sports

Playing sports I love to do
It makes me feel athletic.
I love to score a point.
I like to feel needed when I am playing sports,
I play soccer, basketball, football, and wrestling.
When my team is losing I like feeling the adrenaline
So my team could win.
I hate to let go of my possession of the ball.
Playing sports I love to do.
Without any sports I would be lazy.
I have to be lazy but playing games is what I rather be doing.

John Addison, Grade 6
Magnolia Elementary School, MD

My Grandma Owns a Restaurant

My grandma owns a restaurant.
Trust me, there will be something you'll want!
But when you see the nutrition,
You may want to change your decision:

Kentucky-fried wookie breast,
Pig juice with lemon zest.
Computer wires with zapping gravy,
Chopped tiger liver with french fries that are wavy.
Dragon potluck orange peels,
Fried turkey that still squeals.
Ladybug cluster with barbecue mayonnaise,
And the melted gravel will give you a craze!
Trash barrel bags with Dijon mustard,
Fish bowl algae with Wonder bread custard.

My grandma owns a restaurant,
And trust me, there'll be something you'll want!
Before you leave, you'll remember to pack,
What is left over of your scrumptious snack!

James Coppinger, Grade 5
Mount Hope Christian School, MA

The Babbling Brook

The day I sat down by the babbling brook
Relaxing peacefully, reading my book
Was the day I realized I was lucky
for having the family that I have
It seemed as though the brook talked
It told me of the days when he had family
Of how his family died
Humans ruined them, ruined the lakes, rivers
streams, and brooks
Just think, think of how lucky you are to have family

So, next time you're by a babbling brook
Relaxing, peacefully, reading your book
Just listen, listen to that brook
It just might have a lesson in store for you.

Erin Ryan, Grade 5
Soule Road School, MA

School

School is as boring
as if doing nothing all day
except when lunch
comes around then it's as if
the day completely changes

Jessica Evers, Grade 6
Monelison Middle School, VA

Summer/Winter

Winter
Cold, icy
Sliding, shivering, sledding,
Freezing, white, hot, sweaty
Burning, swimming, playing
Sticky, colorful
Summer

Aileen Maloney, Grade 5
Jane Ryan School, CT

Sprite

Sprite tastes just right.
I will drink it tonight.

Sprite makes me jiggle.
When I drink it makes me giggle.

Sprite puts a twinkle in my eye.
It makes me want to fly.

Sprite tastes great
So go to the store and buy eight.

Justin Kim, Grade 5
Landon School, MD

Normal Brother

I wish I had a normal brother
Sort of like my mother,
And instead of being crazy
I'd rather him be lazy.

You do not know my brother
He's not like any other.
He hates Mom's hugs
But he loves furry bugs.

He isn't very big
And he loves to do a jig.
My brother is a Charlie Brown
And just to tell you, he's a clown.

When my brother is away
It really makes my day.
I wish I had a normal brother
Sort of like my mother.

Michael King, Grade 4
Grace Miller Elementary School, VA

Stay Away from the Water

The ghostship floats
Across the silent water
The crew is long dead
Yet the wheel still turns
The wheel of eternity
The terrible wheel of time
Spinning, Spinning
Lives come and go
Like the waves on the shore
Who knows where the bow may point?
Who shall fall next?
Only the ghostship knows
Who shall be sunk
And those who rock the boat
Or look too long
May fall to the water
Never to be glimpsed
By any but the ghostship
The horrible, eternal ghostship of fate

Dylan Kenseth, Grade 6
Smith College Campus School, MA

Summer

Fun, play, laugh
Eat, drink, swim
Vacation, baseball, football
Having friends over, sleep over
Going to the beach
That is what summer is to me.

Connor Flynn, Grade 5
St Mary's Primary School, MA

Puppies

puppies
pleasurable
playing, barking, chomping
creeping around to catch a mouse
noisy

Delaney Rhoades, Grade 5
Hebron Elementary School, CT

2 sides of them

tiptoeing
shaking what their ma gave them
swaying
glaring
as bright as day as dark as night
2 sides of them
mad
glad
sad
bad
dead alive…
plucking flowers

Juashay Lawrence, Grade 5
C C Burr Elementary School, MA

The Sun, Volcano, Snowflakes

The Sun
Shining up in space
Shimmering with bright color
Casting tons of light

Volcano
Blasting hot lava
Shooting fire everywhere
Burning with magma.

Snowflakes
Cold and endless white
They fall about like feathers
Light upon the breeze.

Adam Rayfield, Grade 6
Scotts Ridge Middle School, CT

Why?

Why do we take the wind for granted
The frigid nights for punishment
When the wind makes the trees whisper
And the coldest nights are never spent
Alone or apart from one another
We all huddle around
A warm cozy fire, talking and laughing
On these nights, love is found
So why do we regret the rain
Or shutters that stick shut all day
For the rain provides a place to dance
And the shutters keep the rain away

Rachel Nolan, Grade 6
Irving School, CT

A Fun Wacky Day

One day it was sunny and warm,
Then all of a sudden there was a storm.
First snow, then rain,
Then came little candy canes.
Marshmallows and chocolate bars,
Cookies in the shape of stars.
Even though it was cloudy and gray,
It still was a fun, wacky day.

Taylor Gomes, Grade 4
Willis E Thorpe School, MA

Sick

Horrid cough and runny nose
Headache and earache
Bad tasting medicine
Your eyes sting when you wake
Sleeping and snoozing
When you walk your bones are stiff
No fun at all
Don't get sick, "sniff"

Tony DiPippa, Grade 5
Trinity Christian School, VA

My Dog Freckles

I have the greatest dog,
Her name is Freckles,
she has the neatest little black speckles.

She has the most energy,
A lot of get up and go,
it's hard to keep up with her, don't you know.

She really likes to play, but
she has sharp teeth and nails,
we end up getting scratched, it never fails.

She's an important part of the family,
we found her at the pound,
and she's the best dog all around.

Sarah Vance, Grade 5
Grace Miller Elementary School, VA

Nature

Nature surrounding us,
The wind blows in my hair.
Water I can see,
As pretty as can be,
Flowing down a mountain of dreams,
Deer are in the meadow,
What can you hear?
Chewing,
From the deer,
Wind blowing,
Water falling,
And outrageous amount of organic shapes,
Mountains and rivers,
What would we do without nature in our lives?
Nature surrounding us.

Samantha Toli, Grade 5
St Mary's Primary School, MA

Snowflakes

A glimmering flake
To the shining cold white ground
Peacefully falling

Megan Rosenberger, Grade 4
C Hunter Ritchie Elementary School, VA

Courage

It is a feeling bigger than yourself.
The man inside of you is filled with fear.
But you keep on going.
You feed off your own fear.
You use it against something.
It doesn't use it against you.
With courage and determination you can do anything.
Courage forces you to never stop.
You will have courage until you drop.

Connor Shea, Grade 5
Booth Hill School, CT

The Weather and Me

The mist touches my soul with warmth,
The sun fills my heart with love,
The wind steals my mind with its cool breeze,
The rain sweeps me away with a gush of fresh water,
All I need is your kindness and friendship to fill my life with joy.

Jamie Downing, Grade 6
Memorial School, MA

Wolf

Wolf
Howling to the golden crescent moon
As if to say
Melt the bullet
Blunt the knife
Striking fear into man, woman, and animal
Like a demon with glowing eyes in the shadows
A horned cattle under the wolf's teeth
The elusive enemy of all shepherds
Wolf

Liam Bruce, Grade 4
Braeburn School, CT

Snap!

A rope wearing thin,
Breaking in,
About to go,
Watch the show,
Instead I show you self control!

Maury Bayer, Grade 6
School of International Studies at Meadowbrook, VA

Cantaloupe

You look like a yellow brain.
You feel like a rock.
When I tap you, you sound like a woodpecker pecking at a tree.
When I cut you open, it sounds like an iceberg cracking.
You look like a pumpkin seed on the inside.
You feel like a snake's belly.
You smell like a rotten squash.
You taste like a grapefruit.
Tell me why your outer-layer looks like a bunch of trees.

Cole Hale, Grade 4
Naquag Elementary School, MA

Amazing Heaven

Yes, all believers will go to amazing Heaven
And meet our great hero Jesus Christ
Walking on gold streets and the lights sparkling so bright
Yes, indeed it's amazing Heaven
More than a billion castles in Heaven for us to stay
But we'd be too busy talking to Jesus
Yes, some will go to Heaven, some will not
But all believers await for the glorious day

Suzanne Adjani-Aldrin, Grade 5
Church of the Redeemer Christian School, MD

My Yard

My yard is…
Fresh air
The sun's warmth
Running around and killing each other
The feeling of a creeping worm in
My hand

My yard is…
My awesome hideout
The smell of dinner cooking
Plunging into the pool
On a hot summer day
Hitting a ball onto the porch

Can't get any better,
Right?
But it does
My yard is…
Setting up my telescope
Staring into the cosmos
Fireworks on a warm July night
Running from imaginary monsters
That is what my yard is.

Shane Cardi, Grade 4
Fawn Hollow Elementary School, CT

Bug in a Mug

There once was a little bug.
It fell into a hug mug.
It was full of tea.
So he started to plea,
But all you could hear was blub, blub.

Dustin Harris, Grade 4
Grace Miller Elementary School, VA

Bon Jovi

Did you know
That my mom loves Bon Jovi
Oh she is in love with the music
Bon Jovi, Bon Jovi,
Is all she sees
When she closes her eyes and dreams.

Courtney Tremble, Grade 4
Grace Miller Elementary School, VA

Fasting

Hungry I am yet I must keep my fast.
It's almost time to break at last.
Boy am I so glad I stayed steadfast.

I thank Allah with glee,
now it is Eid.
Full of happiness and fun,
fasting days are already done!

Huda Khwaja, Grade 5
Home School, MA

Sleep

To sleep you have to be tired. I cannot sleep when I am wired
When I get frighted or excited
I cannot doze for I might get a stuffy nose.
All I hear is tick tock, from that old dumb clock.
My sister has a fit and cries, she makes a mess that hurts my eyes!
I try to keep my poise, but I just can't stand all that noise
I feel the need and try to heed,
But my body just does not want to sleep.

Now finally I get some peace, buried deep, inside my fleece.
Sometimes I dream, about the dress with a seam.
I go to different places, and see new faces.
I start to have some fun but then someone says "hon."
I look around and see a giant mound and what have I found?
A big scary monster, it has black matted fur.
I scream, which finishes the dream,
I start to wake up, and see my little pup.
I drag myself out, and start to pout,
All I want is to go back to sleep!

Rebecca Frank, Grade 6
Corkran Middle School, MD

Don't Let a Tear Fall

The tear stings as it falls from your bloodshot eyes.
It feels as if a piece of your heart
Has just been ripped away and crushed.
You know you can't let a tear fall, where all will see.
You think acting tough will stop the tear from falling.
That one tear could change the course of your entire life.
It could have a negative effect on your life.
You will not let the painful tear fall.
All it takes is one cruel word, one ugly stare,
One hard hit to make the tear fall.
One slip could change it all.
But when you woke up all of the pain was gone.
It was all a nightmare a mere memory that will
Fade with each passing of the day.
All of your troubles are gone
And you are left with a sunny day.
You wonder if you could replay your nightmare just to make sure
It was just a nightmare, it all seemed so real.
Now is the time to just let yourself go, and live your life
As happily as possible.
"Because your life will only be as happy as you want it to be."

Noel Eastham, Grade 6
Blue Ridge Middle School, VA

My Dream

The moon is bright but I'm not grey because no one else can feel this way
As I skate around the rink someone gave a wink
I smile back as they turn with their sack, but I know they felt it anyway
I leave the skate rink at 10 o'clock to meet my family at the boat dock
There they have a tiny boat, so I jump in onto my warm fluffy coat
I look around at the sparkling sky, this is my dream a midnight boat ride.

Madalyn Saunders, Grade 5
Our Lady of Lourdes School, VA

The Apple Trees

Watching those giant monsters
Swaying gently in the breeze
Climbing up the trunks,
Seeing the lovely view
But, what I love most is…
Plucking a huge green ball
Crunch! Crunch!
And tasting the sweet beauty
As I watch from my perch on the tree branch
I see the sun setting
That's what I love most
About apple trees

Anayis Doolittle, Grade 4
Braeburn School, CT

What Is Orange?

Orange is the color of fall —
Carrots, an orange, and a jack-o'-lantern sitting on the wall!
In a blacksmith's forge orange dances in the flame.
Orange is their favorite color many claim!
The orange smell is spice —
The kind you find in a pumpkin pie slice.
Orange makes me feel warm all over —
Just like when I find a four-leaf clover.
The orange touch is hot —
The kind you find in a boiling pot.
Orange is the leader of the hit parade…
Orange is truly a breathtaking shade.

Elly Overton, Grade 5
Har-Bur Middle School, CT

I'm Ready for the Pool

It is time for the time of my life.
It is even more dangerous than using a knife.
I've never jumped in or gone into the deep.
I really just thought it was just too steep.

But today is the day when I'm going to dive.
They have lowered the deep end so I'll give it a try.
I put on my goggles and my swimming cap.
I get on the board and hear it tap!

I won't get scared even though I'm alone.
Why isn't anyone here? But I won't groan.
I'm going to jump, first I look around,
Then I look down and hear no sound.

No waves in the water, there is simply no noise.
I'm ready to dive as I stand here with poise.
I start to jump, here I go.
1, 2, 3, "Oh no!"
As I'm in the air, I'm suddenly aware…
I realize there's no water down there!

Danielle MacDonald, Grade 6
Edmond P Talbot Middle School, MA

Dalmatian Molly (Fish)

Energetic, happy
Swimming, eating, playing
Gills, front flippers, back flippers, tail, spots
Jumping, amazing, surfing
Fast, cool
Molly

Alexander DiMisa, Grade 6
St Bartholomew School, MD

Flag

As I peer down from atop my pole
there are some bad things I see
Though I'm this country's symbol
I'm not sure I'm proud to be

Corruption has taken integrity's place
in government and rule
Sometimes I wonder
what they teach kids in school

What's happening in the world
everything's falling apart
The Earth is on fire
and it hasn't been this way since the start

Pollution in our air
pollution in our mind
Spring from our cars and TVs
all knowledge left behind

Flying high above
I look down at it all
Seems to me
like somebody dropped the ball

Charlie Hill, Grade 6
E W Thurston Middle School, MA

Soccer Field

The green grass all around,
My hair is floating in the breeze.
I kick the ball in the net,
Shoot
Score!

Second half,
I'm in goal.
The sweaty gloves go on my hands,
And the hot goalie shirt goes over my jersey.
A player shoots the ball in the white net,
My team wins!
I save it!

The game is over,
The score is 5 to 3!

Mindy Blanchard, Grade 5
Oakdale Elementary School, MD

Losing a Family Member

As blue as the tear that you cry
Looks like somebody
that just got paralyzed
and wasn't opening their eyes
Smells like that familiar scent
that you've known all your life
Tastes like the bitter sorrow of sadness
Feels like being stabbed
in the back for no reason

Garrett Taylor, Grade 5
St Christopher's School, VA

Brothers

I'm about to make a shout out,
about what brothers do.
I know better than anyone,
because I have 2!
They yell,
    They scream,
        They kick a lot,
and every minute,
They're making a plot!
But always remember,
they love you so,
So don't get angry.
When they throw a ball of snow!

Samantha Dolan, Grade 4
Munger Hill Elementary School, MA

My Flower

My flower's name is Kate
    She's a great mate
She watches me grow
And sometimes while I mow
    She likes to see my plant
    And listen to my chant
My flower is very graceful
    And always playful.

Celia Wilson, Grade 4
Crestwood Elementary School, VA

Desert

On the pebble sand
Snakes are slithering
The sun is rising.

Jodie Lee, Grade 4
Trinity Christian School, VA

Season

In the warm summer sun
In the leaves of autumn's empty trees
In the shivers of winter
And in spring's black striped bees
All can find seasons

Harrison J. Silva, Grade 4
St Mary's Primary School, MA

Spring

I hear with my ears,
birds chirping in the soft breeze.
Then I know it's spring!

Nicole Rogers, Grade 4
St Joseph School-Fullerton, MD

Idea

Trying to get out of my head
trying to break free
when it finally gets out
it comes straight to
ME!

Ryan Kiel-Zabel, Grade 5
C C Burr Elementary School, MA

The Circus

Circus
Fun, exciting
Rope-walking, fire-breathing, clowns
Cotton candy is my favorite
Entertainment

Julianna Kennedy, Grade 4
Trinity Christian School, VA

Snowboard

This is my snowboard
I glide across the snow
It's a new Burton
Of that I know.

This is my snowboard
It's so shiny I see my face.
Colorful design
This is kept in a case.

This is my snowboard
I keep it clean
It always looks new
So it could always be seen.

Chris Wurfbaum, Grade 6
Scotts Ridge Middle School, CT

Memories of Huckleberry

The very best part was walking old Huck,
    down the road to the beach.

Morning breeze tapping my face,
    as crisp as winter frost.

Morning glories awake as always,
blue faces climbing up the fence.

Little ripples touching his feet,
    Huck shaking his honey fur.

Monika Gabriele, Grade 5
St Luke's School, CT

A Wonderful Creature

A Wonderful Creature
in search of its prey.
It flies calmly over trees
and grass
With its wings it makes
a whooshing sound.
Silently it flies overhead
Now quite low to the ground
With a breeze blowing
through it wings
I see a gray and white
Crane.

Kaitlin Gale, Grade 4
Southbrook Academy, MA

The Martyr's Prayer

Oh, Lord, have mercy on their souls,
On they who lit this pyre,
For while I perish in this life,
They, too, will die by fire.

Yes, they believed that they were right,
And I the evil one;
So now I die for being true,
And they for being wrong.

I would not pay obeisance to
Their god they call "The Church,"
For I had started in the path
To many higher works.

The last nail struck, the last beam laid,
I speak my final words.
They go to death and will not rise;
I go to meet my God.

Jennifer Coleman, Grade 6
Martin Barr Adventist School, MD

Just Be Yourself

Just be yourself
Don't have any doubt
Just be yourself
Inside and out
Don't be afraid
Of what others say
It's good for your health
TO JUST BE YOURSELF!

Deanna Leung, Grade 5
Sacred Heart School, MA

The Moon

Way up in the sky
You only see me at night
Shining so brightly

Caitlin D'Amato, Grade 5
Sacred Heart Elementary School, MA

Bears

Bears
Bears
Bears
Hungry bears
Strong, black bears
Tough scary brown bears
Mad bears
Sad bears
Big, funny Grizzly bears
Small, happy Kodiak bears
Polar bears, too
Tiny bears
Angry bears
Don't forget Panda bears
Last of all, best of all, I like Gummy bears

Jasmine Dixon, Grade 4
C Hunter Ritchie Elementary School, VA

Harriet Tubman

Araminta was born near Chesapeake Bay,
In the year of 1820 on a fateful day.
In 1820 Old Rit gave birth,
Bringing baby Minta onto this earth.
When Minta got older she worked as a field hand,
When she was a slave on Brodas Land.
Araminta soon got hired out,
To mean Miss Susan who made her pout.
Minta was sent back to the plantation,
But the north was still her true destination.
Harriet became Araminta's new name,
Which is the name she would gain her fame.
When Harriet was going to get married,
She made a quilt she always carried.
Harriet Tubman then got in a fight,
Because she was to be sold which made her take flight.
Harriet Tubman brought many slaves to see,
What it was like in the north to live and be free.
Harriet's final day came at last,
At the age of 93 she finally passed

Kaycie McCarthy, Grade 6
Daniel L Joyce Middle School, MA

Patchwork Quilt

Grandmother's kerchief
Sits next to grandfather's vest
My mother's satin scarf
And my father's favorite curtains
Sit side by side
My pioneer ancestor's old cotton tablecloth
Is their sweet smelling dresses' neighbor
My great grandmother's white ribbons
Are beside her brother's navy cap
All of these memories, cut and sewn
Into the lovely Patchwork Quilt

Susannah Devenney, Grade 6
Nathan Hale-Ray Middle School, CT

Janitor's Closet

In the Cleaning Superstore it was a perfectly normal day.
Then a man bought me and took me away.
He threw me in the backseat of his shiny car.
We drove and drove and drove and drove,
I could tell we were driving far.

When we reached our destination, he threw me in a room.
There I met my new best friend, a small and dusty broom.
Then I met another mop, a snarl upon his face.
Then one kid made a mess, so I scrubbed up the place.

But I had a question that wasn't answered yet.
So I asked a nearby bucket,
I was in the Janitor's Closet!

Becky Mainzer, Grade 6
Fuller Middle School, MA

It's Music

It's music that wakes me up to a beautiful day
Even if it costs me to pay
It's music that makes every day a special day
Even in the most unexpected ways

It's music that serves as my "guiding light"
Even through the coldest of all nights
It's music that takes a stand for me to fight

It's music that shows as my only love
Even if the world compares it to worst of all above
It's music that gives me a world of my own!

Gaby Go, Grade 5
Church of the Redeemer Christian School, MD

Fireworks!!!!

Pop! Boom! Bam! Majestic fireworks in the sky.
Wonderful colors meet my eye.

Blue, red, yellow, green…
And all the colors in between.

The colors are awesome. The colors are unique.
Just make sure they don't land near your feet!

You see them popping in the sky…
You don't know who lit them you just wonder why?

Why, my friend, are you having a celebration?
This most wonderful day is such a jubilation.

The Chinese invented them; the French employed them.
Now you, my friend, are going to enjoy them.

Pop! Boom! Bam! Enjoy!

Trey Butrym, Grade 5
Davenport Ridge School, CT

The Ugly Old Witch!
There once was an ugly old witch.
Who had a terrible itch.
She always made stew.
That gave her the flu.
And that's what made her twitch.
Carli Cummings, Grade 4
Freetown Elementary School, MA

Computer
Computer
Teaches, shows
Entertains, informs, helps
Computers are really cool.
Knowledge
Rahel Sirack, Grade 4
Sacred Heart School, MA

Idea
It starts out small.
Just a tiny speck,
Until it is fed
Inspiration,
And grows
As years go by,
Like your own child
Until it has grown old,
It fades
And dies,
Yet a new develops.
Ayva Tedstone, Grade 5
C C Burr Elementary School, MA

Snowflake Compassion
snowflake drifting
sun disappearing
moon glowing
glowing, glistening
a blanket of snow
fluorescent light
sparkle alone
one sparkle
moon's best friend
one sparkle
of one snowflake
blowing around
around the corner
to a different yard
a different dimension
a white star
a falling diamond
a snowflake
one sparkle
moon reappearing
snowflake compassion
Harper Glantz, Grade 4
Sinai Academy of the Berkshires, MA

Hippies Again
Put on those bellbottoms and take that necklace that has once been dented.
How about that protest sign that John Lennon once held?
Call some friends and start an invasion of hippies again!
Jonas Von Schmidt, Grade 5
Hindley Elementary School, CT

Blue
Blue looks like a bright, clear, sunny morning in June.
Blue sounds like the ocean waves coming to the shore of the beach.
Blue smells like a blanket a new born baby boy is wrapped in.
Blue tastes like a sour candy in my mouth.
Blue feels like a fuzzy, warm sweater in December.
Blue
Elizabeth Feldman, Grade 4
Helen H Hansen Elementary School, MA

A Change in Seasons
My favorite season is finally here, the signs of it are very near.
Wind whistling in my ear trying to talk to me it is clear.
It whispers secrets, it sings a song, it tells me tales both short and long.
The leaves gracefully galloping like stallions down from the trees
A race to the finish line caused by the breeze.
Crispy and crunchy in my hand, I try to catch them before they land.
Rose red, honey yellow and cinnamon brown surrounding me.
The fresh pumpkin pie aroma is as rich as gold, its taste so bold.
Sitting around a big bonfire warms your heart like a child's smile.
Comfy as can be, I watch scary stories on TV.
These clues I have given for a reason, can you guess this beautiful season?
If you guessed autumn you guessed right, autumn it is, what a wonderful sight.
The place to see, the place to be, New England is the place for me.
Brooke McKean, Grade 6
Madison Middle School, CT

I Am Quiet
Around the world right now there is quiet like a mouse on a cold winter's night.
People always move as fast as cheetahs, racing through the savanna.
But I right now am quiet.
Some people are nervous, like a child who thought she heard a monster.
Mean, like an ongoing cat fight.
Angry, like the wind whirling about.
Gentle, like a puppy after being played with.
But I now am quiet.
I dream about smoothness in the world, like a kimono.
But wherever there is darkness, like ghost roaming a home,
I know there will never be any.
I wish the world could be glittery and beautiful like a tiara,
To be placed on a princess's head.
But with fire and destruction like a red stop sign,
I know it could never be.
I can wish for a fuzzy blanket, like a kitten near a fire, to surround us all.
I wish, dream, and pray,
But only together can we change the world.
So until that day,
I am quiet.
Emma Spector, Grade 5
Memorial-Spaulding Elementary School, MA

Baseball

Baseball is
fun, active, and about teamwork
with a lot of sportsmanship
you play hard and try to win
with glory and fame and
become rich and famous
will you go down in history as a
great player and enjoy the fame
with all the fun baseball will bring
it's a great sport for everyone to love and enjoy
with all the great success one may hold
go out and play give it your best and
play the game of baseball like you know how

Jarred Bryant, Grade 6
Monelison Middle School, VA

Shaving Cream

I told my dad that I was almost finished,
He told me to eat the rest of my spinach.
"Can we have ice cream for dessert?"
Asked my big brother, Bert.
"Can I spray the whipped cream?" I said.
"Okay," said Dad, "But after dessert, it's time for bed."

After I was finished spraying the whipped cream,
I asked my dad, "Do you like how I did it?
Do you like how it's done?"
"Sure," he said,
"If you want to shave your tongue."

Aaron Mackert, Grade 5
Milton L Fuller Elementary School, MA

Mountain Glories

Mountains shine like gold
around me they reflect everything like water
looking into them makes your life flash before your eyes

Kyler Apgar, Grade 5
Francis Asbury Elementary School, VA

Spring Break

Flowers are blooming, birds are chirping,
What a wonderful time!
The weather is changing, we are coming out and playing,
Oh! What a wonderful time!
Insects and animals are prancing around.
Baseball and softball are starting up.
What a fun, terrific time!
But the best part, my favorite part,
The part all kids like is
Spring break!
No school!
No work!
Here comes the fun… I can't wait!

Casey Turner, Grade 5
St Joseph School-Fullerton, MD

Winter

Winter of wonders
A calm snowy day
The feeling is outside
Sledding on a winter dream of feet and feet of snow
The feeling of the impact of a crash in the soft snow
Through blizzards and storms and ice
Skating…on lakes and ponds slip and fall
This is winter with and through all
Christmas Day New Year's Eve
Presents and fireworks
The excitement of it all
Day by day night by night
Everyone waits for the Holy night
New Year's Eve the staying up
All night never ending
Time in the dark
New Years Day a day of
Excitement and wonders
The first hours of the first day of the year
New times to yell and cheer
And that is what winter is all about

Brandon Wood, Grade 6
Whitinsville Christian School, MA

Baseball

Baseball
Fun, exciting
Outing, arguing, injuring
Angry fans
Hoping for victory

Joey Connors, Grade 5
Linscott-Rumford Elementary School, MA

Into the World

There's a sleepy little creature
In the center of the Earth
His favorite time is sunset
And his favorite moon is Rose
He's been so many places
Yet he can't count them all
He thinks the world wouldn't be here
If he didn't enjoy it so much
The clouds all look to him like
Rushing waterfalls
He hears so much more
Than there is to hear
The sky sounds to him
Like a troubled, troubled wise old man
His life is a circle
Never ending at all
There's no holes in his circle
He paints the world with rainbows
And he's learned to ride the wind
The sleepy little creature in the center of the Earth

Juliana Durning, Grade 5
Thoreau Elementary School, MA

Christmas
Christmas
Trees with glittering lights
Freshly baked cookies for Santa
Christmas carols being sung
Delicious burning hot chocolate
The spiky tip of a Christmas tree
Christmas
Matthew Burke, Grade 5
Jane Ryan School, CT

Water Pollution
Water pollution.
Destructive, impair,
Suffering, exterminating,
Decreasing, hurtful, destructive, dirty,
Non-caring, dead, poisoned
Unfit, toxic dump.
Jose Garcia, Grade 6
City View School, MA

My Shy Shadow
My shy shadow,
it is very black.
My shy shadow,
the light it attacks.
My shy shadow,
bad things it has seen.
My shy shadow,
is scared it seems.
My shy shadow,
on the outside is duller.
My shy shadow,
in my world is filled with color
Shelby Devanney, Grade 6
Albert D Griswold Middle School, CT

Dark/Light
Dark
Black, sad
Spooking, scaring, hiding,
Dim, shadowy, glow, bright
Shining, illumination, gleaming
Brilliance, radiance,
Light
Maria Goodrick, Grade 5
Trinity Christian School, VA

Spring
Spring is beautiful in every way
Having fun day by day
but sadly when the sun goes down
It's time to turn the day around
It's a very pretty sight to see,
So can you come and watch with me?
Lizzy Cormier, Grade 4
Brookside Elementary School, MA

The Whites of Winter
Flakes dance gracefully.
Snow smothers the Earth lively.
A white blanket falls.
Sumin Woo, Grade 4
Jacksonville Elementary School, MD

Basketball
B ig men shooting
A ssist to get points
S hooting a three pointer
K nowing the plays
E xciting to see slam dunks
T ime out to put new players in
B asketball is a great sport
A good shooter
L ay-up to the basket
L oud cheers for the team.
Dakota Roy, Grade 4
Freetown Elementary School, MA

Exit Sign
The Exit Sign:
Your ticket to freedom.
Your ticket to laughs.
Your ticket to not learn.
Just thinking about it makes you squirm.

The Exit Sign:
Leading your way to sports
Leading your way to
running
jumping
yelling
screaming.
Leading your way to the new game
you are going to get.

But…
It's not 2:25 yet!
Sergey Dushkin, Grade 6
Fuller Middle School, MA

Birthdays
Presents everywhere, I cannot bear,
I want lipstick, and a football.
And even a candy cake, do I dare?
Blowing out candles all life long,
With joy to me on my birthday.
The guests sing, "Happy Birthday!"
Surprise parties are the best.
It's my birthday today,
One year older and the better I'll get.
Are you coming to my party?
Birthdays, birthdays, birthdays.
Kate Spade, Grade 4
Riderwood Elementary School, MD

Why?
On this day,
I watched the sky turn gray.
The white clouds became black,
and I saw her lying on her back.

It was so easy for me to cry,
and I asked myself why.
She was dead,
my nana was dead.
Erika Scott, Grade 5
Miscoe Hill Elementary School, MA

Penguins
A big parade of penguins
Slipping and sliding
Like their arch enemy the seal
Diving into the icy water
Gathering fish
Ready to feed their chicks
Macy Parisee, Grade 4
Freetown Elementary School, MA

Sunny Day
It's a sunny day
I like to go and play,
and horseback riding
is very exciting,
And every day,
I feed him hay
I love my horse,
of course!
His name is Freddie,
we always get ready
It's a great day,
I'm going to play
So I'll see you later
A-L-L-I-GA-TOR
Devon Cormier, Grade 4
Brookside Elementary School, MA

My Dad
I love my dad

I love his smell.
His smell is like a rose.

Every time I see him
it's like I'm seeing a rose
glittering in the light.

Whenever I hear a song he likes
I think of him and smile.

I love my dad.
Jasmin Cedeño, Grade 5
Clark Avenue Middle School, MA

My Favorite Sister

I have a favorite sister
Her name is Melissa
Who thinks she's in the Hall of Fame
She's tall and funny
Her favorite animal is a bunny
So now you know my favorite sister
Who's nickname is Belissa

Ashley Arndt, Grade 4
Helen H Hansen Elementary School, MA

Breeze

The calm, cool breeze
Slowly passes you by
At the crack of dawn
On a Sunday morning.

As the breeze whirls its way around
the world
It turns dark.
The breeze is gone.

You wake up in the morning.
You can smell the fresh morning dew
Knowing that the cool breeze
Would whirl and twirl its way around you
Again.

Dzenana Karajic, Grade 5
Clark Avenue Middle School, MA

Jake and His Snowflake

There once was a young boy named Jake,
He caught the world's largest snowflake.
It looked like white lace,
Hung in window's place,
Now wind caused it to dance and shake.

Jasmin Wills, Grade 4
St Clement Mary Hofbauer School, MD

Peace in the Glade

The birds are chirping,
The busy bees buzzing,
The sun shines bright on all.
The worms are wriggling,
The ferns are tickling,
I'm sitting in serene shade.
The leafy boughs shield me,
The air clears me,
The soft moss covers the ground.
Then all falls silent,
I remain self-reliant,
Eating an apple in the shade.
How blissful!
How wonderful!
Peace reins in the leafy glade.

Althea Lutwak, Grade 5
Marblehead Community Charter Public School, MA

Opening My Eyes

Opening my eyes for the thousandth time
but this time it's different.
I can finally see through that cloudy mist
that covered up my future.
Questions are tempted to spill out of my mouth.
What will I grow up to be?
How long will I live?
But these questions
will be answered
with…patience.

Corinne Taney, Grade 5
Hindley Elementary School, CT

African Animals

One fine day at
two o'clock exactly
three unfortunate events happened maybe more
Four elephants trampled
five monkeys
Six birds scared
seven lions
Eight hyenas had
nine frightening laughs
Ten rhinos got run over by
eleven springboks
Twelve alligators swapped places with
thirteen polar bears
Fourteen penguins swapped places with
fifteen ostriches
Sixteen galloping gazelles galloped to Paris
Seventeen dolphins washed up on shore
Eighteen giraffes wished they had shorter necks
Nineteen hours of mishap for
twenty days on

Lee Hayes, Grade 5
Wakefield Forest Elementary School, VA

Life

Life is a gift.
Life is a present.
Life is a lovely peaceful dream.
Sometimes you have nightmares
but you always know
life sometimes goes that way.
A smile is all you need
to lift your spirits.
Love is infinite,
you can make as much as you want.
You choose who you love,
at one minute you love,
at the next you don't.
But you have your ups and downs,
trust me things will turn around!

Hayley McManus, Grade 4
Helen H Hansen Elementary School, MA

Water

Water, water —
when I
shake you,
what do I hear?
Water going from side to side,
Water, water,
When I
touch you,
what do I feel?
Soft, liquidity wetness.
Water, water
when I look at you,
What do I see?
A bumpy water bottle with water in it.
Water, water,
when I taste you,
how do I feel?
Refreshed!

Andy Hubina, Grade 4
Hawley Elementary School, CT

Orange

Orange
Like a basketball
Shooting into a hoop
Like a goldfish swimming
In his fish tank like a mom
Squeezing an orange to make
Orange juice

Summer Noveska, Grade 5
Clark Avenue Middle School, MA

The Red Eft

The red eft is fast
Like a blur of flaming red
To eat food it speeds

Matthew Brooks, Grade 4
Grace Miller Elementary School, VA

The Unknown

I'm in the rocket
Seat belts fastened tight
Supervisors pacing nervously,
"This is the night!"

Ten, nine, eight, seven, six
Thunder rumbling
Five, four, three, two, one
Boom!! Towers crumbling

Shooting off into the unknown
More exciting than I knew
Out of Earth's boundaries
A lifelong dream come true

Chaya Wolff, Grade 6
Yeshiva Academy, MA

Nurse

Jael was heading to the medical room where no one dared to go.
I tried to warn, I pleaded for her to stop, but she kept on.
She does not know what is behind those closed doors.

"The Nurse!" I yelled. "The NURSE!" I screamed.
They say she's too scary for your eyes to see.

I heard rumors that she's ten feet tall.
And has eyes all around her head.
She has long arms and fingers with suction cups that suck you in.
Her hair sticks up and is lime green.
I tell you there are things about her I cannot say.

When kids come out, they're never the same.
They seem like robots, it's very strange.

Jasmine Choate, Grade 6
Fuller Middle School, MA

The Jungle

The screeching breaks of the bus, the door gasping for air.
Every day a fight to get in the back.
Shoving and pushing, screaming and yelling, dazing out.
You arrive at school.
Everybody goes ludicrous, a fight to get off the crowded bus, shaking and rumbling.
Finally, peace and quiet…for now.

Alex Tellez, Grade 6
Fuller Middle School, MA

The Dragonfly

As the dragonfly buzzes to the purple wet flowers that shimmer in the daylight
the dragonfly lays itself upon the flowers
the pretty bug shy and depressed
still wondering how the flowers bloom
how the colors sparkle
and how the sky is sometimes blue and sometimes…black
as he is on a flower he feels the soft petals rubbing against his rough skin
but people make fun of his bubbly eyes
but people also see…his sparkling, shining colors
twirling and mixing with blue, purple, and green like a rainbow
you can see the wet and delicate wings
with rain gently dropping upon it like melting ice cream
but he is special in everyone's heart he is the dragonfly

Justine Hawkins, Grade 5
Stadley Rough School, CT

Sundown

The day I was born, all I saw was a colorful horizon,
when it was sundown, my mom was loving, relaxing, soothing at the ending.

One day it was cold with a loving breeze,
one night I saw a solar eclipse,

I woke up one morning,
I heard little birds chirping.

Savon Hicks, Grade 6
Maple Valley School, MA

Gymnastics

Flipping and twisting all around
Almost never falling to the ground
Round and round the bars
You go so high you're almost in Mars
If you stick it the crowd goes wild
Cheering and screaming with your child
It's not called gym-nice-tics for a reason
But who cares cause we bounce around every season
Back handspring, front handspring, back tuck, front tuck
If you fall it's just your luck
Floor
Isn't such a bore
Then comes jumping and squatting on the vault
If you fall then it is your fault
Leaping around on the beam
Everything is just a scream!

Kendall Rochlin, Grade 5
Coleytown Elementary School, CT

The Tree

The old tree stands strong, like a soldier, right in front of me.
Its golden green leaves catch my eye.
The sturdiness of its trunk gleams in the sunlight.
The grass beneath, cuddles to the tree
As a child would to its mother.
The breeze sways the golden leaves back and forth.
The tree I'm looking at brightens the whole neighborhood.
That old tree does, it really does.

Aslan Bakri, Grade 5
Wakefield Forest Elementary School, VA

My Sister

You are always there for me,
　Even when I'm sick at sea.
Loving, caring, helpful too,
　Showing love between me and you.
Getting Band-Aids for giant scrapes,
　We fool around like crazy apes.
In your room we have a blast,
　Our fun times will definitely always last.
We sing and dance and have some fun,
　You share your toys with everyone.
Music, games, making friends,
　Fun and laughter never ends.
I love you and you love me,
　I think that we were meant to be.
At camp and school and at home too,
　I'll always be happy
　Because I'm with you
Basketball, skiing, softball too,
　I always try to win for you.
Now this poem must come to an end,
　It was about my most loved friend, my sister.

Maddi Weinstein, Grade 5
Weston Intermediate School, CT

Happiness

Happiness is the color of the orange blazing sun.
It sounds like the laughing children in Africa.
It tastes like rich chocolate with sprinkles on top.
It smells like a fudge brownie gooey and good.
It looks like a ballerina twirling in the air.
It makes me feel wild.

Kirstyn Arcata, Grade 6
Albert D Griswold Middle School, CT

A World with No Inspiration

It felt like there was no inspiration left in the world.
There was basically none left.
But then, I wouldn't be able to write this poem.
No one would be able to write anything.
The world would be thoughtless.
And our world would be
A World With No Inspiration.

Francie Grasso, Grade 4
St Mary's Primary School, MA

Sadness

Sadness
One of many things we do not need
We need food, we need water, and we need shelter
But we do not need sadness.

After war, there is sadness
After a severe storm, there is sadness
Sadness is everywhere you look.

In the end, my friend
There will be happiness
You'll forget about depressing things
And look on the optimistic side.

John Tusa, Grade 6
Scotts Ridge Middle School, CT

Spring Fun

When you're
out of school and want to have fun,
you can hang out with your friends,
or have ham on a bun. You can
always go out to the movies, take pictures,
or go to the mall. There is so much more!
Maybe you'll stay home and relax,
or stay home and do all of
your chores. (Yuck!)
Right now I am stuck
in school, writing
this poem…
I just can't
wait until
Spring
fun!

Crystal Dong, Grade 5
St Joseph School-Fullerton, MD

He's Real

Sh, sh, sh! I open the door gently seeing if anyone is around. I face right, I face left, yet I can go. One foot at a time, left behind right. The ground is tickling my feet making me almost laugh. Squeak, squeak, squeak the floor sounds like a mouse. Come on, I stop and turn back, I give up. Swoosh, a crunch of a cookie and a sip of milk. I could not believe it was Santa. I could not stand giving up. As I walk slowly back to the stairs I look, someone with a red and white suit on is eating our milk and cookies. The person likes the smell. Well it does smell good. As the man turns around, it's him!

Margaret Hill, Grade 4
Litchfield Intermediate School, CT

Family Guy

I look at the time, 8:00 I run over to a chair and turn on the TV.
I hear the last of the theme song. I watch as Brian the dog talks to the baby Stewie.
I watch as the family talks to one another. I laugh every once and a while, even to the most
random things. I hear Peter the father laugh his weird and funny laugh and I laugh with him,
Then my dad comes in. We laugh together, we talk about how some things make no sense we bond together.
And I love that we bond.

Jesse Tuttle, Grade 6
Swampscott Middle School, MA

Through the Eyes of a Squirrel

Crunch, go the leaves as I scurry by. I'm as busy as a construction worker because I seek food for the winter yet to come.
Up a tree? Yes I must go so I quietly start up the towering oak.
"Ouch!" I shriek as a rough piece of bark juts into my fragile foot. It hurts for a while but I overcome the pain and move on.
Finally, I reach the top branch and feel proud of myself. I turn my head and what a sight I see. Acorns galore. It's my favorite treat so I start to pick some. They're positively sweet.
One…two…three…I think that's enough so into my cheek they go. I hear a thud as faint as a person punching their pillow as the acorns drop out of my mouth and plummet to the ground below.
I swiftly scramble down the tree and retrieve my marvelous acorns.
Again I tuck them into my cheek and I start to take them to my burrow. As I race down my path, I tear through the rainbow of leaves that are peacefully scattered all over the ground.
I stop for a second and look all around me. I can see scarlet, apricot, and bronze colors and I admire them.
Then I take off again like a race car speeding down the track. I smell the fresh autumn air on my nose and remember that this season comes only once a year.
I locate my burrow hidden under a patch of leaves and slide into it.
My large, bushy tail tags along behind me as I travel into my home.
"Home at last," I mumble and take a bite of one of my delicious acorns.
Then I silently curl into a ball and fall asleep.

Max Martel, Grade 6
Madison Middle School, CT

Home Run

The hitter comes up to the plate ready to hit the ball.
The pitcher is waiting ready to strike out them all.
Here is the wind up and then the pitch comes.
"CRACK" goes the bat and then the hitter runs.
The center fielder sees the ball soaring high and far.
The pitcher has a gloomy face and his shoulders are slumped a ton.
The hitter slows down with a grin on his face because he knows he just hit a home run.

Devin Rosen, Grade 5
Memorial-Spaulding Elementary School, MA

Stars

Throughout the day you just see blue skies and a beautiful sun, but at night the magic happens! Slowly you see sparkles appear. You feel as if you can grab them and pull them tight, but as the night thins and the stars disappear as the moon just sits there and says, "I'll hope to see you soon!"

Ashley Timmons, Grade 6
Irving School, CT

John Paul Jones Arena
It is a very special place
when you're inside and having fun
listening to concerts
and watching the basketball games
seeing Cavman repel through the ceiling
going crazy and screaming loud
but yet outside it is a plain old building with big glass panes
and huge white columns that hold the building high

Holden Fockler, Grade 4
St Christopher's School, VA

Sound the Bell
They are not well,
So sound the bell...
They are living in poverty.
Yes, we aren't just talking about
People in foreign countries,
But also right here,
So sound the bell...
Not many people think of parts
Of the USA as poor
But some people are poor in wealth and Christ,
So sound the bell...
Spread the news of the Lord
And they will come aboard the Liberty ship of the Lord
So sound the bell.

Alex Boa, Grade 6
Whitinsville Christian School, MA

I Wish
I wish I was a mermaid.
I could ride on a dolphin,
And feel the water in my face
And bubbles tickle my skin.
To be a mermaid I must have a tail,
But I don't have a tail.
That's why I can only wish!
Mermaids are beautiful and fun.
But am I?
How cool it would be to be a mermaid.
Half-human, half-fish,
I wish I was a mermaid.

Megan Gombatz, Grade 5
West Woods Upper Elementary School, CT

Who I Am
I am a sun, bright and full of life
I am an ocean, peaceful and quiet
I am a rose, pretty and unique
I am a butterfly, colorful and sweet
I am a wonderful fish in a shiny, blue lake
I am a shark, full of anger
I am a lip gloss that shines everywhere
I am like a rat, causing problems

Ana Luisa Faria, Grade 6
Fuller Middle School, MA

A Majestic Eagle
Standing tall and stiff,
on the rocky white and jagged cliffs.

Soaring up high in the air,
to the sky azure and bare.

Using her sharp keen eyes,
she will find something to pry.

Razor and sharp are her talons and beak,
but she is no monster freak!

She is bold, intelligent,
and also very diligent.

Rachel Madeline Sit, Grade 5
Church of the Redeemer Christian School, MD

The Rainbow
Pitter Patter, Pitter Patter
The light rain daintily dripped and dropped
Onto my umbrella.
The radiant reflection of the rainbow from a nearby puddle
Glistened and glowed,
Wanted to show
And flaunt its stunning and dazzling beauty.
Its magnificence was as lovely as a rare flower;
Each member of the rainbow had its own special smile
That shone bigger than the one before.
The rainbow is the queen of all colors,
A princess of the rain, and the heir to the throne of the sky.
As I looked up at the brilliant display,
I dreamed of pots of gold and little leprechauns
And marveled that,
Bursting with brightness, the rainbow
Brought light into the gloomy darkness of the sky,
And the only remains of that sparkling spectacle
Were left to mingle inside my mind.

Minnie Jang, Grade 6
Trinity School, MD

Winter
It's winter now
It's very cold
The winter is young
And summer is old
There's sledding and skiing
Snow angels and snowball fights
It's not summer anymore
So put away you kites
There are no leaves on the trees
I can hear the beautiful Christmas chimes
Chestnuts are roasting
In this wonderful wintertime

Michael Nunziante, Grade 5
Toquam Magnet School, CT

Waiting in Line for the Fountain

I don't like waiting in line for
The fountain
It's almost like climbing a mountain.
I wait and I wait saying to myself,
"I don't have this time,"
And when I finally get to the fountain,
I see grime.
When some people taste the water,
They say, "Yum!"
When I taste the water, I see gum.

I don't like waiting in line,
Some people think it's just fine.
I stand and I stand,
In one big band,
To wait this long,
There might as well be a chair,
To wait so long for warm water,
It's just not fair.

Jacob Meyers, Grade 6
Fuller Middle School, MA

Christmas

Christmas
Colorful presents
Chestnuts roasting
The rip of wrapping paper
Delicious, juicy ham
A bouncy, rubber ball
Christmas

Mason Geary, Grade 4
Naquag Elementary School, MA

Books

I love to read
Because reading is fun
It takes you places
That you've never been before
It can take you to a jungle
Or a bloody murder scene
Or it can take you to another planet
Where everyone there is green
When you're reading a book
Whether it's happy, sad, or gory
You don't pay attention
To anything else but the story
Reading can be fun
For people of all ages
Once you open a good book
You just can't stop turning the pages
Reading takes you places
That you've never been before
Just get one taste of an adventure
And you'll be begging for more

Sade Moses, Grade 6
Salem Church Middle School, VA

Life as a Kid

At one you're just walking
At ten you're getting in trouble.
At fifteen you're talking back
As sixteen you're in a good mood
Next you're in a bad mood
By twenty you should've moved out
Because this poem is about life as a
Kid!

Aaron Harawa, Grade 6
Magnolia Elementary School, MD

Michael

My friend Michael
Loves to ride his motorcycle.
He rides around the town and city
Telling all the girls they're pretty.

David Fox, Grade 5
St Luke's School, CT

Summer

Summer is the best
To go outside and have fun
And to wear light clothes

Tobias Allen, Grade 4
Hebbville Elementary School, MD

Easter

Jesus is risen
Lenten prayers are answered
A time to rejoice!

Erin Shoul, Grade 4
St Joseph School-Fullerton, MD

Repeat

R eproduce
E ncore
P lay again
E cho
A gain
T he end

Melvin Cortez, Grade 6
Edmond P Talbot Middle School, MA

I Don't Know What to Do

I don't know what to talk about
I cannot write a poem
Because I have nothing to say
Unless I am instant messaging at home
So while I'm sitting here wasting my time
I could be on a scuba dive
But no I'm stuck here "writing" a poem
I hope I get out of English alive
This writing thing is really not fun
Hey wait! Now I am done!

Xavier Carter, Grade 6
Edmond P Talbot Middle School, MA

Seasons

Summer
loud, sporty
steaming, swimming, playing
baseball, soccer, snowmen, snow angels
freezing, throwing, snowmobiling
playful, scary
Winter

Kaylee Morton, Grade 6
Captain Nathan Hale Middle School, CT

The Scare of War

In the war I was trying hard
You know me
Still with war scars all over me

Staying behind the sandbag wall
When a small fry took a fall
A tear left my eye
As another bullet
Whizzed through his thigh

So I ask you all to pray
That one fantastic day
We're friends all around?
And leave this brutal killing ground
Fighting for my country
I do not fear
Never seeing my family again
I will shed a tear

War is horrible
Someone who is merely eleven
Could on very short notice
Be sent (hopefully) to heaven

Sean Baker, Grade 5
Soule Road School, MA

Gone

Stepping up to the plate
can't take the
pressure
the crowd was
silent
pitcher slipped the ball
whoosssshhhhhh!
Crack!
wave hand
soaring around the bases
other team put their head
to shame
best
moment
in
life

Daniel Lehrman, Grade 5
Coleytown Elementary School, CT

Please Don't Fight

I can make a difference by not fighting…
I wonder why we fight
A dream no one can withstand —
Your anger takes over your senses and fighting wins the war.
I don't like to fight — at least not anymore
I wonder why we fight
Silly things can do much harm.
Territory, pride, toys, and jealousy
And all this junk in my eye
Is something I cannot deny.
I no longer wonder why we fight.
We fight because God made it that way
And that's the way we live
It's hard not to fight
When your favorite toy is broken
Or maybe someone made fun of you
And made you feel real bad
You just got to hold your head on and hold it very, tight
And remember to do your personal best and please don't fight.

Jake Rudolph, Grade 5
Booth Hill School, CT

Reality

Oh it seems so silly how the taxes get so high
The anger builds that you might just cry.
How the gas starts to get high
you're going to wish cars can fly.
Oh, how we can't change the past but we can change the future.

Johnnae Vernon, Grade 5
Washington Elementary School, MA

Bravery

I am brave.
I have an eye of a tiger,
Fighting a bear I am courageous and strong.
He grabbed me by my neck and threw me to the ground.
I shivered and shut my eyes.
I woke up in the wet, cold grass.
I glanced deeply into the sky, feeling as if I could fly.
I looked at the bear and thought of what he had done to me.
We must get even.
But how?
I could barely stand or walk.
The bear has won.
I tightened all of my muscles,
Another chance has come!
I stood silently, holding my breath.
I took a chance and swung at him.
All my power was in my hands.
But, he fell backwards, dragging me down.
Now I am lifeless, a spirit trapped between life and death.
And in my heart, I know there is still a place where I am alive.
I am brave.

Sammi Tompkins, Grade 5
Weston Intermediate School, CT

Feelings

I felt really weird when I was scared,
Like no one is there to protect me.
I felt like there was no God,
No one to be there by my side.
When I dared to look out into the night,
I wondered why I had that fright.
There must be a God.
To create the moon, stars, trees,
The grass, river, and sun,
Day and night,
Dark and bright.
Who could do
Such a wonder?
The world is like a field of splendor,
The deep blue seas,
The creatures of day and night,
If only we all would be praying saying "Thanks"

Elizabeth Groot, Grade 6
Whitinsville Christian School, MA

Fear

Fear has a red colour.
It sounds like the lion roaring.
It tastes like salt.
It smells like a dead rat.
It looks like a dragon with fire out of its mouth.
It makes you feel scared.

Akua Sarpong, Grade 6
Albert D Griswold Middle School, CT

I Am…

I am a curious girl who always imagines weird things

I wonder what other people usually think
I hear thundering waterfalls and whispering winds
I see wondrous creatures gathered around their king
I want myself to draw it out someday and let everyone see

I am a curious girl who always imagines weird things

I pretend to be the only one that got everything but lost it all
I feel lonely but I will stand tall
I touch the magical land which I've been born
I worry the day it'll be torn
I cry because I feel like it

I am a curious girl who always imagines weird things

I understand life can be easy or difficult
I know things are changing around the world
I dream space is just an imaginary place
I try to change the destination of my fate
I hope someday I will be successful
I am a curious girl who always imagines weird things

Ziyin Mo, Grade 6
Swampscott Middle School, MA

The Freezing Lake

There once was a fat cat named Jake
He went to go take a dip in the lake
He thought he was bold
It was freezing cold
He started to shiver and shake

Heidi Stevenson, Grade 6
Captain Nathan Hale Middle School, CT

Dolphins

Lives in bluish green water
A large ocean that stretches for miles
Or a pool that is very deep.

Tail fins help them swim
Pointy noses, glide through the water
A fin on the top of their body.

Surroundings is water,
And fish, but sometimes people.

Swim through the water using its tail fin,
Up and down, swimming.

High pitch squeaking sound.
Interacts with other living things,
By squeaking.

Nicole Romano, Grade 6
Albert D Griswold Middle School, CT

Snowflake

Snowflake
very icy
falling and blowing down
twirling and whirling so pretty
So nice!!

Amanda Maguire, Grade 4
Brookside Elementary School, MA

School

School
fun, teaching
learn, read, play
I love my school!
Trinity

Sierra Chen, Grade 4
Trinity Christian School, VA

Floor Hockey

In floor hockey you go for the Puck.
Just be careful you don't get stuck.
I ran so fast on the floor,
I practically broke the door,
If you don't run fast,
You will probably be last

Andrew Demers, Grade 4
Brookside Elementary School, MA

Nick the Mighty

He is the sun,
I am the moon,
We bond tighter than anyone else in the universe,
Sometimes we need to separate,
His voice is a lion
Mine, is a deer in headlights
Our mother is the one and only Mother Earth
Our dad is Mars, our brother is Saturn,
Nick and I, can be inseparable
Whispering secrets, that nobody else knows
Sometimes I wonder, what I would be if he wasn't born
I would wish I had a twin
And I would draw him every single day and I would draw him exactly like him,
With so many features
Loving to sing
Loving to act,
And most of all
Loving to play video games,
Born together, living together, dying together
I'm proud to have Nick Hansell
As my twin brother

Kat Hansell, Grade 5
John Ward Elementary School, MA

Blue

Blue looks like the beautiful sky on a warm summer's day.
Blue sounds like the ocean waves crashing against a strong hard rock.
Blue tastes like a blueberry you've just popped in your mouth.
Blue feels like a soft warm blanket your mom put on you while you watch a movie.
Blue smells like a sweet smelling rose that my dad had given me on Valentine's Day.

Cassandra Melo, Grade 4
Helen H Hansen Elementary School, MA

Books

A book is opened, and a world is exposed, its people jumping up and down,
Some are happy living in a city, others in a town.
The page is turned, and the scene is set, in the trees or on a mountain,
Maybe near a bench, or in a park, by a fountain.
A book is more than a document with ink,
It is something to explore, ponder and think.

Willow Hubsher, Grade 6
Scotts Ridge Middle School, CT

My Secret Life

My life is
    with nobody.
        I grow roses!
            And a lot of them.
                The touch of my
                    Fingers make them grow.
                        The light of my hair
                            and smile makes the whole wide world grow.
                                Now the wall is blocking my way to
                                    Let every thing grow!

Keri Traeger, Grade 5
Francis Asbury Elementary School, VA

Watching a Beach

When I go to the beach,
I love to watch
as the sunlight pours
down from the sky
onto the golden sand.
The glittering glass ocean
rests beneath cotton clouds,
with soft winds
making pleasant waves
while washing away
pearl shells.

Tovya Goodwin, Grade 4
South Area Solomon Schechter Day School, MA

Bats

I saw a bat
that sat on a mat
It saw a cat
that chased a rat

Jacob Normand, Grade 4
Courthouse Road Elementary School, VA

Beach!

This Beach:
The constant crashing surf
Waves against the jagged rocks
Seagulls soaring gracefully through the air
Silent movement of the sand
Moving back and forth in the tide
The golden sun sets in the ocean
The smell of salt mist sails
Through the air

Victoria Scata, Grade 5
West Woods Upper Elementary School, CT

Winter

Warm coat, three blankets
hot chocolate and cookies
snowballs and sledding

Yesenia Manche, Grade 5
Charlotte A Dunning Elementary School, MA

My Monsters

In my room, under my bed,
Lived some monsters — black, white, and red.

Then one night when I was asleep,
Out came Dracula and tickled my feet.

He had to leave from under my bed.
When he left, he bumped his head.

Now every monster knows,
Not to go and tickle my toes!

Morgan Jones, Grade 5
St Clement Mary Hofbauer School, MD

Yellow

The leaves are as yellow as the sun.
The sun is as yellow as a star, flashing in the dark.
Yellow is the color of a bee.
It is the color of a bird.
It is the color of a lion.
Yellow is a color of the beautiful yellow flowers;
Like glittering yellow daisies.

John Lagoutaris, Grade 4
Potter Road Elementary School, MA

I Sing Because I'm Happy

Singing for my church on Sunday
Singing for my school on Tuesday
Singing for the world every day
I sing because I'm happy
I sing because I'm free.

Some say I'm a fool
But my voice is a precious jewel
My plan is to cherish it deep in my heart
I'll sing on Sunday, on Tuesday, and every day
For I love to sing.

Jasmyne Dias, Grade 4
Freetown Elementary School, MA

Courage

A force of boldness
An emotion that feels as high as the Eiffel Tower,
When your mind is telling you, "You can do it!"
A suit of armor over the weakest emotions
It is help when you are afraid
Something that builds up inside
A search of refuge to keep you calm
When you look to the sky and have faith
Guidance to bear hardship, danger, opposition
Facing anything that comes against it
Courage is confidence and fearlessness
COURAGE

Megan R. Morabito, Grade 5
Booth Hill School, CT

My Life Is Like a Shape

My life is like a shape.
It has a starting point and an ending point.
It has ups and downs.
Its unique texture describes my personality.
It has twists and turns, where I don't know where to go.
It has different streets.
Where do I turn?
Did I make the right turn?
Do I need to turn around?
You may call this shape "Life."
But I call this shape "Me."

Jessica Martin, Grade 6
St Joseph School-Fullerton, MD

I See You

I am sitting here
I wonder why you stare at me
I hear your popcorn popping
I see you spill your drink
I want electricity
I am lazy
I pretend I'm expensive
I feel you push my buttons
I touch the floor
I worry you will leave
I cry when we watch soap operas
I am tired
I understand you are too
I say good night
I dream about tomorrow
I try to sleep
I hope you come back
I am your television

Harrison Brush, Grade 6
Page Middle School, VA

Morning to Night

morning
sun rising
getting hotter, getting light
Sun, highest, hottest, point
cooling off, quiet
dark, setting
night

Andrew Powers, Grade 5
Trinity Christian School, VA

Blank

Sitting here
Thinking
Still sitting here
Bored the page is still blank
Still bored
Unhappy
Quiet
Tired
Still sitting here
And the page is still blank

Landy Cary, Grade 5
St Christopher's School, VA

Math

Math
Fun easy
Multiply, divide, subtract
Math is my favorite
Decimals, fractions, percent
Data graph
Math

Lorena Tavares, Grade 5
J F Kennedy Middle School, MA

Rainy Nights

Rain was bubbling from the sky!
My clothes were all wet,
But my socks were dry.
Clouds roaring with loud thunder!
It was coming down in spirals,
I just had to wonder.
It was coming close to midnight!
But puddles were still glittering,
And the raindrops were bright.
Then it started to kinda sizzle!
The water was actually…
Coming to a drizzle.
And all else was calm that night!
I was in bed,
And had no more fright.

Jordan Howes, Grade 6
West Frederick Middle School, MD

The Skate Park

Kids all ages riding 'round
grinding up and grinding down
on the stairs and on the rails
falling down with weeps and wails

Skating on the quarter pipe
doing tricks out of sight
ollies, nollies, kick flips too
doing tricks just for you

Harleigh Kaczegowicz, Grade 5
Jane Ryan School, CT

I Made a Mistake

I came to school to do a paper,
I made a mistake…and I came in later.

I went to the playground to play a game,
I made a mistake…and I felt lame.

I went to the bus to get a ride,
I made a mistake…and then I lied.

I went to the cafeteria to eat my lunch,
I made a mistake…and I ate a bunch.

Kellcie Ferreira, Grade 4
Freetown Elementary School, MA

Golfing

G reens that you putt on
O vershoot your ball
L oft the ball
F ind your ball
I n the hole
N arrow fairways
G one when you hit the ball

Devin Fitze, Grade 4
Appomattox Elementary School, VA

Reading

He sits in a chair
Unaware
Of anything around him
Eager to turn the page
To find out what happens next
The book is a porthole
A mind slideshow
Transfixed in the story
He can hear the birds chirping
Or
The fierce battle raging
Making a rainbow with his hands
Turning every page
Like a sponge
Absorbing every word
And
Every detail
Turning the pages of every book
Till the end of time

Kyle Mendelsohn, Grade 5
John Ward Elementary School, MA

I Am the Campfire

I am a flame
I wonder if I will destroy everything
I hear the crackling of wood
I see a small dome and people
I want to be with them, watching myself
I am a burning desire
I pretend to be human, watching a fire
I feel no cold
I touch my brothers and sisters
I worry that I might die
I cry "Tend to me for all eternity"
I am a flame
I understand that I won't live forever
I say "Why?"
I dream to see my future
I try to stay alive
I hope I may see the morn'
I am a dying flame

Hayes Slusher, Grade 6
Page Middle School, VA

Gold Ball

Oh, hanging there,
On that tiny limb,
Of dazzling green hair,
Hanging next to tin.

Oh, gold ball of wonder,
I'm glad you come to stay,
You are what I ponder about
Each and every day.

Christopher Rodts, Grade 6
Village School, MA

Summer

S unny skies
U nbelievably warm weather
M arvelous beaches and vacation spots
M uch time to hang with friends
E nd of school year
R eady for the best summer yet, the summer of 2008

Lindsay Berg, Grade 6
St Joseph School-Fullerton, MD

Down

I can't hold my breath any longer,
So I just let the waves carry me down.
I thought of the smiley faces
That were directed at me today,
And the ones that would reverse tomorrow
Everyone's face is down,
Except for mine.
Because I know where I am,
And where some people would be later in life
My heart full of love,
My eyes full of tears,
I know it was my time
To take a different path,
To keep looking forward never looking back.

Rachel Graziano, Grade 5
Soule Road School, MA

Cats

I love cats!
What kind do you like?
I like many, many cats,
Like fuzzy cats, and cuddly cats.
But those are only two.
Running, purring, licking cats,
And there's still more to go.
Pouncing cats, playing cats, and funny cats, too.
I love cats!
What kind do you like?
Loving cats, crazy cats, hissing cats,
Prancing cats, dancing cats, or grooming cats?
I really wish I had a cat,
One I could call my own.
The one I love the very best
Will always be a kitty cat.

Rachael Perdue, Grade 4
Riderwood Elementary School, MD

America

Looks like men and women serving our country
Smells like dust and dirt
Feels like a cool day
Tastes like sweet cherries
Sounds like people cheering

Aislinn McKoin, Grade 4
C Hunter Ritchie Elementary School, VA

What Is Happiness?

They really just wanted to go home.
They all hear the crashing waves.
Wondering if there is anyone else with them.
Their skin blends with the darkness.

A bright person's face grabs one, two, three.
As the sun shines their pupils get smaller
and they close their eyes tightly.
Thrown to the hard ground.
Torn away from their families, crying…in pain
Brought up to a tall wooden stool,
getting splinters on feet as dark as night.

A slave boy sprints through the night.
From his owner.
Back to his cabin.
"Mama what is happiness?"

Damian Wong, Grade 5
Charlotte A Dunning Elementary School, MA

Peace

Peace is like a quiet place in the house.
Peace looks like a happy face on somebody

It sounds like waves against the hard rocks
It can be like a colorful rainbow but,

Peace is always in my heart

Shaquille Epps, Grade 4
St Augustine Cathedral School, CT

The Perfect Tree

I open the car door
And place my boot on the wet asphalt
That was once covered in white flaky snow.
We walk towards the giant Home Depot
Looking at all the people
That are filled with Christmas spirit.
I see thousands of trees lined up
Next to a giant wall.

I see couples and families,
Workers and shoppers.
We pick 12 trees and
Then there it is, staring down
From the end of the end of the aisle staring at me.
The tree that really is
The perfect tree.

We pay,
Put the tree in the back of my car,
And drive off saying,
"This tree is truly
The perfect tree."

Nunzio Morretti, Grade 6
Swampscott Middle School, MA

Monkey's Day

Swinging in the trees
A banana fills their mouths
They smile with joy

Picking bugs off backs
Ladybugs, ticks, and spiders
It's like their popcorn

Predators chase them
They try hard to get away
Some don't make it back

Sleeping in leaf nests
They worry about the law,
"Eat or get eaten."

Meagan Schwarz, Grade 5
Jane Ryan School, CT

Touchdown!

The center hikes the ball
And the quarterback catches it
He fakes a handoff
And tosses it
The runningback catches it
On the run
Uses misdirection
Spins
Slips out of a tackle
Breaks into the secondary
Turns on the jets
Loses another tackle
Jumps over a diving tackler
Alone
Jumps into a 360
Falls into the end zone
Touchdown!

Wills Green, Grade 6
Grace Episcopal Day School, MD

Detention

One kid spits a spit ball,
Another jumps up and down,
A third is standing on his desk,
The teacher starts to frown.

A fourth kid talks out of turn,
A fifth is just plain bad,
A sixth colors in his textbook,
The teacher's really mad!

A seventh kid sings out loud,
The kids now lack attention,
The teacher is about to blow,
"All seven of you DETENTION!"

Tyler Cook, Grade 6
E W Thurston Middle School, MA

My Friend Forever

I stare in admiration as her tired body is
sprawled across her blue and red plaid bed.
I gaze at her pink belly inflate
and deflate as she snores quietly.
Her tail, white and bushy, wags
happily as she dreams of the impossible.
This is my dog, Downey.

When up and alert, I see her doggy
smile and her wagging tail.
I see her soft brown eyes, her black, moist
nose and white floppy ears. I gape upon
Downey as she tears apart her dearly loved
red squeaky toy. I watch her plump fat body
trudge into the white powder-like snow,
where she comes invisible like a hidden
super power.

When I am alone Downey is there to comfort me
with the silly things that make me giggle. She is the peanut butter to
my jelly and she is the one I can't imagine living without.

Haeree Park, Grade 6
Swampscott Middle School, MA

Harry Potter

There has been a secret for a very long time,
About to be revealed in this very rhyme
About a boy who was a wizard, a Parseltongue,
Talking to snakes and lizards.
His name is Harry Potter, and his friend Ron Weasley.
They're magical and fun, and I've just begun
About Potter, Granger, and Weasley! Hermione,
Very smart, and fun just well, Harry is very famous and here's why, I'll tell…
A dark lord named Voldemort, killed everyone around.
He even tried to kill Harry, not making a sound.
It didn't work. He didn't die. This is not a lie.
Now Ron and Harry and Hermione are working at Hogwarts,
A school of Witchcraft and Wizardry, with lots of magic, dangers and sports.
Between Harry and Voldemort, the battle's just begun,
With Harry and all of Hogwarts, they'll act as one.
Through the Goblet of Fire, the Half-Blood Prince, and the Deathly Hallows as well,
One of them had to kill the other, and one of them fell.
Now Harry has a good life, with Ron and Hermione, too.
They all had a family as their friendship and love grew.

Matthew McDonald, Grade 5
St Joseph School-Fullerton, MD

Santa for Snow

Snow is a blanket on a soft bed
Snow is so soft, you could use it as a feather bed
Snow comes down on the ground like Plop!
When down, snow is calling me to play
Snow is like a frozen smoothie made from the sweetness of nature
But is waiting for the smiling Santa to sled through

Camerin Carroll, Grade 6
School of International Studies at Meadowbrook, VA

Look at Me and What Do You See?

Look at me and what do you see?
A smile as warm as a hug
Eyes as pure as gold
My presence as firm as a rock

I am a sun
Bright, helpful, shiny
I shine so everyone can see what's inside of me
And I rest at the end of the day

I am a Teddy bear
Fuzzy, cuddly, cheerful
Like a mom's heart, so warm and pure
And I give everyone a friend to laugh with.

Sade Samuels, Grade 5
West Woods Upper Elementary School, CT

If You Look Closely

If you look closely you will find
A land that is beyond the mind
All you need to get there is a book you see
So climb aboard and start to read
Books can take you to hundreds of places
All you need is your imagination.
One day I'm in Whoville
The next I'm on Mars
A few months from now I'm on Sassacasar
If you look closely you will find
A land that is beyond the mind

Michaela Daisy Arguin, Grade 4
Freetown Elementary School, MA

The Ocean

The dark waves came crashing down on me,
I got swallowed by the ocean sea
Then I truly saw the ocean around me
I saw fish, seaweed and hollow caves,
But then I had to take a breath
I was really sorry to go
Then again I went to the ocean depth
This time I saw a flounder move to and fro
Then my dad called, "Time to go"
I was sad to leave but I know
I can come back tomorrow.

Eric Tessicini, Grade 5
Soule Road School, MA

Blue

Blue is a quiet calm sky
Blue is a shiny swift ocean
Blue is a gentle happy blue bird
Blue is a big fat whale
Blue is calm still water
Blue is sharp cold ice

Kyle Kelly, Grade 4
C Hunter Ritchie Elementary School, VA

Fireflies

I step outside
a large bright glow surrounds me
The glow is huge
brighter than any flashlight
only one thing could be this bright
Fireflies

A million little bugs flying about
lighting up the dark night sky
glowing like a town nestled at my feet

the fire flies shine bright,
so bright it's almost blinding
And yet, I can't take my eyes away

I watch staring in amazement at the fireflies' acrobatics until,
The sun peaks over the grass covered hills
and the glow vanishes
replaced by the brightness of a new day
The fireflies leave me with a tiny invincible gift

An unforgettable memory

Meagan Peoples, Grade 5
Miscoe Hill Elementary School, MA

Majestic Horse

Swiftly running
through a field,
hooves thumping
loudly.
His long,
silky locks
flow in the wind.
Powerful muscles
ripple down his legs,
eyes
as bright
as the shining sun.
Majestic Horse.

Matthew Channing, Grade 5
Charlotte A Dunning Elementary School, MA

What Is Christmas

Christmas is twinkling stars over Bethlehem,
Jesus is born, angels worship Him!
Christmas is lots of singing,
And Christmas lights are beaming!
Christmas is the sound of bells,
People saying, "I wish you well!"
It tastes so yummy,
Sweet cookies in your tummy!
Christmas is lots of fun,
Enjoyment for everyone!

Lyric Updike, Grade 4
Home School, VA

Change the World

Changing the world
Is a simple thing
All you need
Is love and peace
And a little luck, too

I can change the world of everything
That is evil and that is wrong
And I think
That maybe, you should come along

I can do it, there is nothing to it
But a little bit of smarts
And you must help
Me on my journey from afar

Meaghan Wylie, Grade 6
Weston Middle School, CT

Water

Quickly caressing my body
Calming, quieting
Like a poem
Or the pages of a book
Soft, predictable
Wet

Halley Townsend, Grade 6
Cape Henry Collegiate School, VA

Banana Split

This boy was a bottomless pit
So he made a banana split
This was not fine with Mom
She yelled, "No Tom!"
Then he had a tremendous fit

Nick Garcia-Pennewill, Grade 6
Captain Nathan Hale Middle School, CT

Reading

As I stare to colorful words
I'm dreaming like the character
suspense is filling me
I no longer can see
then as fast as it started
I calm down to find nothing is harmed.
But I do find something new
my still flowing breath.

Jessica Vannelli, Grade 5
C C Burr Elementary School, MA

Snowflakes

Snowflakes —
Graceful and free,
Falling like a bunch of frozen teardrops,
Come watch the snow with me.

Angela Zhang, Grade 4
Mount Hope Christian School, MA

My Goats

Very wacky
Eating everything in sight
Pounding against fences
"Maahing" every second
Drinking Pepsi
Runs away from me
Hooves clacking on the ground
Horns rubbing against trees
Butting heads with each other
Awesome pets

Jessie Whitmer, Grade 5
Mary Walter Elementary School, VA

Fox

Fox
bright orange
wandering past me
such shining brown eyes
amazing

Bethany Stoddard, Grade 4
Southbrook Academy, MA

Mystic Fall

Water falling pounding hard
To see a better place above
To find the treasure behind the fog
Looking up there you see a golden fish
Swimming happily
Mossy rocks fast asleep
Dreaming a dream of
Chicken soup stream
Water falling pounding hard
Wishing to see that better place above

Caitlin Riley, Grade 4
St Mary's Primary School, MA

Out of the Dust

Out of the dust,
Into the wind,
Out of the wind,
Into the day,
Out of the day,
Into the night,
Out of the night,
And this pattern will repeat for life.

Wayne Parlette, Grade 6
Friendship School, MD

My Friend's Kitten

my friend got a kitten
And on the kitten's forehead is an m.
But my friend didn't name it with an m
she named it Daisy
and she likes to play the piano a lot.

Miranda Pinet, Grade 4
Marsh Grammar School, MA

Candy

Candy is sweet
Such a great treat
Not nutritious
But so delicious
Gumball, pixie stix
And lollipop licks
Snickers, Charleston Chew
Hershey's; just a few
My teeth will rot
That's all I've got!

Michelle Iken, Grade 5
J F Kennedy Middle School, MA

The Exit Sign

It's the thing that's glowing red,
Hanging right above my head.
Running towards it
We're almost out,
Thinking of the ways to play,
Before the day has gone away.

Eric Mellusi, Grade 6
Fuller Middle School, MA

A Silly Old Lady

There once was an old lady from Nox
Who wanted to learn how to box
She gave a shout
Then knocked herself out
That sill old lady from Nox!

Madeleine Purcell, Grade 4
Weston Intermediate School, CT

Rain

Today is a rainy day,
I love these days,
You stay in and watch TV,
Maybe even do a craft.
Drip, Drop,
Rain drops from my window pain.
Suddenly rain drops faster, and faster
By the minute.
It stopped,
My family and I go outside and jump
in a big, big puddle full of rain,
from the sky
After that when we come in,
we are dripping rain from
Our head to our toes,
Dripping cold rain on my warm house,
Kitchen floor,
Inside the house we warm up
And watch the rain drop one at a time
Falling from the sky.

Victoria Teixeira, Grade 4
Hawley Elementary School, CT

Water and Silence

Falling, Dripping, Splashing, Bursting
Liquid dancers leaping down,
Gently landing with a plopping sound.
Dropping from a great height and distance…
Silence
Tipping, Leaning, Sliding, Skidding
Beautifully bursting on the rocks they're landing.
Dropping from a great height and distance…
Silence
Twirling, Tossing, Tumbling around
Soaking through the soil
And swimming deep into the ground.
Dropping from a great height and distance…
Silence
Oh, how the water drips, the silence hangs.
The water sings, while the silence rings.
Water falls, bursts, and splashes every day…
Silence
Lingers in an endless amount of ways.

Anna Seo, Grade 6
Wakefield Forest Elementary School, VA

Look at Me!

My hair
dark butterscotch and caramel swirl
shiny, smooth
Cascades down my back
like a glossy waterfall in the jungle
My eyes
shimmering like the sea
with jet black midnight in the middle
Light pools shine,
sparkle and glimmer
Creamy skin
as soft as peaches surrounds me
My lips,
red as cherries
shine and gleam
My face sprinkled with tiny grains of sand

Look at me!!!!!

Jessie Powers, Grade 5
John Ward Elementary School, MA

All Around

Bats are flying down
Cats begin to frown

Cows are sleeping here
Dogs are barking there

Pets are in the yards
Monkeys are reading cards

Andrew Bergeron, Grade 5
Linscott-Rumford Elementary School, MA

Gone*

Tears drench my face as I scream
It's not true…my skin crawls with anger
My legs get weak and I collapse I feel as if he doesn't care
He doesn't care that he left us
I feel the result of 1000 stab wounds
Each one deeper than the last
My heart pounding
My lungs inflating and deflating to the fullest
I try to stifle my tears
But it doesn't help much
Later I sleep
And dream of him
His smile, his scent, his laugh, his love
I wake up
And think it's all a dream
Only to find the reality all
Time passes and I move on
Always thinking of him
And smile because he never
Left like I once thought he did

MyKayla Delgado, Grade 6
Whitinsville Christian School, MA
*In loving memory of Frank J. Deiana, gone but never forgotten.

V.I.C.D. (Very Important Cellular Device)

I am a cell phone
I wonder if my keys will fall out from texting
I hear the tapping of the keys
I see the fingers
I want to be charged
I am a L.G. Chocolate
I pretend to be useful
I feel the fingers on my keys
I touch the charger
I worry about my battery dying
I cry ring, ring, ring
I am a ice blue L.G Chocolate
I understand I.M. language
I say "1 new message"
I dream of saying "50 new messages"
I try to be responsive
I hope I will last forever
I am a cell phone

Kelsey Bridges, Grade 6
Page Middle School, VA

Imagination

Imagination is a creation anyone can make
if you have it, you'll know it's a piece of cake
if you haven't, you should try it
and no one can ever deny it,
so if you're feeling low
just create your own imagination.

Micha Duque, Grade 4
Salem Elementary School, VA

A Pro Athlete Has Been Killed!
I was watching a football game.
My family thought it was cool.
My friends think football is lame.
I think they are a bunch of fools.

The football player had no phone.
At home he was killed by a stranger.
He knew he was alone.
He knew he was in danger.

My friends and I went to the funeral.
He was a talented guy.
His name is Michael Cameral.
Now he is living in the sky.
Thavady Pech, Grade 6
Gerard A Guilmette School, MA

My Little Blue Car
I am driving
    in my little blue car.
I am losing gas
    in my little blue car.
I am going to the gas station
    in my little blue car.
I am filling the gas
    for my little blue car.
I am leaving the gas station
    in my little blue car.
I am going too fast
    in my little blue car.
I am starting to lose control
    in my little blue car.
I have crashed
    in my little blue car.
I have learned a lesson
    with my little blue car.
Jason Daniel, Grade 4
Mount Hope Christian School, MA

Wasted Words
I feel like everyone talks too much,
Words just go on and on,
They just say what's on their mind,
And soon all their thoughts are gone.

If you choose your words carefully,
And think about what you say,
Words mean more to you,
Every single day!

So don't take words for granted,
They are very special you know,
Think about your words carefully,
Before out your mouth they go!
Bridget Curley, Grade 4
Mitchell Elementary School, MA

Things Never Seen
The sun resting on the horizon between water and land,
A mango colored sun glowing against the colorful sky,
With royal purples, vibrant pinks, and vivid oranges.
Yet only the dune grass, blowing silently in the wind saw it.
The first snow, drifting ever so softly onto the ground,
These cloud-white flurries spread a new woven blanket on mother earth,
Making the sleeping land pure white and colorless.
Yet only the abandoned red barn in the meadow saw it.
The strong wind blowing against the old oak trees on a cool fall day,
Their branches swaying, their leaves jingling, making them dance in the wind.
Yet only the silent mother bluebird huddled in her nest saw it.
Caroline Henebry, Grade 6
Chase Collegiate School, CT

Who Shall Avenge Osiris?
Who shall come to avenge Osiris? This little god Horus
Son of the gods Osiris and Isis, He shall come to avenge Osiris

Then Horus got bitten by a scorpion he died all of a sudden
Ra took pity and saved him, He shall come to avenge Osiris

Horus is known as the great hawk and also the sun beetle and avenger
Thoth raised this young god, He shall come to avenge Osiris

Horus should own the throne but Set won't give up
Isis tricks him into making his fall, He shall come to avenge Osiris

Set gets angry and summons his army Horus comes and ends them all
While Set slithers away, He shall come to avenge Osiris

Horus challenged Set to a duel, Set posed for attack as a red hippo
Horus shot his harpoon through him, He shall come to avenge Osiris

Who shall come to avenge Osiris? This little god Horus
Son of the gods Osiris and Isis, He shall come to avenge Osiris
Anamika Huq, Grade 6
Middlebrook School, CT

The Steps to an Amazing Poem
P ick a topic for the poem!
O ff we go to get a paper and a pencil!
E at some Smartfood to charge-up the wonderful poetry side of your brain!
T ry your hardest on it!
R ace to the end…No way, take your time!
Y et another fantastic idea!

C elebrate we're having a poetry contest
O h my, that is a great poem!
N eat work!
T ell your friends you can play with them soon. You are so close to finishing.
E at some junk food now. You've almost finished!
S tart smiling…you finished!
T ell your friends you can play with then now, you finished, congratulations!
   You're so cool!
Michaela Peck, Grade 4
Helen H Hansen Elementary School, MA

Fall

The crunchy, crispy leaves dancing around my feet
Hearing little kids shout, "Trick-or-treat!"
Eating pumpkin pie and cherishing every bite
It's like going to heaven in a quick flight
Watching each light, limp leaf turn auburn and gold
Seeing each bird fly south before the cold
Feeling the brisk breeze brush against my face
Warming up my hands against the blazing fireplace
Hearing each acorn thump upon the roof
Is like the clickity-clackity sound of a horse's hoof
Smelling every spice my mom puts in the bread
Knowing I have to wait puts a pain in my head
On Halloween, I spy the restless kids scurrying to each house
Like a clever cat trying to catch a mouse
The worst day is having fall come to a close
Fall is the best, everybody knows

Daniel Michel, Grade 6
Madison Middle School, CT

Nature

The woods are waving
back and forth while the wind is blowing,
and squirrels are crawling from tree to tree, playing tag.
Raccoons and deer are coming out
to find some breakfast to take
back to their families.

Makellah Mann, Grade 6
Monelison Middle School, VA

Soccer

Teammates, soccer balls, friends too.
You don't wear a normal shoe, you wear a cleat.

You can play in the summer, fall too.
You can play in the winter and spring.

But you can't wear a ring, it is
different than most sports you don't play on a court.

Or a snow covered rink we
play on a field soccer is fun.

Kaeli Serafino, Grade 4
Alice B Beal Elementary School, MA

Spring Chicken

Have you seen a spring chicken?
What does it really mean?
Is it really a chicken?
Does it have springs for feet?
And what about its beak?
Is it curly and metal?
Does it come out in spring?
What do you think?
Hey, why does that chicken have springs on its feet!?

Ashley Hart, Grade 5
Charlotte A Dunning Elementary School, MA

Sunset on Wellfleet

Sunset on Wellfleet
Ocean breezes warm faces
Always remembered

John Welcome, Grade 5
Charlotte A Dunning Elementary School, MA

The Leaves Their Colors Call to Me

The leaves on tree their colors call to me
They call and sing to thee
Come swing come swing from me
Come jump come jump from my trunk
Yellow is the color of warmth and happiness
That falls upon you in the breeze
Brings a smile to your face
It turns first the maple trees

Red is the color of passion and pride
The spark of every hill
It's the confidence of every stride
It gives the forest thrill
Green is the color of life and growth
It shoots up high to the ski
It gives you a boost when slowing down
It makes you feel like you can fly

Orange is the color of hope and trust
It's the sign of a wish to come true
It puts joy in every thrust
It's like a bird singing to you
The leaves their colors call to me.

Miela Mayer, Grade 6
Foote School, CT

That Special Someone

When I first saw you
I was speechless
You looked into my eyes
As I looked into yours
I was lost in your dreamy
Brown chocolate eyes
I melted when you held my hands
Your hands were so soft and smooth
It felt like I was holding a baby's hand
When looking into your brown chocolate eyes
And holding your baby soft hands
I melted away to a very special place
The day you came to me
You told me that you were moving to Georgia
My heart dropped
I felt
Empty,
Angry,
And Alone

Shenelle Smith, Grade 6
Swampscott Middle School, MA

Alexis Nong

Alexis
Sensitive, shy, energetic
Sibling of
Asia, T.J.
Lover of
Field hockey, Bengals, Chad Johnson
Who feels
Joy, loved, enthusiastic
Who needs
My own room, field hockey, friends
Who gives
Friendship, trust, loyalty
Who fears
The drop, death, not having a best friend
Who would like to see
Into the future, my dad more often
Every day be the weekend
Nong

Alexis Nong, Grade 6
Immaculate Heart of Mary School, MD

My Life

I wake up
in the mountains
looking at
the golden sky.
I go down
to the clear
blue water
and realize
this is my life.

Cyrus Carper, Grade 5
Francis Asbury Elementary School, VA

Adult and Kid

Kid,
Little, silly,
Playing, running, moving,
Playscape, daycare, work, store,
Shopping, driving, caring,
Tall, serious,
Adult

Taylor Armstrong, Grade 6
Captain Nathan Hale Middle School, CT

Volcano

Lava shoots
Like a train whizzing out of a tunnel
Brings fear into my eyes
As the lava oozes
Out of the mountain
The volcanic rock rolled down
Like a line drive in a baseball game.

Cole Donelan, Grade 5
John Ward Elementary School, MA

History

History oh, history
I feel you are the one
with everything that happened
and all the world has done
with everything we lived through
and even far before
When the world was at its good times
and when the world was at war
and the landmarks they all stand for you
To remind us of our past
It's what the world did years ago
and what it just did last
and history may seem to some
Just an ugly lie
But to me history is the best
From now to the day I die
and landmarks may collapse
and documents may fall apart
But history will still go on
That's the most important part.

GO HISTORY!

Adam Klesser, Grade 6
Ashford School, CT

Long, Lost, Friend

I sit down
Beside my dog's grave.
Remembering the good times
I had with him.
I remember
One year
When he ate the
Pumpkin seeds,
And when he
Joined us
For a parade.
I see him
Greeting me
Home from school.
At that second
The wind blows.
It feels like a
Long,
Lost,
Friend.

Trevor Gaines, Grade 4
Hawley Elementary School, CT

Sara Sips

Sara sips sarsaparilla silently
Sara's sarsaparilla surely soothes her
Satisfying sarsaparilla is to Sara.

Nathalie Rovira, Grade 6
Benjamin Syms Middle School, VA

What a Beautiful Day!

I really want to say,
The clouds are gone and the sun is out,
It's such a beautiful day,
No time to pout.

Destini Johnson, Grade 4
Hebbville Elementary School, MD

Twins

Look, same
Wrestle, play, trick
Fun, I'm a twin
Clones

Jack Grigsby, Grade 4
Trinity Christian School, VA

How

Who does everyone want me to be,
Maybe, could it be, just me?
But how?
That's what I don't understand,
But how?
Oh, I really wish I can.
How?
Can't you see?
I can't be who you want me to be!
I know what you want me to be.
But,
How?
I don't know how to be me!

Karra Lang, Grade 6
Perryville Middle School, MD

An Ordinary Day

After school
On an ordinary day:
Basketball dribbling,
Slippery noodles.
Thumping bass
Of a stereo.
Cars driving by,
Steamy steak.
Smoke on the grill,
Wind in my face.
A ball hitting a bat,
Kids *screaming* and playing.
Opening of a garage,
Scratch of a pencil.
Doing homework,
Mind exploding.
Mailbox closing,
It's just an
Ordinary
Day.

Alex Simon, Grade 5
Clover Street School, CT

Turtle*

Under a shady tree
The turtle lies down,
Gazes at the pond
Stretches, curls,
Gropes at nothing
Clawing the dirt
Abrupt, head up;
Gazes at the sun
Mindlessly resting
And drowsily shifts
Yawns
A while after
Drowsy turtle
Now asleep
In his comfy shell.

Shinhui Cai, Grade 5
West Woods Upper Elementary School, CT
*Inspired by Valerie Worth

Snow

Snow is falling,
Little dots of white,
Covering the ground like a blanket.
Piles up beside the door,
Buries the cars on the driveway,
And covers the road,
Until the snowplow plows straight through.
Kids run out to play happily,
Building snowmen and having snowball fights,
Until the sun comes out,
And sadly the snow melts away,
And we wait for the next snowfall to come.

Ray Zhang, Grade 5
Toquam Magnet School, CT

Family Vacation

Loving a family vacation
Traveling to places near and far
Having special times together
Going by plane or by car
Loving a family vacation

Alison Condon, Grade 5
Charlotte A Dunning Elementary School, MA

My Peace in the World

The world war has come to an end!
Peace has come; something you can defend.

I feel calm mixed with sad.
The peace will make me hopefully glad.

The trees, the birds, my mom, my dad,
This is all peace, and I'm really glad.

Brenda Price, Grade 4
Quashnet School, MA

People

The light,
The dark.
The right,
The wrong.
The dead,
The alive.
What makes us different?
You think we are different because of skin?
In fact, there are different people
That stand up for what they believe in.
I believe in good people.

Andrew Carver, Grade 4
Nottoway Elementary School, VA

Waddle

Waddle, waddle
Penguins go a-walking,
Slip, slide.
The penguins dash down into the water,
Splash, splash, splash!
They waddle from the water with a rock and a roll.
Penguins go gliding on a wintry stroll!

Kiersten Schiller, Grade 4
Cape St Claire Elementary School, MD

The Sky

When early morning arrives
I lift up my head to look out the window.

The everlasting pool of blue is pink and peach
with specks of faded stars.

As the sun rises higher in the sky
it becomes azure.

The birds fluttered across the sky
as though they looked like they were
swimming in the ocean.

The beaming sun looked lost in confusion
as it sat in the blue pool.

As the sun lowered itself
the sky became shades of red, orange, and yellow.

The stars glittered and the moon
hung proudly in the sky.

Chandler Parr, Grade 5
Church of the Redeemer Christian School, MD

Snow

Snow freely falling.
A white blanket on the ground.
Snow is coming down.

Nick Krasovec, Grade 5
Friendship Valley Elementary School, MD

LB's

Ladybugs are cool.
Ladybugs are black and red.
Ladybugs are cute.

Andrew Brandt, Grade 5
St Joseph School-Fullerton, MD

Responsibility

R esponsibility
E xpert at it
S ensible
P atience
O bedience
N ever say no
S ay you can do it
I have responsibility
B eing happy to do it
I will do it right
L ove your job to help out
I n it to help
T o have fun with it but do it right
Y ou will be happy to do it

Jillian Cooper, Grade 4
Mount Hope Christian School, MA

The Culture in My House

In my house,
Cultures,
Sculptures,
From far away.
Masks from Africa,
Dolls from Peru,
Beadwork from Ghana,
And Native American Kachinas.
Pots and baskets,
Mancala game and an Amazon butterfly,
Exotic ceramic birds,
From Africa and Peru.
Patchwork quilts,
From Amish villages,
And cloth,
From Andean looms.
Treasures from others' cultures,
Loved by us, the Americans,
All thanks to those in other places,
Creating beauty for us all.

Clare Specht, Grade 6
Grace Episcopal Day School, MD

Turtle

Turtle
Slow, protective
Crawling, hiding, swimming
The turtle just hatched
Tortoise

Evan Wang, Grade 4
Sacred Heart School, MA

Evil

Evil. It burns red and orange flames, reeking of chaos and violence.
It destroys your most precious thoughts and memories.
It seeps into your mind, and before you know it can overcome you.
The searing pain compliments the deep sorrow, shrieking in the night atmosphere.
It makes a sound of crisp burning flames.
It looks like your worst nightmare.
It smells like burning charcoal and destruction.
It is poison to humanity.

Christopher Rogers, Grade 5
Newton-Lee Elementary School, VA

Poet

Hard at work the poet sat at his comfy desk.
Etching out a marvelous poem writing and writing all day long.
The poet's pencil is no longer sharp but blunt,
his eraser weak and tired from use.
The poet works harder and harder, putting a picture in our minds
like a masterpiece made of words.
Still hard at work he reads to himself every word on every line,
editing his poem to perfection.
And finally he's done.

Hamish Alexander-Drysdale, Grade 6
Wakefield Forest Elementary School, VA

Barkley

My dog's name is Barkley. He is my pet.
Barkley is the greatest dog that anyone can get.

He licks you to death so you can't breathe.
He snuggles beside you when you're fast asleep.

Although he's a big dog, he easily feels fear
When my mom uses the vacuum cleaner and it's buzzing in his ears.

He's afraid of my cat, too. He won't forget
That she's the queen and my other mean pet.

That's my Barkley, the best puppy
That anyone can get and that any dog can be!

Rachael Murphy, Grade 6
Quashnet School, MA

Fall

I walked outside and feel a tap on my back.
I turn around just to find a leaf acting like a hand.
I keep walking, my feet crunching on all the leaves.
Different hues of colors.
The chestnut brown chipmunk living in my backyard seems like he is late for work.
The wind is whistling like the brakes on a rusty old train.
The blue jays are chaotically cackling their songs.
My freshly groomed dog is barking.
It smells so good outside, like my mom's great Thanksgiving ham.
Leaves are dancing like brilliant ballerinas as they fall from their trees.
This is a fabulous fall!

Chris Adiletta, Grade 6
Madison Middle School, CT

Different Kinds of Pencils
She collects different kinds of pencils,
enjoying so many different designs and colors.
Red, orange, yellow, green, blue, purple, and brown.
But they can't beat her favorite,
professional looking black and silver mechanical pencils.

Some grips are smooth and comfortable,
while others are hard and stiff.
So many different types of grips!
Plastic, rubber, squiggle, encircled, and squared.
But they can't beat her favorite,
professional looking soft, black ribbed grips.

Pencils influence her writings.
She doesn't like to write,
but when she holds her favorite pencil,
a strange but powerful energy comes to her.
Resulting in her writing with such enthusiasm.
Jin Sun Kim, Grade 6
Wellesley Middle School, MA

Candy
Candy
Candy
Candy
Hard candy
Big fat candy
Long, thin, stringy candy
Red candy
Blue candy
Big purple jolly candy
Purple chewy gum candy
Juicy candy, too
Tiny candy
Circle candy
Don't forget soft candy
Last of all, best of all, I like sour candy
Tristan Cleveland, Grade 4
C Hunter Ritchie Elementary School, VA

Where the Flowers Are Never Pale
Let's go to that farmhouse,
you know I've heard a tale
that at that farm there was an old meadow
where the flowers were never pale.

Is it true that fruits are for sale?
I don't have any money.
Oh, you don't either, that's just as well.

How 'bout you — I say let's go.
We could learn about that tale
and see if there really, actually was a meadow
where the flowers were never pale.
Mitchell Losito, Grade 5
Hindley Elementary School, CT

Tornado
Midnight so peaceful,
A whisper of wind,
Sighing with pleasure.
The wind picks up,
Clouds wrap around the mountains,
A small spiral of wind begins to dance in the sky.
Twisting faster and faster,
Leaves whirl in circles,
The ground trembles,
Wind is whipping at forgotten spaces.
Tornado.
Once so delicate,
As a gentle breeze,
Now destructive.
Tim McDermott, Grade 6
West Frederick Middle School, MD

Balloon
The balloon I see is shaped like a sphere
It is in the store right over there

The string is long
I pull it right along

Into the sky the balloon will fly
I am starting to sadly cry

It is quickly flying away
Oh I wish it would stay

How fast it will disappear
No one will ever know it was here
Marisa LoCoco, Grade 5
Linscott-Rumford Elementary School, MA

Small World
Just when I got to a party
my mom always sees her friends.
My mom always looks for
her friends at the party.

She sees a person from a long time ago
Then she always tells me
"This is a small world"
Then I say, "What do you mean?"
She tells me,
"Life is too short"
And I say, "What do you mean?"
Then she always tells me
"That you should be nice to other people."
This is a person she's been looking for
Ever since the last time she came
To my uncle's birthday party.
Oluwatosin Akinmoladun, Grade 6
Magnolia Elementary School, MD

Halloween Night

Halloween night, it can be an enormous fright with Jack-o-lanterns lighting the night
The crisp, clean air blows through my hair as I pass all the signs that say "Beware!"
The pumpkin yells "Come here! Come here!" He just might give me a scare
The children jog from house to house scurrying promptly like a mouse
The ghastly goblins make a toast while they have some fun with their friends, the ghosts
As the children swallow some moist, mellow fruit they hear the owl going "Hoot! Hoot!"
The wind goes running all over the place like a person running in an important race
The candy wrapper tickles my hands and the sticky air head gets caught in my hair strands
The smell of the fresh chocolates soothes my nose
And when I finally look up I see a see a group of groundhogs dart into their burrows
Once the night ends, the kids are as sad as a person whose dog died "I don't want it to be over," one kid cried
When the clock strikes 12, Halloween is officially done but everybody knows they had lots of fun

Hayley Wettenstein, Grade 6
Madison Middle School, CT

The Beach

 I step on the golden sand that is crunching along my feet.
I smell the sweet salty air and the rotten seaweed.
I look along the horizon to see the raft already afloat,
As the waves crash in and out.

My cousins and I sprint to the mountainous rocks,
Tiny barnacles fill the tops of rocks, small but sharp.
The protruding rocks are filled with crawling crabs,
As the waves crash in and out.

I arrive to the water with a smile upon my face. I know what is coming next,
A raft ride!
We head across the shimmering water with a boatload of smiling children
I pass the buoy; it sways in the current back and forth not knowing where it is about to travel.
As the waves crash in and out.

I put on a warm comforting towel,
Ready to leave behind a wonderful day.
I look upon the horizon and see nobody in the water,
As the lonely waves crash in and out.

Lyndsay Giroux, Grade 6
E W Thurston Middle School, MA

Summer

Summer's coming.
The hot, dry sun will beat down upon my back, drying up the mud from Spring's rain.
Summer's coming.
Temperatures will soar like a lonesome eagle flying high above the ground, and sweat will trickle down my body.
Summer's coming.
Families will visit their favorite summertime places,
swimming through liquid diamonds and boating through the great blue ocean.
Summer's coming.
Hot and cold air will fight with thunder and lightning, rain endlessly splattering against the windows.
Summer's coming.
School will close. Cool breezes will dance with the trees, dressed in lush green leaves.
The lawn will be a green ocean, its grassy waves rippling through the wind.
I will bid Spring farewell and welcome Summer with outstretched arms.
Summer's coming.

Joseph Stack, Grade 4
Weston Intermediate School, CT

Green Is

Green is big and green is small.
Green is the grass that sways in the wind.
Gentle like the ocean at low tide,
Ebbing away at the beach with each wave and current.
Green is the great, vast forest by day,
Teasing us with its daunting mass.
Green is the seaweed
Found only at the ocean's turquoise depths,
Stuck in like spears at the bottom of the world.

Green's fragrance is the almost
Perfect spring day;
The sun just a little too hot.
Green's scent is heavy,
Humid summer nights
Lying awake,
The chorusing crickets in the distance,
Expressing their unique sonata
Far, far away it seems.
And finally,
Green is the mint
Atop my chocolate cake.

Sam Robiner, Grade 5
General John Nixon Elementary School, MA

The Sleeping Time

I am a comforting bed,
I wonder if I am soft enough,
I hear the child sleeping at night,
I see I am covered with blankets,
I want to stay and never leave this child.
I am a graceful blanket,
I pretend I am alone at night,
I feel like a protective shield to the child,
I touch and cover the child,
I worry if I will ever wear out,
I cry when the child is sad.
I am a fluffy pillow,
I understand I give softness to the child,
I say "sweet dreams" to the child at night,
I dream of the child's dreams,
I try to comfort the child enough,
I hope I stay where I am.
I am the sleeping time.

Taryn Rowan, Grade 6
Page Middle School, VA

Spring

Spring is
Finally here
With colorful flowers
Slowly starting to bloom in many
Rainstorms

Tucker Bobrow, Grade 5
Coleytown Elementary School, CT

Cancer

I wish I was the cure
For those suffering with all kinds of cancer
Saving
Millions of lives
Rebuilding those families
Who have been destroyed
Bald, weak, suffering and frail

Chelsea Guerra, Grade 6
Scotts Ridge Middle School, CT

Place of Fascination

I'm free here like a bird, to roam when I want
Where I want, my serenity place.
To run my fingers through the softness
The tiny, hot grains are like a warm welcome.
It feels like gritty sandpaper upon my feet
The feeling was pure
Like vanilla ice cream
The land is extraordinary.
You can hear the noises of seagulls,
They are yelling in the distance,
They are fascinating.
The crashing of the blue sparkling water
Crashing on each other,
Competing to reach land first.
Creatures roam where I walk.
All shapes and sizes to imagine.
Some with hard shells,
Some with sharp claws.
This place is peaceful.
This place of all colors.
This place of fascination.

Chelsey Tyree, Grade 6
Monelison Middle School, VA

I Have a Dream

I have a dream to play basketball in the NBA.
Because I have always played
So if I play more I will get better and better
All I have to do is keep believing I will succeed.

In my dream if I fail I will try to play in the NFL.
I have played football for three and a half years.
I know how to tackle but I think if I try.
They will probably just tell me to back off.

I have ideas for the future like a flying car
If I think of inventing a car.
Maybe an engineer is my next choice.

Some who like science, stars, and space
Then an astronomer is my taste.
These dreams that I have may come true
But all I need to do is keep on dreaming.

Davaughn Parker, Grade 6
Magnolia Elementary School, MD

Dogs and Puppies

They eat hard dog food
They are very lovable
Love to lick people
Love to chew rubber items
They bark at people walking.

Sara Weisman, Grade 4
Battlefield Elementary School, VA

Mother Sun, Father Moon

Day has Mother Sun
When she comes up
She makes a beautiful sight.
When she sets
She makes everyone smile.

It's time for Father Moon
He shines brightly,
He is the watchman
Of the night sky.

Taylor Scott, Grade 4
Quashnet School, MA

Fleeting Fantasy

Tonight as soon as the sun goes down
And you lie back in bed,
A little spark of wonder
May kindle in your head.
The spark becomes a full fledged dream
Of falling or flying or fun,
And suddenly your dream explodes
And you are overcome.
But as the sun peeks up above
The cloudless morning sky
Your dream crumples and vanishes
And you're left to wonder why.

Marianne Engelke, Grade 6
Bigelow Middle School, MA

Polar Bears

Furry polar bears,
white as snow with big black eyes,
looking for their den.

Meryl Bucciarelli, Grade 4
Long Meadow Elementary School, CT

The Desert

Dunes of sand all around
Like rolling hills on a barren plain
The slight fragrance of cacti flowers
Mingling with the smell of sand
Coming over the horizon
Cacti in abundance
The outlaws of the desert.

Robert Scaramuccia, Grade 5
St Mary's Primary School, MA

Mom

My mom loves me
as you can see
she is so nice
she makes us rice.

She gives me tomatoes
and mashed potatoes,
she gives me a simple life.

She makes great food,
only if she's in a good mood.
She is very tall
five feet of love
because she's the best mom of all.

Richard Santos, Grade 6
Whitinsville Christian School, MA

Spring

Flowers start to bloom
Eggs are just starting to hatch
Spring, it is here now

Brittany Tran, Grade 4
St Joseph School-Fullerton, MD

The Parade

Trumpets are booming!
I'm clapping.
My mom is also clapping.
People are marching happily!
People are cheering merrily!
All this is because it's Veterans Day!
I honor the Veterans.
The band is playing their good music!
My hands are flowing with the rhythm.
I have a United States of America flag
And I'm waving it proudly!

Sammy Ruiz, Grade 4
WB Sweeney School, CT

The Beauty

A rose reaches up
Peeking up from the white snow
Grasping the sunlight

Brenna McFarland, Grade 4
Trinity Christian School, VA

Sports

S o much fun to play
P lay for fun, not to win
O n the court is where I play
R eady for any sport
T oday I will play
S ports are the best!

Tim Lowell, Grade 5
J F Kennedy Middle School, MA

Skittles

S tealthy since she was a shy
K itten.
I ntensely cute and
T iny but still
T roublesome. At
L east she gets to
E at whenever she wants. I love my cat
S kittles!

Bevin Eastman, Grade 6
Monelison Middle School, VA

I Wish

I wish I could capture
The sun
And use it as a
Backup source of light.
I wish I could capture
A cloud
And get water from it.
I wish I could capture
A star
And gaze at it
All day long
I wish I could capture
The moon
And talk to the astronauts.

Will Sherrill, Grade 4
St Christopher's School, VA

Trojan War

In 1250 B.C.
Greeks set to sea

To rescue a maiden
With arms heavily laden

Odysseus went to battle
And plundered town's cattle

Achilles was slain
Paris to blame

Menelaos to rescue his queen
When he got her he would be mean

A horse was made
Inside men were laid

They slaughtered here
They slew near

They left for Greece
Without much peace

Isaac Sutor, Grade 5
Trinity Christian School, VA

Friendship Fights

I have friends that are friends with me day and night,
but sometimes we get into friendship fights
We don't talk to each other at recess or on the phone,
we only do this because we want to be alone
When we say stuff that's mean and annoying and bad,
sometimes we get aggravated and really mad
We give "the look" to each other and a few rolling eyes,
at least girls solve their problems by talking,
it's punching for the guys
There are two sides, one on mine and one on the other,
sometimes when I get home I'm so mad,
I talk about it with my mother
I hate it! I hate it! I hate it so much,
I wish I could zap them back to nice,
I would have a special touch
Then we start getting nice to each other day after day,
this is the best part to me, I have to say
But now all of our problems have their mends,
I'm happy not because of our problems,
but because we are back to being friends.

Chereen Chalak, Grade 5
Miscoe Hill Elementary School, MA

Peace River

The zebras are as quiet and still
As a soft breeze in the yellow mist on a summer day,
The yellow mist stays floating in the air,
On its way to another river, like a cub moving on in the distance
The other zebras drink water like a river flowing peacefully.

Samantha Roche, Grade 4
Freetown Elementary School, MA

My Feelings

I'm
Only happy.
If you think not,
You are so, so wrong.
My motto:
Laughing and having a good time.
Kids have told me
"Why don't you ever stop smiling"
Or
"You've got the biggest smile I've ever seen."

I'm
Only sad.
I'm a sad bear who has lost her cub.
Rarely happy:
When the cub is found.

You see,
I'm
Not happy,
Nor sad.

Devin Peterson, Grade 4
Hawley Elementary School, CT

Our Green World

I
See
Tremendous,
Towering trees
You can smell the pine,
See the dark, green colors,
Deep brown, as brown as a dark
Chocolate brownie or a dark chocolate
Bar, you can hear the birds chirping, tweeting,
It seems like
A top secret
Code we are
Just beginning
To crack, and
Still today we
Are learning a
Lot more from
These lovely
Flying miracles

Tyler Suarez, Grade 5
St Mary's Primary School, MA

Fall

Leaves falling as we speak.
The whistling wind slow and meek.
The wind in my hair, the sun in my face.
Jack-o'-lanterns staring out into space.
The colorful leaves getting caught in my hair.
Kids playing in the very cold air.
I can tell from sitting out here.
I can tell that fall is here.

Alison Johnson, Grade 5
Lincoln Street School, MA

Racing the Waves

I am a ship
I wonder if it is windy today
I hear seagulls calling out
I see dolphins racing after me
I want to go even faster
I am a ship
I pretend I am the fastest ship in the navy
I feel water lapping at my face
I touch the ocean floor
I worry that I will get stuck
I cry because I want to be out in deep water again
I am a ship
I understand that I am on the water
I say I am fast
I dream to be the fastest ship in the water
I try to go even faster
I hope to be in a race one day
I am a ship

John Lingenfelser, Grade 6
Page Middle School, VA

Summer Breeze

I lay aside the palm tree,
Waiting in the breeze.

It was so quiet,
You couldn't hear a sneeze.

Every night I lay there,
For no apparent reason,

Passing all the time,
And the lonely season.

Carlie Ferry, Grade 5
Soule Road School, MA

My Little Brother

My little brother is as sweet as a mouse.
He always smiles at my house.
He loves me more than candy.
I think that he's just dandy!

Blanca Anavisca, Grade 4
Bensley Elementary School, VA

Ocean

Seagulls bother you
Fish roar by you as you swim
Crabs pinch your feet hard

Connor Aldrich, Grade 5
Hebron Elementary School, CT

The Lonely Owl

The Owl,
Has no friends,
Very gloomy in the twilight.
No friends to play with
Besides the pine cones,
On the arms of the tree,
Darker,
Darker,
Darker,
Goes the moonlight,
Owl still in the tree,
No friends,
Wish, on a star,
It may come true,
Night has come,
Owl,
Time to get to work

Max Parent, Grade 5
Francis Asbury Elementary School, VA

Water

Is cold and icy
It is quite easy to drink
Does not have a taste

Sami Ryan, Grade 5
Jane Ryan School, CT

The Beach

The sweltering sizzling sun shines solely in the sky,
And the waves splash on the shoreline nearby.
With the scorching hot sand beneath my feet on the beach,
Walking over the sharp shells sends an alarming alert to my feet.
The splish-splashing of the ocean waves creates a battle to beat.
Sally skims seashells softly by the shoreline
Amid the buzz of the children playing with the popping paddle balls of mine.
Lighthearted Larry laughs and licks luscious lollipops
While lounging on his luxurious chair made of twine.
I anticipate the ring of the ice cream man's bell signaling a treat
Then watching the waves creep up to destroy my delicate sandcastle feat.
The chatter of the clamoring crab's claws
Causes chaos with the kids,
Hiding from the cackling sea gulls while using our umbrella as a lid.
Relaxing in my large lounge chair, I read an exciting book.
My father asks me to take a walk — along with a look.
I see my father's footsteps in the hard crunchy sand,
And this allows me to follow him so I can take a solid stand.
The day ends too soon with a warbling warning whistle blow;
The lifeguards have signaled that everyone must go.

Andrew Franchetti, Grade 6
Trinity School, MD

Peace Is for Everyone

"Peace can be a state of harmony or the absence of hostility."
Peace is when my brother and I play baseball together.
Peace is when two countries solve their differences with words, not wars.
Peace is skiing in the fresh powder at Beaver Creek
Peace is Al Gore fighting to save the Earth from the fate of global warming.
Peace is jazz music playing softly when I fall asleep at night.
Peace is celebrating differences.
Peace is the end of the War in Iraq.
Peace is for everyone.

Ben Cormier, Grade 5
Marblehead Community Charter Public School, MA

Baseball Glove

I am a fold of leather that is able to embrace a baseball.
If I didn't exist, no one would play America's beloved game.
I am oiled, brutally punched, and I may be thrown against the wall
but I am always used during a person's moment of fame.
Smack!

There's a gold award named after me that only the astounding players own.
I defend the palms of every single player.
I am like a giant web, morphed like a cone.
I am able to salvage the ball from the giant wooden slayer.
Smack!

I make a loud, sharp noise that could be heard throughout the planet.
No matter how important I am, everyone eternally took me for granted.
When a ball hits me, I feel like I have been smashed by granite.
Without me, the whole game would be uneven and slanted.
Smack! I am a baseball glove.

Alex Lo, Grade 6
E W Thurston Middle School, MA

Spring Is Near

S unny, warmer days.
P eople are planting plants and seeds.
R ainy days will help them grow.
I ce has melted.
N o more shoveling.
G rass is growing.

I can ride my bike now.
S now is gone.

N o more Winter coats.
E ach month grows warmer.
A nother sunny day.
R un out and play.

Isaac Hartigan, Grade 4
Helen H Hansen Elementary School, MA

I Wonder

Have you ever wondered what's out there?
Are there rabbits made out of hair?
Is there grass in the shape of a bear?
I wonder what's out there.
Are there stories to be told?
To be published and then sold?
I wonder what's out there.
Is there an endless ocean?
With its waves always in motion?
Does it wash away the suntan lotion?
I wonder what's out there.
Could there be a beach?
Maybe right within my reach?
I wonder what's out there.
I wonder what's out there.

Sydney Ziegler, Grade 4
Riderwood Elementary School, MD

Follow Your Dreams

You've got to follow your passion.
You've got to figure out what it is that you love —
Who you really are.
And you have to have the courage to do that.
I believe that the only courage anybody ever needs
Is the courage to follow your dreams.

Grace Perry, Grade 6
Village School, MA

I'll Be Watching

It is a very sunny and warm day at the garden.
I see beautiful flowers of all sorts.
Children playing in their backyards.
Will the deer eat the flowers tonight?
Will the bees come out in the winter?
I'll be watching!

Abigail Heron, Grade 4
Southbrook Academy, MA

Summer Vacation

Vacation will be great fun this year.
We'll soak up the sun,
And when school ends cheer.
Relaxing on the beach
And hanging with friends
Our fun times will never end.
Drinking cool drinks on the poolside,
Even speeding down the waterslide.
I can't wait for vacation this year,
The beautiful skies will be so nice and clear.
Coming back to school will be our only fear!

Samantha Freund, Grade 6
St Joseph School-Fullerton, MD

My Dog

"Licking, laying and lapping"
My dog is my best friend
and he has always been.
My dog is with me in the hard and good.
My dog is always relaxed
and calm making me enlightened.
My dog is a great friend who comforts
in a time of need.
In some ways he is like a person.
My dog is playful and fun
especially in the sun.
My dog is fun but when his
odor fills the air, I cannot bear.
When he finally gets his bath,
the fur on his back is once again touchable and wonderful.
His barks of joy are loud and clear.
As people watch they scream and holler.
My dog is beyond great and wonderful
he is my best friend.

Chelsea Hayward, Grade 6
Litchfield Intermediate School, CT

My Little Hamster

Running round and round on his little wheel
Watch him eat his seedy meal
Twinkling his pink little nose
He's so cute from his ears to his toes
As my eyes sparkle with delight
he falls asleep and I say good night
Oh, little hamster, have sweet dreams
of fruit and veggies and paper streams
As I pet your fur it twitches
Its brown and gold as millions of riches
Your tiny whiskers brush against my skin
It looked like you had one million ten
Oh, little hamster, your so sweet and chubby
I think your new name is Tubby
Wake up Tubby, it is a brand new day
You're my little hamster and you are cute in every way

Kacey Price, Grade 5
McCleary Elementary School, VA

The Wall
Wall
Flat, rocky
Cementing, building, smoothing
Bundle of reddish colors
Brick
Garrett Small, Grade 5
Soule Road School, MA

Black Hole
A flash appears.
Black hole.
Pitch black.
Like the night
Sky.
Floating in space
Sucking everything
Up,
The planets,
Stars,
Air,
Until nothing but time stands.
Rudy Gelb-Bicknell, Grade 5
C C Burr Elementary School, MA

What I Feel!
I feel good,
I feel sad.
Some things in life are happy,
Some are scary.
Sometimes I feel excited.
Sometimes I feel afraid.
But everything is okay.
Nothing is bad.
I feel good,
I feel sad.
Sometimes in school people are nice.
Sometimes people are unfriendly.
Sometimes I feel dandy!
Sometimes I feel down.
But everything is fine, nothing is bad.
I am alive! Everything will be ok.
Raina Burgos, Grade 4
WB Sweeney School, CT

Ready to Surf
Looking out for giant waves
Aqua monsters coming at me
Crushing down upon me
Holding my breath
Tumbling, tumbling
Light as a feather but packed with force
It passes by
Ready for another one
Augie Barringer, Grade 5
St Luke's School, CT

Zombies
Zombies are old
Zombies are wrapped.
They have toilet paper wound
Around them.
Some are tall, but some are short.
Watch out. They will get you!
Trevor Carter, Grade 4
Bensley Elementary School, VA

Flowers
Flowers, flowers everywhere
One over here, one over there
Some pink, some blue
All so beautiful and new
Roses are prickly
Tulip are tickly
Spring is here, time for sun.
Katie Bower, Grade 4
Weston Intermediate School, CT

Every Day
Every day you shall see the bluebirds fly,
See a smile,
Hear a laugh,
Every day you will be you
You shall feel the joy of the day
Be happy, not sad
Every day, be glad
Shenelle Kelly, Grade 4
Clover Street School, CT

Tia
You are the come and go rain cloud
The swing you play with
The snap of the chips.
You are the nicely picked flower
The rays of the sun
A sweet treat.
You are the hotness of summer
The sound in a trumpet
The bounce in a basketball.
You are the presents on Christmas
The love on Valentine's Day
The luck on St. Patrick's Day.
You are a tough tiger
The little bug I chase
The merry go round I play on.
You are the brightness in morning
The sunset in the afternoon
The shadow at night.
You are the sax I play
The "fame" in famous
The twinkle in my eye.
Josie Williams, Grade 5
St Luke's School, CT

Dreams
Dreams
Can't wake up
Pulls me farther
Into
Darkness
Like TV commercials
One after another
Flash!
They are as
Quick as
Lightning
Not
Connected to
Each other
Hold on to dreams
For when you wake up
They slowly start to fade away
Again
Emma Barnes, Grade 4
Braeburn School, CT

Morning Walk
The bitter frost clings to my cheeks,
As I hold onto Honey's leash.
We walk around,
Our pace is brisk,
For warmth,
My hands become two fists.
My dad leans over,
And grabs her from me,
The leash clicks,
And she is free.
She runs through fields,
She's having a blast,
But we catch up,
Though she is fast.
We walk her over,
To the car.
She's put in back,
We drive away,
But we'll be back,
Another day.
Grayson Kennedy, Grade 5
St Luke's School, CT

My Pet Turtle
I have a pet turtle
He is so slow
He can't jump a hurdle
He is so cute
He can fit in my boot
His name is Moe
I am not kidding he is so slow
Haley Fouts, Grade 4
Crestwood Elementary School, VA

Rain

I hear the rushing wind blowing into my wide open mouth.
I taste the dampness of it, and know it's going to rain.
and sure enough,
I feel little tinkles of water,
Clinging onto my hair,
And running down my arms.
I see the drops getting bigger,
And growing into more groups,
And before I know it I realize,
Without *one* tiny *drop* of rain
The rainstorm would be different.
And it's the same with people.
Without one tiny person,
The world we know would be different.

Angelee Parmar, Grade 4
King's Highway Elementary School, CT

Soccer

Soccer! Sounds like the ocean roaring
Tastes like a river quenching my thirst
Feels like perspiration on my skin
Smells like freshly cut grass
Looks like a sea of players chasing after a ball.

Pablo Francisco Rubio, Grade 5
Church of the Redeemer Christian School, MD

Fall Is Here

F all is here
A ll the kids make piles of
L eaves and jump in the
L eaves

I hope their mothers don't
S ay what a mess of leaves, clean every leaf up.

H igh up in the sky
E very tree is
R eady to let
E very leaf fall off of its branches!

Sonia Gonzalez, Grade 5
Woodlawn Elementary School, VA

Jack

It must be hard
to be a dog.
Always trying
to get attention.
Always begging
for food.
Looking
for bones.
That would make
me tired.
To be a dog.

Kayla Clarke, Grade 5
Charlotte A Dunning Elementary School, MA

Alone

I'm walking through the trees in the woods.
I have on a large coat,
and the bark is frozen.
I found a pond of very thick ice.
I only need some wood to make a fire.
The warmth of the fire will help me live.

Jordan LaDoucer, Grade 5
Francis Asbury Elementary School, VA

Eye of the Beast

As you stare into the eye of the beast
You'll see death itself rise
From the grave and come alive
You'll feel yourself paralyzed
Incapable of moving or screaming for help
All you can do is watch as it gets closer
Feeling the fear trickle down your spine
Then it's there
It starts to suffocate you
You feel your heart slowly start to stop
Right before you close your eyes
For the slumber of your life
You'll slowly utter the words "Eye of the Beast"

Alysha Whipkey, Grade 6
Macarthur Middle School, MD

My Mom

My mom is a hard working woman,
she is just like my dad.
She involves me in after school programs
so she can do her job.
When she is not working,
she is on the phone
with her friends and cousins
and she needs to cook dinner.
I wish my mom didn't work as much.
So I could spend time with her.
When she gets home she is strict as a police officer.
She will be mad as a shark if I don't read,
but she's my mother and I love her.
I miss her every day.
I wish my mom didn't work as much.

Noah Orakwue, Grade 4
Hawley Elementary School, CT

Winter/Christmas

Winter
Cold, white
Playing, sledding, skating
Friends, family, presents, Santa
Reading, opening, visiting
Red, green
Christmas

Rachel Scardina, Grade 4
C Hunter Ritchie Elementary School, VA

Owl

An owl is hooting
Up high in the evergreen
In the dark of night.
Mike Finn, Grade 5
Trinity School, MD

That Pillow

P lenty of space
I n the corner of the couch
L ove it
L ike a cloud surfing a wave
O h how soft it is
W ow, a pillow!
Rachael Allshouse, Grade 5
Wakefield Forest Elementary School, VA

Cycle

Winter is still here,
I wait longingly inside
For Summer Sunshine.

Winter turns to Spring,
One step closer to Summer,
It makes me hopeful.

Summer has arrived,
The Sun warming my shoulders,
It was worth the wait.

I bathe in Sunlight,
It seeps into my being,
But it will not last.

I look to the Sky,
It is dark with Autumn's touch,
Another long wait.
Ezra Dulit-Greenberg, Grade 6
Bigelow Middle School, MA

My Books

These are my books,
They sweep me away,
To faraway places,
And let me stray.

These are my books,
They're thick and thin,
But all still wonderful,
There isn't a place I haven't been.

These are my books,
They crinkle and rip,
I fix them with care,
And I hide them in my pillow slip.
Anna Boucheva, Grade 6
Scotts Ridge Middle School, CT

Ode to Friends

Friends are always there in my time of need
When my heart is about to drown in the river of hopelessness
My friends are there to pick me up
And bring me to the shore of hope

You all have different traits that make you all so perfect in your own special way
Different looks, they don't matter to me
You're all the same at heart
Supportive, caring, friendly

Friends are always there to back me up
And to always say the exact same thing that I want them to
Just like a puzzle piece missing its pieces but your friends just fill them in
You're the sunlight to my day
The highlight, the reason I get up every day
The reason I have good dreams at night

When we're in a fight, I am gloomy. blue, droopy
There is always a mini cloud over my head
The one that screams out BOOM
But when we make up, the sun shines
The grass is new with sparkled dew
All the nastiness, cruelness, and horror are out on vacation

You're my friend
Peaches Memishian, Grade 6
Greenwich Country Day School, CT

I'll Always Miss You CinCin!*

I'll always miss you CinCin, you were the best pet I ever had.
And though you are not with me, I will cry, weep, and mourn,
But nothing will ever change.
I will never forget you, for you were the best friend that I have ever had.

You were a Christmas present, but the best I could ever ask for.
For four years you cheered me up, when I was ever sad.
But now you are gone forever, and my life is just sad.
Now whenever I start to cry, I cannot stop right away.
For now I cannot hear an adorable chirp,
That talks to me and makes me happy.

I always said that when you passed away, I would not know what to do.
And I guess I was right, because I don't know what to do anymore.
Since you passed away, my life has been a wreck.
My heart has been crushed, and I can't stand the pain.

My life has gone downhill, since you have been gone.
I have wept every time I thought about you, only because I love you so much.
Just letting you know, that I'll always miss you.
And do not forget that I will always have room in my heart,
To love, care, and think about you.

Written in tears, Love Kasey.
Kasey Dean, Grade 6
Gilmore Academy, MA
*Dedicated to CinCin.

Sunset
Evening walks outside,
The ending of a great day,
Happiness and peace.
Elena Shand, Grade 6
Worcester Seventh-Day Adventist School, MA

Foxes
Foxes take a notion to stop
When they see a bunny hop
It's called catching prey
Sometimes they can wait all day

When they're waiting they don't move a fur
You may see this odd thing occur
You may see it at your home
Or even when you're on your phone
Kevin Libby, Grade 5
Forest Avenue Elementary School, MA

The Sun
When I look up, I see a glistening sun.
Watching over everyone.
Shining so brightly, big and bold.
In the warmth or in the cold.
It shines brightly for everyone to see.
Suddenly it fades away.
I wish it could have stayed.
Then the moon comes up, standing proud.
But I like the sun, bold and loud.
Sarah Tessler, Grade 4
Weston Intermediate School, CT

Flowers
I sit here
Looking out the window.
I see buds on flowers.
One day these buds will bloom.
They will bloom into big beautiful flowers.
Is that what they were meant to be?
I have so many questions.
When a flower blooms,
Is that like growing up?
Or when it loses its petals,
Does that mean it's
Dying?
These questions may never be answered.
But for now,
I will sit here…
Staring,
Watching the flowers
Grow up
Or
Die.
Devin Luzietti, Grade 4
Hawley Elementary School, CT

The Amazing Deer
I spring gracefully in the meadow.
I fight with the other bucks for does.
I have dark hazel colored fur.
I am the glamorous gigantic antlered deer.
Nathan Champagne, Grade 4
Greylock School, MA

Advice
Dear Friend,
Life isn't always a yellow brick road…
There will sometimes be bumps in it.
When you are stuck in that bump,
You can't give up on yourself.

Life is like the weather…
Which is not always fair.
Like pouring rain which nobody likes,
But you can overcome it with the sun —
And make a happy rainbow.

Life is like a box of chocolates…
You never know what you're going to get.
You can get stuck in the nuts or gooey parts,
But when you overcome it, you get the good chocolates.

Life can sometimes be like a Rock 'n Roll band…
Playing an awesome concert.
But it won't always be like that —
The concert can still be not the best!

Never ever give up on your life!

Trenton Kowalec, Grade 5
Har-Bur Middle School, CT

Allison
Bouncing,
Springing off the walls
Like a bright red playground ball
Each of her words jumping up and down,
Up and down, up and down.
Excited for who knows what,
Smiling all over,
Shining like the sun.
Flying around the couch,
Her famous phrase spills out of her mouth:
Can I call Madison?
Now she leaps like a ballerina
Off of her perch on the couch
And snatches the phone as if it is the only thing that matters.
She is everything,
A hopping frog,
A glittering star,
A soaring butterfly,
Allison
Lucy Beizer, Grade 5
John Ward Elementary School, MA

What Is Basketball?

What is basketball?
Big round orange sun
Sweat runs down your body
Kids spring to get the ball
Players push and shove for the ball
Break in action for water
Crowd roars in close games
Winning a close game feels great
Play for a championship
Advantage goes to a team
Silent at a game winning free-throw
That is basketball!

Brandon Owen, Grade 5
Jane Ryan School, CT

Fire

Burning up this earth
Taking over the green ground
Darkening our world

Brandon Harb, Grade 5
Soule Road School, MA

Glue

Glue, glue
Sometimes blue
Always sticky,
And sometimes icky.

Glue, glue
In schools too.
I got some in my hair,
From a dumb dare.

Glue, glue
I'm going to sue!
Now I'm picky.
And please don't licky!

Oliver Guox, Grade 4
Grace Miller Elementary School, VA

The Storm

Flashes of lightning,
It is a warning from God,
There is no way out!

Daniel Conry, Grade 4
Riderwood Elementary School, MD

Otters

Otters
wet, playful
swimming, splashing, squeaking
happy otter playing tag
Animal

Aaron S. Lewis, Grade 5
Sacred Heart Elementary School, MA

Spring

I smell the budding flowers.
I feel the sun shining on me.
I see the kids playing outside.
I taste the sweet lemonade.
I hear the birds chirping.

Makenna Mont, Grade 4
Freetown Elementary School, MA

The Everlasting Sea

In front of me
Is an everlasting sea
Vast as anything
But next to me

I saw it reaching out to me
Pulling me
Into the depth of the sea
In front of me

All around me
Is an everlasting sea
No one else just me
And the sea

Everywhere I go I see
Me and the sea
Nothing but me
And the everlasting sea

Olivia Hicklen, Grade 5
Soule Road School, MA

Gym

Oh how it smells in there
With all the dirty socks.
Even though it smells like that,
Gym really, really rocks.

Oh how it smells in there
With all the dirty clothes.
I wish it smelled as good
As a beautiful red rose.

Oh how it smells in there
I wish it could end.
The only reason why I like gym
Is because of my best friend.

Priscilla Rodriguez, Grade 6
Fuller Middle School, MA

First Sign of Spring

A little frog leaps
Into the blue spring water
With a cool light breeze.

Taylyn Soult, Grade 6
Monelison Middle School, VA

To Have Life

To breathe. To smell.
Life
To hear. To laugh.
Life
To hate. To love.
Life
To dream. To imagine.
Life

Lea McDade, Grade 5
C C Burr Elementary School, MA

Heavenly Emerald

When I awoke in the morning
in my room filled with peace,
my mind starts pounding with ideas
to do like a drum that won't cease.

I walk to the window and
whisper to myself,
"Am I the only one that
knows about this glorious wealth?"

The emerald sea of clovers is
the sight that I see,
all wet and glittery,
I wonder if I'm still asleep.

I go back to my bed all
covered up in ribbons of silk
I fall back asleep under the
moon as white as milk.

My life has changed,
it truly has.
Now that I've seen heaven,
I can let go of my past.

Danielle Wood, Grade 6
West Frederick Middle School, MD

Fashion

Elegant dresses on the runway,
Designing fashions for every day,
Creating your own unique style,
It could be short, or take a while.

Jordan DeGaetano, Grade 4
Leicester Memorial School, MA

Softball

Try to hit home runs.
Sometimes you throw the ball far.
You can hit the ball far.
Sometimes you might get a strike.
Do not want to have three strikes.

Cassidy Mitchell, Grade 4
Battlefield Elementary School, VA

I Love Fall

I love fall so much
when the leaves fly.

The earth is so colorful
it's like it's covered in orange and red dye!

I can smell the fresh air
as clean as it can be.

No pollution, no germs
Just me and the leaves.

As we watch the sunset
and the moon comes out to play.

Now that is how we spend
our beautiful fall days.

Sarah Prescott, Grade 5
Miscoe Hill Elementary School, MA

Silvery Sails

Silvery sails whipping by,
Furled beneath the darkening sky,
Whitecaps rolling far and nigh,
Silvery sails shining high.

Keenan Brawley, Grade 5
Church of the Redeemer Christian School, MD

Yellow

Yellow is a banana, sweet and gooey
Yellow is a sunset shining so bright
Yellow is fire brightening the dark
Yellow is the moon disappeared in the darkness
Yellow is the sun shining down on me
Yellow is cheese on my cheeseburger

Sierra Reynolds, Grade 4
C Hunter Ritchie Elementary School, VA

Peace

Still, calm
Soothing, quieting, nourishing,
As everyone sees its beauty
Wonderful

Maria Ronchi, Grade 5
Marblehead Community Charter Public School, MA

What Am I?

Ball Point, dancing around the thin, white carpet,
drip, drop my ink splats on the thin ground,
making marks everywhere I dance
Twirling, leaping, making smudges,
My black shoe is pointy
making thin and straight lines,
Can you guess what I am?

Michaela Blum, Grade 6
E W Thurston Middle School, MA

Good-bye to My Jewels*

Good-bye to ye jewels so near,
I must give you up now I fear;
Now with King George's laws
Which have many flaws
I cannot buy you any longer
Great Britain just gets wronger and wronger;
The time is done
When Britain and we were one.
At first the tax
Now the Intolerable Acts
With the ports shut down
Because of Britain's "Crown;"
So I say good-bye to my jewels
Only because of King George's rules.

Kirby Kochanowski, Grade 5
Tenacre Country Day School, MA
*Patterned after "A Lady's Adieu to Her Tea Table"

Seasons

Fall rushes in
Like birds rising to fly
And leaves gliding to the ground
Fall comes cool and windy,
With the smell of pumpkins and apples,
And crumpled up leaves

Then winter slips in
With light snowflakes falling
And ice covering the ground
On a cold empty day,
With children inside
Warming their hands by the fire

Next spring blooms in
Like flowers in parks with bees resting on top
On a warm, windy day
With small, furry creatures running up trees

Lastly summer floats in
Like petals drifting off flowers and seashells in the water
Summer comes softly
Like the breeze at the beach
After being in the ocean.

Rachel Roberts, Grade 5
Weston Intermediate School, CT

What a Monkey He Is

My brother's a monkey
He loves to play around
He also is funny
And can make any monkey sound
He loves bananas as yellow as can be
So come monkey around with my brother and me!

Jared Jonas, Grade 6
Benjamin Syms Middle School, VA

Ringtail Animal
R uns
I gnores others
N eeds food for family
G ets water from nearby ponds
T eases
A muses humans
I mmune to desert
L ong tail
Matt McClanahan, Grade 6
Albert D Griswold Middle School, CT

Spring
During March rain falls
sweet smell of flowers escape
birds chirp and bees buzz
Phillip Edward Ross, Grade 4
St Joseph School-Fullerton, MD

Ocean
Waves curl with no sound,
fish swim on and on,
all this happens without a sound,
dolphins skim across the surface,
all is well in the ocean,
as the waves curl with no sound.
Kevin Boudreau, Grade 5
John F Kennedy School, CT

Summertime Is Coming!
Summertime is coming!
Shorts and tans,
Golden sun and light blue skies,
Water fun all day long.
Birds and bees flying around
A simple bird call,
The buzz of bees.
Hot days are coming,
It will not last so long.
Emma McNally, Grade 4
Quashnet School, MA

The Black Hole
TV is like
a suction cup
once you sit down
to watch it
you can't get up!
Madison Sutton, Grade 4
Munger Hill Elementary School, MA

Dogwood
The dogwood's lovely
The leaves and flowers glisten
The smell is so sweet
Jasmine Hitt, Grade 4
Grace Miller Elementary School, VA

9-10A Team Lax Max Championships
Our first Lax Max game Cobras' jerseys like ours were the same.
They had great and powerful defense, but we had stronger and harder offense.

I scored an awesome goal the joy lit up my soul.
Cobras came back hard and fast, but at the end we won the match.

We moved on to our second game, Yellow Jackets, was their name;
All of them had a frown because they were one man down.

They were small we were tall.
An advantage we had I felt somewhat bad.

Perry Hall we played they were shamed
We had won they are all done.

The Lax Max games we won the teams were all done
Our trophies we got they weighed a lot.
Haley Jackson, Grade 6
Immaculate Heart of Mary School, MD

When I Think of My Mom
When I think of my mom
I see a person as tall as a tree
I see an open heart that cleans and takes care of her kids
I see every night that she gets home worn out
I see an unselfish heart and mind that cares for others like family
When I think of my mom
I hear her soft voice call my name
I hear tiny steps coming soft, quietly, on her tiptoe to her room
I hear a clever person cleaning the house
I hear her slowly falling asleep, snoring
When I think of my mom
I smell her chocolate melting cake, just out of the oven
I smell her new, flowery, sweet perfume
When I think of my mom
I taste her spicy food like her meat and rice
I taste her chocolate melting with caramel
I taste smoothies every morning, strawberry, my favorite, "yummy"
When I think of my mom
I feel loved every time I am with her
I feel sad when I am far away from her
When I think of my mom
Wellyda do Prado, Grade 6
Fuller Middle School, MA

Flowers
Red, yellow, orange, purple, white, pink and violet.
Beautiful, lacy, soft, velvety, bright and fragrant.
Happy, graceful, delicate they make me feel.
Sparkling with dew, early in the morning as the warm sun begins to shine.
With a gentle breeze they bend as if in an elegant dance.
Rose, violet, lily, iris, daisy, daffodil and tulip.
Birthdays, weddings funerals, hospitals, love and just because,
Are a few of the ways flowers brighten all of us.
Shy-Ann Drake, Grade 5
Forest Avenue Elementary School, MA

Why Sudan Is Sudan

I am Sudan,
because of my beautiful skies.
I am Sudan,
because I am the land where my soldiers died.
I am Sudan,
because of my hope and pride.
I am Sudan,
because my sun always shines!
I am Sudan,
because one day all my people will reunite.

Roda Ibrahim, Grade 5
Marley Elementary School, MD

Daydreams

I sit in the hills of luscious green grass.
I lie calmly under an apple tree.
The shade feels good
Cool breezes float over me.
I look into the blue sky; clouds drift
So gentle they hardly look like they're moving.
I look deeper.
I see beautiful flowers, animals, and trees, all white.
It brings me to a different world.
My eyes slowly close until shut.
I sleep peacefully.

Caroline Helmes, Grade 6
Village School, MA

New England Swimming Championships

I am going to Boston
Harvard to be exact
to swim my heart out
you should come too

to where the scoreboard
flashes your name in big neon lights
where medals are earned
big blue ribbons too
you should come too

to where you tighten
your goggles so much
they hurt your face
your heart pumps and knees shake
you should come too

to where your dives
barely make the water ripple
shallow and smooth
you should come too

win, cheer, applause
you should come too

Cami Coppage, Grade 5
West Woods Upper Elementary School, CT

Blue

Blue is the glittering, smooth ocean
Blue is a round, plump blueberry
Blue is the shining, light sky
Blue is a smooth, round flower petal
Blue is the beautiful bluebirds
Blue is round lollipops

Lauren Burnett, Grade 4
C Hunter Ritchie Elementary School, VA

Man's Best Friend

Man's best friend starts off so sweet
When his big black eyes and ours meet;
He is fearful and shy
And he mumbles and cries.
When I take him to go home
He sits in a corner acting all alone.
He slowly grows; he starts to know
Where to go, and that I am not his foe.
We play all day, and he runs as he may
While I watch and gaze.
Time goes by, and he's suddenly nine;
I can't believe how fast is time!
All those years just went on by,
We grew together, friends forever,
Leaving my side never,
For better or for worse.
Now I am eighty, looking out at my childhood,
And I know I wouldn't change it if I could;
I went to sleep with my best friend, as it should be.

Daphne Effinger, Grade 6
Cape Henry Collegiate School, VA

Now and Today

Now is your time
Today is your day
To lift off and shine
And brighten the day
Tomorrow is waiting
But so very far away
Your calling is calling
Now you're off and away
Now is your time
Today is your day
Keep on dreaming
Because hope is never far away
As you rise to the challenge
And continue your journey
Remember the good times, remember the day
That you started your journey
And pushed the past away
Now is your time
Today is your day
Don't let it escape you
Be free — be free today

Lauren Kane, Grade 6
Horace Mann Middle School, MA

Spring

In the spring I like to play,
and it always goes my way.
It's very hot 'cause of the sun,
So I like to have some fun.
I like the breeze,
But it makes me wheeze.
It's my Allergies!

Ryan Bradbury, Grade 4
Brookside Elementary School, MA

What if I Got Lost?

What if I got lost in the mall?
Will people ignore me
if I ask them to take me home?
Will someone kidnap me?
Will I live poor on the street
with nothing to eat or drink,
and ask people for money?
Will I?

As I think of these things,
I grip my mom's hand so tight it turns
sea blue!
My thinking is interrupted by
a really pretty coat
on the rack of my favorite store.
My thinking suddenly changes as my
shopping motto
springs out of my mouth,
"Can I have it, mom? Please!"

Josefina Mendez, Grade 4
Hawley Elementary School, CT

Snowboarding

Snowboarding is really fun,
But it is not a breeze.
Because the fun will be done
If you hit any trees.

Snowboarding is the sport for me.
It really is a blast.
There are a lot of views to see,
Too bad it cannot last.

I see the tall evergreens.
I see the bald oaks.
I see some people eating beans,
And some are drinking coke!

I really, really love this sport
But let me tell you what,
If you jump and come up short
You could get badly cut.

Josh Smith, Grade 6
Captain Nathan Hale Middle School, CT

Spring

Flowers are blooming
Trees are growing back their leaves
Spring is here again!!

Rebecca Lynn Vincent, Grade 4
St Joseph School-Fullerton, MD

Freedom

You look at me
I look at you
Knowing what to do
So we can be free
We see the bar
Knowing we're not that far
We get ready
Knowing to be steady
We get the key
To unlock the door
Opening it a little more
And at last, we are free.

Elaina Audi, Grade 6
E W Thurston Middle School, MA

Life

Life is like a lime…mmm
Tangy and sour. Snap!
Quiet, speechless as a mime.
Bold and noisy like a crime.
Life goes fast without a stop,
Like the time
Because life is a rhyme.

Andrea Segura Ramirez, Grade 4
Bensley Elementary School, VA

The Boston Bruins

Our mascot is a bear
Stands with might anywhere
We hustle and fight
On the ice every night

Shoot score, hat trick
Move the puck with a hockey stick
Roaring fans are there to see
The team win a victory

Sometimes when we lost we are sad
Sometimes when we win we are glad

Alex Vieira, Grade 6
Edmond P Talbot Middle School, MA

Summer

I like summer best
It has wild geese that are big
In the evening sky

Christopher Parrison, Grade 4
Hebbville Elementary School, MD

Dragons

They can be small
Some can be tall
Some can be true
Some can be new
They can even be on a wall.

Christina Lewis, Grade 4
Grace Miller Elementary School, VA

Dinosaur

Thump, thump, roar, roar
Here comes the dinosaur
The people watch in horror
As it steps on all the stores

Thump, thump, roar, roar
Here comes the dinosaur
First the head, then the feet
It's sure to give you the creeps

Thump, thump, roar, roar
There goes the dinosaur.

Kate O'Neil, Grade 5
Forest Avenue Elementary School, MA

Stars

Stars sparkle high in the sky,
While people make wishes,
As they wander by.
Stars are like race cars,
Zooming by fast,
White dwarfs shine bright,
Like a lantern burning its gas.

Every night I look out my window,
Glad to see this wonderful sight.
Of all the shapes and colors,
Shining throughout the night.
But during the day they're sleeping.
Getting ready to glisten high in the sky.

When they're not there,
I get gloomy.
Because they make me perky.
Stars are gigantic, but look so small,
How do they do it?
I want to know it all.

Noelle Murphy, Grade 5
Tilghman Elementary School, MD

Grass

Beautiful green blades
Petite needles shine with dew
Glistening at dawn

Nicholas Di Meglio, Grade 4
Trinity Christian School, VA

Rain

Rain
Rain
Rain
Wet rain
Clear swishy rain
Cloudy misty damp rain
Drizzly rain
Dewy rain
Stormy cold umbrella rain
Puddly droplet raincoat rain
Splashing rain, too
Hard rain
Light rain
Don't forget rain boot rain
Last of all, best of all, I like spring rain

Emily Borst, Grade 4
C Hunter Ritchie Elementary School, VA

Birthday

People, people
Everywhere celebrating
The birth of
Me.
Eating cake and
Bouncing in
Moonwalks while
Everyone is singing
"Happy Birthday" to me.
People, people
Everywhere celebrating
The birth of
Me.

Chris Marshall, Grade 5
Foxborough Regional Charter School, MA

Poems

Can be about you.
Can be about your friends.
Some can be weird
Short; long;
Rhyming; not rhyming;
Funny; silly;
Cool; happy;
Mean; nice;
Emotional; Gross;
Awesome; Scary;
Good
Can make you cry;
Can also be about your life.
Can be about a mess in your desk.
About a place you have been to.
Can be about your summer vacation.
Can be about school, home or field trips.
Poems can be whatever you want them to be!

Ivan Rivera, Grade 4
WB Sweeney School, CT

Halloween

Halloween is the night when
Children dress as ghosts, ghouls, and witches.
This is the night when ghosts come to life
And scare little children.
So, if you see one,
Just say, "Boo!"
They will run away screaming
Just like you might do.
Remember what I say
Because if you don't
And the ghosts scare you
You'll run away screaming
While they have a
Ghost parade!

Cheyenne Smoot, Grade 4
Bensley Elementary School, VA

Spring

Spring
Warm, Bright
Growing, Living, Warming
Spring comes with new life each year
Spring

Emily Peugh, Grade 5
Marblehead Community Charter Public School, MA

A Block L.A.

Sixth period Language Arts,
directly after lunch.
There's quite a lot of kids here,
but we're a spiffy bunch.

There's Janellia, Uche, Jess, Jasmine, Britt,
Emily, Cas, and Karla.
And Christian, Mario, Eduardo, Sergey,
and don't forget about Scott.
(I guess you're right, there is a lot).
But who really cares? We sure do not!

Ms. Bucci is the awesome-est,
but everyone knows one fact:
Some things that go on in here are VERY, VERY wack!

Kirsten Hansen, Grade 6
Fuller Middle School, MA

Two Purple Flowers

Two purple flowers so pretty and sweet,
like a little piece of velvet underneath my bare feet.

When I run through the garden I feel free and like a girl,
spinning and dreaming,

Ready to take on the world.

Jill Holmes, Grade 5
St Mary's Primary School, MA

Golf Course

When I step up to a tee
I hear nothing, but silence.
Although I hear the divots
Whispering, "miss" or "pure."
When I'm on the green
I can hear the contestants' feet
Going in slow motion
Booommm, Booommm.
I can also feel my eardrums
Vibrating when they step.
And if I miss a putt
The letters on the flagpole
Turn into faces and haunt me.
Although whenever I get the chance,
I would do anything to
Get on the golf course and play.

Matthew Naumec, Grade 5
Soule Road School, MA

Peace

It is calm
I won't deny it
Underneath this palm
all is quiet

The breeze blows my hair
The sea tickles my toes
I have not a care
I've forgotten my woes

If only it would stay like this
a peaceful paradise
and I will certainly miss
This peace that will subside

Taylor Gobeil, Grade 6
Southbrook Academy, MA

Florida

Royal palms,
geese and ducks,
hopping toads
on the street.
Blossoms
on the plants,
red ants
marching along
the searing hot driveway
The smell
of sweet
tropical flowers
surround me.
The royal palm trees
sway their huge branches —
taking me away in a dream.

Tara Hegarty, Grade 4
Hawley Elementary School, CT

Ollie

Ollie is a fat, fuzzy, and lazy cat.
He is one, bright orange cat with white little stripes just like a tiger.
Ollie isn't just one of those ordinary cats
He's an adventurous cat!
Ollie sometimes sneaks upstairs
and hides under the bed.
My mom roars at him saying that he shouldn't go up there ever again.
Ollie is a fat, lazy house cat,
but he thinks he's as mighty as a lion roaming through the fields of Africa
When my little sisters leave the front door open,
Ollie goes in for the act and sneaks out
like a city rat and eventually comes back
But if he doesn't come back
I have to go find him no matter what kind of weather.
But then the most terrible thing happens
Ollie's for sale!
you would never imagine how mad I was when someone knocked on our door and
took him away,
When the person was gone with my kitty cat
I cried,
"I will miss you Ollie!"

Sabrina Elhag, Grade 4
Hawley Elementary School, CT

Why…

Why is the Earth so round?
Why does it go around and around?
Why is the moon so bright and help me see at night?
Why is the sky so high?
Why can't I fly? Do you know why?
Why is the ocean so deep and blue and fish so good to eat?
Why does the rain feel so good on a warm summer night?
Why won't girls pick up worms?
Why is grass green and not pink?
I ask myself these things…do you?
Why are some people short and some are tall?
Why do you have blue eyes and I have brown?
Why are some people young and some are old?
Why do babies cry sometimes when nothing is wrong with them?
Why is there war and not peace?
Why do good people die and bad people live?
Why can't there by only love and not hate?
Why do some people not have a home?
Why can't we all just get along?
Why will ice cream make you fat?

Chanllun Thomas, Grade 4
Elk Knob Elementary School, VA

Summer

It is as hot as the sun at 12:00 noon.
I'm melting because of the intense heat.
Summer is like a 2 year old with many moods.
The moods of a 2 year old are like the changing temperatures.
The waves in the water cause the children to splash in the ocean.

Lyndsey Shultz, Grade 6
School of International Studies at Meadowbrook, VA

The Eagle

There once was an eagle who strayed from his nest,
Don't blame him, he didn't know best!

So along the way he hit a tree,
A bear below yelled, "Yippee!"

The bear said to himself, "This will be my lunch."
Then he thought, "It's not that late, I'll make it a brunch!"

But that little brave eagle got up and flew away,
I guess the bear won't have his brunch today!

Matthew Krol, Grade 5
Soule Road School, MA

Summer Camp

One late night at Summer Camp
The sky was clear and the air was damp
A boy named Tim
Snuck out for a swim
He tiptoed into the pool so he wouldn't be heard
I watched him through my window and didn't say a word
Little did he know he was not alone?
There was a toad at the pool side that let out a groan
Then the toad leaped into the water and made a big splash
The boy was gone as quick as a flash!

Monica Machado, Grade 4
Freetown Elementary School, MA

Summer Fun

S unshine in the summer is hot
U nlimited play time
M ountains of things to do
M emorize your reading list
E xercise by riding your bike or scooter
R ace at the park, anytime — anywhere

F unky fun while playing outside
U nlimited sunshine for a lot more fun
N ow that it's spring we are ready for summer fun!

Rosina Toscano, Grade 5
Sacred Heart Elementary School, MA

Peace

Peace is like God's hand taking you to
Him in Heaven

Peace looks like a plate of strawberries
with cream

Peace sounds like someone saying "I love you" and
It can be a couple sharing a big chocolate kiss, but

Peace is always in my heart.

Leonora Torres, Grade 4
St Augustine Cathedral School, CT

Myself

Myself outside
   And
Myself inside I guess is kind of close

My outside appearance is rather bright
With outgoing shoes you see
No hats, not bandannas on my small head
Only headbands and long locks of hair
Family says I'm beautiful
I tend to agree

The outside appearance is what you make yourself
I've done great on me
My outside appearance is lovely
You see

Dancing on a big huge stage tons of people watching me
Being picky with food is what my mind tells me?
Pretty midgety, I tend to agree
Not as short though, as Santa's elves
So nice and warm to everyone I know
But sometimes not to me

My inside appearance is very nice, sort of, kind of, technically!

Brooke Miller, Grade 6
Mountain Christian School, MD

Life Is

Life is like a snowflake, beautiful and fragile
Life is like a runner, quick and agile
Life is like a book, descriptive and warm
Life is like an antique, all ripped and torn

Life is like a memory, happy or sad
Life is like a convict that has done something bad
Life is to cry, so bring out all your tears
Life is living your dream, taking chances, no fears

Jordan Isaacs, Grade 6
Weston Middle School, CT

What's the Point

Mom, what's the point of school?
All you do is work.
I'm not even sure if my teachers aren't dogs!
They bark and bark orders at you
for fun not for work!
I even saw one breathe fire
and eat bugs
Mom, the school lunches are distasteful,
a kid got one with hair,
another with a fin!
So mom please, please!
don't make me go to school
make a monkey go instead!

Kyra Campbell, Grade 6
Monelison Middle School, VA

Christmas Day
Tap-Tap-Tap!
Down I run to the living room floor, where the presents galore, in the room, I explore!
Holidays are fun and exciting, and that's what I adore!

Click! Went all the lights.
Oh my goodness — what a sight!
Excitement rushed through me, as I saw the presents, shiny and pretty, like a puppy chasing its toys.
"Oh boy!" I cried out loud, "Mom! Dad! Come on! It's Christmas Day, I say! Hurray! Hurray!"

The Christmas tree glittered like crystals shining in a cave.
The house was quiet, but all was aglow, the noised filled the air, making Christmas Day brightly grow.
"Chirp!" went the birds, "Swish!" went the wrapping papers.
They roared and lashed, as they flew into the air, while I laughed and danced!

The cookies were eaten, oh dang! I got beaten!
The milk was chugged, to myself I hugged.
From that jolly, old man, who was once here at my house, to drop off the presents, and left without a sound.

Christmas was fun,
I must admit,
Fun and exciting,
And I'll click, "Submit!"

Pamela Anne B. Solis, Grade 6
Litchfield Intermediate School, CT

Ballet
Ballet can take you to a place where your dreams come true and goals are achieved. As you leap into the air you feel as if you can fly and nobody can catch you. A feeling of freedom rushes about you. Your glittering skirt twists and turns as you dance across the floor. Dangling hairs whip your face and you know that you alone are the star of ballet.

Kelly Winterbottom, Grade 5
Har-Bur Middle School, CT

If I Were an Animal
If I were an animal I would be a dragon.
I would blow fire at bullies.
I would fly super speedy in the sky.
I would blow ice at the sky so it would snow outside.
When it's summer then I would dig a giant hole of dirt, big like a beach and put lots of sand and water in it.
Then I would get a big long log and cut it into a surfboard. Then I'd go surf's up!
When I am done I will go under the ocean to find a coral reef to find my friend the Water Dragon.
He freezes the water if bad guys come.
He can make rain and snow and ice.
At the coral reef I saw my other friend the Earth Dragon.
He can turn into any color and he can turn into anything.
Then I went to the volcano. That's where my friend the Lava dragon lives.
He has the power of meteor showers.
Then I went home to sleep.
Today I am going to space.
I saw an alien at space.
I saw a very very huge asteroid.
I saw a special friend the Space Dragon.
He shoots lasers from his eyes and he turns invisible.
Tomorrow I will do the same thing
But I will explore the jungle and the ocean and the earth's core.

Giancarlo Rivera, Grade 4
WB Sweeney School, CT

Silver and Gold

Silver is like clouds, all puffy and gray.
Gold is like the sun, so yellow and bright.
Silver is like a wrench, so shiny and strong.
Gold is like maple syrup, poured over waffles.
Silver is like a diamond, so sparkly and clear.
Gold is like a sun flower, yellow and pretty.
Silver and gold are everywhere.

Jack Brooks, Grade 4
Weston Intermediate School, CT

On This Very Christmas Night

On this very Christmas night,
There was a star shining like a light.

Our Savior, Jesus, was born this day,
In a manger where He was put to lay.

The baby lamb slept next to Him,
To keep Him warm with the light so dim.

Mary and Joseph were by His side,
While the three kings traveled far and wide.

God gave us this holy sight to see,
A special gift for you and me.

Courtney Lanasa, Grade 6
St Clement Mary Hofbauer School, MD

Girl Scout Cookies

The chocolate chips are sugar free
But they might taste the same to you and me
Samoas and All Abouts are really good
You should try them, you really should
A Do-Si-Dos is a peanut pastry
Tagalongs are also tasty
Trefoils are really light
You can even have them at night
Thin Mints are really minty and thin
Try not to drop any crumbs on your chin
Lemon Chalet have lemon flavors
I'll give you one if you do me a favor

Erin Murray, Grade 5
Toquam Magnet School, CT

Memories

As I sit here and write this poem,
Wonderful memories flow through my head.
Memories of swimming in the ocean…
Memories of learning to ride a bicycle…
Memories of playing basketball…
Memories of making new friends…
When I think of these things,
It makes me happy
To just want to share them with other people.

Julien Amrhein, Grade 6
St Joseph School-Fullerton, MD

The Girl on Strings

She has no name, only strings
that are attached to her legs and arms.
No voice and no dreams, only blank.
She is in the dark dancing around like a fool.
The strings make her feel like a joke.
Everyone laughs at her as she walks past them
and she wants to cry, but no water comes out.
She's not happy she only has a frown.
She's angry at those strings
that are attached to her hands and feet.
She has no family, nor friends.
Now she is free, till she is dead.
She is now happy and no longer depressed.

Alexa Ruffin, Grade 5
Francis Asbury Elementary School, VA

History

The discoveries throughout the ages have been amazing
All of our questions have been answered
The sky is the limit with this
History has many twists and turns
There are many things we don't know about
We want to know as much as we can
But I am sure with our new technologies
We will be sure to find out

Jacob Eisner, Grade 6
Wakefield Forest Elementary School, VA

I've Always Wanted to Be a Cook!

I've always wanted to be a cook.
All day over a recipe book,
Adding my special flavor
To dishes people will savor.

Cucumber, lettuce, and tomatoes,
Steak served with a side of mashed potatoes,
Red sauce and noodles,
For dessert I have strudel!

Jillian Lombardi, Grade 5
Foxborough Regional Charter School, MA

Spring

Spring is the season when flowers,
Butterflies,
And plants bloom.
It's the season after
The cold, and snowy winter…the season when everything
Springs to life!
The season when Jesus resurrected.
The season when the world becomes a happier place
Bringing
Everything
To life!!

Ezinwa Nwakma, Grade 5
St Joseph School-Fullerton, MD

Shades of the Sky

Sunset
Orange; Red
Relaxation on a
Fall day
Rainstorms,
Grey, death —
Silence…
Summer day;
Blue…clouds…
Bright sun,
Children have fun
Swamp,
Humid
Mysterious, green, grey?
Somewhere in between…
Midnight…silence, death repeats…
And the endless black, stars are hidden
Tonight…
Early morning;
Peace — From black, to golden, to blue,
In a minute.

David Kwartler, Grade 5
C C Burr Elementary School, MA

My White Cat

My white cat, my white cat
is as funny as a clown.
When she rolls around outside
She looks so very brown.

My white cat, my white cat
is really really cute.
If a man comes with a gun
I wouldn't let him shoot.

My white cat, my white cat
knows something that you should know.
She knows that her name is Munchy,
and that I love her so.

Jonah Fouser, Grade 4
Alice B Beal Elementary School, MA

Playing Outside

Running out on the field.
Walking in the grass.
Talking to your friends.
Humming to yourself.
   run!
   walk!
Hiding from your friends.
Climbing from your friends.
Playing outside is the
most fun thing to do.

Ahmeen Reese, Grade 4
Bensley Elementary School, VA

Recycle to Help the Earth

Recycle soda cans,
Don't leave them on the floor.
It makes the environment dirty,
It is one thing nature doesn't adore.

My family recycles cardboard,
Your family might recycle plastic.
All that matters is we recycle,
Isn't it fantastic!

If you use Campbell's products,
You should recycle the cans.
To help the Earth instead of hurting it,
Recycle all kinds of brands.

Just to remind you,
To be friendly and nice,
It is great,
Like sugar and spice.

Ally Lanasa, Grade 4
St Clement Mary Hofbauer School, MD

Wolf's Eye

My tear shaped eye
Glows with hate and joy
On a rare occasion
You'll hear my cry

And when this happens
You'll learn my history
And when this happens
You'll understand the wolf's eye

Julian Jacobs, Grade 6
Weston Middle School, CT

The Sky

I am like the sky.
We both cry
And chuckle.

We both growl,
We both grumble,
We both shine
With all of our strength.

We can scare people
With our loudness.
We can also caress people
With our calmness.

I love the sky,
The sky loves me.
I am like the sky.

Leigh Anne Kline, Grade 6
Cape Henry Collegiate School, VA

Dogs/Cats

Dogs
playful, loyal
playing, eating, barking
beagle, boxer, siamese, alley
darting, drinking, meowing
mischievous independent
Cats

Matthew Ferguson, Grade 5
McCleary Elementary School, VA

Checkers and Chess

Checkers
Quick, easy
Jumping, crowning, losing
King, pieces, pawns, knights
Checking, moving, winning
Long, complicated
Chess

Ayanna Washington, Grade 4
Clarksville Elementary School, VA

Spring Time

S easonal flowers blooming
P ollen blowing through air
R unning eyes from allergies
I tchy eyes need rubbing
N o relief in sight
G ood grief it's raining pollen

T ime for Benadryl
I can hardly see
M ommy I need the tissues
E very minute I sneeze

Shannon Keith, Grade 5
Sacred Heart Elementary School, MA

What I Saw There

Once I was a bird.
I flew high in the air.
Big, puffy, white clouds
Are what I saw there.
Once I was a deer.
I ran everywhere.
Leaves, trees, and squirrels
Are what I saw there.
Once I was big and white.
I was a polar bear.
Snow and lots of ice
Are what I saw there.
But, what was I really?
Not a bird, deer, or bear.
I was a human, dreaming
Of what I would see there.

Taryn Nugent, Grade 6
St Joseph School-Fullerton, MD

Homerun

The emerald green baseball bat
slices through the darkness of the night
as it flies to the ball.
They meet for a split second —
everything freezes —
as the ball changes direction
and sails over the fence.
Homerun.
Is all you think
Homerun.

Mark Steele, Grade 5
West Woods Upper Elementary School, CT

Awesome Orange

Orange is…
Orange is a Miami Dolphins Uniform
Being played in
Orange is a sleepy basketball
Sitting in a bin
Orange is a speedy fox
Running really fast
Orange is a starfish
Sticking to a rock in the sea
Impossible to remove
Orange is a piece of colored glass
Stabbing painfully into my foot like a spear
Orange is a Fanta soda
Going "slurp slurp" as I drink
I think orange is an amazing color!
Do you like orange too?

Michael Tobin, Grade 5
Spring Hill Elementary School, VA

My Grandmother

My grandmother is awesome,
She surely is a blossom.
She loves me just like she should.
She's still alive,
And I hope it stays that way,
Because I love her and she's here to stay.

Erick Fernandez, Grade 5
Clark Avenue Middle School, MA

Drawing Blood

Oh no it's that day again. We are not going to the bay;
I'm not going to watch a play or be in one.
I'm going to get blood work today.

I've been getting blood work for sometime now. But I hate it.
Oh no, I'm next.

The nurse calls my name. Ouch! Hay that didn't hurt much.
Wonder who said ouch? I'll never tell.

Adrian Lehne, Grade 5
Friendship Valley Elementary School, MD

Spring

Flowers budding all around
Green grass growing on the ground
A nice break from winter is finally here
No snow or cold — the sky is clear
A spring breeze is passing by
I just love spring, I cannot lie
Bees and bugs crowd the field
A praying mantis humbly kneels
Spring is here, oh how good it feels!

Courtney Paris, Grade 5
Church of the Redeemer Christian School, MD

Tree

I look far and beyond,
Watching the year that passes by.
My lime-green children are full grown,
Attached to me, their shadows an abundance
On the flower-filled ground.

My children are losing their color.
They gently fall from my arms onto the ground,
Where they are swept away
By the traveling air.
Only a few remain to me.

They're gone.
A white powder settles on my arms
And buries my children that are on the frozen ground.
It tickles my nerves, freezing my veins.
Like water into ice.

The powder melts away.
It keeps me hydrated as Sunshine gracefully
Reveals herself.
Hundreds of my children attached to my arms.
Full bloom.
I think about the year ahead of me.

Danielle Wall, Grade 6
St Stephen Parochial School, MD

Only You

There is one thing I need that only I know of.
The one thing I need is called love.
Only one person can give me this gift
Then my spirits will lift.
He always asks me what he can give or what he can do
I wish I could tell him, "I only need you."
I am so afraid he is going to be mad
But he does wonder why I'm so sad.
I sit up in my room, hoping he will come to me soon.
He finally asks, "What do you need me to do."
I push away my fears and say, "I only need you."
He sits there and sighs as he watches me cry
Tears of joy because I am so happy to know he loves me.

Abigail Robinson, Grade 6
Salem Church Middle School, VA

Alberto Montrond

He holds a weapon.
He's running his way through
So many hurt people
yelling and screaming.
He's so terrified.
But on the inside he's got the strength.

He watches a bomb fly
through the air.
Next thing you know his car is hit.
He loses his soul forever leaving
us filled with sorrow.

His family cries but we know
that's how life is.
We come, then we go
never seen again.
A true soldier
Alberto Montrond.

Emily Silveira, Grade 6
Swampscott Middle School, MA

Snowflakes

Snowflakes
floating, floating
down and down
dancing all around
you amaze me with
your lovely pattern
you make a white blanket
on the endless field
of green strips
you make the sky look
like a white blank space
Snowflakes

Michael Grinnell, Grade 4
Potter Road Elementary School, MA

Riptide (Sword)

Riptide is ready
Sweaty hands grasp him tightly
Pointy tip aloft

From his owner's hand
He is given a command
Thrust toward enemies

Soon the fight will end
Victory around the bend
He does try his best

He sees opportunities
He knows there's no way to lose
They become winners

Annie Stachura, Grade 5
Jane Ryan School, CT

The Wanderings of Isis

Curse you Set for you killed my husband
And left me weary soon to give birth
Those who don't help me shall feel the wrath of the scorpion
And those who do shall be rewarded greatly

My child is left with you oh kind snake goddess
For I am off to Byblos to find my beloved husband
Hello oh great Queen I will happily care for your son
Leave me to my work I will value him greatly

You take him away, why? You foolish one
Your son was to be a god now he is just an ordinary boy
I will give him my blessings if you give me what is in the pillar
My husband's body I have finally found

I will hide him carefully where no one can find him
But now that Set has ripped him apart I have to find the fourteen pieces
The pieces I have gathered and brought to Anubis
To mummify the body for my husband shall lie in peace

Laura Knapp, Grade 6
Middlebrook School, CT

Dance vs. Gymnastics

Dancing is like a whole different world where you can do anything you want,
Gymnastics is like stretching out a blanket.

Dance is like jamming to your own beat,
Flipping on a gymnastics bar is like flying with the wind blowing in your face.

Dance is a way to express your feelings in a whole new way,
Strong cartwheels are like doing a dance spin.

Dancing is like another form of gymnastics.

I love to dance,
But I also love gymnastics!

Sarah Kuczmiec, Grade 5
Charlotte A Dunning Elementary School, MA

Missing Him Every Day!

you cry your tears you laugh your laughs but you never forget the past.
i miss him every day that passes by just too bad i couldn't say goodbye.
i watched it happen, i cried all day and i prayed that he was ok.
if only my wish could come true he would be here to say "i love you!"

Daniella Procopio, Grade 6
Memorial Boulevard Middle School, CT

Energy

E lectromagnet: travels through space without a medium.
N uclear: due to the splitting of the nuclei of atoms
E lectric: available by flow of an electrical charge through a conductor
R adiant: transferred by radiation
G ravitational: describes attraction between physical objects with mass or energy
Y ou need energy to move

Kailiyah Martinez and Sarah White, Grade 5
Leicester Memorial School, MA

Winter

Feels like fresh crisp air on my skin
Tastes like hot cocoa in my mouth
Looks like someone painted everything white
Smells like pine trees everywhere
Sounds like a deserted town

Neal Sidney Iannone, Grade 5
Church of the Redeemer Christian School, MD

Recycle

Why do people pollute the world?
Though it may save money or time
Why do people pollute the world?
It's getting covered in dirt and grime.

Why do people pollute the world?
The streets are laden with trash
Why not recycle things instead?
Put paper with paper and glass with glass.

So why not get a big green bin
To put all of your recyclables in
And if we recycle these objects quite often
Our cold, hard hearts will likely soften.

Aly Rabin, Grade 6
Bigelow Middle School, MA

The Magic Box

I lie in my bed anxiously awaiting him,
my imagination ready to burst.
I hear his strong footsteps as he gets closer and closer.

The door entering my room creaks
and my father's face appears.
I sit up as a huge smile widens onto my face,
because finally, finally he was here
to speak of the tale of
"The Magic Box."

"I was just about your age when I discovered
the magic box. I snuck up into my attic,
and found myself sitting in a wooden box
lined with red satin"

I can listen to these stories over one million times,
and never get tired of hearing them.
I lived for the nights of "The Magic Box."

Erin Condon, Grade 6
Swampscott Middle School, MA

A Dream

One day I had a dream
of me being in the boxcar championship
The air in my hair, the rattle of the wheels
The doorway of my life has just opened

Michael McKenzie, Grade 5
Wakefield Forest Elementary School, VA

Musical by the Leaves

Crunch, Crunch, Crunch
I walk around my front yard
While leaves are falling to the ground
And pat the ground like a feather
I hear the plopping of acorns
I see acorns and leaves all around me
It feels like a Musical with the leaves pattering down
And the crunching of the leaves under my feet
Pat, plop, crunch, plop crunch, pat
Then the wind starts to pick up
And now it sounds like
Swish, plop, pat, crunch
Swish, plop, pat, crunch
I start to run by making more sounds like
Crunch, plop, crunch, pat, swish
Then my mom calls me in for dinner
And I feel like a conductor leaving the stage
Proud and satisfied!

Megan Ryan, Grade 6
Wakefield Forest Elementary School, VA

Pesky Tests

Scritch Scratch
Erase
this test is hard as concrete
my brain is yelling, "Stop Hurting Me"
the silence pains my ears
I'd do anything to listen to another lesson
I gripped my pencil tightly; my mouth grew dry
this was a difficult problem, I knew I had to try
why do teachers torture us with
these tedious tests?
Blank answer spaces stare me in the face
eraser shavings tickle my nose
When I finally finished; hard work, now done
my test I handed in, not to the teacher
but in the paper shredder pile
my work that had been done
fell into the big machine
and I watched my paper shred
one piece by one!!!

Shelby Elwell, Grade 6
Litchfield Intermediate School, CT

Wild Cats

A lion is as strong as a hurricane
destroying a village.
A cheetah is as fast as a race car
speeding down the track.
A tiger is as ferocious as a shark
trying to catch its prey.
A jaguar is as sly as a thief
trying to rob a bank.

Jared Chin, Grade 5
Memorial-Spaulding Elementary School, MA

Summer
Summer
The bright sunny skies
Playing on grassy fields
I love the summer
Hot
Patrick Freeman, Grade 5
Sacred Heart School, MA

The Wonders of the Ocean
Colorful fish swimming by,
A big bunch of octopi.
Coral that looks like a robot there,
Fish finding homes in the coral lair.
Dolphins splashing up above,
Manatees showing some love.
In the trenches you will find,
Sunken ships that squids will bind.
Wonders of the ocean blue,
There are surprises for you!
Caila McHugh, Grade 4
Trinity Christian School, VA

The Pen
There once was a boy named Ken.
Who had a pretty pen.
Ken threw a fit
Because someone stole it.
So then Ken had to get a new pen.
Meghan Audibert, Grade 6
Captain Nathan Hale Middle School, CT

Sweet Sourpatch Kids Goodness
Yummy! It smells so sweet,
I can't wait 'til I eat.

It makes me feel good.
It makes me feel relaxed.

Squish, squish, squish,
It goes right through my teeth.

Soft, chewy, soft, chewy
I like that it is nice and gooey.

We look so sweet,
We're so colorful and flavorful!

Sweet sourpatch kids are so succulent,
They are also soothing.

Sourness makes me have
an interesting expression
The sugar tastes so amazing!
Liana Flores, Grade 6
City View School, MA

Cherry Blossoms
Cherry blossoms bloom
It is beautiful in spring
Graceful petals fly

When petals fall off
A yapping monkey comes by
To eat the petals
Faustinray Abogadie, Grade 6
Magnolia Elementary School, MD

Spring
Spring is a great time to take a glance,
to see things that dance and prance.
Fawns at dawn, moose and a goose.
Flowers bloom there is no doom.
Birds sing high in the sky.
Baby bunnies go passing by.
So slow down and notice
The wonderful nature around you.
Sophia Fagan, Grade 5
Chalk Hill School, CT

I Am
I am the sparkles in glitter
I am a lover of animals
I am the party in life
I am best friends
I am scruffy
I am Pats, Red Sox, Celtics
I am family
I am sports
I am a fish in a pool
I am a dolphin swimming in the ocean
I am fifth grade
I am fashion
I am pink
I am Kate Drew.
Katelyn Drew, Grade 5
Willis E Thorpe School, MA

Spring
Spring is my thing
The birds sing
And they bring hopes and dreams
Of happiness
The sun is yellow
It makes me feel so mellow
When I lay on my hammock
I never worry or panic
I gaze at the sky
With a twinkle in my eye
For I know that summer
Will soon be here.
Kyle Penniman, Grade 5
Forest Avenue Elementary School, MA

Civil War
The bloodiest war
The North and South fought Bull Run
The North won the war
John Hoffman, Grade 4
Waller Mill Fine Arts Magnet School, VA

Night Lights
The streets all empty,
The sidewalks filled.
Their traffic gone,
Their street lights stilled.

The ladies would smile,
Men tipped their hats.
Each person guessing who from who
And also this from that.

The trodden roads were cracked,
As they shined upon the street.
They lay coolly, and almost still
As if they were a sheet.

The silence coils around the city,
The people gasp at the sight.
As the moon shone yellow beams,
Gleaming with all night lights.
Jillian Schwartz, Grade 5
Lincoln Street School, MA

Night Falls
Bright sun,
Turns into gray sky,
Then night falls.
When night falls,
The sun rises.
When night falls,
The symphony of Chirping Birds,
Turns into the March of the Crickets
Until another dawn.
At dawn,
Night rises
And the sun falls.
Then that sweet pattern returns
Again.
Samuel Duffy, Grade 4
Hawley Elementary School, CT

Dr. Martin Luther King, Jr.
Dr. Martin Luther King, Jr.
Brave, strong
Fought, thought, taught
He wanted more freedom
Civil Rights Leader
Haley Pierce, Grade 4
Sacred Heart School, MA

Silence

It's hard to catch quiet in Colchester.
You might find silence,
but it doesn't stay too long.
You may spot it in the woods,
after a coyote howls at the moon,
but before the growling begins.
You might feel it right after sunset,
yet before the sun rises once more.
You might catch it when the soft wind blows,
but before the horrible storm arrives.
When you hear it, keep it close,
It is an important piece of your world.

Sarah Baseler, Grade 5
Jack Jackter Intermediate School, CT

Harriet Tubman

Harriet Tubman was born one day,
On the Brodas plantation near Chesapeake Bay.

Like Old Rit, her mother, and Ben, her dad,
As a hardworking slave, Harriet was very sad.

At plantations she was sent to, masters showed her hate,
Later back at Brodas's, she got hit with a weight.

Brodas wanted her to be sold, and he hadn't lied,
And then she was told one day that her master had died.

Harriet was tired of work on the plantation,
So she went up North to a free part of the nation.

After her escape, she wanted others to be free,
She brought many slaves north, and they were full of glee.

Next, Harriet Tubman joined the Civil War,
During that time, she became a scout, nurse, and more.

Later, she left the war and delivered food instead,
Then, in nineteen thirteen, she was sadly dead.

Douglas Salvati, Grade 6
Daniel L Joyce Middle School, MA

Dream

If you could dream
about anything
what would it be?
Would there be cats as teachers
and dogs as chefs?
If you could choose your dreams
how would it be?
How would the world be?
Would the world be made out of cheese?
I love my dreams.

Sam Rudman, Grade 4
South Area Solomon Schechter Day School, MA

The Water Fountain

How many more people
Before my turn
My mouth is so dry
It feels like a desert.

Slurping, splashing
Of other people's quenching
Is like an oasis in
The middle of the sand dunes

As I get closer to the oasis
I can almost taste it.
I finally survived and my thirst will be quenched.
When beep beep beep goes the fire alarm.

Alec Ablondi, Grade 6
Fuller Middle School, MA

He Lives

The cross is the symbol of our belief
Since Jesus died on it, we have great relief
By doing this He washed away our sin
So when we die we can go to Heaven

After His death they placed Him in a garden
In the background there was lots of sobbin'
Three days later, three women went to the tomb
To see their Savior in His burial room

When they got there He was gone
They thought enemies had taken Him before dawn
Two ran away to tell Jesus' friends at an inn
But the one who stayed behind was Mary Magdalene

She didn't know Jesus resurrected that day
He told her everything would be okay
She ran to the inn to tell Jesus' friends
It was simple, but amazing, she said, "He lives!"

Joshua Fernandez, Grade 5
Church of the Redeemer Christian School, MD

Strange Dream

Last night I had the strangest dream
It was so strange you wouldn't believe
I ate two tons of vanilla ice cream
I got a stomach ache that made me heave

Kyra Butler, Grade 4
Hebbville Elementary School, MD

Blue

Blue looks like the ocean with precious sparkles.
Blue sounds like the Blue Man Group acting their parts.
Blue smells like the salty water waving on the shore.
Blue tastes like the mint gum refreshing your mouth.
Blue feels like the winter breeze bashing on you.

Carlos Morales, Grade 4
Helen H Hansen Elementary School, MA

Rainbows

The big beautiful sun is shining
Right at the perfect timing
The rain is gone
Beautiful colors on my lawn
And rainbows shine like bells ringing.
Alyssa Andrade, Grade 4
Freetown Elementary School, MA

Meadow in the Spring

Green grass all around.
Wild daisies on the ground.
Birds chirping in trees.
All I feel is a very light breeze.
Chris Hale, Grade 4
Munger Hill Elementary School, MA

My Mouse

I have a pet mouse,
I made him a house,
He is very shy,
I wonder why,
He will make no sound,
When he is around,
OOPS! Look at his tail,
It got stuck in a pail,
He has his own boat,
And his boat can float,
His boat will take him to a far land,
With a language he cannot understand.
Gabrielle Miller, Grade 4
Crestwood Elementary School, VA

First Day of School

What if I have no friends?
What if my teacher is mean?
What if I make a huge mistake
and everybody laughs at me,
Even the teacher?
What will I wear?
Should I put my hair up
in a ponytail
or should I
keep it down?
What will I eat
for breakfast?
Will I be late
for the bus?
So much pressure!
I should calm down.
Anyway, I'm still
in my pajamas.
Oh no!
I need to get dressed!
Help!
Nina Rhyins, Grade 4
Hawley Elementary School, CT

The Sad Night

Once there was a bright fight
over the mountain peak
and
a little girl was watching it
through the thick mist.
'Twas almost dawn and the sunrise did not set
Mother's life was taken away by God.
Every day I pray to God I say "God why 'o why did
you take her life away?" I will keep praying until my life is taken away.
Alec Bleeker, Grade 5
Francis Asbury Elementary School, VA

The Lunch Line

Take a look at the clock, it's 11:40, which means it's time for lunch,
but I hear nothin' in my mouth goin' munch, munch, and, munch.

I have to wait for my meal in this mad long line,
I don't think I'll get to eat, 'cause it's already half past nine.

There's only what…10, 20 more people to go,
dang, I think I could probably catch the late night show.

I'm at the cash register paying with a 5 dollar bill,
I want to eat so bad I just can't stay still.

I'm finally at my seat and about to take a bite
but then they say "Clean up" while they turn out the lights.
Chase Balayo, Grade 6
Village School, MA

I Planted a Seed

I planted a seed and I'm waiting for it to grow,
I water and check the soil for the roots down below.

I planted a seed and I'm waiting for it to grow,
Later it will supply me with apples and a shady place to rest.

I planted a seed and I'm waiting for it to grow,
This patch of green will be an orchard of apple trees when I'm done.
Jill Greenberg, Grade 5
Davenport Ridge School, CT

Ski Music*

This ski area
The always noise of ca-chunk ca-chunk of the old rickety chairlift
The great sound of little kids yelling and whooping
Having a great time learning to ski
The orchestra of music coming from the lodge
The V-O-C-A-B-U-L-A-R-I-E-S of bang, smash, clank of my skis on the ground
The wind whooshing by my face
The thump of people landing on a jump
The rolling drums of racers hitting gates with
The always noise of ski music.
Ben Carroll, Grade 5
West Woods Upper Elementary School, CT
*Inspired by Arnold Adoff

A Very Special Lady

The days that I have mend into regular days,
The school days I have that are lost in the gaze.
The teacher I have so wonderful and kind,
The blessing I have to call her all mine.
The happiness I have to see her big smile,
The sadness I'll have when I leave her in a while,
The joy I have watching her walk in her big booties,
The smile I have when she calls us "Puhtooties"
The wonder I have to know she is real,
The thinking I have, "Does she know how I feel?"
The memories I have, even when we're far apart,
Oh! The feelings I have; she'll always be in my heart.

Lily Mitchell, Grade 4
Riderwood Elementary School, MD

Darkness

Darkness is a black pool of anything.
When you look into it you can make it
a picture of anything you want.
First, I am in a dark, dark galaxy full of imaginary creatures.
Then, I open my eyes and the creatures are gone,
but the galaxy is still there.
Darkness is good when you want to be alone.
All right, my eyes are closed again.
This time, I see people swimming
in the warm, nice, black, cool, galaxy of darkness.

Amanda Lillian Doherty, Grade 4
Helen H Hansen Elementary School, MA

Our Printer Is Bust

Our printer is bust and is covered in rust,
I think it's impossible to fix.
All the long day it prints out in gray,
Although I have tried all my tricks.
It's a stubborn mule and not at all cool
It's certainly going berserk.
The ink from the cartridge was drunk by a partridge
No wonder the thing will not work!

Timmy Greco, Grade 5
Mount Hope Christian School, MA

Night

What is night?
Night is silently staying alive.
A never-ending trail continuing.
Creeping around the sidewalks.
Staying still through every shiver.
Speaking softly in every direction.
Whistling in every tune,
Intimidating, yet so beautiful.
Crickets chirping so loud in the silence.
A renewing process, coming and going.
Watching everyone drift asleep in their beds
This is my night.

Everett Alcan, Grade 5
Jane Ryan School, CT

Spring Melody

Spring is here it's time to jump outside and play, play, play
Swinging and sliding and having fun all day long
Blossoms are blooming
Dragonflies are buzzing
Boys and girls are playing hand in hand
This spring day may never end

Sara Ackermann, Grade 5
Francis Asbury Elementary School, VA

Report Card

My report card is almost here,
The moment of judgment is almost near
I hope my grades are good, like A's and B's,
Not those bad ones like C's and D's.

My report card came out, I got it today,
I opened it up, and didn't know what to say.
I got B's and C's and even some D's,
All of my friends looked at me, and they started to tease.

I told my mom about my awful grades,
How I got B's and C's and not any A's.
She said I was grounded, for only one day,
To think about why I didn't get one A.

My grades are bad, but please, don't fear,
I will get a lot better grades next year.
With A's and B's and no homework that's late,
I won't get C's or D's next year, just wait!

Ryan Lannum, Grade 6
E W Thurston Middle School, MA

My Dream

I'm walking down the street
Ready for another day's work
People all around me
Fans are the ones I love to meet.
Signs all around me
All covered in lights
Big buildings everywhere
I love this great big city.
People in taxis ride by
Trying to make it on time
The theater waits for no one
I love this place, I'm just that kind of guy.
I see my costar down the way
I don't think he can see me.
He's just one among the crowd
But I wave, I can tell I'm on Broadway.
This is my dream
As an actor, my name in lights
I love the crowd, I live for the applause
As I take my final bow, in the spotlight's big bright gleam.

Chad Nowlan, Grade 5
Mapleshade Elementary School, MA

The Hotel

I wish I were a nice hotel
Inviting women and children to come in
Staying in a suite ordering room service
The men can also enjoy the lounge
And there will be no more homelessness
Caitlyn Guirgis, Grade 5
Trinity Christian School, VA

Sweet Music

I sit down and pick
up my guitar.
I strum and the sweet music
hits my ears at the speed of sound.
The more I play
the bigger calluses I get.
Different tunes give
me different emotions.
Just sitting down and playing
my guitar makes me happy.
As your hand gets tired
the more you try to learn
that new chord.
I strum and the sweet music
hits my ear at the speed of sound.
Noah Gopen, Grade 6
Swampscott Middle School, MA

Life After Death

One year to live
Many years
To lie dead

Leaving everyone
Who I've known

Alone

With no soul
Or memory
Just leaving
A part of their hearts

Dead
And empty
Kuba Babinski, Grade 6
Weston Middle School, CT

Shed Bed

There once was a bed
Who had to be fed
He was lumpy
He was grumpy
He lived in a shed.
Charles Brown, Grade 4
Grace Miller Elementary School, VA

Lilly the Mouse

There once was a mouse named Lilly.
She went on a road that was hilly.
She made a big thump,
As she hit the bump,
And that was the end of Lilly.
Emma Gould, Grade 6
Captain Nathan Hale Middle School, CT

Baseball

Do you like baseball?
I do. Whenever I hit the ball
It's like education.
You have to learn how to play it.
You sometimes might strike out.
But hey that's how we play hardball.
Garry Robinson, Grade 6
E Russell Hicks School, MD

Basketball

B ank the ball off the board
A iming for the hoop
S top the team from scoring
K ick the ground if you're behind
E nd the half with a big shot
T rot up and down the court
B ouncing the ball up and down
A sking for a pass
L aughing after you win
L eaving after the game
Matthew Bruce, Grade 4
Leicester Memorial School, MA

It's Raining

The ran sprinkles
Down from
The dull, grey sky.
The water
Dashes down
the mucky, cracked road
With puddles
Exploding when a car
Runs into it.
The water still dashes
And rushes.
The grass is wet,
The mud is squishy,
The wind blows,
The water falls
Off the trees
Like a hose on calm.
It drops on my head.
As I get off the bus
It stops raining.
Nicholas Genovese, Grade 4
Hawley Elementary School, CT

What Is Poetry?

What is poetry?
Is it something,
that comes from the soul?
From our hearts?
From the music of a brook?
From a nodding sunflower?
From a creepy crawly?
So if anyone can answer
please let me know!
Kaleigh Gordon-Ross, Grade 5
Litwin Elementary School, MA

Fun, Furry, Furballs

Kittens can keep people calm.
Kittens can jump.
Kittens can play.
Even with a string of hay.

Kittens are fun to cuddle with.
They are fluffy.
They are cute.
Also some are really mute.

Kittens have feelings like people.
They get happy.
They get mad.
They get sick.
They get sad.

Kittens can play.
Kittens can sleep.
Kittens can crawl.
Kittens can peep.
Brittney Diaz, Grade 6
City View School, MA

Stars

Stars are big and small
You can see them over the wall
They are so very bright
You can see them on the darkest night.
Jacqueline Lai, Grade 5
Sacred Heart School, MA

The Woods

The woods is a magical place,
With lots and lots of open space.
Hunters are the animals' foe.
A fox, a bird, a fish, a doe.
Ponds and rivers with water so clear,
Makes a good drink for foxes and deer.
Go to the woods and take a hike,
Or just go and ride your bike.
Skyler Beatty, Grade 4
Bowers School, CT

A Ride in the Woods

The vanilla ice cream snow
Sparkled in the tree branches.
Cloud-filled sky
Blue as the sea.
Dry leaves crunched under my horse's feet.
Tiny chirping birds danced overhead,
Wild dogs barking loudly,
We sped by them all.
Fragranced pine needles
Green as grass.
The smell of sap from the maple trees
Strong as love.
Newly refined, rust-colored reins ran through my fingers.
The freezing, bitter wind lashed my crimson cheeks.
My horse's gait
Smooth as a rocking chair.
Excitement overwhelmed me as we raced away from civilization.

Leandra Grasso, Grade 6
Two Rivers Magnet Middle School, CT

Summertime

Summertime is really hot.
I feel like a boiling pot.
It's so hot sometimes I cry.
Because I feel like I'm about to die.
Do you think summer is hot?

Ki-Jana Harris, Grade 6
Benjamin Syms Middle School, VA

How Wow?

How wow is a painting?
Depends how creative and colorful it is.

How wow is a new toy?
Depends how exciting and innovative it is.

How wow is a new *Harry Potter* book?
Depends how suspenseful and riveting it is.

How wow is a new sport?
Depends how energetic and full of life it is.

Oodles of things are just OK, but only some things are WOW!

Rachel Garner, Grade 4
Weston Intermediate School, CT

God

I love God because He is good.
I love Jesus because He died on the cross for our sins.
He arose on the third day.
And He takes care of us.
God is perfect.
He loves us.

Zoe Shepard, Grade 4
Agape Christian Academy, VA

Ever Wonder...

Did you ever wonder
where and when you would let go
or soar away?
What might the boundaries of heaven be?
The clouds or the beautiful stars?
If I let myself concentrate, really hard,
I can still hear his voice.
Grandpa is trying to send me a sign
that only my cousin and I can hear.
What if he can hear us, but we cannot hear him?
Sometimes I can feel the warmth and texture of his hands.
I can hear his laughter and happiness.
I picture his face clearly.
He is alive in heaven,
with his angel-like friends,
floating and flying cheerfully from cloud to cloud.
Grandpa is up there over my head, watching my every move.
He is sending me his love and joy.
When Grandpa died, the magic was lost,
but when we reunite, the magic will surely be
stronger than ever before.

Abby Ryan, Grade 6
Swampscott Middle School, MA

Snow!

Snow is like sugar
that falls on the trees
it sails to the ground through a cool soft breeze.
Snow is like flour
so soft to the touch
cookies will need it, but not too much.
Snow is like marshmallows
that float in a cup
but snow sails down, doesn't land with a tup.
Snow is the best thing for cold winter days
but when time is summer it leaves behind tears,
only to come back in the cold winter near.

Rachel Ward, Grade 6
Piccowaxen Middle School, MD

My Messy, Messy Room

I haven't cleaned my room for weeks,
And now my door has a squeak,
I wonder where it's coming from.
It's probably my old set of drums.
I have games, and toys, and balls, and socks.
Hey! I just found my blocks!
Underneath my bed is food.
My mom is in a grumpy mood.

Finally I cleaned my room,
On a hot summer day in May.
And every piece of junk,
Went in the back of my dad's trunk.

Taryn Gilbert, Grade 4
Grace Miller Elementary School, VA

The Fat Cat

There once was a cat named Pat.
He was really, really fat.
Once he ate a mouse.
Then he found a house.
And that was that.
Gary Long, Grade 4
Crestwood Elementary School, VA

Christmas Time!

The smell of eggnog
Lingers in the room.
The pine needles
Falling off the Christmas tree
Lay still on the floor.

I hear the crackling
Of someone taking off wrapping paper.
The soft sound of Christmas music
It is almost like the background music
In the room,

Seeing all the presents
Under the Christmas tree
Made me very excited
To open them.

When the time comes
I rip off the wrapping paper
And enjoy the moment!
Keila Cox, Grade 6
Swampscott Middle School, MA

A Winter Dream

I am on my snowmobile
Going into the trails
As you enter
The trails it's like
A magical world
Of white snow
The green trees
Are covered in white crystal
Snow like white blankets
When you're in the trails
You see many animals,
Footprints, in the snow
Like pathways
To see where they
Have gone.
A cool gust of wind blows
Against your face
Like frostbite
For a quick moment
A winter dream
Is upon your imagination.
Curtis Williamson, Grade 4
Hawley Elementary School, CT

The Bond*

Moonbeams dance across the walk; shadows prance across the floor;
You take my hand and gently lead me, dancing, dancing out the door.

We dance across the grass; we prance along the walk;
Dancing, laughing, singing, then finally sitting down to talk.

We talk about the dew-filled grass; we talk about the nighttime sky;
And we smile as you mention, the bond between you and I.

We smile as you mention it, how it's sturdy and it's strong;
We smile because we both know, it will last so long.

We watch our hands and feet turn red, as it begins to snow;
But we're keeping warm not by heat, but what we both know.
We finally standup, our faces cast a glow;
Not by the rising sun, but by what we both know.

We know it shall go on forever, no matter what fate may send
We know as long as we believe, our friendship will never end.
Rachel Kellner, Grade 6
Memorial School, MA
*Dedicated to Lin G. Forick

Friends

Friends
They are jewels in a mine, towering over the ignorant, dusty rocks.
They are also … meeting together to chat about their good grades on the spelling test,
making plans for recess, whispering secrets during lunch.
Ring! Ring! The jewels are calling each other after school,
clustering on the rug during lessons,
Buddies!
Always excited when a pen pal writes back,
begging mom for sleep overs on Friday and the weekend.
Pals
are two magnets attracting.
It is they who pamper a birthday buddy with bulky packages and good wishes.
But the *best* thing about friendship is…
the heart that will be heavy when your pet fish dies.
Embracing you when your leg is broken.

The best acquaintances you could have, overtaking all the riches in the world.
Friendship is as pure as fresh snow floating to the ground.
The sun drapes friends as if they were chosen.
But the most wonderful thing about friendship is…
the unique, unbreakable bond that connects…
Friends!!!
Julia Faxon, Grade 4
Hawley Elementary School, CT

A Book

B ring adventure from
O ver seas
O ver mountains, time, and space and
K nowing that if the battle ends survival took place in the living room
Carissa Coy, Grade 5
Trinity Christian School, VA

Soccer

Soccer is awesome
Soccer makes me feel happy
Soccer is my sport

Manvir Singh, Grade 5
Charlotte A Dunning Elementary School, MA

Slower

Everything was slower when this country started.
It took three months after the Pilgrims departed.
Americans made a living off of the land.
We cut down what we needed and let the rest stand.

Then came the Industrial Revolution.
That's what really started the pollution.
They left the farms, and factories grew.
The water and air pollution we threw.

We built more and more what the world wanted.
The oceans and forests became quite haunted.
The animals and plants disappeared.
Even the rain forests started to be cleared.

Dirt and pollution filled the air.
People lived on and didn't seem to care.
The earth has gotten hotter.
Animals die like the little sea otter.

The polar ice melts, and the oceans rise,
Soon the polar bear will say its good byes.
How does this end? I do not know.
Maybe we should go back to taking it slow.

Luke Brissette, Grade 6
Captain Nathan Hale Middle School, CT

Where Poetry Hides

Poetry hides
In the projects you never finish
Poetry hides
In dreams and things you never thought could happen
But did
Poetry hides
In those four inch binders
You can only seem to fill with two inches of stuff
Poetry hides
In those brussels sprouts that you push to the side of your plate
Hoping your parents won't notice
Poetry hides
In all those times you fell and got up
Without any tears
Poetry hides
In those hoodies you can never seem to zip
Poetry hides
In life
And love

Jaclynn Unangst, Grade 6
Weston Middle School, CT

My Musical

Come on everyone
Join the music fun

Having instruments and voices
You can make your own choices

Make sure everyone is near
Grab your listening ears

This is a poem from a 6th grade band kid
Playing the flute is exactly what I did

I love being in my school band
Will you give me and my classmates a hand?

Kari Rawls, Grade 6
Pocahontas Middle School, VA

Her Lock

Will not open
Will not budge
Wants her late for class.
Wants her to miss her bus
Will not give in until
She's on her last nerve.
With a hard yank it opens
Allowing her in until
The next day.

Renee Garrahan, Grade 6
Fuller Middle School, MA

Spring Has Sprung

Spring has sprung and it's finally here,
So go on out and give a loud cheer.
Flowers to be grown and yard work to be done,
Just the thought of it sounds like fun.
Jump rope, kickball, it's great exercise,
Just be careful of the beehives.
Whatever you do
Just remember spring is the season for you.

Kendra Curran, Grade 5
Plainfield Catholic School, CT

The Waters of the World

What do the oceans do at night?
Do they tease and tickle the bottoms of the boats?
Do they ripple away in fright from noisy ships?
Or are the beaches like blankets
That keep them cozy and warm?
Is it the noise from the boats
That keeps everyone awake?
Maybe it's just the ocean sleeping
When morning arrives,
The sea awakens from sleep.

Felix Seip, Grade 5
Booth Hill School, CT

Sweet Dreams

Morning dreams of meeting night
Stars take then sun away
Sea leaps onto the horizon
But do not be afraid
Cause night only lasts so long
Enjoy your sleep little child
Sun is tired moon is here to stay
Bailey Armstrong, Grade 6
River Bend Middle School, VA

Puppies

Puppies
Bounding about
Barking, gnawing, sleeping
Noisily frightening squirrels
Playful
Brendan Sweeney, Grade 5
Hebron Elementary School, CT

Mad

I'm so mad.
My face is red.
I almost flew out of my bed.
I even hit my brother Ted.
At breakfast, I yell and scream.
I am even blowing steam.
Because at school, I found out
We have extra HOMEWORK!
Josh Burgett, Grade 4
Waller Mill Fine Arts Magnet School, VA

The River

feel wind rush through hair
running through meadows to river
icky sticky mud
runs between my toes
cool calm water touches knees
while I hold up pants
then a school swims by
bringing fishy smells to noses
but grass smells stronger
can't wait until fall
when river's very pretty
colored leaves around
then comes cold winter
when I skate on chilly holes
the deep parts of river
then spring and summer
splashing, wading, watching
loving to watch minnows
I love my river
my river is my best
my river loves me.
Whitley Drinkard, Grade 4
Appomattox Elementary School, VA

Maryland

Mary's land; this old place is,
With its diamond blue waters,
And scarlet rich light.
Crabs float softly
against crashing, sinking waves.
As well as the constellations
whose stars are crystal clear.
I must go now
But there's so much we haven't explored.
Meet me next time.
I will wait.
Jessica Gaurin, Grade 4
Ridgeway Elementary School, MD

Peace

Peace is like a quiet river near
the waterfall.

Peace looks like a dove flying through
the air.

It sounds beautiful and
It can be laughter of children but,
Peace is always here.
Jose Tabora, Grade 4
St Augustine Cathedral School, CT

Lizzy

I am Lizzy
All cuddly and sweet,
And like other dogs
I love to eat meat.

Surrounding me
My sister lies,
While I look
At the peaceful skies.

I am Lizzy
All cuddly and sweet,
And like other dogs
I love to eat meat.
Rebecca Dryden, Grade 4
Crestwood Elementary School, VA

Spring Break

Children are sitting
On the front porch,
The rain falling on their faces
No canopy to keep them dry
Smiling faces everywhere.
Everybody gone for break,
Too happy, to think of school.
Shira Steinberg, Grade 5
Wakefield Forest Elementary School, VA

Horses

Running gracefully
Galloping through red flowers
Stopping to eat grass
Joseph Dainis, Grade 4
Leicester Memorial School, MA

City and Town

City
Busy, loud
Rushing, shopping, walking
Buses, skyscrapers, houses, cars
Sitting, driving, sleeping
Quiet, peaceful
Town
Connor Lavin, Grade 5
Leicester Memorial School, MA

A White Glow

Two beautiful swans,
Lounging in the waves
Paddling their feet,
Repeating the same steady
Rhythm.
The two swans
Float away
When purple, orange and red colors
Rage into a dark, depressing black.
But two lights
Gliding on the pond
Are the swans
Glowing their bright white.
The swans' white glow
And the night sky
Have their battle,
A war against a million soldiers.
White blocks the stars
Until they all fade away
And the swans rest until
The rise of the sun.
Kieran Lynch, Grade 4
Hawley Elementary School, CT

Between Friends

I'm between two friendships
But don't know what to do
I try to discuss it not fuss
Should I choose one or the other?

Who should I pick?
The one that's right handed or left
Hard headed or friendly
Powerful or not
Maybe they should both go away?
Jominique Eberhardt, Grade 6
Magnolia Elementary School, MD

Winter

Tiny white snowflakes fall from the clouds
Children shout really loud
Snow piling on my window sill
Wow, look at the heating bill!
Hot cocoa just for me
Lots of presents under the tree
Carolers on my front door step
Open the door so they won't get upset
Time for giving
What a wonderful time for living!

Marie Moncata, Grade 5
J F Kennedy Middle School, MA

Nature

The dewy grass twinkles
In the morning sun like the evening stars,
The birds chirp in the increasing heat
Of the golden rays of light,
The beautiful wood of deer and
Flowers fills the air with the crisp smell of nature.
The thick woods tower over the tiny armies
Of thorns and the red petaled roses.
The robins extend their wings and
Stretch before a long day of endless flight.
The babies stay near their mothers
To learn the ways of life before each daily sun sets.

Kaitlyn Sams, Grade 6
Trinity School, MD

Difference

I can make a difference by praying,
because when I pray, God listens to my prayers.
I can make a difference by asking God for forgiveness,
because if I ask for forgiveness, I will receive it.
I can make a difference by believing,
because if I believe in God, God will believe in me.
I can make a difference by being a follower of Jesus,
and because I am a follower of Jesus I can help you
become one too.

Kayleigh Kachmar, Grade 6
Andrew Lewis Middle School, VA

Our Friendship Is Gone

Our friendship is gone,
Like how the wind comes and goes,
It blew every scrap away,
Now what's left is a shriveled pulp,
Our friendship is gone
The sea gracefully and gradually washed it away,
Now what's left is just lonely sand,
Lonely…broken hearted…sand
And in its place it leaves a broken hearted, shriveled
Person

Sara Carnahan, Grade 4
Myersville Elementary School, MD

Waiting

As I'm writing a letter at camp
Whispering each word aloud to myself
Revising my work on punctuation
Checking to see if everything was perfect to go
As I place the letter into an envelope
Carefully attaching an etch to send to my parents back at home
Hoping they'll receive it and write back
I slip it into the camp's mailbox
Making sure it won't get damaged by the pouring rain
Praying that the letter won't become as soggy
As oatmeal when it gets wet
Then one day, as I came back from a hike
I find a letter on my pillowcase
Could it possibly be them?

Victoria Huynh, Grade 6
Wakefield Forest Elementary School, VA

Galaxies

Galaxies galaxies big and small
Planets planets sizes of a ball.

A star of gas in the center
A big planet of rock.

I would love to visit
But could never go.

I just love this galaxy
Our home galaxy the Milky Way.

Tim Thomas, Grade 4
Courthouse Road Elementary School, VA

Friends Forever

Best friends are till the end
that's why I say
we can play another day
for I have
work to do
things to be done
What's that you say?
Today is Saturday!
Gee wiz let's go play!

Olivia Mulrey, Grade 4
Helen H Hansen Elementary School, MA

Stars

Stars are like beautiful flowers
They shine like the morning sun
They brighten the night sky
With their luminous powers
And with the moon they have fun
Although we cannot see them at noon
We know they are always there
Hiding and watching us up in the midday air

Robert Cantor, Grade 6
Tyrrell Middle School, CT

Sadness

Sadness is a puzzle,
That no one can solve.
It makes your heart heavy,
Like a bucket full of mud.

Sadness fills your eyes,
With salty tears.
And makes the anger swell,
Building inside of you.

Sadness is black.
Like a bundle of bad luck.
It makes you sick inside.
And it blocks your mind.

Sadness is grieving.
Especially when a loved one is lost.
But it'll eventually pass,
If you don't look back.
Mara DaVoudi, Grade 6
E W Thurston Middle School, MA

Clouds

There are
all
kinds of
clouds.
There
are
cumulus
cirrus,
nimbus
and finally
stratus.
I love
them all.
They
bring
weather
like
snow,
rain,
hail,
and sleet.
Samantha Collette, Grade 4
Alice B Beal Elementary School, MA

Smile

I'm always smiling,
I can walk a mile and still smile.
My face always has a smile,
Even when I return from my mile.
I always like to smile.
Brad Carter, Grade 5
Grace Miller Elementary School, VA

Spring

Flowers blooming,
Children playing
Such a beautiful sight.
Birds singing,
Squirrels chattering
With a breeze in the sky.
What a start of a beautiful spring.
Danielle Dinneen, Grade 4
St Mary's Primary School, MA

Snow Day

There's a cycle of a snow day
That I think we'll all agree.
That the moment on TV
When it says that school is closed
All of your joy becomes exposed.
Like popcorn in a popper,
Your joy comes out in bursts
And personally I give a shout
And start to run about.
But then when it's over,
I let out a big sigh
And then it's time to go to bed
And kiss the fun goodbye.
Ethan Perkus, Grade 6
Reed Intermediate School, CT

Winter and Summer

Winter
Cold, harsh
Snowing, hailing, freezing
Snowballs, hot chocolate; pool, beach
Sweating, swimming, traveling
Hot, warm
Summer
McKenna Deal, Grade 6
Wakefield Forest Elementary School, VA

Top Lockers

As I hurry down the hall,
I open my locker, very tall.
The top swings open
Then papers fall
Like white snow falling down the wall
I shove them back
Knowing it will happen soon again.

I figured it out,
I now know how.
To control the monster that lives in there
All the papers from 180 days
Now into the trash they fall today,
But the memories will never fade away.
Julia Royce, Grade 6
Fuller Middle School, MA

The Sun

Shining bright above.
Glowing shiny here and there.
Shining everywhere.
Alex Chang, Grade 5
St Luke's School, CT

Summer Time

The sunny sky is shining.
bright and yellow.
the sound of pools
being filled to the tippity top
Danielle Rogers, Grade 6
Monelison Middle School, VA

Good Bye

My cute little cousin
Who's one year old
Lives in California
Where its not very cold

I love when I visit him
I love his cute face
The only thing I don't like
Is time flies like a race

I take one more look
Before I say bye
For I will always remember
His cute little eyes

I get in the car
And cry my last tear
All I can think of
Is see you next year
Lauren Sullivan, Grade 6
Swampscott Middle School, MA

A New York City Street

People walking
Down the street
New York minute
Lots of feet,
Walk down the street,
Taxi cabs
Beep, beep, beep,
Taxi cabs go down the street,
Lots of shops
Up and down the street
Where people buy shoes
So they can walk
Down the street too!
These are some things that you may find
On a New York City street!
Lisa Evans, Grade 4
St Mary's Primary School, MA

What Is Yellow?

Yellow is a star burning bright
In the dark night.
Like a sunflower, following the sun.
Yellow is the sun's rays,
Warm on your skin,
The soft fluffy mane
Of a lion sleeping happily.
Yellow is a sour lemon,
The juices squirting out.
It's the sweet taste of fresh honey.
Yellow is the sound of a cheetah
Racing through the forest.
Yellow is a hawk,
Calling, gliding, happily through the air.
Yellow is swift,
Like a falcon diving for its prey.
Yellow is the smoky smell of a raging fire,
The smell of a wet dog, shaking its fur.
Yellow is exciting,
Like a 3-year-old on Christmas Eve.
Yellow is happiness.

T.J. Simpson, Grade 5
St Luke's School, CT

School

School can be very fun.
Recess in the sun!
Playing, playing all day long!
Jumping rope and singing songs!
Learning math, English, and science
Being with partners or buddies
Together learning social studies!
Reading books and studying
Acing tests and having fun
During recess in the sun!

Anna Laskorski, Grade 5
Foxborough Regional Charter School, MA

Eating

I'll eat some pie,
I'll eat some cheese,
I'll eat some turkey,
Don't make me stop, please!!
If we run out, we'll get some more,
We'll fill the house right up to the door
(Ouch).
As the food goes up, we'll eat it down,
so what do you say, good old pal?
No? No? Is that what you say?
What if it's sugar, we'll have a par-tay!
So much sugar, so much sugar,
So much sugar the world will be better!
Still no you say,
Then we'll sell the food and be rich today!

Jack Schlater, Grade 4
King's Highway Elementary School, CT

Grandmother

O' grandmother
Even though you left the earth
Your love and soul is still inside of me
Guiding me through the patches when my family and I
Are not strong enough to hold our heads up high
And to give people the love
You had for us

Rachel Newell, Grade 4
Alice B Beal Elementary School, MA

Halloween Night

H orrified humans have nightmares
A corns litter the ground like sand grains in a desert
L eaping goblins scare children
L eaves cling to the trees like a climber clings to a mountainside
O wls hoot at the moon
W ind whispers in my ear like kids sharing a secret
E verything is real and yet fake
E yeballs stare at me like a warrior stares at his enemy
N ightfall lures trick or treaters out

N obody goes to bed without a scare
I love Halloween
G hosts and goblins grab goobers
H alloween has many perks
T ime to head home

Ryan O'Hagan, Grade 6
Madison Middle School, CT

Winter's Ending

Winter is ending all too soon.
The icicles are crying while they run down
The long pointy body and hit the ground.
Ski lifts close down and they wish that
They could take one more flight.
Hot chocolate sits on the cupboard shelf
Waiting for next year's winter in a sad mood.
Frostbite is taken away by the warm calm wind.
The snow melts away and says "Bye see you next year."
I wish that I could still hear the trees telling me
To come play with them in the light fluffy snow.
I wish winter were still here and never ended.

Zachary Regenstein, Grade 5
Weston Intermediate School, CT

The Bird of Beauty

Tweet, tweet, tweet!
The robin was the prettiest singer.
She won all the pageants and was the prettiest bird.
Her feathers were the gentlest.
Her beak perfectly shaped.
Tweet, tweet, tweet
The robin was the most graceful singer.

Dylan Hogge, Grade 6
Page Middle School, VA

Horus the Avenger

When Horus was a child he was hidden away. His father, Osiris, was killed because of a test
Then Horus was killed by the evil Set, and Isis called on Ra and he took pity on her dismay

The great Horus was saved but Set found out about Ra and his mystical ways
Now Set was angry and something bad was bound but a gathering came around

Now Horus would become one of the greatest kings, thanks to his mother Isis,
For going to the gathering and tricking Set, and telling everyone about him by turning into a bird with wings

Set, who did not get a chance to be king, gets mad and the fighting situation turns bad
There is no armor or a knight, but instead there are crocodiles in this fight

But at the end of it all, Horus entangles them in chains and his army wins
Set gets even angrier for his terrible flaw — another war begins

This is the last war between them both Set turns into a red hippo and Horus gets a solid gold boat
With a strike of a harpoon to Set's head, the gruesome evil beast is dead

This is how the story ends, Horus wins twice but the battles are not so nice
Set and his army are dead, Set wanted revenge but he died instead

Natalie Danielski, Grade 6
Middlebrook School, CT

The Treachery of Set

There once was a man a very envious man was he
jealous of his brother Osiris, the Pharaoh of Egypt.
Set, the man of envy, was the lord of desert associated
with everything evil. His brother Osiris was the god of resurrection.
Osiris left to go keep peace in other lands. He left the throne
in charge of his lovely wife Isis, the goddess of protection.
Evil Set was befriending his brother. 72 conspirators assist
him in throwing his innocent brother a marvelous party with gifts.
One of Osiris's magnificent gifts was a chest, which soon became his tomb.
It was a beautiful chest laced with gold and a scribes amazing artwork.
Osiris's twisted mind decided to try fitting *in* the chest. It fit him live a glove.
Set and his team nailed the chest shut while Osiris was in it.
Set's plotters and him poured lead into every crack poisoning
Osiris and crucifying him. Poor Osiris was flung into the Nile by Set's doing.
Unfortunate Osiris was washed up near the palace of Byblos. A king admires the
chest and brings it home. Osiris's tomb was carved into a pillar placed in the Great Hall.
As any other concerned wife would be Isis searched
and searched but never found poor Osiris.
As it ends Set took the throne while Osiris was left
To rot in the Great Hall. Set would do anything to cure his painful envy.

Christy Smith, Grade 6
Middlebrook School, CT

Blue

blue is when you fall into dazzling water filled with sweet little fish
blue is when you find a cup with trickling water bursting about in the steaming desert wasteland
blue comes up in your mind when your spine crumbles and stiffens when you accidentally jump
off a really dangerous cliff and you know that you are going to die
blue is when you lay down in the turtle green grass on a hot summer day
and stare up in the sky and doze off to the sound of birds

Daniel Aaron Savitz, Grade 5
Weston Intermediate School, CT

Electric Pages

A book is a television with a string
It's bookmark hanging over the electric pages.
Plugging into my mind for me to enjoy,
I watch it with my imagination.
I read it without a remote.

Benjamin Harrison, Grade 6
Benjamin Syms Middle School, VA

Misunderstood

I've been here, I've been there
I've never fully been in-tune with others
Always shoved into the clutter
This is where I belong
But maybe I was wrong
I was only trying to be me
Trying desperately.

Lost without fear which is worse
'Cause my adrenaline does not work
Want to run faster but I'm stuck
In a frozen trance
You don't seem to see you don't care — I'm invisible
I'm not even leaving a trail of dust behind
Nothing to be remembered by.

They came to apologize — I knew it was another lie
My alarm rang deep inside warning me they're cowards
Coming for me since I lost my power to pull me into their game
Parasite thriving off each other's lies
To make themselves feel better inside
But I would never hide
Even when weak I will always be me.

Maria Koutsouris, Grade 6
Bigelow Middle School, MA

Amanda

A mazing at school work
M y older and annoying sister
A person you might be able to have fun with
N ice to her friends, but not to me
D ummy is her favorite word to call me
A sister that is ok to have

Nick Cirino, Grade 5
Jane Ryan School, CT

Skiing

When I go skiing,
I go by the trees,
Flying down like a buzzing bee.
Zooming, zooming down the mountain I go,
All I can see are the trees and the snow.
When I go to ski,
I always feel glee.

Noah Freitas, Grade 5
Foxborough Regional Charter School, MA

I Am Water

I am water
Swimming through the salty sea
H_2O flowing through the world
Oceans high to the sky
Waves crashing down on me
Boats cruising through the water
Deep Blue waiting for stories to tell
Unpredictable like a deadly attack
Rain pummeling down on my skin
The pool's clear crystal blue water
Hot summer enjoyment in the water
Icy cold on cold days and refreshing on hot days
I am water.

Matt Dennis, Grade 5
Wakefield Forest Elementary School, VA

Summer

Blazing hot, summer days,
The nights just take my breath away.

A dip in the pool, a swim on the beach,
It keeps me occupied every day every week.

It's the end of summer, getting ready for school,
The days turn grayer, and the nights turn cool.

Nadina Moric, Grade 5
Clark Avenue Middle School, MA

Where Did the Dragons Go?

Where did the dragons go,
are they past fields where jeweled flowers grow?
Do they live in snowy mountain tops,
or in cities where traffic never stops?
Are they living in turquoise seas,
or are they at tropical islands in the summer breeze?
Dragons are rare as June snow,
but I believe in them forever so.

Erin Cooney, Grade 6
McCall Middle School, MA

Gymnastics

Rebounding from the ground
Twisting and flipping all around
Swinging and fling around the bars
The judges' score makes you a star
Then I start leaping on the beam
I fall off and start to scream
But the crowd's cheering keeps me alive
I get back up and start to take a dive
Flipping and spinning all around
My feet land perfectly on the ground
I think in my head that was perfectly done
The judges' faces looked very stunned
At the ending ceremony they said, "You have won!"

Emma Boland, Grade 5
Coleytown Elementary School, CT

Winter Days

The
Last leaf
Gripping
Onto the ole'
Sycamore tree
Being stubborn
The blizzard flakes
Fall onto my face
So quietly and
Peacefully
On those
Winter
Days

Mason DiCicco, Grade 4
Braeburn School, CT

The Swing

I sit here serene,
In my tire swing,
With my cares to the wind,
Not worrying about a thing.
Swinging to and fro,
With my toes to the sky,
Running with my dreams,
No boundaries apply.
The sun in my hair,
Grass in my toes,
Going to the place,
My imagination goes.
It's a magical place,
Where I often roam,
The place I like to call,
My home away from home.
So tied to a twisted rope,
Wrapped 'round my old oak tree,
Hangs my tire swing,
That gently cradles me.

Miranda Warzel, Grade 6
West Shore Middle School, CT

Poetry!

If poetry had a taste
It would taste like linguini
With a lobster and croissant at the side.
If poetry were touchable
It would feel smooth like a baby's skin.
Poetry would smell like
A valley full of flowers.
It would sound like a waterfall
Rushing to fill your body
With the sweet sound of poetry
And if poetry was a color,
It would be golden like my soul.

Alexander Chance, Grade 5
Clover Street School, CT

Super Bowl XXXVIII

Super Bowl thirty-eight
Was supposed to be a happy night
It was long and it was late
It ended in a fright

Patriots scored the first touchdown
That made me sad. I was so mad
Westbrook runs to get a first down
Eagles score no longer I am sad

Patriots fumble the ball
Eagles recover now I am happy
Wait! The ref made another bad call
Eagles intercepted. I am clapping

Patriots win, so sad
Super Bowl XXXVIII made me very mad.

Sean Donnelly, Grade 6
Immaculate Heart of Mary School, MD

Too Much Ice Cream

50 scoops of ice cream.
I can't see the top
They are scooping too much,
I just want to yell "STOP!"
Choco mocha cream —
cold vanilla bean
Scooping into
waffle cones
answering
customers
on the phone
"You're
scooping
too high"
I say,
but it's
too late.
P
L
O
P

John Baronas, Grade 5
Sacred Heart Elementary School, MA

Bubble Gum

BUBBLE
Colorful, floating
Popping, floating, explode
Large, round, gooey gob, colorful
Sticky, stretchy;, chewy
Chewable, tasty
GUM

Treyvon Manago, Grade 6
Benjamin Syms Middle School, VA

The Night

The black covers the earth
As mysterious as your dark eyes
A dark swirling cloud of black
Only a few sparkling stars shine
The moon watches over the earth
But light wins his battle
And dawn arises from his slumber.

Michael Amico, Grade 5
Trinity Christian School, VA

Cinderella

Cinderella dressed in blue
Went outside to cry in the dew
Miracle came
And led her to fame
Lost a slipper she did
The king didn't forbid
For the prince to marry who
Fit in that tiny shoe
Prime minister when to see
Just who that could be
Locked in her room
She could only assume
Help was on its way
For that very day
The prime minister found
Just the one who was bound
They got married to stay
For then anyway
And lived happily ever after.

Katherine Holley, Grade 5
Trinity Christian School, VA

Shooting Stars

Like little
light bulbs filled with ideas.
Swiggling
through the sky.

Exclaiming to all
their friends
"follow me!"

Make a wish
while they're sprinting.

Don't tell your wish,
it will come true.

The little stars are like Santa
giving presents.

Stars, stars give wishes.

Hayley Eicher, Grade 4
Braeburn School, CT

Baby Steps

He might be small but he has a big heart.
He is chocolate brown.
He takes small little puppy steps.
He is a two year old toy poodle.
He loves chasing after a little tennis ball.
He is as cheerful as the sun.
He loves seeing other dogs.
He is learning to swim in my aunt's pool.
He has a teddy bear that he curls up to when he sleeps.
He has doggy food breath, and I think he can use a breath mint.
He loves playing in the fluffy white snow.
He loves taking golf balls from my room.
He knows where his container of toys is.
His bark is more of a yelp.
He might be small but he has a big heart.

Jonathan Silverman, Grade 6
Charles E Smith Jewish Day School, MD

Me, Myself, and My Sister

She hits me every day
She's mean, rude, and gets away
She yells and yells and I cry and cry
I get in trouble and she cries with laughter
I always tell her to see me this afternoon
I feel bad when I see her mood
She scares all my friends
And all her friends too
It's weird to say it, but I love her so much
But it wouldn't hurt to leave for a day.

Cydney Dennis, Grade 6
Independence Middle School, VA

Do We See?

It's here
It's there
It's everywhere
This disease is so rare
You don't even sneeze
It is everywhere do we even see?

No, because we're too busy riding Mercedes
Our natural habitat is going away
Do we care?
No, because we're too busy buying gasoline
Animals dying and even our plants
This is sickening
Because it's spreading everywhere.

This disease is called Global Warming
Oil rich people say it's a lie and make an excuse
But Al Gore know more
And is trying to find a cure
If we had more Al Gores
This disease would spread no more.

Zainab Kargbo, Grade 6
Magnolia Elementary School, MD

The Big Race

We have all heard the saying life flies by
But what does that really mean
We all ponder that question
Life is a short time, it seems
Although it is still our unfortunate fate

Don't let life run past you
Because then you are losing your own race
I think of life as a journey
It starts out taking a long time
But then when you finish
You say, wow, that went fast.

Every second,
Every minute, and every day
We come closer to finishing our race
Sitting around doing nothing gets us nowhere
We only have one big race
Don't sprint
Run the speed that is good for you
And I am sure
You will win

Audrey Dannenbaum, Grade 6
Weston Middle School, CT

The Secret Pocket

The Secret Pocket holds all of my treasures
The Secret Pocket holds all of life's pleasures
The pleasures are mine,
They'll stay there for all time
And the love is carried within.

Olivia Plante, Grade 4
Mapleshade Elementary School, MA

Silly Sally

Silly Sally went to the skating rink with her sister Nell,
She sat down to put on her skates,
And when she got back up she fell!

She was so embarrassed she started to yell and scream,
But when she got back up again she seemed so very mean,
So she took her sister Nell home and started to pout,
And when her parents came home they finally worked it out.

Kristie Montooth, Grade 6
Benjamin Syms Middle School, VA

Winter Night

Night, night winter night
Can you feel a chill?
With the rapid winds swaying at night
Going past the bright moon
You feel peace and light going through you
Night, night winter night.

Jonathan Coleman, Grade 6
Magnolia Elementary School, MD

Summer Fun

S wimming happily in the pool
U nder the humid sun
M errily singing and dancing
M oment of fun
E very flower is blooming
R olling down the hill

F riends smiling and laughing
U nited with friends
N o more school

Amara Headley, Grade 5
Sacred Heart Elementary School, MA

Lava

It creeps slowly
Down the mountains
Burning all in its path

Not caring; plant or animal,
Rock or road, truck or toad
Coming to the sea

Steam hisses, waves crash
The sea and lava fight
And build a rocky island

Stephen Whelan, Grade 6
E W Thurston Middle School, MA

The Teddy Bear

Fuzzy and soft
Warm and cute
In the day we play
At night
He hugs me with a gentle grip
Keeping me warm

When I'm not here
He's alone and afraid
As I get older…
He gets lonelier
And he'll fade into a memory…

Brianna Long, Grade 4
Braeburn School, CT

Leaves

The leaves dancing,
singing, whistling and whizzing as they
fly through the air
Then rain falls
like a symphony of sounds
falling out of pace
leaves wet
falling off trees like bowling balls
the weight of rain on their backs.

Keanu Bordoni, Grade 6
Smith College Campus School, MA

Flowers

Glamorous, magenta flowers twirl in sand-colored pots,
Scents of caring colors grasp my sense of smell.
Sleek vehicles are like a blur of bumblebees,
Red dye — the color of a stop sign — winds around a boy's tee shirt.

Lavish standard poodles scramble along a flaming beach.
Swimsuits should not startle.
Memories of this birthplace are sweet and soft,
I can finally remember my life.

Steph Slimp, Grade 6
Wakefield Forest Elementary School, VA

As Cool as Blue

Blue is the ocean, waves and sea
Blue is the frost pecking at me like a pecking bird up high in the trees.
Blue is the eyes of a young girl at play
Blue is the sorrow of homework sitting in your lap
Blue is being relaxed and getting lost in the sky
Blue is watching blue birds fly by
Blue is at the beach watching the waves break.
Blue is the cool breeze whipping at my face
Blue is sadness of tears in a lake
Blue is the morning rise that keeps you awake
Blue is the face my family will make when I dye my hair blue
Blue is the smell of blueberry pie baking in the oven
Blue is the fish swimming in the sea always peering a glimpse at me
Blue is the wind whistling to a show tune

Emily Rocker, Grade 5
Willis E Thorpe School, MA

The Trojan War

It all began in 1250 B.C. when Paris captured Helen.
He did not shackle her in chains but rather used charms on poor Helen.

The Greeks readied their weapons with a terrible hate.
They sailed there in ships and marched up to Troy's gate.

There goes Achilles shot in the heel,
While Hector marched up to a ship's wooden keel.

For ten years it lasted. But suddenly a thought,
Good 'ole Odysseus, the supplies they brought.

Then immediately was formed a wooden horse,
With six men inside ready to kill with no remorse.

The unsuspecting Trojans brought the horse into the city,
As an offering to Athene to celebrate victory.

The spy let them out once inside the gate,
They pulled on its hinges while the army would wait.

They slaughtered the Trojans; they got back sweet Helen.
Many men died for Helen, sweet Helen.

Cameron Woo, Grade 5
Trinity Christian School, VA

Winter

Winter is cold, winter is white,
It smells like rain,
And is all I can think about.

Sometimes winter makes my teeth chatter,
I feel like I could run straight through it,
And not stop.

Winter's snow feels soft,
Like a flannel blanket,
The snow is as white,
As the clouds in the sky.

Now the snow is melting.
And I am getting bored,
Because winter is ending.

Kyle Barrow, Grade 4
Tilghman Elementary School, MD

Baseball

Baseball is a game full of shouts.
You just hate it when they say you're out.
You just get to the bench and sit down.
And you sit there getting booed by the crowd.

Then you go out and take first base.
And suddenly something hits you in the face.
It's a rotten tomato, and you start to get mad.
Then you get to the out field and start to feel sad.

Then there is a whack, and someone has hit.
Then you catch the ball right in your mitt.
The team calls you a hero, and you start to feel glad.
And then you forget how you once felt sad.

Patrick Favre, Grade 6
Captain Nathan Hale Middle School, CT

Delicious Sal's

If you're hungry come down to Delicious Sal's
It's 50% off for all my pals!
And we've got the most rare food in town
Our #1 special is squirrel's frown
From octopus ears
To snail tears
We've got tiger's tentacles
To bunny's spectacles
From monkey horns
To scales of unicorns
We have baked piranha
And some fried llama
Yes, if you're hungry
Come down to Delicious Sal's
It's 50% off for all my pals!

Dara Faleye, Grade 5
Mount Hope Christian School, MA

What We See in the Ocean

It's pretty how the waves
push and pull into each other
as though working together as a family
We see the fish swim and the
starfish that stick to the ocean floor
rocks smile at us as we swim by
We see the turtles swim with the
ocean current toward the shore
where they are going to lay their eggs
We see clown fish juggling pearls
in front of a school of fish
they clap and scream as he finishes his act
We swim on the back of dolphins
toward the Antarctica shore
where we swim with seals and penguins too
Where we get the next humpback
back home we think
it's amazing how all these different kind
of fish can live together under one big
wet roof it would be awesome if I
could live under the sea

Jazmine Goings, Grade 6
Monelison Middle School, VA

A Pure Gold Heart

Is your heart as pure as gold?
Just thinking about it makes you wonder…
Here is how you can tell:
Your heart is loving and caring.
With all your thoughts and dreams it beats with tenderness.
Courage,
And bravery.
That's how you know.
The heart is full.
A pure gold heart.

Allison Sevidal, Grade 5
St Joseph School-Fullerton, MD

Violet

Violet
Mysterious, but lovely,
Billowing, waving, growing
A mysterious flower with a passion for darkness
Lovely flower

Ruscha Banks, Grade 4
Grace Miller Elementary School, VA

Tribute to the American Soldiers

The soldiers were all together one day
They climbed the hill on their way
Over the hill they proceeded to fight
Everybody joined together with all their might
Though the odds were against them ten to one
They put all their strength together, and won

Shannon Stivaletta, Grade 6
E W Thurston Middle School, MA

Excited

If excited were a color
It would be yellow
As yellow as the sun

If excited were a taste
It would taste like lemons

If excited were a feeling
It would feel like rabbits fur

If excited were a smell
It would smell like
A cherry blossom air freshener

If excited were a sound
It would be as annoying
As a younger sibling screaming.

Ashley Goodacre, Grade 4
Naquag Elementary School, MA

Light of Black

I lie on my back on the
black, black sand.
The water is clear.
The sand shows many colors, it is
special special special.

The sunny, cloudless
summer day makes the water
sparkle sparkle sparkle.

I feel the heat of the sand.
I want to bury my feet
and jump in the water to
swim swim swim.

I hear the sound of rushing water,
the laughter of children,
the splashing in the
ocean ocean ocean.

How did it get here?
Will I ever go
back back back?

Omer Zeliger, Grade 5
Mill Pond School, MA

Snakes

They like to slither,
Some are poisonous,
They like to eat mice,
They have venom,
Some are different colors.

Asiah Williams, Grade 4
Grace Miller Elementary School, VA

The Island

Peaceful trees shiver
Hear nature's music play
Birds chirp lovely songs

Bailey Miller, Grade 4
Trinity Christian School, VA

The Zoo

There once was a man from Cebu
He dreamed he was in the zoo
He woke with a fright
In the middle of the night
To see that his dream had come true

Hannah Campos, Grade 4
Weston Intermediate School, CT

Dinner Time!

Yum!
Three little birds eat their way
Through a bright red forest of
Delectable winter berries
As a cool breeze weaves its
way throughout the branches
While the berries are helpless,
Unprotected eggs
Just waiting to be eaten.
Twittering with ecstasy,
The birds fly away like happy
Children with full bellies,
And a squirrel comes along to find
A bushel of
Nothingness.

Alice Langlois, Grade 5
Chestnut Hill Community School, MA

Jesus the Light of My World

Jesus the light of my world, my Savior.
Jesus the light of my world, my friend.
Jesus the light of my world, my teacher.

Jesus the light of my world, my guide.
Jesus the light of my world, my helper.
Jesus the light of my world, my Lord.

Jesus the light of my world, my light.
Jesus the light of my world, my God.
Jesus the light of my world, my Savior.

Michael Beckman, Grade 5
Little Flower School, MD

Spring

Spring fun and dandy
Spring awesome and exciting
Spring so inviting

Katelin Hall, Grade 5
Marley Elementary School, MD

St. Patrick's Day

There once was a leprechaun.
He liked to mow the lawn.
He dressed in green.
Was shaped like a bean,
I liked that leprechaun.

Rachel Lee, Grade 4
Trinity Christian School, VA

Friends

We like to talk about boys.
We love to play with our toys.
We're great at making noise.
We always cheer!
We have no fear!
And although we may fight
It turns out just right.
We call each other all the time.
And this is our rhyme.

Nicole Berry, Grade 4
Grace Miller Elementary School, VA

Jerusalem

I wish I were Jerusalem
The golden city.
Enlightening.
Bringing
Harmony to all religions.
Teaching compassion,
Empathy,
And
Kindness.
Peace.

Shanni Alon, Grade 6
Scotts Ridge Middle School, CT

The Sleeper

Never came
to visit with my
grandma.
He forever
sleeps
in his
grave.
Slipped away
before I
was born.
Only pictures
can help us
see.
I'll never
know him.
I'll
miss him

Emily Lewis, Grade 5
Coleytown Elementary School, CT

Ode to My Family
Thank you, mom,
For giving me birth.
Thank you, dad,
For telling me how to be a man.
Thanks to my brother
For being good and playing with me.
Thanks to my grandma
For helping make socks.
Thanks to my cousin
For cheering me up.

Omar Lira, Grade 4
C Hunter Ritchie Elementary School, VA

Big King Gorilla
Swinging through the jungle
Hiding in the treetops
Eating bananas and berries
Playing wrestle high
Watching out for hunters
Thinking about bananas
Dreaming about being ruler

Olivia Settle, Grade 4
C Hunter Ritchie Elementary School, VA

Soccer/Crowd
Soccer
Fun, awesome
Running, kicking, saving
Friends, coach, fans, cheering
Jumping, yelling, waving
Cool, freaky
Crowd

Nick Blevins, Grade 4
C Hunter Ritchie Elementary School, VA

My Team
In 2004, my team went through an incredible season.
They caught, ran, and scored, for a specific reason.
They did an amazing thing, I say.
They're in the playoffs, hip-hip hooray!
They fought their way through, all the way to the end.
They must have good offense, and they must defend.
They were doing well against the Eagles.
They were going to be pretty regal.
They fought their way, 'til the game was done.
The Patriots had finally won!

Barrett Fitzgerald, Grade 5
Weston Intermediate School, CT

Lighthouse
I am a lighthouse with glowing light shining from my head.
I always stand up and I never go to bed.
Here I stand on a pile of rocks
helping boats to navigate around the clock.

Jacob Ayers, Grade 6
Ashford School, CT

The Windsor Library
The Windsor Public Library is the place to be
If you don't believe me, go and see!

You'll find shelves of books full of pictures
Just take a look

The Windsor Public Library is the place to be
If you don't believe me, go and see!

There are comfortable chairs so you can sit and read
Thousands of adventures and mysteries

The Windsor Public Library is the place to be
If you don't believe me, go and see!

All the books in the series is what you'll find
Your favorite ones of every kind

The Windsor Public Library is the place to be
If you don't believe me, go and see!

Gabriella Levius, Grade 5
Clover Street School, CT

I Fell
I fell in a hole.
Down, down, I go,
I fell in a hole.
It felt like it never would end.
I knew it would never end and still it…
With my last breath I heard my friend say,
"I guess you were wrong."

Ryan Monteiro, Grade 5
Forest Avenue Elementary School, MA

Day of Love
Anyone can do one thing and that is being very caring,
giving to the moneyless living,
helping whom who falls to the ground,
saying sorry to what was done wrong,
but the most important thing is doing all those things
on the day of love.

Carrie Gilboy, Grade 5
Blacksburg New School, VA

Green
Green is the grass and leaves in the summer.
Green is the smell of hot green tea boiling in the kettle.
Green is peace, calmness, and relaxation.
Green is the sound of leaves blowing in the wind.
Green is the smell of fresh grass poking out of the snow.
Green is my room with green over the walls.
Green is the sourness of a bright green apple.
Green is the park and the baseball field just waiting for a game.

Jenna Glazier, Grade 5
Willis E Thorpe School, MA

Spider Man

Spider
Round, black
Makes webs, climbs walls, catches insects
Small, hairy, hero, cool
Catches thieves, saves people, defeats villains
Wears costumes, a brown haired geek
Man

Howard Herring, Grade 6
Benjamin Syms Middle School, VA

New Jersey Beaches

Look at the land by the sea
and the sand that you can see.
There is the boardwalk where you can
walk and talk. Buy some fries; they are so good!
Make sure you wear shoes on the wood…
Now you see how good beaches are
So find a beach not far from you!

Matthew Linz, Grade 5
St Joseph School-Fullerton, MD

Heaven

Heaven is a place where God and souls live on and on.
Where angels watch children play and nuns pray.
Some don't believe but I do and I always will.
When the wind whistles I can hear angels in Heaven singing.
Please believe or there will be no more praying and Heaven.

Kennedy Branco, Grade 6
Edmond P Talbot Middle School, MA

Volcano

Massive sounds coming from the ground.
Lava stirring into ash,
While ash becomes rain.
Smoke rising from above, touching the heavens,
Feeling the earth's surface.
Nothing can stop this, nothing at all,
Nothing can cure a volcano's temper.
Eruptions getting louder and louder,
Ash covering all nature's beauty,
Lava oozing down the edge of the volcano,
And the smoke cloaking the bright blue sky to solid gray.
The mighty volcano.

Francesca Falvo, Grade 5
Wakefield Forest Elementary School, VA

The Clock

The clock in the classroom
goes tick tock tick tock
I feel badly for you
having to keep time
with hands
that you can't control.
I wish you could be free.

Kyle Barrett, Grade 5
Charlotte A Dunning Elementary School, MA

Ten Little Geckos

Ten little geckos heard a dime;
One got greedy, then there were nine.
Nine little geckos went on a date;
One became a big shot, then there were eight.
Eight little geckos had to be driven;
One fell out the window, then there were seven.
Seven little geckos were doing crazy tricks,
One broke his leg, then there were six.
Six little geckos went for a dive,
One drowned in the river, then there were five.
Five little geckos found an oar,
One whacked another, then there were four.
Four little geckos broke their knees,
One needed the medics, then there were three.
Three little geckos got stuck in goo,
One ate himself, then there were two.
Two little geckos had a bun,
One was allergic, then there was one.
One little gecko went for a run,
He found the sewer, and then there were none.

Patrick DesRocher, Grade 5
Ashford School, CT

Earth's Nature

I wish the Earth's Nature would be nice and clean.
When will the Earth's last pollution ever be seen?
With bright and clear days,
And sunshine rains,
And rainbows shining above.

With fish in seas,
Swimming happily, eating weeds.
With natural resources saved
And no animals caged
So they would have free land again.

With lots of snow in winter,
New life in spring,
A hot and wet summer,
And also colorful falls.
With all my wishes, Earth would be the cleanest planet of ALL!!

Gemma Hyeon, Grade 4
St Rose School, CT

Rolling Waves

Rolling waves are here and there,
they roll all over town,
they roll during thunderstorms,
and tornadoes, too
People and animals topple over,
They roll like
wheels on a bike,
Look out for rolling waves!

Jared Finn, Grade 4
South Area Solomon Schechter Day School, MA

Hello Winter, Goodbye Summer

Hello winter, goodbye summer.
Hello to grass with white on top,
Goodbye to green grass you have to mow.
Hello to hot chocolate, as hot as a stove,
Goodbye to ice-cold lemonade.
Hello to fast sledding,
Goodbye to slides as fast as a car.
Hello to skiing and snowboarding,
Goodbye to swimming in blue, clear water.
Hello winter, goodbye summer.

Riley Shay, Grade 4
Long Meadow Elementary School, CT

Crepsley

Crepsley
He wasn't *my* cat — he was *a* cat,
He wasn't *my* brother — he was *a* brother,
He wasn't *my* friend — he was my *best* friend,
Orange and white were never so bright
Till you saw them on Crepsley,
Dull green eyes watching, waiting like spies,
Right on his face — on Crepsley,
His tail
It flowed, twisted and glowed,
Right on his body — on Crepsley,
His paws, oh, his paws, his cute little paws,
They carried, they carried him — Crepsley,
His mouth, oh his mouth, his tiny little mouth,
It ate, it ate for him — Crepsley,
And his nose, oh, his nose, his pink little nose,
Why is smelled, it smelled for him — Crepsley,
My soul, my heart — 'til Death did us part,
Not mine, but his own —
Crepsley

Nick Gilfor, Grade 6
Memorial School, MA

Nathan B. Is Me

I sprang from the earth
Strands of dark chocolate flow out of my melon
When chocolate is scarce there is gold on the front
Six grains of sand on the bridge of my sniffer
Make me come alive
Then suddenly
The clouds and the sky mix together
They become two spheres
They are my peepers
My brain thinks of funny things
The world begins to laugh
My entire complexion is taller
Than the tallest tree
And when you put it together
You get me Nathan B.

Nathan Buchwald, Grade 5
John Ward Elementary School, MA

Waking Up in the Morning

Can't do it just can't do it
Back is hurting
Arms are aching
And the blankets of darkness cover light
Morning takes over night
The black pools of darkness disappear
My eyelids are like clouds blocking my view
And when I wake up in the morning
My dreams
Float
Far

Far

Away

Lost forever

Michael Burnett, Grade 4
Braeburn School, CT

Springtime

Springtime is a time to see bees going flower to flower
I love to hear the birds singing a lot of songs
It's a wonderful day so come and play

You can see a lot of butterflies playing in the sky
I love to hear children playing in the playground
I can see a lot of people running in the grass
I can see the green green grass

I lie down in the grass and look at the clouds
The clouds are so
white
white
white

Kaylyn Greer, Grade 5
Francis Asbury Elementary School, VA

Saint Cecilia

My virtue is love
I sang with my heart and voice.
Two men became believers
When my guardian angle appeared.
I'm the Patroness of Music,
Lots of people sing like me.
I died three days after being struck by a sword.
My body did not decay.
My feast day is the 22nd of November.
 I am Saint Cecilia.

Kaitlyn Hurley, Grade 4
Angelus Academy, VA

Snowflakes

From the moonlit sky
Small white snowflakes are falling
Onto the tree tops

Kristen Kelly, Grade 4
C Hunter Ritchie Elementary School, VA

Snow

Fluffy covering
Lightly drifting from the sky
Falling down my back

Winter wonderland
Always making snow angels
Covering the earth

Making me chilly
Made of crystallized water
Floating from the sky

Canceling school
Sledding quickly down a hill
Drinking hot chocolate

Samantha Meyer, Grade 5
Jane Ryan School, CT

I Am the Floor

I am the floor
dirty and more.
People walk on me,
stomp on me,
and run on me.
I do not like it one bit.
This is why
I would much rather
be a door knob
Can't you see?
So please,
do not spit on me!

Kiah Hottle, Grade 4
Crestwood Elementary School, VA

Someone Special

Someone special that's my daddy
He'll always be there for me

And when he hugs me tight
he hugs me comfortably

I know he's very caring
and very kind too

He always makes me laugh
and he feels just like goo!

He works his hardest to take care of me
and always tries his best,

I know he loves me very much
he's better than the rest.

I love you daddy!

Ashley Lee, Grade 5
Tyler Heights Elementary School, MD

Werewolf

Werewolf, lurks within, the night.
The full moon's bright glow, casts shadows in the darkness, he runs.
Peering at, the intense light of the moon, seeping through trees.
Iron claws, razor sharp, ready to kill any moving creature.
Yellow rotten teeth clamp together, in a tight bond.
Wet dog stench streams through the air.
Silent, hungry, waiting to strike, the monstrous creature is frozen solid.
Then, when the time is right, he'll move, swift, waiting, waiting to make his move,
When the lights go out.

Justin Whitham, Grade 6
West Shore Middle School, CT

The Bad Bat

There was a lonely mansion in the woods that I had bought,
but in that home that I did buy a lesson would be taught.
For when I went to the basement, a dark and scary cave,
A bat came out and said "PURE DARKNESS IS WHAT I CRAVE!"
Then he was let loose in the middle of the night,
I suddenly knew I was in for a fight.
I knew I had to catch him, and so I had to plea,
to the vet "Animal Doctor, I need a dog net now PLEASE!"
A net was what I obtained,
but the animal had a smart brain!
He ran and flew, far away from the city zoo,
and then I had an idea!
"Hey, SCUM!" said I, looking straight in its eyes,
"You're very untrustworthy!
But if you catch me, you will prove that you are very worthy!"
I ran really fast, shivering 'cause of a draft,
then I led him straight into the zoo.
"Oh, mighty beast, you've proved your might,
so sit in this throne, and I'll serve without a fight!"
As he stepped into the throne, which really was the net,
I threw him in the monkey cage, and said "Thank goodness for the vet!"

Arturo McGill, Grade 6
Governor Thomas Johnson Middle School, MD

Playful Pink

Pink is cold cheeks, lip gloss, and Valentine's Day —
Pink feels how you treat your crush in a special way!
Pink is the tulip, lily, and rose flower.
When it is spring, pink has the power!
Pink is a new fleece jacket —
And even a girl's tennis racket!
Pink is a kind of color that shows someone smiled!
Pink is a perfect little bright child.
Pink is a butterfly and bubblegum ice cream that someone's eating.
Pink in the spring is the dawn's greeting!
Pink is ballet shoes, and pink is a heart,
And pink lemonade — with a matching sweet tart!
Pink is the shorts of the children who are playing —
Their swinging movements like trees swaying.
As you can see, pink makes up many a thing,
And if you ask little girls they will shout, "Pink is King!"

Shaylah Renzullo, Grade 5
Har-Bur Middle School, CT

Winter

Winter is one of my favorite seasons!
I have plenty of reasons.
For one, I love to go skiing.
It's thrilling for my entire being!
It is very beautiful to watch the snow fall.
The feeling I get is really peaceful.
After the snow has fallen on the land,
all is covered with a white, fluffy blanket.
It is so sparkly and grand.
Some other great activities are
snowball fighting, sledding, snowman making,
sipping hot-cocoa and homemade cookies for baking.
Winter is not only cold but cool.
Especially if it snows hard and we don't have school!

Cali Robin Schenkel, Grade 5
Toquam Magnet School, CT

Horses

H orses are beautiful
O beying your rules
R unning free and fast.
S taying in the field
E ager to run.
S leeping on the fuzzy hay in the barn.

Aly Sugrue, Grade 5
Charlotte A Dunning Elementary School, MA

Cats and Dogs

Cats
Soft, cute
Snoozing, pouncing, purring
Tabby, Tortoiseshell, German shepherd, Collie
Running, hunting, barking
Energetic, playful
Dogs

Elliott Brooks, Grade 5
Wakefield Forest Elementary School, VA

Spring Is Here

No more winter coats
Caterpillars are creeping
Goodbye winter bite

Amanda Egginson, Grade 4
Charlotte A Dunning Elementary School, MA

Yellow

Yellow is a bright sun
Yellow is a tasty banana
Yellow is a piece of paper
Yellow is a greeting card
Yellow is a new shirt
Yellow is a pair of pants
Yellow is a fancy hat
Yellow is an expensive necklace

Olivia Murray, Grade 4
C Hunter Ritchie Elementary School, VA

Saturn

Oh Saturn with your rings
They look better than some kings
Oh Saturn if you had any mothers
they must have had some colors
Oh Saturn with your beauty
you are such a cutie

Benjamin Tarnacki, Grade 4
Courthouse Road Elementary School, VA

The People Who Serve Our Country

S erve is what they do
O ur men and women serve our country
L oyalty is their middle name
D uty to our country is first
I nspiring others to do good
E ach one of them is often in danger
R eady to serve anyway
S oldiers will always protect our country

Ryan Gigarjian, Grade 4
Helen H Hansen Elementary School, MA

Jerry

When you left
The Earth for good
I cried
Each and every day
But thoughts of you now
Are happy
And I don't frown
But I wish you were with me today

Sarah Morgan, Grade 5
Linscott-Rumford Elementary School, MA

The Turtle

I am the turtle
My feet wander slow as a snail
My body swims like a boy in a swim meet
My teeth snap like a family eating
I am the turtle
My shell is like a comfortable bed
My tail is as short as a minnow
My head looks for food like a mouse in a house
I am the turtle

Mac Ukrop, Grade 4
St Christopher's School, VA

The Leopard

One day a leopard shed a great tear.
She said "My life is quite drear."
"I'm covered with lots,
Of these big ugly spots
And stripes are the fashion this year
Oh dear."

Alyssa Papadakis, Grade 4
Courthouse Road Elementary School, VA

My Seventeen Year Old Dog

Oh how I love my dog
But sometimes she's in a fog
And all she does is sleep.
She never plays or leaps.
She's always looking for a drink
And never misses a blink.
When I get her to play
All she does is lay.
Even though she's lazy all day,
I love my dog anyway!

Amanda Harlow, Grade 4
Grace Miller Elementary School, VA

Isabel

Isabel
Cute, cuddly
Running, barking, playing
Fur, teeth, claws, muscles, ears
Looking, lunging, chasing
Funny, furry
Happy!

Anthony Morabito, Grade 6
St Bartholomew School, MD

What Is a Friend?

Stands up for you
Brave and determined
Caring and helpful
Always there for you
Smile on their face
Strong and immune to insults
Creative and colorful
Stomps off bullies
Hangs out with you
Always by your side
This is my friend!

Nikhil Ramachandran, Grade 5
Jane Ryan School, CT

The Rain

It was raining,
thundering, lighting
the power went off
the house was cold
drip!
drop!
the rain was slowing down
boom!
it thundered once again
clouds clearing up
sun coming out
temperature changing
Finally it stopped!

Lakeisha Graves, Grade 6
Monelison Middle School, VA

Emotions

There are many emotions,
Joyful, sad, mad, terrified,
Silly, jealousy, love, etc.
There are many emotions.
Everyone has one of these emotions.
But everyone has their own emotions.

Vivette Caraballo, Grade 5
Clark Avenue Middle School, MA

Happy Fish

Streaming waterfall
Creates swirling pond where
Fish swim happily

Hayley Burzenski, Grade 6
Our Lady of Mercy School, CT

Unexpected

Lots of people crowd the place,
Trying just to see my face
They're shouting only one word.

My mouth is gaping with surprise
Tears are forming in my eyes.
Trying to push through.

As I walk around and about,
Everybody starts to shout,
"Happy Birthday!"

Now, I finally understand
What a lucky girl I am,
To have such good friends.

Lan Ngo, Grade 6
E W Thurston Middle School, MA

The Dream

I'm soaring over the hills.
I'm in Antarctica having the chills.

I can run faster than light.
I can jump to an unknown height.

I'm floating in space.
I'm in a cyber chase.

I'm seeing plants walk.
I'm hearing dogs talk.

I listen while mermaids sing.
I can fly with a single wing.

As bizarre as it may seem.
It is only a dream.

Joshua Geronimo, Grade 6
St Joseph School-Fullerton, MD

Supercar

S upercar
P retty
O utstanding
R oadster
T aillights are different than other cars
S hiny

C orvette
A ston Martin
R umbling roaring engines
S leek

Jack Bassett, Grade 5
St Christopher's School, VA

Silent Movement

I am beautiful
    and graceful
        with long painted wings.
They take me higher and higher
in the sky.
    I am attracted
        to bright colors
and I stop on many flowers
    as I sip the sweet nectar.
My fluttering wings
    that are quiet but fast
allow me to glide
    in the crisp clean air.
I soar through the air
    like a girl on trapeze.
My wings gently flapping
    up and down.
A spot on one side
    a spot on the other
        I'm a symmetrical beauty.

What am I?

Elizabeth Gallary, Grade 5
Mill Pond School, MA

In the Courtyard

I see a tiny orange goldfish
Gliding through the pond
The rays of light make the pond sparkle.

Richie Fruchterman, Grade 5
Wakefield Forest Elementary School, VA

Fish

Bright and shiny fish
Jumping in the lake
Small ones, big ones
Red ones, blue ones
Many kinds of fish in the lake.

Devin Keane, Grade 4
Freetown Elementary School, MA

Radiant Red

The scent of coconut drifts through the air when red is around.
Like birds singing and cats purring, red is an exquisite sound!
When you touch worn velvet, think of red.
While tasting red strawberries, there is nothing to dread.
Red is a schoolhouse,
And the pants of Mickey Mouse.
Red is the waddle of a chicken and a gobbler,
And my mother's delicious cherry cobbler.
Red is not just beautiful to see,
But it's a safety signal for you and me!
The first color of the rainbow is red.
Red is the hat I put on my head.
Red is also pink's mother!
Red is a color like no other!

Maddy Florian, Grade 5
Har-Bur Middle School, CT

The Sky

The sky is crunched between my teeth
A big thunder hops into the sky
The yellow stripes are pushing through their jail bars
But they will never get out
The jail cops are sweating so much
Making puddles on the ground
Everybody is scared
Beware for the sky is after you!

Krista Nayden, Grade 4
Weston Intermediate School, CT

The Last Play

The quarterback snaps the slippery ball
And drops back to pass
The receivers run out onto the field
Like flies looking for trash
The sweaty linemen push their men back, back, back
The quarterback throws the ball to a receiver with great force
And the receiver catches it with soft hands
He runs down the field
50
40
30
20
10
Touchdown!

Noel Plourde, Grade 6
E W Thurston Middle School, MA

Pizza

Pepperoni
Yummy cheese
Eating and chewing
Gaze at the goodness
Pizza

Colin Gilchrist, Grade 4
C Hunter Ritchie Elementary School, VA

Cardboard Box

I am a pirate,
I'll make you walk the plank,
Or sink your ship with my canon tank,
That is, in my cardboard box.

I am an astronaut,
flying through space in my spaceship,
impressing aliens with my dip and flip,
That is, in my cardboard box.

I'm sure you're thinking,
it's not true, a box, taking you so many places,
no way, it can't happen, no, not ever!

Well I'm here to say that a cardboard box,
a turn of your ship or a pull of a lever,
that kind of magic will last forever!

Tatiana Gilchrist, Grade 4
Fawn Hollow Elementary School, CT

Shadow Dancer

Muscles tensed and nostrils flaring
Flanks heaving and limbs flailing
Hoofs thunder across the prairie
Like a flash of thunder
you leap across the leagues
"Why must you charge on across the land
cantering and cantering on?" I ask.
"To stop is to submit, so I gallop and gallop on."

Jack Jiranek, Grade 5
St Christopher's School, VA

Waterfall

Trees have made way
For the stampede
A stampede of liquid mist
A stampede of rushing water

Feeling frigid
Against my skin

Damp villages of moss
Make their homes
On muddy brown rocks

The trees have made way
For something magical

The trees have made way
For natural beauty

The trees have made way
For a
Waterfall

Alissa Piatelli, Grade 5
St Mary's Primary School, MA

My Brother

You are a sunny day
that can turn into a thunderstorm
and a hurricane in Florida
You are a yellow Ferrari
with black racing stripes
and a small road in the woods
You are a falcon flying
over a mountain range
and a connoisseur of cheese
You are a gentle breeze
In a meadow of grass
and the sigh of the wind
You are the movies:
The Fantastic Four, X-Men
and *The Incredibles*
You are a yew tree
but can turn into a Whomping Willow
and a maple all at once
You are a pirate on the high seas
of the Atlantic Ocean
You are what you want to be

Greg Shindel, Grade 5
St Luke's School, CT

Ladybugs

Lucky, lucky, ladybugs,
red and black with spots,
they look like jewels,
those big midnight dots,
fly through the air,
with hopeful wishes in smooth glide,
as ladybugs slide,
the beautiful bug makes grace,
all around the air,
lucky, lucky, ladybugs,
make a wish today,
search for a ladybug,
and find a way,
just say,

Ladybugs,
Lucky, lucky, ladybugs.

Rachel Rival, Grade 5
McKinley Elementary School, CT

Adam

ADAM
Who is cool, funny, athletic, and smart
Who loves baseball
Who fears nothing
Who needs to win
Who gives 100% in every sport
Who believes in making an MLB team
ADAM

Adam Madison, Grade 6
Chalk Hill School, CT

Secrets

Have you ever looked at the end of the rainbow and found a pot of gold?
Can you listen to the wind as it tells of secrets untold?
The world is keeping the secrets from everyone,
secrets will keep coming and will never be done.

We think we know how the Earth was formed, but how can that be true?
All we really know is what life is like with me and you.
The world is keeping secrets from every living thing,
With feet, claws, flippers, or even with wings.
Can you ever find the first time of peace?
Will the turmoil in the world never cease?
The world is keeping secrets, that is right,
But how can we discover them, even if we try with all our might?

Although we think we know the land, it is just a mystery,
we feel really smart and somehow humans can't see,
that the world is keeping secrets from everyone,
secrets that will keep coming and will never be done.

Kelly Heinzerling, Grade 5
Greenwich Catholic School, CT

Excited

Excited
Smells like warm chocolate chip cookies coming out of the oven
Tastes like the pumpkin pie my oma makes on Thanksgiving
Sounds like people screaming, "Hip, hip, hurray!" in my ear
Feels like I have butterflies in my stomach
Feels like I want to jump out of my body
Feels like I can't talk quietly
Excited

Sophia Hall, Grade 6
Quashnet School, MA

I Am…

I am an adventurous 11 year-old who loves the outdoors
I wonder if I will fulfill my dream to travel to Niagara Falls
I hear the raging water tumble down below me
I see the people gathering to watch with their families
I want to freeze time and stay here forever
I am an adventurous 11 year-old who loves the outdoors

I pretend I am a fish flying freely down the falls
I feel the cold rush of water spitting up at my legs
I touch the cool, calm air around me
I worry that I will never be able to experience this dream
I cry when I think that the beautiful falls could be polluted
I am an adventurous 11 year-old who loves the outdoors

I understand that I can't have everything my way
I say that someday I will come back to this place
I dream of standing underneath the falls and seeing a bright, full rainbow
I try to make the best of my last few minutes here
I hope that I will keep my dreams alive
I am an adventurous 11 year-old who loves the outdoors

Leah Dawley, Grade 6
Swampscott Middle School, MA

A Wonder to My Eye
Flying up in the sky
So very high
It is a wonder to my eye

A comet formed from dust and ice seems frail
As it nears the sun, solar wind forms its tail
It is blown away along its trail

Flying up in the sky
So very high
It is a wonder to my eye
Nadav Ben-Naim, Grade 6
Yeshiva Academy, MA

The Strength That My Grandfather Had
The strength that my
Grandfather had he
Took to World War II
And asked for his lover's
Hand right under the
Moonlight moon

So full of despair
For her lover's hand
Was letting go
And the light was
Pulling him to sleep

He fought and he fought
For his life and for
His lover, but one day
He let go of the grass
Let go of his love's
Hand, and said Good-bye
To the world, and
Said hello to heaven
Naomi Diaz, Grade 4
Alice B Beal Elementary School, MA

Marbles
The rolling marble on the floor
As shiny as the neighbor's door
Roll,
Roll,
Roll,
Away from me
Oh no! It's at the stairs!
Bouncing down like a Super Ball
Swirling colors
Glassy and clear
It may be small
But it is amazing
The rolling marble on the floor
Super-duper, slick and clean.
Daniel Brickell, Grade 5
Foxborough Regional Charter School, MA

The Monkey's Friends
A monkey lives in a tree
By a bush with a flea
His friends are both big and small
From rhinos and elk to his flea dirt ball
He must always remember his tiny little friends
If not, it's the fleas dead end.
Sean Berube, Grade 4
Munger Hill Elementary School, MA

Winter
Looks like a million snow flakes falling down
Smells like snow everywhere!
Feels like ice cubes in the freezer
Tastes like ice cream with chocolate syrup
Sounds like children having fun!
Hannah Conway, Grade 4
C Hunter Ritchie Elementary School, VA

Northside United
When running I get so hot as the sun on a hot summer day.
Oh, the coaches are so mean as a professor giving you an F!
Soccer jumps you off your feet!
When I'm running I could stay in a black hole all day.
Bees swarm around my head while I am playing!
Katherine Barrera, Grade 6
School of International Studies at Meadowbrook, VA

Lucky Duck
I wish I was a duck
'cause ducks have lots of luck.
They do not go to school,
they'd rather swim in the pool.
They also don't wear socks, shoes, or dresses
and they don't have to clean up their messes
People have lots of luck also,
we don't spend our life in woe.
We play games and sleep in a bed
We also have cool hats for our head.
We can read, write, and speak
We don't have wings or a beak
I just noticed we have lots of luck,
now I'm glad I'm not a duck.
Meghan Johansson, Grade 4
Angelus Academy, VA

Christmas
Christmas
White-crowned angel
Fragrant brown cinnamon
Chubby red Santa Claus walking on the roof
Tasty gingerbread men
Soft velvet presents
Christmas
Alex Veith, Grade 4
Naquag Elementary School, MA

As Long as We're Different

I don't think this will work
You and I, are as different
As night and day
Chocolate and vanilla
Peace and war
Winter and summer
Black and white
Long and short
Rich and poor
Boy and girl
Smiles and frowns
Outside and inside
Fire and ice
Soft and hard
Nice and vulgar
A and Z
Ground and sky
I don't think you understand
Me and you
That's our difference

Jennifer Thompson, Grade 6
Harper Park Middle School, VA

No Hope, Just Music

Sitting in a one-race town
White from black,
Black from white.
In shacks we live.
No heat, no a.c.,
We deal with mother nature.

When my trumpet goes up
these sorrowful words come out.

We stand, they sit.
We're poor, they're rich.
Shacks are our houses,
Mansions are their homes.
We have no food,
But we still live on.
Our music raises our hope.
But they tear us down.

We, the Africans, stand up with hope.
No lives
And only MUSIC

Hayley Collis, Grade 5
Washington Elementary School, MA

Fire

It tickles the air
Wild and free when it burns
Dangerous to touch

Will Lehman, Grade 4
Trinity Christian School, VA

A Friend

A friend is nice no matter what
You do or say.
They will have your back and
Never give you away.

Lyric Hinton, Grade 4
Bensley Elementary School, VA

A Day at the Races

A shimmering
body of power and muscles
sleek, sweat-soaked hair
ripples with movement
a banner streaming
from behind
hooves thundering
bright colors flashing
crowds cheering
this is speed

Rebecca Webster, Grade 5
C C Burr Elementary School, MA

Spring Grass

The grass is so soft
The green grass Yum smells sweet
Up come the jonquils

Jalen Carr, Grade 4
Waller Mill Fine Arts Magnet School, VA

I Love You

his beard
tickles
my face
as he kisses
me
goodnight
I smile
kiss him back
give him a big hug
edging him closer
and closer
to
me
his warmth floods my body
never wanting to let go
I say
I love you

Sophia Corde, Grade 5
Coleytown Elementary School, CT

Bats

Bats can eat insects
They're very interesting
Bats are resting shhh!

Victor Flores, Grade 5
Marley Elementary School, MD

The Dark

You creep down the stairs
to prove you're not scared
of what is there
You hear a pipe whistle
like old rusty bikes
You go down and down
to the bottom you'll reach
It stinks like wet dog
and there's a faint, "Drip,"
As you sneeze some dust
you wonder…
Where are the stairs?
the stairs you come down
now don't go up
You find the stairs
You proved you're not scared
Now go upstairs and
prove you're not scared.

Dylan Johnson, Grade 6
Litchfield Intermediate School, CT

Baseball

Baseball is one of the best sports.
It is thrilling!
Baseball is fun to watch,
And so much fun to play.
The only contact is with the ball.
You can slide!
And you can steal!
You can hit,
And you can catch.
Baseball is Hank Aaron,
Jackie Robinson,
And Babe Ruth, too.
Baseball is American, like me.

Matt Guzzo, Grade 4
Riderwood Elementary School, MD

The Sun

It's big and round
It's all around.

It shines so bright
But not at night

It helps grass grow
And now I need to mow.

It gives light
Now that's right.

A lot of sun
Is very fun.

Kerstyn Gross, Grade 4
Freetown Elementary School, MA

Life Is Like a Fork in the Road

Dear Friend,
Life is like a fork in the road…
You have to choose the right way to go.
Believe in yourself —
Go where your heart takes you!
Sometimes a rock will block your path…
But you just have to walk around the trouble,
So it doesn't stop you.
If you take the wrong path…
Go back and try again.
If you get stuck between two paths…
Stop for a minute —
Think about which is the best path.
Discipline yourself to work hard,
So that you can follow the path of success!
Keep on hiking, my Friend!

Matthew Borovy, Grade 5
Har-Bur Middle School, CT

Eleven

The way you grow old is like an onion,
Or the circles on the trunk of a tree,
Or even like little dolls placed inside one another
You're getting older,
And too many birthdays passed
Without anyone even knowing it was your birthday
You don't feel like eleven,
Not right away no matter what.
It takes a few days until you hit the spot
It might feel as though you have
11 years of pennies rattling inside you
Like they would in a tin Band-Aid box,
And even when you don't feel like eleven
You feel like 3 or 2 or 1
And then the pennies are gone.
But maybe you feel 5
And you need to get all curled up
On your mommy's lap because you're scared.
But then you feel eleven again
And the pennies are back!

Marissa Catania, Grade 6
Albert D Griswold Middle School, CT

If I Were to Rule the Universe

If I were to rule the universe,
I'd visit all the stars.
I'd come in contact with different galaxies
And I'd fly all the way around Mars.

If I did control the cosmos,
I'd know about black holes.
I'd be the source of all knowledge
And I'd play quite a big role.

Nora Shapiro, Grade 5
Weston Intermediate School, CT

Invisible

I'm sitting in the dark with no one
to share my thoughts with.
I feel so lonely
because no one can see me.

I'm sitting in the darkness alone and cold.
I wish to talk to someone that I know
but I don't know anyone
because they never see me and
if they did they,
would just pass by me.

I wish I had a friend
to be by my side,
but nobody cares about me
because it's like I was never there.
I feel funny inside
I know what's wrong.

I'm Invisible
and that's all.

Leanna Martinez, Grade 5
Clark Avenue Middle School, MA

Wanting the Sea

Her words were a sigh
You could see in her eyes
That she wished to be not there
But that she wished to feel the sea breeze in her hair
A depression emitted from her deep kindred soul
And she saw the salty waves roll
Life wasn't a breeze
She lived nothing at ease
Time is not fair
When you live with such cares
She should live for the moment
Forget her commitment
Be open
Be loud
Be proud
And she could then swim all of the seas
Be where she wants to be

Amanda Panella, Grade 6
Midlothian Middle School, VA

My Cat

My cat is like a devil on earth.
He makes medusa look nice.
He looks very cute, but if
you even try to pet him
he'll give you five scratches…at least.
Be careful if you ever come to my house.
My cat could be anywhere, around the corner,
in the bathroom or anywhere you could imagine.

Alper Turgut, Grade 5
Wakefield Forest Elementary School, VA

Autumn

While daydreaming, I see a maple tree.
Its leaves are turning crimson and falling to the ground like meteors cascading from the sky.
As the days turn colder the sounds of nature grow stronger around me.
Squirrels scurry seamlessly to collect food for the long winter ahead.
The wind howls like wolves in the night like a chorus on just the right pitch.
More leaves are turning apricot, chestnut and orange.
The leaves paint a pastoral scene of different colors like a painter's collage.
As I walk through the crimson maple leaves, I feel like I'm being followed by a ghostly giant.
When the chestnut oak leaves crunch under my feet, they sound like the smashing of houses.
On some jack-o'-lanterns there is a smile and on others there is a frown.
As the trees lose their leaves and become bare they look like a skeleton's bony hand on Halloween.
When I come into the warmth of my house I see the fireplace flames flicker in the night
And smell the hot chocolate brewing in the tea kettle.
I can feel winter at its heels ready to charge in with full force like a moose charging after his prey.
That is why autumn has a special place in my heart.

Grant Amrine, Grade 6
Madison Middle School, CT

October

As I watch the summer sun fade away into the horizon I know that the mischievous days are coming and horror will strike again. As I slowly walk I can hear the wolves howl, I can see the black cats walk and scare little babies until they have had enough. I can see the witches in their houses making rotten candy to spoil the kids again. As I walk to a house I can see that all angels and good have faded away, like the graceful sun in the dark cloudy sky. The last sign of summer floats away like a leaf in the water. I slowly begin to cry as I see the leaves fall and rot, I can only wait until spring will help me get my desperate frown, to become a smile and light shine on me again.

Mirek Gruszkos, Grade 6
Irving School, CT

What Would She Say?

I have a sister. Her name is Megan. I never know what's going through her head.
She is 18 years old and has autism so that just makes this harder!
This is what I think she would say if she could say what she wanted to say.
"Hi, my name is Megan. I have a sister who talks too much,
a mother who always takes care of me, a daddy who loves me a whole lot,
a step-dad who can talk like Donald Duck, a friend of my daddy's who's very nice, two awesome grandmothers,
and I love my Papa!"

"I go to a special school. I have many friends.
I love playing with my sister's Game Boy.
I hate the vacuum. I hate brooms and I hate the sound of crinkling bags.
But most of all, I love my Papa!"

"I hate it when people talk on the phone. I love playing with phonebooks.
I hate new clothes. I have to have a routine and I draw in scribbles.
But I will always love my Papa!"

"I love things that are soft. I love to play in and drink water.
I love to eat spinach and I scarf down mashed potatoes.
I love to play with my mommy's and sister's hair.
But most of all, I love my Papa!"

"I wish I could be like other teenagers. I wish I didn't have super sensitive hearing.
I wish I could be like everyone else. I wish I could out-talk my sister.
But, most of all, I love my Papa!"

Shannon K. Thomas, Grade 6
Corkran Middle School, MD

Summer

What a sunny day
Kids relaxing on the beach
What a charming day.

Jailene Alonzo, Grade 5
Charlotte A Dunning Elementary School, MA

Honey I Love*

I love a lot of things, a whole lot of things.
Like, I love it when I run, shoot and score.
It makes me feel happy on a hot day when it pours.
I love it on a hot day when it pours.
But honey, let me tell you, I love soccer —
I love the sport of soccer.
And
A cuddly little friend that I love very much,
When she does funny things like that.
It makes me laugh when she acts like a cat.
I just love the way my dog acts like a cat.
But honey, let me tell you, I love my dog.
I love my funny dog.
And
I love the color whenever I may see it.
I love it when it twinkles where I sit.
I especially love it when I have to pick a color to use,
That would be purple that I choose.
But honey, let me tell you, I love purple!
I love the color purple!

Emily Stacey, Grade 4
Potter Road Elementary School, MA
*Inspired by Eloise Greenfield

If I Were a Raindrop

If I were a raindrop.
I'd dance and play in the clouds.
I'd wait and wait for the day a storm came around.
Then all my friends and neighbors,
and all my family too,
would fall and fall
'til we hit the ground,
for you to stop and play in too.
'Til we go up again.

Caitlyn Bender, Grade 5
Newton-Lee Elementary School, VA

Purple Shells

Tiny purple shells
sitting at the bottom
of the sea
just sitting there
waiting for me
to pick them up
and wash them well
then thinking how happy they are
to be purple shells.

Ilana Silverstone, Grade 4
South Area Solomon Schechter Day School, MA

Harriet Tubman

Harriet Tubman was born in Chesapeake Bay,
And she would soon have to be working every single day.
Harriet was hired out to help Mrs. Cook,
But helped her husband instead setting traps by the brook.
When Harriet got hit by a two-pound weight,
Edward Brodas then tried to decide her fate.
The new master, Doc Thompson, started selling his slaves,
So Harriet ran off to the better life she craves.
Harriet decided to work at a hotel in Cape May,
So she can work to free her family and get some pay.
When Old Rit heard that her boys were running away,
She created an uproar on Christmas Day.
Harriet's next trip to the North was with Old Rit and Ben.
Though complaining of the cold, they started a new life again.
In Auburn Harriet peddled vegetables door to door,
Although people would stop her for stories more and more.
Harriet Tubman died at the age of ninety-three.
A bronze tablet was displayed in her memory.

Francesco Albanese, Grade 6
Daniel L Joyce Middle School, MA

The Gray and Brown Hound

One day I saw a hound.
He was big, gray, and brown.
He was a big, old dog.
But he was in the fog.
He was so big and high.
It looked like he was in the sky.
So I brought him home.
And I gave him a bone.

Terrence Walker, Grade 4
Courthouse Road Elementary School, VA

Walking Through the World

As I walked around yesterday
Only myself in my imagination
I wobbled through the rest of the country
And every single nation

I saw a dying species
And an ocean filled with trash
A homeless person on the street
And one with tons of cash

I felt disappointed
With our population that day
I was thinking quite a lot
Though there was nothing I could say

I did see deep blue oceans
And snowcapped mountains so high
Though now I know that my generation
Could be the ones to say good-bye

Caroline Zambelli, Grade 6
Scotts Ridge Middle School, CT

Football/Sport

Football
Enjoyable, exciting
Running, catching, scoring
Football is my future
Sport

Andrew Peters, Grade 6
Immaculate Heart of Mary School, MD

Rain

When rain
falls I watch it
wonder why it's there.
I also wonder where it comes
from. I really want to know
and I think it's not fair. I
dream as I am
watching out
the door

Megan Bollinger, Grade 5
St Joseph School-Fullerton, MD

The Race

There once was a race
The cars were at fast pace
The driver's tire did a hop
Then the race came to a stop
That driver came in last place

Michael Boyd, Grade 4
Freetown Elementary School, MA

The Patriots

The Patriots
The greatest football team of all!!!

they won 17 and 0
one more game to go…
the super bowl

faced off against "Giants"
fought and fought
all night long

the "Giants" stormed the field
Patriots lay beneath their feet
crowd from New England silenced

final score 17 to 14
Patriots' fans, heads down
look toward another year

the village stadium is empty now
my heart is crushed
my head still wonders how
our winning season was shushed

Robert Medeiros, Grade 6
Edmond P Talbot Middle School, MA

The Masked Figure

Under the mask are two eyes
to see with.
Under the mask is a nose
to smell with.
Under the mask are two ears
to hear with,
and under the mask is a mouth
to talk with.
You may not see these wonders under the mask,
but what you can see is what describes the masked figures feelings and personality.
You can see this just by looking at the mask and not anything else.

Johanna (Joey) Trujillo, Grade 5
Rowayton Elementary School, CT

A Deep Dark Forest

A cold dark forest
Not a soul in sight
A blanket of snow on branches and on the ground making little hills
The sun shines and warms
Birds rustle out of nests and fly
Smell the fresh air
Snow forts left from a snowball fight
Tent marks in the snow from the night before
The forest isn't so cold and dark

Harley Redfield, Grade 5
St Mary's Primary School, MA

Sunset

It is a magical sunset in the middle of the summer.
The pink, blue, purple, and orange fill the sky,
As if they are trying to make a perfect picture.
Ah…I take a deep breath in and smell the scent
Of sweet grass, pine trees, and the warm summer air.
They fill my nose like someone filling up a glass of water.
I feel the warm breeze kissing my cheeks and the sun's rays
reaching out to stroke my face.
Happy giggles fill the air as children play tag in their yards.
The caw of a black bird flying high in the sky sings a song of loneliness.
Summer is a medicine for the soul that warms me from head to toe.

Hannah Duda, Grade 5
Booth Hill School, CT

Fall

Fall has arrived, get ready here we come!
People being joyous and frolicking with chums.

Neighbors rake the montage of brightly colored leaves
And the children in the background wailing, "More cider, please!"

Halloween and Thanksgiving are celebrated then, too!
The front lawns glimmer with freshly covered dew.

The sun's always shining, but with a soft chill
And yet, I still feel such ravishing thrill!

Karly Mulligan, Grade 5
Hebron Elementary School, CT

Conserve Electricity: The Earth Is Blowing All Her Fuses
Try and conserve electricity,
Or Mother Earth will blow her fuse.
You must use some simplicity,
And decide how much power to use.

Coal is burned in power plants,
To make the turbines go.
It puts pollutants in the air,
Which will damage Earth, you know.

The coal power plants need,
Is brought in by ship and train.
The pollution they send to the air,
Will make us all complain.

Start conserving electricity,
Give the Earth a break.
Turning off lights and turning down heat,
Will reduce the pollution we make.

Ethan Mullen, Grade 4
St Clement Mary Hofbauer School, MD

When I Got Cody
I'm going out to the store my dad says.
I won't be gone long, you wait here.
I wait
wait
wait
and here's my dad
with a little white dog
a big grin leaps onto my face
the little dog whimpers
and jumps up onto its hind legs
he licks me
and tumbles into my lap
the perfect dog,
my dog,
Cody.

Joshua Baker, Grade 5
West Woods Upper Elementary School, CT

Springtime
The gentle breeze blowing
The droning hum of everything
Seems safe and serene
The air is filled with the aroma of sweet honey suckle

Plants with pinks, purples, red, and yellows
Like my bedspread blues, and white.
As the winter season passes
Flowers emerge
The long wait is over
Spring is here now.

Jenae Addison, Grade 6
Magnolia Elementary School, MD

The Unseen Wind
The wind is like people, whispering,
You can hear it but not what it says,
You can't see it,
But you can watch it flutter the leaves of the trees,
When it grows angry, it's like a crowd of people shouting,
Louder louder and louder,
It doesn't want to stop,
But suddenly,
It stops,
Dies away to nothing but stillness.

William Hansen, Grade 5
John Ward Elementary School, MA

Express Yourself
There are so many ways to express yourself.
Don't be afraid to try,
No way is right or wrong.
You can write or paint,
Sing and dance,
Or play an instrument,
Even act.
You don't have to be great at it,
Or worry about what people might say
Try your best and have fun.
Write a story,
Or paint a masterpiece.
Take a dance lesson,
Audition for a play.
Or even learn how to play guitar.
If you can think of something then try it,
Because you might like it.
Whether you're writing
Painting or singing,
Express yourself because it's fun
And you won't regret it.

Emily Weeks, Grade 6
Blue Ridge Middle School, VA

Animals
Animals
Animals
Animals
Little animals
Big furry animals
Brown, black, white animals
Slimy animals
Scaly animals
Cute, cuddly, warm animals
Vicious, mean, brutal animals
Wet animals, too
Huge animals
Tiny animals
Don't forget flying animals
Last of all, best of all, I like shelly animals.

Graham Walker, Grade 4
C Hunter Ritchie Elementary School, VA

Squirrel

A squirrel,
Plump as could be,
But is still crunching above the birds,
That are also eating on the ground,
The squirrel is hard to see now,
that the sun is so bright,
All I see is a shadow,
I go outside and take a long stare,
At the squirrel,
I wonder if he'll ever leave.

Casie Gale, Grade 4
Southbrook Academy, MA

Stuck Indoors

On my mind is the snow outside.
I want to go out and play.
But I am stuck in school all day,
Learning all day, what a bore!
Snow is falling, what a nice sight,
It's a winter wonderland.
But just looking out the window
Three stories above the snow,
I want to jump out there and play
But I am stuck sitting here.
I want the snow but I can't go.

Eric Sguazzin, Grade 6
Summit Montessori School, MA

Fluffy

There once was a cat.
He was so fat.
His name was Fluffy.
He was so puffy.

His owners were away.
Fluffy wanted to play.
Then he heard a fall
And looked towards the wall.

There stood a mouse
Inside his house
Chasing the mouse
All around his house

Knocking everything over
Even a clover
Back to the wall went the mouse,
And Fluffy looked at his house.

It was a disaster,
And home came his master.
When the house was found,
Poor Fluffy was sent to the pound.

Eileen Zadrozny, Grade 6
Captain Nathan Hale Middle School, CT

Hockey/Figure Skating

Hockey
Aggressive, enjoyable
Skating, checking, fighting
Referees, puck, judges, scores
Spinning, turning, swirling
Graceful, joyful
Figure skating

Ben Wosky, Grade 4
Mapleshade Elementary School, MA

Summer's Coming

Flowers blooming
Bees zooming
Birds singing
School bells ringing
Children playing
Dogs baying
Sun shining
Clouds dying
Summer's coming!

Renee Cooper, Grade 5
Davenport Ridge School, CT

School

S noring in class.
C alling the principal.
H earing lots of numbers.
O ver confusing.
O ver tired after the day.
L ost what I was going to say.

Collin Hall, Grade 4
Munger Hill Elementary School, MA

Princess

My daddy calls me his princess
But I don't have a crown
I don't have a pony
I don't have a big white gown

My mommy calls me her angel
But I don't have any wings
I don't know how to fly
And I don't really like to sing

My siblings call me the devil
But I don't have any horns
My favorite color isn't red
And I don't like to hear people mourn

My name is not princess
There is no halo on me
I am not Satan's twin
Don't you agree?

Kasey Keane, Grade 6
E W Thurston Middle School, MA

Friends Forever!

So kind and honest,
Friends forever,
Someone to rely on,
There to lend a hand,
That's what counts to be friends forever!

Nicole Lynch, Grade 4
King's Highway Elementary School, CT

War and Peace

It's hot outside
Because of bombs —
The air is filled with planes
People are running
Around screaming
It's a day of chaos.
Everybody notices.
It's cool outside
Because it is fall.
The air is calm
People are walking
Down the street
It's a peaceful day
Nobody
Even
Notices.

Pierce Walmsley, Grade 4
St Christopher's School, VA

Hockey

All summer I wait
To lace up my skates
The water is now frozen
The teams are all chosen
Black against white
I skate with all my might
To the left and to the right
I give the goalie a good fight
I shoot once more
And into the back of the net
I score.

Patrick Mulhern, Grade 4
St Mary's Primary School, MA

A Day at the Zoo

Roar! The tiger went
I saw it with big dark stripes
Its cage was the size of a large tent
It had very sharp claws
The tiger ran so fast
Stretching its legs and paws
Against the cage he lies
The metal rattles
His roaring cries!!!

Jason Rosselli, Grade 4
Freetown Elementary School, MA

On the Wings

The wind rushing right by
The sensation of the hunt
How delectable and distracting, the scent of a fresh kill
The pestering squeals of the newborn
chicks as they wait endlessly for their next meal
Watching as the Earth, and your
stress just float away
My strong talons grasp the agonizing
height of an everlasting mountain rock

Samuel Baker, Grade 6
Litchfield Intermediate School, CT

The Leprechaun

Look at that green flash
Look at that flash dash, dash, dash
Look at him run by

Peter Bardascino, Grade 5
Linscott-Rumford Elementary School, MA

A Recipe for Freedom

Get the bowl of miracles put in a pinch of trusting flower
And the yeast of love
Put in the dough of misery and pain
Mix it all together
And put it in the oven of survival and set the time to life
And serve it with a bit of worthiness.

Liam McDade, Grade 5
C C Burr Elementary School, MA

Stratton

My teeth chatter.
I hug myself, trying to keep warm.
The gusty winds push me forward.
The bitter cold wind makes me flinch.

I gaze at all the white fluffy snow.
I glance at the layers of snow,
Resting on the bristles of pine trees.

Here I go!
As I glide rapidly down the mountain,
I feel the strong winds hit my cheeks.
The further I go, the more speed I pick up.
I watch other skiers and snowboarders,
Whiz by me.
The power of speed,
The fun of it all,
Makes me smile.

As I reach the end,
I come to a swift stop.
I wait in line, to go back up,
And take in the joy,
Of this wonderful experience.

Caleigh Lang, Grade 6
Swampscott Middle School, MA

A Summer's Thought

I am summertime
I wonder how long I will last
I hear the children laughing
I see the ice cream melting
I want to live forever
I am summertime
I pretend the blue skies will never go gray
I feel the cool, cold creek
I touch the sun-soaked sand
I worry that fall will sneak up on me
I cry a summer's storm
I am summertime
I understand I will have to go away
I say I want to stay
I dream of winter dying
I try to end school early
I hope the children love me
I am summertime

Darby McCreary, Grade 6
Page Middle School, VA

No One

How terrible it must have been.
No room to move.
Shackled by the wrist.
By the ankle.
By the neck.

No one deserves that pain.
The suffering.
The hurt inside.
Or the humiliation.

Never to see your family again.
Being sold and whipped against your will.
No one should deserve that suffering.
No One…

Lauren Sutton, Grade 5
Charlotte A Dunning Elementary School, MA

Runaway

Every day I think should I stay or go
I don't know what to do I just don't know
There are so many things that are happening now
I feel like a hole that just keeps going down
While I sit there and think about what to do
I wonder what will happen if I do
my mind tells me no, but my heart says runaway
So I pick a few things and I'm on my way
As I'm walking my heart starts pounding
As I cleared my eyes to see my surrounding
Then I say to my self why am I running away
I found out truly that I wanted to stay

Paris Braxton, Grade 6
Monelison Middle School, VA

Much More

Sitting and thinking
Not knowing what to say
Remember when we used to play
You were always there
To tell me what to do
Oh my gosh I'm going to miss you
You are more than a sister
More than a friend
So I want you to know
I'll love you till the end
We might yell
We might fight
But in the end it's all right
Don't want you to go
But I want you to see
You're not just a sister
You're much more to me

Deanna Mazina, Grade 6
Swampscott Middle School, MA

Sword Trees

Trees cry for warmth,
Not swords of white, sharp crystals,
Shouting for a fire,
Birds are alarmed and stay away,
The prisoners with swords,
Are too horrified to shout any more,
Hoping the season will vanish.

Elizabeth Kelly, Grade 4
Jacksonville Elementary School, MD

Blizzards

The snow falls,
Climbs over branches,
Giving them
Cold,
White,
Soft coats,
Hands reaching out,

The snow falls,
Eating,
Swallowing the houses,
As they disappear,
Under a soft blanket of snow.

Yotam Gavish, Grade 5
John Ward Elementary School, MA

Basketball

Basketball is a sport,
My favorite favorite sport,
I really never make a hoop,
But the only thing that really matters
Is that I try.

Katelyn Young, Grade 5
Plainfield Catholic School, CT

Atchoo!

I sniffle and wheeze
And I am ready to sneeze I don't know how long I can last…

Atchoo in the blink of an eye
I got boogies on my tie
now I have to go change.
Get me a hanky or maybe my blanky whatever you think will help.
Maybe two maybe three…
atchoo! I need something big something large whatever you see just hurry.
Nothing seems to work so I think I have a bad flu,
but I think I got it from the zoo.

Ryan Stratford, Grade 5
St Joseph Elementary School, MA

In the Forest

I'm in the forest I'm not scared, what's that a one-eyed deer.
I'm in the forest I'm not scared, aw man sticky honey oh no the bear.

I'm in the forest I'm not scared, aw man there are a million fleas.
I'm in the forest I'm not scared, I really wish I was in my bed please.

I'm in the forest I'm not scared, I practically cheer.
I'm in the forest I'm not scared, I've been here all year.

I'm in the forest I'm not scared, I've been here so long.
I'm in the forest I'm not scared, when will someone come along?

I'm in the forest I'm not scared, I know it's all in my head.
I'm in the forest I'm not scared, it's mosquitoes that I dread.

I'm in the forest I'm not scared, aw forget it I can't escape my fear.

Alexander Rivera, Grade 6
Edmond P Talbot Middle School, MA

What Is Happiness?

Happiness is a warm fluffy puppy, nuzzling in my neck.
It is a big bundle of hope that keeps me going.
Happiness is something only the good get.
You cannot buy it with money and it only grows bigger with a positive attitude.
Happiness is not something you can hold.
It is the best possession.
Happiness is a warm cup of tea that warms my soul.
It is a piece of chocolate melting in my mouth.
Happiness is a good book that you can't put down.
Happiness is a warm crackling fire that calmly puts you to sleep.

Jacob Buttiker, Grade 5
Booth Hill School, CT

Sad

Sad is gray like rain clouds pouring out their sad tears onto us.
It runs through my heart like a broken record repeating over and over again.
It reminds me of when I have to wake up for school on a Monday morning.
It makes me feel all achy inside.
It makes me want to relive my life and make it better.

Nicole Roenicke, Grade 5
Newton-Lee Elementary School, VA

A Sad Case

Crack! The great gavel hits the bench,
his fists in cuffs are tightly clenched.
Guilty! The verdict is a lead weight,
the defendant has now sealed his fate.
His heart pounds like a beating drum,
friendships, fresh air, freedom now done.
He looks to the whites of the jurors eyes,
and knows this end is no surprise.

Choices in life are many not few,
each man knows what he should do.
Reach for the truth as it runs and hides,
far beneath temptation's tides.
We all have just one life to live,
we must take less than what we give.
Leave the world a better place
is the moral and end of this sad case.

Aubrey Fuhrmann, Grade 6
Charlton Middle School, MA

My Escape

My escape from you, my hideout from you,
my closed haven from all of you.

You are my enemies trying to get in,
trying to get into my kingdom, trying to make peace with me.

I shut my kingdom door, shut my curtains,
and turn off my lights.

Knock, knock; a stranger is at my door,
swearing, yelling, and banging the door to MY kingdom.

I sit on my throne; I let you in.
You speak and I forgive…for peace, for that white flag.

I try to explain to you that my room can be anything,
anything I want it to be.
Right now it is my kingdom, and you are my enemies.

It's nine o'clock.
You leave my kingdom and I turn off my lights,
while I lie on my bed.

The war ends now, and the white flag is up.

Stefanie Borneman, Grade 6
Swampscott Middle School, MA

Special Day

Horseback riding is fun every week
so we trot and trot with mystique
I look at her, pretty and unique
her tail and mane has a colorful technique.

Victoria Sellick, Grade 6
Monelison Middle School, VA

My Flow

Well I'm back again and things haven't changed
I'm still getting suspended out of school for 5 days
The class is still giving my teacher pain
Before we come to class she prays.

Oh my gosh they should give me an award
Most of the time I don't try I just do it because I'm bored
I don't need help with writing, with this I am a pro
I just get a pencil and paper and write down what I know.

I don't know one person that can write a poem better than me
They act like it's as hard as performing brain surgery
Now somebody in my class thinks they can do this thing
But when it comes to writing poems I'm not a human being.

With me there's never been a limit
With writing I'm superior, it's like I am in it
This poem is just a fragment of my life
This stuff is so easy, that I don't even have to try.

Malick Monestime, Grade 6
Benjamin Syms Middle School, VA

Nature

Drip drop
Upon my leaves
That turn orange, red and green
I sit there still
Minding my own business
Until kids come and sit upon
My branches
I can't make them go
But I don't mind them
Sitting upon a branch
Of mine

Taylor Filippone, Grade 5
Jacob Hiatt Magnet Elementary School, MA

A Child's Psalm of Life

I think you should not care about your hair,
And put it in some fancy ponytail.
You should go outside and play in muck,
Don't care about your clothes getting dirtied up.
Have fun while you can in the summer breeze,
Learn your math, but don't tease.

You might want to adopt a little pet,
Like a puppy or a bunny, or something that hops.
Don't be afraid to ask for directions if you don't know the way,
But, follow your dreams far, far away!

Obey your mom and dad,
And care about the sad.
Make your hopes and dreams go far,
And obey God's law.

Claire Forehand, Grade 4
Homeschool Plus, VA

Ra the Shining One
Ra, the all powerful god
Created the world
He became the sun
Rising in the east
Blazing in the midday sky
Setting in the west
Ra created the sky
The earth
and all things in the sea
by speaking its name
The sun god grows weary
As people plotted with Apophis,
The serpent of evil
Gods begged Ra to burn Egypt
Ra replied that he would
Send his eye into the world
Sekhmet thinks beer is blood
Drank it
Sekhmet slept peaceful
Great mother born
Matthew Lee, Grade 6
Middlebrook School, CT

Spring
S unshine every day
P ainter's creative getaway
R unning outside to play
I ncredible fun in the incredible sun
N o more heavy coats
G ot to go buy an ice cream float
Afridi Majeed, Grade 5
Sacred Heart School, MA

Ireland
Ireland is nice now.
Beautiful rainbows are great.
Huge pots of gold coins.
Maya Simpson, Grade 4
St Gregory Elementary School, MA

Basketball
dribble it,
pass it,
shoot for the basket,
bounce it,
throw it,
the crowd will cheer you know it,
shoot for 2,
shoot for 3,
shoot for a victory,
off the backboard,
around the rim,
through the net and in you win!
Mariah Machnik, Grade 5
St Mary's Primary School, MA

Spring Is Here
Flying flower to flower,
Can you see the fairy powder?

Hearing the chipmunks sing,
It's a sign of beautiful spring.

Blue birds chirping in a group,
No rose is sure to droop.

Tree buds opening up and having fun,
Stretching out to the great big sun.

Butterflies spread their wings,
Doing a pretty little thing.

"Tweet, tweet," baby robins in a tree,
Saying "Hi" to each and every little bee.

The warm breeze is coming in,
All the puffy clouds have a grin!
Kylie Machado, Grade 4
Freetown Elementary School, MA

My Mom
Her face is like a
story that is waiting to be told.
Her hair is like a
rainbow of different shades of brown.
and in summertime a little red,
Her skin is like a smooth color
of light chocolate.
Her personality makes
you feel warm inside.
She has a smile
that could light up a whole room.
Nerel Belay, Grade 6
Fairfax Collegiate School, VA

Test Shirt
I got a shirt from Texas
It came in the mail.
My uncle sent it to me
Thinking I would be surprised.

I'll call it the test shirt
'Cuz I'll only wear it on test days.
I have a social studies test coming up
I think I'll try it out then.

It seems pretty lucky
Because it has a great big star on it.
I hope I'll ace the tests
When I'm wearing the Lone Star shirt.
Thomas Schneidermeyer, Grade 5
Hindley Elementary School, CT

Gymnastics/My Life
Gymnastics
Exciting, life-threatening
Running, tumbling, flipping
Best sport ever invented
My life
Kelsey Santmyer, Grade 6
Immaculate Heart of Mary School, MD

The Peaceful Day
The warm wind blows in my face
I follow it until I come to a peaceful river
The waterfall flows with softness
I go a little further I see a meadow
With lots of beautiful flowers
I lay on them
Looking at the sky I guess the shapes
Of the clouds
When I hear my mom calling
My name
I say goodbye until tomorrow
Nancy LaFerriere, Grade 4
Brookside Elementary School, MA

Freedom
F airness in a country of hatred
R ights that tolerate different religion
E quality has never been so rejoiced
E ven the children are jubilant
D ay and night — it will never end
O n and on, I still wonder about
M y life without it
Sebastien Philemon, Grade 5
Sacred Heart Elementary School, MA

Who Is the Man?
Who is the man?
who will
Watch *Lord of the Rings* with you
and CUDDLE
who will
hike a 13,300 foot mountain with you
and make sure you you don't trip
who will
Joke about piercing your ears himself
and then go get them pierced with you
who will
Walk into Newton Center
and get coffee with you
who will
Never refuse a kiss
and always be there for you
WHO IS THAT MAN?
THAT MAN IS MY DAD!
Leah Braunstein, Grade 5
John Ward Elementary School, MA

Last Bell of the Year

Please bell ring, the last ring of the year
Please bell ring, your sound I want to hear.
Please bell ring, I want to get out of school
Please bell ring, I want to get to the pool.
The sparkly blue water will be nice and cool.
When I hear you ring
I'll fly out like a bird with wings.

Ring-a-ling-a-ling

Now that you have rung
I'm as free as a bird
To shout and scream wherever I'm heard.

Christopher McGinty, Grade 6
Fuller Middle School, MA

Soccer Ball

This is my soccer ball,
I run up and down the field,
Making fake moves and trying to cheer!
My greatness will definitely be revealed!

This is my soccer ball,
My team pouts and has a good cheer!
We win tournaments and games too!
Maybe soccer will be my permanent career!!!

This is my soccer ball,
The game's about to begin…
My team and I gather in a huddle,
And hope to win!!!

Elizabeth Hagele, Grade 6
Scotts Ridge Middle School, CT

Snowflakes

The soft white snowflakes
Lightly fall on the ice pond
On Christmas Eve night

Alexandra Green, Grade 4
C Hunter Ritchie Elementary School, VA

Red Sox

Finally winners!
Opening day hope,
Yawkey way:
    Juicy Fenway Franks,
    Ice cream running down my chin,
    Peanuts and popcorn and Cracker Jacks,

"Sweet Caroline" pumping up the crowd,
Crack!
A home run by Ortiz,
Into the monster seats,
"I love that dirty water!"

Matthew Rosenthal, Grade 4
Forest Avenue Elementary School, MA

Friends

To have a true friend is great
It is something to appreciate!
Sometimes you guys will fight,
Afterwards you will know being friends is right
Now you know having friends is fine
I am so glad Ava and Bailey are mine…

Stephanie Morton, Grade 4
Helen H Hansen Elementary School, MA

Getting Apples

I don't get it why teachers get apples.
What are they going to do with them besides eat them?
They seem so flattered when they get one.
I mean seriously!
They are not magical!

Kristin Heideman, Grade 4
Munger Hill Elementary School, MA

Friends

You like winter, I like spring.
You like to hum, and I like to sing.
Your hair is brown, and my hair is blonde
Your hair is short, and my hair is long.
You like the ocean, and I like the bay.
We are not the same in any way.

I like baseball, and you like soccer.
I have a cubby, and you have a locker.
I like gloves, and you like mittens.
I like monkeys, and you like kittens.
I like green, and you like blue.
We are different, me and you.
But, I like you, and you like me.
And that's the way our friendship should be!

Chaia Bates, Grade 4
Mapleshade Elementary School, MA

I Hope I Get a Dog

I want a pet.
They are not pests.
My parents said they would get me a dog
But it turned out to be a wet log.
Dogs are cool
Even though they drool.
I like to pet them on the head
And teach them how to play dead.
We would play in the park
And stay until it got very dark.
If I had a dog
I would love it a lot
I hope my parents read this poem
And get me a dog
Instead of a wet log.

Niel Shah, Grade 4
Helen H Hansen Elementary School, MA

Olivia

My dog
Reddish-golden puppy
strong, sweet, rough, crazy
retriever
Maggie Wilcher, Grade 5
McCleary Elementary School, VA

The Fame Game

In the year of 2008
I was at the arena Freestate
We started the soccer game
I played so well and I turned to fame
The opposing team was fast
But that was just the past
Our goalie, Maggie, was diving
Our score was rising
Scoring was the other team
So my team turned mean
We scored right back
After the game we started to slack
My team won the game
Because we were the team of fame
I went to celebrate
My mom said I was great
Maggie Burnett, Grade 6
Immaculate Heart of Mary School, MD

Snow Fight

Snowballs are coming
Flying through the icy air
Dodge, throw, charge
Got him.
Eric Benninghoff, Grade 4
Weston Intermediate School, CT

River

Whispering of the
wind
Rapid water
racing
Shades of gorgeous
green grass
So peaceful and
calm
The water flowing
swiftly along its path
The birds' melodies
cover the air
The sun
so bright
So lovely and pleasing
like a
Pink and white lady
slipper
MacKenzie Holmes, Grade 4
Southbrook Academy, MA

I'm Eleven Today

I want today to be far away already.
Far away like a runaway balloon.
A tiny o in the sky.
So tiny you have to close your eyes to see it.
I'm eleven today.
I'm eleven, ten, nine, eight, seven, six, five, four, three, two, and one.
But I wish I was one hundred and two.
Some days you might need to sit on your mama's lap
Because you're scared.
That's the part of you that's five.
Maybe one day when you're all grown up,
You'll need to cry like you're three.
That's ok.
I wish I was invisible
But I'm not
I'm crying like I'm three in front of everybody.
I want today to be far away already.
Far away like a runaway balloon.
A tiny o in the sky.
So tiny you have to close your eyes to see it.
Alyssa Dale, Grade 6
Albert D Griswold Middle School, CT

My Body

My hair is like a heaven for ticks and fleas.
My legs are like engines equipped with nitrous because I'm so fast.
My hands are like pocketknives because I slice when I please.
My eyes are like spotlights because I can see in the dark.
That's me,
a cat.
Jackson Mitchell, Grade 5
St Christopher's School, VA

Halloween Night

Halloween is a scary night,
When ghosts and goblins give you a fright.
Children in their masks
Collecting candy as their task.
My jacket flaps in the cool crisp air,
As a child walks by disguised as a big brown bear.
The fresh scent of Fall under my feet,
Like hot cocoa so creamy and sweet.
Jumbo buckets filled with candy
Making the youth delighted and dandy.
Jack o'lanterns wink candlelit eyes like old men telling a secret joke,
While I see Dracula swoop by, peering from behind his velvet cloak.
A cat as dark as the midnight sky,
The tangy taste of warm apple pie.
Residents roam around their haunted shire,
In the hearth I could hear the crackle of the fire.
The moon shimmers bright as gold,
Lighting the way home for young and old.
Put away your nightmares and fears
Until Halloween comes around next year!
Melanie Gorton, Grade 6
Madison Middle School, CT

Christmas

Christmas
A gold and maroon ocean of presents drowning a pinetree
Tingling smells of sweet vanilla cookies
The quiet screams of joy and heart dropping excitement
Sweet but bitter splashes of juice from a lemon on a juicy ham
The smooth touch of silky gold wrapping on presents
Christmas

Rachel Ruiz, Grade 5
Jane Ryan School, CT

Storm

The sky is turning dark
And the clouds make their mark.
Gone is the light
Day is turning to night.
Down comes the rain.
The clouds form a chain.
It's like on a beautiful day
When the sun runs away.
The lightning bolts reach down to earth
And nobody knows what this storm is worth.
The storm comes down just like a knife
And brings all the flowers back to life.

Ellie Trudeau, Grade 5
Soule Road School, MA

Phoebe

Phoebe has a
Crazy
I
magination. She can be really
BOSSY!

She *Loves!* her mom but her mom
left? Now [she] is really   D
                              O
                            W
                          N.

Jeremiah Schwartz, Grade 6
Friendship School, MD

Who I Am

I am a girl, joyful and excited
I am Brazil, as happy as the crowd
I am water that drip, drip, drips
I am a happy clown that makes people laugh
I am a shark looking for prey
I am a very nice turtle swimming my way to the sea
I am a star fish, beautiful as the sea
I am a soccer ball that goes back and forth
I am the world that wants to improve on recycling
I am a car that goes faster and faster
I am a loving, kind girl

Lorena Dulco, Grade 6
Fuller Middle School, MA

How I Died

I disobeyed my mother
I disobeyed my dad
I went out into the wild
They were very, very sad

I was chased by many vultures
I was chased by cheetahs too
I was chased by snakes and lizards
Who had escaped from the family zoo

I was standing in some quicksand
Quickly I started to sink
I ended up with darkness around me
Now I'm dead I think!

Andru Monteiro, Grade 4
Helen H Hansen Elementary School, MA

You and Me

You are you and I am me
You like the sand I like the sea
I like dogs you like cats
I like Barbies you like Bratz
I like movies you like books
I want to be an athlete you want to be a cook
I like green you like red
I like sleepovers you like your own bed
I like soccer you like tennis
I like salad you like lettuce
I like art you like math
I like showers you like baths
I like sneakers you like heels
I like hippos you like seals
I like summer you like spring
We don't all have to like the same thing!

Dakota Stephens, Grade 6
Blue Ridge Middle School, VA

Buttercup Blossoms

Look at the yellow look at the green,
Have you seen something so delicate and green,
It is a buttercup blossom glowing in the night,
You can see it day and night,
Buttercup blossom

Erin Walsh, Grade 5
St Mary's Primary School, MA

Dog

My dog is like a teddy bear
I sleep with at night,
but he kisses me because he loves me.
His fur is soft and gentle when I pet him.
His sound is so loud when he wants something.
My dog is so small and fluffy,
but he is just so gentle.

Anna Beth Starr, Grade 6
Trinity School, MD

A Walk in the Snow

Snow is falling on the ground
with a peaceful perfect sound.
See the wreath on the door,
You will start seeing more and more,
A nice long walk in the cold,
In my hands my gloves I hold.
Now it is getting colder
I think I might get a very cold shoulder!
I'm on my way home,
While writing this poem,
On a winter walk to my friends I talk,
On a cold winter walk!

Megan Barnes-Neal, Grade 4
Mount Hope Christian School, MA

Ocean

The giant splashing waves
The bright blue
And light green water
The slimy seaweed
The shells
The clams
The salty smell
The whooshing sound
The sailboats sailing
The fishers fishing
The surfers surfing
The tides going out
The awesome ocean
The tie-dyed masterpiece!

Amara Lutwack, Grade 5
C C Burr Elementary School, MA

That Was a Day

This morning,
The sun climbed the sky,
As the moon faded away.
The sun smiled,
As it looked me in the eye.
I went outside, with my pride.
I saw a flower, waving at me,
And cheering me on.
The bush trembled with excitement,
As I walked by.
The tree danced with me,
Through my yard.
An eagle soared past me,
As it screeched with happiness.
The beach sand, tickled my feet.
The ocean fought me, till a final defeat.
I saw a clam, peeking its head out.
Day by day, day by day.
That was a day!

Chantal Gaudreau, Grade 5
Soule Road School, MA

No School!

I don't want to go to school
I would rather go in my pool

I don't care what they say
As long as I skip the day

School makes me lose my cool
School makes me look like a fool

I want to get out
For I'm about to shout

School is boring
I'm like a lion roaring

It is a bummer
I can't wait for summer

James Wagner, Grade 6
E W Thurston Middle School, MA

Wilt Chamberlain

Wilt Chamberlain, big and tall
Wilt Chamberlain, he does it all
He handles the ball
He shoots; he scores,
He runs
He dribbles,
Anything he does, he does with the ball!

Courtney Rhan, Grade 4
Salem Elementary School, VA

Seasons

Winter,
as white as
polar bears on clouds.
The icy windows
slowly change
to spring,
and tell you to go
outside and play.
Then you hear a
SPLASH!
and you know that
summer's here.
You cool down in the pool,
until the leaves
begin to fall,
FALL!
What fun it is
to rake the beauty
from the trees.
You hide and run and play and…
Winter's here again.

Miri Michaely, Grade 5
C C Burr Elementary School, MA

Dawn

Dawn
swallows up
any darkness
for it's
midnight snack
sunlight
blazes proudly
as it
peeks through
my window
an alarm clock
of singing
that has
no snooze button
wakes me
at the crack of
Dawn

Hannah Berggren, Grade 5
Coleytown Elementary School, CT

Boots

Boots
Comfortable, warm
Walking, running, dancing
Through school hallways
Uggs

Alyssa Farren, Grade 6
Quashnet School, MA

Beauty

As a snowflake
Falls on the tip
Of a panda's nose
I imagine walking

Through bamboo in the jungle.
I listen

Oh, what's that I hear
It's a leopard I start to run
I can't get away…
Poof I awake.

Sadie Ulmen, Grade 5
Francis Asbury Elementary School, VA

Seasons

Spring
Green, alive
Brightening, developing, warming
Leaves growing, leaves decaying
Changing, dying, raking
Brown, sleepy
Autumn

Jessica Coyle, Grade 5
Leicester Memorial School, MA

After

After waiting for hours,
After sucking on 14 watermelon sours,
After imagining I have powers,
After making sand towers,
I think the bus is on the way!
After having to say,
Later can we swim in the bay?
After walking the right way,
After running over the speed limit,
I see it's only been 5 minutes!

Jaimilee Dresser, Grade 5
Charlotte A Dunning Elementary School, MA

Teddy Bear

Whoosh, leaves chatter
lying there in the lonely night

brrrrr
holding myself, held on tight

aaah-shooo
shivering, seeing that no one's there

brrrrr
awaiting for my teddy bear

Teddy bear, bear, bear, bear
ahh-shoo-bless myself

Dana Le, Grade 5
Jacob Hiatt Magnet Elementary School, MA

Castaway

I can't feel it.
Deep inside.
Under all of the joy and fun.
The castaway of all the shadows,
has decided to make their mark onto me.
Onto me.
Not you,
just me.
The castaway is scared.
Not angry yet,
just scared.
And as I torment it into shadows,
I stay in peace.
Selfish peace…
As my castaway heart continues to shatter.

Amber Nickerson, Grade 6
Monelison Middle School, VA

Birds

Birds, high in the sky
Jumping on the clouds
Resting in your nest

Adrienne Matuté, Grade 4
Courthouse Road Elementary School, VA

Our Unbreakable Love

My dear love my dear love,
Our unbreakable love shall last forever.

Even the angels of heaven are jealous of our love,
For even the demons of hell are jealous.

For there is no one better than you.
Our love shall last forever.
My dear love why did you leave?

It was the angels of heaven are jealous.
My dear love my dear love.
I am nothing without you when you are gone.
All because of jealous hearts, you died.

Kevin Jemiolo, Grade 4
Alice B Beal Elementary School, MA

School

I spy the school
As I hear the buses park.
I feel a whole bunch of worksheets around me.
I smell the classroom air freshener,
As I taste the end of my pencil.

Jack Eastman, Grade 4
Crestwood Elementary School, VA

Snake

The long wavy body of the snake slithers silently
through the leaves,
trying to find food,
with its head bobbing back and forth
and tongue hissing
to make the other animals aware
of how dangerous he is.

A dwarf mouse jumps out of the leaves;
the snake wastes no time
and wraps its tail around its prey.
When the squealing finally stops,
the snake slurps it up.

Hunting accomplished.
Now for some sleep
in a hollow log.

Alexandra Whelan, Grade 6
Trinity School, MD

Shannon Bobbit

Tennessee player, Shannon Bobbit;
Quick little point guard; like a hobbit.
Only 5'2", but she handles the ball alright,
When she runs down the court,
She goes out of sight!

Emily Freedland, Grade 6
Village School, MA

Spring

Lilies all over
No more four leaf clovers
It's time for spring
The bells will ring
Finally spring has arrived
I do hope the flowers survive
Somewhere over the rainbow
I know
Butterflies fly
And birds sing
Now I know spring has begun

Cassie Gaudio, Grade 4
St Dominic School, CT

Summer/Winter

Summer
joyful, relaxing
calming, warming, playful
extremely hot, cold icicles
sled, snowboard, ski
freezing, frostbite
Winter

Sophia Nistico, Grade 5
Jane Ryan School, CT

Swimming! Fish Swimming! Fish!

Tiny fish!
Huge fish!
There swimming
There swimming
Fast! Fast! Fast!
Racing for survival
Chomp! Chomp! Chomp!
Oh no tiny fish all gone.

Alex Potocki, Grade 5
C C Burr Elementary School, MA

Knots

Knots are like shoelaces
Tie them hard and they
Will never come apart.
Just like families:
If you tie your love very tight
Your love will never
Come apart!!

Monica Stemski, Grade 5
St Joseph School-Fullerton, MD

Rainbow

Rainbow
Colorful light
Brightens a rainy day
Makes me smile 'til it hurts so bad
Color

Natalie Racoosin, Grade 4
Waller Mill Fine Arts Magnet School, VA

Mixed Up Seuss

If you go to the darkest, dreariest, smeariest place,
There you will find the twoslur resting his case.
He will lower a pail with great ease
and a sign that says, "a nickel please."

You drop in a nickel or two,
And he will tell you the story of Horton and Bartholomew.
He will say, "this is for you and you only,
So don't go around telling people baloney."

The story begins.

Horton was standing around one day,
When Bartholomew passed by pushing a cart with great care.
The cart held a grinch with no heart, a hare, and 499 hats to spare.
Horton decided to tag along.

Bartholomew was going to see the Lorax
Because he wanted a truffala to feed to a grebe.

When they got the seed to feed to a grebe,
They then met a hen
Who became their friend
And that was the end.

Adriana Meredith, Grade 5
Forest Avenue Elementary School, MA

The Pearl

T iny seed pearls were all the pearl divers would find.
H ow exciting when Kino finds "The Pearl of the World."
E nvious villagers tried to steal Kino's Pearl.

P reventing villagers from stealing the Pearl Kino's family went to the hills.
E vil doctor fought Kino for the pearl.
A fter Kino shot the gun, he was mortified.
R age consumed Kino because he killed his infant son.
L onging for his old life, Kino hurls the pearl into the sea.

Kyle Kreidler, Grade 6
St Joseph School, MA

Sunset

I am the sunset!
You know me for my many colors
converting the aqua sky scarlet, rose, and lilac.
I go to sleep at dusk
and rise at dawn.
You can't touch; you can only feel my gentle breeze blowing past you.
I can see the whole world when I drift by the tan houses, and the turquoise lakes;
in the winter I can smell the burnt wood from the fireplaces,
and in the summer I can smell the delicious steaks cooking on grills.
I drink the cold rain falling from the sky
like a child drinking a glass of lemonade on a hot summer day.
At night I hear the quiet owls beginning their song
and the wolves howling for the moon.

Paige Linardi, Grade 6
St Stephen Parochial School, MD

Sunsets

The sun is like a flashlight slowly dying out,
Gold and oranges painting the sky.
The daisies' fragrance flows through the summer night,
The air almost sweet to taste.
The grass is soft beneath my hands.
Like a song of praise for the sun setting,
The robins hum a soft tune.

Kirsten Eddy, Grade 6
Trinity School, MD

Riding the Waves of White

At my house, in the afternoon,
I went snowboarding down a snow typhoon.
The wind was blowing, I taste the snow,
I touched my board, and I was ready to go.
I went down the hill as fast as a jet
and I could hear the wind go whooosh.
At the end I hit a rock and broke my board,
so you better be careful when you go to snowboard!

Collin Dunn, Grade 6
Litchfield Intermediate School, CT

James

Pumpernickel is a hawk,
Soaring high above the world
Seeing all.
He is an oak tree, being blown in the wind
And birds sitting on him.
He is a tiger
Waiting to pounce
To get his afternoon snack.
He is a guitar that keeps on going.
He is the person that will never stop arguing,
That will talk and talk and talk
Until his point is made.
Pumpernickel is a back road in the country
Seeing sights
And seeing wonders.
He is the protector of his hair
Fixing it every second
Of every day.
Pumpernickel is salsa
All spicy and hot
With nachos.

Ian Buckley, Grade 5
St Luke's School, CT

Baseball

My favorite sport is baseball
I hit the ball and it looks like a cannon ball
I start running around the bases
It get to the fourth one
Home run!

Travis Welch, Grade 5
McCleary Elementary School, VA

Holly

Caring,
Silly,
Loving,
Wishes to help animals,
Dreams of helping kids in need,
Wants to help find a cure for the sick,
Who wonders why people kill other people,
Who fears of getting killed,
Who is afraid of being embarrassed,
Who likes boys that are cute, sweet, nice, funny,
and play a sport,
Who believes in succeeding,
Who loves pizza
Who loves to play softball,
Who loves to do cheerleading,
Who loves to help people,
Who plans to be a mom,
Who plans to go to college,
Who plans to be a veterinarian,
Who plans on living a good life.

Holly Nalley, Grade 6
E Russell Hicks School, MD

Falling

I am a falling leaf
I wonder where I'll be
I hear the wind singing softly
I see no sign of glee
I want to someday be free
I am a falling leaf
I pretend to be a blue bird flying swiftly through the sky
I feel a rain drop on my stem
I touch the ground
I worry of drowning in a creek
I cry freely, but really weak
I am a falling leaf
I understand I might be crushed or stepped on by a geek
I say "I hate flying," but maybe you want me to be
I dream I'll someday never fly again
I try to imagine when
I hope the wind will die down then I'll touch the ground again
I am now free!

Sharice Murrell, Grade 6
Page Middle School, VA

Fireworks

Crackle, crackle!
Boom, boom!
Hear the fireworks burst,
As they light up the sky above.
What a beautiful sight,
On this very special night.
Pop! Bang!
I love fireworks.

John Hogge, Grade 6
Page Middle School, VA

Brothers

My brother is the best
But sometimes he's a pest.
He thinks it's lots of fun
When he eats my only bun.

Kezia M. Allers, Grade 4
Hebbville Elementary School, MD

Edmund Campion

Queen Elizabeth favored me,
cause I went to Oxford University,
1578 was my ordination date,
the time when the Queen began to hate,
and death became my only fate.
In secret I had to dwell,
with George Eliot on my trail,
while saying Mass,
I was found it came to pass,
A miracle or two attributed to me,
as well as courage and humility.
Taken to Tyburn and tortured first,
martyred, burned and thrown away,
to remind the world of what,
Christ did for us on Good Friday.

Crispin Ferris, Grade 4
Angelus Academy, VA

Golden Fields

Golden fields of straw
Roll across the land
Like waves hitting the shore

Kathleen Baptista, Grade 5
St Mary's Primary School, MA

A Toucan's World!

T he coolest thing you will ever see
O ur toucans are endangered
U nique birds
C ool colors
A wesome birds
N ature's artwork
S hea Dorsey is a toucan lover!!!

Shea Dorsey, Grade 5
Chalk Hill School, CT

Birds of a Feather

Birds of a feather
In the sky.
Birds of a feather
Fly so high.
Birds of the weather
Ready to explore.
Birds of the weather
Flying more and more.

Catherine Walbrecher, Grade 6
St Joseph School-Fullerton, MD

Lemony Snicket

L ucky man
E xtraordinary author
M uscular man
O rdinary person
N ot happy
Y ounger sister

S eries of Unfortunate Events
N ever nervous
I ncredible man
C areful person
K nobby knees
E xciting stories
T oo hyper

Brandon Mills, Grade 4
Appomattox Elementary School, VA

Penguins

Penguins black and white,
Going down slopes on bellies.
Penguins catching fish.

Nathan Lowry, Grade 4
Long Meadow Elementary School, CT

Waterfalls

I see waterfalls
their roaring waters spray me
drops run down my face

Alyssa Curcio, Grade 4
Trinity Christian School, VA

The Rhythms of Music

There are
Many rhythms
To music
Jazz has
Smooth rhythms
Blues have
Calm rhythms
Rap has
Jumpy rhythms
And rock has
Bumpy rhythms
But
Poetry has
The best of all

Michael Hourihan, Grade 4
St Mary's Primary School, MA

Forest Nights

The nice, cool wind blows
On animals in the night
When running in the forest.

Samuel Sandler, Grade 4
Grace Miller Elementary School, VA

Ocean

Waves tossing, turning
Angry winds howl in your ears
Salty smells linger

Emily Hall, Grade 6
Our Lady of Mercy School, CT

Dark Jungle

My heart beats like an earthquake,
But when I stop and calm myself down,
Things in me seem like a jungle.
And my heart looks like hot pepper.
But for me to calm myself down,
Is to just let my anger go.

Paul Awah, Grade 6
Magnolia Elementary School, MD

Notes

Notes
That say sorry
Hi and bye
Want some gum
Here is some candy
don't show anybody
What do you want to talk about?
There are Love notes
There are Get Well notes
Read this
Read that
Notes

Samantha Delaney-Burke, Grade 5
Milton L Fuller Elementary School, MA

What Is Poetry?

Poetry is when
The lines
Flow like a river,
Poetry is when the words
Fit in like
A puzzle
Poetry is when
The stanzas
Are larger
Than a yardstick or
Smaller than a little inch worm
Poetry is when
Your feelings
Of something
Pour out like a
Waterfall
And poetry
Is when
Something you like
Is on paper

Emily McDonald, Grade 5
C C Burr Elementary School, MA

Bullies

Bullies are bad
They make people sad,
Bullies kick
They make me sick.
Bullies are rude,
They always have an attitude
Bullies are rude to others
I hope they're not rude to their mothers
Bullies can be tall or small,
But they are still mean to all
Bullies should be nice
Even to mice!

Brianna Sullivan, Grade 4
Helen H Hansen Elementary School, MA

My Dad Bike Riding

I see my dad turn round the bend;
"One more block, Dad, it's almost the end"
He's coming closer to our house;
His pedals are squeaking like a little mouse;
His ride is over;
He could sleep like a log;
He's drunk enough water to fill a bog;
I want to give a hug to my sweaty dad,
But I would have to take a shower,
And that would be bad,
He's still breathing hard;
I could hear him from a mile
Now I'll stop bothering him,
and let him rest a while,
My dad did a ride that required lots of power,
I gave him a hug,
Oh well, now I'll have to take that shower.

Brett Mayville, Grade 5
John Ward Elementary School, MA

October Night

As I walk up and ring the doorbell to trick or treat
I find a bowl of candy at my feet
I can't help but smell a freshly baked pumpkin pie to eat
The wind whispers in my ear like a friend telling me a secret
And hollers like a father OCTOBER IS HERE
The silver moon sparkles in the night
Filled with children full of fright
Ghostly jack-o-lanterns stare into my eyes
Then POP out comes a big surprise
A russet acorn falls from a tree
I can't help but think what's going to happen to me
I speed away as fast as time
I am relieved
And I am now fine
I trudge back home like a camper to her tent
Halloween is over and
It has been a great OCTOBER

Eliza Lynch, Grade 6
Madison Middle School, CT

Frederikke

You are a snowstorm ready to burst
A cloud drifting across the sky
And a radiant rose
You are drose
A cheerful blue jay
And ice cream from Gudhjem
You are a running river
A snowy tundra
And a shiny bronze medal
You are Farmor's special gravy
A giggle you get out of reading jokes and riddles
And Scooby Doo
You are the color pink
A perfect playful circle
And the tallest roller coaster in Tivoli
You are a jumpy seesaw
The unstoppable motor of a speed boat
And a sweet clementine
You are a princess
A dog as energetic as 1000 wind-up toys
And, most importantly, you're my cousin

Danica Jensen, Grade 5
St Luke's School, CT

One Spring Morning

As the morning glories open the sun is rising.
The clouds open up like big huge puffy pillows.
The pond has the sunbeams coming down on it.
As the little frog stares up he goes croak!
Then he gets pulled under!
Blub blub blub blub blub blub bye bye little frog.

Emma Pereira, Grade 5
Francis Asbury Elementary School, VA

Rain into a Puddle

I am rain
I wonder when I will fall
I hear my family screaming
I see my friends falling
I want to be with them
I am a puddle
I pretend to be dancing in the road
I feel people stomping in me
I touch the road
I worry about myself
I cry while I run into a stream
I am a river
I understand why people swim in me
I say have fun to all the boaters
I dream to be one of them
I try to be happy
I hope children are having fun playing in me
I am rain

Lindsay Macey, Grade 6
Page Middle School, VA

A Trip to the Moon

Count down, 5 to 1, in a ship headed for the moon, a lone dust moon, in space, we are running a race,
Exploring many wonders, along this rocky road, running and jumping, along the dusty plains.
Time to go, to and fro, down the dust plains of the lone moon, heading back to the ship.
Loaded with cargo, in the spaceship, floating and controlling the ship, making it float along space…
Smoothly floating along space, dodging all the craters, having a blast.

Andrew Ciampa, Grade 4
Summit Montessori School, MA

Autumn

The butterscotch leaves fell gracefully to the ground
I saw a ginger pooch dance with the garnet, topaz, and emerald leaves.
Outside you could sniff the crisp apple cinnamon pie wavering in the air.
The aroma made my mouth water.
The pie was wonderfully baked.
Warm, fresh, lime green granny smith apples, flaky crust, topped with vanilla ice cream.

As the sun sets the breezy, brisk night becomes spooky with the sounds of owls hooting, crickets cricketing, and wolves howling.
The noises were as scary as being in a creepy graveyard all alone with a full moon and shadow everywhere!
Children dressed in costumes rustling in the ruby and poppy colored leaves fallen from the trees.

The feeling of the smooth frosty pumpkin felt like a cold damp doorknob which sent and icy cool chill up my spine.

Night falls and with it comes a silvery night and all you can hear is the whistling wind
and the crackling of the fire as you drift off to sleep and say quietly…good night autumn.

Lauren Squires, Grade 6
Madison Middle School, CT

The Heart

Heats are made for loving things like your family or a sport you "love" to play and other things like food, pets and etc. Hearts are also used to doodle when you're bored and don't know what to do, just draw heart's all over your notebooks of spare papers but also hearts are the major component in your body that helps pump your blood to all the organs and keeps your body alive and running.

Julia DiGiuseppe, Grade 5
Har-Bur Middle School, CT

Autumn Time

Autumn time
Strawberry leaves
The scent of pine cones touching my nose, tickles
Within the berries, I see olive green with coral black spots
Flaming red berries
Crispy, crunchy, bay brown leaves
Smelly swamp with green moss
Autumn time, this is autumn time
Autumn time
The colors of autumn are like a color wheel
The sound of leaves crunching as I step on them is just like the sound of someone crumpling paper
Twigs snapped like I snap my ruler on the desk really hard
When fall comes to an end
Trees start to cry as they lose their leaves one by one
Autumn time
This is definitely fall
I can tell for sure
Because of the autumn air

Jennifer Stowe, Grade 6
Madison Middle School, CT

Keep on Moving*

Keep on moving don't stop
Because if you stop
Your dreams or desires will never come true
Believe in your dreams
Keep on moving until you are at the top
Don't listen to the down keepers and what they say
Ignore them and you will feel good about every day
Keep on moving
Believe in yourself
Keep on moving don't stop
Keep on moving until you are at the top

Mark Wilson, Grade 5
Clover Street School, CT
*Inspired by Gwendolyn Brooks

Don't Even Bother

I hate her from the bottom of my soul.
From her blue eyes
to her white teeth.

It's all too perfect.
Behind that perfect smile
lays a hideous smirk,
and behind those perfect eyes
is a shine of malice.

I used to look up to her like everyone else.
But not anymore.
Because I know what she is.

And yet I'm not afraid
because I know she'll never hurt me
because I know her words are lies
and that my friends will keep me safe.
And we can laugh together at her lies
because we know just what she is.

Ellen Brooks, Grade 6
Swampscott Middle School, MA

Alphabet Alliteration

A wesome alligators ache	**N** utty nuts noisy
B lack bowls bounce	**O** dd octopus obeys
C razy cooks cook	**P** ink Panther picks
D irty drum dances	**Q** uick quilt quacks
E ager egg eloping	**R** ed rakes run
F eisty feet fat	**S** unny snake snarls
G reen grape growls	**T** urquoise tiger trots
H airy hippo hiccups	**U** gly umbrella underground
I cky igloo ice skates	**V** aluable villages visit
J umpy jaguar jumps	**W** onderful willows walk
K ind kangaroo kisses	**X** -rayed xylophones x-ray
L ime leopards leap	**Y** ellow yak yelps
M etallic monster makes	**Z** any zebras zip

Brian Morcone, Grade 6
Chalk Hill School, CT

The Three Long Months

As the time grows near,
I get ready to have my next operation.
I have had not one, but five.
I feel nervous and scared.
What's going to happen to me?
I have the surgery, and the recovery is long,
three months to be exact.
I meet some great people: Ingrid is awesome, and
eleven year old Lexi is a very nice girl.
She is there for the same reason as me.
I finally go home after three long months;
I get to sleep in my own bed, play with my own toys,
and even go to my own school.
No more tutor, no more Ingrid, no more halo.
I am sad, but excited; I get to go home. Hooray!
Now Melissa is having surgery.
She needs support and I am that.
I calm her down and tell her it is going to be okay.
The worst three months of my life are over.
No more halos, I'm done with them.
Good bye and good night.

Natali Masarskaya, Grade 6
Swampscott Middle School, MA

Chocolate Chip Cookie Dough Ice Cream

As I was driving to the ice cream store,
I imagined what delicious dessert would be there.
The longing I had for ice cream was making my head sore.
Chocolate chip and cookie dough, what a wonderful pair!

I thought about how many scoops I would get,
So many, piled so high, making its deliciousness show.
I hope that they will provide the best amount yet
Of the heavenly key ingredient, cookie dough.

Bring on the rich and chunky chocolate chips.
The melting ice cream makes my cone have an odd taste.
To make sure I get all I can get, I lick my lips,
Making sure no wonderful ice cream goes to waste.

As I came out of the crowded store and away from the din,
I took a lick and my mouth suddenly broke into a grin!

Laura Schammel, Grade 6
Immaculate Heart of Mary School, MD

I Love a Bakery

In bakeries,
I can smell the cake with the trains on top
I can touch the big glass case with all the treats inside
I can see humongous chocolate chip cookies
They look so delicious!
I can hear the bells on the door when it opens.
I wish I could taste the jelly and cream donuts
to see if they are scrumptious.

Katelyn Pillar, Grade 4
Crestwood Elementary School, VA

Dog Hog

There once was a dog
That acted like a hog
He was stupid enough
To fall in a bog
Swam and swam but
He did not turn into a hog.

Kaci Hill, Grade 4
Plainfield Catholic School, CT

Dancing

Drum, drum, drumming
There I go
Like a kangaroo
Black tights
Purple artist collective shirt
When I leap,
I'm a soaring eagle.
Heart zooming fast as a
Cheetah running.

The room was as hot
As a pot of popcorn,
Bubbling over.

Gabrielle Fearon, Grade 4
Braeburn School, CT

Seasons

Seasons are unique
All seasons are colorful
Each one is special

Flowers are blooming
Green grass is everywhere
Many birds chirping

Going to the beach
Diving into the water
Hot and sunny days

Leaves crunch underfoot
Jumping into crisp leaf piles
Many colored leaves

My cheeks are rosy
Snow gently falls on my face
Snowmen line the streets

Victoria Kirkman, Grade 4
St Rose School, CT

Simon Cowell

A famous judge Simon Cowell
Always had to say something foul
He is on American Idol
And he is looking for a new title!!

Madison Scalley, Grade 6
Captain Nathan Hale Middle School, CT

Scarred for Life

I scout out the deserted area for prey.
In the distance I see a zebra it's fat, big and it will last for a week.
But it was very far away.
I start sprinting over then I hide behind a tree…
good it's still there.
I start sprinting again but faster so fast I couldn't see.
Then before I knew it a dome fell out of the sky and protected the zebra.
And now my face is so implanted on this dome.
Hoooooooray. (Sarcastic)

James P. Casali, Grade 6
Litchfield Intermediate School, CT

Friends

F riends are cool, cooler than ice.
R un together, play together, walk together, so nice.
I t rains today and tomorrow.
E ven rains the day after, to bring more sorrow.
N ever forget my wonderful friends, I'll see them tomorrow, tomorrow, hooray!
D one for today, okay, okay.
S o don't worry, I'll see you the next day.

Tatyana Geneste, Grade 5
Davenport Ridge School, CT

The Soldier

The soldier, fighting for who he loves, the ones he cares about
The soldier, brave and true, head raised high; love and pride all inside
All the freedoms we cherish taken for granted in our daily lives
My heart split in half for the one I love,
If only he had been with me before he died,
He is gone, gone forever,
I'm breaking down inside
If only I had been by his side when my brother died!

Nick Burleigh, Grade 5
John F Kennedy School, CT

A Cyber Christmas

'Twas the night before Christmas and through the 'net,
E-mails and e-cards were flying as fast as a jet.
People all over the world sending cyber holiday cheer,
Sending winter greetings without the smallest fear.
Kids in their chat rooms, talking to friends,
And people typing up merry greetings to send.
Companies sending Christmas bonuses through PayPal and such,
Making sure they don't make a typo and send a bit too much.
Then when it gets late and the kids are sent to bed,
The adults use the laptop and get their e-mails read.
While they update their blogs and website with a Christmas theme,
Santa Claus lands on the roof with his reindeer team.
The grownups click, they type, and then chat,
While Santa eats cookies and gives his belly a pat.
Then he leaves the presents under the tree
For good little children like you and me.
And if you were a little naughty, instead of coal,
You'll get a new computer that your parents will hog and control!

Kate Delossantos, Grade 6
St Clement Mary Hofbauer School, MD

Harriet Tubman

Harriet Tubman was born a hardworking slave,
And she always was caring and very brave.
Harriet was hired out at the age of six,
To a mistress, Miss Susan, who gave her many licks.

She grew stronger still hoping to escape one day,
And live in a world were blacks and whites have their say.
Without warning Harriet was hit by a weight,
It was the start of her journey to change her fate.

Harriet found out that she was going to be sold,
It was because of her injury, so she was told.
Harriet made her final decision to flee,
Because her life would only be worth living if free.

Harriet's journey took her many long dates,
But she finally got to the freedom states.
As a conductor on the Underground Railroad,
Harriet took fugitive slaves North, load after load.

She led hundreds of people out of slavery,
Because Harriet was a woman of great bravery.

Meghan Ryan, Grade 6
Daniel L Joyce Middle School, MA

The Doorknob

Hands, they touch me every day
Every person opens the door
Can't I have a say?

"How 'bout 'scuse me, Mr. Doorknob, can we open the door?"
Instead, with a flick of their wrists, I'm turned again
When I'm locked, and people try to get through
They can't
And they turn me
Too much

Then they put a key in
Do you know how weird it is to have a key in your belly?
It puts a shiver down my spine — every time
And they turn
Déjà vu

I should start a petition
I would

If I could move

Josh Malett, Grade 6
Weston Middle School, CT

Stars

Looking at the stars
The designs in the dark sky
Only here 'til, gone

Philip Tor, Grade 5
Charlotte A Dunning Elementary School, MA

The Humble Soldier

I am a soldier fighting at war
My knees are weak and my shoulders are sore
I'm not sure I'm worth much anymore
I'm just a soldier fighting at war

I was shot down just the other day
Some people came to take me away
And that is when I heard them say
"This graveyard's growing every day"

My soul is gone, so now it's free
And all America's lost is me
So here I'm buried beneath a tree
But my heart is content 'cause America's free

Bethany Wasilik, Grade 4
Pemberton Elementary School, VA

The Beach

The light sand falls right through your hand
The turquoise water crystal clear
The seashells hard and bumpy along the shore
A calm place to go
Nice and quiet
Peaceful all around

Stephanie Schofield, Grade 5
St Mary's Primary School, MA

Like an Angel

Like an angel up in the sky
A big beast flying under me
Carrying me through the obstacles
The sweet smell of hay
Is in the air with me
The horse lands
The magic is over

Alyssa Dawidczyk, Grade 5
Charlotte A Dunning Elementary School, MA

Look at Me

Look at me, what do you see?
Dark brown hair
Light brown eyes
Light pink lips
Calm as a gentle wave
I'm a sunflower
Tall, bright, happy feeling
I can brighten your day
When you are feeling down
And a mouse can hide under my leaves.
I'm a dolphin
Cheerful, always full of energy, exciting
Like a wave moving gracefully side to side
And always gentle to any human I meet!

Alicia Anachasian, Grade 5
West Woods Upper Elementary School, CT

Liberty

L ying down at the face of freedom
I nventing a new way of society
B eing brave no matter what
E veryone wants it, and dies for it
R ejoicing an everlasting echoing plea
T ying down the faces of reality
Y elling and pleading for the humanity

Justin Flattery, Grade 5
Sacred Heart Elementary School, MA

Rollercoaster

I am a rollercoaster
My track is shiny blue.
My drop is 500 feet tall.
My cart is decorated with flames.
I am a rollercoaster
I have eighteen loops.
I have fifty corkscrews.
My cart goes so fast that
Wind hits me at 100 miles per hour.
I am a rollercoaster.

Jonny Najarian, Grade 4
St Christopher's School, VA

Sun

Brightens your mornings
Is always there to greet you
Sky's magic light bulb

Danielle Epstein, Grade 5
Jane Ryan School, CT

Watched

By hundreds of people,
The skydiver jumps into the air
Flying through the sky leaving a trail
of clouds behind him.
Watched
By no one,
The leaf falls from the tree
Flying around in circles
Before it hits the ground
And no one even looked.

Malcolm Ilnicky, Grade 4
St Christopher's School, VA

Halloween

Halloween
Spooky warlocks, witches, and wizards
The sweet candy in my bag
The footsteps of the ghouls
The chocolateness of the Hershey Bar
The wrappers of the eaten candy
Halloween

Kristian Raczkowski, Grade 5
Jane Ryan School, CT

Spring and Fall

Spring
Beautiful, peaceful
Flowering, blooming, raining
Flowers, birds, leaves, school
Falling, changing, playing
Crisp, leaves
Fall

Emily Kreidler, Grade 6
St Joseph School, MA

Telescope

This is my telescope
Through it I see far
I find constellations
Of each little star

This is my telescope
Silver and thin
I observe our Milky Way
And the things within

This is my telescope
It can't see far past the moon
I hope they invent
A better one soon

Holly Storm, Grade 6
Scotts Ridge Middle School, CT

Agenda Book

Will you fail?
Or maybe succeed?
The agenda book
Is here indeed

Are you organized?
Or unprepared
Bring your agenda book
Don't be scared

People will joke
And laugh at you
But you'll be the one who
Is passing grade school

You'll stop by McDonald's
Suit and tie…
Some people we gaze
Some workers will sigh

When employed
You will see…
That your company
Is owned by me!

Tré Paquette, Grade 6
Edmond P Talbot Middle School, MA

Rainbows

They are very nice
Are pretty and colorful
Sparkle in the light

May Blithe, Grade 4
Battlefield Elementary School, VA

Cross

C rucified my Lord,
R ight in front of everyone.
O utstanding example of His love for us.
S ad, for only a moment
S mile, that he died so that we may live.

Zachary Campbell, Grade 6
Monelison Middle School, VA

Boxing

Ding! Ding! Ding! The bell rings
Now it's time to do my thing.
Bam! I socked 'em right in the eye.
But then he got me back, in my thigh.
He swung again, but I blocked it.
Then, I swung my fists.
Hit 'em in the head.
He fell down,
The referee counted to ten
The match was over so…I win!

Austin Makohon, Grade 6
Page Middle School, VA

Dad

Mark
Kind, playful
Cooking, working, talking
A really good person
Dad

Alice Yuen, Grade 4
Sacred Heart School, MA

Cats

Stalking through the grass,
Ears perked up,
Eyes wide.

Rustling in the grass,
A mouse scurries along,
The cat jumps up,
Then all is silent.

As I walk up the steps,
The cat is waiting at the door,
With a mouse at its feet,
Looking up at me,
Waiting for praise.

Cherie Lepak, Grade 6
Albert D Griswold Middle School, CT

Passage to the Unexpected

I open a door.
To my surprise,
it leads into another.
I only see the corner,
of skillfully carved wood.
I glare.
It taunts my curiosity.

Day and night,
looking for explanations.
"Why is it bolted shut?"
I finally lose patience.
While unscrewing it
"I wonder if there is gold or money."

Instead of the gold,
I expected to find.
It's hollow.
The area is not useless though.

I secretly hide my own valuables.
Then bolt it shut.

Alan Swierczynski, Grade 6
Foxborough Regional Charter School, MA

One Chance and One Chance Only*

a perfect round
baseball
and a little
luck
can make a
difference
bottom of the
ninth
stepping to the
plate
glances at the
sky
takes a little
stride
with everything but
fear
smashes the white
ball
and it's history

Tyler Galske, Grade 5
West Woods Upper Elementary School, CT
*Inspired by William Carlos Williams

The Flag

We all look to
The symbol of our people
The seal of our peace

Joseph Vazquez, Grade 5
Charlotte A Dunning Elementary School, MA

The Concert

It was a scorching hot and pitch black night
I could feel the sweat drip off my face
I had come to the Tweeter Center
The place where performances are held
I had come to see the famous rapper
Will Smith,
And he was going to sing
I suddenly hear people screaming
At the top of their lungs
Then I hear the familiar voice
Yes it was indeed Will Smith
I smell cheap perfume
From the lady next to me
I see girl dancers
Dancing
The music was so loud and funky. I just had to dance.
And my body is aching because of it.
Then the concert is over and we go home
In the car my Dad hands me a piece of paper,
With an autograph of Will Smith on it
I will never forget this day

Justin Trudell, Grade 5
Foxborough Regional Charter School, MA

Sawyer

Sawyer is my crazy dog
He loves attention and the backyard
He jumps and barks
He chews up everything
When will his rampage end?
Yet through all of this I know
That if he could tell what he truly thinks
He would be saying
How much he loves us
When I hear my dad talking
About when he comes home
After a long day at work
He sees Sawyer jump up in joy
Now Sawyer knows he has the reassurance
He'll need at the moment until we have to go again
When I walk through the door
Sawyer realizes that he loves me so much
That he'll tackle me to the ground
When that happens I forget all the bad stuff that he did
All I remember is how much I love him
And all the ways he has affected my life

James Mitchel, Grade 6
Grace Episcopal Day School, MD

My Family

When I'm with my family
it makes my day bright.
I hope I could stay with them
Until midnight.

Charles Egypt, Grade 4
Courthouse Road Elementary School, VA

Clouds

Shapes roam the blue sky
Dances in the sky all day
A white, puffy sight
Ryan Cranston, Grade 4
Trinity Christian School, VA

Dove

Soaring through the sky,
A white wonder landing on a branch,
It chirps with joy and interacts
With only the others it could trust.

So quietly and graceful,
This peaceful bird,
Even though small,
Fun to be around
In the air flies a dove.
Melissa Nenninger, Grade 6
Albert D Griswold Middle School, CT

Butterflies

Butterflies fly high.
Butterflies are beautiful.
Blue, yellow and pink wings.
Kelsey Cardenas, Grade 4
Long Meadow Elementary School, CT

Benedict Arnold

B ritish aide
E nlisted man
N ever finished school
E nergetic
D ied in England
I njured
C aptain of militia
T raitor
Shyon Ambrose, Grade 5
Lake Shore Elementary School, MD

Two Common Pets

Kitten
fluffy, short
pouncing, shedding, shredding
fur, claws, tail, paws
running, fetching, sleeping
cuddly, soft
puppy
Kate Flinchum, Grade 5
McCleary Elementary School, VA

Leap!

Hop, hop, hop. That's what a frog does.
Hop, hop, hop. Let's leap, leap
and bounce, bounce all night long!
Ramon Gracia, Grade 4
Bowers School, CT

The Greatest Empire

The war cry of soldiers strikes fear into the hearts of the enemy.
The feeling of defeat weighs them down, like a film of iron.
Death and impending doom is all that crosses the enemy's panic stricken mind.
Tiny doubt changed their fate completely.
The last things they saw were the glinting blades of Roman swords.
The enemy, completely, totally obliterated.
The winds of sorrow whip across the barren landscape.
This ruthlessness made Rome the greatest empire.
Alex Furbank, Grade 5
Wakefield Forest Elementary School, VA

Life

Life is what we were given by God
Whose only son Jesus, who will again descend
People and creatures are what God gave life to
And some people still waste their lives with "newly" cool cars too
Some people skip school and some people use it
It is a blessing that God gave us a choice on what we want to get
This is my opinion on life, so don't think I'm dumb
It is your choice to cherish your life with God
Or waste it with the material things that are to come
Life
Leroy Hyson II, Grade 5
Church of the Redeemer Christian School, MD

Sijo

I am looking through the window out at the courtyard.

I see a beautiful garden and nature around me like a person who is happy.
The stone turtle watches the pond like a guard
As bubbles burst and lily pads slowly glide through the water!
Anne Rutherford, Grade 5
Wakefield Forest Elementary School, VA

The Rainbow

Cerulean is the bubbles that leak from the waves
Saffron is a blazing tangy orange

Blackthorn is the cloudy midnight of the apparition
Pewter is the click of a new nickel

The coarse blaze of timber wolf is a group of storm clouds, running to strike
Periwinkle is the twilight, signaling the encroaching night

Lilac is the color of the breaking dawn
Scarlet is the flare of an open wound

Mustard is the color of a field of grain
Violet is the color of a shriveled prune

Aqua is the pure clean depths of an oasis
Magenta is a Valentine's card

These colors are only a few
Riley Meachem, Grade 6
Scotts Ridge Middle School, CT

Burning Logs

Smoke in the blue sky
Wood burning with orange fire
Making peaceful warmth

Drew Wilkers, Grade 4
C Hunter Ritchie Elementary School, VA

No Matter the Size

There once was a dog, a very fat dog
His stomach bulged and wobbled while he walked
Blumb, blumb, blumb,
He rand down the hall
As he went for the ball,
With his skinny stick legs
And his bowling ball body
He waddled like a penguin,
And gave me a kiss, I hugged the big tuft of fluff
And that was it
It's not only his body that's big,
But also his heart
I love this dog,
Big and wide
This dog is mine no matter the size

Natalie Wihbey, Grade 6
Litchfield Intermediate School, CT

The Woods

Green Pines a-rustling,
Song birds singing.
The blue sky hushes,
As clouds go by.
Let the earth feel your presence as you walk along.
Singing the whispers of a new tune.
Yell it out loud,
Let the world hear,
How beautiful the woods are,
Only you can see.
And the river whistles along
Like your dad when content.
Sliding,
Slipping along,
Singing its song.

Berta Warner, Grade 6
Smith College Campus School, MA

Chocolate Chip Cheesecake

Splash! Splash!
A wonderful piece of cheesecake melts in my mouth,
Like an ice cube on a hot summer day,
Oh! The wonderful sound of it, the sound of joy!
Oh! The delicious cake of joy charging like a
choo choo train in my mouth to my taste buds,
And every time I don't take a bite, my mouth turns to freight!
Every time I take a bite,
My taste buds go to heaven and come back down.

Joseph Velez, Grade 6
City View School, MA

A Feis

The music starts, I am ready to dance
I point my toe and my stomach thumps
Steps flow from my brain to the tip of my toes
Excitement lifts me up into the air
My wild, curly wig is bouncing as I am moving
Crossed Tippy-toes
I am done with the dance
I bow with pride
My smile is lighting the earth
The results are called as my heart bounces like a kangaroo
"Number 13," I hear over the microphone
"I have won!"
My eyes glisten in the stage light
Holding the trophy in my hand
Thinking about the times I haven't won
All the disappointments
Watching someone else hold the trophy
But, today I have done it
Winning at the Feis

Julia Murphy, Grade 5
Booth Hill School, CT

My Little Red Robin Friend

The little bird sat perched up high,
sitting in the tree I always passed by.
I climbed onto a branch, there the view was best;
and there I saw three tiny eggs in the red robin's nest.
Every day I stopped at the brown oak tree,
hoping three tiny heads would poke out at me.
I went one day and saw the red robin bird,
a sweet sad song was all my ears heard.
I peered into the nest, but there was nothing there:
the little baby birds had gone off somewhere.
I looked at the robin, with its big brown eyes,
seeing sadness and grief and hearing all her cries.
A glisten of hope was in my voice,
to help the little red robin was my choice.
I would search the whole town: every hill, every tree.
I'd search and look until I found all three.
After I had told her what I would do,
she whistled and sang as if she knew too.

Leigh Hamlet, Grade 6
Whitinsville Christian School, MA

Early Morning

I wake to the sounds of beautiful birds singing,
As they slowly swoop down onto old mossy-green trees.
The orange sun slowly drifts up into the newly blue sky.
As I walk outside, the wet grass tickles my ankles.
I can feel the cool breeze swiping across my face,
And the warm sun soaking into my skin.
I sit under the old oak tree to enjoy the
Spring sunrise.

Emma Berry, Grade 5
Coleytown Elementary School, CT

The Raven

A raven glares with beady eyes,
Looking to and fro as it flies.

It comes around to look at me,
I didn't look back; afraid of what I'd see.

The raven held his ground as though,
He thought he was a giant crow.

I felt as if I was so small,
Trapped inside a narrow hall.

It dove down low into my eyes,
What a dreadful surprise!

I'm so glad it was just a play,
And that raven was really made of clay.

Paul Miller, Grade 5
Hindley Elementary School, CT

Life

Life is about people.
Life is about family.
Life is about music.
Life is about love.
Life is about stars
in the night glowing.
Life is about living.
Life is about friends.
Life is about animals.
Life is about school.
Life is about everything
That is important to you.
What is your life about?

Yasmin Qudah, Grade 6
Magnolia Elementary School, MD

Rainbows

Rainbow shining
In the sky
Could be low
Or could be high
Bouncing round
From cloud to cloud
Oh, that rainbow
Majestically proud
I squint my eyes
For how bright it is shimmering
Almost brighter
Than the stars are glimmering
Fills my heart
With lots of love
For the rainbow in the sky above

Hallie Fuchs, Grade 5
Burr Elementary School, CT

Trojan War

Around 1250 B.C.
The Trojan War began,
Helen, a beautiful woman,
Captured by Paris, a man.

Greeks built a wooden horse
Men were hid inside
Soon it was pulled in Troy
The men came out, many died.

Some went to the gate
Comrades then entered in
They took Helen on a ship
Sailing back to her kin.

Micah Nagel, Grade 5
Trinity Christian School, VA

Hitting

My first homerun
my old friend
pitching to me
he used to be
on my team
gives me one
right down the middle
the ball
going whoosh through the air
then I smacked it
the bat goes clinck
to dead center
just clears the fence

Josh Berthiaume, Grade 5
Sinai Academy of the Berkshires, MA

Animals

Squirrels climb up big trees
They will always eat acorns
Their tails are furry

Frogs jump all around
Slimy, bumpy skin on them
Flies will be their lunch

Turtles have a shell
They will never win a race
On their back is home

Rebecca Cerone, Grade 5
Jane Ryan School, CT

Winter Finally Came

When it is snowing,
I stay inside all day.
I'll have a good time.

Emeka Okafor, Grade 4
Hebbville Elementary School, MD

Black Cat

There once was a big black cat
Who loved to itch her back
She found a flea
Fell down on her knees
And asked him not to come back.

Zachary Brown, Grade 4
Waller Mill Fine Arts Magnet School, VA

Easter

You get chocolate
Nice people give it to you
Easter is such fun.

Shane McWilliams, Grade 4
St Joseph School-Fullerton, MD

Spring

In spring, I see flowers
They are in the showers
In March there's lots of rain
Growing flowers down the lane
I always want to run
But only in the sun

Nick Cloutier, Grade 4
Brookside Elementary School, MA

Empty Hallways

As I walk through
the empty hallways
I hear silent
noises stepping
of feet and
drippings of leaks.
The radiator
creaks as
the lights
flicker and
EEEKKK!
The fuzzy
buzzes from
the broken intercom
run through
my mind
like a steak on a grill.
Empty hallways
Empty hallways
Empty hallways

Alec Sanford, Grade 6
Fuller Middle School, MA

Spring

Spring comes in full bloom,
Showers fall from the gray sky,
Bringing flowers life.

Charli Holland, Grade 4
Hebbville Elementary School, MD

Misty Sea

Misty sea deserted and blank
Like someone erased the ships,
White caps to prove
They had once been great
They now rock gently to lull the world to sleep.

The sea birds settle
So do the nettles
To feed their young alike,
As the wind slashes
Through the air
As sharp as a wetted knife.

Adina Ripin, Grade 4
Old Saybrook Middle School, CT

Yellowstone Park

I went on vacation last summer,
It was fun, but the car ride was a bummer.
Our cabin was the first thing we saw,
And when we got inside, it was rather small.

The waterfalls were rushing,
And the geysers were gushing.
The canyons were amazing,
But the heights were dazing.

The rodeo was quite a show,
With cowboys being tossed to and fro.
The elk and deer were running wild,
While the buffalo and wolves were fairly mild.

The hydrothermal pools were colorful and deep,
And into Yellowstone Lake they would seep.
As we left, going through Wyoming,
We stopped to see Mount Rushmore while we were going.

Drew Walker, Grade 6
Immaculate Heart of Mary School, MD

My Dream Restaurant

My dream restaurant,
is located in Vermont.
The food critic orders a steak,
it takes a long time to make.

One lucky customer who walks in the door,
receives a free s'more shaped like a dinosaur.
Our dishes have many unique flavors,
which everybody wants to come and savor.

At my eatery we master the clam bake,
and also triple fudge chocolate cake.
This great place is in Vermont.
It is my dream restaurant.

Varun Rao, Grade 5
Foxborough Regional Charter School, MA

Randy Moss

My least favorite player is Randy Moss.
In the big game against the Giants he dropped every toss.
Wide Receiver is his position.
And he thinks he has good intuition.

Joey Delillo, Grade 6
Captain Nathan Hale Middle School, CT

Youth

Youth is laughter and letting the good times roll
Youth is frolicking, skipping, and tumbling
Youth is smiling bright and showing glee
Youth is the start of your winding road
For youth is life's whipped cream;
The fluffy scrumptious topping
That you are told to savor
But instead swallow
In one tasty gulp.

Jessica Campbell, Grade 5
Hindley Elementary School, CT

Fireworks

P-O-P
They go as they light up
The sky like a star.

B-O-O-M
You hear as they separate
In different colors in the night sky.

C-R-A-C-K-L-E
Goes the sparks
As they fly down
In all sorts of colors.

Fireworks, fireworks, fireworks.

Kaitlyn Toth, Grade 5
Friendship Valley Elementary School, MD

When Flying Cows Attack

There once was a farmer who was wearing armor
Because the cows were about to attack!
Every time he turned around,
The cows jumped right on his back.
The sheep jumped on his arm.
Then he thought, "I have to leave this farm."
But, before he could, the goats joined in, too!
They rammed him in the leg.
He jumped so high he reached the sky.
Then BUMP! He landed on his back!
But, of course, again the cows started to attack!
Then, the sheep, the goats, and everything else
Jumped on the cow's back!
So, the farmer got up and ran away.
So, in his house he went and there he did stay.

Emily Rodgers, Grade 4
Mapleshade Elementary School, MA

Water vs Flame

Water
cold, liquid,
freezing, pouring
ocean, lake, volcano, fire pit
scorching, flaming, scarring
warm, colorful
Flame

Brian Arsenault, Grade 6
Captain Nathan Hale Middle School, CT

Days of Autumn

Cold breeze starts to blow
Bright colored leaves fall off trees
Walking in the woods

Jacqueline Bourassa, Grade 4
Leicester Memorial School, MA

College

C ollege is where I want to go
O nly smart kids can get in
L iving in dorms is the best part
L earning is okay too
E xtremely hard work
G etting in won't be easy!
E njoying college won't be hard!

Andrew Leal, Grade 5
Wakefield Forest Elementary School, VA

Guilt

A weight
 A heavy
   heavy
    heavy,
     weight
Upon your shoulders
Eyes seem to follow you
The same question
ruuuuuuuuns
through your head
again and again and again
"Why did you do it?"
your brain taunts you
You feel like you are in a maze
The light of freedom dances away
from you
You know the only way out is
The Truth

Meghan Cum, Grade 5
Sinai Academy of the Berkshires, MA

Shadows

Darkness of the day
It is a mirror of you
Afraid of the dark.

Luke Doris, Grade 6
Scotts Ridge Middle School, CT

A Recipe for a Light Bulb

Take a gallon of problems,
And stir with frustration. Add a pinch of chance,
And a bottle of failure.

One cup of
Thought, one ounce of possibilities.
For best results (and to prevent injuries) leave until calm (optional).

A tablespoon of discovery, and
Then pour the mixture into an anxious mind.
Do not forget the final ingredient: one large-sized AHA!

Stir until understood. The final result?
One luscious, juicy,
YES!
(If followed carefully, this recipe never fails.)

Bill Shen, Grade 5
C C Burr Elementary School, MA

Skiing

Speeding, rushing down the shimmering white, cold slope.
Rush of colors sliding past my cold, black eyes.
Leaning, trying as hard as hard can be to keep balance,
while it seems like I'm going 100 miles per hour!
The wind whipping my face, as if trying to murder me.
This wind as big as a tornado, passing unknown faces,
these faces, as it seems, came out of nowhere.
And hearing the little metal skis sliding over the snow,
as fast as they came they were suddenly gone, out of sight!
I am feeling such strange emotions,
the weird thing is that half of me wants to stop and that is my brain.
But, then my heart tells me to just go and go and go
and never to stop, not knowing where I am going.
But while I am deciding between my heart and my brain
I am starting to feel scared and then also free
as if in a plane heading 800 miles per hour
rushing toward the ocean,
falling, falling
gone
But most of all I feel free,
free as a bird soaring through the skies.

Nick Hansell, Grade 5
John Ward Elementary School, MA

The Ballet Dancer

A gasp filled the air as the stunning ballerina entered the theater.
Her rose colored slippers seemed to glide on stage.
She was as swift as a fox and as graceful as a swan.
A gentle smile stretched across her blood red lips.
The tinkling music was like her story and the emotion in her eyes was her character.
She seemed as light as a feather and as gentle as a fairy.
She reminded me of a Degas painting but "oh" so much more.
As she performed I was transfixed, and perplexed by her merry personality.
She was truly a ballet dancer.

Alexandria Hickey, Grade 5
Har-Bur Middle School, CT

Yellow

Bright, shining, bursting out
Sunshine on my face
Cool lemonade when I come in
From playing on a hot summer day
The weak rays of the sun rising up at dawn
A bittersweet lemon sitting on the table
The color of the sandy beach
After a light rain,
A yellow flower blooming on wet, moist grass

Annmarie Fallon, Grade 4
Waller Mill Fine Arts Magnet School, VA

Beads

Beads can be:
Colorful
Different shapes
Hearts
Big, small, large
Swirly, curly,
Tiny, thin
Smooth, rough
Pointy, shiny
Have lines
Straight, bumpy
Dark, light
Some have words on them!
Beads can make different things that are unique!

Harli Kettle, Grade 4
WB Sweeney School, CT

Monkeys

Monkeys live in the jungle deep.
They travel all day to invade my sleep.
Running, swinging, screeching on high
They hurt my ears and make me want to cry.

Funny, agile little bundles of activity
They don't do well in captivity.
Monkey see, monkey do
They make my worst nightmares comes true.

Collin Peterson, Grade 5
Foxborough Regional Charter School, MA

Colds

Everyone knows colds aren't fun, coughing, and sneezing,
You feel like you weigh a ton.
Snot goes flying everywhere,
Sometimes it even lands in my hair.
My mom brings me chicken noodle soup,
And then I get a cold ice-cream scoop.
The thermometer lands on my tongue,
It really hurts my aching lung.
Throwing up is never a bore,
My muscles are so very sore!

Alexa Davis, Grade 5
Coleytown Elementary School, CT

My Fish*

Inside the Aquamarine Shelter
We walked down a long blue path.

With tanks full of
All different kinds of fish
Big fish small fish
Of every color
With every eye in sight
Every fish is staring at you
And the way they look at you
You can read their minds saying
PICK ME! PICK ME!

And that is when we saw the
Green, blue, and red goldfish
Looking straight at me
Tossing his fins like he is saying
ME! ME! PICK ME!

And we did.

Eric D'Souza, Grade 5
West Woods Upper Elementary School, CT
*Inspired by Sharon Creech

Who Am I?

I am a soccer ball, round and rolling a lot
I am a computer that memorizes everything
I am a Toyota car that drives on the streets
I am a gentleman that respects everyone
I am a president that leads my country
I am a goldfish that swims under the water
I am a sun that's giving light to the world, especially my country
I am a Haitian who likes to go to the carnival
I am a nightingale that likes to sing on the tree

Marc Henley Celoy, Grade 6
Fuller Middle School, MA

The Tree's Battle

The tree trunk merely tremored
as it battled the storm.
However, its branches tapped and its leaves loosened,
then leapt, and lunged,
And its limbs bent and broke.

Zap!

The tree burned, covered in flames
shriveling leaves and covering branches.

Tap, Tap, Tap,
Suddenly cool.

Saved by the rain.

Matthew Thompson, Grade 6
Trinity School, MD

The Might of the Dragon

Mighty dragon,
free to fly
from
the storm.
Blowing
a fiery rage
black
with smoke.
You
see your friend,
the falcon.
But,
the war-song
does not bring
remorse.
The
nearest tower
brings danger.
Mighty dragon,
beware of the unknown.

Logan Thomason, Grade 5
Francis Asbury Elementary School, VA

Food

Food, food, lots of food
breakfast, dinner, dessert and lunch,
and occasionally a brunch.
Noodles, pizza, chicken and more,
ice cream, canolies, brownies galore,
chips, fruit, pie and cake.
Cook, broil, fry or bake.
Food, food, lots of food.
All of our lives depend on food,
and it puts us in a good mood.
Whether it's big, small or in the middle,
add entertainment, like a fiddle.
You can eat at a restaurant or at home,
and eat in China, Mexico, or Rome.
Food, food, lots of food.

Nora Walker, Grade 6
Swampscott Middle School, MA

Created Colorful

Colors, colors everywhere.
In your eyes and in your hair.
Movies made in black and white
have suddenly changed to colored sights.
Grass at your feet and treetops seen
are made of lush and beautiful green.
And clear skies on cloudless days
are made to match the bright blue bays.
So when you look at skies and trees
remember who created these.

Katie Lutero, Grade 6
Culpeper Christian School, VA

Morning Dew

Morning Dew
The way the morning dew
Sits on the grass is like
Glitter on paper.
Like snow gently falling
From the sky.
Morning dew is like a
Cloud gently rising.
Morning dew a circle of life.
Morning dew what would
We do without it.

Josh Bloem, Grade 6
Whitinsville Christian School, MA

The Underworld

A cavern,
A burnt-out light,
A dead polluted river,
The Underworld.
A fire blown out by the wind,
A burnt piece of toast,
A hot, blackened coal,
The Underworld.
A trash can full of hopes,
A dream abandoned,
A cave full of dread,
The Underworld.
A bombed home,
An apartment for the dead,
A cold, dark jail cell,
The Underworld.

Grace McAden, Grade 5
Raleigh Court Elementary School, VA

Day at the Beach

The sun rises and says hello
We jump into our suits
And run to the beach

Waves racing up the shore
Then admit defeat
And sink back into the sea

Sea shells and crabs make their home
In the rough, golden brown sand
Seaweed lies in the sun and on rocks
Sunbathing

When its time to go
A shower of fireworks
Bids us farewell
And the sun sinks down
And says good-bye

Teresa Lally, Grade 6
E W Thurston Middle School, MA

Winter

Winter is shimmering bright,
At night, it is very white.
In winter, it is cold,
With fluffy snow to hold.
Snow is as thin as a sheet,
All folded tidy and neat.
People have red noses,
And dead, reddish roses.
The wind blows as trees dance in gowns,
Like white snow in romance.
Black, slippery ice,
Snow, pretty and nice.

Madison Kustom, Grade 5
Booth Hill School, CT

Her Touch

Her eyes
watch
staring at me
with joy
and support
The twinkle
in her smile
shows
she cares and always will
The happiness
in her laugh
brings me to life
Her touch
is gentle
gentle as a feather
The strongest feeling
she gives off
The gentle touch
of
Love

Isabelle Calderon, Grade 5
Coleytown Elementary School, CT

Poppy

I hold his hand
He holds mine
He looks at me
Stares
He says I love you
With a big wink and a smile
Our hearts say it with no words
I kiss him
He kisses me
I leave
But
Our hearts stay together
Forever

Edward Houseworth, Grade 5
Coleytown Elementary School, CT

Turkey Bowl

Two years ago I went to the Turkey Bowl
Colleen and I were very cold
We asked her dad for chocolate that was hot
Colleen went to find out spot

Our hot chocolate was ready
I was not holding steady
We looked for Colleen to go to sit
I wanted the end seat. I had a fit

Her dad stumbled into me
The hot chocolate spilled, how could this be?
My pink puffy jacket was all wet
I wasn't happy and I started to fret

My hot chocolate was on the floor
I asked her dad for some more
He said "No, now is not a good time,
Or you will have to wait in a big line."

Cori Kosko, Grade 6
Immaculate Heart of Mary School, MD

Buddy Boy

Buddy Boy is a cutie
His little white paws look like booties

He loves his treats, he does a trick
He jumps up and he lick, lick, licks

His color is brown
He has no frown

He sleeps all night
All curled up tight

He's sort of small
Not very tall

He doesn't play
But that's okay

I love my buddy, he's my friend
I'll always love him till the end!

Rebecca Lawson, Grade 4
Helen H Hansen Elementary School, MA

The Nut Dog

One time I was going to eat a peanut.
Then I said, "Oh no, here comes that crazy mutt!"
Then I dropped it and the dog took the small nut.
I better go before he eats it all.
When I came in he played with his ball.
He ran and I said, "Get back here Carl!"

Sage Rabito, Grade 4
Brookside Elementary School, MA

Beginning

Yesterday's memories are in the past,
And there is no need to be aghast.
You must keep living
Because bad days come and go
Like the shimmering winter snow.
As you must know,
Today is a new beginning.

Forget your mistakes
For there is nothing at stake.
Try because today is a new way.
Put everything behind you
And try something new
Or maybe experience a new point of view,
Just don't go back to yesterday.

Kristyna Murphy, Grade 6
Mapleshade Elementary School, MA

Who Are You?

Who are you
To make fun of people of wisdom
But not of sportism
And popularity?
Who are you to judge who they are from their looks or doings?
Because to them they see themselves as sporty
And popular.
How they see themselves in their own eyes
Is more important
Than the untruthful judgment
Of you.

Kymbre Doan, Grade 6
Two Rivers Magnet Middle School, CT

Darkness

It is one of those dark nights.
There's no one outside.
But it's really windy.
I am alone in my house with no lights.
While watching a frightening movie called *Hide*.
Then I hear a name…Cindy.

After that a loud noise banged in my room.
I didn't check because of the movie I had seen.
I heard it again and got even more scared.
I was scared because it hit me with a broom.
I called my mom, she came as fast as a beam.
She checked everywhere, maybe the person that stole was poor.

One of the windows was open.
My mom didn't call the cops.
Why did someone do this,
It was my bedroom window that was broken.
My mom hugged me and I saw her tears drop.
She said she loved me and gave me a kiss.

Luis Gonzalez, Grade 6
Gerard A Guilmette School, MA

Cafeteria

The cafeteria is a jungle
Wild animals scrambling for food
Grunting
Like wild boars
Stampeding
To the line
Devouring
Their prey
Cleaning
Their paws
And then returning to their dens.

Kiana Orr, Grade 6
Benjamin Syms Middle School, VA

Anger

I feel a fire
Lit in my soul
Making me feel anger.
In a flash
I try to scream out the
Anger
I have flowing through my veins.
I hold it back
With raging temper,
Tasting burnt,
Crispy
Ashes…
It fills my mouth
With a taste
That has
A shocking experience.
I want to scream
The anger out loud
But…
I already
Did.

Erin A. Burbank, Grade 4
Hawley Elementary School, CT

A Winter Breeze

A winter breeze
It calms me down
It moves the fluffy snow
The breeze makes it swirl
Like a small tornado
When I go outside
The soft breeze skims my cheek
That makes me get the chills
The light winter breeze
Will swim around the air
It makes me think
And think real hard…
Does anyone else appreciate
The winter breeze?

Timothy Benjamin, Grade 6
Whitinsville Christian School, MA

Luna

Her hair so gracefully curled on her fuzzy little back
Her stomach is white and in the shape of a moon
And what color is she now you might ask, and the answer to that is black
You tell her, come get a cookie, *she'll be next to you soon*
Her eyes are brown with a hint of black
Her paws so scuffed up and pruned
With her small tail spiraled back
And to top it off her claws are beautifully groomed

Morgan Fleming, Grade 6
Scotts Ridge Middle School, CT

Basketball

When I play basketball it feels like I can run coast to coast nonstop.
When I have the ball I feel like I can shoot from anywhere on the court.
I love playing it.
It is my favorite sport in the world.
One day I hope to go to the NBA!!!

William Rogers, Grade 6
Monelison Middle School, VA

I Wish

I wish I were a cure for every existing disease,
All of the sick would stop suffering
And they would live long, happy and healthy lives
There would be no more mourning families,
Suffering from the loss of their loved ones

If I were a cure for every existing disease,
Everyone would have a chance to forget about their worries and have fun!
Nobody would have to lie down in a hospital bed all day long,
Watching the world go on without them

I wish that I could be that one spectacular thing,
That saves all of those poor people
from suffering

Ciara Carruthers, Grade 6
Scotts Ridge Middle School, CT

Dogs

Dogs, is there anything better?
You wake up when they lick your face.
They paw at you to feed them.
"C'mon Buddy, lets go play."
But you know that soon, it won't be day.
As time winds down, you start to cry.
And your friend look's at you, like he's saying,
"Why?"
You try to hide your tears, but it's too hard.
So you go to get a tissue and then go to bed.
But, when you lie down your pillow's breathing.
You turn around and realize, your pillow is trying to comfort you.
You stroke their soft fur and gently whisper, "Good Night."
And just like that, you drift off to sleep with your BF right by your side, FOREVER.
'Cuz you know that he won't leave you.

Jake Farrell, Grade 6
E W Thurston Middle School, MA

Wrestling for Life

Wrestling is the best,
Some people might wear a vest.
The Gold they want to claim,
So they don't have to feel the shame.
One wrestler named the Undertaker,
Is the one who is the gold taker.
Another wrestler Edge,
Likes to live on the edge
And, to cheat always
In a lot of ways.
Tall, small, skinny, fat,
Wrestlers with pants, wrestlers with a hat
I love wrestling and this is a fact
But, watch out! You might get sacked!

Chuta Sano, Grade 5
Charlotte A Dunning Elementary School, MA

Friends

Friends are there 'til the end
They are like a helping hand
They are always there when you're down
They would get up and become your clown
Friends are there whenever, and for whatever
But most important forever
They are like angels from above
They are the reasons I live, laugh, and love

Erica Stemski, Grade 6
St Joseph School-Fullerton, MD

Day

I must get out of this
Monotonous gray den of night
And into that precious blend of colors
That dance and fly against the morning sky.

Once I am free, from branch to branch
I will leap with limbs spry and sprightly.
Up the damp gray trunk, while sunlight rushes down
I will bolt like the winter sun bolts across the ice.
Only at the top will I pause, to watch the hasty
Waters frothing below.

Through forest and meadow I will run.
I will sing a song that is of the bluebird,
Sing loud and listen, for if I am still,
Perhaps the bluebird will return my call with his
Sugared ballad.

Up hill and dale I shall climb, Up again, and down again,
Into lush valleys, over violet hued mountains.
I will rush to the top of the tallest mountain and
Gaze triumphantly down upon the sun's golden domain.
I will let the liquid warmth wash over me
I will let the day stroke my cheek.

Christina Ruggiero-Corliss, Grade 6
Smith College Campus School, MA

Jillian

Jillian, Jillian, where do I start…
She's cute, funny, kind and smart.

I love her, I love her, she is the best
She's my little sister, the baby of our nest

She can sometimes be wild
And still be so mild

When she doesn't get her way
She could cry all of the day

I still love her so very much
My heart is what she will always touch!

Michelle Doherty, Grade 4
Helen H Hansen Elementary School, MA

Dream Come True

I'm in my room dreaming of him
In my sleep we talk and laugh
About the things we should have done
I'm in his arms and oh how it feels so warm
I can smell his clothes and feel his prickly hair
I think I found another part of my heart
Just like a jigsaw puzzle.
It's a dream come true like I found the man on the moon.
Yes, it's true it's not a myth, he left me when I was young.
But I feel that now there's a chance for daughter and father.
Time should go back, where love can sink in.
Bonding time…I do not want to wake up.

Shealon Ferguson, Grade 6
Benjamin Syms Middle School, VA

I Am a Hoping Star

I am a hoping star in the sky,
I wonder do people see me when they look up at the sky,
I hear the planes flying in the sky,
I see the other stars around me,
I want to be a human,
I am a star who want's to be gone,
I am a star who want's to be out having fun with friends,
I feel hurt and sad,
I touch my face,
I worry why I am the way I am,
I cry very loudly,
I am a star,
I understand that I'm a star,
I say that I just have to except this,
I dream of being happy,
I try to wish every night.
I hope my dreams come true.
I am a hoping star!

Jayla Foster, Grade 6
Page Middle School, VA

If Only the Clouds Hadn't Cleared

There was an old man with a beard,
Whose shiny bald head got quite seared.
He stood in the sun
And thought of the fun,
If only the clouds hadn't cleared!

Julia Guyer, Grade 4
Trinity Christian School, VA

Spring

The birds are singing
The colorful flowers bloom.
The fresh air is cool.

Arnelle Fonlon, Grade 4
St Joseph School-Fullerton, MD

The Flowers Blossom

The flowers blossom
Beside Fall's leafy
Path.
They are soon to find
Winter's wicked wrath
As they freeze like
Icicles in the killing, chilling wind
They remember
Spring's warm, fond, love.

Ben Tidswell, Grade 6
Smith College Campus School, MA

The Boston Tea Party

One night in 1773,
The colonists dumped some British tea,
When the British ships refused to flee,
Out of the Boston Harbor.

Later called a tea party,
Cost Boston months of misery,
After the party there was no glee,
Because the British closed the harbor.

Paul Poling, Grade 4
Angelus Academy, VA

Silent Day

Today was not like any other day.
The birds weren't chirping and
The dogs weren't barking.
The cars weren't beeping and
The people weren't arguing.
It felt like I was alone and
No one was there.
The thought of someone behind me
As I looked through the window
Passed through my head
Today was a silent day.

Jeremy Villanueva, Grade 6
Swampscott Middle School, MA

Toast

T oast is very crunchy.
O range and grape jam
A lmost cooked to a golden brown
S atisfies the craving in my stomach
T oast is my favorite breakfast food.

Kayla Podell, Grade 6
St Joseph School, MA

Florida

Florida
Hot, humid
Swim, relax, play
The place to be
Sunshine State

Stephen Novick, Grade 4
Sacred Heart School, MA

Birds

Birds, so peaceful
as they leap
from tree to tree.
Skip on stones
and use their wings
to fly up in the trees.

Whitney Lenardson, Grade 4
Appomattox Elementary School, VA

Cold

nose dripping
fingers frozen
lips chapped
teeth chattering

soup simmering
chocolate running
throat satisfied

fire blazing
sports flicking
light dancing

cold gliding away

Emma Sinkoff, Grade 4
Sinai Academy of the Berkshires, MA

St. Clare of Assisi

I lived in Assisi
With Agnes my sissy
My parents gave me permission
To become a nun. I started a mission.
My feast day is August 11
Have you guessed who I am
I am St. Clare of Assisi

Allison McCrumb, Grade 4
Angelus Academy, VA

Snowflake

Snowflake, snowflake, falling down,
Landing on me like a crown.

Snowflake, snowflake, such bright white,
Like a beacon in the night.

Snowflake, snowflake, small and fragile,
Falling down, very agile.

Snowflake, snowflake, why do you go,
When you'll be back I do not know.

Christopher O'Shea, Grade 6
E W Thurston Middle School, MA

Thorns of a Rose

The last time I saw you
Was six years ago
We were little girls
Playing in the snow

Two years later
We were still together
We made a promise
For now and forever

And then that happened
Three years passed
You had to move
We said our last

I was heart broken
You probably were, too
I miss the days
Of me and you

We were best friends
Everybody knows
That we stuck together
Like the thorns of a rose

Atang Agwe, Grade 5
St Joseph's Catholic School, MD

Volcano

You sit still as a mountain,
You don't say a word.
For years you sleep…
Until Mother Earth shakes you awake!
You stir, then, BOOM!
You explode!
You are no longer,
As still as a mountain
You speak with a loud voice,
YOU HAVE AWAKENED!

Brittany Hughes, Grade 6
Benjamin Syms Middle School, VA

Football

Working is tough
On Mon, Wed, and Fridays all I do is practice
running fence to fence
Knowing what I have to do to be the best
I'm trying to practice hard and tough
Now is game time and I'm ready
"Good luck says the sun"

Denzel Thomas, Grade 6
School of International Studies at Meadowbrook, VA

Different

He looked
In the mirror
A geeky freak
Stared back
The one
Who made everyone
Stay away from him
The one
Who was mayor of the nerd herd.
The one
Who was treated differently from the rest.
But when you give it a lot of thought
Maybe some Loser like him
Isn't that different.
Maybe he's different like that
Because people tell him that.
If you just give the person a chance
maybe
just maybe you'll find a way

Emily Charash, Grade 4
Hawley Elementary School, CT

The Unknown Hallway

The Unknown Hallway where secrets are held.
The Unknown Hallway holds monsters as well.
The Unknown Hallway the teachers will never tell
what is held in the dark hallway.
I'll just never find out!

Scott Jacobs, Grade 6
Fuller Middle School, MA

The Sock Stealing Troll in My Washing Machine

There's something in my washer
I don't know what it is
all I know is it eats my socks
and makes a growing "hiss."

At night I hear the buzzer ring.
I know it's time to empty the thing.
To my notice I hate to admit
I feel a hole in my laundry basket!

Jordan Charette, Grade 6
Edmond P Talbot Middle School, MA

Carryann

Once I had an angel in my head.
And every night she'd tuck me in my bed
She'd always tell me to have good dreams.
When she looks at me her eyes gleam.
And she wears a beautiful white hat.
She's my aunt that died did I mention that?

Makayla Nickles, Grade 4
Brookside Elementary School, MA

The Roses

When it is summer and the sun is high up
The roses climb up the clean soil.
The roses would laugh and have fun.
For the sun is by,
To keep them company.
They are of course loyal.
When it is night
The sun wouldn't come down without a fight.
Then the roses would say hi to the shiny moon
And sadly say goodbye to the sun.
The tiny roses were fleeing and had fled,
For the winter is coming by.
Oh what a shame.
Winter is as cold as the North/South Pole.
So the roses say goodbye
And better luck finding us until next summer.

Arno Cai, Grade 5
Soule Road School, MA

Honeydew

Honeydew
Hamster
Talented, cute, furry, small
Lover of Abby, seeds, and water
Who feels cats are evil
Who believes she should get more food
Who wants to see a giant carrot, the outside, and no more cats
Who says squeak
Resident of Abby's house

Abby Bryant, Grade 5
Catoctin Elementary School, VA

My Christmas

I love putting up our Christmas tree.
I try to make it as decorated as can be.

Ornaments and lights everywhere!
There may be a nutcracker here or there.

And at the top, I'll put a star,
That you can see from afar.

Then when I'm finished, I'll go to bed.
When I awake, I'll eat some gingerbread!

Allyssa Ahnn Pingul, Grade 6
St Clement Mary Hofbauer School, MD

Just Listen

My family moved out in the west
No friends at all

So I just played in the field
I like being alone

I love feeling the cold breeze
                    I just lay out on the fresh green grass
                                        and look up at the blue sky God
                                                            created
But I do have one friend
                my shadow.
                        All you have to do is listen!

Emilee Jones, Grade 5
Francis Asbury Elementary School, VA

The Big Bang

I hear a sound like a bullet being fired from a gun. Bang!
I listen to the echo throughout the ballpark,
I swing the bat, and feel the bat shatter in the
Grip of my hands.
I smack the ball,
I catch a glimpse of the ball   Going,   Going, Gone!
I hear the fans screaming, and shouting my name,
And I smell the glorious smell of the ballpark.
I feel the grass all bouncy and freshly cut.
We win, a fantastic feeling flows through my body.
I see my teammates lining up to high-five me.
I want to take a bottle and trap this feeling, then whenever I feel sad I'll open the bottle.
And voilà I feel this sensation, it's indescribable,
Like a tingling feeling through my body. This is my first ever home run.
When I get home after a big celebratory dinner with my team,
I go to check out the scores around the country.
As the headline appears word by word I see it's talking about me,
"Redsox's rookie hits first home run." I was so happy.
I had that feeling again.

Daniel Thorne, Grade 6
Charles E. Smith Jewish Day School, MD

Monday

Beep! Beep! Beep!
Monday already?

I try to ignore the clock's ear-piercing alarm but it's too loud.
Reluctantly I get up…

…Only to lie back down. Why me? Why today? Can't I just stay in
bed for a few more minutes (or hours)!

From downstairs my mom tells, "Time to get up!" There goes my second alarm clock.
My dog must also want me up I realize, when she starts jumping on me and licking me.

Fumbling through clothes I think and know,
Mondays will always be Mondays.

Alex Balleza, Grade 6
Swampscott Middle School, MA

Zahyria

Zahyria is a very clever chick.
With ideas that always seem to stick.
I'm determined and smart
And always willing to start
On any challenge weather thin or thick.

Zahyria Temple, Grade 6
School of International Studies at Meadowbrook, VA

Fireworks

Fireworks flash and fireworks glow
Each time we see them
It's a wonderful show.

Fireworks zing and fireworks zoom
Fireworks bang and
Crackle and boom.

They dazzle and sparkle and fly in midair
Every time we see them
We stop and stare.

Christopher Lucci, Grade 5
Friendship Valley Elementary School, MD

My Wish

Wishing on a star
   Wondering where you are.

Inside my house
   As quiet as a mouse.

Shuddering in my tears
   Because of all my fears.

Holidays pass by
   I hope my wish did not die.

Every day
   I hope it's okay.

So I still miss you
   Although my wish came true.

Melanie Goodall, Grade 5
C Hunter Ritchie Elementary School, VA

My Love

My love for you is soft and warm
like a newborn baby in my comforting arms
a kiss from you makes my whole world spin
turning and spiraling from now until then
your hugs are tender to every touch
in your arms I love it so much
my love for you is one in a million
focusing on you is my number one mission
   I love you

Sierra McDade, Grade 6
Salem Church Middle School, VA

Snow

Snow, snow, snow so white
I saw it snowing late last night
A wonder of nature I know it is
It's fun to play in with the other kids
It can be peaceful or destructive
When it's destructive I feel so sad
That something so beautiful can be so bad
That's what I think about snow

Evan Perkins, Grade 6
Whitinsville Christian School, MA

Hunting

Hunting is the sport for me
The main focus is always safety
Always treat a gun as loaded and hot
Keep the muzzle pointed where people are not
Be sure of your target and what's beyond it
Never take an over-hill shot from where you sit
Protect your game from moisture, dirt, and heat
These things will destroy the meat
Do not kill more than you can eat
That would be a waste of meat

James Roman, Grade 6
St Joseph School-Fullerton, MD

Colors of Fall

F rilly ruby leaves.
A lways golden bees.
L ittle scarlet foxes.
L ow hanging willow trees like tearful children.

C ool breezes blow as cold as glaciers.
O range sky like the color of pumpkin pie.
L ogs huge and auburn hollowed for animals.
O verly excited owls outside of our oasis.
R osy red cheeks running restlessly in the cold.
S kunk cabbage smells seriously horrible.

Nick Bartoli, Grade 6
Madison Middle School, CT

I Am…

I am more powerful than gravity
I am fragile, and not to be trifled with
I am in hiding until the time is right
I make you feel bubbly, jittery, and at the same time sick
A brick wall will not stop me
I won't stop until I get what I want
I am what people fear, but adore
I am your worst enemy, but your best friend
I am strong, but can rip like paper

I am LOVE!

Rebecca Marks, Grade 5
Weston Intermediate School, CT

A Special Meadow

I walk through a luscious meadow,
Clouds roll on and on over this meadow.
Watching the flowers blow,
And the little animals toe to toe,
I stand there blown away,
Thinking "Am I near heaven or away?"
This meadow full of life and fun,
Just blows my mind away, into the sun.
Where my soul lifts,
Up high, my thoughts drift,
Why can't the world be a little this?

Briana Ball, Grade 6
Quashnet School, MA

Basketball

B asketball is a team sport.
A sk your teammates to pass the ball.
S core points to win the game.
K eep the ball on your team.
E ach team knows its strategy.
T ry your best.
B oth teams play fairly.
A ll the players try hard.
L ove your team.
L ove your coach.

Jessica Gardiner, Grade 5
Little Flower School, MD

The Bay

Today is a vibrant sunny day
Families picnicking by the bay
Kites are flying, seagulls soaring
And best of all, kids exploring

With faithful Tipsy at my side
I sail and slice through the tide
Wet spray drenching my face
Salty air I can taste

Winds roaring in gusts
Striking sails with great thrusts
To save my fair ship
I hiked out like a whip
My mind now at peace
I set off toward the east

Ropes snug in hand
Eyes focused on land
I make a tack
To head on back

Sunset drops in an orange sky
I glance at sea with a mournful sigh
And sorrowfully wave a simple goodbye

Oscar Morris, Grade 6
Weston Middle School, CT

Music

Music is a melody that brightens your day.
Music is a door; you are free to express yourself.
Music can change lives, it whispers to your heart.
Music is a comfort to those who welcome it warmly into their lives.
Music flows freely in the air, like a gentle mist on a summer's day.

Sandra Webb, Grade 5
Wakefield Forest Elementary School, VA

Baby Blues

A baby brother?
You're kidding me.
There's no more room on this family tree!
I can't put up with diapers and endless crying;
If you go through with this I'll end up dying!
What? My room is my personal space!
Can't you find it another place?
They went through with it;
The baby is here.
He wails so much I can barely hear.
There's no more room for me anymore;
Paying attention to me is one heck of a chore.
Now they want me to babysit him;
The chances of that are pretty slim.
My parents are now out on a date;
I get to sit with him and wait.
I guess I'll go make sure he's all right;
Now he's holding my finger very tight.
He looked up at me and for the very first time
He gave a toothless smile;
And all the things I've sacrificed for him have become worthwhile.

Laila Serpe, Grade 6
Cape Henry Collegiate School, VA

Tasty Chicken Strips

Pop! pop! Goes the strip in the pot as they fry and fry
until there are no more pops!

I love chicken strips, so soft and fresh!
I love chicken strips, so soft and fresh!

The strips are so tender that they taste so scorching hot and crunchy.
They taste so good when you taste the fresh white meat.
The tasty part is the smoky flavor.

I love chicken strips, so soft and fresh!
I love chicken strips, so soft and fresh!

The silliest thing to pick from is the selectable sauce.
The sweetest sauce to pick from that I'd choose would,
be the sweet savory honey mustard sauce.

At the end before I eat never forget to dip your strips in the sauce,
before you eat Yum! Yum! It's all gone I'm sad, but
now I know here to have such a hot tasty meal.

Jekeira Pitts, Grade 6
City View School, MA

Red Maple

I am fire
Blazing
red,
orange,
yellow.

I am a hand,
reaching out
to touch
you.

I am an angel,
soaring
in the sky.

I can be
millions
of things
if you
think
about it.

Jacob F. Hartman, Grade 4
Memorial-Spaulding Elementary School, MA

Sadness

Looks like a horse rider who fell off his horse.
Sounds like an angel that can't go home.
Tastes like an apple that was rotten.
Feels like a teardrop going down your cheek.
Smells like something you would not like.
Please don't get this feeling.

Kelsey Sluss, Grade 4
Waller Mill Fine Arts Magnet School, VA

Penguins

Penguins live in the Arctic
Making them feel like ice cubes
They see through the clouds of white precipitation
Streaming through the sky as though
Buffalo are on a rampage
Penguins have black feathers
As dark as the night sky
White feathers as white as fine cotton
Their only two predators;
The killer whale and the elephant seal
Both as wild as the gusting wind
Prowling around penguins
Making their continuous journey
To their nesting grounds
The breeze licks them like a dog as they waddle
Knowing they have to endure everything again
On their way back

Thomas Schutz, Grade 5
Booth Hill School, CT

Jose Armando Morales

J oyful
O utgoing
S mart
E xpressive

A mazing
R efreshing
M arvelous
A ssertive
N eat
D andy
O riginal

M iracle
O utstanding
R emarkable
A rtistic
L aughter
E xplorer
S urvivor

Jose Armando Morales, Grade 4
Helen H Hansen Elementary School, MA

Candy

Candy is a thing hard to resist.
You eat it and you want more.
Candy is something you can have every day.
There is chocolate, sour, sweet and bitter.
But most of all I like sour candy because it tastes very good.

Monica Warner, Grade 5
John F Kennedy School, CT

Baseball Glove

You put your hands inside of me
And hit my face with a ball
It tastes bad, covered in dirt
And red leather bumps.
But then you save me and pull the ball out of my mouth
And I try to thank you
But I can't because I am silent.

Then I try to yell
Don't torture me anymore!
But you don't listen.
You make me eat the ball again. I spit it out.

You throw me onto the ground.
The freshly cut grass.
But you pick me up, and drop me on the bench
With a great big bang
And I listen to the loud crack of the bat!
And even though I'm silent
I scream "Thank you."
Because I am a baseball glove.

Collin Timmerman, Grade 6
E W Thurston Middle School, MA

Sasha

Sasha is my puppy,
Her face is so cute,
She's ten times faster than a guppy,
She plays with a flute!!!

Grace Heacock, Grade 4
Ridgeway Elementary School, MD

Life!

When you live, you learn
and when you learn you succeed.
When you succeed you can explore
the places life takes you
and may life take you many places!

Trejon Edmonds, Grade 4
Salem Elementary School, VA

Ice Cream

Drip, drip
Delectable, delicious
Ice cream
Dripping down my arm
It drips, I lick
Vanilla, chocolate, strawberry
3 scoops
Melting slowly, slowly dripping
Going from cold to warm
I can't stop licking
Delectable, delicious
Gone!

Grace Martell, Grade 4
Munger Hill Elementary School, MA

Super Hero Seal

The seal was sitting there
watching the waves
The waves were crashing monsters
To be surfing them I would be scared
But the seal was sitting there as
brave as a super hero

Alyssa Nolin, Grade 4
Freetown Elementary School, MA

Sunset

The bright sun shines on
The ocean of the calm beach
Sunset comes slowly

Maria Makinde, Grade 6
Immaculate Heart of Mary School, MD

Energetic

Sitting in this class
Rather be out in the grass.
Playing hard all day.

Dylan Farnella, Grade 5
Trinity School, MD

Mouse in the House

There once was a mouse in the house,
my cat chased that mouse
throughout the house
he ran as fast as the speed of light
only looking like a blur
ready to catch that mouse,
he could already taste the victory
he stopped for a moment to smile at me
but continued to hunt
for that mischievous mouse
when all of a sudden…
Boom!
Clash!
"Meow!"
…that was what I heard
thinking that my cat had a big fall
but as it turned out,
he ran into a wall
my cat never did catch that mouse
but it's not about winning or losing
it's about playing the game.

Olivia Judd, Grade 6
Litchfield Intermediate School, CT

What Is Black?

Black is the dullness in your heart,
That contains the dark arts.
Black is gothic in your mind —
It leaves all the sunny behind.
Black is poison in your throat,
For which there is no antidote.
Black is almost always fright —
It makes you feel all tight.
Black is darkness and fear.
It is growling in your ear.
Black is a shadow casting far —
Also the color of a dead star.
Black is coldness everywhere!
It is silence in the air!

James Boland, Grade 5
Har-Bur Middle School, CT

My Penguin

My penguin looks so fancy
in his hat and suit and tails,
A cummerbund from Macy's,
and a tie from Bloomingdales.

He always looks so dapper
in his handsome black tuxedo,
but when he goes swimming,
he wears nothing but a speedo!

Emily Derkosrofian, Grade 6
Charlton Middle School, MA

Lago Mar

I eagerly wait
all year long
for the day
that I will be back

At Lago Mar,
a hotel by the sea.

I imagine swimming
at the sparkling shore
or dipping into a
lagoon pool.

I dream of playing
table tennis and shuffle board,
mini golf and volley ball, or
sitting and tanning on the sand.

I count the days
until the morning I will wake

In Lago Mar, that splendid hotel
by the sea.

Elizabeth Sullivan, Grade 6
Swampscott Middle School, MA

Papelbon

The best in the bullpen is Papelbon
Everybody likes to call him Jon
After the game
It was the same
As every big win
He did not sin
They played his music
And he got to it
He went into a trance
And began to dance
Jon is the star
And I think he will go far

Patrick Keohane, Grade 5
Sacred Heart School, MA

Monday Mornings

Monday morning are very rough
but I can get through
because it's not that tough
people help me through the day
because they have no delays
I sleep and turn and seek
But I always have to take a peek
Monday morning is sometimes fun
I'm happy when it's all done.

Michayla Young, Grade 5
Sacred Heart Elementary School, MA

Summer

The summer is fun,
There is a lot of sun.

Splash! You jump in the pool,
Instead of going to school.

You get to hang out with friends,
You don't want the summer to end.

The sky is so blue,
It looks like new.

When school starts again,
There is no end.

The birds fly so high,
Up in the sky.

You get to play outside all day,
The sky never gets gray.

The summer is fun,
There is a lot of sun.

Kassidy Campbell, Grade 5
Foxborough Regional Charter School, MA

Night

The crickets sing now
A glowing sphere in the sky
It is all silent.

Elise Lenzi, Grade 4
Charlotte A Dunning Elementary School, MA

I Am

I am disciplined and determined.
I hear the line screaming from the reel.
I wonder if I'll acquire a 50 pounder.
I see the splashing water.
I want to reel in a huge fish.
I am disciplined and determined.

I pretend that I just won the striper cup.
I feel like I will catch a world record.
I touch the slimy scales of a 50 pounder.
I worry about him not fitting in the boat.
I cry about the thought of the breaking line.
I am disciplined and determined.

I understand I may not get him.
I say, "I will."
I dream about big bass.
I try to catch a significant one.
I hope I will apprehend a monster bass.
I am disciplined and determined.

Nicholas Hentschel, Grade 5
Hebron Elementary School, CT

So Cruel

Working in the cotton fields
That was horrible.
A brave person wouldn't cry
Running away
Never coming back
I would hate that to happen to me
Getting whipped,
So cruel, how rude, so cruel.

Rayven Mitchell, Grade 5
Charlotte A Dunning Elementary School, MA

Nathan

Nathan
The one who cares
The one who gives
The one who is fair
The one who truly lives

His smile is like a golden sun
Shining down on us
He was always a bunch of fun
Unlike a piece of dust

We must never forget
The one who loves
The one who plays
The one who is kind like a dove
The one who will be here through all the days
His smile is like a golden sun
Shining down on us
He was always a bunch of fun
Unlike a piece of dust

I know we will never forget Mr. Bach Jr. himself
The one and only
Nathan

Rebecca Hellman, Grade 5
Cunniff Elementary School, MA

Summer

I love school, but summer is cool,
Snowballs, and swimming in the pool.
The temperature's warm, the days are long,
Makes you want to burst out in song.

School is okay in the winter I guess.
When the temperature is cold then learning is best.
But when it gets warm I just want to play,
And have no schoolwork to get in my way.

Don't get me wrong I really like school,
But there is a time and place for everything cool.

Jessica Miller, Grade 6
Krieger-Schechter Day School, MD

Wrigley

Excited, fat
Jumping, eating, smiling
Tail, eyes, paws, fur, friend
Barking, running, scratching,
Cute, beautiful
Happy!

Willem Servaes, Grade 6
St Bartholomew School, MD

March

Spring up off your feet
to see the wonderful scenes
that happen in March.

Sara Tolentino, Grade 4
St Joseph School-Fullerton, MD

A Puppy at the Pet Store

I bought
the puppy
at the pet store

that you
were probably
saving up
your money for

I truly am
sorry but
he is
just so cute
and so cuddly

Micah Greenspoon, Grade 4
Sinai Academy of the Berkshires, MA

Outside

Clouds of
Gray
Rumble,
Over the sky.
Which at one point today
Was as blue as the Caribbean Sea.
Wet, Cold,
Drops of rainfall.
Slowly
They gently touch the ground.
It splatters
Into a puddle
Of cold wet,
Water,
With a small but weak noise.
Wet branches
Sag
In the wind,
They sing a song of sad sweet sorrow

Jamie Calandro, Grade 4
Hawley Elementary School, CT

Colors

Red is the color of the fierce fiery sun.
Orange is a summer of endless sunsets.

Yellow is lemonade with a pinch of mint by the poolside.
Grass green is the front lawn with dandelions dancing in the breeze.

Cerulean is the bright salty sea reflecting the sun.
Pink is the color of laughter with friends.

Deep purple is my bed sheets and curtains in my place of quiet.
Silver is my earrings that dangle from my ears like wind chimes.

Gold is a gold chain necklace swinging around my neck when I walk.
White is the fluffy whip cream that floats in my hot chocolate.

Black are the eyes on my cat that stare back at me with a beacon of light.
Brown is the color of my long flowing hair in the breeze.

Colors can be strange and unexplained.

Cassandra Canavan, Grade 6
Scotts Ridge Middle School, CT

Red

Red is the USA flag waving in the air.
Red is an apple being bitten.
Red is my face after being embarrassed by my dad.
Red is the cheering at a Red Sox game.
Red is the pledge of allegiance being said at my school each morning.
Red is the softness of my pillows while I am sleeping.
Red is me playing in the heat of the summer.
Red is me eating raspberries because Melissa lets me have some.
Red is me hurrying to get water after eating too much spicy salsa.
Red is me seeing the clown nose on *Wife Swap* last night.
Red is me singing Christmas carols with my cousins on Christmas.
Red is me laughing so hard because my dad said something funny.
Red is me thinking if the Red Sea is really red.
Red is me saying to my family, I love you.
Red is me going to New York and seeing all the I heart New York shirts
Red is me being a doctor and fainting because I see blood.
Red is my cousins and me getting a fever.
Last but not least
Red is Thorpe School's mascot, Thorpie!!!

Becca Horn, Grade 5
Willis E Thorpe School, MA

The Ronnie Dream

I want to play basketball; I want to be a star.
Like Kobe, Lebron, now you can add Ronnie's name to that star.
Or, I could just do the music thing, like Michael, Luther, I was born to sing.
I'm sorry, now I know that this is my dream.
I forgot to tell y'all when I was born, I was a king with a big ole castle and everything.
I'm sorry I put you down this path, because I'm still livin' the dream
And when I wake up we can all have a laugh.

Ronnie Brooks, Grade 4
Washington Christian Academy, MD

The Sun

The sun, with prominences on its edge,
The moon reflecting it, in the shape of the wedge

This beautiful star, shining its hardest,
Pluto the dwarf planet, orbiting the farthest

It's the source of any living thing,
The atmosphere surrounding us, almost shaped like a ring

Sunspots, flares upon the sun,
Firing heat, like a gun

It can be as hot as melting metal,
Or heating up like a kettle

The sun is oh so far away,
But just one ray could brighten our day

Light and heat is what it will give,
Without the sun, we could not live

This beautiful star lies in space,
The fiery ball has no face

In such a long time it will be gone,
No more mornings of beautiful dawn

We all need this beautiful star,
Although it looks so big, it's really far!

Paige Steinberg, Grade 5
Weston Intermediate School, CT

My Messy Bedroom

My messy bedroom,
has spilled water everywhere,
and my sister going zoom, zoom, zoom,
with underwear on her hair!

There are movie stacks,
on my backpack,
with the dust bunnies going and going,
and overflowing.

My bed unfolded,
the trash all molded,
my dirty clothes tumbled over,
with on top my dog named Rover.

You don't want to see
my messy room,
so you might as well
grab a broom!

Jordan Baker, Grade 4
Henry B Burkland Elementary School, MA

Lost

Birds are flying
Trunks having ivy
You hear rain go pit pat, pit pat
Crows flocking over the field
Leaves on the floor like that's a big deal
Bridges on a trail
I wonder if we'll ever get there

Karina Gandulla, Grade 5
Jacob Hiatt Magnet Elementary School, MA

Morning Music*

This house
The always noise
Stressing
From the early morning chatter
At home
Between TV talking
And the electronic toothbrush
Cha-cha-chaing

I turn on my iPod
Listening
To the soothing sound
Of "Lean on Me"
Then the roaring car
And we drift off
To school

Morning music

Sean McCluskey, Grade 5
West Woods Upper Elementary School, CT
*Inspired by Arnold Adoff's "Street Music"

Football

Football is so much fun,
I can play it in the sun.
I go outside on sunny days,
and kick the ball in silly ways.
I love my football, it is my friend,
I take it to bed and this is the end.

Andrew Carter, Grade 4
Courthouse Road Elementary School, VA

Ode to the Snowflake

Oh, snowflake
you're so pretty
I'm sure you know winter
is coming soon
oh snowflake you're so
peaceful and white
but when I say winter
I don't mean to scare you
so have fun and stop
hiding in the clouds

Taylor Foley, Grade 4
C Hunter Ritchie Elementary School, VA

Tia

I have a cat named Tia.
She is like a baby tiger
learning to survive.
I love to entertain Tia by racing her.
She's like a puma,
she always wins.
I get most of my exercise from her.
I have been taking care of
her ever since
I was 3 years old.
She gets annoying at night.
She sleeps on my bed
and claws me.
She's a living pocketknife.
I love her most when
she watches television with me.
Sometimes she understands
what's going on in the show,
She's my little baby fur-ball.
I love Tia!

Devin Matté, Grade 4
Hawley Elementary School, CT

Spring

Spring is here
Spring is here
Time to cheer
Because you feel the breeze
Come upon your face
And birds singing with grace
And trees provide a home
For furry and old
And Spring is the boldest season
Of them all!

Isaiah Walker, Grade 4
Crestwood Elementary School, VA

Snowflake

What is a snowflake?
Is it a figment of the sky?
Is it a blessing from above?
Will we ever find out?
A snowflake is so delicate,
So light.
Its body is so cold,
Yet it makes you feel fuzzy.
When a snowflake falls.
It's like a baby is born.
So we don't know what it is,
Or why it makes us feel fuzzy.
But we do know it's there,
And it's happy.

Charlotte LeClue, Grade 5
Toquam Magnet School, CT

Spring Time

S ummer hot day
P atting on the sand on a beach
R aking the leaves
I ce cream in your mouth
N apping with the windows open
G iggling with your friends at the mall

T ime to have fun
I nto the pool
M aking lemonade
E ating at cook outs

Jalissa Batista, Grade 5
Sacred Heart Elementary School, MA

Our Flag

From the moon,
To the sand dunes,
From the bottom of the ocean,
To swaying in motion,
Visible in far away places,
Shown on familiar faces,
From the people who fly it,
To the people who fight by it,
What a Grand Old Flag.

Jimmy Degnan, Grade 5
Hindley Elementary School, CT

What Is a Dad?

Caring toward his children
Very playful anytime
A hard worker
Always helps his son with problems
Stays by you
Takes care of you
Brings you toys
Always there for you
Very buff
Has a good job
That is my dad!

Nate Gibson, Grade 5
Jane Ryan School, CT

Sun

Sun, sun
You bring such fun
Underneath your glare I run.
You shine above the lakes and rivers.
When you're not out I get the shivers.
High above, you brightly shine.
I feel as if your light's all mine.
Sun, sun, you shine so bright.
Warm me with your glowing light.

Sarah Lagan, Grade 5
St Joseph Elementary School, MA

24 Hours a Day

24 hours a day wind smashing swiftly
against the horizon only for me to
witness the break of day.
In the distance I see the sun and the
moon cross, only for me to witness
night fall.
Then it happens all over again,
24 hours a day.

Isaiah Fontaine, Grade 5
Clark Avenue Middle School, MA

Dreams*

Hold tightly to your dreams
Because a lost dream
Is like it's raining without clouds

Hold tightly to your dreams
Because a life without dreams
Is like a world without color

Savannah Carrington, Grade 5
Clover Street School, CT
*Inspired by Langston Hughes

The Girl at School

There was a girl at school
Who thought she was so cool
Until one day
She dropped her tray
So now she feels like a fool

Kerline Joseph, Grade 5
Sacred Heart Elementary School, MA

Baby Deer

Small helpless
The deer walks
Uneven legs
Falling over

Chomping on grass
That is fresh
And wanting
A drink of water

Nearby pond
Calling to the deer
She runs
To the pond, thirsty

Refreshed
Tired
The deer falls
Asleep.

Kate McLaughlin, Grade 6
E W Thurston Middle School, MA

I Am

I am an enthusiastic girl who loves to cheer
I wonder if I can twist down from a stunt
I hear the scream of the crowd when we win
I see a trophy that I want to earn
I want to be as good of a cheer coach as mine
I am an enthusiastic girl who loves to cheer

I pretend to cheer at professional football games
I feel the outrage of the coaches when we lose
I touch my maroon, gold, and white pompoms
I worry about rejection
I cry when a football player gets hurt
I am an enthusiastic girl who loves to cheer

I understand that listening keeps me safe
I say nothing is impossible
I dream about being in a *Bring It On* movie
I try to do my best in competitions
I hope that I will be as successful as other pro cheerleaders
I am an enthusiastic girl who loves to cheer
I am Lindsay Nicole Diamond

Lindsay Diamond, Grade 5
Clover Hill Elementary School, VA

Clear Round

The announcer finally comes on
And broadcasts the last ride of the day.
Everyone's hoping for my clear round,
I race through the timers,
calculate the careful approach for the first fence,
and soar over it.
I draw near the second fence, close,
a slight rub, but the pole stays up.

I feel the power beneath me,
the heavy breaths of the horse.

Over the last fence
As I ride to victory at Rolex Kentucky.

McKenna Oxenden, Grade 6
Trinity School, MD

The Leaf

A little leaf left among the dirt
Then a kind wind lifts the leaf into the air
But fails
Once again the leaf is left
Then the wind tries again!
This time the leaf is brought to where
the sky separates into two
and the angels sing the heavens to sleep
Where God's gates open and all is calm
And just to think it started with a kind wind
and a little leaf left among the dirt

Carolyn Scharl, Grade 5
Soule Road School, MA

A Dog's Life

I'm running on the street,
My heart has a powerful beat,

I run and chase my tail,
'Til dad comes out and puts me in jail,

Humpf! I think as I sit in my crate,
So boring, not fun. it's not so great,

Next morning dad again lets me out,
I sniff him with my little pug snout.

Before I go out on another adventure,
I get some water, the perfect thirst quencher,

The door flies open, I go outside,
I mark my yard, and I do it with pride.

Justin Rosenthal, Grade 4
Forest Avenue Elementary School, MA

Begin a New Day

Help to save the Earth,
Give our world a new birth.
Begin to recycle all your paper goods,
This will save the trees deep in the woods.

Turn off lights when they're not in use,
This will save electric juice.
Turn off the water after taking your shower,
You will conserve lots of power.

Don't dump oil in the bay,
This will help the fish live another day.
Catch a ride with your friend,
This will help the air to mend.

Pick up your trash when you're at the beach,
Many people this will teach.
Pollution could ruin our Earth forever,
So help the world get it together.

Chloe Bialozynski, Grade 4
St Clement Mary Hofbauer School, MD

Sounds of Peace

Peace to me is a quiet and tranquil sound in the night.
Alone in your soft bed of flowers.
Here, there is nothing but the sound
Of the animals crawling around your room.
The spider is spinning his web.
Mouse is trying to find the garage,
To get away from owls.
Sleep tight in the peaceful night.

Gregory Kalagher, Grade 4
Quashnet School, MA

The Memory of a Veteran

As he feels the wind
On his scarred and gnarled face,
He remembers days
Long ago, so very, very long ago,
About that horrible war.

Before the bombing
Of Pearl Harbor in Hawaii,
Before the work camps
And Hitler's reign of terror,
And the death of many boys.

When he fought in it,
When his friends died around him,
But he still fought on,
And he remembered D-day,
And the surge of hope he felt.

He remembers when
The allies raided the eagle's nest,
And, at last, caught Hitler.
The joy was incredible,
Because World War Two was over.

Jeb Forehand, Grade 6
Homeschool Plus, VA

Books!

Books,
Books,
Books fall open,
You fall in,
You go to a magical,
Mystical world.
The spine is your holder,
The worlds are your sea.
Each word is like a fish,
With rich bountiful flavors.
Then you fall out,
The book falls shut.
So you are left wondering,
Until next time.

Nolan Griffin, Grade 5
C C Burr Elementary School, MA

Ice Cream

I s there any for me?
C ooling on a hot summer day
E veryone wants some!

C an I have vanilla?
R eally good
E very day I could eat
A ll the ice cream in the world
M ore please!!!!

Caitlin Dye, Grade 5
J F Kennedy Middle School, MA

My Love

I really love my girl
She's the only one in my fantasy world
When she hugs me my soul soars like a bird
Her voice is the greatest thing I ever heard
When she leaves my face fills with gloom
When she comes back my joy comes back into the room
When she died my tears fell down like rain
Now I know nothing will never be the same
Now I don't have anybody to love
I can hear her calling me from the heaven above
I don't have anybody in my world to start
But I still have a cold memory stored down deep inside my heart

Davonte King, Grade 6
School of International Studies at Meadowbrook, VA

The Beach House

O Lord, You who art so dear Who deserve all thanks for this house
Because so seldom am I here I often think I will see at least one mouse

First the suntan lotion from head to toe
Then off to the ocean so fast we go!

I like making castles of sand I think it is really fun
But sometimes things get out of hand my mom is happy when I'm done

I like swimming with the fish this is really cool
O Great! Fish is my favorite dish You see, I eat from this huge pool

I sit out in the sun not wanting to run
Because I just ate another Cinnabon knowing I really should have stopped at one

Not eager to share my boardwalk fries they are so very delicious
But I give in to the cries and realize that they are not so nutritious

Adrianna V. Jews, Grade 5
Church of the Redeemer Christian School, MD

Frost Fur Squirrel

Dashing up and down the old oak's branches,
Like two tiny balloons,
He stuffed his cheeks with nuts and seeds
Here comes the frost fur squirrel…
Hundreds and hundreds of seeds and nuts
"I must hide these where no one would think to look,"
Squeaks the frost fur squirrel
Rapidly racing through the tall towering trees
As if he were a rabbit and a dog was hot on his trail,
The frost fur squirrel found his luck to be
As empty as a burnt down house,
An abandoned muskrat den lay in the ground
Swiftly sniffling the air he scented a stale fragrance
Assuming the muskrat moved…
He spit the seeds out of his mouth to store them in this new hiding place
Perhaps it will be a perfect winter for this little squirrel.

Bailey Cotrona, Grade 6
Madison Middle School, CT

Cantering
My heart stops,
The feeling takes my breath away.

My legs feel like rubber
Against her warm body.

The world blurs around me,
And everything disappears.

The echoing voices are silenced
The only thing I can hear is the pounding of her hooves.

This feeling is like no other,
I wish to keep going until the end of time.

Alyssa Resar, Grade 5
McDonogh School, MD

Winter
In winter,
Snow covers the ground and hides rooftops,
Geese fly south and snowballs fly everywhere,
Sleds slide down hills,
While parents drink eggnog by the fire,

In winter,
White smoke floats out of chimneys,
And rests like clouds above,
The sky turns a pale white,
While the sun is distant,
It looks like a giant blanket,
Has covered the roads and cars.

Grayson Harrison, Grade 5
Tilghman Elementary School, MD

An Ode to Christmas
Christmas is time for fun in the snow.
It's time to give presents to people you know.

It's time for the adults to laugh away,
And for the children to play all day.

Gifts unwrapped with eagerness and joy,
At the idea of getting a particular toy.

Christmastime is like a decorated tree,
With so many people and things to see.

The Christmas season is here at last!
It's time to go out and have a blast.

So long, farewell, I bid thee adieu.
I have so many things to attend to!

Drew Merryman, Grade 6
St Clement Mary Hofbauer School, MD

Fireworks
A crowd gathers on the frosty field,
Huddling together for warmth

They hold their breath,
Waiting for the first streak of light in the dark sky

Suddenly, something rockets up, high enough to reach the stars
It explodes, green sparkles light up the sky

More and more keep coming,
So bright it hurts my eyes,
So loud I cover my ears

Then, it is over,
A few last sparkles dance slowly to the ground,
The sky is empty,
The night is quiet,

And people slowly make their way back home

Rose Murphy, Grade 6
E W Thurston Middle School, MA

School Yard Play
Children screaming,
Teacher's whistles blowing
Up the ladder
Down the slide
Feel the mulch in your shoes
When you hit the ground.

Ian Goulet, Grade 5
Foxborough Regional Charter School, MA

What Is Poetry?
Poetry is…
Periods and question marks, none
Expressing yourself in every way
Writing whatever you want
And thinking of your life

Poetry is…
Thinking of ways to rhyme or not
Having a writing sore on your finger
Because of how much writing you do
You would never want to stop your imagination…
As it is floooooowing.

Kyle Page, Grade 4
Fawn Hollow Elementary School, CT

Excitement
Looks like entering an amusement park
Smells like fresh made cotton candy
Feels like winning a contest
Tastes like popcorn and icees
Sounds like kids going out of control

Catie Harper, Grade 4
C Hunter Ritchie Elementary School, VA

Spider Web

When I see a spider web,
I think it is so neat.
To think a tiny spider
Made it with its own
Eight feet.
I think it's kind of scary
When a fly comes buzzing near.
For when the poor thing gets so stuck
It begins to quiver with fear.
Then the spider breaks its neck
And sucks its blood 'till it's dry.
And that's the very sad ending
Of poor old Mr. fly.
When I see a spider web
I think it is so cool.
Except for the part when it kills the fly,
I think that's kind of cruel.

Natalie Mitchell, Grade 4
Munger Hill Elementary School, MA

Dogs

The dog sits
Still as a tower,
Gold glittering
Soft as a bundle of hair,
Peering in the window at fluffy bunnies.
Red at night, and brown in light.
Swift as the wind,
Running free in the heat of summer

Gregory Savino, Grade 4
Potter Road Elementary School, MA

True Desire

My eyes are wet
It's not sweat
I'm not cold
No one will ever know
That my heart has true desire
It's like a big fire
I feel left out
But my heart's in the game
I think it's running out of flame
Why is it dying out on me?
Will it ever believe?
I deserve a second chance
I'm falling down
My face hit the ground
I'm turning cold
And I'm getting old
When push comes to shove
I need my heart
Was it there from the start?

Chantel Hargrove-Stephens, Grade 6
Benjamin Syms Middle School, VA

My Favorite Star

As they shine so brightly
They seem to send a message

Each star has its own story
And they always like to tell it

But my favorite story
Is the one from the star

That I know so well
Because I know she's watching over me

And it stays as a reminder
To show how much we loved her

Timothy Scully, Grade 5
Soule Road School, MA

Desert

The blazing heat goes
Setting over the horizon,
The sun shines no more

As everything darkens,
The more calm and serene it gets
Sand whips from wind

Jessica Rende, Grade 5
Jane Ryan School, CT

Spring Break

I can't wait to go away,
get a break for a while,
because when I'm at school,
there's not much fun.
I get to be in the sun
and enjoy it while I'm there,
but the week soon ends,
got to go to school again,
I wish it would never end.

Kyleigh Middleton, Grade 6
Monelison Middle School, VA

Spring Is Here

Trees are blooming!
In the air,
Colors are shining,
Everywhere!
Richer the grass
Warmer the air
Just because
Spring
Is
Here!

Brenna Jagodzinski, Grade 5
St Joseph School-Fullerton, MD

Winter

Frost on the windows
Snow billowing in the air
Winter has arrived

Kathleen Welch, Grade 6
Spring Hill Elementary School, VA

Sports

Dribble, shoot, score
Shoot, score, run
Score, run, kick
Run, kick, pitch
Kick, throw, punch
Throw, punch, flip
Punch, flip, *SPORTS*

Morgan Winship, Grade 6
Chalk Hill School, CT

Whispering Waterfall

Look at it
rushing down the river
it's glistening shine upon the riverbank
reflecting against the sun.

Listen to it clashing
against the rocks
rushing down the stream,
it splashing and clashing in the sun
down the beautiful stream.

Hear the wind whispering
"the stream is all yours"
but for now
I need to let the stream
whisper for it's own.

Hannah Bulie, Grade 5
Hindley Elementary School, CT

Sometimes I Wonder

Sometimes I wonder,
why I love you
sometimes I wonder,
why I hate you
sometimes I wonder,
why we argue
sometimes I wonder,
why you lie to me
sometimes I wonder,
do you love me
sometimes I wonder,
why we go out
sometimes I wonder,
why I love you

Lexxus Jeffries, Grade 6
Monelison Middle School, VA

A Day at the Beach

At the beach
Sandcastles, shining shells,
Loud motor boats, and the big blue ocean

It's a bright sunny day
No clouds in sight
The vibrant sun makes the water
Sparkle, sparkle, sparkle

Sounds everywhere
Waves crashing to the rocky shore
Laughing and screaming of children

The shock from the hot beach
To the cold water stirs up a thought
Why is the water so cold and the day so hot?

The cool breeze makes a relaxing day
The beach is an amazing place to be

Maegan Moran, Grade 5
Mill Pond School, MA

Dog's Favorite Part of the Day

Nose nudging endlessly,
Walking warily around the house
with paws pressing against the patio floor.
Irresistible eyes with a longing look.
The dog begs to go out.

Jogging joyfully and effortlessly,
The dog enjoys its daily run.
Muzzle panting profusely, "Heh, heh, heh."
Padding finally into the house with heavy breath,
He moves to his mat where he rests.

Michael Bernal, Grade 6
Trinity School, MD

Regionals

I smell chlorine in the air
I peer down at the pool water, cold and still
I get ready to jump off the diving board
I hear the whistle scream
I can hear the cheers of parents loud

I finally dive into the water
I have been waiting for my time to shine
I feel like a dolphin finally reaching its goal in life
I feel the water jump right back at me as I dive in

I can only think of one thing as I start to swim
That I repeat over and over again in my head
"Go as fast as you can!"
Until I find myself out of the water
Giving high-fives to everyone.

Karla Bachiller, Grade 6
E W Thurston Middle School, MA

Clothes

Clothes, clothes, it's like they have a personality.
Clothes, clothes, do they bring you humility?
Clothes, clothes, it's like they talk.
Clothes, clothes, I wonder why they don't walk.
Clothes, clothes, are they warm or are they cold?
Clothes, clothes, are they new or are they old?
Clothes, clothes, are they good or are they bad?
Clothes, clothes, are they ripped a tad?
Clothes, clothes, do they give you a bad name?
Clothes, clothes, do people think they're lame?
Clothes, clothes, they tell so much.
Clothes, clothes, they have the magic touch.

Noah Jones, Grade 5
Trevilians Elementary School, VA

My 'Lovable' Locker

Locker, Locker, I do not like you
Picking on me is all you ever do.
Although you store all my stuff
Trying to open you is very tough.

Today, tomorrow, my whole year through,
I will never stop avoiding you!
Oh locker, oh locker, how I dislike you!

Kassandra Cruz, Grade 6
Fuller Middle School, MA

Christmas

I smell the delicious
Aroma of turkey being
Soaked and cooked in
Scrumptious juices
I feel the fluffy couch
That I am sitting on
And the comforting heat
From the fire in front of me

I hear my older family members
Chatting away their worries

As I sit in near-silence
I wonder what I will get in a glittery wrapped box
A book, a toy
Maybe even a note
From the jolly old man in red

I wonder when I will fall asleep
When sleep will bring
The wonderful sensation of rest
For my body
As I slowly drift
Drift into sleep

Aisling Dennehy, Grade 6
Swampscott Middle School, MA

Red Bird

In snowy tree so tall
Fiery cardinal sits
Staring distantly
Kathryn Phillips, Grade 6
Our Lady of Mercy School, CT

Mom

Mom, oh, Mom
what wonderful things you do.
You cook and clean
Oh boy! We all love you!
You are the mother of all times
you are the family tree
I can't help but smile,
when you look at me!
You are the one who is there
through all bad times,
you are the one who held me
when I kicked and whined.
The heroes of this world
are the mothers that rule all,
they pick you up when you're down,
they make you stand proud and tall!
Olivia Schrader, Grade 5
Litwin Elementary School, MA

Friends and Enemies

Friends,
silly, crazy,
laughing, enjoying, fascinating,
friends, mall, back stabbers, drama,
scuffing, hating, fighting,
mean, jerks,
Enemies
Courtney Hill, Grade 6
Captain Nathan Hale Middle School, CT

Blu

I have a fish his name is Blu.
He swims around his bowl.
Bubbling wherever he goes.
He loves his food.
He creeps up and gobbles it up.
Blu chews then swallows.
Just like we do.
He's a fast fish.
He moves as fast as lightning.
Blu likes the things we get him
He thinks they're really fun
His favorite toy is blu shell.
He pushes it to and fro.
His favorite color is blu
He is a blu fish.
That's why I named him Blu.
Gabriel Suazo, Grade 4
Marsh Grammar School, MA

Dance

D oing dance is our passion
A udience applauding our dance as we shine on stage
N ever-ending classes pay off in the end
C ostumes of all different kinds feathers, sequins, fringe, and more
E ntering a competition, butterflies fluttering in our stomachs
Kelsey Hyland and Brittany Bowes, Grade 5
Leicester Memorial School, MA

Why Music

Music is a stormy cloud of notes everywhere.
It is like inspiring someone of something.
The D is singing high like a person.

Music is wonderful, witty, worried and wacky anything you want
it to be. I am so full of music I can sing low notes at once and can make
sounds that you want like bammm, whooshhh and dinggg.
Phillip Mack, Grade 6
School of International Studies at Meadowbrook, VA

The Army

The Army is like sadness, all wrapped up in one big ball.
The green on the uniforms make the men and women look brave.
The sweat running down their faces, giving them a fierce look in their eyes.
The hard cold nights shivering as some of them hide under their beds.
The sounds moving through the air mixed with wind and death cries.
The taste of their food scorching down their throats.
The smoke from the explosions being thrown at them, making them choke.
Their confidence roaring out loud.
The road is rough, walking and running through every type of matter.
But even doing all of this, it's done for you.
Amber Consani, Grade 5
Newton-Lee Elementary School, VA

The Land of Sweets

Once upon a time there was a land of sweets,
There was bubblegum and fairy cakes,
A chocolate river flowed over peanut butter cups,
The volcanoes spit chocolate chunks when there were earthquakes.

The trees were made of cotton candy,
And the peppermint bark drip honey,
Flowers are sugared strawberries,
The snow was icing sugar so it was never sunny.

Cherry pie mountains,
And cupcake bushes,
Candy cane grass,
And soft marshmallow rocks to rest your tushes.

Springs spurt Pixie Stix,
A Cocoa-Cola sea,
With whipped cream foam,
And it's all for me!!!
Megan Evershed, Grade 5
St Luke's School, CT

Easter

Easter is school's off.
Easter is candy, eggs, and chocolate bunnies.
But Easter is more,
Easter is happiness, sadness, and joy.
Easter is white, a celebration.
Easter is black, a funeral, a time for mourning.
Easter is a time where Jesus died on the Cross
for us and rose up again.
The tomb was left an empty eggshell, a symbol of Easter.
The people were scared, worried, confused
That the person before them was not Jesus.
But he said to them,
"Be not afraid, for I Am God's only Son."
And with that He rose up to Heaven.

Jesus sacrificed Himself to save us from our sins.

So when you think about Easter
think about old-fashioned cartoons,
Black and White,
a Celebration a Funeral
happiness, sadness, joy.

Easter.

Ellie Profaci, Grade 5
St James Academy, MD

Mother's Day

Mother's Day
My mom's smile when she sees breakfast
Eggs and bacon cooking on the stove
My mom saying thank you, thank you for breakfast
Some of my mom's bacon
The pink and red petals of beautiful flowers
Mother's Day

Taylor Starkey, Grade 4
Naquag Elementary School, MA

My Pool

Water rippled with people in it,
The non-calm splashing,
The filter's many noises,
The water sprayer spraying across the pool,
The smell of the chlorine in your nose,
The smell of the snacks,
Yummy
The taste of the water when it touches your tongue,
Yuck
The taste of the snacks,
Yummy
The feel of the freezing water,
Burr.

Corey Miller, Grade 5
Foxborough Regional Charter School, MA

Happiness

Happiness is the sound of laughter.
Happiness looks like a thousand smiling faces.
Happiness smells of daisies in an open field.
Happiness tastes like strawberries in the summer.
Happiness feels like the green grass when the wind blows.
Happiness must just be great.
How I wish the world had it.

Caitlynn Shafer, Grade 4
Waller Mill Fine Arts Magnet School, VA

Leprechauns

Leprechauns dancing all around.
And look what they found.
A big pot of gold.
And then they take and hold.
It's over their heads and then
march across the ground.

Matthew Peck, Grade 4
Charlotte A Dunning Elementary School, MA

A Cold, Snowy Night

I have snow memories in abundance
From my childhood especially
But none are compared to tonight
Freshly fallen snow with no prints
The stars are shining bright like just polished jewels
Reflecting light on the snow
But oddly enough
The moon is absent from the party

Sara Prince, Grade 6
Wakefield Forest Elementary School, VA

When I Think of My Cousin

When I think of my cousin
I see a bright light in the sky like his face
I see a lion scaring a weak mouse like I scare him
I see glitches because he destroyed my game
When I think of my cousin
I hear him shouting like a madman from a hospital
I hear him asking for chocolaty cookies on the shelf
I hear him breaking my toys like a lion to meat
I hear comical talking about cars
When I think of my cousin
I smell his food like banana cream
I smell his baby shampoo from his hair
I taste his baby powder that he never puts on when awake
When I think of my cousin
I taste banana and strawberry cream that he eats every hour
I taste half fresh grapes with salt
When I think of my cousin
I feel very warm because he always puts on tons of clothes
I feel soft and cozy like his skin
I feel smooth sand because he likes to play with it
When I think of my cousin

Simran Pabla, Grade 6
Fuller Middle School, MA

My Running Dream

Gliding over dew dropped ground, I float away from daily stress and past a sleeping landscape under a blue morning sky. Sparkling like diamonds, the spring flowers fill the air with a delicate aroma.

Slap! Slap! My feet hit the damp earth and my hair blazes back as the wind whispers through the trees. Two birds join my peaceful dash chirping their joyful songs overheard.

The salty taste of sweat is fresh on my tongue and my legs have turned to jelly. In the last moments of my run, I hear a familiar voice piercing the air.

Hey Liv, what's the answer to number 5?
Oh well, back to reality.

Olivia Nordland, Grade 6
Litchfield Intermediate School, CT

Flying Through the Wind

When I go outside on a windy day
the wind makes me feel like I'm on a boat gliding through the air 100 miles per hour or
like I'm growing wings and flying through the air at 100 miles per hour, or
I am jumping off a cliff but not falling.
Flying through the wind.

Andrew Murphy, Grade 5
Charlotte A Dunning Elementary School, MA

Kids

We sing and dance and laugh and play
Although sometimes obnoxious and little rude,
We can be kind hearted, and helpful too!
So don't be surprised when a kid asks you "Is there anything I can do?"
To you our baggy jeans are such an insult, but to us, it's in style! So relax, it's what we do!
We burp and talk in slang, and to you it's like another language, but to us it's like a second nature.
We are very adventurous, but maybe just a little confused, so sometimes, we might need a little push.
We may grow up, we may not. But that's up to us, not you adults.
But how we play, and how we act, how we talk and how we dress,
that's all up to us, and there's nothing you can do.
So don't try to change us, outside or our insides, we are who we are.
We're kids, what do you expect?

Kelsey Carvalko, Grade 6
Irving School, CT

Am I Asleep

The whistling tone of the wind sends a shiver through my spine. The sound tells me it's freezing out, my but figure is completely numb. Yet my lips are blue crystals of coldness, they are my only sense that I'm still here, that I'm not in a dream, a section of my imagination, or dead. The taste of the trees can only be described as darkness, as the taste of a million painful dreams, of a choking oak. Behind me, the trees are spiraling into the top of the world, grasping for the clouds far, far above me. The ground has the soft soil texture; as if it were a silk pasture, flooding over me. The wind is still dancing its dance, and chanting its chant while I try to warm myself. I close my eyes, which are truly useless for the sky is as dark as my nails, my heart, and my eyes. Although it's so dark, I can still see a magnificent spider crawling across a rock in the middle of the walkway — the walkway, an exit, a passageway, an escape route from the horrible depth of the forest, the unbearable cold, and the saddening, soothing song of the wind. I stand on my wobbly legs. I feel as if my legs have just come alive after hundreds of years of rejuvenating sleep. With my first step, I fall right to the ground, a pain of pins and needles shoot up my leg, or as I describe it, sand in my shoes. Sand in my shoes, like when you sit on the ground for too long, exactly what I was doing. My pale toes inch forward, taking baby steps towards my destination. The moon is hardly more than a sliver of silver, but the black of my pupils and my irises soak up the little light there is in left in the sky.

Becca Morey, Grade 6
Two Rivers Magnet Middle School, CT

Springtime

Spring is here, it's time to rejoice!
Spring is here and that means no more winter!
Spring is when the sunny days come.
Spring is when the snow and bad weather has vanished.
Spring is when cherry blossoms and exquisite flowers bloom.
Spring is when it rains unexpectedly, but it won't ruin the day.
Spring is when most birthdays are to be celebrated.
Spring is when animals come out of hibernation!
Spring is when animals play in the good weather.
Spring is the most jubilant season of all!

Dayane Torres, Grade 5
Davenport Ridge School, CT

What I Have in My Pocket

What I have in my pocket is a mountain of clutter
Twenty three spoons and eight sticks of butter.
A hammer and nails and some watering pails,
A cat with ten paws and seventeen tails.
What I have in my pocket is a mountain of clutter
When I empty it out it just makes me shudder.

Elizabeth Doub, Grade 4
Boonsboro Elementary School, MD

I Am Your Creation

When I look at Your creation and everything You've made
I can't help it but to give You praise
I am thankful Lord, that You made me part of your creation
And that I'm allowed to serve You in this nation

My heart is touched by Your amazing grace
And every day I will run this great race

My prayer Lord is to be light
To this dark world and each day
To serve You with honor and joy

Thank You for the gift of being a drummer
Is the best way to give You honor

When I'm in Your house jamming away
I start thinking of the day I'll see You face to face

Keep my heart humble in all my ways
So I can serve You for the rest of my days

Gabriel Cardenas, Grade 5
Church of the Redeemer Christian School, MD

Mr. Bully

Dear Mr. Bully, you always pick on me
Dear Mr. Bully, there's other fish in the sea.
It's an eye for an eye and my eye's always black
You always give me nuggies when I turn my back.
I've tried all year to be your friend
Please bring this bullying to an end.

Victor Mariens, Grade 6
Fuller Middle School, MA

An Autumn Breeze

An autumn breeze is not a freeze,
It is nice and cool.
An autumn breeze is fun and inviting,
Even though you cannot swim in a pool.
I still love autumn;
It might be cold to some people,
And you can't wear any shorts,
But you can still roll around in the leaves
And still have hot cocoa when you are done for the day.
I love autumn;
An autumn breeze is not a freeze.
I love autumn

Megan Williams, Grade 6
Whitinsville Christian School, MA

Jar of Dreams

The empty jar,
filled with dreams,
the clear jar,
the most miraculous thing.

The colorful ribbon,
purple, yellow, pink,
the colorful ribbon,
slowly slips away.

The golden cover,
twists and turns,
so don't the dreams inside,
they flutter above me,
slowly drifting down,
then,
suddenly disappear.

My head explodes with wonderful thoughts,
I fall down on my knees,
and thank God for my wonderful,
LIFE.

Nichole Gouveia, Grade 4
St Mary's Primary School, MA

Rainbow Day

Today,
As I watch the rain come to an end,
I begin to get excited.
I know,
That soon,
A rainbow will appear outside my window.
Rainbows,
In my opinion,
Are beautiful.
The colors blend together so marvelously
No words can explain it.

Melanie Orent, Grade 4
King's Highway Elementary School, CT

Basketball

3 seconds left
What will he do?
Will he pass?
Or will he shoot?

2 seconds left
What will he do?
Will he call timeout?
Or drive to the hoop?

1 second left
What will he do?
Will he win?
Or will he lose?
KJ Grubiak, Grade 6
Cape Henry Collegiate School, VA

Ways to Clean Our Earth

We want the Earth to stay very clean,
So here is what you do.
Stop the world from polluting,
The following ways are true.

To recycle you need cans and bottles,
So you can throw them in the trash.
You can also use cardboard and paper,
And don't forget the glass.

The Earth is not an ashtray,
And neither is the bay.
Do us all a favor,
And stop smoking today.

I hope you use my advice,
And try these helpful ways.
It would be a big help to all of us,
So stop polluting these days.
Nicolette Ficca, Grade 4
St Clement Mary Hofbauer School, MD

Art

Art you sketch
Paint a lot
Study facts
And take a class
Go here
Go there
Having fun
Art is
Challenging
To make when
It's all done!
Paige Ferreira, Grade 5
St Mary's Primary School, MA

Green Money

There once was a bunny named honey,
Who always tried to be funny.
She was very sweet,
She wanted to eat,
A stack of the old man's green money.
Samantha Carey, Grade 4
St Clement Mary Hofbauer School, MD

Summer Fun

S pecial for all kids
U sually happy to get out of school
M ostly outside playing or having fun
M aking sandwiches for a picnic
E nergetic kids ready to play outside
R eading for the summer reading list.

F un to play with family and friends
U sually not ready to go back
N o, school has started again
Veronica Reyes, Grade 5
Sacred Heart Elementary School, MA

Woods

It is very dark
The animals creep me out
It is so scary

Dead trees hang freely
I don't like running in there
I can't see a thing
Colin McMenamey, Grade 5
Jane Ryan School, CT

Chipmunks

Chipmunks chew on nuts
Chipmunks live in giant trees
Chipmunks fear humans

Little and very cool
Sensitive to everything
Scared of giant birds

Playful all the time
Smart enough to escape prey
Trees are their headquarters
Tom Switzgable, Grade 5
Jane Ryan School, CT

Flowers

Flowers bloom pretty
It's just a great sight to see
While birds fly up high
Andrea Galaviz-Garcia, Grade 4
Hebbville Elementary School, MD

Stars

Stars glow up so high
Bright, beautiful specks of light
Making dreams come true
Anna Ford, Grade 6
Our Lady of Mercy School, CT

Baseball

Every time I hit a ball,
That goes up really high,
It seems to fly like a bird,
In the big blue sky.

Then it soars down to the ground,
And into my brand new mitt.
Then the opposing team cries
Losing their winning hit.
Bobby Tremblay, Grade 5
Soule Road School, MA

Bullies

They strut around
Prowling the playground
Searching for their next victim

Their goal?
To make you feel inferior
To make themselves feel powerful
To make you feel tiny
To make themselves feel like a giant

But they don't realize the truth
The powerless ones are themselves
They are the ones that are small
Sarah Heinzmann, Grade 6
Scotts Ridge Middle School, CT

Seasons

Seasons are lovely.
Summer, winter, fall, and spring.
Four lovely seasons.

Summer, my favorite.
Pretty, sunny, summer days.
Sunlight shines brightly.

Spring, the second best.
Scented, pretty, pink flowers
Children run freely.

Fall, the third best.
Brown and orange falling leaves
Raking crinkly leaves.
Holly McPartland, Grade 5
Jane Ryan School, CT

A Busy Autumn

A busy autumn has many sounds
The hum of bees and leaves falling to the ground
The winding wind whistles in my ear
The sweet chirping of birds like a church choir you can hear
The roar of the lawn mower driving about
And the frightening scream of children followed by a pout

A busy autumn makes a huge mess
Leaves and sticks all over the yard cause people great stress
The scraps of nuts left behind are like cans in a garbage dump
People stepping on them with a loud thump
Rocks and gravel silently sift down below
Finally the day ends with darkness following the last soft glow

A busy autumn has many a fright
As kids dress up as monsters and go off in the night
Ghouls and goblins refuse to be tame
Houses are egged, who is to blame
Jack-o-lanterns glisten in the darkness
Scaring people is their ultimate test
Scarecrows shivering in the cold
Keeping crows away from the corn that grows
This is the busy autumn I see all around you and me

Sarah Morsches, Grade 6
Madison Middle School, CT

Dogs and Cats

Dog
playful, furry
barking, running, jumping
Shih Tzu, Pomeranian, Himalayan, Siamese
purring, sleeping, eating
lazy, relaxed
Cat

Katie Konieczny, Grade 6
St Joseph School, MA

A Dog's Tail

My feet thump across the long prickly grass
The sun streams down in rays,
soft and warm
the scent of bugs
and other things
lingers through the air
So clean and pure
a calling reaches
my fluffy sensitive
ears and I bark softly
in reply.
I run into the arms
of my faithful owner
I am content.

Madeline Bove, Grade 6
Litchfield Intermediate School, CT

L'Ardeche

Glimmering waves
shining in the vivid sun
stony shoreline at my feet
tall rocky mountains to stare at
with dark, cool caves of exploration
Looking up, I watch, watch, watch
staring at the daring people
Jumping from the tall mountains
into the glimmering water forty feet below
I hear the playful birds and laughing kids
echoing from the caves
The splashing swimmers
The ripples in the water
from the vibrant fish
I'm eager for a swim
into the calm, calm, calm, water
Spotless with sparkles from the sun
As I swim an extended distance
to a gigantic and pebbly mountain rock
I wonder, will I really jump off this?
Will I make it through?

Melanie Barbini, Grade 5
Mill Pond School, MA

Pretzels

Bread twisted with white cubes,
It lies down,
broken and complete,
with two eyes and a mouth,
and three holes.
looking like glasses.
With two it could look like a jack 'o lantern
with a huge face
When broken it can be many different things
but a tasty snack to me and you.
Pretzels.

Matthew Hickey, Grade 5
Charlotte A Dunning Elementary School, MA

Water Tracks

The water sleeps softly,
Before I jump in.

I carve a track through the water,
From my kicking feet.

Pushing off the wall,
From one end of the pool.

I get to the other side in 20 seconds,
Pushing off again.

I'm out of the water dripping water on the floor,
Leaving another track.

Izzy Donabed, Grade 6
E W Thurston Middle School, MA

Daisy

Walking in the house
Daisy charges towards me.
Leaping right into my arms.
As hyper as a
monkey flinging bananas.
Crying and demanding to go on a walk.
Cheering when I say yes.
Bark! Bark!

Vvvviiiuuummm!
the Frisbee soars
A dog flies through the air
Like a cheetah chasing a disk.
Lovely in the sunlight.
Clever enough to watch for cars.
Thrilled when we get inside
An awesome dog who is my friend!!!

Rashida Solomon, Grade 4
Braeburn School, CT

Oh How I Wish

Oh, how I wish
I had a sibling
Not younger
But older
Not a boy
But a girl
To help me with my problems

Oh, how I wish
I had a sibling
Not older
But younger
Not a girl
But a boy
To prank the family

Oh, how I wish
I had these siblings
Both boy and girl
Both young and old
To help with problems
Or maybe a simple prank
And we'll always be the best of friends

Nora Perlmutter, Grade 4
Alice B Beal Elementary School, MA

Summer and Winter

Winter
breezy, icy
snowboarding, caring, giving
skateboarding, airsofting, paintballing
steamy, sporty
Summer

Kevin Mahoney, Grade 4
Brookside Elementary School, MA

Night Sky

Through a curtain of black, stars twinkle so bright
They dance to the rhythm of the wind in the night
The moon plays the music of the Milky Way
While the planets sing, hum, and sway
Other constellations do the same when they hear the harmony's cry
From one end of the galaxy to the other you can hear the sweet song,
Of friends in the night getting along
Thunder soon rolls in to join the tune
It creates a new beat to play with the moon
But alas, the joy must come to an end,
So we wait till night to perform again

Amanda Richter, Grade 6
Scotts Ridge Middle School, CT

Daisy

Daisy is sweet, she's lovable too.
Daisy is a dog not like me or you.
I play with her a lot, just like you would do.
Daisy likes to chew on her chew toys and make them go squeak, squeak, squeak.
Daisy even has a nickname that is D.
Even though she's a dog she feels like a puppy to me.
She likes to stay inside with me more than going outside with her doggy friend Chloe.
She jumps on my legs when I get home from lots of things.
It's a doggy way to say "Hello"
That's why I love Daisy.

Jillian Penfield, Grade 4
Miscoe Hill Elementary School, MA

My Life

Sometimes I feel happy about living in Boston.
But sometimes I don't.
I left a lot of memories and feelings in Haiti,
Feelings and thoughts that I can't even talk about,
Memories of happiness and fun.

I don't feel the freedom that I used to feel.
I used to laugh when I play.
I don't feel as comfortable as I used to around my friends.
They don't understand me as well as my old friends.
They don't understand how I feel.

They don't know what I have been through all my life.
I have been through trouble.
I have been through sadness and happiness.
I also have been through the most important thing, love.
Love is a very important thing in my life.

Love means care.
My mom always gives me love.
She makes me feel secure.
I am not scared when I am around her.
It is just because of love.
I love my country and I will never forget the life and the friends that I had.

Anne Therrie Toussaint, Grade 6
Swampscott Middle School, MA

When Bells Toll*

When bells toll — it calls us to pray.
When bells toll, it's time to say,
To say what abuses and bothers us
In our daily life, alas!

When bells toll — it's a sign again,
Again to recall who left us, amen!
To light a candle, to cross, and to ask
For pity from the Lord and the burden of task.

When bells toll — it's a joy for the youth
In wedding's celebration to find a truth.
To start a new fate coupling the rings
To share love and duty, and the hope that it brings.

And only for me when the bells start to toll
John Donne is the man I always recall.
Recall his deep wisdom and appeal for esprit
When bells toll, remember, "it tolls for thee!"

YoElena Tkebuchava, Grade 4
Memorial-Spaulding Elementary School, MA
*Based upon John Donne's "For Whom the Bell Tolls"

Gardening

Whatever I touch dies.
It's actually no surprise.
I've killed any plant you name.
My mother says I'm going insane.
I've planted loopy lilacs
Deranged daffodils
Moldy marigolds
Rotten rosemary
Soggy sweet peas
Cruddy carnations
Gross gardenias
Frumpy forget-me-nots
And many more!
This gardening stuff is so dumb!
I guess I didn't inherit my mother's green thumb.

Victoria Sayeg, Grade 6
E W Thurston Middle School, MA

Border Collies in a Field

Three black and white forms bounding through the grass
Beautiful, graceful, runners, each other trying to pass

They imagine they are herding sheep
The instinct of their breed runs deep

Circles and circles and circles and still not getting tired
Barks ring through the air like gunshots being fired

At last they are called in to get a treat
Now they are normal dogs lounging on couches while they eat

Ava Siegel, Grade 4
Helen H Hansen Elementary School, MA

Family Feast

I sat down, I placed my order
First the dazzling drinks came out
Slurp, slurp, swallow
And those drinks were as cold as Alaska.

Then the appealing appetizers
There were so many words to describe them like:
Hot, sizzling and delightful
Crunch, much, crunch, swallow
More and more food was on its way

Later on the final mouth-watering meal had arrived
"Dig in," I said
Crunch, munch, swallow
Crunch, munch, swallow
I was as stuffed as a pig
"No more
No more," I said
That's enough food for a perfect day
We will just have to save the delicious dessert for tomorrow!

Alexa Beatrice, Grade 6
Swampscott Middle School, MA

The Floor

I am the floor
I like to be clean
without trash on me.
It hurts when you put your hard feet on me.
So please be careful, clean,
helpful, easy and friendly
with your nice clean floor.
And one more thing,
tell your custodian to keep me shiny clean,
so he can see his face!

Marlon Cooley, Grade 4
Crestwood Elementary School, VA

Yummy Yummy Crummy Food

Yummy, yummy crummy food
it's everywhere you see,
it's here, it's there and everywhere
it's a pity it's not free

I like to eat and eat and eat,
but only yummy food,
sometimes duck or octopus,
but never while they're stewed

All the food at Burger King,
is just as good as here,
except it's what they don't have,
that gives me the most fear.

Navi McSharry, Grade 5
Foxborough Regional Charter School, MA

Spring

The clouds have powers,
to bring down showers.
You can play,
almost every day.
In the sun,
you can laugh and run.

Arieanna Blanchette, Grade 4
Brookside Elementary School, MA

The Great Bird of Maine

In the state of Maine
There lives a bird
The eagle

White head just like snow
Black body just like a shadow
The great golden talons
The orange striking beak
There lies the eastern beast

William Fuller, Grade 5
St Mary's Primary School, MA

Cookie

I have
eaten one
of the
cookies

you made
which were
probably for
dessert

forgive me
but they were so
delicious
so crunchy
and warm.

Ian Phair, Grade 4
Sinai Academy of the Berkshires, MA

Happy

Winter has past
Spring has come at last
Kids are out playing
While adults are in singing
Babies are not whining
While grown-ups are dining
Teenagers are having a party
While grandparents are having a jubilee
This is the reason why spring is
my favorite season.

Emily Hunter, Grade 5
Southbrook Academy, MA

The Puppy

The puppy is tan
The pound found him in the Fan
The puppy has brown eyes
The puppy has a frown
He likes the ball
He likes the fall
He is always by my side
He will be there by and by

Juliana Gecker, Grade 4
Crestwood Elementary School, VA

Cotton Candy

Cotton candy is like a cascade of sugar
in your mouth.
It flows so serenely
through your mouth
and is a great treat
to have on the weekends.
It is fluffy, pink,
and it feels like a small pillow…
…Until it gets stuck in your HAIR!!!

Carter Clements, Grade 5
St Christopher's School, VA

Snow

Snow is so cold,
And it's all over the sidewalk and road.
Snow is very pretty and white,
but if you're out too long
You might get frostbite!!

Alanis Santiago, Grade 6
Benjamin Syms Middle School, VA

Spring

This season
It's warm and cool
and hot and sunny
Roses are blooming
Orchids are beautiful
and Lily's are pretty
It's Spring!

```
        L
        E
        T
        T
        H
        E
        B
I          G!
   R      N
     D  I
      S S
```

Tamare V. Adrien, Grade 5
Sacred Heart Elementary School, MA

Butterfly

B eautifully flying
U p,
T owards the sky.
T he children are
E ntertained by their
R adiant colors
F lying to
L ands unknown.
Y early

Bennett Green, Grade 5
Trinity Christian School, VA

Spring

Sun shines from the east.
Beautiful new plants growing.
Everyone is glad.

Luke Birdsong, Grade 4
St Joseph School-Fullerton, MD

Bee

If I were a bee
I'd pollinate plants and
I'd help fruit and flowers grow and
I'd produce honey and
sting if I had to

Thomas Clawson, Grade 4
St Christopher's School, VA

How I Hate Cafeteria Food

Oh how I hate cafeteria food;
The milk is always sour,
And it always puts you
In a more sour mood;
All their snacks I'd like to include
In my list of hated food;
All the condiments and shaved ice
Taste like they're made of mice;
I'd have told all this to the lunch lady
When she arrived;
Except for little Jimmy,
Some think he may have survived.

James Potter, Grade 5
Ashford School, CT

Chocolate Milk

CHOCOLATE
Brown, gooey
Eatable, crunchy, chewy
Mushy, gob, wet, white
Smooth, drink, slurp
Tasty, low fat
MILK

William Marshall, Grade 6
Benjamin Syms Middle School, VA

Jupiter

While Jupiter rotates quietly in space,
Sixty-three moons revolve above its face.
All of these moons seem to hover,
So many of them, are there more to discover?
With comets and meteors running across the sky,
They are barely visible to the naked eye.
The comets and meteors seemingly race,
While Jupiter rotates quietly in space.

Akiva Garfield, Grade 6
Yeshiva Academy, MA

How to Eat a Poem

Don't use a fork
Knife or spoon
Use a pencil
And a paper
As your plate

Stuff similes down your throat
And devour the details
Lick your lips and fingers
To show that you want more

Then scoop out the metaphors
From inside the big bowl
And munch them down
Until you can hardly breathe

Ask Mom to "Pass the personification, please"
Then shovel them down
Now everything's gone
But you want more
So pick up your pencil and paper

And write some

Alexandra McNamara, Grade 6
Weston Middle School, CT

My Dogs

I call to my dogs
And they come running, panting, sniffing, and grunting.
They drop the ball at my feet
I pick it up and with all my might throw it into great flight.
The ball then lands bouncing and rolling
And they all dive for it
Moaning and groaning.
Finally one of them picks it up in his mouth
And comes flying back
With the others right on his trail.
Again he drops it and again I throw
This one going farther and farther until it lands in the pond.
Where no one will ever see it again except for maybe a frog.

Connor Beauregard, Grade 6
Scotts Ridge Middle School, CT

A Spring Storm

As the sun ran away,
The clouds invaded the sky.
Like an evil army,
They cast shadows over the sunny hills.
A bolt of excitement!
Thundering surprise!
A screech of lightning echoed through the night
As buckets of rain poured down into the flooding streets.
Boom! Boom!
As the battle fought on,
A small light appeared in the clouds.
It was hidden away, desperate to come out.
It was bright, it was pure,
It was spring.

Raquel Leslie, Grade 5
Willis E Thorpe School, MA

Moving In

Boxes, boxes, with stuff pouring out
Filled with things I don't care about
Stuffed with papers, letters and more
Most of the stuff is such a bore

Boxes, boxes cover half the floor
From the old computer to the office door
Enough to fill an entire store
With nothing but boxes, boxes, and more!

Brooks Hood, Grade 5
St Luke's School, CT

Going to France

When I get off the plane
The lights of Paris hit my face
A cool breeze blows
The lights of the Eiffel Tower gleam in the distance
I run to the baggage carousel
As usual my brother doesn't do anything to help
He just sits on the cart
We go to the next plane to fly to southern France
We get there
Do the same thing we did at the first baggage carousel
We get to our house and sleep
The sun emerges over the hill
In a month we do the same thing going in the other direction

Charles Hennessey, Grade 6
Grace Episcopal Day School, MD

The Unknown

The wind blows as if it was being called.
The globe turns as if we don't know it
The sun shines every day.
And who calls and, turns and makes these things shine?
Nobody knows,
Yet.

Wyce Nasiri, Grade 5
Charlotte A Dunning Elementary School, MA

Thanksgiving

T hankful
H appy for family
A wesome food
N ice day for a visit
K indness
S pecial friends

Elijah Aguirre, Grade 4
Freetown Elementary School, MA

The Clock

The clock
Always there
Its tick-tock filling the room
Louder, louder
It seems to get
Distracting me from work
"STOP! STOP!"
I want to yell
But it continues to tick away
The clock

Bianca Aridou, Grade 6
Fuller Middle School, MA

Summer Fun

S wimming around the pool
U mbrellas to be cool
M any people go to the beach
M ajestic carnivals you can see
E nergetic kids play around all day
R ain falls sometimes

F riends go visit other friends
U nbelievable passages you can enjoy
N umerous kids stay home watching TV

Ashley Dominguez, Grade 5
Sacred Heart Elementary School, MA

Chamber of Fear

I heard you say
Loud and clear
Filled my head
With sorrow and fear
I knew you meant it
But I wasn't sure why?
I felt like I
Could fall and die
Your golden eyes,
And bronze waved hair
I cannot help
But to stop and stare
My love, my loss
Can you hear?
I have to get out
Of this Chamber of Fear

Arminda Ferreira, Grade 6
Home School, MA

What Is Yellow?

Yellow is the sun on a hot summer day, topaz,
corn on the cob, and crunchy leaves in the fall.
Yellow feels fuzzy like a tennis ball!
Yellow is the stripes of honey bees, a duck's bill, and a daffodil.
Yellow is little stars twinkling in the sky one by one.
The color yellow shouts, "Get ready for fun!"
Yellow is the electricity going through your house,
And the yellow beam guides from the lighthouse.
Yellow is the brightest color of the rainbow.
The feeling of yellow makes your heart glow!
Yellow's father is precious gold that a rich person finds in his pocket.
Also, grandmother's favorite locket.
When there's a smile on your face you hear yellow…
Yellow is a very special fellow!

Holden Robinson, Grade 5
Har-Bur Middle School, CT

Science Rocks!

S is for states of matter: solids, liquids, gases and plasmas
C is for chemistry: involves the use of chemicals
I is for intelligence: there are a lot of smart scientists
E is for experiments: the method scientists use to find or prove theories
N is for nano: scientific word for *very small*
C is for calculating results: the aftermath of an experiment
E is for energy: in earth, wind, fire, and you!

Ryan Levin, Grade 4
Clover Street School, CT

Hot Cocoa!

The first sip of hot cocoa of the year
I blow away the steam it floats away
and vanishes into air

The cup gets closer and closer faster and faster
I am racing my sister
I burn the picture in my head
As to always remember it
The picture of the snowman on the mug and tree in the back

This is a keeper
I glue the picture to my scrapbook in my head
And flip through the pages
Seeing all eleven pictures
The same mug and tree
But hands are bigger
And nails are pink

My lips touch the steaming chocolate drink
I take a huge gulp the marshmallows cool it down
I swallow its milky and warm
I feel it sliding down my throat and plop it goes into my stomach
The first sip of hot cocoa of the year
I burn the picture in my head

Melissa Stephens, Grade 6
Swampscott Middle School, MA

Home Is…

Home is where my mama makes
Delicious steak with white rice and beans
Home is where my mama makes
Awesome tacos
(I think that they're better than Taco Bell!)
Home is where my mama makes
The best chicken pie, it is the best
And she makes it so yummy.
Home is where my mama makes
The famous oh-my-gosh burger
So delicious, greasy with ketchup,
Mustard, Mayo, lettuce, tomato, onions
And pickles!
Home is where my mama makes
A special dessert — a big double chocolate cake
Home is where my mama makes
My favorite cereal cinnamon toast crunch
So good and cinnamony.
That's my mom's food schedule!

Christian Ortiz, Grade 5
Clover Street School, CT

Nature

Respect Nature
It keeps you alive
Water, plants, and air
Help you survive
Respect Nature

Megan Amico, Grade 5
Charlotte A Dunning Elementary School, MA

My Perfect Day

Not every day is perfect
I know this to be true
Sometimes when it turns out bad
It can really make me blue

I wake up in the morning
And get ready for school
My mom has to wake me
Which isn't really that cool

Eating breakfast gets me going
Off to school in a car
Up the street we go
The drive is not that far

Learning all day was fun
But I'm glad it is over
Lots of stories to share
With those who really care
As nighttime comes
The day is almost through
My perfect day has ended oh, what a view

Andrew Noviello, Grade 5
St Mary's Primary School, MA

Papa

My Papa fought in World War II,
Knowing exactly what he had to do.
He's really important to me.
He was in the war against the Japanese.
He's inspired me for a long time,
And he is very kind.
He made a little house with parachutes, for the rooftop,
I think the parachutes really made the house pop.
He kept track of all the planes,
Of when they left and when they came.
He's the best, I love him so,
And that I want you all to know.
Now he sits and watches the ball game,
And I think that will always stay the same.
He is as great as ever,
And what he did in the war I'll always remember.
He helps this land that's yours and mine,
And that's what makes him so divine.

Amber Drouin, Grade 6
St Joseph School, MA

Everlasting Love

He looked so different with his eyes closed
I kept praying he would come back to life
But he didn't
I felt his stomach to see if he was breathing
But he wasn't
I tried to be brave and not cry
But I started to sob
I went in the other room and tried to pull myself together
It did not work
It has been almost a year since that day
I always wish he was still here
But he's not
Nothing, not even death,
Can stop how much I love my OPA

Michaela Castelline, Grade 5
Charlotte A Dunning Elementary School, MA

Wishes

When I wish…
I never tell anybody what I wished for
I close my eyes and think very hard
But not too hard
Because it might hurt the wish
A wish is so special
It takes me a long time to think of one
I got my wish
But I won't tell you what it is
I blink my eyes only three times and twirl around
I send my wish far away to come true
And in my heart my wish will always come true

Rebecca Bernstein, Grade 4
Weston Intermediate School, CT

Shadows

Your partner for life
Dark and mysterious things
Always beside you

James LaLone, Grade 4
Trinity Christian School, VA

Just if I Could Fly

Why can't I just fly?
All the way to the huge moon
For a huge party
Everyone will be welcome
What a great day it would be!

Tyler Choate, Grade 5
Wakefield Forest Elementary School, VA

Wind

Whispering through the trees
Disturbing all of the bees
Howling through the night
Using all of its might
Wind pushes upon the weather
But yet is light as a feather
Wind is as strong as can be
Flows farther than the eye can see

Clair Huffine, Grade 4
Mary Walter Elementary School, VA

Candlelight

The candles flicker in the night breeze.
The crickets' song fills the night air.
The gentle hum of their consistent song,
    calms the tense silence.
The stars illuminate the night,
as street lights point out guilty children,
    late in bed.
People murmur in the pleasant evening,
as nature sleeps when the dark settles in.
Night

Anna McAnnally, Grade 5
Raleigh Court Elementary School, VA

Footprints

Beautiful sparkling
Blue water
Flowing onto
The shore
Brilliant black shadows
And amazing green
Trees
Gold desert sand
There are footprints
I wonder where they lead…

Kyle Lawrence, Grade 5
St Mary's Primary School, MA

Delta

Once my dad was at the trash,
when he heard a cry
He went around the corner
to find a little pup

He immediately took it home
and showed it to my mom,
They decided to keep the little dog
until it died.

Then my mom had me and my sister
we loved the dog so much
When we got older, our dog
kept loving us so much

Till this very day
our dog is still alive
but she is getting older,
my Delta is so precious

I don't want her to go.

Rachael Berthiaume, Grade 5
Lincoln Street School, MA

Split Second

The ball is snapped,
As all receivers scatter.
I drop back on coverage,
And look at the quarterback.

His eyes glimpse left and right.
I hear the sound of footsteps behind me.
It's my chance.

The ball is thrown up.
It goes, heading right to me.
It stares at me,
Spinning round and round.

In a split second, it's above my head.
I lean up and it lands in my hands.
I run, not looking back.
The twenty…
The ten…
Touchdown!

Sam Walker, Grade 6
Swampscott Middle School, MA

Spring

Birds chirping softly
Flowers slowly start to bloom
Spring is here at last

Shannon Guenette, Grade 5
Leicester Memorial School, MA

The Hit

I can see
the white ball
clearly in the
nighttime sky.
I feel like
I'm flying
as I round
first base.

I make my
one mistake.
I look for
the ball.
The center fielder
has it.

He throws it,
I slide.
I can hear
the umpire yell,
"Safe!"
My teammates cheer.
The crowd cheers.

Ben Rotner, Grade 6
Swampscott Middle School, MA

White Little Flurries

Snow is falling down,
Slowly twisting, turning down.
Just like white flurries,
Carpeting the ground with white,
Everything looks very nice.

James Callaway, Grade 5
St Luke's School, CT

Three Kings

Hanukkah is here
It is hardly dark outside
Shepherds celebrate

Connor Davis, Grade 4
Freetown Elementary School, MA

The Locker

He walks right up and does his code.
In the building of 31 Flagg Road.
He grabs his things and slams me tight,
then he walks into the dim light.

Soon again I see him later,
at least he's not a locker hater.
But then again he walks right off,
I'm left for the summer again.

James Golden, Grade 6
Fuller Middle School, MA

Why Did She Have to Go?

Everywhere I go, my grandma's on my mind.
What should I do with me being depressed?
I loved her so much, and she was so kind.
Having her on my mind I feel so blessed,
    Why did she have to go?
I saw this picture in the sky.
As I opened my eyes everything looked lit,
I closely looked and it was my grandma that was way up high.
I started to cry a little bit.
    Why did she have to go?
My mom asked what's wrong.
When I started to cry.
I was confused, I was going back and forth like a ping pong,
But it was time to say goodbye
    I loved her so much why did she gave to go?

Davian Cabrera, Grade 6
Gerard A Guilmette School, MA

Secret

There's a secret place I've been longing to find
That's deep inside my head
It's filled with wild creatures
And trees that hide the sun

The clear waters wash over the sand
As the frogs hop along the lily pads,
While deer run away
And dash into the woods

Once I find it
I will stay there forever
With the animals accompanying me
Until they die

Grace Heilman, Grade 5
Friendship Valley Elementary School, MD

To Look into a Soldier's Eyes

To look into a soldier's eyes you see the whole them
You see the horrors that are never told.
You see the pain they've been through.
You see how badly they miss their family and friends.
You see how badly they want this war to end.
To look into a soldier's eyes you see their soul.

Kathleen McWatters, Grade 6
E W Thurston Middle School, MA

Honey

What is sticky and sweet
that everyone loves to eat.
It comes from a yellow bee
some people put it in tea.
It is called sweet Honey!!

Emily Daniel, Grade 6
Monelison Middle School, VA

Hear that Basketball Cheer

Yes, the time is here, that basketball cheer
Your team is in the finals, which comes once every year.

The round orange ball, the cheer of the crowd,
This is a game to think in your head, not aloud.
That sound in your head, the way your heart pounds,
That sweet, sweet feeling, when your feet leave the ground.

Now you've taken flight. The hoop is near,
Listen to the opposing fans, sigh in fear.
The time is now,
Your team's season is on the floor,
You slammed it through with no remorse.

Now listen to this crowd roar,
As if a lion would for more.
You are the king, this is your court,
Brighten up, you love this sport.
Though this championship game was over, you had fun,
And you feel like it just begun, don't forget you won!

Don't worry, there is always next year,
And you'll once again be #1.
Hear that basketball cheer!

Tyrae Sims, Grade 6
City View School, MA

Trail

The crack, crunch, and drop
of twigs and rain, crunch and drip
All in the wide trail.

Tyler Hatfield, Grade 5
Jacob Hiatt Magnet Elementary School, MA

The Sound of Music

Music is a puzzle
Fitting every one of my emotions.
Wanting to feel soothed and relaxed
I listen to a part of the puzzle.
It calms me like I was floating weightlessly up to Heaven.
When feeling happy and overflowing with energy
I listen to music that makes me feel like a squirrel
Who drank 100,000 cups of coffee.
Another puzzle piece shifts my emotions
My worries fall asleep and leave me free from stress.
The puzzle also has a dark side
That makes me feel full of hatred
Like a house burning to ashes.
Sometimes when I am listening to the puzzle
I feel like a man banned from his own kingdom.
Music is a puzzle
Each piece fits one of my emotions.
Each emotion has its own rhythm.
That is why it is called the sound of music.

Cary DeYoung, Grade 4
Hawley Elementary School, CT

A Sleeping Storm

A fool skipped up the dark, gray path,
with a large unpleasant sigh.
He sat down for a picnic,
with his sandwich made on rye.
He skipped a stone across the creek,
as he thought about tomorrow.
He fell into a silent rest,
with dreams that brought much sorrow.
The world began to twist and curl,
and trees began to snap.
Hail the size of children,
fell from the heavens to his lap.
He now began to tremble,
with the hurricane soon to come.
He now must run from the thunder,
his feet were turning numb.
But now he awoke from the terror,
with his body curled into a heap.
He now realized what had happened,
it had all been in his sleep.

Mitchell Reynolds, Grade 6
West Frederick Middle School, MD

The Man with No Hair

There once was a man with no hair
Who didn't like big black bears
The bear liked to bite
So the man had a fright
He ran away and smashed into a chair.

Anthony Carpino, Grade 6
Captain Nathan Hale Middle School, CT

Lily

You are a piano
A musical ear
An ocean
You are a cheetah sprinting
A Z3 zooming
A cool pool
You are an Abercrombie girl
A kite soaring
An iPod blasting
You are a fashionable girl
A chatty person on the phone
A rush of warm water
You are a sweet maple tree
A brown-eyed girl
A late sleeper
You are dark chocolate
A Pulitzer girl
A Juicy jacket
You are a phone texter
A slippy slide
Lily is a lovely lily

Charlotte Robinson, Grade 5
St Luke's School, CT

Roller Coasters

Roller coasters are fast and bumpy
But make sure you don't eat a lot or your throw up will be lumpy
Be careful where you sit
So you don't sit in someone's spit
Then they will shut down the ride and people will be grumpy.

Chris Holguin, Grade 6
Monelison Middle School, VA

Sky Hunt

Soaring high in the sky of Congo,
The clouds unveil a jungle clearing where the prey garrisons.
Other falcons, call, signaling the time to strike.
To the whipping, whistling wind my streamlined body pays no heed.
Bloodlust kicks in as the leaves and mist come up to greet me.
WHAM!!
The sweet taste of meat and victory fill my mouth.

James Pavlick, Grade 6
Litchfield Intermediate School, CT

Winter Town

The angels are singing for Christmas, it's near.
The lake is frozen stiff as the children skate on it.
The houses are covered with snow that glitters bright lights.
The moon is pearl white as it enjoys the pretty sight.

The children are inside, tucked in, all warm.
The wind hollers WOOOSH! This is the start of a winter storm.
For they say the wind whispers secrets to anyone that comes near.
Listen close. Just hear.

The town streets are covered in white, the snow from winters past.
The wind sings again, for it has started its midnight blast.
A snow storm has come; it has done so for so long.
For this is Winter Town, it snows all year long

Arianne Ureta, Grade 6
Scotts Ridge Middle School, CT

The Courtyard

A joyful sun mosaic on the stone wall adds life to the courtyard.
A grey fox with beetle brown eyes stands guard as a stone turtle hides in the ivy.
Will it always be so pretty and yet so unique?

Caitlin Barbieri, Grade 5
Wakefield Forest Elementary School, VA

My Best Friends

My brother and my sister are fun to be around
We laugh, we play, we jump, we joke, and we love
My brother is the lighthearted, energetic, little clown
Who jumps around all day and night.
My sister is the kind, gentle, butterfly
Sitting on a big pink rose.
They are, no doubt, my very best friends,
I mean what could be better than hangin' out with little sis and bro.

Emma Crowley, Grade 5
St Luke's School, CT

Christmas Tree

Christmas tree, so big and wide,
Filled with ornaments, lights, and charm,
What was life like for you
When you were still at a tree farm?

My life, child, was very dull,
I wanted to be picked when I grew,
So I always waited in the cold
Hoping to be chosen by someone like you.

Tell me, glowing Christmas tree,
Were the other trees all nice?
Were they kind or mean or in between —
Warm, or cold as ice?

Those trees, child, were competitive,
They tried to look their very best,
Every tree's dream, you see,
Is to be favored above the rest.

I'm glad you're here, Christmas tree so bright,
You make our house calm and cozy!
I love it here, child, where everyone smiles,
Thank you so much for choosing me!

Erin Curran, Grade 6
Wayland Middle School, MA

Snowflakes

Falling from the sky
Making a cool white carpet
Covering the ground

Peyton Helou, Grade 4
C Hunter Ritchie Elementary School, VA

Apple

So crisp and tart you are an apple, apple
On the outside you look like a pebbly yard
On the inside you look like a flat, sandy beach
On the outside you feel like a glossy book cover
On the inside you feel like wet wood
Tell me apple, how boring does it get
Sitting in a bowl for days on end?

Miranda Waltz-Peters, Grade 4
Naquag Elementary School, MA

Winter

Winter is for fun
Winter is not for the sun
Winter is for play
Winter means it's getting close to Christmas Day
Winter is for sledding
Winter is for skiing and snowboarding
Winter is for having fun with friends
Winter fun just never ends!

Jacob Newton, Grade 4
Mount Hope Christian School, MA

Love

Love is pink.
It sounds like birds chirping in the forest,
It tastes like milk chocolate melting in your mouth,
It smells like the beautiful red roses growing in the garden.
Love looks like hearts beating loudly.
It makes you feel like there are butterflies in your stomach.

Sabrina Ortiz, Grade 6
Albert D Griswold Middle School, CT

Sunset

All the colors, so beautiful
Red, orange, yellow,
The kids gaze in amazement.

They see all the glowing fireflies floating around.
I know they want to catch one,
But the pull of the sunset keeps them still.

I almost fall off the porch,
But I hold onto the railing.
I just want to reach out and touch all the colors.

It is getting late and
All the children are falling asleep.
The sun says her good night
By disappearing.
The Earth is at rest.

Amanda Ignacio, Grade 6
Trinity School, MD

My Life as Me

Every morning is the same thing.
I wake up and get my things.
I go to school.
And I wish I was in my pool.
I want to go home.
So I can eat whipped cream foam.
I will go play baseball.
Then I'll kick around a soccer ball.
I will ride my ripstik.
Then I'll do a kick flip.
Then I will finally do my homework.
And I'll have an evil smirk.
I'll torment my sister.
And I'll make her call me mister.
I will watch a movie.
And I'll drink a strawberry-banana smoothie.
I'll watch TV before I fall asleep.
And I'll start counting sheep.
I'll wake up in the morning and start again.
And I'll do it all over again and again.
And that's my life as me.

Sam Reyna, Grade 6
Corkran Middle School, MD

Radio

If I were a radio
I'd blast my music out loud
I'd send out the news worldwide
and yell the winner of the lottery
I'd be in a car or in a house
I'd be shiny and new or
dull and old but everyone would like me

Sean Menges, Grade 4
St Christopher's School, VA

The School Day

Desk, chair, student,
Chair, student, teacher,
Student, teacher, pencil,
Teacher, pencil, pen,
Pencil, pen, bus,
Pen, bus, car,
Bus, car, locker,
Car, locker, classroom.

Nicole Franco, Grade 6
Chalk Hill School, CT

Dog Named Bog

There once was a dog named Bog
Who wanted to be a frog;
Bog tried to bounce,
But a large cat pounced;
So Bog tried to bounce no more.

Jordan Parent, Grade 5
Ashford School, CT

Nature

Sky,
Big and Blue,
Covers all of us
Surrounds us fully

Trees,
Large and Big,
Small and Tiny
Gives us lots of shade
to cool us down

Grass,
Small and Green
with little ladybugs
and grasshoppers

Flowers,
Little and Big
Blue and Red
bees buzzing around

Erin Murphy, Grade 4
Odyssey Day School, MA

Powerful

Hero
Powerful, friend
Saving, trusting, thinking
Icon, cape, boots, weapon
Planning, practicing, fighting
Evil, powerless
Villain

Peter Kingsbury, Grade 6
Captain Nathan Hale Middle School, CT

Dream

Out of the dust of dreams*
Into the air of love
Around the sea of waves
Over the hills of mountains
Back to the dust of dreams

*Line written by Langston Hughes

Maggie Blumenthal, Grade 5
Rowayton Elementary School, CT

I Wish to Float Upon a Cloud

I wish to float upon a cloud
Looking over the world
I wish to pass the stars so bright
That glisten and glimmer all night
I wish to float upon a cloud
Circling the midnight moon
To watch its beauty and all its delight
See its crater face that reflects so bright
I wish to float upon a cloud
To dream and think all day
No more resting on the ground
No more of a valley but a cloud
My wish to fly
My wish to be free
I wish to float upon a cloud…
At least until 3:00.

Jessica Ganim, Grade 5
Booth Hill School, CT

Bats

Bats whooping through the air,
Throw a rock and they'll be there.
Chasing bugs through the night
But when it's day they're out of sight.
Whooping through the shadows
In the cool crisp air.
Their enemies are owls
And they're always on the prowl.
Hear the bats through the night,
See them sleep at first light.

Madison Compton, Grade 4
Grace Miller Elementary School, VA

A Missed Friend

She had always been my friend,
Many memorable times,
It was hard to comprehend,
But she had to move sometime.

One day the moving truck came,
I said my final good-byes,
I had nobody to blame,
I just wanted to ask "Why?"

Walking to school without her,
It just didn't seem quite right,
And the whole day was a blur,
With her not being in sight.

My friend cannot be replaced,
No matter where she will go.
She can never be erased,
She's my best friend and it shows.

We have since then kept in touch,
I hope that will never end.
I still miss her very much,
She is always a missed friend.

Katie Sabin, Grade 6
Captain Nathan Hale Middle School, CT

Pencils

They help me with my homework,
They help me with my schoolwork,
They help me ace my test,
So I can get some rest.

They take away my mistakes,
So my grades aren't at stake.

They write my amazing stories,
And express my open mind.

They let me write this poem,
So we can all think about,
What we'd do without pencils.

Evan Nelson, Grade 5
Forest Avenue Elementary School, MA

Butterflies

Butterflies are a wonderful sight,
Only when they are fluffy and light.
I hope they don't fly away,
Off in the brush and in hay.
Into the beautiful sky to glide,
I just do not hope that they will hide.

Emma Claire Connor, Grade 4
Trinity Christian School, VA

What If?

What if there were no schools
And all people became fools
What if the 13 colonies
All of a sudden were myths
What will happen if all wars
With guns, cannons, and lasers were no more
What if there was no black, white, or mixed
But people all the same in no different look
Will life become easier
And much more friendlier
Or will it go in ruins
And would Earth become dark
What if? What will happen?
Or if it really could happen
If something was different?

Roderick Renfrow, Grade 6
Salem Church Middle School, VA

Nothingness

I can't think of anything else in the world
My mind is blank like a piece of paper with no words
and my life is like a pond with no water
My parents are gone
I have nothing left
I don't see the morning I don't see the night
I see nothingness.

Erin Thomas, Grade 5
Francis Asbury Elementary School, VA

The Whale

I swim between coral.
I bump into rocks.
See scuba divers and eat fish a lot.
My tail is so long it flips over boats.
As I swim by I see other whales dead and a float.

Sarah DeMatteis, Grade 6
Litchfield Intermediate School, CT

Guitar*

In the shine
Of the stage light
The guitar is noticed
By all
Hit by the pick
At every concert
Making music
That runs through your soul
Oh how I love
That feeling under the lights
You shine like the sun
The guitar is music

Michael Griffin, Grade 5
West Woods Upper Elementary School, CT
*Inspired by Valerie Worth

God's Nature

View the nature God has made,
We could not make with aid.
He made the winter and the spring,
You'll never know what it will bring.
He made all plants and trees,
Even the bumblebees.
He made rocks and clay,
God filled every bay.
He planted each strand of grass,
He made all fish — trout and bass.
This world was made before Adam and Eve,
A world like this, we could never retrieve.

James Gilchrist, Grade 4
Trinity Christian School, VA

Raindrops

Raindrops have names
Only when they rain
But I saw one
So I caught one
But then I missed one

Jordan Bibens, Grade 4
Courthouse Road Elementary School, VA

Drifting Away

Floating away,
Drifting away,
In the gentle breeze
I feel so enchanted
As I drift away
Passing the city
Humming to myself
A beautiful melody
Dazzling throughout my mind.
But as I lay
In my bed dreaming,
Such a wonderful dream
Of drifting away,
I start to fall
On the cold wet ground.

Katelyn Goldstein, Grade 5
Friendship Valley Elementary School, MD

Sometimes

Sometimes if you look straight up into the sky
It feels like the world is going right by.
The clouds so white and the sky so blue
You may even see the birds smile at you!
Sometimes if you look straight down to the ground
You may see rocks, some sand and grass.
The grass is so soft you may fall asleep
So rest there a while, do not make a peep!
Sometimes we forget to enjoy the world each day
So remember, it's where we live it's where we stay.

Haley Gagnon, Grade 4
St Dominic School, CT

The Lion

In the circus, there was a lion,
He wished he was a Hawaiian.
One day he escaped,
To the ocean landscape.
'Cause the animal was a sea lion.

Sarah Dugay, Grade 6
Captain Nathan Hale Middle School, CT

My Teacher

My teacher is nice
She helps me with my homework
She's very helpful

Muhammad Khalid, Grade 5
Marley Elementary School, MD

Scary Night

The moon peers through the pine trees,
The snow crunches under my feet.
I feel a shadow coming towards me,
My stomach starts to constrict.

I can only think of home,
While shivers are rolling down my back.
My lips are turning blue,
I'm feeling very frightened.

The crickets are very loud,
Playing their soulful song.
A plane booms overhead,
Too many scary sounds.

Suddenly, it's quiet.
There are no more sounds…
I make my way toward home
So I can then be warm.

Michelle Janco, Grade 4
Fawn Hollow Elementary School, CT

Candle

A candle
with a flick
and it is fierce yet tamed
it is vibrant and dear
it makes a sound
but no one you can hear.
There is more to the eyes
that meets the ear.
A candle can say so much
but be very careful,
do not touch!
A lot can happen
with a blink or a stare.
But it all just happens
without a care.

Lori Crawlle, Grade 5
Sacred Heart Elementary School, MA

First Fishing Trip

Out to sea my father and me in the freezing cold waters
It was 6:00 in the morning there were sons but no daughters.

I was about to cast out my fishing rod when a thought came to me
About catching a 32 pound fish in the middle of the sea.

I took a deep huge breath while casting my rod
And putting one foot forward I prayed to God

I felt a little nibble and my face filled with glee
I reeled in my rod as fast as it let me

The fish was a real fighter and I knew the time was near
As I finished reeling in my rod I was overcome by fear

Then when I reeled him in I relieved a sigh
He was a 28 pound fish and I exclaimed, "Oh my!"

Kevin D. A. Hood II, Grade 6
Immaculate Heart of Mary School, MD

Rainbow

These are the most beautiful sites to see.
They can also be very blurry to see because it's fading.
Rainbows have lots of colors!!!
You don't get to see them a lot in the sky.
They also appear after it rains.
The rainbows are supposed to represent happiness.
The rainbows can make kids and adults happy.
It can also be a very big surprise to anyone who sees it for the first time.
I wonder how rainbows appear from the sky.
I saw a lot of rainbows before in one day.
I love to see rainbows because they are pretty and bright.
They can also make you calm if you are angry.
They can also remind you of finding a pot gold.
The only time it does not show is when it is cloudy or dark out.
They can shine right into the window.
You can also get lots of ideas to draw just from looking at rainbows.
Some rainbows could have your favorite color in it.
I would love to see these beautiful sights of color every day.
You can make lots of cool things like bows with color!!!
Rainbows remind me of leprechauns.
They also make me feel lucky!!!

Courtney Volza, Grade 6
Irving School, CT

Sauntering on the Beach

As I amble through the blazing mushy sand
I hear splashes from the turquoise waves brushing upon the sand
Seeing all the sweaty people trying to cool off in the frigid ocean water,
The occasional nippy breeze helping to block out the hot air,
Unfortunately it is not effective,
As for me I prefer lying on the soft and cozy beach towel getting a beige tan.
I love going to the beach.

Josh Campbell, Grade 5
West Woods Upper Elementary School, CT

Just Because

Just because you were old
You had to go.
Just because you were sick
You came and went.
Just because you were a part of my family
You loved and you were loved.
Just because you were my great grandfather…
I wanted to say just because I gave you this name
I wanted to remember you just the same.

I love you Grandpa Eeka.

Zachary Chapman, Grade 5
St Mary's Primary School, MA

Alien Invader

No one could escape,
From the dumb alien apes.

They started their invasion yesterday,
But everyone is so scared they're jumping in the bay.

But I'm not scared I'll take them on,
I said who's with me, but everyone was gone.

So I went up to that stinky king ape,
And I yelled at him; look at what you did to my tape.

He cried with a whimper and I said go home,
But come back next year and I'll give you a lawn gnome.

Dylan Carver, Grade 6
Captain Nathan Hale Middle School, CT

Beach Music*

This beach
The
Always
Noise
Of
Rowdy waves as they pull up to shore and drive away
Running shells,
Scraping rocks,
Twirling grains of sand.
Vocabularies of:
WHOOSH!
SHHHHH!
CCCHHH!
Hot sand moving under my feet!
Combinations:
as blimps overhead sway gently in the baby blue sky,
a band of rolling bottles,
scraping shells that all-day hurt my ears.
With the always noise of the beach:
Beach music!

Christina Burgio, Grade 5
West Woods Upper Elementary School, CT
Inspired by Arnold Adoff

Which One?

"I want this one!"
"No, this one," my brother and I were arguing.
My mom said, "We are cutting down this one."
"It's too small," I nagged.
"It will look big in the house."
"Timber," I yelled as the tree came down.
We hauled the tree down the hill
and tied it to the roof of the car.
Turns out it was the perfect size for our house.
I guess it's just a mother's instinct.

Cameron Byrne, Grade 6
Swampscott Middle School, MA

New Hampshire

N orthern Hemisphere
E ast of Vermont
W hite Mountains

H istory of the United States of America
A merican Revolution
M aine is a neighbor state
P urple lilac and purple finch
S ummer resort
H istory of New Hampshire
I ts motto is "Live free or die"
R hode Island is south of New Hampshire
E njoy the Granite State

Sarah Tsan, Grade 4
Sacred Heart School, MA

Bang!

Clank!
Swoosh!
I ran past first base at Community field,
the dirt in my eyes,
the cool spring air rushing at my face,
as the screams of the crowd make me keep on going.
I ran through a cloud of musky air as I dashed past second!
I raced by so fast I skated and slid on the run,
dirt in my mouth!
I raced past third. I started to slow down when I hear,
"Push it! Come on girl! You can do it!"
I sped up just when, like a distant shout only I heard,
"Keep plugging in!" it said.
Just as I rounded the corner,
a loud noise like a buzzing of a bee or a honking of a horn.
I blinked 3 times and…
Boom! I fell…I fell!
I started moaning. "Timeout!" calls the coach.
"No she's out!" calls the Ump.
Thump. I woke up thinking,
Softball's a lot of fun.

Rindi Losee, Grade 6
Litchfield Intermediate School, CT

Family Matters

I spend most of my time with my family, although sometimes it is a deed,
    So I thought I would write a tribute to each of them, for everyone to read.
My dad likes to play outside with me, as long as I play fair,
    And at night he likes to sit around the house, in nothing but his underwear.
My mom is very beautiful, and as bright as she can be,
    But as smart as she is, I don't know know why she won't do my homework for me.
She works all day, makes dinner, washes and folds our clothes,
    And when we do something good or bad, she seems to always know.
My oldest brother Matt thinks he is really cool, and likes to toss me around,
    Sometimes we stay up late playing video games together, when he is not out on the town.
My older brother Jon can be annoying, but he is probably my best friend,
    I find it funny, when he and his friends see girls and try to act like big, bad men.
My baby sister Natalie is really super cute, and makes me laugh out loud,
    She likes to sing and dance around in pretty dresses, and hang out with the older crowd.
We have a puppy named Elsa, she is as dumb as a box of rocks,
    She runs all through the house and the yard, ripping everyone's socks.
The family rabbit, Bun-nard, is black and white with floppy ears, and lives in a two-story Hutch,
    All day long he plays with his empty orange juice bottle and really nothing else much.
So there you have it, as this poem is about to conclude,
    A portrait of my family members, a day in the life of Jude.

Jude Barlow, Grade 6
St Joseph School-Fullerton, MD

Spring

S urprises are around every blade of green grass!
P ansies, daffodils, daisies, roses, morning glory, tulips, and poppies are all spring flowers.
R adiant nature all around us, with a raindrop on every leaf.
I cannot describe the beauty of this season. Sunshine, flowers, and blue skies!
N ever say that you are bored, because there are over a thousand different things to do!!!
G o to someplace relaxing, beautiful, sunny, and awesome on any free day or spring vacation!

Claudia Chick, Grade 5
Foxborough Regional Charter School, MA

Look at the World

Look at our world. Embrace it with love and care, for it gives so much to us.

Look at the sun. As it falls upon your somber body, you feel indescribable warmth growing slowly inside you, reality seems to fade into mist, and your soul yearns for the heavenly light which gives you the strength to live your life with pride and dignity. Without it we'd live our lives in a web of depression and shadow, where the meaning of life is gone.

Look at the sky. When you look at the never ending blanket of blue you feel as if anything is possible, all your dreams and hopes seem to be just within your reach. You then wonder why the sky is blue, but knowing inside it symbolizes the frantic tears of pain and loss you and others have cried at night.

Look at the flowers. Although you glance as you walk by, the image is meaningless. But just stop a moment and witness what they really can be. They give us a pleasurable sweetness within; watch them grow, they cower from the world in fear of what will come, but one day they will awake.

Listen to the birds. They chirp a soft engaging tune that seems to melt away all the pain. You hold your breath, for you are afraid that one resentful movement could shatter the peacefulness and wonderment of this moment.

So don't you see the holiness of this world we're in? Given so much, but we don't give a care, we destroy it all, bringing death and sins, but wait, this can all end, you'll see what I mean. Words will never do my friend, just stop and take a single moment to look at the world we're in.

Kaitlyn Winkler, Grade 6
Fairview Elementary School, VA

Where I'm From

I am from a condo on the back of Piave Street
from screaming babies in separate cribs
I am from the one room I shared
with two siblings both 1 year old
I am from mommy I can't take it
from when their diapers smell like mold

I am from toys and games
that were all over the floor as we aged
from cribs disappearing and beds appearing
I am from the rattle of Josh pulling the blind
from kalabunga when I jumped off the top bunk
I am from Zach are you out of your mind

I am from bye mommy on the first day of school
From learning and playing
I am from summer this year is going to be so cool
I am from getting older from being stronger and bolder

I am from Africa and Ghana
from get out the way as we rushed
to the hospital as blood just gushed
I am from the lip I tore
from when my face hit the floor

Zachary Conduah, Grade 6
Roger Ludlowe Middle School, CT

My Camera

This is my camera
With it I film my friends, relatives, and families
It brings me joy and I have lots of fun
It captures my memories.

This is my camera
I make films with it
They can be funny, scary, or filled with action
When I show them to people they think it's a hit.

This is my camera
Every time I use it my videos get larger
I would use it all day and all night
But I can't find my camera charger.

Jack O'Neill, Grade 6
Scotts Ridge Middle School, CT

Christmas

Colored lights that brighten my day
Fresh pine from the newly cut trees
Sparkling snow falling gently on the ground
Minty candy canes
Soft blanket of snow
Christmas

Sara Chille, Grade 5
Jane Ryan School, CT

Shopping

S hopping always makes me happy
H uge bills are given to the cashier to pay
O nly certain stores please me
P eople pushing just to get what they want
P eople wandering everywhere
I really love Hollister and Abercrombie
N ever leave your money at home, you will need it
G oing shopping always puts a smile on my face

Tiffany Monteiro, Grade 5
Jane Ryan School, CT

It Has to Be Written

It has to be written.
Every single whip.
How slaves died.
whipped so hard
their skin hanging.
The salt,
The maggots,
The pain, suffering, humiliation.
It has to be written.
Everything.

J.C. Proia, Grade 5
Charlotte A Dunning Elementary School, MA

Fall Football

Fall
Red, yellow
Falling, gliding, surfing
Rakes, branches, cleats, balls
Hitting, tackling, running
Muddy, scratched
Football

Luke Miller, Grade 4
C Hunter Ritchie Elementary School, VA

Clouds

Clouds have many shapes and sizes
They can be in the form of a bunny rabbit
Or a shoe
A dragon, a dolphin, or a monkey, too
You can lay in the grass and watch them float by
Or sit on a park bench and watch them while enjoying pie
Clouds are special
And they float by fast
So always look up whenever you pass

Aubrey Pruzinsky, Grade 6
Irving School, CT

Will Smith

There once was a boy named Will Smith.
All he would do on his shows is kiss.
He thought he was so funny.
When he got some girls he called them all his honey.

Samantha Roy, Grade 6
Captain Nathan Hale Middle School, CT

The Five Eared Cashier

There once was a boy with five ears,
Who wished for a job with many fears.
He chose to apply
For the F.B.I.
But instead became a cashier.

Trevor Banavige, Grade 6
Captain Nathan Hale Middle School, CT

Baseball

Red Sox win, Red Sox win
Come on Josh Becket, let's get that win
Ball, strike, ball
Come on, ump, give us that call
Hit, foul, bunt
Wow, that catch was like a stunt!
Pitch, swing, hit
That bat just split
First, second, third, home
This is the end of my poem

Mario Maturi, Grade 6
Whitinsville Christian School, MA

Falling Snow

Sweet, soft, snow,
Falling from above,
White crystals all different sizes,
Falling, falling, falling, from above.

Kaylee Custis, Grade 6
Page Middle School, VA

Horse/Cat

Horse
brown, walk
running, galloping, trotting,
quarter, pinto, chine, American
playing, purring, jumping,
black. furry
Cat

Adrianna Huffman, Grade 5
McCleary Elementary School, VA

Rain

Gently the rain falls
Calming my mind, soul, and heart.
I love the moist rain.

Stephanie Culotta, Grade 5
Trinity School, MD

Flowing River

A flowing river
Traveling calmly and peacefully
Down a waterfall

Matthew McCloskey, Grade 6
Our Lady of Mercy School, CT

The Snowy Florida Dream

Come on Timmy, come on Jo!
Let's go play in the snow!
We can go sledding and build igloos too,
Have snowball fights and shout out woo!
Wait!
Hold on.
There's just one problem with that.
We live in Florida so how 'bout that!?

Catherine Cuddy, Grade 6
Summit Montessori School, MA

His Face

Wrinkles
carved
in his face,
his back arched
leaning
against his cane.
Looking up
feeling the connection
we used to have.
Eyes
halfway closed,
tears
being held back
by the bags
formed
under his eyes.
Setting a rose
over my chest
he slowly steps back
lifting his cane,
walking away…

Taylor Harrington, Grade 5
Coleytown Elementary School, CT

Baseball

Best sport in the world!
I like the New York Yankees.
Yankees are the best!

Michael Mills, Grade 5
St Joseph School-Fullerton, MD

Baseball

B ases are getting touched
A wesome players getting big hits
S tolen bases in the game
E rrors happening in the game
B alls getting hit out of the park
A wesome game everyone says
L osing teams are always getting mad
L oving baseball is my favorite thing.

Dakota Walenten, Grade 4
Freetown Elementary School, MA

Mountain

My soft green grass in summer.
People walk up and down me,
And when they run,
It tickles!

My trees light up in fall.
People jump in my leaves,
And when they rake,
It scratches me!

My flowers are blossoming in spring.
People roll down my side,
And when they dig up my flowers,
They scar me!

A white cap on my head in winter.
People ski down me,
And when they fall,
It hurts!

Throughout all the seasons
I stand tall
I never brake
And I never fall.

Jennifer Feldman, Grade 6
E W Thurston Middle School, MA

Mia Hamm

Soccer player
Kicks, scores, competes
World's greatest goal scorer
Champion

Alyx Patey, Grade 5
Sacred Heart School, MA

Life

Life, life, life is grand,
always so fragile as known to man.
Life is exciting and is an adventure,
life takes your breath away,
life, life, life is so grand!!!

Dayn Roberts, Grade 4
Salem Elementary School, VA

My Cat Strudels

Strudels
Unintelligent, sleek
Purring, running, pawing
Tail, claws, fur, reflexes, muscle
Leaping, pouncing eating
Funny, black
Scared Cat!

Ashley Arcidiacono, Grade 6
St Bartholomew School, MD

My Pet

My pet is a clown fish, he is not really a fish,
He does not swim and swish.
My fish takes a walk,
And we sometimes have a little talk.
He can make every sound in the world, except a fish.
He can eat off a dish.
I named him Clown because he makes me laugh.
He is good at math and drawing a graph.
But yet this is my pet,
That I have not gotten yet.

Kristina Eikens, Grade 6
Boonsboro Middle School, MD

Skiing

Swish swish go my skis as I head to the jump
Swish swish
I look at my surroundings
Big snowy white trees
Looming over me like a giant shadow
Swish Swish
As I see the huge jump
It reminds me of how nervous I am
Swish Swish
Skis straightened I go on the jump
I bend my knees
Whoosh
The wind whistles in my ears
Crack
My knees buckle but I stay up
I did it!

Quinn Mayville, Grade 5
John Ward Elementary School, MA

Ten Little Monsters

Ten little monsters having a party;
One ate some grime and then there were nine.
Nine little monsters having a party;
One added some weight and then there were eight.
Eight little monsters having a party;
One went to heaven and then there were seven.
Seven little monsters having a party;
One had a smoothie mix and then there were six.
Six little monsters having a party;
One started singing "I Will Survive" and then there were five.
Five little monsters having a party;
One went to the store and then there were four.
Four little monsters having a party;
One ran into a tree and then there were three.
Three little monsters having a party;
One went "moo" and then there were two.
Two little monsters having a party;
One said he's done and then there was one.
One little monster having a party;
He went on a run and then there were none.

Kaitlyn Lyons, Grade 5
Ashford School, CT

A Stormy Night

On a cold stormy night in a faraway land,
A small little drop beats its rhythm
With a thundercloud band,
Floods an ant home with a heavy plop
And in the fast and stormy wind
One thing barely, rarely, scarcely bends.
For in the cold rain
A big proud tree
Drops all its soggy leaves in defeat.
But one creature outside on this cloudy day
Thanks the storm for its non-delay;
Since a small wiggly worm
chews through its loot
Eating its crisp, ripe, delicious fruit
And that is all that's left to say.
The storm is over, gone;
The meadow is quiet
And all is calm.

Michael Varga, Grade 5
Ashford School, CT

School

S ocial study
C ounting
H undred chart
O ne other thing you have to do homework.
O ne other thing you have to do is raise your hand.
L isten

Amanda Mercado Rivera, Grade 5
Bensley Elementary School, VA

I Am an Artist

I am…an artist
I wonder about…being an artist when I get older
I hear…my pictures come to life
I see…my pictures in expensive antique stores
I want…my pictures to be famous
I am…an artist

I pretend…I am an art teacher
I feel…the need to draw when I'm bored
I touch…my masterpiece's feelings
I worry about…what I'll do with my other paintings
I cry…happily when I do better and better each time
I am…an artist

I understand…the true meaning of A-R-T
I say…"I LOVE ART!"
I dream…to have the whole world know who I am
I try…to be the best I can
I hope…to be in lights
I am…an artist

Alexis Ross, Grade 4
Munger Hill Elementary School, MA

Sad Times, Mad Times, Good Times

Sad times, mad times, good times
Sad moments
Brother screaming
Try my best in school
Hard to see myself
I try to find me
Clean to help my mom
Dad always gone
Miss my dad
Have no friends
Love my family
My uncle passed away
Miss my uncle
People say they hate me
Sister taking my stuff
Do chores
I am spoiled
Seeing my teacher smile
People saying they won't be my friend
Hanging out with my family
Having these feelings

Kayla Startz-Ibrahim, Grade 5
Jack Jackter Intermediate School, CT

Pennies

Pennies
Copper circles
Isn't worth much alone
until joined with many more
Money

Kyle Foster, Grade 5
Jane Ryan School, CT

The Black Death

A girl named Beth
Died of the Black Death
She died in 2 days
People were amazed
It went all over Europe
But people could not endure it
They say it was caused by rats and fleas
Dear God don't let me get it please!

Gracie Lawler, Grade 4
Angelus Academy, VA

Soccer

Kick, score, dribble
Goalie, dive, save
Skills and thrills
Rainbows, scissors, crossovers
Beckham, Henry, Adu
Go up the steps
Success
World Cup

Alex MacDonald, Grade 5
Milton L Fuller Elementary School, MA

King of the Sea

My gigantic tail propels me through the dark waters
    at amazing speeds

I have huge fins
    that pierce the surface and send a harpoon of fear
    through anybody who is watching

I can kill fish with one fatal bite
I can smell blood from miles away
My two huge marble eyes roll up into my head when I am attacking
    only adding to the terror

I am curious and always willing to take a taste
I can kill almost anything in the sea
I am one of the most feared creatures on Earth

I am the King of the Sea
    and what makes me king is my teeth
    jagged like mountain tops
    and as sharp as knives

I am fun to look at
    but not fun to be around

Jackson Smith, Grade 5
Mill Pond School, MA

The Great Outdoors

Nature
You are the tree in my yard
You are each one of the billion blades of grass that make up my backyard
You are the forest outside
The vineyard down the road
The mud after it rains
The rocks in my garden wall
The creek that runs through the valley
The pasture in which the cattle graze
You are the bird's nest and the fox's den
You are the leaf pile in the autumn
The snow in the winter
The flowers in the spring
The beach in the summer
You are the most beautiful thing I have ever seen

Jamie Cuffe, Grade 6
Greenwich Country Day School, CT

Harvest Moon

A field of wheat sways gently.
A delicate wind tickles the air.
An ebony night looms overhead.
Stars dance and gleam bright.
The essence of blackness hovers in the air.
The Milky Way, like a wavering carpet illuminates the wheat below.
And…a pumpkin, as big and bright as the sun, climbs into the sky.

Laura Franklin, Grade 6
Scotts Ridge Middle School, CT

Life Is Like a Baseball

Life is like a baseball
Sometimes smooth
Sometimes bumpy when you hit the laces
Sometimes you're forgotten
Sometimes you're thrown away from your owner
But always you will land in a soft glove

Chris Bouchard, Grade 6
Albert D Griswold Middle School, CT

Dancing Shadows

When the sun is low, just above the horizon,
the dancing shadows come out to play.

Twist and turn, then 'round and 'round,
they dance, they sing, they fall.

Then pop back up and start again.

Black images below the rising pink sun,
but when it turns that goldfish color they scramble and run.

Back at home they belong, they sleep, they wait until the sun
is low just above the horizon,
then those dancing shadows come out to play again.

Julia Cohen, Grade 4
Weston Intermediate School, CT

Hear That Fish Jump

Can you hear that fish jump?
Can you hear it through the air?
Can you hear the fish jump,
casting your first try, you get your first bite.
You can see you got a good grip on him,
and you can feel him struggling in the water.
He's jumping, jumping,
but he gets off and you just see him,
just swimming there
and he's looking at you,
he swims away into the weed brushes,
waiting for you,
to choose a bait.

Francisco Rodriguez, Grade 6
City View School, MA

My Cat Named Angel

Running through the yard
Hiding in bushes
Eating cat food, birds, and mice
Playing inside and out
Watching out for other animals
Thinking about having fun
Dreaming about playing with me

Kathryn Cooke, Grade 4
C Hunter Ritchie Elementary School, VA

I Love You Oh Lord

I love you oh Lord,
You're stronger than a sword.
We have great hope,
You left us with a pope.
You're the greatest of all
And You will not fall,
I'm waiting for that little call.
You're our King.
You'll give us a little ring.
To earth You came,
From then on things were never the same.

Caroline Payne, Grade 4
Angelus Academy, VA

Submarine

A tin can
Exploring a deep dark ocean
A rusty rocket
With bright yellow eyes

The coral reef admires the
Iron shark
As it passes through the bottom of the big blue.
Fish scatter
As the shadowy figure
Passes them.
Working gears and
Foul smelling fuels make this magical torpedo...
A submarine

John Caruso, Grade 5
C C Burr Elementary School, MA

Pumpkin

My kitten's name is Pumpkin Lohr,
From him I have one more chore;
I have to clean his litter box,
I'd rather get in a fight with an ox;
It smells really bad,
I'd rather change the diaper of a young lad;
Pumpkin is orange and white,
He is a really cute sight;
He is quite small,
A little bigger than a doll;
Pumpkin keeps me up at night,
Sort of like a glaring light.

Caitlin Lohr, Grade 6
Quashnet School, MA

Black

Black looks like the dark shadowy night of dawn.
Black sounds like owls patrolling the night.
Black smells like witches polluting the air.
Black tastes like licorice on Halloween evening.
Black feels like Halloween every day.

Jacob Santos, Grade 4
Helen H Hansen Elementary School, MA

My Poetry

My marvelous poetry hides
My feelings
Also my emotions
The wishes I pray for
That may never come true
My real feelings for others
My creative imagination
It hides millions of things
My memories
My goals to success
My future
It is all my poetry's magic

Jimmy Craig, Grade 4
Hawley Elementary School, CT

Elvis

There is a singer named Elvis.
Who liked to shake his big pelvis.
He sang with his lip curled up,
Always saying, "I'm all shook up."

Kersten Stelmach, Grade 6
Captain Nathan Hale Middle School, CT

Winter

The snow on the trees
Flutters with the gust of wind
And rests on the ground.

Tucker Nosal, Grade 4
Grace Episcopal Day School, MD

Help!

Some animals are frail:
They deserve our care
It's only fair!
Animals like a bear
Don't really care,
But the little nestling turtle
Needs protection
For their eggs' survival!
Let's help!

Kevin Soellner, Grade 5
St Joseph School-Fullerton, MD

Guitars

Guitars
Guitars
They're colorful
They make beautiful noise
They come in many different shapes
and sizes
Guitars
They're wonderful

Yordy Martinez, Grade 5
Clark Avenue Middle School, MA

FLA

Florida's awesome!
I love being in the sun…
It is amazing!

Emily Meyerl, Grade 5
St Joseph School-Fullerton, MD

Ashlinne Watkins

A mazed by my
S inging. And I'm
H aving a great time
L istening to my voice
I n this place.
N o one's to be found,
N or here or there
E mptiness around me to sing aloud.

W ishing I was
A t my dad's
T o run and
K ick a ball really far away.
I n my mom's house I sit,
N othing to do but
S itting, sitting, sitting, no playing, at all!!

Ashlinne Watkins, Grade 6
Monelison Middle School, VA

My Dog

Her fur is so shiny in the sun
Like a coyote's shadow
On a starry night

Nose as wet as water
Getting me all soaked
Sniffing the air

A little black fox
With small black claws
As fast as a cheetah

Whines like fifty
Babies crying

Hears like an owl
Has five million
Teeth

Pointy ears like a cat
Tail could shatter all the
Windows

Whiskers twitching like
Mice scurrying

Susanna Clark, Grade 4
Weston Intermediate School, CT

Spring

Flowers popping out
a time to play in the sun
at the first real bloom.

Nicholas Menikheim, Grade 4
St Joseph School-Fullerton, MD

Burning

Bright and
Yellow
The sun comes out
On a hot summer's
Day,
Nobody even looked up
To notice the clouds come in.
Chilled
By a gust of wind,
Everybody went outside
To see the snow
Drop to the ground.

John Szymendera, Grade 4
St Christopher's School, VA

Pictures

Smile at you,
laugh and frown,
make faces too,
I Love Pictures

Rebecca Phillips, Grade 4
Center School, CT

Sailing

Deep blue endless sea
Calm relaxing ride
Waves and water about

Spencer Walker, Grade 6
Our Lady of Mercy School, CT

Splash of the Past

Tugging at my arms and knees,
The past gains a better grip.
Holding on with all my might,
My fingers slowly slip.

Down I plunge into the past,
When I held my head up high.
Still the thought of a new school,
Nearly made me want to cry.

My arm is then gripped by the present,
Who brings me to the top of the sea.
We look around just to spy…
The joyful future waiting for me!

Haily Yelle, Grade 5
Soule Road School, MA

Panda Bear

This poor panda bear
he is an orphan and I feel bad for him
if only his mother really did care
he has no more kin

he is only two months old
he is a tiny baby
his paws are so very cold
a foster mom maybe…
his real mother was sold

I feel very bad for him
he has no more family,
no more kin

why should he suffer I ask
he is all alone and I wish I could help him
its like he has to hide his identity under a mask
he has no more kin

Kajsa Lundeen, Grade 5
Hindley Elementary School, CT

Fish

There are many fish down in the sea,
So they swim and dance, and jump with glee.
God made them all different colors and sizes,
Some fish are used after contests as great prizes.
You can buy them as pets,
You can buy them in sets.
Listen to their soft swish, swish,
So please help these lovely fish!

Lauren Osterhoudt, Grade 4
Trinity Christian School, VA

Go Home

Gross and disgusting
Physically and emotionally hurt
For their race beliefs
And color of skin.
slaves
Physically hurt
The whip,
Pure evil.
How, why, where, what,
So many questions
Family, friends, home
So many losses
Beaten and whipped
Until mortal flesh bleeds out
Of constantly whipped cuts
Undressed in front of public and friends,
Emotionally hurt
Slaves
Only wanting to go home.

Jacob Kaufman, Grade 5
Charlotte A Dunning Elementary School, MA

A Day Saved

Loud footsteps
Look to the left, there
A dark monster,
What we call

A BULLY!

Rumbling sound
Under the ground,
As 'he' walks towards the boy.

The boy's heart turns from sunshine to stone —
Pain and fear on his face
Sadness and anger (and fear) in my heart.

The moment calls —
Find the teacher
She stops the creature.

I say to the boy, "I like your jacket" —
Blue with *Patriots* across the back
And now a smile across his face
A compliment to take the edge off his wounded heart.

Hannah Peterson, Grade 4
Helen H. Hansen Elementary School, MA

Go Fall!!

Fall is a time to prance in the leaves,
Scarlet and gold fall from the trees
If you don't' think prancing in leaves is fun,
Once you see what you've missed, you know you were dumb!
Dead leaves that are crunchy crisp,
Sound like walking on potato chips.
The air feels cool as you walk along,
As if Mother Nature turned a fan on.
The smell of fresh cut grass from the season's last mow,
Will soon be replaced by the arrival of snow.
Towering trees with branches now bare,
Must wait until spring for leaves to be there.
The birds flock together like a swarm of bees,
Silently soaring South on the cool fall breeze.
This season is short and winter is near,
So I'll stop to enjoy the best time of year!

Brandon Hirshfield, Grade 6
Madison Middle School, CT

Peace

Peace is like a dove floating in the air
Peace looks like a smile on someone's face
It sounds like a wave of an ocean and
It can be noisy but,
Peace is always here.

Briana Castro, Grade 4
St Augustine Cathedral School, CT

Horses

Horses
Big, smelly
Showing, eating, living
Through rain, snow, and hail
EQUINE
Kellie Dionne, Grade 6
Quashnet School, MA

Summer

Around the corner from spring
Before fall and winter
To have fun in the sun
Like never before
About the best season ever
Except when it rains
From the crack of dawn
Till broad daylight

Summer is the best season ever
Stephanie Abadom, Grade 6
Albert D Griswold Middle School, CT

Summer Sunrise

It is silent
    The gorgeous sunrise
    dances across the
blue-green ocean
        Orange,
        yellow,
        pink,
        purple,
        and gold
reflect on the
        water and
        make the whole world
            sparkle
                sparkle
                    sparkle
the colors taint the
    puffy
        clouds
and the salty ocean sprays
my face waking me
    from my dreamy sensation
Kyra Robins, Grade 5
Mill Pond School, MA

Precious Load

Careful hands lift with a precious load
The hands spread out.
One white wing comes out, then another,
A beautiful bird comes out.
It's our sign of peace,
A dove.
Xavier Brown-Rose, Grade 6
Memorial School, MA

Blue

Blue looks like the sky over a beautiful ocean.
Blue sounds like the victory of winning first place in gymnastics.
Blue smells like a blueberry scented marker in art class.
Blue tastes like fluffy cotton candy at a big carnival.
Blue feels like tears in your eyes at a funeral when someone dies.
Richy Gibbs, Grade 4
Helen H Hansen Elementary School, MA

The Colors

Gold is the color of a trophy you worked hard for.
Silver represents a newly glistening nickel

Red is one of the honored colors on the American flag
Indigo is the color of a non-polluted lake

Green show the color of leaves on a nice day in the fabulous summer
The bright dazzling sun shows the color yellow in the middle of a fantastic day

Black is the color of the mysterious night.
Orange represents the amazing vivid sunset

Dark red shows the color of a beautiful rose
Light blue is the color of the miraculous amazing sky

White is the color of the puffy clouds floating in the sky on a nice day
An intriguing captivating newspaper represents the color gray

These are some of my favorite colors what are yours?
Michael Zhu, Grade 6
Scotts Ridge Middle School, CT

Set

The jealousy rages on within me, so we shall kill the pharaoh, states my decree.
The man who can speak to all the gods, I will kill him with all the odds.
He comes to my royal feast, but yet to realize his life will cease.
Finally when I bring in my chest,
It proves to me that I'm the best.
For he shall fit in perfectly, and it will be time to pay his royal fee.
The fee of pain, the fee of sorrow
The fee that won't let him see tomorrow.
The second he is in, the box will close shut and we will seal it up,
With molten lead making it an inescapable bed.
Me and my band of devils swarm the chest,
And swore to kill anyone who is to protest.
We sweep up the chest and run towards the river.
Excitement making me quiver, we dump the chest down the Nile,
When eventually it can't be seen for over a mile.
That was it I had succeeded, although the witnesses pleaded,
Not to kill my brother.
I didn't listen to them, not one or the other
Though my brother had won noble and brave,
His new chest has become his grave.
Later on I became Pharaoh, one of the greatest of them all if I do recall!
Ryan Cunningham, Grade 6
Middlebrook School, CT

The Lion and the Lamb

Lion
ferocious, majestic
hunting, crouching, pouncing
predator, teeth, prey, wool
bleating, grazing, snoozing
soft, peaceful
Lamb

Allison L. Mills, Grade 5
Church of the Redeemer Christian School, MD

Reptiles

Reptiles are green
And sometimes mean
Some of them are small
So we can not see them at all
Frogs, toads, and snakes
Like to live by the lakes
Water, grass, and sunshine
Can make a reptile feel just fine

Tyler Goldman, Grade 5
Foxborough Regional Charter School, MA

Summer/Fall

Summer
Hot, fun
Swimming, running, biking
School, teachers, students, vacations
Writing, reading, studying
Cool, warm
Fall

Bryan Reinaldo, Grade 4
C Hunter Ritchie Elementary School, VA

Blue

Blue is a cloudless sky
Blue is a calm, peaceful ocean
Blue is a baby blue jay
Blue is a perky dolphin
Blue is a small pond
Blue is a tropical fish in the sea

G. Suhrie, Grade 4
C Hunter Ritchie Elementary School, VA

Cameron

Cameron
Nice,
Friendly,
Funny,
Wishes that he had $1,000,000,000,000
Dreams of having a nice paid and great job
Wants to play for the Philadelphia Eagles(NFL)
Wonders if space ever ends

Cameron Cox, Grade 6
Monelison Middle School, VA

Dancing Free

As I dance by the mirror I see
A body looking into me
I see her dancing free
I can hear other voices
"Look up," "Keep your arm bent"
But I know it's me, dancing my life out
Trying hard to keep in class, but I can't
My body keeps moving in every which way
I can't resist but sway, as I hear the music
I just can't resist
I see other bodies as my sweat starts to drip
I feel as though I can
Can try harder
I try to think
But I can't
As I see in the mirror an image of me
It makes me excited to know I am free
I try another leap
As my body starts to seep
I know I can do it
I am free

Taylor Potasky, Grade 6
Smith College Campus School, MA

There Once Was a Small Bear Named Ben

There once was a small bear named Ben.
He consumed a very large hen.
He got extremely fat,
As giant as a vat,
And someone thought he ate big men.

Jesse Cabral, Grade 4
St Rose School, CT

A Place of Fire

I am fire
I wonder if my light will burn
I hear kids playing
I see darkness
I want to last forever,
I am scared.
I pretend to be water, only for a little while
I feel so lonely
I touch the ground, the grass
I worry if I shall not last
I cry of joy
I am happy
I understand I will die down
I say good-bye
I dream of living freely
I try to end the cold
I hope for happiness around me
I am fire

Tia Javellana, Grade 6
Page Middle School, VA

The World!

The world is great
the world is good
everybody just needs to appreciate
there's not need to hate,
it's not right to fight
the world is big
the world is tall
people are happy
people are sad
every body just needs
to get a long.

Da'Shana Gordon, Grade 4
Bowers School, CT

Katydid

Echoing is the
Sweet sound of the katydids
Clacking in the grass.

Sharon Hull, Grade 5
Trinity School, MD

Horses

Horses
strong, soft
jumping, running, walking
through fields and tracks
animals

Cassidy Robert, Grade 6
Quashnet School, MA

Softball

My dad is the coach.
I will hit a long home run.
They will not catch it.

Allyson Westfall, Grade 5
St Joseph School-Fullerton, MD

Dog

Dog
Playful, husky
Runs snuggles, sleeps
It loves to eat
Demon

Kayleen Lenihan, Grade 4
Sacred Heart School, MA

Books

Books
big, adventurous
exciting, interesting, captivating
everything you could need
Story

Alexis Jones, Grade 5
Sacred Heart Elementary School, MA

Two Generations Back

Baby soft hands
soft,
sweet,
caring, listens
to my
every word
her kiss, falls
on to me leaving a mark
in my heart
her eyes saying
only one thing
I love you
her hand falls upon mine
looking into my eyes
a little smile takes shape
she may be
gone
but she still takes
place in
my heart

Sydney Sussman, Grade 5
Coleytown Elementary School, CT

My Parents

When they chose me, on that long night
the happiness in that room shone
I didn't know, but it felt right
Now the love we share has grown

The extensive love that we give
Always makes me smile
Without it there, I could not live
It is all worth my while

Adoption is love
It's how my family formed
With God's help from above
My heart soared

Until I reach Heaven, till the very end
Love is something I will always send

Ami Crist, Grade 6
Immaculate Heart of Mary School, MD

The Chocolatey Day

Today, today is a very chocolatey day.

It is raining chocolate everywhere
And it's coming from right up there

I can't wait to stick out my tongue
To enjoy that lovely taste.

Maryann Rainey, Grade 5
Wakefield Forest Elementary School, VA

Wings on the Ground

Preparing for the ride,
Grooming, tacking up.
Put on boots and a helmet.
Ride with pride.

Mount the horse.
Walk to warm up.
The letters mark,
The boundary of the course.

You walk along,
You're all warmed up.
Ready to trot,
To ride you must be strong.

The horse will work,
They will carry you with pleasure,
Just give them the right commands.
And remember every horse has a quirk.

Lauren Marshall, Grade 6
Captain Nathan Hale Middle School, CT

Freedom

F ree to do what we want
R ight to work where we want
E ducation for all the children
E ager people with homes of their own
D omestic animals and pets
O ne person alone
M oms that care for you.

Danielle Ferrell-Roberts, Grade 5
Sacred Heart Elementary School, MA

Sun

Sun, sun, sun
So big and bright
The sun is such
A beautiful sight

Sun, sun, sun
I love you so
You lead me where
I need to go

Gregory St. Laurent, Grade 5
Litwin Elementary School, MA

Confident

My friends say I should TRY my best,
My family says I should TRY my best,
My coach says I should TRY my best,
BUT…
I say that I should DO my best.

Jack Book, Grade 5
Hindley Elementary School, CT

Shark Tooth

The little boy went to the water park
When he found a big shark
He thought it would be cool to go to the store booth
But the clerk said, "You're too young to buy a tooth
You can't even go to the phone booth"

Rishul Marwah, Grade 6
Chalk Hill School, CT

Spring Is Near

Spring is near,
Have no fear
All we have to do
To make our dreams come true,
Is…
Jump out of bed,
Spring is ahead!
We have to plan our day,
Make it just the right way
First, we'll go outside,
And plant flowers long and wide
Then we'll paint Easter eggs
And place our friends on our bike pegs
We'll walk to the beach to fly our kite,
And watch the sun go down making a dimmer light
At night we'll catch some fireflies,
And listen to the wolves' cries
Spring is here, spring is here
Spring is here,
What a wonderful year.

Emily McComb, Grade 5
Willis E Thorpe School, MA

Bats

What's that?
I hear a soft fluttering of wings
Above my head in the pale moonlight.
It sounds like paper flying in the wind.
Then I realize they are bats!
They're outside at night looking for food
Like a bird looks for worms.
Then I walk away in the darkness
As the bats enjoy their midnight snacks.
Then when I walked into my house I told my brother
Do you know what bats eat?
His reply was how should I know it's too dark to see.

Eric Plaut, Grade 5
Coleytown Elementary School, CT

Out of School

Lying in bed looking all red
head aching, body shaking
Sneezing, wheezing, feeling queasy
While the other kids are learning I lay here burning
I am out of school…and sick

Isabella Pontbriand, Grade 6
Southbrook Academy, MA

Spring

Do I await spring?
or does spring await me?
Do flowers and leaves
Robins and trees,
all come out when I do?
Or is it winter's fault
and spring is off
fighting and bringing it
to the freezing forces
of Winter?
I start to fear that
Winter could last forever.
But when I see the
Robins all playing
around and hoppin'
I know that spring's right around the corner

So let's hope
that spring has a longer stay
while winter's on its way.

Hanna Rosenfield, Grade 5
West Woods Upper Elementary School, CT

The Squirrel

I live in a hole
In a tree
In the woods.
I don't need a jacket or coat or a hood.
This is because my fur is so warm
So it protects me from cold winter storms.
My home's filled with nuts
From bottom to top.
If you listen carefully
You can hear them go POP!
My tail is so fluffy and my fur is so gray,
I cuddle up with my tail every day.
I live in a hole
In a tree
In the woods.
In fact I live in a squirrel neighborhood.

Emma Llanos, Grade 6
Scotts Ridge Middle School, CT

Winter

I look around and all I see,
Is a snowy blanket falling over me.

The trees are so white, all around,
As I realize how much snow is on the ground.

It's now starting to freeze
As biting winds blow a frigid breeze.

Hanna Bareihs, Grade 6
Wakefield Forest Elementary School, VA

Four Seasons

The first snowflake falls,
An excited little pup jumps,
It's its first winter,

Newborns trample land,
There's a new feeling of life,
A new beginning,

By the beach I sit,
Waiting and waiting for this,
Here it is: summer

Leaves changing color,
Now an adventure begins,
Fall is returning,

One year has just passed
Seasons will come then go,
Time and life has passed

Hannah Borden, Grade 6
Middlebrook School, CT

Summer Is Great!

In the sunny sky,
I see nice kites
And see very nice children too.

Simone Dickens, Grade 4
Hebbville Elementary School, MD

Fifty Cent

Yo, my name is fifty cent,
I'm brothers with a dollar,
My cousin is a penny and
A nickel is my father.

My mom's a cash register,
She keeps us all in place
I'm friends with John F. Kennedy,
Because he's on my face!

Dom-Dom Clicka-Clicka
Dom-Dom Clicka-Clicka
Dom-dom wicki-wick
Cha-ching!

I love the paradise
Of bein' with my brothers,
Because I'll always know
That we'll have each other!

And when I'm in your pocket,
It is not that much fun,
Especially when you put me in with
Week-old chewing gum!

Matthew Ashman, Grade 4
Forest Avenue Elementary School, MA

Colors That Surround Us

Pink is the color of a thorn rose you give to a valentine
Red reminds me of your face when you are mad

Black is the color of the unforgiving forest at night
White is the color of the blanket that covers your lawn in the winter

Blue reminds me of the flag we pledge to
Yellow is the color of a pitcher of sour lemonade on a scorching summer day

Green is the color of cool thick grass in the summer evening
Brown reminds me of a freshly opened Hershey's bar

Tan is what you see in the beaches of sand in Florida
Orange is the color of a freshly squeezed glass of orange juice.

Gray is the color of the gloomy sky on and overcast day
Gold is what you see from a rare brick

Which color makes your day bright?

DJ Jancin, Grade 6
Scotts Ridge Middle School, CT

When I Think of My Mom

When I think of my mom
I see her happiness when I get a B or higher
I see her energy when she goes to parties with her friends
I see her cleaning when she is mad at someone in the house
When I think of my mom
I hear her screaming at my brother when he doesn't take out the trash
I hear her talking nonstop when she's mad
I hear her talking to her soap opera
I hear her telling me to clean the house
When I think of my mom
I smell her fruity Jennifer Lopez perfume
I smell her delicious homemade rice and greasy chicken
I smell her nasty smell of smoke
When I think of my mom
I taste her salty "arroz con chuleta"
I taste her homemade "limbe de leche con canela" that tastes like cinnamon
I taste her chocolate cake
When I think of my mom
I feel her soft, smooth, baby blue shirt
I feel her curly hair
When I think of my mom

Kassandra Figueroa, Grade 6
Fuller Middle School, MA

Red

Red looks like the beautiful sunset over Boston on a warm summer night.
Red sounds like the crack of Red Sox bats.
Red smells like smelly red fish in the lobster traps of Boston Harbor.
Red tastes like cotton candy at the always crowded Topsfield Fair.
Red feels like putting on a Bandaid, but it'll just be fine.

Joseph Piana, Grade 4
Helen H Hansen Elementary School, MA

Thoroughbred

A velvet muzzle pushes my pocket.
Tangled tails are brushed out
As I stroke a wiry mane.
One neigh and my heart is stolen.

I throw a saddle on
And his hooves hit the ground like an earthquake.
Muscles ripple and his tail streams.
What a beauty unknown —
His coat is light like snow,
His mane is black as a crow.

A touch with my hand;
That feeling comes again.
His power overtakes me
Whoosh — over the fence.

He is
My Thoroughbred.

Chloe Just, Grade 6
Trinity School, MD

Who's My Mother

Is my mom black or white?
Is she my type?
Does she like to walk?
Does she like to talk?
Will she like a lot?
Or will she not?
Does she like to have fun?
Will she call me Hon?
Will she make me food?
Or will she be rude?
Will she love me in pain?
Will she give me fame?
Will she kiss me?
Will she miss me?
Is she small or tall?
Is she nice at all?
WHO IS MY MOTHER!

Autumn Durham, Grade 4
Helen H Hansen Elementary School, MA

Dakota

Dakota
Intelligent,
Honest,
Hard working,
Wishes to become a famous singer,
Dream of living in a world where no one did anything wrong,
Wishes to be able to believe everything anyone said.
Who wonders why everyone dies so young.

Dakota Claytor, Grade 6
Monelison Middle School, VA

Boston Red Sox

In center there is a man named Jacoby
He runs very swift to rob the homerun
Then there is Dustin Pedroia at second base he's the master
When he takes away hits you can tell that he's having fun
Now there's David Ortiz some call him Big Papi
Sometimes he will play at first base
He has a fast bat with all his home runs
You can tell the ball is gone when you look in his face
And now I'll tell you about their pitcher Jon Lester
Than Andy Pettitte, he is much better
His pitches will make you strike out
Especially his fastball which gets out like a jetter

Daniel Bullock, Grade 6
Captain Nathan Hale Middle School, CT

What Is the Seashore?

The seashore is…
Feeling the water up to my ankles
Seeing shells come in and out of the water
Noticing a starfish stuck to a rock
Imagining mermaids giving you 3 wishes and her gold

The seashore is…
Your feet stuck in seaweed
Seeing little crabs everywhere
The noise of people walking in flip flops
The smell of sand with every blow of air

The seashore is…
Family being with you
Vacation with the ones you love
Swinging and Splashing in the water
Fish so young and tiny they look like
Little lines of joy.

Danielle Gallagher, Grade 4
Fawn Hollow Elementary School, CT

The Back of the Room

I don't want to sit in the back of the room
It will surely seal my everlasting doom
I cannot see the board
I feel like I'm ignored
I do not want to sit in the back
I always hit the flower rack
I set next to a goofy kid named Jack
Who always trips over his backpack
I do not want to sit in the back of the room
I think I will explode with a boom
I do not think it's fun
The person sitting next to me is burning in the sun
I do not want to sit in the back…
Excuse me sir but what did you say?
You said I can sit in the front today?
No thank you, I will sit in the back of the room.

Andrew Darsch, Grade 5
Litwin Elementary School, MA

Waves

The waves rise and fall
I can feel the mist they leave
Sacred and not there
Andrew Ippolito, Grade 5
Coleytown Elementary School, CT

Snow

Snow in Alaska
Freezes from the frosty air
On cold winter nights.
Danielle Bellefeuille, Grade 4
Munger Hill Elementary School, MA

My Attitudes

I am competitive
  Like a soccer ball on the field
I am caring
  By loving my pets

I am stubborn
  To my dad
I am troubled
  When I don't clean my room

I am loving
  To my parents
I am helpful
  When I clean the basement

I am bold
  When I go in front of the class
I am gullible
  When you say aliens are real

I am open minded
  When a new girl walks in
I am competitive
  Like a soccer ball on the field
Jordan Plumhoff, Grade 6
Blue Ridge Middle School, VA

Sunshine

The sun is shining,
It's at my door
When I let it in
I always beg for more.

It's dark again
And I am left alone.
The black is grim
And depressing so.
Can't wait to see the light again.
Annabelle Krupcheck, Grade 6
Holten Richmond Middle School, MA

Heartbeat Time

Time goes by and the feathers fall
Nothing's lost at all,
As the clock talks to one through twelve,
I wait, watch, and listen
The only thing that moves,
Is the feathers and the clock
Tick tock goes the little clock
Tick tock tick tock
The noise is the heartbeat of the clock
The feathers fade and time,
Slips ever so slowly,
Nevertheless,
Time goes by and the feathers fall.
Elizabeth Mastrio, Grade 5
Soule Road School, MA

I

I am air
Free with writing
Full of bright ideas
Can be a messy tornado at home
Ready for anything life throws at me
Sarah Thomas, Grade 5
Wakefield Forest Elementary School, VA

My Grandmother

Grandma,
Eccentric and exotic,
Ballroom dancer, investor.
Missed.

Grandma,
Fun and entertaining,
Stained glass maker, gardener.
Remembered.

Grandma,
Elegant and classy,
Gourmet chef, jewelry maker.
Cherished.

Grandma,
Stubborn and tenacious,
Cancer victim.
Gone.
Colleen Curtis, Grade 6
Swampscott Middle School, MA

Sun

Sun shines so brightly
Sun lights up a whole classroom
Sun comes out today
Kristine Paz, Grade 5
Jane Ryan School, CT

A Small Red Apple

A small red apple,
Hung high up on a tree.
I looked up at it,
And it looked down at me.
"Come down, please," I said,
And what do you suppose?
That small red apple,
Dropped right on my nose!
Esmeralda Guzman, Grade 5
Marley Elementary School, MD

The Bakery

I walk into the bakery
  I just had to stop
I walk into the bakery
The bakers hurrying around the shop.

I walk over to the display case
  Pies, strudels and cakes
I walk over to the display case
All kinds of things, including cupcakes.

I walk up to the counter
  Pick out what to order
I walk up to the counter
  It only costs a quarter.

I walk out of the bakery
Leaving a good smelling shop
I walk out of the bakery
  Next time, again, I'll stop!
Lyla Rossi, Grade 4
Crestwood Elementary School, VA

Mollygolly

Mollygolly oh so jolly
Did you know that she's part collie?
She runs around all the day
Smelling things along the way
I love her and she loves me
Especially when she licks me
When she goes, I'll be sad
But I'll think about good times we had
My best dog Molly
Emily Ryan, Grade 5
Mill Pond School, MA

Me and Fun Things

I do a lot of fun things
I play on the swing
I play tackle football
I play with a basketball
Abdou Campbell, Grade 4
Hebbville Elementary School, MD

I Owe Christmas

I owe Christmas for all of the times
My family got together and talked till bedtime.

We'd laugh and sing and eat together,
Until it was cold, like outdoor weather.

We'd tell stories, and do as we pleased.
The laughter and happiness would never cease.

It's my excuse for being crazy,
For playing video games, and being lazy.

We eat so much we just want to burst,
And when the cake comes out, I want to be first.

Then we gather 'round the Christmas tree.
It's the loveliest sight you'll ever see!

Then until next year we say our goodbyes.
The ceremony is over and I want to cry!

Laura Paulina Vega, Grade 6
St Clement Mary Hofbauer School, MD

I Wish

I wish it was summer yes I do.
I wish I had money so do you.
I wish I had a puppy that will come true
and I wish I lived in a big house morning or noon.

Daniela Rodrigues, Grade 4
Bensley Elementary School, VA

Kitchen Music*

Slice
Bang
Sizzle
So much depends
Upon
Kitchen music
Making food:
Burning hot tacos
Fish smothered in sauce
Sizzle, crack
From boiling water
Ketchup
Mayonnaise
Mustard
Relish
Do you like food?
Bing!
Bang!
Bam!
I like to call it:
Kitchen Music

Joey Harrell, Grade 5
West Woods Upper Elementary School, CT
*Inspired by Arnold Adoff

Swimming

As I jump into the pool
The water goes over me
The cool water feels refreshing
When I start swimming, the water surrounds me
I come back up for air
Leaving the underwater world for a while
Then I go back underwater
As I swim the water rushes over me
I feel free
Eventually I will have to escape this freedom, though
But for now, I enjoy it
I wish I could never leave
That I could stay here forever
It is time for me to leave now
As I get out of the water
I slowly walk away from the pool
The aquamarine water is waving goodbye
As I leave the underwater world

Langley Parker, Grade 6
Grace Episcopal Day School, MD

Piggy

You look at her one time and then you turn around
by the time you think about it she's in the dirty ground.
You wash her over and over
Then you let her free
you turn around to look and the piggy is dirty!
You wash her off again and put her on a leash.
You start a bonfire to have a piggy feast.
She sees what you are doing
thoughts race through her head
however she has no intention of being dead.
She sees the fire growing big and hot.
She then decides to run because bacon she is not.

Mary Hall, Grade 5
Church of the Redeemer Christian School, MD

How to Munch on a Poem

MMMM — a fresh poem
Straight from the oven
First, chow down on the amazing adjectives
Next, nibble on some nutritious nouns
Now, swallow some scorching syllables
And fork down some vivacious verbs

Munch down on some marvelous metaphors
Sip some stupendous sentences

Wipe the sound droplets on your shirt sleeve
Lastly, lick up some luscious letters
Now
Go back for seconds!

Isabelle Schwartz, Grade 6
Weston Middle School, CT

Stray

I walk.
My paws feel sore,
Atop the hard gravel.
I leap.
Soaring over a hill of sky,
the wind, whipping
my ears back.
I land.
Like a bird
That has paused life for awhile.
I feel
the cool breeze greet me,
and the sand between my toes.
I taste the salty sea, and the air
Is full of arguing seagulls.
I run to a house, and they say,
In a kind but stern voice,
"Here is a treat, come in."
And these humans, the heroes to me,
let me in, and I say, "This is home."

Ellie Guzewicz, Grade 4
King's Highway Elementary School, CT

Spring

Butterflies floating
In the gentle summer breeze
Sucking up nectar.

Blue jays flying high
Far above all the people
Feeling almost free.

Robins eating worms
Filling themselves to the brim
Making themselves plump.

Rabbits hopping fast
Swiftly jumping to safety
Warming their burrows.

Christopher Costantini, Grade 5
Jane Ryan School, CT

Yelling at Air

I yell at the air
Because my anger is fierce

I think I might cry
So I start to scream

Then I realize that
I need to be happy
I should not be mad
Life is a gift
Do not waste it being sad

Casey Moriarty, Grade 5
Soule Road School, MA

The Terrible Two in You

Your blonde hair the sun
Your pale skin
Your smile so white, could make anyone in a million miles smile
Your blue eyes are puddles
Sometimes kids splash in the puddles
Making rivers stream down your face
That terrible two in you
The one who loves to see my tears of fake sadness
The one who savors my pain
The one who interrupts any sentence with the famous phrase:
I HATE YOU
But under that terrible two is also you
That understanding look has been on your face forever
As Uncle Rob plays the guitar you hide behind the door
Listening, just listening
Your adorable clothes, wiggles outfits
You scream, you cry and whine
You're loving, you're sweet and you're understanding,
You listen, you laugh, you care
I Love you the way you are!!!

Jenny Flaumenhaft, Grade 5
John Ward Elementary School, MA

Far

One day I'll be a star, I'll go really far!!! People
don't know I'm strong, all they know is that I can be wrong.
Why do I have that reputation? All I want to see is me walk across that
stage on graduation day. I'll be rich off my diamonds and pearls,
No McDonald's, no Burger King, and No fried onion rings,
Just bling bling and just doing my acting thing.
If you really knew me, you could see right through me.

Sade Samuels, Grade 6
Magnolia Elementary School, MD

The Infuriated Tempest

I sit in my room killing minutes,
To try to finish my assignment,
The sky becomes crammed with infuriated clouds.
The clouds blanket the sun with an ominous quilt.
As I grasp a pencil and sketch to my heart's content,
The vivid afternoon sky darkens like a small child's face wrought with disappointment.
The clouds wept, descending icy cold drops.
It drizzles, and rains, then pours,
As the rain rages onward, I sit inside snugly and comfortably.
The clouds simmer with fury and release a shattering thunder clap. Boom!
My heart leaps and fear flows in my throat.
Lightning screams across the evening sky.
But I sit in my cluttered room, feeling minuscule and delicate in this huge world.
The evening sneaks along
The tempest is drained. The world is silent and placid.
The outside world lies there, drenched and shaken.
I snooze in my cluttered room, my haven,
Feeling delicate and minuscule, in this huge world.

Michael Cohen, Grade 6
Charles E Smith Jewish Day School, MD

Time

Time's the one thing that can change the world.
Time's the only
thing that holds us back from doing what we wish.
If time is so important then why do we abuse it so?
Why do we have time I do not know.
But I do know that without time
everything would go…
WRONG

Jimmy Kavetas, Grade 4
King's Highway Elementary School, CT

If I Were in Charge of the World

If I were in charge of the world
I'd cancel parsley,
Arts and crafts,
Britney Spears, and the Cartoon Network.

If I were in charge of the world
There'd be more loops in rollercoasters,
No smell of skunks in the backyard,
And definitely skydiving every day.

If I were in charge of the world
You wouldn't have baby playgrounds,
Annoying brothers and sisters,
Brussels sprouts or asparagus,

If I were in charge of the world
There'd be absolutely NO going to the dentist.

Diana Atoui, Grade 5
Charlotte A Dunning Elementary School, MA

Writing

When in writing,
Take a pencil or a pen,
And let your imagination begin.
Write what you think, write what you know,
Write what's inside you, and let it show.

There are no limits, there are no rules,
Write where you want — at home or at school.
Expository, narrative, or even a poem,
Writing's a way to let your feelings be known.
Use silly or fancy words, just let them be heard!

Follow your dreams, follow your heart,
Let your career as an author start.
All you have to do is write, write, write,
And your stories will be a glorious sight!

So I'm telling you to grab your creativity, and grab your soul,
Follow this advice and your writing will always be bold.

Joanna Rizza, Grade 5
Middlebury Elementary School, CT

Glory

A soldier is brave.
A soldier is strong.
They fight for our country all day long.
A soldier has trained.
A soldier has taught.
They fight for the freedom that they now brought.
A soldier is nice, they don't leave us behind.
They fight for our country and that is so kind.

Allon Guseynov, Grade 4
Helen H Hansen Elementary School, MA

If I Were Rich…

I sit on my swing
thinking how wonderful would be my life if I were rich.
I would imagine myself driving fancy cars,
while the wind blows through hair.
My face would be on magazines,
and directors would beg me to be in their movies.
Just how sweet would life be if I were rich?
But then I realized if I was rich,
the drag of people following me everywhere.
If I were to make one mistake on TV,
I would be very embarrassed and really humiliated.
I looked to my side, and heard birds sing.
I was blown off from my imagination.
I saw my neighbor smiling towards me,
and at that second I realized that;
my life doesn't need to change because I'm rich in my heart!

Vanessa Santacoloma, Grade 6
Salem Church Middle School, VA

Untitled

Dragon dragon flying by
Like a bird flapping her thick wings proudly
Like a hungry red lion flying for food
Like a big red chair with wings and legs
But most of all,
Like a huge fiery dinosaur
Flying by

Amanda Xia, Grade 4
Thoreau Elementary School, MA

The Joys of Christmas

My family and I have an artificial tree.
They won't decorate it without me.

My presents looked like a pot of gold!
When I saw them, my heart was sold.

Christmas is more than presents alone.
A baby and a bright star to us were shown.

The angels sang loud as a rock n' roll band,
To welcome Baby Jesus to our land.

Charles Chilton, Grade 6
St Clement Mary Hofbauer School, MD

Signs of Fall

The wind slowly whistles its toneless sound to all who will listen. It's the first sign of fall.
The daily frost glistens peppermint green on the grass as it slowly melts in the glowing morning sun.
A symphony of birds chirps madly like they're enjoying a last talk with each other
before they have to fly south for the winter where a new journey awaits them.
The feelings of autumn travels with the breeze and soon spreads to the people as the chills surprise them on the street.
The ground is littered with tangerine pumpkins soon to become jack-o-lanterns
whose variety of smiles and stares are those like a handmade portrait that is happy
but gives the feeling that it is always watching you.
Beautiful trees tower over me as the time of fall sets upon them like an invisible hand overpowering them,
putting them into a sleep as silent as stone.
Pine cones plunge off the branches, while hazelnut acorns soon follow them to the ground where they will stay forever more.
The only remaining things on the trees are the painted leaves that have been with them since last spring
and like loving parents holding onto their children, they do not let go.
The leaves slowly jump one by one toward the ground, though their journey is over,
new leaves will be back next spring.

Sam Carley, Grade 6
Madison Middle School, CT

Just One More Thing to Wonder
Way Down Under the Sea

Just another thing to wonder about the deepest part in sea,
The farthest we've ever gotten farther than ten times me.
Down all the way under the deepest part in the sea,
What lives so far down there a mermaid or a beast?
Suppose in a family of beasts 100,000 yards long, jellyfish with an obvious killer sting,
or a tiny, silky otter with gills that if you touch will bite.
Or a shark as big as a football field that can shock and kill but yet harmless to things.
Will there be mermaids in the sea?   Maybe a fable but not to me.
There might be a snake with the head of a whale, and a body that slithers
on the ground and takes up ten yards that swings on reeds and swims in circles.
Or maybe a duck with gills and wings which holds green and yellow feathers.
And when it swims it dives deep down under.
Or a beautiful oyster that swims and is very big in size. Or maybe just a cave full of creatures from fables.
So if you ever wonder what's deep down under read this and let the wonder be yours.

Jillian Lurie, Grade 4
Helen H Hansen Elementary School, MA

Fingers of Fall

The fingers of fall that touch your head, creating an eerie feeling of dread.
From the brisk branch of a tree you try to run and flee.
You turn your head as you fall; you realize it is only the fingers of fall.
Soon the other plants join the mischief of the night.
Acorns suddenly dropping as is surrendering their soul, the mud and leaves consume them whole.
More and more join this silent parade.
Leaves are soon changing their skins, taken and kidnapped by the wind.
Icy coldness goes through the branches.
They whisper a distant sound, as though a voice drifting down.
The dying thorns grip your ankle; wrapping you into a tangle.
The fumbling fingers blowing in the breeze search for their next victim to seize.
A nightshade and a witch hazel plant, plan secretly and they create a wire,
Soon you shall descend into the gripping, bony clutches of the Fingers of Fall.
As if the trees and leaves are possessed by a spirit, it seems you are the only one to hear it,
A long cry down this forest hall, it mutters "Beware of the Fingers of Fall."

Winston Crumb, Grade 6
Madison Middle School, CT

The Library

The library is a great place to be
You can check out books for free
The librarian will let you have books to borrow
And you do not have to return them tomorrow

The library also has tapes, CDs, movies and maps
You can even sit and read to someone in your lap.
Everyone, all ages are welcomed the same
To get a library card you have to write your name.

Activities are offered to you
They have all kinds of things for you to do.
You can find all subjects to read
They have books that even tell you what you need.

In the library you can study
You can also invite a buddy.
peaceful and quiet the library stays
It is opened on most days

Now I hope you enjoy the library as much as me
Remember; return your books on time to avoid a fee!

Caroline Cottrell, Grade 4
Mary Walter Elementary School, VA

Living on a Poem

What is it like to live on a poem, you say?
I hope I will find out someday.
It could be hard and very weary.
It could be cold and really teary.
Maybe it's warm and smooth and soft,
Maybe it's like sleeping on a huge, straw loft.
Whatever it's like to live on a poem,
I think I'll just live at home.

Nicole Williams, Grade 4
Trinity Christian School, VA

Sisters We Are

Strong and sweet, sisters we are.
Laughing and playing, sisters we are.
We're like the leaves in different seasons.
Break up in autumn, and make up in spring
Hold strong in summer, and fight in winter.
But we always hold together, sisters we are.

Isabella Randazzo, Grade 5
Weston Intermediate School, CT

A Dumping Friend

My friend, Don, wants to rob a store.
"Just a couple dollars, that's all, no more."
The cash register might get a scare.
Well when he does I won't be there.
'Cause jail is a place for robbers and crooks!
I'd rather stay home reading law books.

Justin Vanover, Grade 6
Ashford School, CT

Remember!

Believe in yourself like a pro.
Follow your dreams then you'll know.
Live while you can and you will soon be…
…a singer on MTV.
Time goes by way too fast.
No need to worry if you'll last.
Live your life how you want it to be not how others want it
Soon you'll see.
No one is Perfect just like you.
Remember this is a hint on what you do!

Mollie Ghiabi, Grade 6
Roland Park Country School, MD

Look at Me, What Do You See?

Look at me, what do you see?
Am I rain?
Am I a red Nintendo?
Or am I Mesprit (a Pokémon)?

I am rain.
Helpful, powerful then…dangerous.
Mostly I benefit all.
I am also a torrent
But beware I can be moody.

I am a red Nintendo.
Fun, nonstop, but I am breakable.
I am energetic and exciting.
But don't yell at me for I may shatter.

I am Mesprit (a Pokémon).
I have strong willpower, and I am shy and rare.
I have a strong mind
But I am still very timid.
No one can replace me.

Look at me, what do you see?

Elena Lynch, Grade 5
West Woods Upper Elementary School, CT

Hope

Hope is…
an umbrella keeping your dreams from getting damp

Hope is…
an elephant crushing my problems into the ground

Hope is…
a sun brightening your day

Hope is…
an airplane flying you away from worries

Austin Seiler, Grade 5
Clover Hill Elementary School, VA

Picture Perfect

Beautiful sunset
glaring over the water
creating a dazzling sight

Then comes the night sky
with twinkling stars
Hard to see because
of the glistening smiles
on the faces of Sarah, my cousin
and Kaitlin, my sister

The only sound is the waves
crash,
crash,
crashing against the boat
causing the anchors to jingle

I can feel the amazement
conquering all my thoughts except

Wow!
Shannon Lawton, Grade 5
Mill Pond School, MA

As Time Stands Still

A soft breeze flows gently
Through the trees
Bringing the scent of
Fresh pine to my open window
I gaze into the night sky
Watching the bright stars
Twinkle like millions
Of flickering candles,
Oh so far away
I lean back and listen
To the rustling of leaves
As a cool April wind
Kisses my face
Time stands still and I wonder
Who is running the rest of the world
Lindsay Pattavina, Grade 6
Nathan Hale-Ray Middle School, CT

Feelings

Excited
Smells like vanilla frosting on a cake
Tastes like a toasted marshmallow
Sounds like a surprise
Feels like I can't breathe
Feels like a small chinchilla's fur
Feels like I'm in a small room
Excited
Lori Freda, Grade 6
Quashnet School, MA

The Trojan War
from Helen's Perspective

It was 1200 B.C.
As bloody as can be
I was captured
And they fought for me.

I was Troy's queen
And was taken away
"Help!" I called
One day they will pay.

They hid in a horse
But then fell asleep
They got attacked
Now I shall weep.

I was saved
But people died
They went to save me
And some survived.
Caroline Howard, Grade 5
Trinity Christian School, VA

The Time of My Life

Have you ever been a shopaholic?
I must confess, my secret to you
Blush, eyeliner, gloss, or lipstick
I always have to buy one or two

Purses; Chanel, Coach, Louis Vuitton
Blouses, skirts, jeans, galore
I will shop 'till my money is gone
I will never miss another store

Earrings, bracelets, necklaces, all
I've gone everywhere
Now I need to go to another mall
I wish I was a millionaire!
Alyssa Audet, Grade 6
Edmond P Talbot Middle School, MA

Wolves

Some people call them mutant canines
But I think they're majestic creatures
Running through the leaves
They give their scraps to cubs
How much they whine and starve
Their very powerful jaws
Yellow and dirty but magnificent
Searching for prey and water
Cubs need to rest but only one saying
Survival of the fittest
Joey Raymond, Grade 4
Brookside Elementary School, MA

The Lion Cub

The cub's fur is as soft as a pillow
He is as gentle as a lamb
As he lays there,
He dreams of what he will do tomorrow
Samantha Cabral, Grade 4
Freetown Elementary School, MA

Blue!

Blue is a fish
She is big.
Blue has fun with me
Blue died when she was two
Blue was cool!
Nathan Moesta, Grade 4
Marsh Grammar School, MA

That's the Real West

Our friendship is a little stronger
Because we hold each other longer
That's the real west

The sun is a little brighter
Because we hold each other tighter
That's the real west

The sky is a little bit bluer
Because our friendship is truer
That's the real west

There is a fresher wind blowing
And true personalities are showing
That's the real west

More giving, less taking
More truth, less faking
That's the real west
Meredith Gosnell, Grade 6
Weston Middle School, CT

What Is Baseball?

What is baseball?
From inning 1 to 9
Exciting after every pitch
Intense at every minute
Energetic after every out
Amazing every moment
Pride is taken for everything done
Nail-biting 9th inning
Hoping your team will win
Competitive at every game
Shocking 1st inning
That is baseball!

Chris Steigler, Grade 5
Jane Ryan School, CT

A Dog's View of Life

I love my food
I'm always in a good mood
I'm always playing
But sometimes I may be laying
My owners are so great
They always give me food on a plate
Night is the best
Because that's when I get to rest

Bryce Cushing, Grade 5
Charlotte A Dunning Elementary School, MA

I Remember

I remember the good days and the bad days.
I remember my first birthday. #1
I remember my first fall. Ouch!
I remember my first dentist visit. Numb.
I remember the first day of school. So fun!
I remember blowing bubbles on the sidewalk. So bubbly.
I remember being alone. So lonely.
But most of all I remember you!

Jazmon Martin, Grade 6
Monelison Middle School, VA

Disney World

I love Walt Disney World because,
Of all of the things you can see,
Like Mickey and Minnie,
It has all of the rides that you can dream,
When you go there you really believe,
In everything that you see,
It's a perfect place for the whole family,
Mickey the mouse gives a high five to me,
The night time sky is always bright,
When it is fireworks time,
But time flies by,
Like a bird getting pulled by the wind,
Sometimes it is fun at the pool,
Because the water splashes and cools you off,
That's why I love Disney.

Kyle Abbott, Grade 6
E Russell Hicks School, MD

The Day America Shut Down

I am sent home from school.
I am scared.
Not knowing what is going on.
My mom is driving my sisters and me quickly home.
My mom looks worried.
We get home and I rush inside the house.
I turn on the TV.
Now I know what's going on.
I start to cry.

Matt Farrell, Grade 6
Charles E Smith Jewish Day School, MD

Gymnastics

G old medalist
Y ou have to put your all into everything
M ajor deductions for form
N o whining allowed
A lways pushing forward
S o much fun!!!!
T ough tumbling tricks
I ntense conditioning and training
C horeography is important in floor and beam
S uper Olympians like Nastia Liukin and Paul Hamm

Makenna Collari and Mary Brown, Grade 5
Leicester Memorial School, MA

Old Orchard Beach, Maine

The cool, cool breeze from the ocean,
The lovely, lovely smell of salty sea water,
The sea glass at your foot,
The crashing waves you hear far away,
The sand so cold from under your feet,
Looking at the beautiful sunrise at 5:30 a.m.
The slimy, ugly, green seaweed is floating
In the crystal blue waters sparkle, sparkle, sparkle,
The wet sand that imprints your feet,
Digging to make cold puddles,
Making sand castles, for people to see,
Tanning in the sun's warmth.

Elizabeth St. Pierre, Grade 5
Holland Elementary School, MA

White Glue

Life is white glue with your responsibilities
And problems sticking to you
Stick to what you think is true to you
Because if you're in white glue,
You can't get out with just a pout
Because you're stuck in white glue
Up and down and all around your responsibilities
Good or bad stick to you
My problems your problems
We will try to get out of this
White Glue!!

Didjana Celkupa, Grade 6
Albert D Griswold Middle School, CT

My Dog Spartan

So black and hairy, big and strong.
So bold and brave, tough as nails.
Yet so kind and caring, just as if I was his very own.

Watching over me as my father does.
Protecting, caring, with both our lives at stake.
But yet never stopping for a break
'Til the job is done correct
It is always done perfect.

Sam Bevins, Grade 5
Milton L Fuller Elementary School, MA

Heaven

We miss you so much.
We couldn't make you stay.
There are lots of people
that go there each and every day.
God saw you drift away.
We know you look over us
from danger and pain.

Lindsey Strople, Grade 5
Milton L Fuller Elementary School, MA

The Changing Seasons

Spring
Warm, breezy
Flowers blooming, running, frolicking
Meadows, flowers, oceans, sand
Swimming, surfing, boogie-boarding
Hot, beautiful
Summer

Kevin Cunningham, Grade 6
Cape Henry Collegiate School, VA

PM School Bell

RING!! There it goes!
Everyone running down the rows.
People screaming and yelling, "Yay!"
And then other people saying, "Hey!"

Everyone with happy faces,
Just looking at all the running paces.
Pushing, shoving, 'till outside,
It seems as if someone had cried.

"Stop running!" yell the teachers,
But only because that rule features
Once everyone gets outside
Then that is when I wave bye-bye.

Kaillee Sanquintin, Grade 6
Fuller Middle School, MA

My Doggy

This is my doggy
He's black and white
He has floppy ears
My best friend at night

This is my doggy
With him I feel happy
His fur is so soft
As he cuddles with me

This is my doggy
He always sits still
He's just a stuffed animal
To always cherish him, I will

Keanu Rivas, Grade 6
Scotts Ridge Middle School, CT

What Is Blue?

Blue is the color of a blueberry,
A first place ribbon, ocean waves, and the dress of the tooth fairy!
To my nose —
Blue smells fresh — like an ocean breeze and clean clothes!
A sunny sky is blue,
As are juniper berries, the Connecticut flag, and the color of a new canoe.
When I taste blue I taste pie and brightly colored lollipops.
When I touch blue it feels…smooth, silky, and comfy like flip-flops.
Blue is the color of my grandmother's sapphire ring,
Jeans, and the color of a blue jay's wing!
Blue look like snowflakes falling from the sky,
The icing on a birthday cake, and a baby boy's blanket that stops him from his cry.
Think of the world without blue,
It would be depressing, lonely, and gray — like living in the world without you.

Tessa McNaboe, Grade 5
Har-Bur Middle School, CT

Nature

N othing boring about it
A lways something new to explore
T errific and adventurous so that you can hardly wait to learn about it
U nbelieveable things that you can easily find in your own backyard
R elearning facts is even fun in nature study
E very day you can learn about it and never get bored!

Mike Cerny, Grade 4
John F Kennedy School, CT

The Lake

The birds chirping, the frogs ribbiting,
people say what's that, I say it's the lake.

The calm waters at dawn meet ruff waters at midday
It's the lake.

The bass jumping, or the loons singing,
It's the lake.

The Mosquito's biting, the sun is setting on the lake
I hear a loon, and watch the vibrant sun slowly sink down until it disappears
I hear nothing, except a faint frog ribbiting.
It's the lake.

I see the clouds rise and rise, until they die.
It's just another wonderful day at the lake.

Matt Pucci, Grade 6
Thomas Blake Middle School, MA

Yellow

Yellow feels like the sun against my face.
Yellow smells like fresh lemonade on a hot day.
Yellow sounds like sour Pop Rocks crackling in my mouth.
Yellow looks like my third place gymnastics ribbon at a very special meet.
Yellow tastes like cheese in the perfect sandwich.

Isabella Hobbs, Grade 4
Helen H Hansen Elementary School, MA

Bamboo the Panda

Fluffy furry panda swinging near a tree
Looking at the people "oh what a sight to see"
Chewing on his bamboo happy as can be.
The zoo's fun to visit, it's the place for me.

Elizabeth McCabe, Grade 6
Litchfield Intermediate School, CT

I Am

I am comical and polite
I wonder if I will be a comedian when I'm older
I see me as being really polite and nice
I want to pull pranks on my parents
I am comical and polite

I pretend that I am a pro motocross rider
I feel brave and mighty when I get on my bike
I touch the extremely soft foam on my seat
I worry that I will crash and get injured
I cry when I plummet off my dirt bike
I am comical and polite

I understand that I have to do my homework
I say that I have to do my best in school
I dream that I'll do better in school
I try to do my best in school
I hope I will get a 100% on my next test
I am comical and polite

Camden Mund, Grade 5
Hebron Elementary School, CT

The Whining Basketball

Boeing, boeing goes the basketball.
"That hurts!" he said.
"This is dangerous,
You're going to get me all dirty!"
Says the basketball.
The shoe says, "Stop whining!

You do it all the time, you never cry then."
Says shoe.

"But they like to dunk me and throw me from half court,
At the end of the quarter."
Says basketball.
"When you bounce me up and down the court,
I get tired and I also get happy when the game's over
Because I don't get hurt"
Says the basketball.
The basketball went bong, swish and bang.
"Stop! Are you trying to kill me?"
The basketball said.
"I like to bounce my basketball
On the back porch,"
The player said.

Antwone Clarke, Grade 6
City View School, MA

Wind Chimes

I am outside making music
Wind bosses me around
But I don't care
I make music

I come in all shapes and sizes
While I'm outside
Kids are playing so happily
Like I was there
At least
That's what I think

Birds sail over my head
Storms are crazy, they drive me insane
But that's why I'm a wind chime
And make music in the air

Looking down on everyone is what I like
And some days, I long to be a kid
Playing and having fun
Though I know, every kid must turn into an adult
And that's not what I want

I want to be myself, no one can change me, I am a wind chime

Kerri Noble, Grade 6
Weston Middle School, CT

Spring Is in the Air

Blossoms blowing off the trees
Blossoms blowing in the breeze

Spring is in the air
Time to curl my hair

Let's go to the fair
Since spring is in the air

When spring is in the air
The sky is like a beautiful ocean

Alexis Powers, Grade 4
Courthouse Road Elementary School, VA

Snow

Dancing snow falls all around
But never makes a single sound.
It *plays* until it hits the ground
Though still it *laughs* and *jokes* around.

In the night the moonlight glow
Reflects the beauty of the snow.
I only wish that I could stay
But I turn my back and walk away.

Josephine Federici, Grade 5
Weston Intermediate School, CT

Late for School… Again!

Oh no, I'm late!
It's already ten of eight!
I must rush
or I'll miss my bus,
I brush my teeth with care
and quickly comb my hair,
how long I have,
I cannot say,
HEY! No one told me
it was Saturday!!!

Nicholas Raposo, Grade 6
Edmond P Talbot Middle School, MA

Older Brothers

Older brothers, older brothers,
Are as annoying as head lice

Older brothers, older brothers,
Even though they can be nice.

Older brothers, older brothers,
I don't get why they are mean.

Older brothers, older brothers,
Are as cloudy as a dusty screen

Older brothers, older brothers,
They are sometimes nice

Older brothers, older brothers,
Just forget the head lice.

Older brothers, older brothers,
They aren't really that clean.

Older brothers, older brothers,
But they aren't really that mean.

Nathan Tsatsos, Grade 4
Munger Hill Elementary School, MA

School Clocks

Ticking the time away,
Every minute of every day.
Students waiting anxiously,
Thinking just the same as me.
Waiting for the end of the day to come,
So we can go home and have some fun.

So when the clock says it's time to go,
We run out as if there's a big show.
When we come back the next day,
Again we watch it tick the time away.

Sara MacDonald, Grade 6
Fuller Middle School, MA

Dinner

Dinner
Cooking slowly
Warm delicious smell
Eat with my family
Remember my thanks
Clear dishes
Dinner

Will Rabinow, Grade 5
J F Kennedy Middle School, MA

Books Are What?

Books are keys,
Keys to open doors,
Doors to life,
I like reading,
Some hate it,
I'm a mystery,
Others are comics and cartoons,
Even nonfiction if they wish,
Books open doors to life like a key,
I will always love to read,
For then I will know the meaning of life.

Ravi Viradia, Grade 6
Irving School, CT

Stars

A beautiful light
Shining in nighttime's darkness
The sun's substitute

Liam Garrity, Grade 5
Booth Hill School, CT

Florida

F antastic place to be
L ots of things to do.
O ranges grow there.
R oller coasters are in Disney World!
I ncredibly warm there
D oes your family go every year?
A t Disney World you have a ball!

Mikayla Miller, Grade 4
Brookside Elementary School, MA

War and Peace

War is red burning wood
   Peace is a nice furry kitten.
War is a blazing battlefield,
   Peace is a nice cool breeze.
War is a blistering hot humid feeling,
   Peace is the wonder of giving birth.
War is a terrible walkway of doom,
   Peace is a blissful walk in heaven.

Tommy Dauphinais, Grade 4
Quashnet School, MA

One Day at the Park

One day as I was walking
In the middle of the park,
I saw a beautiful dog
And he began to bark.
I tried my best to pet him
As he chased after a ball.
I tried to catch him
But all I did was fall.
As I was trying to get up
I started to cry and cry
I looked around for the little dog
And cried and cried and cried.
I did not see where he went
It was getting pretty dark
I had to get up from the ground
Then I heard him bark.
He was hiding behind a bush
I saw him peaking at me
I saw 2 eyes and a nose
His tail was hard to see
But I know it was wagging.

Rosjenee Shelton, Grade 6
Irving School, CT

Ms. Bridget

Soft white leather seats
As smooth as sheets
Hard light blue sides
That rush up against the tides

Light black fast motors
Just like all the other boaters
Rusty old brown anchor
That could hold down a tanker

Always out on the sea
Where having fun is the key
Fast she always goes
Breaking the oceans rows

Danny Young, Grade 6
E W Thurston Middle School, MA

I Saw God

the moon was gleaming
that glorious night
the night when I saw God
He took me above the clouds
in one of the clouds He opened a door
and I saw Heaven
so every night
I say my prayers
so I can go to Heaven

Rebecca Cavin, Grade 5
Francis Asbury Elementary School, VA

Glum

Glum is like soldiers
Fighting in the war
Sad when they passed away
Motionless when it strikes fear in your heart
Embarrassed when you see them
Risk their lives for you
Smells like burning ash on a campfire
Feels like a pale cold face
Lying on the ground losing heart beat
Sounds like a gunshot piled over with gunpowder
Glum is like a broken soul.

Dameion Russ, Grade 5
Clover Street School, CT

Apart

It was made to happen, but still it breaks my heart
Just to live with knowing that it all fell apart.
I will never let it go, I'll always take it hard
Just being honest here, it took me off guard.
Fast like a bullet, burns like the sun
Just the thought of everything makes me wanna run.
Feels like everyone's watching me as I pay this toll
It seems like I live in a child's fishbowl.
At nights I hide out in my room, my pillow soaking wet
My life is feeling dark, but I'm not caving yet.
I'll wait to see the day, bright or stormy weather
The day that somehow things get put back together.

Jennifer Macneil, Grade 6
North Reading Middle School, MA

All About Casey

You are the curls of a spiral notebook
  The reflections of the blue Caribbean water
    When blushing, you're a strawberry tree.
You are a Lamborghini on nitric
  A sudden rumble of an earthquake
    A dart of a hungry shark.
You are a Whomping Willow with thousands of branches
  "Swift foot" or "Cat feet" stalking
    The innocent person getting away with everything.
You are the glue of the Richbourgs
  The queen of the family
    A hungry dog whining.
You are the face of a puppy
  The heart of an angel
    But, the attitude of a bossy kid.
You are the final slam dunk of a basketball game
  Pele's last goal in the World Cup
    Number 1 in my heart.
You are the prisoner who wouldn't sit still
  The one star always out first
    The one person who is always littler than me.

Kyle Richbourg, Grade 5
St Luke's School, CT

Vermont Wonders

As the sun sets over the lake, the sky turned pink,
Orange, purple like the sky had been painted
By a multicolored paintbrush! As the singing
Birds call fades away to the chirping march of the
Crickets and croaking frogs. The moon shines
in the sky shining like a giant flashlight, its
reflection reflects off the lake like a giant mirror.
You're in your bed snoozing under the cozy covers
dreaming about tomorrow. The stars are
Shining like miniature flashlights. Then the sun
Comes up, painting the sky blue, yellow, and green
As if it were a paintbrush. I love Vermont and so will you!

Peter Buck, Grade 4
Hawley Elementary School, CT

When I Think of My Mom

When I think of my mom
I see her happiness all the time
I see her watching her favorite soap opera, "Eterna Magia"
I see her smile just like a clown
When I think of my mom
I hear her singing just like a bird
I hear her vacuuming the dusty floor
I hear the birds in her garden singing like angels
I hear her loud opera voice
When I think of my mom
I smell her spicy turkey sandwich
I smell her grape conditioner and shampoo
I smell her flowery, strong perfume
When I think of my mom
I taste her juicy mango fruit
I taste the saucy mini pizzas she makes
I taste her orangey orange juice
When I think of my mom
I feel her soft tan skin
I feel her smooth, soft hair
When I think of my mom

Nichollas Souza, Grade 6
Fuller Middle School, MA

The Dog

Itching, scratching, barking too,
May be too much trouble for you.
Digging holes, burying things,
Bones, toys, and diamond rings.
This animals is really cute,
But sometimes it can be a brute!

This pet knows how to fetch a stick,
And it loves to lick and lick.
It responds to "Come here boy!"
And it squeaks its squeaky toy.
This pet may be sloppy like a hog,
But this animal is simply a dog!

Maddie Dudek, Grade 5
Foxborough Regional Charter School, MA

bedtime bunnies
little, soft, fluffy
cute bunnies lay down and rest
warm and cozy they sleep

Emily Goodwin, Grade 6
Charlton Middle School, MA

Puppies
Puppies
cute, small
barking, sleeping, eating
they are very playful
Dogs

Binah Saint-Loth, Grade 5
Sacred Heart Elementary School, MA

My World
Elm bark is my skin
Hard saplings are my bones
My mouth that talks
In the living wind
Is the door that leads the world,
My breath is the smoke of chimneys
Rising up to join the clouds
My heart is the fire of the
Circling stones and my eyes, my
Spirit and my dreams belong to those
I trust and love

Justin Le, Grade 4
Alice B Beal Elementary School, MA

Rose
Glamorous bright rose
Spreading out her petals wide
Magnificent rose

Kaylee Rose Danaher, Grade 5
Hebron Elementary School, CT

Snow
White lacy fragments of the sky
Blanketing the ground
Tiny weightless cotton balls
Bits of heaven brought down
It's fun to throw them up
And watch them flutter all around
No two alike
The glittering diamonds
Touch without a sound

Nathan Casey, Grade 6
Whitinsville Christian School, MA

Butterflies
Butterflies can fly.
They are very beautiful.
I love butterflies.

Jamie Teramani, Grade 5
St Joseph School-Fullerton, MD

The Wolf Statue
Here I am stuck in a frozen gaze
The sunny glistening glass at the courtyard
It is a nice, quiet, peaceful place in our school

This is one of the sights I will never forget as my hand slowly writes
Forming words, the wolf statue seems to be moving his head towards me
He is staring me down
His red eyes capture me.

I try to turn away, but he has caught me like a trap,
But finally I pull away with my last bit of strength that I have
Then I realize I am free, free as a Bluejay in the cloudy beautiful sky.

Zachary Kilby, Grade 5
Wakefield Forest Elementary School, VA

Can Man Be Grateful?
Can man be grateful for what he has done?
Find formulas for math or a cure for AIDS.
Can he be grateful?

Can man be grateful and not hate someone of different skin color?
Or hate them because of their genes?
Can he be grateful?

Can man be grateful to someone he loves?
Or hating them because his love is not true.
Can he just be grateful!!!

Nehemiah D. Boone, Grade 6
Magnolia Elementary School, MD

Math
Math is fun!
Math is great!
Math gets me up and ready!
Are you good at math?
I'm good at math!
I can do adding!
Can you?
My teacher and I like math a lot!
I am quick at adding.
Are you?
When math is over, I say see you another day!
I just finished math and I am sad because I love math a lot!
If you don't like math, please don't say that!
I love math!
Math as a subject is wonderful!
Sometimes we play math games on laptops because we earn it!
In math we play math games like time Bingo!
That is the best game of all!
If you are not good at math think about giving it another chance and you will like it!
Trust me!
Math is fun!

Jadyn Gamache, Grade 4
WB Sweeney School, CT

Proud Water

Twirling
Racing
Swift as a hawk
Graceful and glittering
Before your eyes,
I am water
Strong and flowing.
You may say I am boasting
But who says I don't have the right?
Might but light
I flow before you
To the left and to the right
And become a great sight
To behold.
I am older than you
And your grandfather too
I come form the mountain's' great throne.
I'll stay here through
This world's great plight
I will survive
I will definitely fight.

Simon Wolfe, Grade 6
Bigelow Middle School, MA

Cloudy Days

Darkness
Wet puddles
Thundering and hovering
Staying inside
Cloudy days

Conor Fanning, Grade 4
C Hunter Ritchie Elementary School, VA

Reading

Still as a tiger when he sees his prey
Eyes glued to the page
My mind is the book when I open it to the world of adventure
Reading like nobody is around me
Shivering from the scary setting
My eyes are on one paragraph then another
I flip the page like a bird turning the corner to keep on flying
It starts all over again

Mimi Daniell, Grade 5
John Ward Elementary School, MA

Life's Depression

Roses are red, violets are blue.
I might be blue if I'm thinking of you.

A gentle breeze came by.
Took my tears from my eye.

I am sad, and this is no impression.
I am going through a life's depression.

Nicholas Grant, Grade 4
Courthouse Road Elementary School, VA

Cheetahs

Cheetahs are cool, cheetahs are neat,
Cheetahs are very elite

Cheetahs are nice, cheetahs are great,
Cheetahs dominate

Cheetahs live in the wild,
Sometimes they give birth to a child

Cheetahs are fast,
Cheetahs are never last

Cheetahs eat mice,
Cheetahs give good advice

Ryan Comeau, Grade 5
Foxborough Regional Charter School, MA

Leaves

Fluttering in the breeze,
past the other leaves,
minding its business,
falling with super ease.
Soaring,
floating,
something special,
red,
orange
yellow,
the colors of fall.
But so rhythmic,
floating,
falling,
breezing by.

Noah Floeser, Grade 5
West Woods Upper Elementary School, CT

Brady

Football star Tom Brady
He walks around town showing off his lady
He wants to win with his heart and soul
But that's too bad he lost the Super Bowl.

Casey Doran, Grade 6
Captain Nathan Hale Middle School, CT

My Pomeranian Dog, Prince

Prince is a lovable cute dog
You are my chocolate with golden mahogany fluffy fur
You always land on your feet
It almost seems you have eight lives
You are very young
One year old to be exact
I love my little chocolate

Kani Jackson, Grade 4
Crestwood Elementary School, VA

The Wind

Slowly,
Silently,
Quietly,
Whispers,
In its hushed tone.
Never knows,
Where it goes,
Only goes,
Where it knows.
The wind,
Slowly,
Silently,
Whispers,
In its hushed tone.

Rachel Wheeler, Grade 4
St Mary's Primary School, MA

Changes

Changes in life,
And changes in dreams,
There's change everywhere
It might seem.

Some changes are good,
Some changes are bad,
Most changes are often,
Misunderstood.

Even if you think,
Bad can't change to good,
You're wrong with changes,
Because as I repeat:
Most changes are often,
Misunderstood.

Some changes can change,
So just open up your eyes,
Because all of changes…
Can always be an exciting,
SURPRISE!

Meredith Nerreau, Grade 5
Burr Elementary School, CT

Lacrosse

Shoot score
Lacrosse stick pads
Metal goal
Soar
Save goals
Win
Drink Gatorade
After the game you grin

James Farrell, Grade 5
Trinity Christian School, VA

Baseball

B ases getting stolen by fast players
A bout to drive a player home from third
S triking the best player out
E rrors in the infield
B atter up
A big hit to drive all the players in
L oud cheers for the home team
L oving baseball every day.

Riley Costa, Grade 4
Freetown Elementary School, MA

Stream

A fresh water stream
Trickles over gray pebbles
In the faint moonlight

Kendall Blizzard, Grade 6
E W Thurston Middle School, MA

Wish, Wash

Wish, wash, wish, wash
The water rushes by
Whoosh said the trees
Waving at me
Cold as a cucumber
Is the sea
As big blue waves
Are heading toward me

Lea Vedovelli, Grade 4
Litchfield Intermediate School, CT

Live

Come to me
And you will see
The paradise beside the palm tree
Lie on the silky sand,
Clump less,
A blanket on the seabed
Bathe in the crystal clear water,
Quietly tumbling ashore
Venture at sunset, shall I,
To the top of the yellow-green palm tree
Beside the paradise
Overlook the land,
The barrier repelling
Rural from Urban
The barrier uncrossed by my footsteps
Join me
In my heavenly haven
Join me
In the paradise
And learn
To live

Laura Kenney, Grade 5
St Mary's Primary School, MA

Seasons

A ray of sun,
A drop of rain,
A hint of falling snow,
A drifting leaf,
And all of these,
Are the seasons
That we know.

Erin Kelly, Grade 4
Jacksonville Elementary School, MD

Automobile

A utomobiles can be used for racing
U p and down go the speeds
T rucks, cars, and SUVs
O ff-roading, dragging, and NASCAR
M any styles of racing
O pen the pits
B ecause the racing is about to start!
I love to
L isten to the
E ngines roar!

Alan Nicholas Chretien, Grade 4
Freetown Elementary School, MA

A Tree

A tree, a great big brown tree,
As tall as can be, even taller than me,
I sat by its trunk, when suddenly I sunk,
I thought about my case,
When I saw a face,
It was yellow and mellow,
Red and dead, sad but still mad,
And a finger so pointed,
You might get a chill,
So I suggest you take a very strong pill,
And think of a pretty windmill.

Danielle DeCanio, Grade 5
Weston Intermediate School, CT

Easter

Easter eggs hidden,
Baby bunnies, hop, hop, hop,
Little children play.

Jordan Mosco, Grade 4
St Joseph School-Fullerton, MD

Sensory Beach

I spy the azure sea
As waves crash upon the shore.
Hard, hot sand burns my feet,
Banana Boat sunscreen on my pores.
As I swim, I taste the salty sea.

Diane Bivins' 4th Grade Class
Crestwood Elementary School, VA

We Are the Champions

It is the championship game, our biggest game.
If we win, we'll bring home the trophy.
If we lose, we go home empty handed.
We're down by one, with only ten seconds left.
Score a basket, we win.
Miss the basket, we lose.
We inbound the ball and I get the pass.
The clock ticks down to only five seconds.
I dribble toward the basket, it's now 3,2,1.
I get the shot off just before the final buzzer.
The ball is in the air, soaring, then floating.
It feels as if time has slowed down.
The ball drops into the basket. Swish!
The crowd erupts with roars and cheers.
I jump with excitement because now I know.
We are the champions!

Tim Costin, Grade 6
Swampscott Middle School, MA

Beaches*

so much depends upon
a beach
with white smooth
sand
and loud crashing waves
boom boom boom
whoosh whoosh whoosh
over flowing with castles
dazzled with shells and sea glass
on a hot summer day.
so much depends upon
a beach
with annoying
sounds of seagulls
caw caw caw
over flowing with the sound of children
screaming and laughing
ha ha ahhh ahhh yippee
on a hot summer day.

Madison Hunter, Grade 5
West Woods Upper Elementary School, CT
*Inspired by William Carlos Williams

Painting the Cat

When I paint I tend to splat.
Then it gets all over the cat.
The cat turns red, yellow, and blue.
Green, pink, and orange too.
When this happens she has to take a shower.
So I'll put the water on full power.
Dry, dry, dry until we're done.
Then back to painting to have some fun.

Kara Ploss, Grade 4
Helen H Hansen Elementary School, MA

Apple Tree

A green seedling pokes its head out of the earth,
Gazing up into the deep blue sky,
Watching the clouds roll by and by.

Roots reach out to grasp the earth,
Stretching down farther for years to come,
Drinking in water that has trickled down from the clouds above.

Branches stretch out to touch the sky,
With leaves rustling in the spring wind,
Apple blossoms are blooming while bumblebees collect pollen.

For now it is a full grown tree,
Looking at young ones just like me.

Julie Peterson, Grade 5
Soule Road School, MA

Cooking What I Love to Eat

I love to eat and love to cook
I started as a baby and grew up like a hook
Did you know this miracle happened today
I finally made a Creme Brulée

Derika C. White, Grade 4
Hebbville Elementary School, MD

Life Is Blooming

Flowers blooming in the sun,
Dance, sing, shout, it sure is fun!
Live life, breathe air,
Wiggle your pedals until you can't wiggle anywhere.
Stop and think of where you are,
And soon realize
You're in a car…
Driving up north on the highway of life,
Think it, feel it,
And everything will be all right.

Mary Brown, Grade 5
Hindley Elementary School, CT

My Room

My special place is in my room
No loud noises or booms
I call it serenity, peace, and silence too
I go to my room to escape from the world
There is nothing in my room to scare me off
My room is peace, my room is quiet
And to think all of this is just a door away from the real world

Max Dodge, Grade 4
St Christopher's School, VA

Sky

The sky is so high, it makes me want to fly,
So very high
Up in the sky.

John Genest, Grade 5
Milton L Fuller Elementary School, MA

Baseball

People sliding to catch the ball
Players running to get on base
Pitchers pitching
Stealing bases
Outfielders catching fly balls.

Infielders sliding to stop the ball
Players going for a double play
Basemen running
Hitters bunting
Baseball is here to stay.

Zackery Pike, Grade 4
Freetown Elementary School, MA

War Ship

In the old days,
We had wars on ship,
Hardly anyone survived,
As cannons fired,
Men would die,
And ships would go down,

I heard of a pirate named Charlie Blade,
Taking down all British ships,
His was an untouched ship,
That would only come out at night,

His ship was like a monster attacking,
Under the moon,
When the sun came out,
They would return to their cave,
On the coast of France.

Raymond Weisman, Grade 4
Tilghman Elementary School, MD

My Favorite Things

The movement of birds
and the rhythm of words
The clickety-clacks
of trains on the track
Lava lamp bubbles
Swedish fish — doubles!
Long-paged books
Bright colored hooks
Fire places, bright
and twinkling lights.
The number twenty-three
plus, great climbing trees
Sports where you kick
Hamsters that lick
The blue colored Smurfs
Fresh ironed shirts
Musicals that soar
with seven encores

Meg Merlino, Grade 5
J F Kennedy Middle School, MA

Checkered Flag

The checkered flag is black and white
And when I see it
It is such a sight
I go around the track so fast I feel so bad for the boy that's last
I tried my hardest as I always do
But sometimes you might lose
This the day that you won't see the flag first
But I come around the track with such a burst
I was the first to see the checkered flag this time
That first place trophy is all mine.

Austin Cederquist, Grade 4
St Mary's Primary School, MA

Jamaica

Jamaica is a great land of beauty surrounded by the Caribbean Sea.
It is a land filled with fruits and vegetables
like juicy red plums and luscious mangoes.

Jamaica has hundreds of acres of land
Many filled with sugarcane fields and tall trees with coconuts
We are known for our white sandy beaches and generous hospitality.
This is my Jamaica.

Kadeem Sweeney, Grade 5
Toquam Magnet School, CT

Mrs. Gimler

The days have gone past
Unbelievably really fast

The first day I walked in
I did not know what to expect

Inside the little classroom
I saw a friendly teacher getting a lot of respect

Dunkin' Donuts runs a part of her day
How could she possibly get through without at least three a day

She's small and compact, but stands ten feet tall
She believes in strong work ethics, and instills good morals for us all

She wears many hats two or three at a time
She juggles her busy life, but you'll never hear her whine

She's a lot like my mother, she guides us each day
To make the right choices that we carry along our way

New people step into my life each and every day
But Mrs. Gimler left a footprint on my heart that will never wear away

So thank you Mrs. Gimler for all the love you shared
You stood out among other teachers because of the way you cared.

Kayla Sepe, Grade 5
Foxborough Regional Charter School, MA

The Beach

I come out of the car to see
The beautiful blue waves crashing over the rocks
The dolphins stuck their heads out of the water
And talked to me
I dipped my head under
Only to see seven little fish look back at me
The soft wet sand took my feet under
The salt you can smell from miles away
What a beautiful day
I put my ear up to the seashell
It said to come and play
But sadly, it was the end of the day.

Haley Rice, Grade 5
Soule Road School, MA

Frozen Soldiers

Marching through the land
timidly preparing for battle.
Hesitantly asking the captain for a rest.
Eluding their enemies like
a mouse eluding a cat.
Swoosh!
They are posing sculptures.
Their chiseled faces cold as frigid water,
They speak to each other by moving their limbs.
They roar with agony as their limbs crumble.
They stay there, waiting
for a battle that will never come.

Jack Pacheco, Grade 5
Chestnut Hill Community School, MA

Hope

What happens to people without hope?

Do they die without hope
Many years later?
Or do they live a sad life
Crying their eyes out?
Do they live in a room
With white padded walls?
Who would want to live that life?

Maybe they turn to stone
And birds sit on their chest.
Isn't that a sad life?

Maybe their hearts will slow down
As they hear their funeral march
In that empty void in their mind
Where hope used to be?

Or do they drop like a fly
And venture on as a spirit
Looking for their lost hope?

Katelynn Stanley, Grade 6
School of International Studies at Meadowbrook, VA

The Last Period Clock

The clock it goes tick, tick, tock.
No student will move or even talk.
It's 2:24 and the clock won't budge.
I wonder if it's filled with sludge!

I grab my bag and start to heave
it onto my back cause it's 30 seconds 'til we leave.
I look at my friends they are nice and kind.
I wonder if they know what's on my mind.

I feel like I'm in a learning prison.
Does anyone know the second hand has risen?
There is 5 seconds to spare and I want to go home,
back to the place where I'm allowed to roam.

I want to get out of this horrible building thing,
then I finally hear the "go home" bell ring!

Cassie McKinnon, Grade 6
Fuller Middle School, MA

His First Day

Today was the day my brother was leaving.
We were all up early getting prepared.
His high school goal he would be achieving.
I hope and pray that he is not scared.

As he leaves us to become the person he wants to be.
We sit outside and wait for our new midshipman.
We watch the ships sail out to sea.
As we sit in the sun and try to get a tan.

The midshipmen are brought in
While the jets fly over.
We wait for the induction to begin
And I agree he is a great achiever.

As I see a good luck clover
I know he will be fine and now the day is over.

Caroline Doyle, Grade 6
Immaculate Heart of Mary School, MD

Summer Fun

S unny days on the beach
U nder an umbrella resting
M aking a water slide
M aking up games
E veryone gathers around and has a good time
R unning around in the yard

F ire crackers exploding
U nder a tree relaxing
N ever ending summer vacation

Sophia Lopez-Peña, Grade 5
Sacred Heart Elementary School, MA

A Question Mark

Is the thing
That leads you
Down the strange
Path of
Maybe?

Grace Ledgard, Grade 5
C C Burr Elementary School, MA

If I Was a Monkey

I leap from vine to vine,
I climb to the tallest branches,
see rain forest and eat bananas.
My call is so loud
you could hear it in any crowd.
As I finish a banana
I watch the peel fall.

Shianne McClintock, Grade 6
Litchfield Intermediate School, CT

What Is Fawn Hollow?

Fawn Hollow is…
A nice and caring place
Students learning Math and more
And there are also playgrounds too

Fawn Hollow is…
A beautiful place
Where teachers work and teach
We read, write and play with each other
There are funny kids too

Fawn Hollow is…
A creative place
There is a library
A gym and a music room
Maybe you can go there too

Taylor Rodrigues, Grade 4
Fawn Hollow Elementary School, CT

Fall

Leaves drift to the ground
Everyone dances around
Kids rake a great huge pile
When they jump people smile

Anna Keller, Grade 5
Lincoln Street School, MA

Moon

M idnight bloom of glinting happiness
O nly out at night
O ccasionally full — but will
N ever fade away from our hearts

Karin Leupold, Grade 5
J F Kennedy Middle School, MA

Stars

Glimmer, glow, shimmer,
in the flashing night.
Shine like the golden sun,
all night long.
Shimmer, shine, glow,
through out the globe.
Glitter without fear.
Glimmer like the one you are.

Glitter, shimmer, glow,
let all know who you are.
Shimmer and shine,
like there's no tomorrow.
Glitter, shimmer, shine,
with friends by your side.
Glitter and shine,
with family near.

Glimmer, shine, glow,
Cameras capture your attitude.
Glow and pose,
The cameras will make you a
Star!

Sarah Sotelo, Grade 5
McKinley Elementary School, VA

Secret

I watch my mom
Walk into the store
Something catches my eye
It tempts me to look
I see the open sun roof
I stand on my seat
And push myself up
There I was sitting
On the roof of the car
The wind blows
Against my face
I look and see my mom
Walking out of the store
I collapse into the seat
And I am safe
She gets in
"What did you do"
And I just smiled

Jonathan Joyce, Grade 6
Swampscott Middle School, MA

Autumn Leaves

I love autumn leaves,
in orange, brown, and yellow,
watch them fall, deep down

Romina Montes, Grade 5
Marley Elementary School, MD

A Tear in My Heart*

I felt like the world was tearing apart,
But no one else could see
All of the dreadful changes
That were happening to me.

My whole family was ripped away
And arguing way too much.
I tried to share my feelings,
But I had no souls to touch.

It's been seven years since the news,
And still the gash is there.
I get reminded every day,
Like it's a real nightmare.

There is a tear in my heart
That is impossible to sew.
A tear that keeps on ripping
And continues to grow.

Sophia Malonson, Grade 6
E W Thurston Middle School, MA
*About divorce

Jasper

Jasper is a bunny
He really is funny
He chews
Peoples' shoes
He twitches his nose
And licks his toes
Jasper is a bunny
And really is funny

Michaela Sullivan, Grade 5
Mount Hope Christian School, MA

The Summer Sun

The sun is bright and shining.
It glistens and gleams all day.
At night it bestows away,
And goes to sleep the next day.

Jake Smith, Grade 5
Occohannock Elementary School, VA

The Winning Catch

There are ten seconds left
In the fourth quarter
The quarter back throws the ball
It slowly glides through the air
Then falls falls falls
And softly lands
In your hands
For the winning touchdown

Owen Foley, Grade 4
Munger Hill Elementary School, MA

Food

People like to eat food.
It puts them in good moods.
Hamburgers, fries, milkshakes there on top.
People just eat like they never wanna stop.
If you are good to the critic you'll be a hit.
Watch my greedy brother eat every bit.

Samaria Moss, Grade 4
Courthouse Road Elementary School, VA

Autumn

Take a walk with me
There are such amazing sights to see
Hawks soar like kites on a breeze
Squirrels swiftly scamper up the trees
Take a walk with me

Come with me on Halloween night
Jack-o-lanterns cast a spooky light
There's so much candy to be eaten
Ghosts and goblins run up to houses Trick or Treat'n
Come with me on Halloween night

Join me on an autumn day
Chipmunks run around like children and seem to play
Leaves swirl like a tornado and then disappear
Autumn's always an amazing time of year
Join me on an autumn day

Sit with me by a crackling fire
Amber flames dance higher and higher
The scent of smoke softly streams up my nose
The heat of the fire gives warmth to my toes
Sit with me by a crackling fire

Peter Freund, Grade 6
Madison Middle School, CT

Cuddles

Cuddles I loved you,
I do not care if you are gone,
You will always be in my heart.

With those soft and downy feathers,
And those beautiful colors,
You will be with me through all times.

You made me cry, but that was fine,
Because I know you will always,
Love me back.

Through the times we had together.
You were always so wonderful.
There will never be another bird like you.

Alyson Flahive, Grade 4
Alice B Beal Elementary School, MA

The Choir

Choir
Singing
Loud noises
Beautiful   noises
Rhythmic   Inspiring
La
La

La
La

Laaaa la La
I love to sing   Laaa
The choir sounds good
Like a chorus of angels singing
The Director swings his arms
The song comes to an end
Everyone starts to clap
The choir

Kenny Lawson, Grade 6
Grace Episcopal Day School, MD

Travel Music*

This Journey to their new home:
the always noise
projecting from the
   cats:
soft pat, patting from furry feet
and meows from cats
who protest in all
   vocabularies of
growl, screech, hissing
cat language
   combinations
as the hail starts to erupt
   angry cats
scratch up trees
screeching loudly
assaulting creature
   ears with the
always noise of
this journey to their new home:
   travel music

Maggie Underwood, Grade 5
West Woods Upper Elementary School, CT
*Inspired by Arnold Adoff

Who Am I

I may be slow since I have a home on my back
and I always go places forgetting to pack
I am not fast
but I know I'll last
and I have nothing to hurdle
since I'm a turtle.

Christopher Francois, Grade 5
Sacred Heart Elementary School, MA

Starfish Island's Heroes

Starfish-man
funny, silly,
slinking, stretching, exploding
both friends and heroes —
stretching, inventing, thinking,
smart, intelligent,
Brain-kid

Michael Gilbert, Grade 6
Ashford School, CT

Hockey

The love of the game
Willing to take consequences
To the ice we fall on
To the snow that falls on your jersey
There is no sallies to this game
You must play for the love of the game
You must play for the love of the game
And just for the love of the game

Johnathan Spear, Grade 4
Alice B Beal Elementary School, MA

Bike Riding

I step onto my bike,
My helmet snug on my head,
waiting for the adventure.
Ready
Set
Go.

I push forward,
Pedal a few times,
falling into the adventure,
Excitement in my bones.

I keep on pedaling.
Faster.
Faster.
All my worries gone.

Speeding like a roller coaster
going up, down, around
in this marvelous adventure.

Matt Bonazzoli, Grade 6
Swampscott Middle School, MA

Petals

White petals
Flutter in the breeze
A pollen glaze
Spreads out on the flower
So soft and smooth
An elegant fragrance in the air
Glaring in the sun

Brian Tracy, Grade 5
St Mary's Primary School, MA

Yet Some Beauty Remains

In winter, once the land was an unbroken forest of snow.
Now dump trucks spread their salt over roads where forest is no more.
But yet some beauty still remains as I walk behind my house in the woods.

In spring, once the meadow was sprinkled with wildflowers.
Now houses stand where their colors once bloomed.
But yet some beauty still remains when I find a secluded clearing in the forest.

In summer, once the sun shone in full glory.
It does still today, but hidden behind clouds of smog.
But yet some beauty still remains on a warm day by the ocean's edge.

In fall, once every tree bore leaves of red, orange, or gold.
Now more are brown, killed by our pollution.
But yet some beauty still remains deep in the countryside, on a farm of colorful oaks.

Of the summer sun, the autumn leaves, the spring flowers and the winter snow,
We see only a fraction of what our ancestors beheld.

Darby Levin, Grade 5
Krieger-Schechter Day School, MD

Fall's Here

It's getting colder,
Days are becoming shorter,
Wind whistling, leaves skipping along the sidewalk,
It can only mean one thing,
FALL'S HERE!

Plump pumpkins line the farm,
Trees mutate their leaves like an artist gathering fresh paint,
Coffee-colored nuts litter the ground like a small child's toys,
It can only mean one thing,
Fall is here!

Colossal, charcoal geese fly high over, heading south,
Squirrels scurrying around, burying their acorns deep into the heart of mother earth,
The black bear, as dark as night, settles in and prepares for the long rest ahead,
It can only mean one thing,
Fall's here.

Jackson LaBoa, Grade 6
Madison Middle School, CT

Scientist

S igmund Freud's study of the mind
C arl Young's interest of the mind
I saac Newton's discovery that light is made up of the colors of the rainbow
E instein's equation $E=mc^2$
N ewton's magnifying telescope
T homas Edison and his light bulb
I rving Langmuir was a chemist and a physicist
S uccessfully launched liquid fueled rocket Robert Goddard
T homas Edison's favorite invention: the phonograph

Anthony Iandoli and Timothy Peltier, Grade 5
Leicester Memorial School, MA

Ice Cream

There are so many flavors it's hard to decide,
Chocolate, vanilla, and Dublin Mudslide.

There are sundaes and hand-dipped, soft serve and splits,
Even frosty milkshakes topped with small chocolate bits.

So how should I have it, in a cone or a cup?
It doesn't much matter just fill it right up.

Try adding different sauces; it's all up to you,
Like hot fudge, caramel, and marshmallow goo.

Don't forget the toppings they make ice cream fun,
Whipped cream, nuts, and cherries bring smiles in the sun.

It's cool and refreshing and quite a delight,
What a tasty treat on a steamy, summer's night.

Cristina Montemorano, Grade 4
Mary Walter Elementary School, VA

Bedtime

"It's time for bed" my mother said.
I said "all right lets not fight."
I climb into bed as the clock strikes ten.
As I say goodnight to the stars, and the cars.
A shadow comes over me so I forget my prayer.
I cover my head as if I was scared.
I suddenly realize I'm getting a hug.
We laugh and give each other a shove.
I finish my prayers without being scared.
My mother turns off the light as I smile.
I'm left in the dark with only the clock to see.
Sorry to say but that was a dream.

Talia Balakirsky, Grade 6
Krieger-Schechter Day School, MD

Graduation Day

On the platform during graduation day,
I was feeling terrified, happy, and sad.
How would I make it through the day feeling this way?
Having my family and friends there made me glad.

I was standing next to my friend Paige,
Trembling and nervous as can be.
My teacher called me up to the stage,
Looking out I saw everyone cheering for me.

Then, we were off to a party at a pool.
This was the last time we'd all be together.
Singing, laughing, and dancing, it was cool,
I will never forget my friends from Cromwell, EVER!

When it was time to go, I turned to wave goodbye,
I had a smile on my face, and a tear in my eye.

Ali Feathers, Grade 6
Immaculate Heart of Mary School, MD

Caly

Is very smart but thinks she knows everything,
Always tries to fix things when they go wrong,
Loves talking to people like she's never talked before,
Tells the funniest jokes around,
Sings very well, like a dove in the morning,
Likes to make everything as perfect as possible,
Throws the best parties in the whole wide world,
Thinks boys are mean, weird, and gross.

Julia Albino, Grade 4
Long Meadow Elementary School, CT

Parts of Art

When I woke up again
To finish my work
The only thing I saw
Was the small line of a new beginning.
When I lowered my head
All these pictures started surrounding me
Then I knew what to draw
I finally made the small and gentle line
But it wasn't good enough
To make the picture perfect and alive
It was too hard
To make the eyes
But can I do it?
I know I can
It is just a matter of time
To make the picture complete
I finally made the eye
It was a horrible sight
But it was the best eye I can make
Now I must wake up
Now I must draw

Aric Huang, Grade 5
John Ward Elementary School, MA

Dogs

Dogs
Dogs
Dogs
Funny dogs
Striped, spotted dogs
Small, thin schnauzer dogs
Playful dogs
Happy dogs
Hairy, shiny, pretty dogs
Black tan German dogs
Golden dogs, too
Tiny dogs
Big dogs
Don't forget long dogs
Last of all, best of all, I like weiner dogs

Brianna Hughes, Grade 4
C Hunter Ritchie Elementary School, VA

Autumn Nature

Lost and scared in the woods my footsteps crunch the crisp, golden, autumn leaves.
The deer swish around me like running water in a stream.
I grasp an acorn. It feels like the prickers of a cactus plant.
Alone in the woods fall is so lonely.

I trip and land on some slippery, olive moss but don't seem hurt.
It is like a soft, furry blanket that protects me when I'm cold.
I look around and see lazy, lanky, limp leaves of the oak trees floating down like a feather dropping from a bird.
While the branches of the bumpy, brown bark bite my back I swiftly move away toward the crumbling rock wall to rest.
Fall is so lonely.

The bitter, black berries are bulging under the shadow of the midnight moon.
Next to the monstrous tree trunks that feel firm and rigid creaking stringy branches reach out like fingers coming to grab me.
The scent of musty, moldy, decaying leaves fills the air and causes me to sneeze.
The wind moans like a hurt animal, while a fog rolls slowly in surrounding me.
Fall is so lonely.

Shawn McAuley, Grade 6
Madison Middle School, CT

Colors

Colors are the building blocks of life, they build imagination, like bricks build a building because everything is something and colors make up everything, "WAP" when you close a book you lock the colors out because even sound has a color and even though you can't see them they are there. Much like germs on a window and we are always with flying colors because with every emotion we have our own color when you're mad you have colors it can be red or green or even purple, as well with cravings or feelings but to sum up life there are three things, the devil who is red, the heavens who are white, and the third one is COLORS.

Aleah Rippeon, Grade 6
E Russell Hicks School, MD

Yellow

Yellow is like the sound of an egg yoke sizzling on the stovetop,
Yellow is like the smell of a newly ripened yellow banana,
Yellow is like the taste of a fresh squeezed lemon in a cold glass to make lemonade,
Yellow is like the feel of the bright, powerful sunlight beating against my back and shoulders.

Paige Schmincke, Grade 4
Long Meadow Elementary School, CT

Autumn Leaves

Maroon and scarlet maple leaves falling off the humongous oak trees.
Don't forget dandelion and sky blue they are colors of autumn too.
The chestnut marvelous maple leaves make a magnificent crunch.
The leaves falling off the trees are like snowflakes falling of a gigantic comfy cloud.
I can smell the fresh scent of pine from the pine trees.
Leaves aren't the only objects parachuting off of the giant birch trees,
there are also russet acorns and sugar pine cones that might hit your front door.
The red dogwood berries look like a puny version of cherry tomatoes.
Have you noticed how the leaves leaping off the trees act like they're running around because winter's coming.
There are so many mountains of massive mushrooms.
The towering trees hovered over me.
The gigantic willow trees look like a larger version of a mushroom.
I love hearing the great tweets of the little blue jay.
I hope no one makes a fright cause in fall it's Halloween night.
Beware of ghosts and goblins running around scaring people all through the town.
Get out your rake to clean up the mess.
Now you know about the leaves in autumn all around the ground.

Amber Schultz, Grade 6
Madison Middle School, CT

The Nurse

She welcomes me in.
She bandaids my skin.
I sit on the bed
and she feels my head.
I come in when I don't feel right.
She makes me laugh, she's like a bright light.
She helps me when I'm in need,
even when my knee starts to bleed.

She is the Nurse!

Erika Sales, Grade 6
Fuller Middle School, MA

Cars

So we start the car,
And head off the tar.
We told the man that wanted to race,
To stay at a steady pace.

So off we sped,
Against our opponents that were made of lead.
We raced with our hearts,
Hoping to get ahead.

We went up a jump,
But when we came down I heard a big thump.
I sat there on the edge of my seat
With my foot on the gas,
Hoping to get to the finish line in Mass.

We won the race and got a trillion dollars,
And then became English scholars.
We put the trophy in its case,
And I said to myself that was a good race.

Devan Valdes, Grade 6
Captain Nathan Hale Middle School, CT

Teachers Are Like Fishermen

Us the students are the fish, the homework is the
Bait, the teachers are the fishermen oh why this
Cruel fate?

Here we wait at S-R-M-S day in and day out
Finally we're home…but there's still homework
No doubt.

This bait would seem offensive possibly even
Rude but lest we take it line and sinker our recess
Is pursued.

This cycle will repeat till we are 18, oh great here
Comes college I guess it's time to scream

Max Scroggins-Lee, Grade 6
Scotts Ridge Middle School, CT

Race Cars

Race cars are so cool that I drool.
I love the smell of gas that smells like fries.
Tires that smell like steak.
They make me want a lot of food.
Race cars can be a lot of fun and money.
But when they go round and round
they make me very dizzy.
So next time I will watch them instead of playing!

Aaron Gettel, Grade 6
E Russell Hicks School, MD

Leaves!

Leaves are colorful!
They fall off of the trees.
They are beautiful when you step on them.
They make a noise that goes crunch crunch!
They are pretty.
They are blue, red, brown and green.
In the fall you will have to rake them!

Kayla Mejias, Grade 4
WB Sweeney School, CT

A Halloween Fall

There was an old, ugly monster named Dean,
Whose daughter was dressed up for Halloween.

His daughter was screaming for she needed his help,
So he came running when he heard her loud yelp.

She said, "I saw a ghost behind that tree there.
It was really horrid and it gave me a scare."

Her father went looking to find her fair ghost,
But all that he found was a sheet and a lamppost.

The two of them laughed as loud as can be.
Then they fell to the ground in front of that tree.

Keegan Lowensen, Grade 5
St Clement Mary Hofbauer School, MD

Life

Life is like a boat
that takes you places.

Life is full of sorrow
and happiness.

Life is curiosity
waiting to be discovered.

Life is a door
filled with dreams.

Life is a wonderful thing.

Katherine Keller, Grade 5
Foxborough Regional Charter School, MA

The Flame of Hope

The flame of hope is in our hearts.
It was planted in the spring,
When all bloomed and thrived and grew,
And the flame had everything.
But the heat of summer soon arrived,
And the flame was dying down.
The land was dry with a searing heat;
The flame barely made a sound.
Of course, autumn was much better;
The trees shaded it from the sun,
But the leaves let rays of gold escape,
So, gladly, the flame wasn't done.
But when no one could predict it,
Winter's icy grip reached out,
And a cold threatened to end it,
But the flame simply stayed stout.
The flame of hope is in our hearts.
It was planted in the spring.
And though obstacles have tested it,
The flame has survived everything.

Trevor Jennings, Grade 6
Grace Episcopal Day School, MD

Ireland

Leprechauns will hide,
Ireland is the coolest place,
St. Patrick lives there.

Amira Corbett, Grade 4
St Gregory Elementary School, MA

Think

What makes me stop and think?
Will I have friends till the end?
I think about the war in Iraq
And all the unlucky soldiers that go there
And all the ones that don't make it back
Then I think back on my life.
I say, "I have a good life these days."

Ross Anjos, Grade 4
Munger Hill Elementary School, MA

Peace Is a Butterfly

Peace is a butterfly
flapping its wings.
Peace is not like war.

War is a butterfly
Trapped in a web
full of spiders.

Peace is a butterfly
flapping its wings.

Adam Halbrook, Grade 4
Quashnet School, MA

Dog

Sounds stir sleep;
yawning and stretching.
The barks burst bubbles
and hair hangs in halos
while tail tussles with teeth.
The teeth tear toys
and ears eat echoes.
She slurps her favorite drink
after chomping and munching
on foods she can eat.
Her nose nudges knees
as she places her paws
on patches of pavement.
She barks at bullies
but provides tail wags
when family or friends come over.
Just another exciting day
in the doggone-doggy world.

Edmund Seyfried, Grade 6
Trinity School, MD

Life's What You Make It

Life's what you make it.
So make the best of it.
You don't know what you
Have until it's gone.
So cherish all you have.
You won't get what you
Want until you try.
You won't find what
You want if you never look.
So take a minute to search
High and low while you can.
'Cause Life's what you make it
And nothing more.

Angelica Strickland, Grade 6
Salem Church Middle School, VA

The Sun

Bright burning sunshine
Burning my eyes as I write.
Glazing at the Earth
Making it warm and healthy.
I look at it blindingly
Staying in one spot while the
world spins around.
As the sun sets south I
Stay north.
As the sun rises
Like a sprout looking sparkly
At a beach sunset. Now the
Sun is gone.

Ryan McIntyre, Grade 4
Hawley Elementary School, CT

Ireland

Shamrocks everywhere.
Tourist come to look yearly.
Language is different.

Andrew Royes, Grade 4
St Gregory Elementary School, MA

A 'Special' Dream

There once was a man from Peru
Who dreamed he was eating his shoe,
When he woke up,
He looked at his tongue,
And there was the bottom of his shoe,
He was mad he had only one shoe,
So he ate the other one too,
Now he needs new shoes,
So he bought size twos,
Then his mother caught him in bed,
With a ladder near his window stead,
I bet he wishes he was dead,
But it was all in his head.

David Gallant, Grade 5
Plainfield Catholic School, CT

Sour Cream Dumplings

Laid out on the table
Little round balls of dough
With sour cream inside
I take a bite
And my mouth has a party
Sour cream spurts out
But only if you're lucky
I take one after the other
Never seeming to stop
Everybody eats a million
With apricot jam on the side
Suddenly, they are all gone
Only the smell remains
Wafting in out of the kitchen
Out on to the sidewalk
And pretty soon
The whole town
Has the smell
Of sour cream dumplings

Wolfie von Furth, Grade 6
Smith College Campus School, MA

Silly Lilly

There once was a girl named Lilly.
She was very silly.
She went to the ball,
And had a great fall,
And that was the end of silly Lilly.

Taylor Lariviere, Grade 4
Freetown Elementary School, MA

Life Under the World

I am waking up to a new day
I wonder if I will get a new neighbor
I hear the sounds of restless children
I see nothing but the occasional foot
I want to be free
I am afraid
I pretend I am fresh and new
I feel unwanted
I touch the same things every day
I worry for the new friends I have
I cry for my family
I am leaving my home
I understand I am not pleasant to the touch
I say I will not perish alone
I dream I will be with my family, in the end,
I try to avoid others
I hope to be left alone
I am a single piece of chewed gum

Tori Fitzgerald, Grade 6
Page Middle School, VA

If I Was a Boy

I'd have a new life and my name would be Troy.
Id' have cool clothes, if I was a boy.

I would have new friends and a lot of joy.
I would get a cute girlfriend, if I was a boy.

All of my sister's things would be destroyed.
I would bug her a lot, if I was a boy.

I would hang out with guys and have pride and joy.
I would play football at recess, if I was a boy.

For Christmas I would get an even better toy,
Like a monster truck, if I was a boy.

Melanie Humeniuk, Grade 6
St Clement Mary Hofbauer School, MD

Hawaii

Hawaii is so nice
Being there is like paradise

I love going to the beach
I never hear the gulls screech

I love to see the pretty palm trees
My mom agrees

The waves are so tall
They always make me fall

You should go and visit the Aloha State
Don't be late

Samantha Kominiarek, Grade 5
Foxborough Regional Charter School, MA

The Beach

One day in Ocean City
I went to have some fun
The day was so pretty
I soaked up lots of sun

My dad and I took a walk
Down the shore we strolled along
Hand in hand, we talk
Waves crashed to make the ocean's song

As we walked I found a crab
It pinched me on the thumb
I threw it at my dad to grab
It left my finger numb

Even though it hurt for awhile
It's a day with my dad that makes me smile

Brynly Wilson, Grade 6
Immaculate Heart of Mary School, MD

God's Love

Gods love is real
His love is my strength and my shield
His love saved me of my sins
His love is the only love that lasts forever.

His love is great beyond all understanding
His love shows me the right way to live
His love comforts me when I am sad
His love is perfect in all ways.

Alfonso De Diego, Grade 5
Church of the Redeemer Christian School, MD

Missed Me

As I rub my horns against this tree
the beautiful mountains and water I see
My horns feel good against the rigid tree
with beechnuts and berries surrounding me
I drank too much water and now I gotta pee.
And sadly a hunter just shot at me.
Haha you missed me!
Even though, you still have a gun and
now I shall flee.

Evan Shortsleeve, Grade 6
Litchfield Intermediate School, CT

The Blizzard

The particles of snow aimlessly swirl and twist around the sky.
Slowly drifting closer and closer towards the earth.
Eager children waiting for the wonderful white snow to fall,
Look up into the many layers of winter white clouds,
Waiting, hoping what the weatherman said was true.

Gabriela Goldsmith, Grade 6
Scotts Ridge Middle School, CT

Rainy Monday

It's a rainy Monday
But I'm still
Outside
Writing this.
As I watch the
Big
Oak Tree
It looks like a soldier
That just came out of the shower.
A couple wet
Leaves stay standing
But the rest are
Limp.
Now
I look at the green grass,
It droops from
The heavy dew
That lay upon it.
It's a rainy Monday
That's why
I'm writing this.
Casey Harkins, Grade 4
Hawley Elementary School, CT

What to Wear

How 'bout this
No, no this
No, that won't work
I think I've tried everything
Huummmmmm…
How 'bout I mix it up a little bit
This with this
Oh and maybe that with that
Ya!! Perfect!!
Time for bed!!
But, but Huh??
Come on!!
So I guess I did that for nothing!!
And I still have nothing to wear!!
Amanda Ray, Grade 6
Edmond P Talbot Middle School, MA

Stars

Stars shine so bright.
Just like a delight.
I can't wait till I see stars shine so bright.
So I can see the light.
Ashley M. Darwick, Grade 4
Munger Hill Elementary School, MA

Wildcats

Stalks along the ground
Climbs tall trees to watch and wait
Pounces on its prey
Sammy Powers, Grade 4
Trinity Christian School, VA

Mosquitos

Mosquitos are buzzing everywhere.
On the ground or in the air.

They suck blood to fertilize their eggs,
These weird creatures have six spiny legs.

They've been around since the beginning of the Earth,
So next time you think about them, think about how much they're worth.

You itch and scratch everywhere,
You say they are the most annoying things in the air.

I know they're gross but this is how they thrive,
Without any blood they wouldn't reproduce and survive.
Parker Riordan, Justin Feldman and Robert Anderson, Grade 5
Blueberry Hill Elementary School, MA

The Flip Trick

"Smack!" The course of my fingers hit the mats,
Next up is my feet.
Dizziness comes upon me,
But my mind comes back to earth,
Like the feeling after a morning shower, refreshed and new.
Sweat trickles down my face…
When I swallow, it is like a gallon of salt crawling down my throat.
At times I fall but I am cradled by a field of mattresses.
When I flip, it all flashes in one big picture,
The blue and brown mats are the only thing taken.
Chatter is filling the trapped air,
It reminds me of recess.
"Flop!" My whole body crashes to the floor as always.
I shoot back up and heave myself over for the millionth time.
Megan Deacon, Grade 6
Litchfield Intermediate School, CT

Paint It Black

Black is licorice found in a candy shop,
And it is also the uniform worn by a cop.
Black is an 8 ball found on a pool table,
And the beautiful stallion found in a stable.
Black tastes like dark chocolate that I desire!
It is the color of charcoal in a glowing fire.
Black feels mysterious and sinister…
It's the feeling one gets when they have a disease no one can cure.
Black is the clothes on a man whose hobby is stealing,
When playing cards, black is the spades and clubs you are dealing!
Black's a color found on a bruise,
And also the print of the Connecticut news.
Black is what I see when I look into space,
And the color of the lawyer's leather suitcase.
Black is the opposite color of the snow in December —
Black is a color I'll surely remember.
Jacob Rochford, Grade 5
Har-Bur Middle School, CT

Metaphoric Me!

I am the ocean.
Undiscovered,
deep, never shallow.
Full of songs my waves create.
Hidden treasures beneath my sandy skin.
I am clothed in the sun's reflection,
and warmed by its blazing rays.
Dive into me.
Explore my world of curiosity and beauty.

Madison Purcell, Grade 5
Sarah Noble Intermediate School, CT

Summer

Summer, summer, summer
It's beautiful
What is so beautiful about it?
The warm weather, the beautiful flowers,
Summer, summer, summer
No school, relaxation,
Summer fun,
Vacations,
The fun never ends
Summer, summer, summer
Have no fear summer is here
Have fun during the summer break
Summer, summer, summer
Always ends
But the fun never ends
Summer

Romesa Mustafa, Grade 5
Friendship Valley Elementary School, MD

Loss

Loss is when something goes away
Forgotten and alone
A hole in your heart that will never be repaired
Good or bad
For better or for worse

Something that makes happiness drain away
And sadness pour in
Damaging you forever

You go on and live life
Because nobody feels your pain
A loss can last a lifetime
Even though it can hit in a moment

Something that is gone
And can never come back

My grandmas

Julia Muller, Grade 6
Weston Middle School, CT

The Garden

The gorgeous
Petals droop down on to the
Bright green stem.
The brilliant red flowers
Shine like
The luminous
Moon in the velvety pitch
Black sky.
The rain drops go
Pitter patter on the soft, delicate,
Glasslike petals
And they burst with the silky
Soft rain.
Then…it stops, quiet, stillness, no sound,
Just the sweet sound
Of the wind rustling through the petals.
The strange yet
Beautiful array of the many unique flowers
Shine like a
Fantastic glittering new rainbow in the
Bright blue sky.

Jenny Lupoff, Grade 5
Coleytown Elementary School, CT

The Shark

Glides gently through the water.
Stealthy.
Silent.
Deadly.
The king of the ocean,
Dominates all the other creatures,
Treats its dominions with no mercy.
Powerful.
Unforgiving.
Its teeth are like jagged razor blades,
Tearing through flesh and bone.
Its eyes stare through the water at its soon to be prey
Nothing can overcome its wrath.

Peter Tortora, Grade 6
Scotts Ridge Middle School, CT

A Typical Monday Morning

Everybody stopped, turned, and stared at me,
What was wrong?
Was there something on my face?
Did I really dress that badly?
Could it have been another wacky hair day?

I turned around and sure enough,
23 5th grade eyes were on me,
At that moment I felt bare.

It's not like I was a new kid or anything,
It was just a regular Monday morning.

Charlotte Ferguson, Grade 5
Hindley Elementary School, CT

Drip Drop

I'm wet
I quickly spin 'round and 'round
Blown by the wind
Pushed to the ground
I'm now falling, falling oh so fast
Quickly go to the ground with a splash

Ally Bisegna, Grade 6
Village School, MA

Chocolate Frosted

The best time
of the week,
when my dad and I are
having our
Saturday morning
doughnuts.
Chocolate frosted
for me,
Boston cream pie
for him.
Finally,
time together
to talk.
Feeling safe,
his arm around
my shoulder.
Just dad and I,
together,
eating
doughnuts.

Leo Andriuk, Grade 5
Coleytown Elementary School, CT

An Astronaut Launch

Getting ready for launch!
I heard in a staticy voice,
Making sure I make the right choice.
THREE!
TWO!
ONE!
BLAST OFF!
Shooting so high
Up in the sky
Afraid I might die
Cry! Cry! Cry!
Through the atmosphere
I lost all my fear
Floating through space
At a very slow pace
On cloud nine
I'll be fine
Getting home just in time!

Brendan Cooney, Grade 4
Freetown Elementary School, MA

Gerger

There once was a cat named Gerger.
Who loved to eat a burger.
He tried chalk.
Then couldn't walk
Poor old Gerger.

Alex Shenk, Grade 4
Crestwood Elementary School, VA

Flowers

Flowers
Pink, red
Bloom, stand, worship
Flowers make me smile
Roses

Erika Dyer, Grade 4
Trinity Christian School, VA

Jumping in a Pool

Run
On the cold wet gravel
Stop running
Lifeguards screaming at you
Almost there
Suddenly
You slip
You fall in the pool
Water pushes against you
Cold
Freezing
I told you so
Screams the lifeguard
Jumping in a pool
Such a rush of excitement

Osebo Akhigbe, Grade 6
Grace Episcopal Day School, MD

My Dream*

My dream is to be them
My dream is to be them
To be a soccer star just like Beckham
Him is me, him is me
I said him is me, him is me
23, 23 that's all they say
But 19, 19 why would people care!
Talking trash, scoring goals and
Pass the ball that's what we do
Soccer isn't just some silly sport
It's life I said
It's L-I-F-E LIFE!
My dream is to be them
My dream is to be them

Akbar Maliki, Grade 5
Clover Street School, CT
*Inspired by Will.I.Am

Your Dreams*

Hold tightly to your dreams
Because a lost dream is like
A brother who doesn't care

Hold tightly to your dreams
Because a life without dreams
Is like a constant battle against yourself

Hold tightly to your dreams
Because a life without dreams
Is like fighting a family member;
Something you would never want to do

Spencer Royce, Grade 5
Clover Street School, CT
*Inspired by Langston Hughes

Dancing Dogs

Dancing dogs are fun to watch
dogs will be dogs and dance to
entertain.
My dog is still a great dancer and
entertains me too.
I do think he was born to dance
but nobody believes me.
If there were dog dancing contests
he'd be number one.
He's the best dancer.
At least that's what I think,
but maybe you don't think so
That's why I think dancing should
be for party dogs.

Shane O'Leary, Grade 5
Miscoe Hill Elementary School, MA

Helping Hand

One day I saw a man
Who needed a helping hand

The man was working on his car
He was gone so far

So, I gave him a helping hand
He said what a nice girl I am

Ty'Sheona Cook, Grade 6
Salem Church Middle School, VA

The Rodeo

The cowboy is brave as a lion
I would never do that
He is strong as an ox out in the rodeo
The cowboy is a skilled craftsman
Riding his horse on the way to victory.

Clint Almeida, Grade 4
Freetown Elementary School, MA

The Worst Day

It was Monday and I was tired,
Then I found that my cereal had expired.
So then I walked to school,
And slipped on ice like a fool.
This day has started off so bad,
I could tell I was going to be mad.
At my locker realized my best friend was on vacation,
In class, got yelled at for not meeting the expectation.
The next thing was a boring lesson,
It was a reading on Thomas Jefferson.
When I left school and arrived home,
I got bored and began to roam.
I started my homework but fell asleep,
And I knew I'd dug myself deep.
I slept all night to a magical dream,
But horror awoke me, I started to scream.
Why, why does it have to be me,
I'm having bad luck, as you can see.

Kyle Arruda, Grade 6
Edmond P Talbot Middle School, MA

Waffles

There are so many waffles out there,
There are so many waffles to share.
There's chocolate chip, blueberry, and strawberry,
And ones that are plain, but none that are hairy.
Some people eat one waffle,
I think that's awful.
I like to eat two while tying my shoe.
People have waffles for breakfast,
Some, for lunch, I like to eat them a whole bunch.
Waffles are great.
Waffles are fun,
But now the day is done.

Lianne Copertino, Grade 6
Salem Church Middle School, VA

Who Am I?

I am a radio, talking all the time to my friends
I am a mountain that's always upward
I am a lovely flower, bright like the moon
I am a diamond shining the world
I am a carnival dancing, singing
I am a colorful pencil who loves to write
I am the rain that does not stop falling from the sky
I am a lip gloss shining everywhere

Maria Gabriela Costa, Grade 6
Fuller Middle School, MA

American Idol

The worst American Idol singer is Sanjaya.
I'm glad American Idol said "good bye a."
He doesn't deserve fortune and fame,
Because his voice is so lame!

Marisa Mucha, Grade 6
Captain Nathan Hale Middle School, CT

Colors of the Rainbow

Red is a rose, all pure and bright,
Red is a cardinal, its wings in flight

Orange is a scrumptious fruit, juicy and sweet,
Orange is lovely, surely a treat

Yellow is an acerbic lemon, sour and tart,
Yellow is a wonder, a work of art

White is an intimidating ghost, all around the room,
White is a fabulous wedding, a bride and groom

Green is the forest, majestic and tall,
Green are the leaves, except in the fall

Blue is the vivid day sky, over the ocean so deep,
Blue is the alluring night sky, above us as we sleep

Purple is royal, the luxurious cloth on a crown,
Purple is your face when you hang upside down!

Emily Everlith, Grade 5
Hebron Elementary School, CT

Damp Puff Balls

Clouds floating as if they were marshmallows
cotton swabs gliding upon the baby blue sky
the wrinkly wonderful wads of white taking a stroll
sparkly wet rain drops
fall from the brilliant clouds
I feel as if
I were in a rainy wonderland
the cool damp grass
now tickling my dirty feet
the smell of scum from the pond across the road
bit my nose
the clouds now bursting
with an orange and red glow
saying goodnight.
I think to myself
what a peaceful day
gazing upon the horizon
nature is so relaxing!

Kimberly Higgins, Grade 6
Litchfield Intermediate School, CT

Moonlit Sky

I saw the moon up in the sky
It shone on down into the night
It glistened on the lake so blue
I heard the song the angels sing
I stayed all night till the rooster crowed
And waited until night came again

Duncan Harker, Grade 4
Courthouse Road Elementary School, VA

Civil War

A merica
M onitor Merrimac
E qual rights
R ed, white, and blue
I ndependence
C ivil War
A braham Lincoln
N ation

F reedom
L iberty
A bolished
G eneral Robert E. Lee

Ashley Cordner, Grade 4
Waller Mill Fine Arts Magnet School, VA

I Am

I am
I am a tornado
I wonder why
I hear kids screaming
I see her cry
I want her to play
I am lost
I pretend I know
I feel scared
I touch my heart
I worry about a lot
I cry myself to my home
I am love
I understand only what I can
I say "I love you"
I dream of you
I try to understand
I hope you will stay with me
I am a survivor.

Abygail Brown, Grade 6
Page Middle School, VA

Spring

Flowers blossoming
Cries of baby animals
Warm radiant sun

Julia Breed, Grade 4
Leicester Memorial School, MA

Colorado River

The Colorado River
deep and blue,
freezing cold at forty-two
through a thousand miles of canyons
and right straight through five states.
The Colorado River
I think it is so great!

Thomas Ziegenmeyer, Grade 4
Salem Elementary School, VA

Rain

Drip,
　Drop,
　　Drip,
The rain tapped on the roof like a person knocking on the door,
　Tip,
　　Tap,
　　　Tip,
Trickling down, falling from the sky
Like crystals,
　Shining,
　　Sparkling,
　　　Shimmering,
Breathing and blowing air in my face,
　Dripple,
　　Ripple,
　　　Dripple,
Like waves gently hitting the ocean floor, soaking my hair,
　Swish, Swash, Swish,
It simmers down to a gentle stir,
　Drip, Drop, Drip

Sammy Segal, Grade 5
John Ward Elementary School, MA

Forgotten Life

I'll never see once more the sunshine that heats my heart each lonely day.
And see the black ink shadows fall on great big trees.
Never smell the morning flowers, or taste the honey on my lips.
The fire that was burning in my chest is fading quickly.
I'm here in mindless heaven now with my soul in deep thought.
Forgotten life that seeks no past.
My life is gone in nothing less then nothing.

Nikita Safronov, Grade 5
Charlotte A Dunning Elementary School, MA

That Old Indian Flute

That flute, that old wooden flute,
You took my heart away with your wonderful joyful song,

The song that you play goes with the awakening of the sun into sky at dusk,
You flute, you take a very good idea of mine and change it into a painting,

That old Indian flute makes my dreams come alive when
I hear the joyful song, of the Indian flute.

The little girls and boys are put to sleep by your song,
Your song makes me rest in peace, that flute, that old Indian wooden
flute, that has a song that puts people to rest in peace,

That flute, that old wooden flute, that makes me happy.
My grandmother plays the flute, to rest me in peace at night,

That flute, that old wooden flute that has a very big history, is that flute.

Kristina Davignon, Grade 6
Memorial School, MA

Sports

Colts, Chiefs, and Cardinals too,
So many teams you don't know what to do

Shooting, blocking and dunking galore,
Don't get injured because you'll want to play some more

Practicing hard, shooting a goal,
Up against your bigger sibling, so go win some more

Dreaming 90 (mph), really is 10 (mph),
Acing the ball, go do it again

Flying majestically in the air,
Landing on the ice, you can't compare

The goalie's in your face, the crowd is cheering
You want some space, so get leaving

Esther Fuzayl, Grade 5
Krieger-Schechter Day School, MD

They Need to Learn

Europeans free from their king
no longer are the Africans
The ship rocking sending people
over the edge
Loaded on the auction block
to their owner sold
Pain from the whip
blood slithering down their back
Bruises from picking
crops all day
Respect only from people
of their own kind
They would rather die then
to stay away from their
home and family
They need to read
They need to write
They need to learn
About history.

Chris Wilson, Grade 5
Charlotte A Dunning Elementary School, MA

The Lovely House of God

A rainbow is its door,
And creatures of the earth its floor.
The moon its window pane,
The steps are made of mountain chains,
The owner's name shines as bright as the sun,
The gutters are the scales of fish,
The trees of earth and all the rocks form the walls.
The lovely house of God!

Brielle Stovall, Grade 5
Jacob Hiatt Magnet Elementary School, MA

Summer Fun

S kipping on the chalk ground
U niting with family and friend
M eeting new BFF's every day
M erry-go-rounds going around and around
E veryone having fun chasing BFF'S
R unning energetically

F un, fun, fun three cheers for fun
U SA is the country, we honor on Independence Day
N othing could be this fun, just summer.

Malaika Saint Juste, Grade 5
Sacred Heart Elementary School, MA

Christmas

Christmas
snowflakes falling from the sky
the fresh smell of warm milk
and chocolate chip cookies
I hear the sounds of bells ringing on the horse's sleigh
I taste the warm hot chocolate running down my throat
And I touch the icy cold snow piling up from the ground
Christmas

Ashley Koss, Grade 5
Jane Ryan School, CT

Ballet

Her movement is fluid and effortless,
as graceful as a swan.
Her body flows like the wings of a bird in the wind
or grass swaying in the summer breeze.
"Ooh, aah, wow," the crowd sounds
with every leap, turn and pirouette.
Ballet is music that is peaceful and relaxing
like a lovely lullaby soothing a little baby to sleep.
Ballet is freedom in the air
with leg stretched straight to the sky.
Angelic, soft, and tender,
Ballet is as mesmerizing as an eagle in flight.

Robyn Howard, Grade 6
Trinity School, MD

Skies*

In the sky
in the blue
I am always watching you.

In the soil
though I never spoil
I am always watching you.

In your heart
I know you're smart
and I am watching you.

Amanda Donelan, Grade 5
West Woods Upper Elementary School, CT
*Dedicated to Grandpa, who is loved

The Black Foot

Small shapes
Dart through
Tall grass.
Shiny eyes
Appear
Through
The undergrowth.
The black footed
Ferret is hunting!
As silent as a mime,
It sneaks toward
Its prey.
Wallop!
A prairie dog
Falls limp
Under the
Viselike grip
Of the cunning hunter
The black footed ferret
Has hunted.

George Murray, Grade 4
Braeburn School, CT

Rainbow

A rainbow fills the air.
It is going across the gray sky.
The day is quiet and peaceful.
I see red, yellow, and a little bit of
blue and green.
I feel so special!

Caroline Costello, Grade 4
Southbrook Academy, MA

Tornado

Wind twirling tumultuously
Tornado…Everyone look out!
Until it's too late.

Anna Mackay, Grade 5
Hebron Elementary School, CT

Flowers

Pushing strong and bright,
Flowers peek through spring soil
All around the meadow

Maxwell Bechtold, Grade 6
Our Lady of Mercy School, CT

Bugs

Creepy, crawly
Eat, fly, die
I like big bugs
Beetles

Sabrina Patton, Grade 4
Trinity Christian School, VA

Animals

P uppy dogs
R unning like a tiger
E ating like a cat
C ats like milk
I guanas are reptiles
O wls sleep during the day
U nicorns have corn in their name
S nakes have no arms or legs

Shaina Peters, Grade 4
Ridgeway Elementary School, MD

What a Starry Starry Night

What a starry, starry night!
The wind blowing,
The trees swaying in the wind.
What a starry, starry night.
The stars shining in pretty patterns,
The constellations sparkling brightly.
What a starry starry night!
How peaceful it is in the night.
Pretty patterns in the wind.
What a starry, starry night!

Linda Lauzier, Grade 4
Mount Hope Christian School, MA

Candle

Candle
Flaming, sparkling
Melting, glowing, burning
A halo of gold surrounds it.
Waxed wick.

Emily Straley, Grade 6
Scotts Ridge Middle School, CT

Spring Sprung

A mazing
B irds flying up in the sky
C hirps from the little birds
D aisies sprung in the grass
Spring sunny, beautiful, and warm!

Gianna Lionetti, Grade 6
Albert D Griswold Middle School, CT

Octopus

It's disgusting, wet
And has eight legs
I was dared to eat it —
Not knowing what it was
Don't try octopus
No matter what
Because you are
What you eat

Keyana Dorsey, Grade 4
Munger Hill Elementary School, MA

The Past

We have many questions about
what came before us.
So we study history.
We are limited to
what those before us
have chosen to share.
We still are yet to discover
every detail about the past.
We hope to discover
new things about ourselves
and the study of the past.

Olivia Lafferty, Grade 6
Wakefield Forest Elementary School, VA

Your Turn to Shine

All that glitters,
In the spotlight,
Your turn to shine and you'll be fine.
Let your heart be light,
Star light star bright,
Make the season be bright with light.
Comfort and joy, oh boy!
As you frolic and play,
Sparkle and shine,
Being warm and welcome,
When you're holly and jolly,
When you rise and shine,
When you're out and about,
When it's two by two,
Wishes and dreams,
Double the fun!

Lena Syed, Grade 4
E Ethel Little Elementary School, MA

Bugs Bunny

There is a character named Bugs Bunny,
I don't find him very funny.
He is just a silly gray rabbit,
And a humongous nitwit.

Devin Ellsworth, Grade 6
Captain Nathan Hale Middle School, CT

Christmas

C ookies are great for Christmas
" **H** appy Holidays" you hear
R ed and green are Christmas colors
I love Christmas
S anta comes every Christmas
T oys and lots of toys you get
M erry Christmas
A lways enjoys seeing family
S anta and his reindeer are great

Taylor Boehn, Grade 5
Jane Ryan School, CT

Spring

Peep! Chirp! Squawk!

The sound of baby birds
walking in the wood
shatters the silence of morning.

The scent of tulips and daffodils
floats fragrantly across the springtime sky.

Kites, with their small pilots below,
ride the wind
through a battlefield of trees and towers.

In the marsh, frogs form a midnight melody
of croaks and groans,
summoning the day to a close.

Elissa DeStefano, Grade 6
Trinity School, MD

The Land of the Books

I lie in my bed with the sheets half off
Preparing to go on a vacation
To go where my wonderful book takes me
I carefully open the bound papers
To enter the Land of the Books
A fuzzy gray and white feline
Lays on the snow colored mattress
I hear nothing except the voices of the characters
My hands are so weak,
Barely able to hold the book
I am motionless
But my eyes move like sprinklers
As they reach the end of the page
And every so often
My hand jerks toward the book
and slowly lifts up,
the black and white page
The corners of my mouth turn up at funny remarks
And raindrops rain down my cheeks when a character dies
I never want to leave the Land of the Books

Julia Feinstein, Grade 5
John Ward Elementary School, MA

Nervous in Basketball

I am on the court shooting the game winning shot.
The ball goes up and I go down.
I cannot look!
Tell me what happens.
Swish…
What?
It went in!
Yes!
We won the game!
I always knew we could win!

Thomas Conlon, Grade 6
Southbrook Academy, MA

Dogs/Cats

Dogs
Dogs are cool
Dogs love to play with people
Cats are fast and flea bags, dogs play with people
Cats like to eat a lot
Cats sleep
Cats

Justin Umstot, Grade 4
Ridgeway Elementary School, MD

Ice Cream Cake

Thinking of an object, actually food.
Not chicken, not even a chocolate milkshake.
I don't think you'll get it, and I'm not trying to be rude.
This is taking too long. I'll just tell you,
Ice Cream Cake!

Ice cream cake is so tasty!
I would swim in it — if it melted into a lake.
This poem is almost done so don't be hasty
So sweet and cold — that's why I love ice cream cake!

Gerald Paradela, Grade 5
Sacred Heart Elementary School, MA

Mom

Do not stand by my mom's grave and weep
She is not there she does not sleep

When the moon shines at night
I think of her smile big and bright

Even though she can't push me in the shopping cart
She is number one in my heart

I think about her with every step I take
And with ever shot I make

I know my mom is watching over me
If I think about her in sports she is the key to victory

Do not stand by my mom's grave and cry
She is not there she did not die

Steven Johnson, Grade 6
Quashnet School, MA

Halloween

Children running about
The scent of sweet smelling candy in the air
Listening to giggling children
Sweet chocolate melting in my mouth
Fuzzy wolf costumes
Halloween

Marisa Gnandt, Grade 5
Jane Ryan School, CT

Why Am I Here

Why am I here, why do I care
all I do here is sit here and stare.

I sit in a chair, looking at a wall,
wishing I was not in here at all.

I look to my side, and see a
   big
      bed
   of flowers,
I'd like to go out and smell them,
but I just sit here for hours and hours.

But I sit in a chair, looking at a wall,
wishing I was not in here at all.
Oakley Roach, Grade 5
Francis Asbury Elementary School, VA

Ireland

Ireland's a country.
Leprechaun's gold is magic.
Shamrocks give you luck.
Marly Frederique, Grade 4
St Gregory Elementary School, MA

A Summer Night

A summer breeze blows gently,
as fireflies softly glow.
Crickets chirp, owls hoot,
and trees sway to and fro.

Stars shine in the nighttime sky,
the moon is very low.
Summer nights are wonderful,
and beautiful, I know.
Isabella Husu, Grade 5
Davenport Ridge School, CT

Caves

Quiet and lonely
Deserted and very dark
Bats glaring at you

Sometimes there's a glow
Sparkling, gentle, white crystals
The whole cave turns white

Other times there's echoes
Voices bouncing off the walls
In wide tunnel space

It's bad to be lost
Not knowing where you should go
Be careful in caves
A.J. Norton, Grade 5
Jane Ryan School, CT

Winter

White snow lays quietly on the frozen ground
The water is running in the small stream
Snow crunches softly underneath me
Small robins tweet from time to time
Thorns want to claw me as I walk by
Large logs want to trip me as I walk over them
Everything is still

It smells of pine trees
Deer tracks were planted quietly in the snow
Distant woodpeckers peck at a tree
Across the stream trees stand alone with no leaves
I kneel upon a smooth snow covered rock
Bright red berries are scattered among the trees

A squirrel bounces softly in and out of the trees
Different sized trees are covered in a thick coat of bumpy brown bark
Leaves are swaying quietly in the whistling wind
Moss is growing slowly up the lovely trees

Where snow has melted dead leaves lay in its place
Pale green grass grows on the side of the stream
Small trees and plants surround me
Years from now I hope the forest will still be able to keep growing
Sorrell Bourgeois, Grade 5
Tyngsboro Elementary School, MA

The Sun, the Moon and the Milky Way

The moon is a gentle man.
Dancing with the sun.
If you look up you can see it.
So in the dark of night
Look up at its shining light.
But be careful not to look too late.
Look before it skates away.
   Across the Milky Way:

The Milky Way is a gentle man.
Dancing with the moon.
You can see its trail of stars.
Very, very clear.
Look up at it in the dark of night.
But if you look too late
It too will skate away.
   In the light of the shining sun:

I will tell you the sun is a woman
There is something that I must explain.
You cannot look up at the sun
Like you look up at the moon and the Milky Way.

And that is what I know about: the Moon, the Sun, and the Milky Way
Sarah Quagliariello, Grade 5
Coleytown Elementary School, CT

Falling Leaves

They crunch under my feet,
And tangle with my hair
As they gently glide down.
Swiftly, yet gently they touch the ground,
Mingling with the dirt.
The sunset casts a gleam of light on them
Making the whole ground gold.
Every morning when I wake up
I see the glowing leaves gliding off the trees
Just as snowflakes fall from the sky

Hannah Barbash-Taylor, Grade 6
Memorial-Spaulding Elementary School, MA

Tommy

Tommy's a swing reaching towards the sky
His weather is partly sunny
He is a calm ocean, but sometimes choppy with waves
Tommy is a jeep — vroom, vroom
A blue jay with windmills as wings
A rectangle, skinny and tall.
Tommy is a teddy graham.
A piano, soft, but then loud
Sweatpants, comfy and cozy.
Tommy is rap music,
Blues so mellow and so calm,
He is Prison Break, suspenseful and mysterious.
Tommy is shepherd pie with so many ingredients.
He is Einstein, and a gold medal too,
Watching ESPN every day.
Tommy's blonde hair is the sun's golden rays.
His blue eyes are a child's happy face on Christmas Day.
His smile lights up the room with delight.
Tommy's the peacemaker, always breaking up the fights.
He is the caregiver.
Tommy, I love you so very much!

Jessica Quindlen, Grade 5
St Luke's School, CT

God Bless Arizona

God bless Arizona,
You're a place I love so much,
With your prickly cactuses I'll remember not to touch

God bless Arizona,
Where the sun shines all day long,
Where the cowboys come and go,
Singing their sad, sweet songs

God bless Arizona,
I hope to come again,
With your sparking wildlife,
In me you've got a friend

Sally Todd, Grade 6
Thomas Blake Middle School, MA

Hope

Shivers, creeps and goosebumps,
Strong cruel white men
whip until blood comes.
Unbelievable sights,
Dogs like monsters
come to eat you.
All slaves are wealth,
All hope to get free.

Carolina Felix, Grade 5
Charlotte A Dunning Elementary School, MA

No More

No more will I hide,
From what I want to say,
And no more will I hurt myself,
By not reaching for what I feel I need,
No more will I keep it in,
All that I've been meaning to say,
And to feel so many things,
But to at the same time feel completely empty,
And to need so many answers left unanswered,
But to not even know,
What the true question you're asking is,
To not be happy with the true you,
But still be asking who is the real me,
To not be able to answer the simple questions,
That you're asking yourself,
But no more will I ask questions,
I will just answer all that I ask,
And when I find the answer,
I will find who the real me is,
And then no more will I need to hide my feelings,
Or will I?

Taylor Goodman, Grade 6
Bates Middle School, MD

The End of the World

Screaming children, crying babies,
Everyone hiding, even the Navy!

Meteors crashing onto my house,
Everything dying, even a mouse,

Look at the sun, it's coming too close!
A huge black hole, who's its next host?

This is a disaster, as you can see,
It's the end of the world, help me, help me!

I wake up screaming, I bump my head,
I've been sleeping in class, my face is all red,

The teacher's so angry, he must think me a pest,
Oh no, I've just slept through the math test!

Thomas Maye, Grade 4
Forest Avenue Elementary School, MA

Cars

Cars,
Cars,
Cars,
Revving cars,
Racing cars,
Jumping, flying, flipping cars,
Crashed, new, noisy cars,
Those are just a few.
Rusty cars,
Fast, slow, shiny cars,
Dull, dirty, artistic cars,
Funny cars, too.
Clown cars,
Clean cars,
Don't forget Chevy cars.
Last of all,
Best of all,
I like Toyota cars.

Patrick Nolan, Grade 4
Riderwood Elementary School, MD

Homework

H orrible
O minous
M uch unwanted
E vil
W retched
O verwhelmingly
R ancid
K ey to boredom

John Dolan, Grade 6
Wakefield Forest Elementary School, VA

Words with Meaning

Waking from
A frightful dream
Can change
Your life's
Devotion
Simple things
Can change
Your life
Forever
Don't fret
Your destiny
Of misery
Just wait
And grow out of it
Like
Growing out of clothes
Then just
Go Free

Emily Kopacz, Grade 5
John F Kennedy School, CT

Without Me

They were sledding,
without me
again.
They didn't bother
to invite me.
They whispered
and laughed
and I was sure,
it was about,
me.
I stood,
hidden
behind a clutter
of brambles.
Watching,
spying,
and they
did not know
I
was
there…

Alia Metke, Grade 5
Coleytown Elementary School, CT

A Hard Life

It's winter and the snow is falling
So hard you can't see.
A fox runs across the field
Showing off her sleek fur
So welcoming and warm
She belches out her cries of hunger.
Then you see two little cubs
Running up to her.
You can feel her pain,
Trying to find food for them all.
But when spring comes
You bet you will see her again.
She will be happy with her cubs
Running and dancing in the field
With happiness and joy in their hearts.

Cecilia Nygren, Grade 5
Soule Road School, MA

A Lost Dream*

Hold tightly to your dreams
Because a lost dream
Is like a person with no love.

Hold tightly to your dreams
Because a life without dreams
Is like a person without a soul.

Jevaughn Campbell, Grade 5
Clover Street School, CT
*Inspired by Langston Hughes

Deep in the Forest

Birds sing quietly in
the distance
All is peaceful,
Leaves fall to the moist ground
under a pine tree.
Butterflies flutter near by.
They are outlined in
black with wings of red,
orange and yellow.
Soothing songs of the birds
make your heart
feel at
home.

Amelia Burke, Grade 4
Southbrook Academy, MA

Wintertime

Wintertime is fun
When cousins come to visit
Snow ball fights,
A cup of hot chocolate,
Warms your body!

Jeremy Piper, Grade 6
Benjamin Syms Middle School, VA

Lucky Pencil

Lucky pencil so pointy and big.
You help me get A's on my history quiz.
Lucky pencil so pointy and big.
Wait you're no longer pointy.
Sharpen, sharpen, sharpen,
Now you are pointy.

Vanesa Guevara, Grade 5
Clark Avenue Middle School, MA

Weather and Trees

Rain
Leaking from up high
Comes down from clouds when heavy
Makes the ground mushy
Snow
Falling from above
They soon create a blanket
You then can have fun
Sun
Heating from up high
You may become very hot
Now you need to cool
Trees
Towering above
Shades of light green and dark brown
Branches break in storms

Charlotte Kendall, Grade 5
Jane Ryan School, CT

Aunt Barbara's Old House

Stranded at my aunt's house branded a fool
the eagles are a swoopin' and the geeses are a poopin'
it can be very scary when the moon is full.

The giant trees out the window that touch the night sky
the owls with their big glowing eyes
put together look like a monster that could make anyone cry.

It leaks and it creaks and I can't tell you why
The light switches are impossible to find.
Just a few more days to keep my pants dry.

Nick Cabral, Grade 5
Pasadena Elementary School, MD

Why We Don't Eat Ice Cream in Winter

We don't eat ice cream in wintertime,
Like we don't drink hot cocoa in summer.
If you do consume ice cream in the wintertime,
Your teeth will chatter,
Like wind up teeth.
You'll have a brain freeze,
Your brain will be frozen just like ice.
And you would have to wear a jacket, scarf, and gloves,
Just to enjoy ice cream in the wintertime.

Hannah Frobenius, Grade 5
Tilghman Elementary School, MD

Guitar

I love to be played
I can talk to you with my music notes by my amp
I have to get tuned once in a while or I sound weird
My strings get plucked and go DOING
I get bored when I sit down idle in your corner.

Lexi Rogers, Grade 6
Page Middle School, VA

Trees

I sit under an apple tree,
a place that's surely just for me.
A place where I am all alone,
a place that I can call my own.

Trees are wonderful, wonderful things,
They let us breathe, they make birds sing.

On trees, you find branches and leaves,
That swish so beautifully in the breeze.
You also find some bugs and berries,
Birds like owls, crows, canaries!

Mother Nature's been really smart,
to make this wonderful work of art.
A work of art that's like no other,
So please, let's thank our Nature Mother!

Sophia Plant, Grade 4
Hemenway Elementary School, MA

The Glory of Day

The sun is rising,
Day is coming,
Night is leaving.
The stars are falling,
People are waking,
The cheerful light of day is here.

Tyler Myles, Grade 4
Helen H Hansen Elementary School, MA

Slaves

Helpless, African
serving, running, weeding
captured, powerless, working
escaping, telling, farming
tormented, fight
African American

Kylie Zonghetti, Grade 5
Charlotte A Dunning Elementary School, MA

Lucky Leprechaun

Oh, Lucky Leprechaun,
Tricky as you are,
I hope you know tonight
He's out — the big bad Jaguar

There's no tricking him this time,
For he's a friend of mine.
He's been trained to hunt you down,
No matter rain or shine

And when he gets you ('cause he will)
I'll find all your gold,
And when I do, you'll go bye-bye,
Well that's what I was told.

Emily Hogge, Grade 4
C Hunter Ritchie Elementary School, VA

Winter Thoughts

I step outside and everything is still
My feet go, "crunch, crunch, crunch"
Behind me are the imprints
Of my steady growing life.

We never know what could happen
In the future that we wish for,
But enjoy everything you have right now
Before it disappears before your own eyes.

I look behind again and again
To see how far I've gotten.
But I have been too much of a worrywart.
All I've taken is one little step.

Erica Oh, Grade 6
E W Thurston Middle School, MA

Come Home Soldier

Come —
Oh I
Miss you,
Easy for you to die.

Home —
Oh I want you
My loved one,
Empty am I.

So long…
Oh please come home,
Love you
Dearly,
I need you
Eager,
Ready to have you home.

Isel Fitzgerald, Grade 6
Grace Episcopal Day School, MD

In the Land That Is Gold

In a land that is gold,
There is an apple tree.
In a land that is silver,
There is a tree of pears.
In a land of diamonds,
There is a vine of grapes.
And in the land of fruitless greed,
There is a seed of hope.

Jenna Froland, Grade 5
St Luke's School, CT

Ice/Fire

Ice
cold, hard
freezing, crackling, sharp
forming, cracking, disintegrating, moving
burning, destroying, cooking
hot, painful
Fire

Mitchell Leonard, Grade 5
Jane Ryan School, CT

Gymnastics, Gymnastics I Love

I love gymnastics
I said I love gymnastics
love to flip front and back
love to do cartwheels and back bends
love to show off like I never did before
love to swing like a monkey on a rope
love to make new friends
love to meet new teachers
and show them all my skills
because I love gymnastics!

Bryanna Clarke, Grade 5
Clover Street School, CT

Summer Days

The sun shining like ice cold lemonade
Clouds disappear like ice cream
Birds in a bird bath people in a pool
Wow I love today it is beautiful,
I love summer days they're so fun
Hold on one sec let me put my hamburger on a bun
Hey I am back all I hear is the little duck quack,
Hey put some more burgers on the grill rack.
I am sitting here swinging away
Oh my goodness we have to say goodbye to the day.
As I was leavin' a duck got close but I gotten closer so it just fled,
Well bye little ducks got to get ready for bed.

Donna Koger, Grade 6
E Russell Hicks School, MD

If I Were a Wave

If I were a wave, I'd come crashing down along the silent, calm shore.
My turquoise claws would scratch the soft white sand.
The fish would move over and under my skin.
I would be a safe haven to many marvelous sea creatures.
I would be majestic and powerful.
I would be king to all creatures living in me.
Every second I would be scratching the sand.
Will I ever stop?
Who knows?
I don't.
If I were a wave.

Evie Chodock, Grade 5
Weston Intermediate School, CT

The Thoughts You Think When Your Father Is Dead

I try to grasp the thought that inside that box is my father.
I want to hear a desperate cry for help,
a cry that would signal life, that death was a mistake.
I understand that cry will never come.
That cry drifted away in the morning breeze.
I try to grip my conflicting emotions of anger and sorrow.
I feel alone; this is a time even my conscience is confused.
I try to understand what my father thought as he drew his last breath.
My mother comforts me, tells me no one will ever know.
The teardrops fall from my face.
They felt so safe inside my eyes, so peaceful.
They fall and land with a splash, too tiny to see or hear.
I suppose that tomorrow will be just like today,
another day of sorrow, anger, and confusion.
I have to stand on my own two feet and put on a fake smile.
When I go home I will feel safe, safe from other people, safe from myself.
I lock away that smile until tomorrow.
Two weeks ago I was a breath away from him, safe in his embrace.
I never knew that would be the last time I would hear his deep voice,
the last time I would hug his large figure,
and the last time I would say, "I love you. Goodbye."

Danielle Baker, Grade 6
Swampscott Middle School, MA

Imagination

My imagination…
what a great sensation.

It's fun and it's boring.
Or just plain old ignoring!

It's about anything I want it to be.
It can be about cats, bats, or just some rats.

It's time for me and my imagination,
imagination.

Sophia Shepard, Grade 4
Courthouse Road Elementary School, VA

Springtime

March is the season when winter goes away,
And when spring is here to stay.
Springtime is the brightness of the year,
It's when the birds chirp merrily in your ear.
The season offers a variety of rain and shine —
That's what makes it so divine!
Spring is the time when the grass is so green,
And when the air seems so clean!
Spring brings the baby blue eggs in a robin's nest.
Spring is the season that brings out nature at its best!

Brooke Barney, Grade 5
Har-Bur Middle School, CT

Let's Go Let's Go We Are Half Way There

My heart is beating, yours ain't.
Hurry up, I'm about to faint!
Let's run into Mom's fast car.
Before I feel like the place is too far.
Let's go, let's go, we're almost there!

Drive fast, drive fast!
For shall I have last.
I try to figure out and think —
And I would get flash futures and start to blink.
Let's go, let's go, we're almost there!

Yes, yes we are halfway there.
Now when I see it I really care.
From faraway I've seen some slides.
And also lots of beautiful rides.
Let's go, let's go, were almost there.

I know the fun place now, It's Water Country.
When I see everything I just go and it's funny —
I went to a huge pool, it has a huge wave.
All the kids go there it's the new rave.
Let's go, let's go, yes we're already here.

Idaliz Moreno, Grade 6
Gerard A Guilmette School, MA

Inside This

Inside this baseball all dark and solid
Flying through the air soaring forever

Always waiting
"Clunk" goes the bat and down it goes
Scraping, bouncing, leaping
Hitting the dirt

Then hitting a soft pad
Picked up and thrown soaring again
Then hitting another pad

"Out" I hear

Finally soaring again forever and ever
"Clunk" goes the bat again
Soaring this time through the air

Farther and farther I go
Suddenly I bounce on cold metal
Slipping and fall down into the dark, cold, green bush

Waiting, just waiting forever

Michael Kuzbel, Grade 5
Newton-Lee Elementary School, VA

Horses

Horses galloping
Grazing to eat golden grass
Wandering the plain.

Bryanna Haskell, Grade 5
Foxborough Regional Charter School, MA

I Am

I am Lynda-Rose
I am 10
I am a year older every April 5th
I am soon to be 11
I am Italian
I am smart
I am on Cole Road
I am a big yellow house
I am big birthday parties every April 5th
I am ice cream by the beach each summer
I am Maine with Emily and family every year
I am vacations to places near and far
I am a singer dancer actress and model
I am Jeter Potter and Mr. T
I am dance 24/7
I am kind
I am nice
I am brave
I am fun and funny
I am friendly, I am ME!

Lynda-Rose Vecchiarello, Grade 5
Willis E Thorpe School, MA

The Sun

The sun shines every day it makes a path throughout the sky.
It spins around the world, but we only see it as steady as a plastic Barbie doll.
Every summer day the sun glistens with beams of light above us.
People play, people swim, people gather feelings as the sun shines above us.
Then no matter what season when the day comes to an end the sun retakes its path
from where it came from and its luminous feeling rolls down and is put away for the day.

Jamie Tanzer, Grade 5
Coleytown Elementary School, CT

A Sport's Affection

The definition of a sport has changed over the years because of thugs such as Ron Artest and Mike Vick
But the definition is when a winner devotes his or her body to the gym, diamond or field
Then your heart and soul follows your body
It is like you live in the diamond, gym or the field
This shows your love and passion for the game
But that is not all, this exhibits your love and passion of life
This shows that you always want to get better at life
A sport is not just a game

Chris King, Grade 5
Blueberry Hill Elementary School, MA

Zebra Conflicts

I gaze across a vast wasteland while in the distance the lion snarls and I fear that I am next.
The water hole is crowded I squeeze between the giraffes,
These are constant struggles for a Zebra like me
But there is something more difficult I face every day
Am I black with white stripes or white with black stripes
YOU DECIDE!

Jack Murphy, Grade 6
Litchfield Intermediate School, CT

Tractor Ride

I step up onto the slippery hay
The titan tractor trembles on this fall day
As I meander along
I see squirrels collecting nuts; they're as busy as a movie theater on opening night
There is a smell of fresh air surrounding me
The dandelion yellow maple leaves scatter on the ground and form what looks like a puzzle
The matchstick-like twigs snap under the tractor's roar
As I pass the pretty pumpkin patch
I see kids screaming with joy as they pick the perfect oblong and apricot colored pumpkin for Halloween
The wind howls like a coyote in the night
The white frost covers the ground like a blanket covering a cold child
I can almost taste the piping hot cinnamon apple pie as I pass the store
The colorful blue jays and cardinals chirp
The goldenrod flowers gleam
The formidable tractor pulls to a stop
The ride is over
What a great October day

Nicole Schwartz, Grade 6
Madison Middle School, CT

Born
You are born
into the world

You can see
You can hear

As you get older
You say mama and dada

But when you die
You go to heaven silently

Gwendolyn Thomas, Grade 4
Courthouse Road Elementary School, VA

The Day of the Purple Heart
One day in the biggest battle of the Vietnam War,
I stand not knowing death would be on this day.
The soft wind sang, "you're ready."
I get into battle and the guns fire and fire,
I look over my shoulder, my friends are against a wall,
A Vietnamese soldier fires a shot.
I jump in front of the bullet.
When it hits me, I see my whole life flash before me.
When I hit the ground my skin is pale, I am cold.
My friends were spared but I was not.
This is the day of the Purple Heart.

Connor Bailey, Grade 4
John F Kennedy School, CT

Forever
It is flowing all over graciously.
Covering over all the erroneous thoughts.
Marine water is crossing left and right.
It brings you into a wonderful world

Calmly and gently bringing the sunset down
A place more spectacular than earth,
To a place beyond the heavens.

Make a splash in this perfect water.
Float on the dream,
Take a step back from the world.
Swim in the calm life living journey.

Dive down where all is placid and serene.
Feel the soaking sand.
Feel like being in a lax place for eternity.

Leaving this wonder,
It is a terrible thought.
No more idealness.
I can't imagine ever leaving this forever.
Goodbye I must say,
Forever.

Anna Giannuzzi, Grade 4
North Street School, CT

The Clock
Your face is white,
Your numbers clean,
Your hands are strong,
Your rule supreme.

You tick and tock,
We hear the chime,
We work and play,
'Till the ends of time,

We listen to:
The sound you make,
At the end of the day,
Until daybreak,

As the seasons change,
We grow older,
You stay still,
But your face gets colder.

We feed you energy,
And watch your hands,
We clean your face,
You rule the lands.

Adina Friedman, Grade 6
Lenox Memorial Middle and High School, MA

Yellow
Yellow bees
Yellow trees
Yellow yellow things

Yellow flowers
Not that many hours
Until I go to yellow world,
Somewhere I go almost every day,
My own little fairyland.

Where I pick yellow flowers
next to the leaves that I play in,
under the trees where bees fly around me.

I love it, I love it, I love it

A bunch of yellow yellow things.
All right here in this world
full of nature,
that I call my own.

Yellow bees
Yellow trees
Yellow yellow yellow please

Kate Aiello, Grade 5
Miscoe Hill Elementary School, MA

This Is Where You'll Find Me

This is where you'll find me
A grassy rice field
The soft Indian breeze
Pushing my hair back
Here I am beautiful
The red-hot-flaming sun
Warms me inside
I open my eyes and look far
The green is infinite
My eyes could walk forever on it
A stray dog trudges along the dirt path
Not disturbing the tranquility
Here I feel calm and serene
Time flies by, waiting for no one
The moon silently creeps up on me
The light brightening the scene
I look up and see a star
Slowly they all appear, one by one
As abundant as the grass
Here I am lulled to sleep
By the peace
Khushwant Dhaliwal, Grade 5
St Luke's School, CT

Brave

B rothers working together
R isking life every day
A stounding, great, and caring
V eterans ready to fight
E veryone thanks them, too
Christopher Vixama, Grade 5
Sacred Heart Elementary School, MA

Celtics

C onsistent all the time
E ast's best record
L arry Legend's Legacy
T he leagues best record
I nterceptions by Rondo
C onfident all the time
S till holds the most titles
Dylan Porcaro, Grade 4
Leicester Memorial School, MA

Swamp

Swamp
murky ground
a quiet creepy
gloomy creature-filled land
trees looming overhead
around you
Swamp
Nathaniel Rowe, Grade 5
J F Kennedy Middle School, MA

Ireland

Shamrocks are all green
Pretty lucky leprechauns
Beautiful country
Richelene Pierre, Grade 4
St Gregory Elementary School, MA

My Brother

My brother Johnny is very cute,
And always filled with joy.
He has a passion for tools,
From hammers to screws.
Every day he cries his head off,
Just to go to Home Depot.
He loves when people play with him,
It puts a smile on his face.
He likes to feel loved,
And welcomed.
He has gorgeous blue eyes,
And cute chubby cheeks.
Angela Tournas, Grade 5
Toquam Magnet School, CT

Anger

Anger
Is like fire.
Anger burns like the sun.
It tastes
Like a whole bottle
Of hot sauce.
Sounds like screams
Pouring through the air.
It is like a thunderstorm.
It's cold like ice.
Anger smells like
Burnt tomatoes.
Anger,
Like the worst thing in the world,
It's your family
And your friends
Gone
Forever.
Jillian Gibney, Grade 4
Hawley Elementary School, CT

Friends

Friends are like brothers and sisters
You never had.
Some are funny.
Some are mean.
Some are nice
And feel like they are
The right friend.
Miguel Chicas, Grade 4
Bensley Elementary School, VA

The Land of the "Free"

America, the land of the free,
Or so it's called.
What about the bad things,
The hard times,
The sorrows and the woes?
Hate crimes,
Racist acts,
It always happens
To the misunderstood!
What is freedom?
What is not?
Is it hurting your friends
Just because they're different?
Or is it respecting each other
And finding the similarities?
America, the land of the free,
Or so it's called.
Noah Elkind, Grade 6
Silver Spring International School, MD

Spring

Spring is the time when
it's warm, warm, warm
Spring is the time when
the plants grow, grow, grow
Spring is the time when
winter goes, goes, goes
Said Kantarevic, Grade 5
Clark Avenue Middle School, MA

A Man from Japan

There once was a man from Japan.
Who hit his head on a pan.
He fell on the floor.
'Cause someone opened the door.
Now he's in a cat scan.
Brianna Raphino, Grade 4
Sacred Heart School, MA

What Is the Sun?

What is the sun?
A warm welcome in the morning
A sunny smile
A hot day in August
A bright star
A natural gift
An energy boost for the plants
The hot sand on the beach
What would make a puddle boil
The sunrise in the morning
The sunny days outside
That is the sun!
Christina Ricitelli, Grade 5
Jane Ryan School, CT

My Family

My family is great,
Even after we debate
I have three brothers, including me is four
I have to listen to screaming
When I'm told to clean my room
I get mad when my brother does not help me, that's true
My parents say "No"
When they don't know what's up
When they do, they say "Yup!"
I am writing this poem to let you see
What my family means to me.

Jordan Hunter, Grade 5
Clover Street School, CT

Baseball

Baseball is a game that can get intense,
There is also a lot of suspense.
Make sure you tie your laces,
Before you start stealing bases.
When I'm not playing, I am in the dugout,
And that's when I love to shout.
When I run,
I think it's a lot of fun.
I love when the bat yells whack and crack,
Then I go to the concession stand,
For a delicious snack!

Sean Burke, Grade 5
Toquam Magnet School, CT

Look at Anna, My Twin

Eyes sky blue
Hair sugar brown
Lips red like a strawberry.

She's an ice skate
Always sharp like a butcher's knife
Her blade cuts a smooth path across the rink
She makes herself
Look graceful like a swan on ice
Always with a friend.

She's a jump rope
Worn from play
Full of fun
Ready for you, too, on a sunny day
Tough like a jump rope
She sticks up for me.

She's a breeze
She cools me off when I am angry
But sometimes she blows things off course.
That's Anna, my twin!

Beatrix Bradford, Grade 5
West Woods Upper Elementary School, CT

On the Trail

We are walking,
walking down the trail.

The mud is squishing,
squishing between our boots.

We are walking,
walking down the trail.

All the birds are flying,
flying from tree to tree.

We are walking,
walking down the trail.

We all do this until it is time,
time to head back.

Amanda Edson, Grade 5
Jacob Hiatt Magnet Elementary School, MA

The Shade of the Willow Tree

The weeping willow gives me shelter,
protection from the cold,
brisk wind.
Sitting at the foot of the tree,
I wonder:
Why does the willow tree cry?

Weeping willow,
have you seen poor people
looking for food and shelter?
Do you know about the wars,
hate, and pain?

Someday,
some time,
everyone will love one another.
No one will be cold,
lonely,
or hungry.
But that day will not be
for a long time
and until then
I will find refuge under the willow's branches.

Scott Walker, Grade 6
Swampscott Middle School, MA

Illuminating

Night
Mysterious, dark
Frightening, illuminating, chilling
Owls, moonlight, sunrise, butterflies playing, blinding, working
Beautiful, active
Day

Rebecca Pranger, Grade 6
Captain Nathan Hale Middle School, CT

School

Sometimes school is cool
but I'd rather be in a pool.
The teachers are crazy
their hair all wavy.
The gym is the BEST
it beats all the rest.
But when it comes down to
Field Day in May...
The teachers are fun
see them while they run.
But later we sadly say...
"Goodbye for now, see you tomorrow!"
Nicolette Kyeremateng, Grade 4
John F Kennedy School, CT

Winter

Blanket of snow
Will never go!
The coats are furry
Vacation comes in a hurry!
Bare trees
Good-bye bees!
Santa's coming
Kids are humming.
Blue and white
Snowball fight!
Meredith Galaid, Grade 5
J F Kennedy Middle School, MA

Sunflower

Petals so bright
Rays of sunlight
Center so rough
Feels funny to touch
Stem as green
As the grass

I hope this flower lasts
Rachelle Joyal, Grade 5
St Mary's Primary School, MA

Living, Hoping, and Dreaming

When you live, you hope
When you hope, you believe.
When you believe, you dream.
And when you dream...
May you follow your dreams.
Tion Edmonds, Grade 4
Salem Elementary School, VA

Winter

It's cold in winter
And when it is cold enough
It can also snow
Chris Corbin, Grade 5
Marley Elementary School, MD

Autumn Is Coming

Autumn's coming I can smell it in the fresh air,
Amber leaves crackle beneath me like a crackling fire
My cousin chipmunks chirp a song,
Sounding as though they were playing a flute with tiny fingers
Tremendous tall trees tower above me,
As I race to my maple standing like a soldier ready for battle
Bitter blueberries burn my tongue as I stuff some into my cheeks
Squirrels scramble to cozy nests at tree tops,
While I crawl in my den among snarled maple roots
Icicle like air sneaks down to my skin like a spy,
Sending a shiver down my spine
I wrap my fluffy tail around myself preparing for sleep
But I tell you, autumn has begun, I smell it, it's here.
Victoria Primavera, Grade 6
Madison Middle School, CT

Snowflakes

Snowflakes dance throughout the night.
They stick their landing on my roof.
When I get up in the morning they've already gotten the trees dressed.
As I go out to play they tap on my head as if to give me a message.
Their combination of six arms and legs are stretching out to me.
While I am putting my head on my pillow to go to sleep
I can see the snowflakes out of my window diving into the winter sky.
Oh snowflakes you are so wonderful.
Alexa Werner, Grade 5
Weston Intermediate School, CT

Waiting

The polar bear waits by the shore every day,
Just waiting, waiting,
For some hope of the meaning of life.
She dives into the ocean, with sea foam spraying around her,
To catch some fish for herself and her starving baby,
But almost drowns.
She gazes out to the horizon with her sharp black eyes,
Eager to catch a glimpse of perhaps one speck, one minuscule dot of white,
But blue surrounds her, and she is trapped.
And every day,
She wonders if this day will be her last.

The mother waits by the hospital from morning to night,
Just dying, dying,
To hear good news of her son —
That he is well,
That he is alive,
And that he is surrounded by angels.
She prays that the medicine will take away his pain,
But the door never opens to bring her with reports of life, or even death.
No hope, no opportunity.

The clock is ticking, ticking on life...remember that.
Grace Chuang, Grade 6
Colvin Run Elementary School, VA

Freedom

Freedom is white like the clouds in the sky
and also like snow on a cold winter's day.
It paces through my mind as I know I am free,
it reminds me of the times soldiers come home from war.
It makes me feel happy like getting a hug.
It makes me want to smile!

Devan Barlock, Grade 5
Newton-Lee Elementary School, VA

I Am Star

I am star
I wonder if I can come to Earth
I hear cars and kids at night
I see I'm very high in the sky
I want to see people up close
I am star
I pretend to be the sun and moon
I feel sad
I touch other stars
I worry if people want to take us
I cry when I'm all alone
I am star
I understand I can't come down to Earth
I say I will try to come down
I dream of becoming a shooting star
I try to fly over the sky
I hope to be a bigger and better star
I am star

Bristy Moore, Grade 6
Page Middle School, VA

Bananas

Sweet sweet monkey food
The shape of the crescent moon
Color of yellow

Robert Soriano, Grade 5
Charlotte A Dunning Elementary School, MA

School

S tudents walk into St. Luke's
C hildren learn how to obey the St. Luke's honor code
H elping my teachers hand out computers
O vercrowded by high schoolers
O pen doors to our classrooms
L ots of great friends!

Matty Novick, Grade 5
St Luke's School, CT

Universe

Universe
galaxies, planets
never ending space
and stars light years
away

Anya Peterson, Grade 5
Marblehead Community Charter Public School, MA

Winter Wonderland

It was cool and refreshing like October rain.
The snow was a friendly nature.
The snowflakes danced lightly on my face.
Melting in relaxation.

This wonderful day could never stop.
Outside was a storm of whiteness.
Flurry to flurry. Frost to frost.
Seemed like the snow crystals were at their brightest.

Marshmallow fluff surrounded me.
The icy blast was just a mere breeze.
It's climbing, spiraling, jumping, and looping.
Whipping past branches in freeze.

I would never return to the warmth of the fire.
That action is just so last week.
Snowy days and chilly weather.
That's all the things that I seek.

Winter is just the greatest.
For me, no sun and sand.
I just can't wait for the next…
The next winter wonderland.

Robyn Michal, Grade 6
Blue Ridge Middle School, VA

Buddy

His eyes shimmer with positivity and hope,
Almost like glowing, honey-colored flames.
You can tell from his eyes that he can act as solemn as a pope.
But you also see he can be fun and active.

His coat is as black and mysterious as the midnight sky.
It shines and gleams with healthiness.
The color makes him look like he is a sneaky spy.
It smells of dirt and nature.

He's a klutz when he trips down the stairs,
But he is smart when he is hungry.
He chases the squirrels in pairs,
But understanding and relaxed when you talk with him.

My dog is like a friend.
He's an equal in my world.
He's my friend to the end.
He's my guardian angel.

As you now see,
My hilarious, loving, dog Buddy,
Is very special to me,
And he can never be replaced.

Samantha Coulombe, Grade 6
Captain Nathan Hale Middle School, CT

Alone

Everyone left me
I'm all alone
I go outside and listen
to the rain drips on the tree fall
as if it were crying
the stream's water croaks like a frog
the animals in the forest
crunch the leaves beneath them
as they run away from me
the wind carries the leaves far away
so far away I can't see where
I wonder if anyone
is on my side anymore
the branches of the trees rustle together
as if they are playing together
the wind suddenly picks
everything up next to me
then I realize
I'm not alone
anymore

Katie Machata, Grade 4
King's Highway Elementary School, CT

The River

The river is calm
The river is very blue
I swim and play here
Noah Costa, Grade 4
Trinity Christian School, VA

Grace

There was an old woman named Grace
Who ran in a six-person-race.
She ran extremely fast.
Grace fell and got a cast
And now her face is a disgrace.
Emily Fisher, Grade 4
St Rose School, CT

Dear Teacher

Dear Teacher,
   I know where it is,
   I definitely know it,
   It is —
   Above the dresser
   Near the clock
   Beside the lamp
   Below the mirror
   With my backpack
      Or else — my little sister
   Threw it out on purpose —
   Oh man!
Bobby Scandura, Grade 6
Albert D Griswold Middle School, CT

Stormy Day

In a summer storm
Rain, thunder, and lightning strike
With their great power
Adam Bechtold, Grade 6
Our Lady of Mercy School, CT

Shadow

My shadow
Creeps behind me
Like my own twin
But every time I
Talk to him he never says a thing.

My shadow
Can be
Big or small
I don't know how he does it

He can even disappear
But only when light's not here.
Justin Lee, Grade 5
C C Burr Elementary School, MA

Tiger

The Bengal tiger
It roars an angry warning
We run away fast.
Jonathan Jeyachandran, Grade 5
Trinity School, MD

Ocean and Beaches

Swimming in the cold
Scorching sand beating your feet
Immense azure waves
Jared Eaton, Grade 5
Hebron Elementary School, CT

Fear

Scary
Overwhelming feeling
Hair stands up
Scary thoughts and dreams
Run away to someplace safe
Joshua Darnell, Grade 6
St Joseph School-Fullerton, MD

Music

Music
Jumpy and loud
Always tapping my foot
Makes people happy when they're sad
Glad times!
Shana Foley, Grade 4
Waller Mill Fine Arts Magnet School, VA

When I Am Asleep I Am at Peace

When I am asleep I am at peace
I close my eyes and I dream.

I dream of prancing ponies
In a wide open field,
They graze and play tag.

When it is morning and I awake
I still feel sleepy.

But my night's peaceful dreams
Will be with me all day.
Ally Downey, Grade 4
Quashnet School, MA

Hobbies

Dancing
up beat, random
exciting, exhausting, jumping
hip hop, jazz, mud, race
riding, speeding, crashing
crazy, nerve-wracking
Quading
Ashley Downs, Grade 6
Captain Nathan Hale Middle School, CT

My Favorite Place, the Ocean*

Where the waves meet the sand
And where the seagulls land
My favorite place the ocean

A salty taste in the afternoon air
Living free without a care
My favorite place the ocean

Where dolphins jump
And seahorses bob
My favorite place the ocean

Where shells are found
And rocks are round
My favorite place the ocean

A peaceful place
The wind in your face
My favorite place the ocean

Children's footprints in the sand
As the sea comes and swallows them
I think of the beauty in my favorite place
the ocean
Grace Murray, Grade 4
Southbrook Academy, MA
*Dedicated to my Grandmother Mimi

Baseball

My family and I went to enjoy another ball game.
I heard myself cling to my seat
I was attracted to the game.

It was the bottom of the ninth,
Our team was losing 10-9.
There was a runner on first base;
Two outs when I heard the stomping from the next batter.

His bat looked big and bad.
With the ball, he began to bang the ball foul.
The batter's plan was to beat the other team badly.
The pitcher was ready for his part by firing with all his power.

He threw the ball.
BAMM!
A home run so horrifyingly huge was hit.
The crowd cheered
So did I.

As we left the park, I heard the bounce of the home run ball.
Looks like I have a souvenir.

Robert Howard, Grade 6
Trinity School, MD

What God Did

He died,
He cried,
He lived for me.
He gave His only son you see.

Shed His blood upon the cross,
God, the Father, had a terrible loss.

When judgment day comes near,
Our hearts will fill with cheer
And a little sadness,
Which will soon be filled with gladness.

Christina Day, Grade 6
Southern Maryland Christian Academy, MD

Mom and Dad

I love my mom and dad
They are always there when I am sad.
They make my day
They make me want to play
I love them in every way.
When I get hurt.
They take care of me.
They can see when I am hurt
Or if I'm OK.
They are the best in every way.

Kalyn Rockman, Grade 4
Helen H Hansen Elementary School, MA

8th Grade Hallway

I feel like an ant today,
Walking through the 8th grade hallway
They are so scary, so tall, so big,
But I'm a small person, I'm just a kid.

I walk through the 8th grade hallway
As a 7th grader now,
I feel more confident doing this,
I am so proud, I say, "Wow!"

I have finally become an 8th grader today
But I will not scare the 6th graders away,
For they will soon know how I felt that day,
When I first walked through that 8th grade hallway.

Athena Ziogas, Grade 6
Fuller Middle School, MA

I Am Christmas

I am sunset.
I wonder if the man below me is happy.
I hear the lonely cricket's song.
I see the night, stretched out so long.
I want to stay, yet I fade away to darkness.
I am moonlight.
I feel something will happen soon.
I touch the mist so cold.
I worry I will soon go out.
I cry farewell, and shine through the darkness.
I am the northern star.
I understand tonight is special.
I say follow me, to three kings on camels.
I dream people will remember me.
I try to see the child in the stable.
I hope that I have helped lead them on.
I am the star that lead three wise men to Jesus.
We are Christmas.

Sidney Ripley, Grade 6
Page Middle School, VA

Rain Drops

It comes from the sky.
Like a butterfly.
I like to dance in the rain whenever I am lonely
But when it's gone I'm lonely again.

Tyler Smith, Grade 4
Courthouse Road Elementary School, VA

Winter

Winter is my favorite season
All I see is white
I hear the crunch of my very new snow shoes
Hitting Colin with wet snowballs that felt like dog's drool,
Protecting my mom and dog by building a snow fort
When I look back a gust of wind came and knocked it all down.

Liam Fortuner, Grade 6
Litchfield Intermediate School, CT

Inside My Desk

Inside my desk
The folders are gossiping,
The math books
Comparing equations.
Inside my desk
The pen shows off his colors,
The loose papers
Wanting a home.
There's a bundle
Of
Unfinished stories,
Leaving off
Where they stopped
And a pad of post-its
Wishing, wishing,
That it will be found.

Maggie Kinabrew, Grade 4
Braeburn School, CT

The Flower

The beautiful red flower,
Watch it sway in the wind,
As the morning begins.
Watch it dance in the wind,
As the sun peeks over the horizon.
As the wind dies down watch it
F
A
L
L
Gently into the hands of Mother Earth.

Christian Collins, Grade 6
Homeschool Plus, VA

My God

Wow!
Is what I have to say
The Lord is here
Right in my soul
I love how I can talk to him
In my own little world
And I don't have to impress him
When I speak
Even when I'm weak
Or at my peak
He's always there, just for me
I can't describe my love for my God
So please do as I say
Bow down to him
Ask him for forgiveness
Thank Christ
For he died on the cross
Just to save your life
That's just the beginning of life

Mirela Caron, Grade 6
Whitinsville Christian School, MA

Little Blue Butterfly

Little blue butterfly floating carelessly in the breeze,
Gliding from flower to flower to savor the sweet nectar they hold,

Landing ever so gently on the petal, trying not to break it,
You blend perfectly in with the pale blue sky,

Your fragile wings
Lifting you with the slightest breeze,

You land on a swaying tulip,
Loving every sweet drop of nectar that passes your lips,

Oh little blue butterfly,
Come dance with me in the wind.

Brendan Jones, Grade 6
Memorial School, MA

The Highest Peak

Do you see a mountain peak
The glimpse of trees
The sound of animals just crying out and running around
A cold feeling of new snow as if just came down to the Earth
The reflection of an island of snow using the water like a clear mirror
With the gray clouds that just follow your every move like it was your shadow
As the mountains tower over you
Highest peak

Andrew Taylor, Grade 5
St Mary's Primary School, MA

When Fall Begins

A breeze swishes by and whistles to me.
I step outside, my foot crackles as I step on leaves
it sounds like popcorn in the microwave.

A mighty oak stands above,
the thin branches stretch and reach out.
Shadows of skeletons appear on the ground.

Cranberry, cinnamon, and hints of yellow;
crash to the ground.
The leaves scurry and leap as a mighty wind passes by.
The leaves form a giant pile that looks like the massive Eiffel Tower.

The fresh smell of pine is welcoming like
my grandma's warm pumpkin pie.

The beaming scarlet dogwood berries are shown in the bushes.
I sit quietly listening for a chirp of a morning blue jay.
A blue jay flies over to the brilliant berries.

All of these amazing parts fall,
bring cheer to all.

Jillian Gelmetti, Grade 6
Madison Middle School, CT

The Train

Roaring like a wild boar
blowing smoke across the land
never sits but only stands
it runs across a metal track
goes around then goes back.

Jacob Hershman, Grade 4
South Area Solomon Schechter Day School, MA

Stars

Stars all shine on their own,
not one of them have the same tone.
They all just shine day, after day,
but try and hear what they say.
Shine brighter and brighter every day,
but don't ever try and shine the same way.

Emily Wilson, Grade 4
Helen H Hansen Elementary School, MA

Life Is Like a Rubber Ball

Life is like a rubber ball.
It goes up and comes down.
There is a chance you might hit something.
But when it lands, there is nothing to worry about.
Life is like a rubber ball.

Simone Billingslea, Grade 6
Albert D Griswold Middle School, CT

Relish

You look like a glump of wet paper with green slime,
You sound like a drop of water falling in a puddle,
You feel like slime with globs of glue,
You smell like sweet candy in my mouth,
You taste like pickles chopped up with sugar.

Lily Hoerner, Grade 4
Bowers School, CT

The Middle

One of three kids in the middle I am
Squashed between two sisters, OH MAN!

My life is not easy because one is five
Some days I'm lucky to even be alive

The other is fifteen and thinks she's 'all that'
In my personal opinion, I'd say she's a brat

My parents are patient but some days are tough
Sharing computer time can get pretty rough

I do have a dog who thinks I'm cool
She wags her tail, and shakes her wet drool

Maybe one day I will honestly think
Life as a middle child doesn't really STINK!

Dean Laughter, Grade 6
E W Thurston Middle School, MA

Water

A sapphire gem,
On and on it goes,
Held in the hands of the world
Running like a young dog through the woods,
Crashing to the sand,
Splash!
Immortal for life,
A blue sky cloudless,
Reflecting life as we know it.
Stones withering away with its power,
A mirror for the Gods,
Water.

Sean Doran, Grade 4
Potter Road Elementary School, MA

Home

Home is a sweet smell
When I walk in the door.
Home is a place
Where lip smackin' good corn bread is made
Home is a place
Where I can play basketball
And I can hear the ball
Koosh through the net
Home is where I play
The Playstation 2 with my brother
Home is where I eat
Sweet snacks
Home is where I watch TV
Home is where
I play games on the computer
Home is where I sleep
On a soft, warm comfortable bed
Hoping for the next day to come
Like waiting for the candy store to open

Jahliil Parrott, Grade 5
Clover Street School, CT

Starlight

Starlight gleams deep upon the depths of the sea.
Nighttime sky paints it black
Soft calls of seagulls drift along the sky.
Sand as soft as velvet cloth blows around the grassy turf.
A golden crisp maple leaf imprints his story along the sand.
This does not appear to me.
I'm staring at a more beautiful sight.
The stars —
Elegant diamonds —
Nighttime fireworks
I am their spotlight
Then —
I drift away.

Lucas Reppucci, Grade 4
Hawley Elementary School, CT

The Four Seasons

In the spring, the flowers bloom.
Summer is going to come soon.
The bees collect honey.
The birds fly around.
The butterflies don't make a sound.
In the summer it is very hot.
I go to the pool.
That keeps me cool.
In the fall some leaves turn brown.
A lot of colors fall to the ground.
I play in the leaves.
I feel the cool breeze.
In the winter it is very cold.
I like to drink hot cocoa.

Travon Liles, Grade 4
Bensley Elementary School, VA

The Bird of Freedom

What is that soaring in the sky?
It's the Bald Eagle of course
Being so very shy,
Soaring in that sky.
As I hear him say
"I'm the bird of freedom."
Then I look with a close eye
And see the Bald Eagle
Looking down at my
Neighbor Lucy and me.
We only imagine
His feathers running
Through our little fingers.
Then we hear the sound
Of a beautiful
Bald Eagle.

Samantha Baskin, Grade 5
Soule Road School, MA

Baby Jesus

Sshh! A baby rests in a manger.
His eyes are soft,
how tired he must be!
He rests his head and falls asleep
in mommy's arms.
All is quiet,
what's this?
Three men who seem to glitter
under the moon lit sky
approach the baby with gifts
of gold, frankincense, and myrrh.
All gather around the baby
as He, the Lord
goes to sleep.

Nicole Catarius, Grade 5
Sacred Heart Elementary School, MA

Spring

Colorful flowers
Baby birds chirping loudly
Soft, fresh breezes blow

Olivia Downer, Grade 4
Leicester Memorial School, MA

Two Shoes

There once was a boy with the blues.
Because he had two smelly shoes.
When he took them off.
The people would cough.
Then all of his friends he would lose.

Erin McGowan, Grade 6
Captain Nathan Hale Middle School, CT

Football Season

Hard helmets clashing together
Bodies flying in the air
Sweaty men pushing each other
Even their brother
They're diving for touchdowns
Kicking field goals
Fumbling the ball
And throwing interceptions
I hate to see it all end.

Kyle Santos, Grade 4
Freetown Elementary School, MA

Louis Armstrong

The music master is Louis Armstrong
He can play the trumpet well and long
He's the one who invented scat
He makes other musicians seem flat.

Aaron Sachs, Grade 5
J F Kennedy Middle School, MA

Me

Let me introduce myself
I am night
My eyes
Are the dark clouds in the sky
My hair
Is the midnight sky
My skin
Is the sun
Gleaming through the solar system
I am as fast as a shooting star
Racing across the sky
I am as powerful as a comet
Crashing into earth
This is who I am
I am me

Josh Kirson, Grade 5
John Ward Elementary School, MA

Free

Free, free, free at last
running out of school really fast
summer is now here

Justin Wines, Grade 6
Monelison Middle School, VA

Beach

The beach is so fun,
when you're in the sun.
Don't forget your suntan lotion,
when you're swimming in the ocean.
It's fun to play in the sand,
where there's now green land.
The fish in the sea,
makes me feel happy.

Makeda Berhane, Grade 4
Angelus Academy, VA

Summer Fun

S wimming at the pool
U mbrellas in the air
M oney for ice cream
M onths away from vacation
E njoying the sun
R eading books for a report

F un time at the beach
U nder the deep blue sea
N ow the day is over

Juliana Rocha, Grade 5
Sacred Heart Elementary School, MA

God

God created me, my classmates, and you!
I look at how God made me,
the things that He gave me
such as my home, the stairs,
things to cook with, a floor to step on
and carpet to keep my feet warm.
I thank God for doing wonderful things.

Narlita Fox, Grade 4
Agape Christian Academy, VA

Haunted House

In my house I think it is haunted
By monsters I am wanted
They may feed me or maybe
They will eat me instead
Now I am scared
Because in my house
There is a man made of lead
Under my bed.

Jaylen Garner, Grade 5
Plainfield Catholic School, CT

Parents

Parents
Proud, thankful
Caring, trusting, protecting
Happiness, strength, love, loyalty, gratefulness
Remembering, changing, observing
Fun, helpful
Happy!

Christian Redmond, Grade 6
St Bartholomew School, MD

The Breath of Life

The soft patter of rain as it hits the earth
The sunlight that flows through the air like a waterfall
The golden mix of color at the setting sun
The dancing trees twirling in the wind
The sweet breeze of a cool, spring morning
The snow that wraps around the ground in a blanket
The rumble of the earth as an earthquake begins
The booms of an angry storm thundering closer
The flashes of light that color the cloudy sky
The stars that twinkle like diamonds overhead
The rainbow that shines over our world

Olivia Watson, Grade 5
Weston Intermediate School, CT

A Baby Named Jesus

Mary gave birth to a special son.
I bet she called him, "Honey bun."
Mary and Joseph had to run,
To have a baby named Jesus.

They travel from Nazareth to Bethlehem.
They thought they can't, but they really can
He lay in a manger with hay in his hand.
She had a baby named Jesus.

The wise men wished, the wise men prayed.
When He grows up He'll save the day.
If you go to heaven, He'll come with you to play.
Mary's so proud for her baby named Jesus.

Gabby Goulette, Grade 4
Mount Hope Christian School, MA

Night

Night is a mystery,
Shrouded in darkness,
Some people alone,
Believe night can play songs of happiness,
Night's song of happiness,
Relieves anyone with luster and despair,
Night's song of happiness can fill the air with a soothing breeze,
Which can calm a devilish soul wandering in the night.

Milo Sherwood, Grade 5
Clark Avenue Middle School, MA

Stars

Stars, stars shining bright,
Talking and dancing with the moon all night.
Colorful stars red, orange, yellow
You stars always look so mellow.
Bright stars watching over the town
I wish I could just pull one down.
I am sad to think you are so far away
But you're still out in the sky every day!

Avalon Mercado, Grade 5
Soule Road School, MA

I Once Had a Bird Named Tweety

Who flew with joy in the sky,
my aunt gave her to me,
I loved to watch her fly.
Tweety was as sweet as can be.
She was the prettiest of them all.

Was soft, silky, and yellow feathered.
She died at the bottom of her cage.
Drooping down, sick and weathered.
Which made me depressed, lonely with rage.
She was the prettiest of them all.

Tweety was a fancy parakeet,
Her eyes would shine so bright.
She would climb with her pink little feet.
Her soul took a flight, into the bright sunlight.
She was the prettiest of them all.

My heart, once full of joy, came to a crumble of sorrow.

Dyanarah Fermin, Grade 6
Gerard A Guilmette School, MA

It Never Ends

It never ends,
    This everlasting place
I am in search for
    The very end of space.

Traveling in a rocket,
    Rushing past the stars,
I even saw the rover
    That was navigating Mars.

Outer space
    Large and scary
What if I find aliens
    That are green and hairy?

The wonder,
    The mystery,
Just around the bend.
    Some day, some day, I will find the end.

Aviva Mühlmann, Grade 6
Yeshiva Academy, MA

Dawn Strikes

Sun rises, moon sleeps.
Twinkling stars blanket the moon.
Dawn strikes, the world wakes.
Hannah Hunt, Grade 4
Weston Intermediate School, CT

Winter

Cool frozen air dancing in circles
Wind howling like a coyote
Animals locked up in holes
Snow covering the landscape
Everything is as still as statues
Trees as skinny as bones
Nothing is moving
The water smooth and icy
Rocks looking like giant snowballs
The sky dark and sad
Winter is here,
Winter is here
William Davies, Grade 4
Weston Intermediate School, CT

Antonyms

Big small
Short tall
Tired wound
Silent sound
Drink eat
Hands feet
Ugly pretty
Dull witty
Ceiling floor
Window door
Nice mean
Whisper scream
Buy sell
Sick well
Type write
Blind sight
Scared plucky
Unfortunate lucky
Old new
Me you
Eileen Walsh, Grade 5
Little Flower School, MD

A Beautiful Sight

The moon's light
The sun is bright
I hope the stars shine tonight
Because if they don't I'll be sad,
but I will not get mad.
Because you know what they say
there will be another day
Devon Pierce, Grade 5
Sacred Heart School, MA

Anger

Anger is a black hole inside you, eating up your happiness.
Anger is a whirlwind of darkness, turning your smile to a frown.
Anger is the thing that makes you growl and want revenge.
Anger will slowly devour you until you are a monster.
After anger is done with you it will just toss you aside
and take another victim.
Thaddeus Cullina, Grade 5
Booth Hill School, CT

Life

A baby first opens its eyes,
Unknowingly entering a world of lies
And as it grows, many challenges it will face,
For life is just one big race
Full of disappointment and sadness,
Enough to drive many to madness
And as that baby grows,
So does the amount it knows
Of the horrors around him,
Of the death and loss of limb
And when he is fully grown,
Confidence has yet to show
But eventually, he sees a sparkle in life, one that isn't all bad,
And that life has many pleasures to be had
And now it is with this knowledge that he is aware of everything around him,
Of all the death, and loss of limb
He has grown,
And confidence has finally shown.
But nevertheless forests continue to fall, and houses will burn,
Disasters will descent and we must learn,
That it *must* STOP!
Henry Tracey, Grade 5
Weston Intermediate School, CT

How the Greeks Won the Trojan War

The Trojan war began when Trojans stole from the Greeks.
Kin Menelaus' beloved Helen from Sparta, a queen.
The Greeks were fed up with other things the Trojans did,
And fought against the Trojans who they considered mean.

Here is something else that made the Greeks upset,
The Trojans decided to charge them in a very unfair way.
Each time the Greeks used the Channel in Aegean Sea,
A hefty toll to the Trojans the Greeks had to pay.

After many years of fighting the Greeks developed a plan.
To build a wooden horse where soldiers would go in and hide.
Then they left the horse outside the Trojan wall,
The Trojans pulled it in, not knowing what was inside.

The plan worked very well and while the horse was in Troy.
The Greek soldiers crept out late at night from this wooden horse.
They burned the city and killed the sleeping Trojans,
And this is how the Greeks won the Trojan war of course!
Sarah Hantz, Grade 5
Trinity Christian School, VA

Anger

I feel it all the time
Hatred, anger, fear
They have become part of me
They feel like horrible beasts
Crawling around inside me
When I cry the tears cloud over an inky black
My face at times become rigid
But only because I feel no need to share my emotions
When I share my thoughts or feelings
it's only half of what I really feel inside
People always think I must be sad
But my anger is boiling and when they ask it surges out
It feels like the anger runs in my veins when they ask
I feel good letting it out but almost immediately I hate myself
for not controlling the anger then my face goes rigid again
But I am always afraid of getting too mad and losing control
I stay away from people for that reason
But who said life was fair…

Matteo Murrelle, Grade 5
Mary Munford Elementary School, VA

The Ocean

An ocean of bright colors and flawless creatures
Wandering through the free sea
Taking in every bit of its space
Before stepping into the real world

A place of relaxation and beauty
Where creatures can live in peace and harmony
Taking in every bit of being free
Before stepping into the real world

My favorite place in the world
The ocean

Nadine Moujahed, Grade 6
E W Thurston Middle School, MA

Just

Feelings,
Their lives,
Family,
Friends,
Hopes,
Dislikes,
Differences,
Alike,
Courage,
And fate,
Slaves,
Who fought,
And fought,
And fell, and fell,
Just
To go home.

Andrew da Costa, Grade 5
Charlotte A Dunning Elementary School, MA

Twin Towers

T errible things happened
W hen the airplanes hit the towers
I nside where many people were dying but
N ever would you

T hink something so tragic could happen
O n such an amazing place, a place
W hich was the tallest in the world and
E veryone was in disbelief but it was the truth because
R ight then millions of people were killed and devastated,
S ometimes you never know and that's what kills me.

Danielle Berube, Grade 5
Har-Bur Middle School, CT

People*

People come,	They are gray,
People go	They are plain
I just stay,	I'd like to say,
Don't you know	They drive me insane
I am still,	Just sit,
Day and night	Just stay
People look,	Stay still,
But see no sight	Never play
I am there,	They lead me to boredom,
But no one sees	So I try to ignore 'em
Won't someone care,	I kick them,
Oh please, Oh please	I throw them,
	I skip them,
	But wherever I look,
	I always find them

Rachel Davis, Grade 5
Forest Avenue Elementary School, MA
*A poem for two voices

Feelings

If you're mad
do not be bad.
Try to be glad
or you'll feel sad.

You go to the park
and you scrape your knee
and you feel so unhappy.
You have no more glee.

Don't let it get you down
when you fall on the ground.
Think about things that make you feel good
or else you'll have a bad childhood.

Sam Shah, Grade 4
Helen H Hansen Elementary School, MA

Happy Times

Your happy times are mine.
We play, laugh, and enjoy ourselves.
We celebrate things together,
Birthdays and holidays.
Tell deep, dark secrets.
Hang out together.
Laugh until we cry.
Make scrapbooks,
Take pictures.
Share our personal belongings.
Enjoy happy times together.

Cassie Murphy, Grade 5
Tilghman Elementary School, MD

Fireplace Fire

When icy winds are far outside
where's the one place you should hide?
It warms you up like the Sunday choir.
Yes, indeed, it's fireplace fire.

The world's eighth wonder has to be
what a fire can bring upon thee:
for, how can a crackling blaze of smoke
bring all joy to all the folk?

It warms you from the inside-out.
You cannot complain. You cannot pout.
It makes you calm. It rests your soul.
It protects you from the winter cold.

Haley Bain, Grade 5
G W Carver Elementary School, VA

Goodbye to Noogie

Goodbye to Noogie
It's such a sad day
There's no time to play
It's time for goodbye

Noogie the gerbil is gone
He was such a class clown
He'd give all the kids noogies
From sunup to sundown

He left during science
Which was always his worst
It seemed impossible to be so soon
It wasn't even afternoon

So from this day on
We will always remember
Noogie the gerbil in our hearts
…forever

Sydney Hess, Grade 5
Newton-Lee Elementary School, VA

Football

F abulous fun
O bstacles
O bsessed
T ouchdowns
B est sport
A bsolutely amazing
L argest watched sport
L ong passes

Nicholas Reynolds, Grade 4
Lynch Elementary School, MA

Cancer

You take away many,
And make people cry,
You snatched my grandfather,
And change people's lives.

You invade the community,
And haunt every hospital.
Yet through your potential
You make things possible.

You give scientists new goals,
To work for a cure,
When they find a medicine
Their joy will be pure.

You strike randomly,
You are not fair,
But you remind people to love
You make stories to share.

Alicia Ouyang, Grade 5
Dayton Oaks Elementary School, MD

Twin Towers

The bombing of
911 was a   horrible tragedy
this day was   the opposite of
magic. No one   was smiling on
this horrifying   day. Everyone
hated this   person who
thought is was   okay. Smoke
could be seen   very far away.
"Crash!"   everyone heard
when a plane   rammed it.
Everyone was   frowning and
there was not   one grin. A devils
face was seen   in the smoke.
Perhaps the   man in the plane
thought it was   a joke. Bombing
of 911   was very sad. It
certainly made everyone very very mad.

Sam Corman, Grade 5
Har-Bur Middle School, CT

Spring

Spring is in the air
No more snow
Birds chirping everywhere
The parks are aglow
No more clouds
Instead more snow cones
Brings sweetness to every pair

Rafael Morales, Grade 5
Litwin Elementary School, MA

Exit Sign

Glowing red above the floor
Makes us run towards the door
It's time to leave
It's time to go
I want to leave
Did you not know?
Glowing red above the floor
Making us run towards the door.

Bradley Monahan, Grade 6
Fuller Middle School, MA

MLB

Major league baseball
Hope it lives on forever
Go, Orioles, go!

Timothy Coffman, Grade 5
St Joseph School-Fullerton, MD

Working Their Hardest

They are pushing, pulling, and lifting,

With all their strength,
Working in the mornings,
Sleeping during the nights.
Up at three in the morning,
Pulling on their boots,
Getting ready for work.
Pouring their fuel,
Starting their powerful engines.
Dipping their nets,
Cawling them crabs.
Sweating like pigs,
Drinking some sodas.
Dropping their anchors,
Back to the dock.
Tying up the boats,
Unloading their crabs.
Getting some money,
Going home,

It's the end of the day.

Greg Kemp, Grade 5
Tilghman Elementary School, MD

Dreaming

Dreaming is a lullaby
Sweet to my soul
Wanting to be let out
But has to stay in control
Dreaming is a wanting wish
Serving a dish of dreams
Creating things you may never have
Like flying on butterfly wings
Like dancing with stars in the sky
Like laughing with all your friends
With no trouble involved I really cannot lie
About Dreaming being a lullaby
I don't know why we Dream
But it is so sweet to me
I feel like I could drift away
And Dream all day
But I know dreaming is a gift we have
Dreaming is a lullaby
Sweet to my soul
Wanting to be let out
But has to stay in control

Colleen Christman, Grade 6
Whitinsville Christian School, MA

Archaeologist

An archaeologist digs up things from the past
The people in museums keep them so they last
To dig, they use a special tool
This fun job is very cool
Although they do find artifacts
They have to learn some very hard facts
They do love wells
And they do find cells
From a long, long time ago
They found a town
Way way down
Underneath the ground
So as you can see
Archaeology
Is important to me!

Libby Bieri, Grade 4
Waller Mill Fine Arts Magnet School, VA

To Be a Bird

If I were a bird
I would be tired
flapping my wings
all the time
Finding scraps of food
while migrating south
oh it must hurt
to be a bird.

David Welch, Grade 5
Charlotte A Dunning Elementary School, MA

My Life

My life is fun.
My life is joyful.
I love my mom.
I love my home.
Life is awesome.
Don't take life out on a friend.
So be a friend not a foe!

Bradley Dougherty, Grade 4
Helen H Hansen Elementary School, MA

Tomorrow

Tomorrow;
Not knowing what lies ahead,
Not caring or thinking about what could happen,
We move on.
Who knows if tomorrow is there?
It is not set in stone.
Do we think about our actions?
Or say, "I'll fix it tomorrow."
You hear about the sudden deaths of the people around you.
You are not destined to live another second.
Every step you take,
Everything you do,
It may be your last.
Tomorrow;
Does happiness really await?

Dorothy Hastings, Grade 6
Grace Episcopal Day School, MD

The Cuddly Penguin*

under an iceberg
a penguin swims
propelling itself through the water
flying like a torpedo
flipper by flipper
dark, black and pearly white
then it stops
looks around
remains quiet
keeps on swimming
between the waves
lapping against him
not looking back
he still swims in his skin
next to the melting ice.

Nicholas DiLullo, Grade 5
West Woods Upper Elementary School, CT
*Inspired by Valerie Worth

Fish

Fish are every single color
They sway from side to side
They're very fast in the water
And when a shark is around, they go to hide.

Nicole Smith, Grade 5
Sacred Heart Elementary School, MA

Storm

The bright blue sky is quickly transforming into a dim cluster of fog.
The grey clouds quickly spread like a virus of sadness.
It starts drizzling tiny droplets of water.
The storm is sadly crawling toward our little town.
Lightning hits the ground and a bright flash distracts our eyes.
Lightning is the sun; its bright light reaching as far as the universe can possibly stretch.
Thunder pounds in the air as if it was playing very loud drums.
Continuous flashes come and go throughout the time.
Little children walk to bed hoping that tomorrow will be a sunny and beautiful day.

Jessica Fanclik, Grade 5
Booth Hill School, CT

I Never Learn Anything in School

I never learn anything in school
Sitting in class is a waste of time
I feel like I'm back in preschool
I'm wasting away my lifetime
First I go to social studies
Countries, capitals, laws, and ancient history
Wars, battles, peace treaties
What do they have to do with me?
Next my schedule drags me to math
Fractions, decimals, and percents
Numbers lead me down the path
But none of this makes any sense
Science awaits me next
Volume, density, and the earth's crust
I read about them in my text
Too bad passing is a must
Two periods a day of English
Reading, writing like this poem
So much time when will it finish?
To pass MCAS we need wisdom
Lunch is pretty cool, but I still say and believe that I never learned anything in school!

Phillip Varao, Raymond Phuong and Andre Pereira, Grade 6
Edmond P Talbot Middle School, MA

Basketballs

When I play basketball I think of a hoop and an alley-oop or a referee 2 shots 2 shots!
Or ten basketball players scurrying down the court
That's what I think of basketball.

Raymond Snow, Grade 5
Charlotte A Dunning Elementary School, MA

Seasons

The seasons are like life, the leaves are like the people.
In spring they're born, in summer they grow,
In autumn they grow old, and in winter no one will know.
The leaves are like people, the tree is mother sun, and the seasons are life, and nothing is done.
The west wind is heaven, the east wind is heck.
The life is short, but peaceful, but the difference of the cruel life of people.

Rayna Feldsher, Grade 5
Krieger-Schechter Day School, MD

Live

Life is a bird
It just goes by
I wish it would last
Until the end of time
Life is a bird

Cheyenne Dellasanta-Swann, Grade 5
Charlotte A Dunning Elementary School, MA

I Am Me

I am cheese pizza
I am nonstop energy
I am a sonic boom that just hit the earth
I am silent after bed
I am a Coca Cola-holic
I am a basketball on the court
I am four and a half feet of fun
I am home relaxing on my bed
I am James
I am chocolate ice cream in a cup at Goodies
I am a math boy
I am someone cool
I am a skier
I am best friends with Matt P.
I am an unusual person
I am tired after Laser Quest
I am colorful
I am everybody's "it" in gym
I am dominoes ready to topple over
I am Princeton Street
I am Me

James Poirier, Grade 5
Willis E Thorpe School, MA

Let It Out!

Your feelings are inside you
And only, only you.
No one can control them
Or tell you what to do.
But let out what you've kept inside
Inside for so, so long.
Let it out! Let it out,
And you cannot go wrong.
Let it out! Now you'll feel good.
So happy that you've told
What's been bottled up inside of you
You've let your tale unfold.
Let it out! Let it out,
Your feelings need to show.
If you spin your hidden tale,
Your happiness will grow.
Let it out! Let it out,
You'll feel as good as new.
Remember — there's ONE person in charge of your life,
And that one person is *you.*

Chloe Mandell, Grade 5
Weston Intermediate School, CT

Peeps Rule

An ode to peeps
peeps are so tasty,
their marshmallow goodness can't be beat.
When you put them in the microwave they go KA-BOOM.
So yummy in my tummy
They come in so many different kinds of color shapes and sizes.
Peeps are the best marshmallow treat in the world.
Peeps rule!!!

Ryan McGrath, Grade 5
Charlotte A Dunning Elementary School, MA

In the Cave of Darkness

On the street corner
In the shadow of a tall abandoned apartment building
There's a patch of complete darkness
Utter darkness
As my gaze falls upon the patch of black shadows
I see…
Nothing.
But wait!
There's something,
Someone,
Crawling from his inner sanctum of darkness
His name is no one, his life is a mystery
He lives deep within the cave of darkness
Takes comfort from its safety
No one ever sees him
Except when he chooses to be seen
He thrives on his patch of shadows
Not ever surrendering himself to the world
Never opening himself up
Simply sitting there, closed
In his darkness, away from the rest of the world

Ross Cohen, Grade 6
Weston Middle School, CT

Spring

Spring is coming,
It will be here soon,
I have fun in the spring.
The pool opens,
And we have spring break,
I play softball in the spring.
It rains and thunderstorms a lot.
I like the sounds of the thunder and the rain.
The rain sounds like the jungle,
And the thunder sounds like a drum being beat on,
But it does not snow in the spring,
I go to my granny's,
And help pick up sticks,
I ride bikes with my granny,
When spring is coming.

Brittany Burns, Grade 5
Tilghman Elementary School, MD

Friendship

Friendship is a fire that burns in your heart,
without it your heart turns to coal
a big lump of ice asleep in your breast,
never to awaken again.
but with friendship the fire can keep glowing bright
yellow and orange and blue.
your friends are your love
and your life and your hope,
hold them tight, keep them close
and together you'll have friendship
forever.

Jesse Granger, Grade 6
Monelison Middle School, VA

Summer

Rising up to stare at the brightly glowing sun.
Strolling to the beach to ride a tide.
Glaring at aqua blue water, while swallowing ham on a bun.
It feels sensational on a summer morning to squint your eyes and look outside.

Brendan Masi, Grade 5
Hebron Elementary School, CT

Index

Author Autograph Page

Author Autograph Page

Author Autograph Page

Author Autograph Page

Author Autograph Page

Author Autograph Page

Author Autograph Page

Author Autograph Page

Author Autograph Page

Author Autograph Page